International Relations Theory and the Asia-Pacific

International Relations Theory and the Asia-Pacific

G. John Ikenberry and Michael Mastanduno, Editors

COLUMBIA UNIVERSITY PRESS
NEW YORK

Columbia University Press
Publishers Since 1893
New York Chichester, West Sussex

Library of Congress Cataloging-in-Publication Data
International relations theory and the Asia-Pacific / G. John Ikenberry and Michael Mastanduno, editors.
p. cm.
Includes bibliographical references and index.
ISBN 0–231–12590–9 (cloth : alk. paper) — ISBN 0–231–12591-7 (paper : alk. paper)
1. East Asia—Politics and government. 2. United States—Relations—China. 3. China—Relations—United States. 4. United States—Relations—Japan. 5. Japan—Relations—United States. I. Ikenberry, G. John. II. Mastanduno, Michael.

DS518.1 .I58 2003
327'.095—dc21

2002034994

∞

Columbia University Press books are printed on permanent and durable acid-free paper
Printed in the United States of America

c 10 9 8 7 6 5 4 3 2 1
p 10 9 8 7 6 5 4 3 2

CONTENTS

ACKNOWLEDGMENTS

This volume began with a series of workshops, held at the University of Pennsylvania and Dartmouth College in 1998 and 1999, that brought area specialists and international relations theorists together to explore the prospects for stability in the Asia Pacific region. We are grateful to the John Sloan Dickey Center for International Understanding at Dartmouth and to the University of Pennsylvania for financial support. Two anonymous reviewers for Columbia University Press provided helpful comments and suggestions. We thank Jackie Lee for preparing the index, and Leslie Bialler at Columbia University Press for his persistence and good cheer.

G. John Ikenberry, Washington DC
Michael Mastanduno, Hanover, NH
January 2003

LIST OF CONTRIBUTORS

G. John Ikenberry is Peter F. Krogh Professor of Geopolitics and Global Justice at Georgetown University.

Michael Mastanduno is Nelson A. Rockefeller Professor and Chair of the Department of Government at Dartmouth College.

Thomas J. Christensen is Professor of Political Science at Massachusetts Institute of Technology.

Avery Goldstein is Professor of Political Science at the University of Pennsylvania.

Alastair Iain Johnston is Governor James Albert Noe and Linda Noe Laine Professor of China in World Affairs at Harvard University.

David Kang is Associate Professor of Government at Dartmouth College.

Masaru Tamamoto is Senior Fellow at the World Policy Institute in New York.

Henry R. Nau is Professor of Political Science and International Affairs at George Washington University.

John S. Duffield is Associate Professor of Political Science at Georgia State University.

Jonathan Kirshner is Associate Professor of Government at Cornell University.

Robert G. Gilpin is Professor Emeritus of Politics and International Affairs at Princeton University.

Dale Copeland is Associate Professor of Politics at the University of Virginia.

William W. Grimes is Assistant Professor of International Relations at Boston University.

Thomas U. Berger is Professor of Political Science at Boston University.

International Relations Theory and the Asia-Pacific

Introduction

INTERNATIONAL RELATIONS THEORY AND THE SEARCH FOR REGIONAL STABILITY

G. John Ikenberry and Michael Mastanduno

Since the end of the cold war, the problems and prospects of the Asia-Pacific region have drawn increased attention from students of international politics and foreign policy. Interactions among the major powers of the region—the United States, China, and Japan—have taken on a particular significance. Scholars seeking to explore these renewed relationships in a dynamic and uncertain international context face a double challenge.

One challenge is to bridge the gap between the rich comparative and foreign policy scholarship on China, Japan, and the United States, on the one hand, and the wider world of international relations theory on the other. The two worlds of area specialty and international relations theory often do not meet. As a result, policy debates about the stability of Asia-Pacific relations tend to be under-theorized, while theoretical arguments about the region are often undertaken without the benefit of historical or comparative perspective. The contributors to this volume begin with the premise that the theoretical insights of international relations need to be brought more closely into contact with the rich history and complex reality of the Asia-Pacific region. Since there should be a payoff for both worlds, the chapters below are motivated collectively by this goal of helping to bridge the gap and bring theory to bear on the international politics and economics of the region.

In doing so, a second interesting challenge emerges. International relations scholars, particularly those trained in the United States, employ theories that emerged in the context of the Western historical experience. American international relations theories are deeply rooted in Western philosophical traditions and debates, with an intellectual lineage traced back to Hobbes, Rousseau, Kant, Locke, Marx, and others classic thinkers. It is not immediately apparent—nor should it be taken for granted—that these theories or intellectual constructs are relevant to understanding Chinese, Japanese, or Korean calculations and behavior. This volume necessarily raises the question of the usefulness and fit of European-centered theories for the Asia-Pacific region. In this sense as well, we believe that the encounter between the Asia-Pacific region and international relations scholarship can only illuminate and enrich both realms.

At a substantive level, the central concern of the volume involves the prospects for stability in the Asia-Pacific. The region itself provokes this concern. The Asia-Pacific is a mosaic of divergent cultures and political regime types, historical estrangements, shifting power balances, and rapid economic change. It is not surprising that some scholars find the international relations of the Asia-Pacific as ripe for rivalry. It is plausible to imagine security dilemmas, prestige contests, territorial disputes, nationalist resentments, and economic conflicts swelling up and enveloping the region.

The key regional actors are China, Japan, and the United States. China is a rising power that is simultaneously transforming its domestic politics and economics, extending its regional influence, and demanding the respect and recognition of other major powers. Japan is an economic great power that thus far has neglected to develop the commensurate military power and diplomatic initiative typically expected of a traditional nation-state. The United States is the dominant power and a formidable presence in the region, although some question its long-term commitment in the absence of the Soviet threat or an equivalent global challenge.

The working premise of this volume is that stability in the broader Asia-Pacific region is in large part a function of the behavior of, and relationships among, these three major powers. For this reason, the volume concentrates on interactions among China, Japan, and the United States. Each chapter analyzes the foreign policy behavior of one or more of these states and/or relations among them in an effort to make claims about the prospects for regional stability. Some of the chapters focus on security relationships, some on economic relations, and some on the interaction of the two. Taken as a whole, the chapters do not promote any particular theoretical perspective. They draw instead on the full diversity of theoretical approaches in contemporary international relations scholarship to illuminate interactions among these three critical players.

If "stability" can be defined broadly as the absence of serious military, economic, or political conflict among nation-states, then existing theories of international relations indeed offer far-reaching and divergent claims about the sources of stability in world politics. The realist research program offers at least two candidates: balance of power theories and hegemony theories. The first two sections of this chapter survey these theories as they are drawn upon in the chapters that follow. The authors in this volume do not agree fully on whether a stable balance of power or hegemonic order is possible in the Asia-Pacific, or on whether shifting power distributions and competing hegemony will render the region unstable. The authors do agree that the distribution of power—hegemonic or balanced—is not in itself sufficient to generate either stability or instability. Perceptions, institutions, and relations of interdependence also matter, as they give more precise shape to the understanding of national interests and security threats.

Other chapters in this volume examine elements of order and stability that might best belong to liberal and constructivist theoretical traditions. Several of the authors argue that history and memory are crucial factors in shaping how China, Japan, and the United States view and react to each other. The Asia-Pacific region contrasts with that of Europe; in the latter region, states seem to have overcome nationalist hatreds to arrive at political reconciliation and even a grand vision of regional integration. Nothing remotely so ambitious exists in the Asia-Pacific, where suspicions and resentments rooted in history continue to dominate the forces of political reconciliation. To take one example, it is striking how different Japan's self-perception is from the perceptions of Japan held by many Chinese and Koreans. The objective circumstances of regional power are not able to explain the divergence in perceptions, and for some authors the divergence in perceptions is the critical variable.

Liberal theories of international relations emphasize the role of international institutions and economic interdependence in promoting cooperation and political stability. The authors also explore these factors in the emerging Asia-Pacific region. Their analyses deepen our understanding of how institutions and interdependence matter. Several of the authors argue that institutions—particularly domestic institutions—actually aggravate regional relationships by fixing into place differences in state-society relations and structures of political economy. These same institutions can also create rigidities that make it difficult for countries to adapt to changing international and region economic circumstances—and this too can be a source of conflict.

In sum, the contributors to this volume draw on a wide array of international relations theories to suggest that the sources of stability and instability in the Asia-Pacific are found in security relations, economic relations, and at the intersection of the two. The region continues to hold the potential for traditional security conflicts that result from dynamics such as major power rivalry, competing territorial claims among sovereign states, and the operation of the security dilemma. However, as many of the chapters suggest and as the concluding chapter argues explicitly, the role of the United States is a crucial variable that will continue to determine whether security conflicts are managed effectively and whether stability endures.

The potential for regional instability and conflict is also embedded in the "low politics" of domestic and international economic relationships. Greater economic interdependence in the Asia-Pacific has brought the promise of both prosperity and disharmony. Economic liberalization has become a regional engine of growth, but at the same time has disrupted the social and political character of "embedded developmentalism" within the states of the region. The confrontation between the Asian developmental state on the one hand, and the forces of globalization on the other, have political consequences that remain uncertain domestically and internationally. The Asian financial crisis of 1997–98 highlighted that regional stability requires the effective management if not outright resolution of this dilemma.

It is important to appreciate the intersection of these economic and security challenges. In a booming regional economy, there are incentives for state and societal actors to downplay international security and domestic political conflicts in order to concentrate on the positive sum benefits of deeper integration. But in times of slower growth and economic uncertainty, security problems become more exposed and loom larger. Security conflicts, in turn, have the potential to disrupt the economic interdependence upon which prosperity depends. For states in the region, then, economic and security relations interact to create vicious or virtuous cycles. The challenge for statecraft is to achieve the latter and avoid the former.

The remainder of this introduction explores five theoretical approaches to the question of stability in the Asia-Pacific: balance of power, styles of hegemony, history and memory, domestic and international institutions, institutions and stability, and economic interdependence. We emphasize the contributions our authors make in utilizing these theoretical perspectives to explain contemporary relations among Japan, China and the United States and to illuminate the uncertain future of the Asia-Pacific

THE BALANCE OF POWER AND ASIAN STABILITY

Will Europe's past be Asia's future? Aaron Friedberg posed this question in an article in 1993/94 and essentially answered in the affirmative.[1] He argued that Asia lacked many of the characteristics, present in Europe, that could lead to stability after the cold war, including widespread commitments to democracy, socio-economic equity, post-nationalist political cultures, and robust regional institutions. Asia, as opposed to Europe, seemed far more likely to emerge as the "cockpit of great-power conflict."[2]

This thesis is not uncontroversial, and has its supporters and detractors.[3] It is an important starting point for the analysis of this volume for two reasons. First, it raises the policy issue of critical importance, i.e., that of the sources of future stability and instability in the region. Second, it points to the critical theoretical issue of whether the traditional tools of international relations theory, and in particular a standard realist depiction of the international system, have relevance in understanding this region after the cold war. Friedberg, in effect, suggests that late-twentieth-century Asia may be understood in much the same way as late-nineteenth-century Europe, with traditional great powers conducting economic and strategic rivalries in a multipolar setting.

The chapters in this volume engage Friedberg's thesis explicitly and implicitly. They highlight factors that lend credibility to the concerns he expresses. But they also reveal pathways to greater stability in Asia-Pacific security relations that a standard neorealist analysis might overlook.

Tom Christensen's chapter (the first) suggests that we should take seriously the prospects for great-power security conflict, particularly between China and Japan. He argues that in Asia the basic realist logic of the security dilemma is compounded by ethnic hatreds, historical enmity, and long memories. Chinese elites are fearful and suspicious of Japan and take reassurance neither from Japanese statements nor from Japanese behavior. These attitudes place the United States in a difficult position, because attempts to strengthen the U.S.-Japan alliance alarm China—but so, too, would any weakening of that alliance, since it would suggest to China the prospects of a more independent Japan. For Christensen, the regional security challenge is serious, but not insurmountable. He suggests that confidence-building measures and security regimes might ameliorate the security dilemma over the long term, and also that U.S. diplomacy might be used more effectively to moderate the tensions in this delicate set of relationships.

Avery Goldstein's analysis (ch. 2) of late-twentieth-century great-power politics in the Asia-Pacific recalls explicitly late-nineteenth-century great-power politics in Europe. He sees China developing a grand strategy similar to that practiced by Bismarck—an effort to engage and reassure other major powers in order to provide space for Chinese development as a great power without alarming or provoking more powerful rivals, individually or collectively. Chinese elites, in Goldstein's account, are striving less for Chinese hegemony and more to temper U.S. preponderance and bring about a peaceful transition from a U.S.-dominated order to one that is more genuinely multipolar.

David Kang (ch. 4) proposes yet another perspective, and one that challenges the whole idea that European models and theories of interstate interaction are relevant in the Asian context. Kang suggests that the long history of Asian international relations has been less war-prone than that of Europe, and one key reason is that Asian interactions have operated according to a different organizational logic. He observes that European interstate dynamics have been characterized by formal equality (i.e., sovereignty) but informal inequality. Asian relationships, in contrast, have traditionally been based on formal inequalities but informal equalities. The organization of a regional system around the recognition by other states of Chinese hegemony played an important stabilizing role historically, and Kang explores the potential for stability in the contemporary Asia-Pacific region as China once again rises to be a major factor in the geopolitical equation.

Other authors also see encouraging signs for stability in Asia-Pacific security relations. For Alistair Iain Johnston (ch. 3), the potential to "socialize" Chinese officials into the norms and practices of the existing international order is far greater than neorealist analysis would suggest. Johnston uses Chinese participation in the Asian Regional Forum (ARF) to demonstrate that international institutions can in fact shape the behavior of Chinese officials in ways that are conducive to international stability. Dale Copeland (ch. 10) makes a similar point by focusing on international economic relations. He argues that by providing China with expectations of positive future trading relationships, the United States and other major powers can, in effect, reassure China by signaling that the international environment is more benign than malign. Finally, Henry Nau (ch. 6) combines realist and constructivist insights to argue that the United States, Japan, and certain other states in the region live in a democratic security community that mitigates, if not totally eliminates, military rivalries among them. And, although these countries face significant internal and external differences in relations with China, their superior military power helps to assure that conflicts with China are handled in political and diplomatic terms rather than as direct military confrontations.

There are other stabilizing forces in the security arena as well. Friedberg's argument assumes a rapid transition to multipolarity, and that "the United States will be less inclined to project its power into every corner of the globe."[4] However, the international structure has not shifted decisively to multipolarity, and as a unipolar power the United States has reaffirmed its commitment to "deep engagement" in Asia and to the effort to manage crises in the interest of regional stability.[5] Domestic politics may eventually force the United States to reconsider its forward political and military presence in the Asia-Pacific. But, as of the end of 2001, it seemed clear that U.S. officials continued to view the region as a vital area for U.S. security, to define U.S. regional interests in terms of an engaged defense of the economic and security status quo, and to conceive U.S. regional strategy as one of sustained engagement.[6] The potential for the United States to play an enduring role as a stabilizer of the Asia-Pacific region is explored in the concluding chapter.

STYLES OF HEGEMONY AND STABILITY

Polarity is one way to think about the stability of the Asia-Pacific; hegemony is another. The region is marked by a variety of sharp power asymmetries, and whatever future political order emerges in the region will be one that is at least partly defined by the divergent political capabilities of the states within the region. But if the region is to be organized by a hegemonic power, the most important question may be: whose hegemony? Whether the Asia-Pacific is ultimately dominated by a Chinese, Japanese, or American hegemonic order is of significant consequence.

Theories of hegemony tell us a great deal about the underlying logic and motivations of hegemonic leadership. A hegemonic state, with a preponderance of power and a long-term view of its interest, has both the capacities and incentives to create and manage a stable political order.[7] But, hegemonic theories also acknowledge that the distinctive internal characteristics of the hegemon itself—its political institutions, culture, and historical experiences—will inevitably shape the ways in which the hegemon builds political order. John Ruggie's often cited counterfactual observation that a postwar order organized under German hegemony would have looked very different from the order actually organized under U.S. hegemony is apt.[8]

U.S. hegemony is already manifest in the region—and it reflects a distinctive national style. Overall, American hegemony can be characterized as reluctant, open, and highly institutionalized.[9] The reluctance is seen in the absence of a strong impulse to directly dominate or manage weaker and secondary states within the American order. The United States wanted to influence political developments in Europe and Asia after 1945, but it preferred to see the postwar order operate without ongoing imperial control. In the early postwar years, the United States resisted making binding political and military commitments, and although the cold war drew the United States into security alliances in Asia and Europe, the resulting political order was in many respects an "empire by invitation."[10] The remarkable global reach of postwar U.S. hegemony has been at least in part driven by the efforts of European and Asian governments to harness American power, render that power more predictable, and use it to overcome their own regional insecurities.

Likewise, American hegemony has been relatively open. The United States is a large and decentralized democracy, which provides transparency and "voice opportunities" to other states in the order. This creates possibilities for political access, incentives for reciprocity, and the potential means for partner states to influence the way hegemonic power is exercised. There are many moments when Asian and European allies have complained about the heavy-handedness of U.S. foreign policy, but the open character of the American political system reduces the possibilities of hegemonic excess over the long term. The United States has also sought to build its hegemonic order around a dense set of international and intergovernmental institutions. These institutions reduce the implications of sharp power asymmetries, regularize cooperation and reciprocity, and render the overall hegemonic order more legitimate and stable.[11]

Despite the robustness of American power, the ability of the United States to extend the frontiers of its liberal hegemonic order further into Asia is problematic. If China emerges as a hegemonic contender in the region, it will resist integration into the U.S.-centered order. Conflict between the two hegemonic competitors will become likely. Moreover, Henry Nau makes the argument in his chapter (ch. 6) that a stable and legitimate political order must be organized in a way that is congruent with the domestic principles of political order. If this is so, it reinforces the view that the region will not soon be fully organized around U.S. hegemony. The polity principles of China are sufficiently different from the United States to anticipate Chinese integration and the consolidation of an extended American system into Asia. It could be argued that the successful integration of Japan into America's postwar order is evidence that the complete commonality of domestic regime principles is not necessary. Japan rose to become an economic giant wielding a different developmental model yet it remained firmly integrated into the American system, and contrary to the expectations of many, it did not become a hegemonic challenger. Perhaps China will follow a similar path. But unique cold war circumstances and the American security relationship with Japan—not relevant in the case of China—make it unlikely China will follow Japan's lead and become a compliant associate member of the American hegemonic order.

But what if in the future China itself rises to become a regional hegemon, assuming that the United States steps back from its regional commitments and adopts more of an "offshore balancer" role? What would a Chinese hegemonic order in Asia look like? The authors in this volume suggest different possibilities. Kang's essay (ch. 4) provides the most explicit image. Drawing on the evidence of earlier Chinese imperial eras, Kang argues that the tradition of Chinese regional domination across the centuries was quite stable and peaceful. This order—unlike European notions of interstate order—was organized around deference and status hierarchy. The various Asian states acknowledged China's superior position within the region—as a matter of status and ranking—and in return the other states were given respect and autonomy within their own sphere. If one could project this image into the future of the Asia-Pacific, Chinese hegemony would be largely benign, at least to the extent that the other states in the region understood and accepted the hierarchical organization of the order.

Goldstein (ch. 2) depicts China as striving not necessarily for hegemony but clearly to be among the great powers. If China subsequently were to emerge as *the* dominant regional power, then the neo-Bismarckian strategy that he outlines suggests that Chinese hegemonic leadership would be driven by conventional notions of power politics. Chinese hegemony would be organized not around a distinctively Asian imperial tradition, but around a more classic European strategy of building "hub and spoke" relations with other important regional actors.[12] The stability of a China-centered order would be based on China's ability to induce or coerce cooperation from neighboring states, rather than on some notion of political or status deference.

One hallmark of American hegemony is its organization around international institutions. American order building between in 1944–51 saw the unprecedented creation of multilateral and bilateral institutions to manage postwar security, political, and economic relations. One might infer from its current behavior that a Chinese hegemony would not emphasize this institutional impulse. Iain Johnston (ch. 3) does argue that some Chinese officials are eager to get involved in regional and global institutions, and this involvement is having an impact on their orientations and attitudes. But there is little indication in China's existing rhetoric or behavior to suggest it would pursue the creation of institutions with the same enthusiasm manifest in U.S. diplomacy. This absence of an institutional agenda may simply reflect, of course, that Chinese hegemonic ambitions are at an early stage. Alternatively, it could be evidence of the view that Western democracies are more inclined to create and operate within multilateral institutions than are Asian non-democracies. State socialist regimes may perceive multilateral institutional entanglement as a threat to their domestic standing—in effect, a future Chinese hegemon may realize what Johnston observes, i.e., that international institutions can have a subtle and corrosive effect on autocratic authority and cohesion.

Although Christensen does not make such a claim, the evidence he presents might be used to support the view that Chinese hegemony would be more coercive than benign. Given Chinese perceptions of the international environment, a hegemonic China might feel itself threatened and insecure, much like revisionist historians depict the Soviet Union in the early cold war era.[13] Chinese hegemony under those circumstances would be aimed at building and utilizing military power to deter or pacify seemingly dangerous neighbors and dictate the terms of Asia-Pacific relations. This, of course, is precisely the concern of many Koreans and Japanese, and the prospect of a coercive Chinese hegemony makes their countries more eager to see U.S. leadership sustained in the region.

This alternative depiction of an Asia-Pacific dominated by China serves to remind us that hegemonic power is not in and of itself sufficient to create or define the character of a hegemonic order. The ideology, internal institutions, and national political character of the hegemonic state will be critical in determining how political order emerges and is maintained.

This observation is even more relevant in thinking about Japanese hegemony. The chapter by Masaru Tamamoto (ch. 5) makes a strong argument that Japanese hegemony is not even possible—even if the objective material capabilities and conditions existed. According to Tamamoto, Japan has fundamentally redefined its political identity and ambitions so as to make any type of hegemony unthinkable. Japan has moved so decisively beyond the territorial and military-dominated great-power orientation that defined Japan's foreign policy until its defeat in World War II that it will remain satisfied playing a junior role in America's regional and global system. Indeed, from a contemporary Japanese perspective, Japan has devised a brilliant solution to its regional dilemmas: the United States solves Japan's security problems—keeping estranged Korea and China at bay, and leaving Japan to perfect and protect its internal political culture and society. Tamamoto argues that Japan really doesn't have a foreign policy, or if it does, it is channeled through Washington, D.C. Japanese hegemony is essentially unthinkable because Japan's external orientation is deeply embedded in its transformed postwar political identity.

The chapters by Thomas Berger (ch. 12) and Robert Gilpin (ch. 9) suggest not necessarily a Japanese drive for hegemony, but at least a greater willingness to attempt to shape regional economic order. During the 1980s and into the 1990s, the spread of the Japanese developmental model to other countries in the region was the cutting edge to the Japanese effort to build a congenial regional order. Unable to assert itself in the security sphere, Japan sought to build economic alliances and production relationships in and around Southeast Asia. This style of regional domination pushes political and security concerns to the background and concentrates on establishing interlocking trade and investment relationships—tied together with the replication of the Japanese MITI model of government-business relations. Berger argues that the spread of the Japanese model was rendered all the more pervasive because it entailed the spread of an economic ideology—a way of thinking about the state, markets, and economic development.

Any effort by Japanese officials to organize a regional political economy seemed to have stalled by the end of the 1990s. But the question remains of whether the Japanese style of regional domination, organized around the export of the Japanese model, has a distinctive style of interaction. Is it a robust and stable approach to building regional political order or is it likely to be conflictual and unstable? Berger's analysis suggests that the adoption of Japanese style developmental capitalism brings with it cross-cutting effects. On the one hand, the spread of the Japanese model in Asia serves to diminish geo-territorial rivalry by creating incentives for states to give priority to economic objectives. On the other hand, the spread and success of developmental capitalism has the potential to fuel new conflicts based on uneven development and the inequitable distribution of economic success.

The Asian financial crisis of 1997–99 certainly put the future of a Japanese-centered regional economy to the test. The Japanese government sought to provide some support to its distressed regional economic partners by proposing an expanded regional financing institution—making the Asian Development Bank a leading source of regional financial support. But Washington resisted this proposal. At the same time, Japan's own inability to expand its economy and provide a market for distressed exports in the region undercut its regional leadership standing, while the crisis in general called into question the desirability and viability of the state-led Japanese model. Gilpin's chapter suggests, however, that it would be premature to proclaim the death of either the Japanese model or of Japanese economic prowess. He foresees the re-emergence of U.S.-Japan economic conflict based on the continued incompatibility of their national styles of capitalism. His analysis raises the broader issue of whether a dynamic regional economy organized around the competition between American and Japanese styles of capitalism would be likely to contribute to or detract from regional political and security stability.

The articles in this volume underscore the domestic underpinnings to hegemonic leadership. The styles of hegemonic leadership are clearly derived from distinctive cultural identities and political institutions. Moreover, the capacities of the United States, China, and Japan to play a hegemonic role in the region also depend on their ability to absorb imports and accommodate the interests and demands of other states within the regional hegemonic order. Charles Kindleberger argued in his classic book on the great depression that "the British were unable and the American unwilling" to play a leadership role at the moment of economic crisis in 1929. In Asia today, the conclusion we might draw is similar: China is unable and Japan is unwilling to play this role. This leaves the United States with the opportunity to sustain and expand its incomplete hegemonic project in the region, at least in the near future.

HISTORY, MEMORY, AND STABILITY

Most of the bloody wars in history have been fought in Europe, fueled by deep hatred, explosive nationalism, and power rivalries. It is striking, therefore, that over the last half century, European states have found ways to bury old animosities and work together to create a unified political order. Old adversaries have managed to move beyond their conflicts. The European postwar experience suggests that recovery, prosperity, and reconciliation can progress sequentially in a regional setting. The Asian experience, in constrast, suggests that political reconciliation is a far more elusive goal.

One of the focal points of lingering suspicion and animosity is Japan. The fear of resurgent Japanese militarism and aggression continues to resonate in Korean and Chinese elites and publics. The *Yomiuri Shimbun* presented polling data several years ago that reflected this ongoing suspicion of Japanese power. Asked if they thought Japan might become a great military power again or that it already is one, Japanese public opinion was overwhelming: 74 percent said they did not think Japan would ever again become a great military power, while 18 percent said that it may become one. In contrast, among Koreans, 56 percent strongly believed that Japan may become and 26 percent thought it already was a military power. PRC respondents were roughly divided on whether Japan would again become a military power.[14] The difference between Japanese self-perception and the views of others is remarkable. At the same time, of course, and as Christensen's analysis suggests, Japan views the intentions and capabilities of its neighbors—most importantly, China—with greater suspicion and anxiety than the Chinese themselves consider justified.

How did Europe conquer its intra-regional hatreds and reconstruct political order on the continent, and is there a lesson in this experience for Asia? Some observers discuss this question in terms of symbols and apologies. Certainly the Koreans and Chinese are dissatisfied with the way the Japanese have dealt with their wartime aggression and atrocities. Various scholars have seen important differences in the ways Germany and Japan have dealt with war guilt and postwar political engagement in their respective regions.[15] Others have pointed to the different ways, and degrees to which, the wartime regimes were overthrown and reconstructed. The Emperor remained in Japan but the symbols of militarism in Germany were thoroughly removed. Finally, some contend that the security crises of the cold war manifest themselves differently in Asia and Europe. German reintegration was more necessary and institutional "solutions" to this integration (which are discussed in the next section) were available in Europe, such as the Coal and Steel Community and NATO. Japan had no obvious partner—as Germany had with France—to bind itself to and force reconciliation.[16]

To what extent and how quickly will Asian states move beyond their predicament? Tamamoto argues (ch. 5) that it is possible to move on. Indeed, from a Japanese perspective, one may plausibly argue that the problem has already been solved. Japan has changed its entire foreign policy to overcome these problems, while Japanese elites have found their own unique solutions. The peace constitution and the elaboration of a vision of Japan as a "civilian" great power is part of this solution. The willing subordination by Japan of its military to the U.S.-Japan alliance is also part of the adjustments that Japan has made to lower the level of regional animosity. Japan has agreeably put itself in the "penalty box" of world politics, and is content to remain there. But Tamamoto argues that Japan's self-containment within constitutional restraints and alliance institutions is not simply strategic. It is also a manifestation of real transformation of Japanese society.

Berger also raises issues of the social construction of Japan's political identity in the region, arguing that the export of its political economic structures is also an aspect of postwar reconstruction and repositioning of Japan in the region. Tamamoto and Berger are both of the view that social structures and political identities can change. Johnston is also sanguine in regard to the possibility of long-term shifts in elite thinking that runs to the heart of a country's foreign policy orientation. Christensen seems less optimistic on this score—and his evidence regarding the propensity of Chinese elites to view Japan with suspicion and hatred is a sobering counterpoint to more encouraging assessments that the Asian past can safely be put to rest.

INSTITUTIONS AND STABILITY

There is a widely shared view that institutions foster political stability. Liberal institutionalists argue that international institutions or regimes facilitate cooperation by reducing obstacles—such as uncertainty and transaction costs—that stand in the way of mutually beneficial agreements between states.[17] Liberal theorists of democratic peace argue that democratic state structures foster norms of conflict resolution and provide institutional mechanisms that inhibit violence in relations with other democratic states.[18] Theories of political development also argue that the expansion and deepening of political institutions within a country is fundamental to political development and vital in creating stable political order.[19] In all these ways, more institutionalized political orders are generally seen as more developed and stable.

The chapters in this volume suggest that the politics and economics of the Asia-Pacific complicate this general view of institutions and stability. Some authors confirm the conventional wisdom by arguing that the *lack* of institutions is a key problem. The region is not ripe for international institutionalization, and that makes stability more problematic. Other authors suggest that it is the *clash* of institutions that is the problem—divergent institutional structures of state and society exacerbate economic competition in the region and diminish the possibilities for a cooperative multilateral regional political order. And still other authors argue that it is the *stickiness* of domestic institutions that undermines stability—domestic institutions stubbornly resist change and fuel regional conflict.

One of the most striking aspects of the Asia-Pacific region is the absence of well-developed, multilateral institutions. It is not that regional institutions don't promote stability, but that the region doesn't seem to promote international institutions. John Duffield (ch. 7) attempts to explain the puzzle of why European states have spent the better part of fifty years intensively creating an increasingly dense and multifaceted array of regional economic and security institutions, while Asia remains largely bereft of such institutions. He offers and combines several explanations for this contrast, including China's role in Asia during the cold war; the absence of equal sized Asian great powers intent on mutually constraining each other; the U.S. inclination in Asia toward exercising hegemony through bilateral alliances; and the legacies of estrangement and stubborn antagonisms among Japan, Korea, and China.

Berger traces the absence of strong regional multilateral institutions to the spread of the Japanese developmental state model. "Unlike the nations of the European Union . . . the Asian Developmental States are deeply reluctant to pool sovereignty, and as a result regional multilateral institutions such as PECC and APEC have been remarkably weak and under institutionalized, dependent on consensus decision making, and limited to offering nonbinding resolutions and promoting informal communication between the region's leaders."[20] The statist orientation of Asian economic development tends to resist the upward transfer of authority that is implied in more extensive regional institutionalization.

It could also be argued that what is missing in Asia is a regional identity, which Europe clearly has had for centuries, despite its many wars. Asia is more geographically scattered: it is really a series of unequal island nations, geographically close enough to antagonize each other but not close enough to generate institutional solutions to the problem of order. Europe is a single piece of land with a single civilizational heritage. Asia is an assortment of islands and abutments that resist the imaginings of a single civilization or political community. If European-style regional institutions require European-style geography and identity, the Asia-Pacific region will always fall short. If regional multilateral institutions can be anchored in a more heterogeneous environment, the future of institutions in Asia is more promising.

Johnston provides evidence of the difficulty of building regional wide security institutions. Chinese participation in the ARF is consequential, Johnston argues. Chinese leaders learn more about the security intentions and capabilities of other states in the region, and over time these officials are socialized into a common discourse and shared expectations. Institutions do matter, even thin ones with little direct authority or binding commitments. But the ARF is not NATO. There is very little prospect of moving toward a more truly operational regional security pact. The AEF may hold the potential for a useful dialogue, but is hard to imagine that the French would have reconciled themselves to German rearmament simply with the instituting of a Franco-German dialogue. It was the enmeshment of German military authority and capability within a wider European and Atlantic organization that provided the necessary reassurances. Binding security institutions were responsible for the reduction of the security dilemma among the traditional European rivals.[21]

The bilateral security alliances between the United States and Japan and Korea may be playing a similar, if more limited, role in the Asia-Pacific. The United States-Japan security treaty eliminates the need for Japan to develop a more capable and autonomous military force, and this in turn reduces the likelihood of a security dilemma-driven arms race between Japan and China. The bilateral alliances also make the American presence in the region more predictable and durable, which has a stabilizing impact on the wider set of regional relations.

Overall, regional dialogues and bilateral alliances do not constitute the type of institutionalization of power that grants West European relations political stability. The implication is that the Asia-Pacific will either not enjoy the same stability that Europe has created, or it will devise it by noninstitutional means.

When our attention turns from international institutions to domestic institutions, the implications for stability are no less troubling. If institutions are understood broadly to comprise the extant patterns of state-society relations, then what is most distinctive in the Asia-Pacific is the clash of institutions. This is true in two respects. First, as Henry Nau argues (ch. 6), the stability of a political order is connected to the prevailing principles of domestic political order. The legitimacy of an international order hinges on its congruence with the ideas that inform the organization of political authority within the countries that make up the order. If this is true, the prospects for stability within the Asia-Pacific region are not bright. Democratic institutions may facilitate cooperation and stability among a group of democratic states. But the Asia-Pacific region is not distinguished by the presence of a group of established liberal democracies. The heterogeneity of political types is most striking: China, Japan, and the United States seem destined to follow different pathways of political development. Nau suggests that China and Japan are both in political transformation. Their emergence as mature constitutional democracies is not yet in sight, although Japan clearly has moved significantly in this direction. But if stability requires homogeneity of regime types, and even more the presence of aged liberal democracies, stability will remain elusive.

But second, even if their were homogeneity of political regimes in the Asia-Pacific, the economic institutions remain very heterogeneous. Even if all the countries in the region were democracies, there is reason to argue that a stable peace might still be impossible because the political economies of these countries retain significant differences. Gilpin's chapter (ch. 9) centers on how the divergent institutions of capitalism can produce conflict and instability. According to Gilpin, the structures of government and business in the United States and Japan exhibit radically different logics and organizational patterns. In contrast to the United States, the Japanese have retained the neo-feudal institutions of state-led, organized capitalism. Highly organized and exclusive business conglomerates tied to government ministries and large banks run the country, manage markets, and resist change. Like an onion, the layers of social and political organization that support and reinforce this system run deep and ultimately go to the core of the Japanese system. Gilpin sides with revisionist scholars in arguing that the differences between Japanese and American capitalism are as fundamental as they are deeply embedded.[22] A clash between these different styles of capitalism is likely if not inevitable. For Gilpin, institutions matter, but they do not promote stability. Rather, they fix into place antagonistic systems of capitalism that tear at the fabric of regional order.

Domestic institutions also complicate regional stability through their tendency to resist change. In this view, it is not the divergence of institutions that aggravates regional relations, but their inflexibility. Both William Grimes (ch. 11) and Berger offer a version of this argument. Grimes argues that the domestic political order in Japan does not allow it to easily adjust to external economic change. The alliance of the LDP, bureaucracy, and organized business creates a set of mutually reinforcing interests that resist change. Reform agents have a difficult time finding a foothold in the Japanese political landscape. Japan's protracted economic slump and banking crisis have brought into the open the structural institutional character of the country's political gridlock. Countries that can't adjust tend to export their economic problems to others, creating economic conflict in the process. The failure of Japan to move quickly to put its economic and banking house in order and play a leadership role in stabilizing the other countries in the region is a chronic source of regional instability.

Berger makes this point in a more general way, arguing that all the countries in the region that have adopted the Japanese model are also struggling today. To some extent, Berger claims, the spread of the Japanese model has shifted attention away from political and security controversies in the region toward an emphasis on economic development. But it has also created new conflicts—both by creating divisions between Asian and Western capitalist orientations, and by spreading rigidities across the region. The developmental state has not been adopted uniformly across the region—variations are many and important. But the similar features outweigh the differences, and if a stable regional order requires far-reaching adjustment by Japan and the other Asian tigers, and ultimately a transformation to a new political economic model, the stickiness of state-society relations will remain a formidable obstacle.

ECONOMIC INTERDEPENDENCE AND STABILITY

Although the Asia-Pacific lacks well-developed, multilateral institutions, economic interdependence within the region has been robust and growing. Trade and financial links between the United States and Japan expanded rapidly throughout the postwar era and especially during the 1970s and 1980s. By the end of the latter decade, as the value of the Japanese yen soared, Japanese direct and portfolio investment poured into southeast Asia and stimulated increased regional trade. China's emphasis on economic modernization and its willingness to allow particular provinces to experiment with capitalist development opened China to the world economy in general and to the Asia-Pacific region in particular. Regional trade, investment, and financial flows have contributed to the overall dynamism of the region, and to the formation of regional economic zones such as the East Asian Economic Caucus and APEC and to the development of subregional zones such as the Hong Kong-South China-Taiwan triangle.[23] Jeffrey Frankel's careful analysis of regional economic blocs finds support for the widely held view that economic relations among APEC states are an outstanding example of market integration.[24]

International relations theorists have long debated the relationship between economic interdependence and the prospects for conflict among states. Liberal theorists argue that interdependence decreases the incentives for conflict and war, in part because states become reluctant to disrupt or jeopardize the welfare benefits of open economic exchange, and in part because domestic interest groups with a stake in interdependence constrain the ability of the state to act autonomously. These arguments can be traced to Kant and nineteenth-century British liberals, and have been given recent expression by American IR scholars.[25] Realists counter that interdependence can just as easily inspire conflict by heightening the inequalities, insecurities, and vulnerabilities among states. This argument can be traced back to Rousseau, who argued that interdependence breeds "not accommodation and harmony, but suspicion and incompatibility."[26] Latter day realists have echoed and extended this basic sentiment.[27]

Several of the chapters engage this debate in an effort to contribute both to theory and to our understanding of the prospects for regional stability. Dale Copeland (ch. 10) steers between the stylized liberal and realist positions to suggest that it is not interdependence itself, but the expectations of future interdependence, that heighten the incentives for conflict or harmony. He revisits the conflict between Japan and the United States during the 1930s to show that Japan's diminished expectations for international economic benefit led it to view the option of war as more attractive. This logic is carried to the contemporary U.S.-China relationship, and Copeland suggests that China's propensity for international adventurism will be influenced by the extent to which it is reassured that positive economic relations with the United States will persist. Put differently, the peace-generating effects of interdependence are rather fragile. They depend not so much on the existence of interdependence, but on the necessarily subjective assessment by states of whether it will continue or diminish. Moreover, Copeland's assessment of the prospects for stability can be taken as optimistic only to the extent that one believes the U.S. executive can maintain, in the face of domestic and congressional pressures, a positive economic strategy with consistency over the long term.

As noted above, Gilpin's analysis of the contemporary U.S.-Japan relationship suggests a pessimistic assessment. Gilpin shows that these two powers are highly interdependent, but that their fundamentally incompatible domestic structures led to sustained conflict during the 1980s that threatened to spill over from the economic to the security arena. The conflict was muted during the 1990s, he suggests, by the combination of U.S. economic recovery and Japanese economic stagnation. But for Gilpin the structural incompatibility of "national styles of capitalism" is key. An economic downturn in the United States or a robust Japanese economic recovery can reignite the economic conflict of the

1980s, but without the buffering effect of the common external threat posed by the Soviet Union.

Jonathan Kirshner (ch. 8) suggests that monetary cooperation will be necessary in the interdependent Asia-Pacific, but will be especially difficult. The complexity of financial and currency markets make adherence to international monetary agreements difficult to monitor. Even if states are able to reach monetary agreements, those agreements are fragile because they require states to adopt domestically unpopular measures such as deflationary policies. Kirshner suggests that the natural conflicts generated by monetary interdependence can be mitigated by strong security ties. The United States and Japan can overcome the conflict generated in the monetary area if they treat China as a common security threat. But to do that, of course, suggests that monetary politics between the United States and China or Japan and China will remain a source of conflict. Additionally, trade policies may be a source of Chinese-Japanese tension, as each seeks to pursue its objectives in the region by cultivating the economic dependence of smaller states.

The chapters below suggest that interdependence also has the potential to foster instability at the domestic level, as states struggle both to extract benefits and to insulate themselves from the vagaries of global market forces. The conflict between state and market is especially intense in the Asia-Pacific because key countries in the region have embraced a development model that situates the state as a gatekeeper between the international economy and domestic society. As Berger shows, the "developmental" state not only facilitated the pursuit of export-led growth but also established a regulatory environment domestically that afforded protection to and encouraged long-term commitments among national firms and their workers. Economic interdependence and liberalization, especially in the financial sector, has undercut the ability of the state to maintain the social contract at home.

Several chapters explore various aspects of this dilemma with a sensitivity to the implications for international relations theory. Grimes demonstrates that Japan is ill-prepared to meet the challenges of the current international environment. During the cold war, its foreign policy was deferential to that of the United States and its export-led growth strategy placed a premium on bureaucratic management rather than political initiative. After the cold war and in the wake of liberalization, both dimensions of Japanese policy have been called into question. Japan faces economic stagnation at home and an uncertain foreign policy environment in its region, and its political system seems immobilized and incapable of providing leadership and initiative. For Grimes, Japan's response provides a test of "second image reversed" theories, which hold that international pressures will force structural changes in domestic politics.

Both Kirshner and Berger argue that contemporary market forces threaten state autonomy and have the potential to undermine state capacity. As Berger notes, the Asian financial crisis "throws into question the dominant model of state-society relations in the region." For Kirshner, the crisis poses a challenge to realist theories, which should expect states to re-assert control of the domestic economy and the ability of market forces to influence it. For Berger, the challenge for constructivism is to explain the origins and spread of the developmental model, and to isolate the changes in interest and identity that might lead to its demise.

Domestic responses to the expansion of interdependence have the potential to reinforce instability at the regional level. For example, the Asian financial crisis could pit the United States against other regional actors, either because U.S. officials are seen as imposing austerity on strapped Asian populations, or because Asian governments reassert strong controls over economic transactions in defiance of U.S. conceptions of international economic liberalism. Second, Berger points out that the developmental state led to an emphasis on economic performance rather than traditional geopolitical influence in state strategies. The withering or collapse of the developmental state reopens the question of whether Asian countries, Japan in particular, will aspire to normal power status.

CONCLUSION

The maintenance of economic and strategic stability in the Asia-Pacific region will require careful management. In the short term, that opportunity will continue to fall largely to the United States. Over the longer term, it remains to be seen whether U.S. or an alternate hegemony, a traditional balance of power system, a more institutionalized regional economic and security system, or some other mechanism will emerge as the principal guarantor of stability.

The chapters that follow also suggest that the more intense engagement of IR theorists and Asian area specialists will bring benefits to both. The focus on relations among Japan, China, and the United States, for example, generates for Christensen a more complicated appreciation of the security dilemma, and for Kang a conception of order not typically found in mainstream international relations theory. The benefits flow from theory to Asian practice as well: Johnston's reliance on socialization theory yields new insights about Chinese behavior, Kirshner's use of a realist framework anticipates novel patterns of regional economic cooperation and conflict, and Nau's combination of realism and constructivism suggests an alternative conception of the prospects for stability among the major Asian powers. Arguments in these and other chapters indicate that "Western" theoretical frameworks have much to say about international relations in Asia—but also that variables such as power distribution, hegemony, international regimes, interdependence, and political identity must be sufficiently context sensitive in order to capture the complexity of those relations.

The chapters that follow are organized according to whether their primary concern is regional strategic or economic stability. The chapters by Christensen, Goldstein, Johnston, Kang, Tamamoto, Nau, and Duffield analyze the prospects for stability in security relations. Kirshner, Gilpin, Copeland, Grimes, and Berger are primarily interested in regional economic stability and in the links between economic and security stability. The concluding chapter by Ikenberry and Mastanduno knits these concerns together and analyzes the special regional role of the United States.

ENDNOTES

1. Aaron Friedberg, "Ripe for Rivalry: Prospects for Peace in a Multipolar Asia." *International Security* 18, no. 3 (Winter 1993/94): 5–33.

2. Friedberg, "Ripe for Rivalry," p. 7.

3. Richard K. Betts, "Wealth, Power, and Instability: East Asia and the United States after the Cold War," *International Security* 18 (Winter 1993/94); Gerald Segal, "East Asia and the Constrainment of China," *International Security* 20, no. 4 (Spring 1996): 107–35; and Robert S. Ross, "The Geography of the Peace: East Asia in the Twenty-First Century," *International Security* 23, no. 4 (Spring 1999): 81–119.

4. Friedberg, "Ripe for Rivalry," p. 6.

5. See *U.S. Security Strategy for the East Asia-Pacific Region*, Office of International Security Affairs, U.S. Department of Defense, February 1995, and Joseph S. Nye, Jr., "The Case for Deep Engagement," *Foreign Affairs* 74, no. 4 (July–August 1995): 90–102. This view is echoed in the last Defense Department strategic report on East Asia of the 1990s, *The United States Security Strategy for the East Asia-Pacific Region* (Washington, D.C.: Department of Defense, 1998). For a recent reflection on the Nye Report, see Joseph S. Nye, "The 'Nye Report': Six Years Later," *International Relations of the Asia-Pacific* 1, no. 1: 95–103.

6. The thinking of the George W. Bush administration is signaled in the findings of the so-called Armitage Report, which reaffirms the importance of America's forward deployed security commitment to the region. See "The United States and Japan: Advancing Toward a Mature Partnership," *INSS Special Report*, October 11, 2000. See also Dennis C. Blair and John T. Hanley, Jr., "From Wheels to Webs: Reconstructing Asia-Pacific Security Arrangements," *The Washington Quarterly* 24: 7–17.

7. Robert Gilpin, *War and Change in World Politics* (New York: Cambridge University Press, 1981).

8. John Gerard Ruggie, "International Regimes, Transactions, and Change: Embedded Liberalism in the Postwar Economic Order," in Stephen Krasner, ed., *International Regimes* (Ithaca: Cornell University Press, 1983).

9. G. John Ikenberry, "Institutions, Strategic Restraint, and the Persistence of the American postwar Order," *International Security* (Winter 1998/99); and Ikenberry, *After Victory: Institutions, Strategic Restraint, and the Rebuilding of Order after Major War* (Princeton: Princeton University Press, 2001).

10. Geir Lundestad, *The American "Empire"* (New York: Oxford University Press, 1990).

11. For a contrasting view of American hegemony that emphasizes its exploitive and domineering character, see Chalmers Johnson, *Blowback: The Costs and Consequences of American Empire* (New York: Metropolitan Books, 2000).

12. A recent description of Bismark's grand strategy is Josef Joffe, "Bismarck or Britain? Toward an American Grand Strategy after Bipolarity," *International Security* 19, no. 4 (Spring 1995): 94–117.

13. For example, Walter LaFeber, *America, Russia, and the Cold War, 1945–1996* (Eighth edition, New York: McGraw Hill, 1997).

14. *Yomiuri Shimbun*, May 23, 1995.

15. Ian Buruma, *Wages of Guilt: Memories of War in Germany and Japan* (New York: Meridian, 1995).

16. A version of this argument is Joseph E. Grieco, "Realism and Regionalism: American Power and German and Japanese Institutional Strategies During and After the Cold War," in Ethan B. Kapstein and Michael Mastanduno, eds., *Unipolar Politics: Realism and State Strategies after the Cold War* (New York: Columbia University Press, 1999), pp. 319–353.

17. Robert Keohane, *After Hegemony* (Princeton: Princeton University Press, 1984).

18. Michael Doyle, "Kant, Liberal Legacies, and Foreign Affairs." *Philosophy and Public Affairs* 12, (1983): 205–235.

19. Samuel Huntington, *Political Order in Changing Societies* (New Haven: Yale University Press, 1968).

20. Berger, chapter 12 of this volume.

21. Daniel Deudney and G. John Ikenberry, "Realism, Structural Liberalism, and the Sources of Western Political Order," in Kapstein and Mastanduno, eds., *Unipolar Politics* (New York: Columbia University Press, 1999), pp. 113–137.

22. For example, Chalmers Johnson, "History Restarted: Japanese-American Relations at the End of the Century," in Johnson, *Japan: Who Governs? The Rise of the Developmental State* (New York: Norton, 1995).

23. C. Fred Bergsten and Marcus Noland, eds., *Pacific Dynamism and the International Economic System* (Washington, DC: Institute for International Economics, 1993).

24. Jeffrey A. Frankel, *Regional Trading Blocs in the World Economic System* (Washington, D.C.: Institute for International Economics, 1997).

25. Robert O. Keohane and Joseph Nye, *Power and Interdependence: World Politics in Transition* (Boston: Little, Brown, 1977); Richard Rosecrance, *The Rise of the Trading State* (New York: Basic Books, 1986).

26. Stanley Hoffmann, "Rousseau on War and Peace." *American Political Science Review* 57 (1963): 317–333.

27. Robert Gilpin, "Economic Interdependence and National Security in Historical Perspective," in Klaus Knorr and Frank Trager, eds., *Economic Issues and National Security* (Lawrence: University of Kansas Press, 1977).

PART I

Security, Identity, and Stability

Chapter 1

CHINA, THE U.S.-JAPAN ALLIANCE, AND THE SECURITY DILEMMA IN EAST ASIA

Thomas J. Christensen

Many scholars and analysts argue that in the twenty-first century international instability is more likely in East Asia than in Western Europe. Whether one looks at variables favored by realists or liberals, East Asia appears more dangerous. The region is characterized by major shifts in the balance of power, skewed distributions of economic and political power within and between countries, political and cultural heterogeneity, growing but still relatively low levels of intraregional economic interdependence, anemic security institutionalization, and widespread territorial disputes that combine natural resource issues with postcolonial nationalism.[1]

If security dilemma theory is applied to East Asia, the chance for spirals of tension in the area seems great, particularly in the absence of a U.S. military presence in the region. The theory states that, in an uncertain and anarchic international system, mistrust between two or more potential adversaries can lead each side to take precautionary and defensively motivated measures that are perceived as offensive threats. This can lead to countermeasures in kind, thus ratcheting up regional tensions, reducing security, and creating self-fulfilling prophecies about the danger of one's security environment.[2] If we look at the variables that might fuel security dilemma dynamics, East Asia appears quite dangerous. From a standard realist perspective, not only could dramatic and unpredictable changes in the distribution of capabilities in East Asia increase uncertainty and mistrust, but the importance of sea-lanes and secure energy supplies to almost all regional actors could also encourage a destabilizing competition to develop power-projection capabilities on the seas and in the skies. Because they are perceived as offensive threats, power-projection forces are more likely to spark spirals of tension than weapons that can defend only a nation's homeland.[3] Perhaps even more important in East Asia than these more commonly considered variables are psychological factors (such as the historically based mistrust and animosity among regional actors) and political geography issues relating to the Taiwan question, which make even defensive weapons in the region appear threatening to Chinese security.[4]

One way to ameliorate security dilemmas and prevent spirals of tension is to have an outside arbiter play a policing role, lessening the perceived need for regional actors to begin destabilizing security competitions. For this reason, most scholars, regardless of theoretical persuasion, seem to agree with U.S. officials and local leaders that a major factor in containing potential tensions in East Asia is the continuing presence of the U.S. military, particularly in Japan.[5] The historically based mistrust among the actors in Northeast Asia is so intense that not only is the maintenance of a U.S. presence in Japan critical, but the form the U.S.-Japan alliance takes also has potentially important implications for regional stability. In particular, the sensitivity in China to almost all changes in the cold war version of the U.S.-Japan alliance poses major challenges for leaders in Washington who want to shore up the alliance for the long haul by encouraging greater Japanese burden sharing, but still want the U.S. presence in Japan to be a force for reassurance in the region. To meet these somewhat contradictory goals, for the most part the United States wisely has encouraged Japan to adopt nonoffensive roles that should be relatively unthreatening to Japan's neighbors.

Certain aspects of U.S. policies, however, including joint research of theater missile defenses (TMD) with Japan, are still potentially problematic. According to security dilemma theory, defensive systems and missions, such as TMD, should not provoke arms races and spirals of tension. In contemporary East Asia, however, this logic is less applicable. Many in the region, particularly in Beijing, fear that new defensive roles for Japan could break important norms of self-restraint, leading to more comprehensive Japanese military buildups later. Moreover, Beijing's focus on preventing Taiwan's permanent separation from China means that even defensive weapons in the hands of Taiwan or its potential supporters are provocative to China. Given the bitter history of Japanese imperialism in China and Taiwan's status as a Japanese colony from 1895 to 1945, this certainly holds true for Japan.

In the first section of this article I describe why historical legacies and ethnic hatred exacerbate the security dilemma in Sino-Japanese relations. In the second section I examine Chinese assessments of Japan's actual and potential military power. In the third section I address how changes in the U.S.-Japan relationship in the post-cold war era affect Chinese security analysts' views of the likely timing and intensity of future Japanese military buildups. I argue that, for a combination of domestic and international reasons, the United States faces tough challenges in maintaining the U.S.-Japan alliance in a form that reassures both Japan and its neighbors. In the fourth section I discuss why certain aspects of recent efforts to bolster the alliance through Japanese commitments to new, nonoffensive burden-sharing roles are potentially more provocative than they may appear on the surface. In the fifth section I detail how China's attitudes about Japan affect the prospects for creating confidence-building measures and security regimes that might ameliorate the security dilemma over the longer term. In the sixth section I discuss the relevance of my analysis for U.S. foreign policy in the region and why, despite the problems outlined above, there are reasons for optimism if trilateral relations among the United States, China, and Japan are handled carefully in the next two decades.

WHY CHINA WOULD FEAR A STRONGER JAPAN

Chinese security analysts, particularly military officers, fear that within 25 years Japan could again become a great military power. Such a Japan, they believe, would likely be more independent of U.S. control and generally more assertive in international affairs. If one considers threats posed only by military power and not who is wielding that power, one might expect Beijing to welcome the reduction or even elimination of U.S. influence in Japan, even if this meant China would have a more powerful neighbor. After all, the United States is still by far the most powerful military actor in the Western Pacific.[6] However, given China's historically rooted and visceral distrust of Japan, Beijing would fear either a breakdown of the U.S.-Japan alliance or a significant upgrading of Japan's role within that alliance.[7] This sentiment is shared outside China as well, particularly in Korea. Although at present Chinese analysts fear U.S. power much more than Japanese power, in terms of national intentions, Chinese analysts view Japan with much less trust and, in many cases, with a loathing rarely found in their attitudes about the United States.

THE HISTORICAL LEGACY

Japan's refusal to respond satisfactorily to Chinese requests that Tokyo recognize and apologize for its imperial past—for example, by revising history textbooks in the public schools—has helped to preserve China's natural aversion to Japan.[8] Chinese sensibilities are also rankled by specific incidents, such as Prime Minister Ryutaro Hashimoto's 1996 visit to the Yasukuni Shrine, which commemorates Japan's war dead, including war criminals like Tojo.[9] Although some fear that

Japan's apparent amnesia or lack of contrition about the past means that Japan could return to the militarism (*junguozhuyi*) of the 1930s, such simple historical analogies are relatively rare, at least in Chinese elite foreign policy circles.[10]

Chinese analysts' concerns regarding Japanese historical legacies, although not entirely devoid of emotion, are usually more subtle. Many argue that, by downplaying atrocities like the Nanjing massacre and underscoring events like the atomic bombing of Hiroshima and Nagasaki, Japanese elites portray Japan falsely as the victim, rather than the victimizer, in World War II. Because of this, some Chinese analysts fear that younger generations of Japanese citizens may not understand Japan's history and will therefore be insensitive to the intense fears of other regional actors regarding Japanese military power. This lack of understanding will make them less resistant to relatively hawkish elites' plans to increase Japanese military power than their older compatriots, who, because they remember World War II, resisted military buildups during the cold war.[11]

Chinese analysts often compare Japan's failure to accept responsibility for World War II to the more liberal postwar record of Germany, which has franker discussions of the war in its textbooks, has apologized for its wartime aggression, and has even offered financial payments to Israel.[12] Now a new unflattering comparison is sure to arise. During their November 1998 summit in Tokyo, Prime Minister Keizo Obuchi refused to offer an apology to China's President Jiang Zemin that used the same contrite wording as the rather forthright apology Japan offered to South Korea earlier in the year. This divergence in apologies will probably only complicate the history issue between Tokyo and Beijing.[13]

It may seem odd to the outside observer, but the intensity of anti-Japanese sentiment in China has not decreased markedly as World War II becomes a more distant memory. There are several reasons in addition to those cited above. Nationalism has always been a strong element of the legitimacy of the Chinese Communist Party (CCP), and opposing Japanese imperialism is at the core of this nationalist story. As a result, Chinese citizens have been fed a steady diet of patriotic, anti-Japanese media programming designed to glorify the CCP's role in World War II. Although far removed from that era, most Chinese young people hold an intense and unapologetically negative view of both Japan and, in many cases, its people.[14] As economic competition has replaced military concerns in the minds of many Chinese, China's basic distrust of Japan has been transferred to the economic realm. Japanese businesspeople are often described as unreliable, selfish, and slimy (*youhua*). As a result, despite five decades of peace and a great deal of economic interaction, chances are small that new Japanese military development will be viewed with anything but the utmost suspicion in China.

Elite analysts are certainly not immune to these intense anti-Japanese feelings in Chinese society. These emotions, however, have not yet affected the practical, day-to-day management of Sino-Japanese relations. On the contrary, since the 1980s the Chinese government has acted to contain anti-Japanese sentiment in the society at large to avoid damaging bilateral relations and to prevent protestors from using anti-Japanese sentiment as a pretext for criticizing the Chinese government, as occurred several times in Chinese history.[15] But Chinese analysts' statements about the dangers that increased Japanese military power would pose in the future suggest that anti-Japanese sentiment does color their long-term threat assessments, even if it does not always alter their immediate policy prescriptions. Because they can influence procurement and strategy, such longer-term assessments may be more important in fueling the security dilemma than particular diplomatic policies in the present.

CHINESE ASSESSMENTS OF JAPANESE MILITARY POWER AND POTENTIAL

In assessing Japan's current military strength, Chinese analysts emphasize the advanced equipment that Japan has acquired, particularly since the late 1970s, when it began developing a navy and air force designed to help the United States contain the Soviet Union's growing Pacific Fleet. Chinese military writings highlight Japanese antisubmarine capabilities (such as the P-3C aircraft), advanced fighters (such as the F-15), the E-2 advanced warning aircraft, Patriot air defense batteries, and Aegis technology on surface ships.[16] Chinese analysts correctly point out that, excluding U.S. deployments in the region, these weapons systems constitute the most technologically advanced arsenal of any East Asian power. They also cite the Japanese defense budget, which, although small as a percentage of gross national product (GNP), is second only to U.S. military spending in absolute size.[17]

Despite their highlighting of Japan's current defense budget and high levels of military sophistication, Chinese analysts understand that Japan can easily do much more militarily than it does. While they generally do not believe that Japan has the requisite combination of material capabilities, political will, and ideological mission to become a Soviet-style superpower, they do believe that Japan could easily become a great military power (such as France or Great Britain) in the next twenty-five years. For example, although these analysts often argue that it is in Japan's economic interest to continue to rely on U.S. military protection in the near future, they do not think that significantly increased military spending would strongly damage the Japanese economy.[18] They have also been quite suspicious about the massive stockpiles of high-grade nuclear fuel that was reprocessed in France and shipped back to Japan in the early 1990s. Many in China view Japan's acquisition of this plutonium as part of a strategy for the eventual development of nuclear weapons, something, they point out, Japanese scientists would have little difficulty producing.[19] Chinese security analysts also have stated that Japan can become a great military power even if it forgoes the domestically sensitive nuclear option. Chinese military and civilian experts emphasize that nuclear weapons may not be as useful in the future as high-tech conventional weapons, and that Japan is already a leader in dual-use high technology.[20]

In particular, Chinese experts recognize that Japan has practiced a great deal of self-restraint in eschewing weapons designed to project power far from the home islands. For example, in 1996 one military officer stated that despite the long list of current Japanese capabilities mentioned above, Japan certainly is not yet a normal great power because it lacks the required trappings of such a power (e.g., aircraft carriers, nuclear submarines, nuclear weapons, and long-range missile systems).[21] For this officer and many of his compatriots, the question is simply if and when Japan will decide to adopt these systems. For this reason, Chinese analysts often view Japan's adoption of even new defensive military roles as dangerous because it may begin to erode the constitutional (Article 9) and nonconstitutional norms of self-restraint (e.g., 1,000-nautical-mile limit on power-projection capability, prohibitions on the military use of space, and tight arms export controls) that have prevented Japan from realizing its military potential.

Interestingly, many Chinese analysts do not consider economic hard times in Japan to be particularly reassuring. On the contrary, in terms of intentions, some fear that economic recession and financial crises could improve the fortunes of relatively hawkish Japanese elites by creating a general sense of uncertainty and threat in Japanese society, by fueling Japanese nationalism more generally, and by harming relations with the United States (Japan's main provider of security). In terms of capabilities, some Chinese analysts argue that Japan's technological infrastructure, which would be critical to a modern military buildup, does not seem affected by Japan's recent economic woes.[22]

FACTORS THAT WOULD ENCOURAGE OR PREVENT JAPANESE MILITARY BUILDUPS

Although almost all Chinese analysts would fear the result, they have differed in their assessment of the likelihood that Japan will attempt to realize its military potential in the next few decades. The more pessimistic analysts have argued that this outcome is extremely likely or even inevitable. Their views are consistent with the predictions of balance-of-power theories, but they do not agree with the analysis of some Western experts on Japan who believe that cultural pacifism after World War II, domestic political constraints, and economic interests will steer Japan away from pursuing such a strategy.[23] Even the more pessimistic Chinese analysts are aware of these arguments about Japanese restraint and do not dismiss them out of hand, but some view such obstacles to Japanese military buildups merely as delaying factors in a long-term and inevitable process. Other more conditionally pessimistic and cautiously optimistic analysts place greater faith in the hypothetical possibility of preventing significant Japanese buildups over the longer run, but have expressed concern over the hardiness of the delaying factors that could theoretically prevent such buildups. The most optimistic analysts have argued that these factors should remain sturdy and will prevent Japan from injuring its regional relations by pursuing a more assertive military role.[24]

The vast majority of these optimists and pessimists believe that, along with the domestic political and economic stability of Japan, the most important factor that might delay or prevent Japanese military buildups is the status of the U.S.-Japan relationship, particularly the security alliance.[25] The common belief in Beijing security circles is that, by reassuring Japan and providing for Japanese security on the cheap, the United States fosters a political climate in which the Japanese public remains opposed to military buildups and the more hawkish elements of the Japanese elite are kept at bay. If, however, the U.S.-Japan security alliance either becomes strained or undergoes a transformation that gives Japan a much more prominent military role, Chinese experts believe that those ever-present hawks might find a more fertile field in which to plant the seeds of militarization.[26]

THE CHINA-JAPAN SECURITY DILEMMA AND U.S. POLICY CHALLENGES

For the reasons offered above, most Chinese analysts fear almost any change in the U.S.-Japan alliance. A breakdown of U.S.-Japan ties would worry pessimists and optimists alike. On the other hand, Chinese analysts of all stripes also worry to varying degrees when Japan adopts greater defense burden-sharing roles as part of a bilateral effort to revitalize the alliance. These dual and almost contradictory fears pose major problems for U.S. elites who, while concerned that the alliance is dangerously vague and out of date and therefore unsustainable, still want the United States to maintain the reassurance role outlined in documents such as the 1998 East Asia-Pacific Strategy Report.[27] Especially before the recent guidelines review, the U.S.-Japan alliance had often been viewed in the United States as lopsided and unfair because the United States guarantees Japanese security without clear guarantees of even rudimentary assistance from Japan if U.S. forces were to become embroiled in a regional armed conflict.[28]

Before 1995 some U.S. elites argued that the alliance was overrated and that it had prevented the United States from pursuing its economic interests in the U.S.-Japan relationship. Some even argued that the United States should use the security relationship as leverage against Japan in an attempt to open Japanese trade and financial markets to American firms.[29] In this view Japan had been able to ride free for too long on the U.S. economy because of Washington's concern over preserving an apparently unfair alliance relationship.

Since the publication of the critically important February 1995 East Asia Strategy Report (also known as the Nye report), U.S. leaders have been expressing very different concerns about the U.S.-Japan relationship. The Nye report, and the broader Nye initiative of which it is a part, placed new emphasis on maintaining and strengthening the security alliance and on keeping economic disputes from poisoning it. The report reaffirms the centrality of U.S. security alliances in Asia, places a floor on U.S. troop strength in East Asia at 100,000, and calls for increased security cooperation between Japan and the United States, including greater Japanese logistics support for U.S. forces operating in the region and consideration of joint research on TMD.[30]

Despite the Clinton administration's decision to insulate the U.S.-Japan security relationship from economic disputes, there has been a widely held concern that, purely on security grounds, the alliance could be dangerously weakened if Japanese roles are not clarified and expanded and if the two militaries are not better integrated in preparation for joint operations.[31] Japan's checkbook diplomacy in the Gulf War was considered insufficient support for U.S.-led efforts to protect a region that supplies Japan, not the United States, with the bulk of its oil. It also became clear during the 1994 crisis with Pyongyang over North Korea's nuclear weapons development that, under the existing defense guidelines, in a Korean conflict scenario Japan was not even obliged to allow the U.S. military use of its civilian airstrips or ports. In fact, if the crisis had escalated, Japan might not have provided overt, tangible support of any kind. Even U.S. access to its bases in Japan for combat operations not directly tied to the defense of the Japanese home islands was questionable.[32] Aside from the obvious military dangers inherent in such Japanese passivity, Japanese obstructionism and foot-dragging could undermine elite and popular support in the United States for the most important security relationship in East Asia. It appeared to many American elites that the cold war version of the U.S.-Japan alliance could be one regional crisis away from its demise. Such concernsdrove the Nye initiative, which was designed to clarify and strengthen Japan's commitment to support U.S.-led military operations. Fearing instability in Japanese elite and popular attitudes on defense issues, Washington also wanted to increase the number of functional links between the two militaries to tie Japan more firmly into the U.S. defense network for the long run.[33]

Chinese security analysts followed these trends in U.S.-Japan relations with great interest and concern. Before 1995 most pessimistic Chinese analysts predicted and feared Japanese military buildups largely because they sensed the potential for trouble, not strengthening, in the post–cold war U.S.-Japan alliance. Those analysts posited that, given the lack of a common enemy and the natural clash of economic interests between Japan and the United States, political conflict between the two allies was very likely. This conflict could eventually infect and destroy the U.S.-Japan security relationship, which in turn could lead to the withdrawal of U.S. forces and eventually Japanese military buildups. In this period some Chinese analysts also discussed how domestic factors such as U.S. neo-isolationism, rising Japanese nationalism, the inexperience and lack of security focus in the newly elected Clinton administration, and domestic instability in Japan could combine with worsening U.S.-Japan trade conflicts to speed the alliance's demise.[34]

By mid-1995 it seemed to an increasingly large group of Chinese analysts that U.S.-Japan trade conflict was being contained and that the Clinton administration was paying more attention to international security affairs and to Asia in particular.[35] Key contributors to this growing confidence in U.S. staying power were the Nye report and the failure of the automobile parts dispute between Tokyo and Washington to escalate.

The news for China was not all good, however. By spring 1996 the Nye initiative had led to harsh reactions in China, exposing the subtle challenges facing the United States in managing the U.S.-China-Japan triangle. China's cautious optimism about trends in the U.S.-Japan alliance turned to pessimism, as concerns about future Japanese military assertiveness grew rapidly. But the new reasons for pessimism were quite different than in the period before 1995. The fear was no longer potential discord in the U.S.-Japan relationship, but concern that the United States would encourage Japan to adopt new military roles and develop new military capabilities as part of a revitalized alliance in which Japan carried a greater share of the burden and risk.[36]

On April 17, 1996, President Clinton and Prime Minister Hashimoto issued a joint communiqué that called for revitalization of the alliance to better guarantee the "Asia-Pacific region." In the communiqué and in the guarantees reached in the days preceding it, Japan guaranteed base access for U.S. forces and committed itself to increased logistics and rear-area support roles. The two sides also agreed to cooperate in the "ongoing study" of ballistic missile defense.

The joint communiqué was issued one month after the most intense phase of the 1995–96 Taiwan Strait crisis, during which the United States deployed two aircraft carrier battle groups, including one based in Japan, off of Taiwan. The crisis and the joint communiqué triggered fears among Chinese experts about U.S. use of Japanese bases in future Taiwan scenarios. It also suggested that Japan might soon begin scrapping various norms of self-restraint and begin expanding its military operations into the Taiwan area and the South China Sea. In addition to focusing on new logistics roles for Japan and the potential for future joint development of missile defenses, Chinese observers believed that the joint communiqué expanded the geographic scope of the alliance from the area immediately around Japan to a vaguely defined, but clearly much larger, "Asia Pacific."[37] As one leading Chinese expert on Japan recently argued, the

U.S. presence in Japan can be seen either as a "bottle cap," keeping the Japanese military genie in the bottle, or as an "egg shell," fostering the growth of Japanese military power under U.S. protection until it one day hatches onto the regional scene. Since 1996, this analyst argues, fears about the "egg shell" function of the U.S.-Japan alliance have increased markedly, while faith in the "bottle cap" function has declined.[38]

In September 1997 Chinese analysts' concerns turned to the announcement of revised defense guidelines for the U.S.-Japan alliance. These guidelines put in writing many of the changes suggested in the joint communiqué. New and clarified Japanese roles in the alliance included those logistics and rear-area support roles mentioned in the joint communiqué and added "operational cooperation" missions for Japan's Self-Defense Forces in time of regional conflict, including intelligence gathering, surveillance, and minesweeping missions. Although Washington and Tokyo quickly abandoned the provocative term "Asia Pacific" following the issuance of the joint communiqué, the 1997 guidelines are not entirely reassuring on this score either. They state that the scope of the alliance covers "situations in the areas surrounding Japan," but that the definition of those areas would be determined by "situational" rather than "geographic" imperatives. This only confirmed conspiracy theories among Beijing elites regarding the potential inclusion of Taiwan and the South China Sea in the alliance's scope.[39] Following the issuance of the revised guidelines, Jiang Zemin announced that China was now on "high alert" about changes in the alliance.[40]

Chinese analysts view aspects of both the joint communiqué and the revised guidelines as troubling in the near term, mainly because they can facilitate U.S. intervention in a Taiwan contingency. They believe that the United States is currently largely in control of the U.S.-Japan alliance's military policy. But they view Japan as having both stronger emotional and practical reasons than the United States for opposing Taiwan's reintegration with the mainland and a greater stake than the United States in issues such as sea-lane protection far from the Japanese home islands.[41] More pessimistic Chinese analysts often state that Japan's material interests have not changed much from the 1930s to the present. They believe that, because Japan is still heavily dependent on foreign trade and investment, it could again choose to develop power-projection capabilities designed to protect its economic interests in the distant abroad. Vigilant about this possibility, Chinese analysts have reacted negatively to even mild new Japanese initiatives away from the home islands (such as sending peacekeepers to Cambodia or minesweepers to the Persian Gulf after the Gulf War).[42]

In 1998 Chinese concerns focused on Japan's September agreement to research theater missile defense jointly with the United States. The initial proposal for joint development of TMD was made by Washington in 1993, long before the Nye initiative had been launched. It was later folded into the initiative, but Japan still seemed reluctant to commit itself to the project.[43] After five years of U.S. coaxing and Japanese foot-dragging, Tokyo finally agreed to joint TMD research after the launch of a North Korean rocket across Japanese territory on August 31, 1998. Although Chinese analysts do recognize the threat to Japan from North Korea, they still believe that development of U.S.-Japan TMD is also designed to counter China's missile capabilities, which the People's Liberation Army (PLA) and civilian analysts recognize as China's most effective military asset, especially in relations with Taiwan.[44]

TAIWAN, THE U.S.-JAPAN ALLIANCE, AND THE OFFENSE-DEFENSE FACTOR

The importance of the Taiwan issue in Chinese calculations about TMD and the revised guidelines cannot be overstated and, along with the brutal legacy of World War II, is perhaps the most critical exacerbating factor in the China-Japan security dilemma. The nature of the cross-strait conflict is such that the usual argument about the offense-defense balance and the security dilemma applies poorly. That argument, simply stated, is that the buildup of defensive weapons and the adoption of defensive doctrines should not fuel the security dilemma and spirals of tension because such capabilities and methods are not useful for aggression.[45] Defensive weapons are stabilizing because they shore up the territorial status quo by deterring or physically preventing aggressors from achieving revisionist goals, whereas offensive weapons are destabilizing because they threaten that status quo.[46]

What makes offense-defense theories less applicable in the China case is that Beijing's main security goal is to prevent Taiwan from declaring permanent independence from the Chinese nation, a de facto territorial condition that Taiwan already enjoys. In other words, the main threat to China is a political change in cross-strait relations that would legalize and freeze the territorial status quo. China's main method of countering that threat is a combination of military and economic coercion. In cross-strait relations Beijing considers traditionally defensive weapons in the hands of Taiwan and any of its potential allies to be dangerous, because they may give Taiwan officials additional confidence in their efforts to legitimate the territorial status quo. In fact, given that China seems willing to risk extreme costs to deter Taiwanese independence, and, if necessary, to compel a reversal of any such decision by the Taipei authorities, and that Taiwan has fully abandoned Chiang Kai-shek's irredentist designs on the mainland, Taiwan's ability to attack the mainland, strangely, may be no more worrisome to China than Taiwan's ability to fend off the mainland's attacks on Taiwan.[47]

Given the Chinese concerns over Taiwan, future U.S. and Japanese TMD, if effective, and if transferred in peacetime or put at the service of Taiwan in a crisis, could reduce China's ability to threaten the island with ballistic missile attack, the PLA's main means of coercing Taiwan. Particularly relevant here are the ship-based systems that Japan and the United States agreed to research jointly in September 1998. China worries for the same reason that most Americans support the choice of a ship-based TMD system.[48] As one U.S. commentator applauds, ship-based systems "can be moved quickly to other regions to support out-of-area conflicts."[49] The "upper-tier" navy theater-wide system, which the United States has proposed for the future, would not only be highly mobile, but because it was originally conceived to provide wide area defense for geographically large U.S. military deployments, would, if effective, also have a "footprint" that could cover the island of Taiwan. Chinese arms control and missile experts note this possibility with some concern.[50] Like their U.S. and Japanese counterparts, Chinese analysts have serious doubts about the likely effectiveness of such a system, particularly given the proximity of Taiwan to the mainland and the ability of China to launch a large number and variety of missiles. Nevertheless, they still worry about the psychological and political impact the system could have on Taipei's attitudes about seeking more diplomatic space and on U.S. and Japanese attitudes about cross-strait relations.[51]

When complaining about how specific aspects of recent changes in the U.S.-Japan alliance might influence cross-strait relations, Chinese analysts tend to focus on the potential problems of a future U.S.-Japan TMD system rather than on the less dramatic operational support roles specified for existing Japanese Self-Defense Forces in the revised guidelines (i.e., intelligence gathering, surveillance, and minesweeping). Chinese analysts' concerns about the joint communiqué and the revised guidelines tend to be more abstract, focusing on the fuzzy "situational" scope of the alliance or the possible erosion of Japanese norms of self-restraint in military affairs. However, although it appears unlikely that they would be deployed near Taiwan in a crisis, the systems of the Japanese Self-Defense Forces mentioned in the revised guidelines also could prove helpful to Taiwan. In particular, if Japan ever decided to deploy minesweepers there, this would have the potential to reduce the PLA's ability to coerce Taiwan in a cross-strait crisis or conflict by playing the purely defensive role of helping to break a real or threatened PLA blockade on shipping. For these reasons, the apparently mild operational support roles Japan agreed to in the revised guidelines may also contribute to Beijing's hostile reaction to recent trends in the U.S.-Japan alliance.[52]

U.S.-JAPAN ALLIANCE TRENDS AND POTENTIAL CRISIS-MANAGEMENT PROBLEMS

If the United States and Japan eventually decide to move from joint research and development to deployment of ship-based U.S. and Japanese TMD systems (at least several years from now), Japan would have the capability to involve itself in a cross-strait crisis in a meaningful way, even if it had no intention to do so when acquiring the system. Under such circumstances, in a future Taiwan Strait crisis involving the United States (short of a shooting war), U.S. leaders would be tempted to ask for Japanese assistance in missile defense near Taiwan in preparation for potential PLA attacks. The United States then might place Japan in the difficult position of choosing whether to help the United States in a Taiwan crisis. Such a decision by U.S. leaders would be most likely to occur if they believed that defensive Japanese roles would not be overly provocative to China.

There may be no positive outcome from such a request. If Japan chose not to help the United States in such a purely defensive role, especially if that refusal placed U.S. forces at added risk, this would have severely negative implications for the U.S.-Japan alliance. But, if Japan chose to help, the results could be worse still. Given the anti-Japanese sentiments in Chinese elite circles and popular culture, Japan's direct involvement in any form in a cross-strait crisis short of a shooting war could have a particularly detrimental impact on crisis management. Although U.S. intervention in such a crisis would be quite provocative to China in and of itself, it is safe to assume that Japanese intervention would be even more likely to lead to escalation.[53] Even if the crisis did not escalate, any hope of building a stable, long-term China-Japan security relationship could be lost. The ability of the United States and China to recover from such a standoff would likely be greater than the ability of China and Japan to do so.[54]

Although missiles are the PLA's likely weapons of choice in a cross-strait conflict or coercion campaign, it is at least imaginable that Beijing could choose less aggressive tactics than missile attacks (such as real or threatened mining of ports or shipping lanes in and around Taiwan) to deter or reverse Taiwan's diplomatic adventurism.[55] A lower-level coercive strategy may be more attractive in certain instances, particularly if Taiwan's alleged violation of Beijing's prohibitions were much less clear-cut than an outright declaration of independence.[56]

The new plans for operational cooperation in the revised guidelines were almost certainly created with Korean scenarios, not Taiwan, in mind. And for several reasons, they seem much less likely to play into a Taiwan Strait crisis scenario than would a future Japanese ship-based TMD capability. But, for theoretical purposes, it is worth considering how such Japanese missions could affect a future Taiwan crisis to demonstrate how misapplied logic about offensive and defensive weapons could lead to avoidable escalation in the Taiwan Strait context.

From Taiwan's perspective, the mere threat of mine-laying would require extensive sweeping to reassure both shipping interests and military commanders.[57] In such circumstances, if for military or political reasons the United States decided that Taiwan's own minesweeping equipment should be supplemented with ships from the U.S.-Japan alliance, future U.S. decisionmakers might be tempted for either military or political reasons to ask Japan to send minesweepers to assist in such an operation. On the military side, current U.S. minesweeping capabilities, particularly those in the theater, are weak, which might make Japanese assistance look attractive (the Seventh Fleet usually has only two minesweepers at the ready in the Pacific).[58] On the political side, if the potentially provocative nature of defensive missions, especially Japanese ones, is not fully appreciated, then U.S. leaders might request Japanese support as a high-profile demonstration of burden sharing. As in the TMD scenario, Japan would then be put into the difficult position of either sending Japanese ships to the front lines of a Taiwan crisis, thus greatly increasing the risk of escalation (less likely), or risking severe damage to the U.S.-Japan alliance by refusing to play an even purely defensive role (more likely).[59]

CHINESE ATTITUDES AND THE PROSPECTS FOR REGIONAL CONFIDENCE BUILDING

An important prerequisite for resolving a security dilemma is for the actors involved to recognize that one exists. A core factor that underpins the security dilemma is the general lack of empathy among the actors participating in a security competition. Beijing elites may be no better or worse than their counterparts in most other nations on this score. Although they may not use the technical term "security dilemma," Chinese analysts recognize the potential for arms racing and spirals of tension in the region. They even recognize that Japan might build its military out of fear, rather than aggression. China actually supported Japanese buildups in the 1970s and early 1980s in response to the development of the Soviet navy.[60] In 1994 several analysts argued that China did not want North Korea to have nuclear weapons because this might cause Japan to develop them.[61]

Beijing also has demonstrated an ability to understand that others might see China as a threat.[62] But, while many Chinese analysts can imagine some states as legitimately worried about China and can picture Japan legitimately worried about other states, it is harder to find those who believe that Japan's military security policy could be driven by fears about specific security policies in China.[63] Chinese analysts, especially in the past two years, seem to agree that China's overall rise (*jueqi*) is a general source of concern for Japan. They tend not to recognize, however, that particular Chinese actions or weapons developments might be reason for Japan to reconsider aspects of its defense policy. For example, when asked about concerns expressed by Japanese officials about Chinese weapons developments (such as the increased numbers and improved accuracy of Chinese missiles) or provocative Chinese international behavior (such as missile firings near Taiwan or bullying of the Philippines over the Mischief Reef), Chinese analysts generally dismiss these expressions as "excuses" (*jiekou*) designed to facilitate Japanese hawks' predetermined plans for military buildups. As the work of Western experts on Japanese security policy demonstrates, these Chinese analysts are very wrong to hold this belief.[64] If such views continue to prevail in Beijing, China is unlikely to take actions to reassure Japan in either bilateral or multilateral agreements.

A different and even more troubling Chinese perspective on China's potential influence on Japanese defense policy has also gained frequency in the past two years. Perhaps because of the relatively high economic growth rates in China compared to Japan in the 1990s, some Chinese experts have expressed more confidence that China would be able to defend its security interests against Japan, even in the absence of a U.S. presence in the region. Although they hardly dismiss the potential threat of a Japan made more assertive by a U.S. withdrawal, they seem relatively confident that China's strength and deterrent capabilities could influence Japan's strategy by dissuading Tokyo from significant Japanese buildups or, at least, later military adventurism.[65] From the security dilemma perspective this attitude may be even more dangerous than the view that China can pose little threat to Japan. If increasing Chinese coercive capacity is seen as the best way to prevent or manage anticipated Japanese buildups, then the danger of China taking the critical first step in an action-reaction cycle seems very high.

There are some more hopeful signs, however. Some Chinese analysts, usually younger experts (appearing to be in their forties or younger), with extensive experience abroad, do recognize that Chinese military strengthening and provocative actions could be seen as legitimate reasons for Japan to launch a military buildup of its own. Given the age of these analysts and the increasing number of Chinese elites with considerable experience abroad, the trends seem to be heading in a positive direction on this score. On a sober note, more than one of these empathetic experts has pointed out that Chinese experts who take Japanese concerns about China seriously are often viewed with suspicion in government circles and sometimes have difficulty when presenting their views to their older and more influential colleagues, particularly in the military.[66]

CHINA'S VIEWS ON MULTILATERAL SECURITY REGIMES

One possible way to ameliorate the security dilemma is through multilateral regimes and forums designed to increase transparency and build confidence. For various reasons, Beijing has viewed multilateral confidence building with some suspicion. Many Chinese analysts emphasize that the increased transparency called for by such institutions can make China's enemies more confident and thereby reduce China's deterrent capabilities, particularly its ability to deter Taiwan independence or foreign intervention in cross-strait relations.[67] Especially in the early 1990s they worried that multilateral forums and organizations might be fronts for great powers, and that confidence-building measures might be aspects of a containment strategy designed to keep China from achieving great power status in the military sector.[68]

That said, China has not shunned multilateral forums. China has participated in the ASEAN Regional Forum (ARF) since its first meeting in 1994, and in 1997 Beijing hosted an ARF intersessional conference on confidence-building measures. Although Beijing has prevented any dramatic accomplishments at ARF meetings on important questions such as the territorial disputes in the South China Sea, the precedent of such Chinese participation seems potentially important.[69] As Iain Johnston and Paul Evans argue, although still in their nascent phases, these developments should not be dismissed as mere rhetoric or showmanship. China is capable of participating in meaningful multilateral accords, as is demonstrated by its recent agreements on border demarcation and confidence-building measures struck with Russia and the former Soviet republics in Turkish Central Asia. Moreover, there is in Beijing a small but growing community of true believers in the benefits of arms control, confidence-building measures, and multilateralism more generally.[70]

The reduced fear of U.S. domination of the Association of Southeast Asian Nations (ASEAN) and of ASEAN collusion against China, combined with the increased fear of developments in U.S. bilateral diplomacy in the Asia Pacific since 1996, have convinced many formerly skeptical analysts that some form of multilateralism may be the best alternative for China given the risks posed by U.S. bilateral business as usual.[71] Given that China both fears and has little influence over various aspects of current U.S. bilateral diplomacy (such as strengthening the U.S.-Japan alliance or the U.S.-Australia alliance), accepting a bigger role for multilateral dialogue, if not the creation of formal multilateral security institutions, may be the least unpleasant method of reducing the threat that U.S. bilateralism poses.[72] So, in this one sense, the revitalization of the U.S.-Japan alliance may have had some unintended positive results by encouraging China to consider more seriously the benefits of multilateral forums that might reduce mutual mistrust in the region.[73] This phenomenon runs counter to psychological and social constructivist theories on the security dilemma that emphasize how accommodation, not pressure, is the best way to make states adopt more cooperative postures.[74]

The acceptance of formal multilateral dialogue has not spread from Southeast Asia to Northeast Asia because of mistrust between China and Japan, and between the two Koreas. But there are some fledgling signs of hope. In January 1998 Beijing agreed to trilateral track-II security talks with the United States and Japan. However, Chinese analysts have argued that the time is not yet right for a formal trilateral security forum given the tensions over the revised U.S.-Japan defense guidelines and the TMD issue, the lack of basic trust between China and Japan, and the fear that China would be isolated in a two-against-one format in which it engaged the U.S.-Japan alliance as a corporate entity.[75] One should not rule out the possibility of official trilateral talks over the longer term, however. If Beijing is sufficiently concerned about U.S. transfer or codevelopment of TMD with regional actors, it might agree to official trilateral dialogue with the United States and Japan to try to head off such an outcome.

U.S. POLICY OPTIONS IN THE U.S.-CHINA-JAPAN SECURITY TRIANGLE

Given the central role that the status of the U.S.-Japan alliance plays in both pessimistic and optimistic Chinese scenarios for Japan's future, there is little doubt that maintaining the U.S. presence in Japan is critical to countering the security dilemma in East Asia. If a Japanese commitment to a more active role in the alliance is essential to the survival of the alliance over the long haul, then some adjustments are necessary, regardless of Chinese reaction. In fact, given how pessimistic Chinese analysts would likely be if the alliance were to dissolve fully, they should understand that the Nye initiative is much better for China than U.S. policies before 1995 that encouraged drift in the alliance and lack of confidence in the U.S. security commitment in East Asia.

Certain new Japanese responsibilities in the alliance seem to have high payoffs in terms of U.S.-Japan alliance stability with few costs in terms of sharpening the China-Japan security dilemma. Increased Japanese logistics roles and guaranteed base access in time of conflict, both relatively nonprovocative measures for Japan's neighbors, should remedy some of the disasters U.S. officials predicted when they evaluated the alliance during the 1994 North Korean nuclear crisis. Japan's general commitment to participate in certain military support functions, such as minesweeping and surveillance, also seems like a good idea, as long as the United States does not become overly reliant on Japanese assistance in this area. For political reasons, it would seem wise for the United States to establish and maintain sufficient capabilities of its own so that it could pick and choose when to request Japanese assistance. In a cross-strait crisis, the United States would likely want to minimize Japanese participation and forgo it entirely at the front. In addition to the reasons offered above, if China's actions inadvertently brought about Japanese intervention, given Japan's reputation throughout the region, Tokyo's involvement could be exploited domestically and internationally by Beijing elites in ways that Saddam Hussein might have capitalized on an Israeli intervention during the 1990–91 Gulf crisis and Gulf War. Washington was able to forgo Israeli assistance because the United States and its allies could secure military dominance without Israeli help.

One unwise way for Japan and the United States to try to reassure China would be to exclude Taiwan explicitly from the scope of the U.S.-Japan alliance. China has pressed Japan and the United States to do this. Both have refused because neither wants to encourage irredentism by the People's Republic against Taiwan by excluding in advance the possibility that they would come to Taiwan's defense if the mainland attacked Taiwan without provocation. This is almost certainly a major reason why the scope of the alliance in the revised defense guidelines refers to "situational" rather than "geographic" conditions. Despite considerable Chinese pressure, Japan has not even agreed to parrot President Clinton's "three no's" policy, declaring only that Tokyo does not support Taiwan's legal independence. But, even if Tokyo did state the other two "no's," this would not be the same as excluding Taiwan from the scope of the U.S.-Japan alliance, which would be a radical, and I believe, potentially destabilizing policy position.[76]

A better way to reassure China without totally abandoning Taiwan or the notion of missile defenses in Japan would be for the United States to consider developing TMD without Japanese assistance. In 1998 Chinese analysts consistently pointed out that U.S.-Japan coproduction of TMD carries a fundamentally different and more provocative political meaning for China than if the United States produced such systems without Japanese help as part of its global strategy to protect U.S. troops deployed abroad. Despite the North Korean threat to Japan, U.S.-Japan codevelopment of TMD in Asia still seems primarily designed to counter China. Codevelopment with Japan also triggers many fears in Beijing about the fostering of future Japanese power that U.S. development of TMD without Japanese assistance would not.[77] For example, following the North Korean missile launch across Japan, which solidified Tokyo's decision to pursue TMD research, Tokyo announced plans to develop an independent spy satellite capability to observe foreign missile activity. If implemented this plan will weaken the effectiveness of, and may even contravene, Diet resolutions prohibiting the use of space for military purposes, an important restraint on future Japanese military power. Like TMD development, the satellite decision suggests the possibility of a more independent and unfettered Japanese military establishment for the future.[78] Chinese analysts also point out that mobile Japanese TMD could provide a "shield" for the "sword" of more offensive Japanese forces and, if extremely effective, it may also be able to protect the Japanese home islands from Chinese missile retaliation, thus reducing Chinese defensive and deterrent capabilities and blurring the political distinction between offensive and defensive weapons.[79] Finally, agreeing with the literature on the technical indistinguishability of offensive and defensive systems, some Chinese analysts argue that Japan can adapt some of the technology involved in TMD for offensive purposes.[80]

American TMD development is part of a global strategy designed to protect U.S. forces and U.S. bases, which are threatened by the increasing quantity and accuracy of missiles in the hands of potential adversaries around the world.[81] As such, American TMD should not be bargained away in negotiations with any particular state or group of states. Decisions on American TMD should be based solely on difficult questions related to the potential effectiveness of the system against enemy missiles, the relative cost to potential adversaries of developing methods that can defeat the system, and the opportunity costs of developing TMD systems in the defense budget.

But decisions about whether the United States should develop and eventually deploy the system alone or with other countries (and with whom) should be left open for consideration and perhaps for negotiation. This should hold true especially in areas like Northeast Asia, where geography and technology might allow potential adversaries to develop cheap and potentially provocative countermeasures against such systems. If the United States and Japan were willing to reconsider joint development of TMD, they might be able to exploit Chinese concerns to encourage Beijing to participate in a formal trilateral security dialogue and to begin to consider a bit more transparency in its murky military sector. Moreover, Japan and the United States may be able to gain more active participation from Beijing in discouraging further North Korean development of missiles and weapons of mass destruction. Given that Tokyo seemed at best only vaguely committed to joint development of TMD until the August 1998 North Korean rocket launch, such a security payoff, if deliverable by Beijing, might be sufficient to convince Japan to rely on U.S. advancements in TMD technology and to wait for eventual deployment of the systems to U.S. bases in Japan.[82] Such an outcome, arguably, would also have a positive effect on U.S.-Japan alliance longevity, because Japan would have added incentive to allow the U.S. navy to remain in Japanese ports for the long run.

In addition to lowering China's more general concerns about Japan, the United States could benefit in other ways from developing TMD without Japanese collaboration and from developing more organic capabilities for the Seventh Fleet. The United States would be better able to avoid scenarios in which it might be tempted to request Japanese support in these areas in time of crisis or war. Japanese agreement to supply such support in many instances cannot be assumed. Moreover, by maintaining a minimum dependence on Japanese capabilities, the United States would be better able to pick and choose when Japan's participation in a conflict would do more political harm than military good.

Of course, my prescriptions about TMD and other U.S. naval capabilities carry costs. If the United States develops TMD without Japan, for example, it will have to forgo Japanese technology and Japanese money. I am not in a position to analyze the importance of the former, but on the latter score, speculation about Japan's expected contribution places it somewhere between several hundred million and several billion dollars over the next several years. This hardly seems irreplaceable.[83] Mine-clearing equipment is not among the navy's most expensive items. For hundreds of millions of dollars, the United States could greatly enhance its organic capabilities in the Seventh Fleet. The main problem is the leadership challenge involved in selling policies based on abstract threats, such as future regional spirals of tension in East Asia, to the American public and Congress.[84]

Even if sustainable only for the next ten to fifteen years, the U.S. strategy of carefully calibrating increased Japanese activities in the alliance should have high payoffs. If the United States can avoid an escalation of Sino-Japanese security tensions in this time frame, several objectives could be achieved. First, the very nascent efforts to create regional confidence-building measures and regimes that encourage transparency will have time to bear fruit, as will Tokyo's and Beijing's recent efforts to improve bilateral ties and high-level contacts.[85] Second, more cosmopolitan government officials and advisers should rise through the ranks in China as a generation of Chinese experts with extensive experience abroad comes of age. Third, China more generally will have time to undergo the next political transition as the "fourth generation" leadership replaces Jiang Zemin's generation, perhaps carrying with it significant political reform. Given the strong popular sentiments in China about Japan and Taiwan and the dangers of hypernationalism in the democratization process, it would be best for the region and the world if China transited political reform without the distractions and jingoism that would likely flow from a Sino-Japanese security competition.[86] Fourth, the process of Korean unification would be significantly simplified if it were not accompanied by a Sino-Japanese military rivalry. Fifth, the region, including both Japan and China, will have time to recover from the current economic crisis without simultaneously worrying about intensifying security competition. As the interwar period showed, a combination of domestic instability and international tensions can lead to extremely unfortunate political changes within countries and in the relations among them. Moreover, if security relations are less tense, the financial crisis might provide an excellent opportunity to increase overall regional cooperation. Sixth, Tokyo will have more time to reconsider and rectify its treatment of the legacies of World War II.[87] Seventh, it would be best for long-term regional stability if Japan's own strands of hypernationalism were kept in check during Japan's post–cold war political transition following the demise of the Liberal Democratic Party's monopoly on power.

We can be fairly certain that new Japanese military roles will exacerbate the atmosphere of distrust between Japan and China. It is more difficult, however, to speculate about what exactly China might do differently if Japan adopts certain new roles. For example, if Japan appears headed toward eventual deployment of ship-based theater missile defenses, China might try to develop ballistic, cruise, and antiship missiles, and perhaps antisatellite weapons faster and more extensively than it otherwise would to acquire the ability to destroy, saturate, or elude the capability of these defensive weapons.[88] Moreover, one could speculate that, if China felt it necessary to diversify and improve its nuclear deterrent in the face of proposed U.S.-Japan TMD, Beijing might abandon its commitment to the Comprehensive Test Ban Treaty in order to test warheads for new delivery systems. China might also be less cooperative with the United States on weapons technology transfers, with implications for security in South Asia and the Middle East. On the most pessimistic end of the spectrum, China might try to speed reunification with Taiwan or press its case in the Diaoyu/Senkaku Islands dispute with Japan in potentially destabilizing ways, fearing that U.S.-Japan TMD or direct Taiwanese participation in a regional TMD system might make it more difficult to tackle those issues after the systems become deployed.

These possible scenarios are based on counterfactual arguments that would be difficult to prove even if one or more of the policies above were actually adopted by China. For example, given the Taiwan problem and the vast superiority of the United States in military power, China is likely to develop its missile capability to a significant degree regardless of the details of U.S.-Japan TMD cooperation. It will be difficult to discern the relative impact of specific policies on the trajectory of that development. But U.S. security policy in East Asia and much of the post–cold war security studies literature on the region have been built on counterfactual arguments that, although impossible to prove, are almost certainly correct. If one is willing to entertain the notion that a continued U.S. presence in East Asia, especially in Japan, is the single biggest factor preventing the occurrence of destabilizing spirals of tension in the region, one should also be willing to entertain the notion that the form this presence takes will also have important implications for Japan and its neighbors.

CONCLUSION

Given China's intense historically based mistrust of Japan, Beijing's concern about eroding norms of Japanese self-restraint, and the political geography of the Taiwan issue, even certain new defensive roles for Japan can be provocative to China. The United States should therefore continue to be cautious about what new roles Japan is asked to play in the alliance. This is particularly true in cases where the United States may be able to play the same roles without triggering the same degree of concern in Beijing.

By maintaining and, where necessary, increasing somewhat U.S. capabilities in Japan and East Asia more generally, not only will the United States better be able to manage and cap future regional crises, but also it ideally may be able to prevent them from ever occurring. By reassuring both Japan and its potential rivals, the United States reduces the likelihood of divisive security dilemma scenarios and spiral model dynamics in the region. In so doing, the United States can contribute mightily to long-term peace and stability in a region that promises to be the most important arena for U.S. foreign policy in the twenty-first century.

ACKNOWLEDGMENT

This chapter originally appeared as an article of the same title in *International Security* 23, no. 4 (Spring 1999): 49–80. For helpful comments I am grateful to Robert Art, David Asher, Paul Giarra, Bonnie Glaser, Paul Godwin, Avery Goldstein, John Ikenberry, Iain Johnston, Peter Katzenstein, Jonathan Kirshner, George Lewis, Li Hong, Michael Mastanduno, Thomas McNaugher, Robert Pape, Barry Posen, Theodore Postol, Edward Rios, Richard Samuels, Harvey Sapolsky, Stephen Van Evera, Cindy Williams, Xu Xin, four anonymous reviewers, and the members of the Brandeis University International Relations Seminar, the China Study Group at the Foreign Policy Research Institute in Philadelphia, the National Security Group Seminar at Harvard University's John M. Olin Institute, the Security Studies Program and MISTI China seminars at MIT, and the Penn-Dartmouth conferences on "The Emerging International Relations of the Asia Pacific Region." I would like to thank the Olin Institute's East Asia Security Project for its generous research funding. I am also grateful to Kristen Cashin for administrative assistance.

ENDNOTES

1. Aaron L. Friedberg, "Ripe for Rivalry: Prospects for Peace in a Multipolar Asia," *International Security* 18, no. 3 (Winter 1993/94): 5–33; Richard K. Betts, "Wealth, Power, and Instability," *International Security* 18, no. 3 (Winter 1993/94): 34–77; Stephen Van Evera, "Primed for Peace: Europe after the Cold War," *International Security* 15, no. 3 (Winter 1990/91): 7–57; and James Goldgeier and Michael McFaul, "A Tale of Two Worlds," *International Organization* 46, no. 2 (Spring 1992): 467–492.

2. For the original security dilemma and spiral models, see Robert Jervis, "Cooperation under the Security Dilemma," *World Politics* 30, no. 2 (January 1978): 167–174; and Jervis, *Perception and Misperception in International Politics* (Princeton: Princeton University Press, 1976), chap. 3.

3. For writings on the destabilizing influence of offensive weapons and doctrines, see Stephen Van Evera, "The Cult of the Offensive and the Origins of the First World War," *International Security* 9, no. 1 (Summer 1984): 58–107; Van Evera, "Offense, Defense, and the Causes of War," *International Security* 22, no. 4 (Spring 1998): 5–43; and Sean M. Lynn-Jones, "Offense- Defense Theory and Its Critics," *Security Studies* 4, no. 4 (Summer 1995): 660–691.

4. My understanding of the Chinese perspectives reflects more than seventy interviews, often with multiple interlocutors, that I conducted during four month-long trips to Beijing in 1993, 1994, 1995, and 1996, and two shorter trips to Beijing and Shanghai in 1998. My interlocutors were a mix of military and civilian analysts in government think tanks as well as academics at leading Chinese institutions. The government think-tank analysts are not decisionmakers, but they advise their superiors in the fol-

lowing key governmental organizations: the People's Liberation Army (PLA), the Foreign Ministry, the State Council, and the Chinese intelligence agencies. For obvious reasons, the individual identities of particular interviewees cannot be revealed.

5. In fact, even optimistic projections for the region are predicated on a long-term U.S. military presence. See, for example, Robert S. Ross, "The Geography of the Peace: East Asia in the Twenty-first Century," *International Security* 23, no. 4 (Spring 1999): 81–118.

6. One might argue that the geographical proximity of Japan alone would make a new regional power a greater threat to China than the more distant United States. In any case, the decision over what poses a larger threat—a distant superpower or a local great power—cannot be reached by analyzing the international balance of power alone. As in the Chinese case, the assessment of which country poses the greater threat will be based on historical legacies and national perceptions. I am grateful to Stephen Walt for helpful comments on this point.

7. For the classic study, see Allen S. Whiting, *China Eyes Japan* (Berkeley: University of California Press, 1989).

8. It is possible that the concerns expressed by Chinese analysts discussed below about Japan and the United States are purely cynical tactics designed to prevent the rise of a new regional power by affecting the debate in the United States and Japan. Such a "spin" strategy could also help justify at home and to regional actors more aggressive Chinese weapons development and diplomacy. Although I believe this probably was the intention of some of my interlocutors, given their large number, the diversity of opinions expressed on various issues over the five years of my discussions, and the controversial positions I sometimes heard expressed on issues such as the Tiananmen massacre or the Chinese missile exercises near Taiwan, I find it difficult to believe that Beijing, or any other government, could manufacture such complex theater over such an extended period of time.

9. Also in that year Japanese rightists built structures on the Diaoyu/Senkaku Islands, which are contested by both Japan and China. Many Chinese analysts saw Tokyo's complicity in their activities, especially after the dispatch of Japanese Coast Guard vessels to prevent protestors from Hong Kong and Taiwan from landing on the Japanese-controlled islands.

10. See Yinan He, "The Effect of Historical Memory on China's Strategic Perception of Japan," paper prepared for the Ninety-fourth Annual Meeting of the American Political Science Association," Boston, Massachusetts, September 3–6, 1998. For example, my interlocutors generally did not believe that a militarily stronger Japan would try to occupy sections of the Asian mainland as it did in the 1930s and 1940s.

11. The problem of Japan's lack of contrition was raised in nearly every interview I conducted. See Zhang Dalin, "Qianshi Bu Wang, Houshi Zhi Shi" [Past experience, if not forgotten, is a guide for the future], *Guoji Wenti Yanjiu* [International studies], no. 3 (1995): 6–11. For a critical Japanese perspective on the textbook issue, see Saburo Ienaga, "The Glorification of War in Japanese Education," *International Security* 18, no. 3 (Winter 1993/94): 113–133. The Chinese view on the generational issue in Japan is similar to the Japanese pacifist view. See Kunihiro Masao, "The Decline and Fall of Pacifism," *Bulletin of the Atomic Scientists* 53, no. 1 (January/February 1997): 35–39.

12. For published Chinese comparisons of postwar Germany and Japan, see Su Huimin, "Yi Shi Wei Jian, Mian Dao Fuzhe: Deguo dui Erci Dazhan de Fansi" [Take lessons from history and avoid the recurrence of mistakes: Germany's introspection about World War II], *Guoji Wenti Yanjiu* [International studies], no. 3 (1995): 12–16; and Sun Lixiang, "Zhanhou Ri De Liang Guo You Yi Shili zhi Bijiao" [A comparison of the postwar right-wing forces in the two nations of Japan and Germany], *Waiguo Wenti Yanjiu* [Research on foreign problems], no. 2 (1988): 1–10.

13. Nicholas D. Kristof, "Burying the Past: War Guilt Haunts Japan," *New York Times*, November 30, 1998, pp. A1, A10.

14. In 1993 government scholars pointed out that, in many ways, China's youth is more actively anti-Japanese than the government. They pointed to student protests against Japanese "economic imperialism" in 1986 as an example.

15. Interviews, 1996. See also Hafumi Arai, "Angry at China? Slam Japan," *Far Eastern Economic Review*, October 3, 1996, p. 21. It is clear that compared to students and other members of the public, the Chinese government was a voice of calm during the 1996 Diaoyu/Senkaku affair.

16. Pan Sifeng, ed., *Riben Junshi Sixiang Yanjiu* [Research on Japanese military thought] (Beijing: Academy of Military Sciences Press, October 1992), pp. 388–392 (internally circulated).

17. Multiple interviews, 1993–98.

18. In 1992 an internally circulated analysis of Japan's military affairs points out that Japan could easily spend 4 percent of GNP on its military without doing fundamental harm to its long-term economic growth. The examples of much higher levels of spending in healthy economies in the United States and Europe during the Cold War are cited as evidence. Ibid., p. 499. Similar positions were taken by active and retired military officers in 1996 and 1998.

19. This was a particularly sensitive issue in 1993 and 1994, and remains so today.

20. Multiple interviews, 1996. For written materials, see Gao Heng, "Shijie Junshi Xingshi" [The world military scene], *Shijie Jingji yu Zhengzhi* [World economy and politics], no. 2 (February 1995): 14–18. For a similar Western view on Japanese "technonationalism," see Richard J. Samuels, *Rich Nation, Strong Army: National Security and the Technological Transformation of Japan* (Ithaca, N.Y.: Cornell University Press, 1994).

21. Interview, 1996.

22. This was a consistent theme in interviews from 1993 to 1998, and was repeated in 1998 during the financial crisis.

23. For the realist view, see Christopher Layne, "The Unipolar Illusion: Why New Great Powers Will Rise," *International Security* 17, no. 4 (Spring 1993): 5–51. For the argument that Japan will likely not remilitarize, see Thomas U. Berger, "From Sword to Chrysanthemum: Japan's Culture of Anti-Militarism," *International Security* 17, no. 4 (Spring 1993): 119–150; and Peter J. Katzenstein, *Cultural Norms and National Security: Police and Military in Postwar Japan* (Ithaca, N.Y.: Cornell University Press, 1996).

24. The simplest versions of the most optimistic and most pessimistic forecasts about Japan's future were offered most frequently during my first three research trips from 1993 to 1995. After the Taiwan Strait crisis of 1995–96, one hears less often the most optimistic liberal argument that economic interests will trump security interests

in the post–Cold War world. Following the 1995 Nye report, one hears the simplest versions of the pessimists' scenarios less often because they were often predicated on fragility in the post–Cold War U.S.-Japan alliance.

25. Interviews, 1993–98. See also Pan, *Riben Junshi Sixiang Yanjiu*, p. 501. This book states in typical fashion, "Of all the factors that could compel Japan's military policy to change, U.S.-Japan relations will be the deciding factor." See also Wang Yanyu, ed., *Riben Junshi Zhanlüe Yanjiu* [Research on Japanese military strategy] (Beijing: Academy of Military Sciences Press, 1992), pp. 308–310 (internally circulated); and Liu Shilong, "Dangqian Rimei Anbao Tizhi de San Ge Tedian" [Three special characteristics of the current U.S.-Japan security structure], *Riben Yanjiu* [Japan studies], no. 4 (1996): 18–30, at p. 27. One article bases its optimism largely on the author's belief that, despite economic frictions, the U.S.-Japan alliance is stable. See He Fang, "Lengzhan Hou de Riben Duiwai Zhanlüe" [Japan's post–cold war international strategy], *Waiguo Wenti Yanjiu* [Research on foreign problems], no. 2 (1993): 1–4.

26. For an early discussion of the two very different potential paths to Japanese buildups, see Cai Zuming, ed., *Meiguo Junshi Zhanlüe Yanjiu* [Studies of American military strategy] (Beijing: Academy of Military Sciences Press, 1993), pp. 218–233 (internally circulated).

27. For the logic of reassurance in official U.S. defense policy, see the Pentagon's *United States Security Strategy for the East Asia-Pacific Region* 1998, which states: "In addition to its deterrent function, U.S. military presence in Asia serves to shape the security environment to prevent challenges from developing at all. U.S. force presence mitigates the impact of historical regional tensions and allows the United States to anticipate problems, manage potential threats, and encourage peaceful resolution of disputes."

28. This common view often ignores the clear benefits to the United States of the Cold War version of the alliance. The United States was guaranteed basing in Japan, and 70–80 percent of those basing costs were covered by the Japanese. Without this basing, the United States would have great difficulty maintaining its presence in the region. For a cost analysis, see Michael O'Hanlon, "Restructuring U.S. Forces and Bases in Japan," in Mike M. Mochizuki, ed., *Toward a True Alliance: Restructuring U.S.-Japan Security Relations* (Washington, D.C.: Brookings, 1997), pp. 149–178.

29. See Eric Heginbotham and Richard J. Samuels, "Mercantile Realism and Japanese Foreign Policy," *International Security* 22, no. 4 (Spring 1998): 171–203, at p. 179.

30. The Nye report, named for former Assistant Secretary of Defense Joseph S. Nye, Jr., is *United States Security Strategy for the East Asia-Pacific Region*, Office of International Security Affairs, Department of Defense, February 1995. For an insider's look at concerns about how acrimonious economic disputes were harming the alliance, see David L. Asher, "A U.S.-Japan Alliance for the Next Century," *Orbis* 41, no. 3 (Summer 1997): 343–375, at pp. 346–348.

31. For discussion of these issues, see Mike M. Mochizuki, "A New Bargain for a New Alliance" and "American and Japanese Strategic Debates," in Mochizuki, ed., *Toward a True Alliance*, pp. 5–40, 43–82, especially pp. 35, 69–70.

32. For the importance of the 1994 Korean crisis in officials' calculations, see Kurt M. Campbell, "The Official U.S. View," in Michael J. Green and Mike M.

Mochizuki, *The U.S.-Japan Security Alliance in the Twenty-first Century* (New York: Council on Foreign Relations Study Group Papers, 1998), pp. 85–87.

33. For discussion of these issues, see Bruce Stokes and James Shinn, *The Tests of War and the Strains of Peace: The U.S.-Japan Security Relationship* (New York: Council on Foreign Relations Study Group Report, January 1998). For the fear among U.S. officials that the Japanese public was moving away from support for the alliance in the 1990s, see Campbell, "The Official U.S. View."

34. In particular, three military officers whom I interviewed in 1994 stressed these themes. For fears about Democrats and neo-isolationism, see Cai, *Meiguo Junshi Zhanlüe Yanjiu*, p. 223; and Liu Liping, "Jilie Zhendanzhong de Meiguo Duiwai Zhengce Sichao" [The storm over contending positions on U.S. foreign policy], *Xiandai Guoji Guanxi* [Contemporary international relations], no. 6 (1992): 15–18. For a similar argument made before Bill Clinton was elected president of the United States, see Li Shusheng, "Sulian de Jieti yu MeiRi zai Yatai Diqu de Zhengduo" [The disintegration of the Soviet Union and U.S.-Japan rivalry in the Asia Pacific], *Shijie Jingji yu Zhengzhi* [World economy and politics], no. 7 (July 1992): 56–58. For an article about the emphasis on trade and the lack of strategic focus in Washington, see Lu Zhongwei, "Yazhou Anquanzhong de ZhongRi Guanxi" [Sino-Japanese relations in the Asian security environment], *Shijie Jingji yu Zhengzhi* [World economy and politics], no. 3 (March 1993): 23–35, 42.

35. Multiple interviews, 1995. For a published work arguing along these lines, see Yang Yunzhong, "Meiguo Zhengfu Jinyibu Tiaozheng dui Ri Zhengce" [Further adjustments in America's Japan policy], *Shijie Jingji yu Zhengzhi* [World economy and politics], no. 7 (July 1995): 61–65.

36. For elaborations of these arguments, see Thomas J. Christensen, "Chinese Realpolitik," *Foreign Affairs* 75, no. 5 (September/October 1996): 37–52; and an excellent article by Banning Garrett and Bonnie Glaser, "Chinese Apprehensions about Revitalization of the U.S.-Japan Alliance," *Asian Survey* 37, no. 4 (April 1997): 383–402. From various conversations it is still my strong impression that Beijing would be more fearful of a U.S. pullout if it were to occur. But this is no longer viewed as an imaginable outcome for the foreseeable future in Chinese foreign policy circles, so most analysts seem unwilling to discuss at length their views on such a hypothetical scenario.

37. Interviews, 1996. See also Liu, "Dangqian Rimei Anbao Tizhi de San Ge Tedian," pp. 20–22; and Yang Bojiang, "Why [a] U.S.-Japan Joint Declaration on [the] Security Alliance," *Contemporary International Relations* 6, no. 5 (May 1996): 1–12.

38. Liu Jiangyong, "New Trends in Sino-U.S.-Japan Relations," *Contemporary International Relations* 8, no. 7 (July 1998): 1–13.

39. See "The Guidelines for U.S.-Japan Defense Cooperation," in Green and Mochizuki, *The U.S.-Japan Security Alliance in the Twenty-first Century*, pp. 55–72, at p. 65.

40. Interviews, 1996 and 1998. The Jiang quotation comes from a Reuters news service report on October 18, 1997.

41. Interviews, 1996 and 1998. Taiwan is a former Japanese colony (1895–1945). It is near international sea-lanes that are important to Japan. In addition, Chinese analysts

argue that, for straightforward reasons relating to relative national power, Japan has a strategic interest in preventing Taiwan's high-technology and capital-rich economy from linking politically with the mainland. Moreover, some Chinese analysts view Taiwan as having geostrategic significance for Japan as a potential ally because of its location near the Chinese mainland. Another issue fueling mistrust of Japan is the feeling that Taiwan's president, Lee Teng-hui, who attended college in Japan and who speaks Japanese fluently, may be more pro-Japan than pro-China. For a particularly alarmist argument along these lines, see Li Yaqiang, "What Is Japan Doing Southward?" *Beijing Jianchuan Zhishi* [Naval and merchant ships], no. 6 (June 6, 1997): 7–8, in Foreign Broadcast Information Service Daily Report China, September 4, 1997. For a more sober analysis, see Yang Xuejun and Li Hanmei, "Yingxiang Weilai Riben Dui Wai Zhanlüe he Xingwei de Zhongyao Yinsu" [Important factors influencing future Japanese foreign strategy and conduct], *Zhanlüe yu Guanli* [Strategy and management], no. 1 (1998): 17–22, at p. 21.

42. This argument was made particularly forcefully in my interviews with three military officers in 1994. See also Pan, *Riben Junshi Sixiang Yanjiu*, pp. 502–503; and Wu Peng, "Riben Wei he Jianchi Xiang Haiwai Paibing" [Why Japan insisted on sending forces abroad], *Shijie Jingji yu Zhengzhi* [World economy and politics], no. 12 (December 1992): 46–50.

43. For the earliest discussions of joint U.S.-Japan development of TMD and Tokyo's resistance to the plan, see David E. Sanger, "New Missile Defense in Japan under Discussion with U.S.," *New York Times*, September 18, 1993, p. A1. A year and a half later, the language on TMD in the 1995 Nye report belies Japan's reluctance to agree to joint research, stating that the United States "is exploring with Japan cooperative efforts" in TMD.

44. Interviews, 1998. See also Wu Chunsi, "Tactical Missile Defense, Sino-U.S.-Japanese Relationship, and East Asian Security," *Inesap Information Bulletin, no.* 16 (November 1998): 20–23.

45. Jervis, "Cooperation under the Security Dilemma."

46. Although scholars differ on specific definitions of what constitutes a destabilizing offense and a stabilizing defense, all definitions in the current literature focus on states' capacity for fighting across borders and seizing enemy-held territory as the measure of the offense-defense balance. See, for example, Van Evera, "Offense, Defense, and the Causes of War"; and Charles L. Glaser and Chaim Kaufmann, "What Is the Offense-Defense Balance and Can We Measure It?" *International Security* 22, no. 4 (Spring 1998): 44–82.

47. For the various reasons why I believe China would risk war, perhaps even with the United States, to prevent Taiwan's independence, see Christensen, "Chinese Realpolitik."

48. See "U.S., Japan Agree to Study Missile Defense," *Washington Times*, September 21, 1998, p. 1; and "Japan Makes Missile-Defense Plan High Priority," *Washington Times*, November 6, 1998, p. 12.

49. Richard Fisher, quoted in Rob Holzer and Barbara Opall-Rome, "U.S. Anticipates Approval from Tokyo on Joint TMD," *Defense News*, September 21–27, 1998, p. 34. See also Peter Landers, Susan Lawrence, and Julian Baum, "Hard Target," *Far*

Eastern Economic Review, September 24, 1998, pp. 20–21. For a discussion of China's more general concerns about TMD, see Benjamin Valentino, "Small Nuclear Powers and Opponents of Ballistic Missile Defenses in the Post–Cold War Era," *Security Studies* 7, no. 2 (Winter 1997/98): 229–232.

50. Statements by Chinese arms control and missile experts in the United States in August 1998, and discussions with one active and one retired military officer in China in November 1998.

51. Interviews with civilian analysts, November 1998.

52. Demonstrating that they are much less sensitive than TMD or other aspects of the Nye initiative, minesweepers would usually only be discussed by my interlocutors after I raised the issue.

53. I base my conclusions about the particularly provocative nature of Japanese intervention more on a general understanding of Chinese attitudes toward Japan than on extensive interview data. In the relatively few interviews in 1998 in which I raised this issue, responses were mixed, and included the following arguments: Japanese intervention would be particularly provocative and likely to lead to crisis escalation; Japanese intervention would be only somewhat more provocative than U.S. intervention alone; and U.S. intervention alone would be sufficient to spark escalation, with or without the Japanese.

54. Of course, in a shooting war across the Taiwan Strait, calculations may be quite different because presumably such an event would severely harm Sino-Japanese relations in any case.

55. For an interesting discussion of a scenario involving a PLA blockade of Taiwan, see Paul H.B. Godwin, "The Use of Military Force against Taiwan: Potential PRC Scenarios," in Parris H. Chang and Martin L. Lasater, eds., *If China Crosses the Taiwan Straits: The International Response* (New York: University Press of America, 1993), pp. 15–34. In 1998 a Chinese military officer said that missiles are a much more likely PLA strategy than mine-laying, but the blockade possibility cannot be ruled out entirely.

56. In fact, for our purposes we can assume such a low-level Taiwanese provocation because, under current U.S. policy (President Clinton's "three no's"), a greater provocation would likely preclude a U.S. response. The "three no's," pronounced by President Clinton in Shanghai, are no [U.S.] support for Taiwan independence; no support for two China's, or one China, one Taiwan; and no support for Taiwanese entrance into international organizations for which statehood is a prerequisite.

57. According to one study, about 90 percent of minesweeping operations have been in areas with no discernible mines. See Captain Buzz Broughton and Commander Jay Burton, "The (R)evolution of Mine Countermeasures," *Proceedings of the Naval Institute*, May 1998, pp. 55–58.

58. The United States' general weakness in minesweeping is widely recognized. Although the United States recently has developed new minesweeping and mine-hunting equipment, much of it is based in the United States and would require a significant amount of time to be sent to the theater. A new naval plan, "the fleet engagement strategy," backed by former Secretary of Defense William S. Cohen, calls for increased "organic" mine-hunting and minesweeping capabilities within battle groups that would involve airborne (helicopters), surface, and submarine-based capabilities. It

is unclear how effective these initiatives have been in providing U.S. forces in East Asia with readily available capability in a crisis. See ibid.; "Cohen Expected to Respond This Week to Navy Brief on Mine Warfare," *Inside the Navy*, August 17, 1998, p. 3; and "Cohen Directs Navy to Add $53 Million to Develop Minehunting System," *Inside the Navy*, August 31, 1998, p. 1.

59. Although it demonstrates the potential problems of even Japanese defensive cooperation in the U.S.-Japan alliance, fortunately there are a lot of rather large "ifs" in the above blockade scenario. Even if most of these came to pass, one would hope that U.S. leaders would be wise enough to recognize the above dangers and would not put Japan into such a difficult dilemma.

60. For example, an internally circulated analysis of those Japanese buildups does not suggest opportunism or aggressive intent. See Pan, *Riben Junshi Sixiang Yanjiu*, chap. 14, and pp. 414–415.

61. Interviews, 1994.

62. For example, Beijing at times has tried to reassure Southeast Asian nations about its desire to settle the Spratly Islands disputes peacefully. Even if these are merely cynical tactics designed to buy time for China to concentrate on the Taiwan problem or develop force projection to handle the Spratlys dispute later, they demonstrate Beijing's ability to conceive of Southeast Asian fears about China.

63. For example, one book takes seriously Japan's fear of the Soviets during the Cold War, but places Japan's concern about China under the heading "Japan's Imagined Enemies," see Pan, *Riben Junshi Sixiang Yanjiu*, pp. 413–416. For another example, see Zhan Shiliang, "Yatai Diqu Xingshi he Zhongguo Mulin Youhao Zhengce" [The Asia-Pacific situation and China's good neighbor policy], *Guoji Wenti Yanjiu* [International studies], no. 4 (1993): 1–3, 7.

64. See Michael J. Green and Benjamin L. Self, "Japan's Changing China Policy: From Commercial Liberalism to Reluctant Realism," *Survival* 38, no. 2 (Summer 1996): 34–58.

65. The increased frequency of such statements over time may be one effect of China's relatively high rates of economic growth in the 1990s in comparison to Japan.

66. In separate interviews in 1994 a military officer and a civilian analyst lamented that the vast majority of Chinese are incapable of thinking in ways empathetic to Japanese concerns about China. In 1996 a civilian analyst complained that too many Chinese leaders and security analysts are unable to separate their analyses of 1930s Japan and 1990s Japan.

67. Multiple interviews, 1993–98. In fact, one military officer was even quite critical of China's last round of military exercises in March 1996 because he was afraid that China revealed too much about its military to a vigilant and highly capable U.S. defense intelligence network.

68. China has worked in the past to block the creation of formal multilateral reassurance regimes in East Asia, such as the Organization for Security and Cooperation in Europe, that might lead to condemnation of China's development and/or deployment of its force-projection capabilities. As Jianwei Wang argues, China has been more open to multilateralism in the economic realm than it has been in the security realm. Jianwei Wang, "Chinese Views of Multilateralism," in Yong Deng and Feiling

Wang, *In the Eyes of the Dragon: China Views the World and Sino-American Relations* (Lanham, MD: Rowman and Littlefield, 1999).

69. For example, at the July 1994 ARF conference and in earlier multilateral meetings with Southeast Asian representatives, China blocked any meaningful discussion of territorial disputes involving Chinese claims. See Allen S. Whiting, "ASEAN Eyes China," *Asian Survey* 37, no. 4 (April 1997): 299–322.

70. See Alastair Iain Johnston and Paul Evans, "China's Engagement of Multilateral Institutions," in Johnston and Robert S. Ross, eds., *Engaging China: The Management of an Emerging Power* (London: Routledge, 1999); Johnston, "Learning versus Adaptation: Explaining Change in Chinese Arms Control Policy in the 1980s and 1990s," *China Journal* 35 (January 1996): 27–61; Johnston, "Socialization in International Institutions: The ASEAN Regional Forum and IR Theory," paper prepared for the conference on "The Emerging International Relations of the Asia Pacific Region," University of Pennsylvania, May 8–9, 1998. See also Rosemary Foot, "China in the ASEAN Regional Forum: Organizational Processes and Domestic Modes of Thought," *Asian Survey* 38, no. 5 (May 1998): 425–440.

71. Interviews, 1996 and 1998. See also Wang, "Chinese Views on Multilateralism," in Deng and Wang, *In the Eyes of the Dragon*; and Wu Xinbo, "Integration on the Basis of Strength: China's Impact on East Asian Security," Asia/Pacific Research Center working paper, February 1998.

72. Interviews, 1996 and 1998. For an excellent analysis of ASEAN concerns and hopes about China, see Whiting, "ASEAN Eyes China." For Chinese reactions to changes in the U.S.-Japan alliance along these lines, see Zhou Jihua, "RiMei Anbao Tizhi de Qianghua yu Dongya de Anquan" [The strengthening of the U.S.-Japan security structure and the security of East Asia], *Riben Xuekan* [Japan studies], no. 4 (1996): 41–42; and Zhou, "Military Accords Create Suspicions," *China Daily*, October 7, 1996.

73. Interviews, 1996 and 1998. I was impressed that multilateral options, previously often discounted by my interlocutors, were now raised as legitimate alternatives to U.S. bilateralism without my prompting.

74. In the psychological literature on the security dilemma, one is not supposed to try to solve security dilemmas by applying pressure but by reassuring distrustful states. See Jervis, *Perception and Misperception*, chap. 3. In Alexander Wendt's constructivist approach, not only do tough policies merely reproduce realist fear and cynicism, but also gentle persuasion and appeasement are prescribed for even truly predatory regimes, such as Hitler's Germany or Stalin's Russia. See Wendt, "Anarchy Is What States Make of It," *International Organization* 46, no. 2 (Spring 1992): 391–425, at 409. In fact, recent work on Chinese foreign policy since Tiananmen suggests that the fear of material sanctions and social stigmatization helps explain a broad range of cooperative Chinese foreign policies from a general, more constructive regional strategy to accession to important international arms control institutions, such as the Nuclear Nonproliferation Treaty and the Comprehensive Test Ban Treaty. See Yu Bin, "China's Regional Views and Policies—Implications for the United States," and Hu Weixing, "China and Nuclear Nonproliferation," both in Deng and Wang, *In the Eyes of the Dragon*. See also Johnston and Evans, "China's Engagement in Multilateral Institutions."

75. These themes were still emphasized by my interlocutors in November 1998.

76. On the importance of Taiwan in the calculations regarding the scope of the U.S.-Japan alliance in the 1997 defense guidelines, see Michael Green, "The U.S. View," in Green and Mochizuki, *The U.S.-Japan Security Alliance*, p. 75. For more elaboration on my preferred position on U.S. strategy across the strait, see Christensen, "Chinese Realpolitik." For elaboration on the three no's, see note 56 above.

77. Multiple interviews, November 1998. Of course, Chinese analysts are concerned about U.S. development of TMD as well.

78. Many Chinese experts believe that the United States' encouragement of Japanese military development and foreign policy assertiveness will unwittingly fuel Japanese confidence and nationalism (a process that has already begun according to Chinese analysts), and that eventually U.S.-Japan security relations could still deteriorate. See, for example, Liu, "Dangqian Rimei Anbao Tizhi de San Ge Tedian," p. 3. In 1998 several Chinese analysts argued that Tokyo agreed to codevelopment of TMD in part to prepare a more independent Japanese defense capability for the future. I am grateful to David Asher, Bonnie Glaser, and Iain Johnston for helpful discussion on Japanese plans for satellites. For a Chinese statement linking the Japanese plans for satellites with the plans for U.S.-Japan joint development of TMD, see "China Concerned about Japanese Satellite Plan," Beijing (Associated Press), December 30, 1998. On the connection to the North Korean missile launch, see "Support Growing for Spy Satellite System," *Mainichi Shimbun*, September 8, 1998, Politics and Business Section, p. 2.

79. Another possible way to reduce some Chinese concerns about joint U.S.-Japan development of TMD would be to pursue a land-based theater high-altitude air defense (THAAD) system instead of a ship-based navy theater-wide system. If effective, a THAAD system could provide the Japanese home islands with missile defense, but because THAAD is immobile it could not travel to the Taiwan area or other regions, and therefore would be less likely to exacerbate Chinese concerns about real or perceived Japanese support for Taiwan independence. China still would be concerned about its deterrent capabilities against Japan and about general advancement in Japanese military technologies and assertiveness, but at least the fears about Taiwan would be somewhat reduced. But possibly because of high-profile test failures of THAAD in the United States, the United States and Japan have chosen to pursue the more provocative ship-based systems.

80. The Japanese sword and shield argument was made in China by a retired Chinese military officer and a civilian analyst in November 1998. The offense-defense indistinguishability issue and the ability to protect Japan from Chinese retaliation was raised by Chinese arms control and missile experts in the United States in August 1998. In 1998 an active military officer argued that U.S. transfer of TMD technology to Japan would likely violate the missile technology control regime. For critiques of offense-defense theory on the issue of distinguishability and responses to them, see Jack S. Levy, "The Offense-Defense Balance of Military Technology: A Theoretical and Historical Analysis," *International Studies Quarterly* 38, no. 2 (June 1984): 219–238; John J. Mearsheimer, *Conventional Deterrence* (Ithaca, N.Y.: Cornell University Press, 1983), pp. 25–26; Lynn-Jones, "Offense-Defense Theory and Its Critics"; Van Evera, "Of-

fense, Defense, and the Causes of War"; and Glaser and Kaufmann, "What Is the Offense-Defense Balance?"

81. See Paul Bracken, "America's Maginot Line," *Atlantic Monthly*, December 1998, pp. 85–93.

82. For Japanese reticence on TMD, see Asher, "A U.S.-Japan Alliance for the Next Century," pp. 364–366.

83. There are no official published estimates of Japanese contributions to TMD. For some speculation, see Holzer and Opall-Rome, "U.S. Anticipates Approval from Tokyo on Joint TMD." The article states that Japan might pay up to 20 percent of the cost for developing a TMD system covering Japan. According to Landers, Lawrence, and Baum, in "Hard Target," such a system could cost about $17 billion over the next several years. I am grateful to Cindy Williams and Eric Labs for their help in analyzing the costs of additional mine-clearing equipment.

84. For a discussion of problems in marketing strategies, see Thomas J. Christensen, *Useful Adversaries: Grand Strategy, Domestic Mobilization, and Sino-American Conflict, 1947–1958* (Princeton: Princeton University Press, 1996), chap. 2.

85. China and Japan exchanged visits by their defense ministers in 1998. In late 1997 there was a meeting between Premier Li Peng and Prime Minister Hashimoto, and in November 1998 there was a summit between President Zemin and Prime Minister Obuchi.

86. Even if China does not reform politically, a perceived "Japan threat" could still prove dangerous, because it could affect negatively the nature of Chinese authoritarianism. On the dangers of democratization, see Edward Mansfield and Jack L. Snyder, "Democratization and the Danger of War," *International Security* 20, no. 1 (Summer 1995): 5–38.

87. As Nicholas Kristof argues perceptively, the worst outcome would be if Japan became more militarily active before it reached a higher degree of understanding with its neighbors. See Kristof, "The Problem of Memory," *Foreign Affairs* 77, no. 6 (November/December 1998): 37–49, at pp. 47–48.

88. China has been building up these capabilities at a relatively fast pace in recent years, but in 1998 my interlocutors, however genuinely, said that joint U.S.-Japan TMD would lead China to increase the pace of this development.

Chapter 2

AN EMERGING CHINA'S EMERGING GRAND STRATEGY

A Neo-Bismarckian Turn?

Avery Goldstein

Like many of the world's states, at the dawn of the twenty-first century China faces radically different foreign policy challenges than it faced during the cold war. Unlike many others, however, China's leaders must not only cope with a transformed international system, but also manage their country's emergence as a true great power. In response to these twin challenges, in the late 1990s Beijing began to stake out a new grand strategy.[1]

On the one hand, the new approach reflects the shifting constraints of an international system in which bipolarity has given way to a period of unipolarity that many (especially the Chinese) expect will eventually give way to multipolarity.[2] Bipolarity had presented rather clear-cut choices to an economically impoverished and militarily backward China facing serious threats from the world's superpowers. Unipolarity, if enduring, would present similarly tight constraints and simplify strategic options for China since it would continue to lag far behind what, by definition, would be a global hegemon. By contrast, multipolarity is expected to provide more room for strategic creativity, though also added uncertainty about the source and nature of future threats. The grand strategy described below has resulted in part from China's attempt to cope with the currently stark challenges of unipolarity as well as to exploit the opportunities a transition to multipolarity may present.

On the other hand, the new strategy also reflects China's growing capabilities (economic and military) that may presage its rise to a position as one of the great powers within the multipolar system expected to define international politics by the middle of this century. Greater power enables China to play an increasingly influential international role while it worries others who see such activism as potentially threatening. As explained below, the shift in Beijing's foreign policy approach that emerged during the late 1990s was in part a response to the adverse reaction China's rise was eliciting, a reaction that earlier insensitivity to such concerns had exacerbated.

Although China's new grand strategy reflects changes in the international system as well as in China's capabilities, it also bears the imprint of three important continuities. First, while the system's polarity changes, its ordering principle does not; anarchy endures, as do its consequences for state behavior. Second, while military technology yields ever more wondrous hardware and software, thus far the so-called revolution in military affairs has not reversed the verdict of the nuclear revolution; vulnerability to swift, massive punishment endures, as do its consequences for the uses of force. Third, despite playing a new role on a changing world stage, China finds itself performing in the same old theater. Because China is moving up, but cannot move out, geography and history combine to pose daunting problems for the country's foreign-policy makers. Although China faces no pressing great power threat along its borders (indeed not since at least 1800 has its periphery been less threatened) there are no guarantees that today's favorable circumstances will continue indefinitely. China finds itself surrounded by great, or potentially great, powers (as well as a number of minor powers) with whom it has a checkered history. None may be enemies today, but prudence requires a strategy for coping with the potential problems a deterioration in relations with any of them might pose tomorrow.[3]

What grand strategy makes sense for a rising, but not dominant, power surrounded by potential adversaries who are nervous about its intentions? With the qualifications noted below, the approach emerging in Beijing can be labeled "neo-Bismarckian."[4] This term is used only to suggest broad parallels in strategic choice that reflect an underlying similarity between the position in which Germany found itself as a rising power in the late nineteenth century and China's position as a rising power today. For each country, the need to reduce the risk that others would try to abort their ascent has shaped foreign policy. In each case, leaders have attempted to pursue national interests by making their country an indispensable, or at least very attractive, partner for the system's other major powers, thereby reducing the chance that potential adversaries would unite in opposition.[5] But the parallel should not be overstated, as explained below, because of substantive differences between historical eras more than a century apart, as well as differences in the two countries' national attributes.

I begin with a brief discussion designed to place China's present strategy in context. In this first part of the chapter, I consider the different expectations about China's behavior that one might infer from major strands of international relations theory, distinguish China's current strategy from some logical alternatives these theories suggest, and clarify the important differences between China's strategic choices and those identified with Bismarck. The second part of the chapter more closely examines the Chinese case. To highlight the sense in which current policy marks a significant change and to identify the sources of this change, I offer a stylized overview of China's evolving grand strategy during and immediately after the cold war, followed by a presentation of the key elements of China's neo-Bismarckian approach.

A RISING CHINA'S CHOICES

International Relations Theory and China's post-cold war role. The logic of a wide variety of major international relations theories suggests that China's growing power in a post–cold war system that the United States dominates will produce recurrent conflict as an ever more capable Beijing pursues its national interests. So many such theoretical arguments anticipate that a self-interested China's rise will have disruptive and potentially dangerous international consequences that trouble seems overdetermined. Robert Gilpin's system-governance thesis and A.F.K. Organski and Jacek Kugler's power transition thesis suggest that a rising Chinese state seeking greater status, benefits, or simply influence in international affairs should be expected to mount a challenge to the system's reigning American hegemon. Kenneth Waltz's balance-of-power theory predicts a determined Chinese effort (building up its capabilities and searching for like-minded allies) to counter the dangers unchecked American power may pose under conditions of anarchy. Stephen Walt's balance-of-threat theory suggests that such Chinese efforts are likely to prompt regional states, worried about China, to respond with their own search for arms or allies, efforts that could in turn intensify China's concerns according to the logic of the security dilemma whose dynamics Robert Jervis has limned. Perspectives that do not focus on power relations yield similarly bleak expectations. Michael Doyle's democratic peace thesis suggests that an authoritarian China's foreign policy will be little constrained by concerns other than self-interest and power. Also, the international system's democratic great powers will be unlikely to refrain from confronting an undemocratic great power or to rule out recourse to the use of military force against it. Neoliberal institutionalist arguments about the effects of regimes or multilateralism point in the same troubling direction. Because international institutions are so weakly developed in East Asia, as opposed to Europe, there are good reasons to doubt their effectiveness in constraining a rising China's assertiveness that the other theories deem likely. Only theoretical perspectives highlighting the self-interested restraint that might accompany China's growing economic interdependence and the sobering strategic consequences of nuclear weapons offer more benign expectations.[6]

In short, most strands of international relations theory anticipate that a rising China will be a disruptive actor challenging American dominance. Initially, China's post–cold war foreign policy did seem to conform to this disturbing expectation. However, the shift in China's strategy in the late 1990s reminds us that such theories merely identify broad constraints confronting states. Understanding international outcomes requires not merely identifying such constraints, but also how particular states respond to them. This is a question that can only be answered by investigating each state's distinctive experience. In China's case, during the early 1990s there were troubling signs that it was indeed adopting the sort of assertive foreign policy many expected. But by mid-decade, the accumulating costs and risks of the challenger's role began to encourage Beijing to adopt the more subtle, though no less self-interested, approach I label neo-Bismarckian.

Grand strategic alternatives. I distinguish China's current grand strategy from four broad alternatives. First, under a hegemonic grand strategy China would strive to maximize its power relative to all rivals by diverting as much national wealth as possible from civilian economic needs to military modernization, and attempt to exploit its power advantages wherever possible to consolidate territorial and resource gains. Second, under a balancing strategy China would strive to offset the threatening dominance of others by a more modest effort at military modernization along with attempts to collaborate with states sharing its security concerns. As noted below, until 1996 this was the post–cold war strategic alternative China embraced. Third, under a bandwagoning strategy China would make little effort to cultivate its own military capabilities hoping to score relative gains, but instead would strive to accommodate the preferences of the system's dominant state, hoping to realize the absolute gains of increased international economic exchange and to enjoy the security benefits the hegemon would provide as a collective good. Fourth, under an isolationist strategy China would invest in military capabilities only insofar as they were essential to the minimal goal of ensuring the inviolability of the country's territorial and political integrity (e.g., a minimal nuclear deterrent combined with daunting conventional defenses along the country's periphery), while seeking to maximize economic independence through autarky.

China's present strategy differs from each of these four alternatives. It finesses questions about the longer term—whether, for example, a rising China will one day be a regional hegemon, a global peer competitor of the other great powers, or perhaps continue to lag far behind the system's leading state. Instead it focuses on the problems a rising China faces and attempts to manage current threats to vital interests. To cope with the challenges posed by a preponderant

U.S. and suspicious neighbors, the strategy combines a subtle realpolitik effort at developing national capabilities and cultivating international partners (one designed to avoid the provocative consequences of a straightforward hegemonic or balancing strategy) with a level of international economic and diplomatic engagement designed to maximize the benefits of interdependence (one designed to avoid the vulnerability consequences of bandwagoning or the opportunity costs of isolationism).

China's Grand Strategy: Historical Analogies? In thinking about China's current international role, others have looked to history rather than theory for guidance. Some have suggested analogies between China today and rising powers in the past. Of these, the most disturbing are those that draw parallels with some of the twentieth century's most disruptive international actors—Wilhelmine or Nazi Germany, Imperial Japan, and the Soviet Union.[7] I instead have suggested that a more helpful historical analogy may be a somewhat less troubling one—Germany in the era of Otto von Bismarck. Like China, it was a geopolitically central rising power whose current and projected future capabilities naturally drew the attention of the system's other major actors. This broad similarity in the countries' international circumstances accounts for a rough similarity in their grand strategic design. Nevertheless important differences between the two cases account for important differences in strategic content. The historical analogy is a loose one and must be heavily qualified.[8]

Three qualifications are in order. First, Bismarck's era was a long one, and his strategy evolved over time. Although certain fundamentals endured (devising means to cope with Germany's unfavorable geopolitical circumstances that precluded English-style aloofness, yet trying to maximize strategic flexibility rather than embracing clear alignments), between the 1850s and 1880s the strategy's purpose changed. In the 1850s and 1860s, the chief goal was to preserve a precarious Prussia's emergence as the leader of Germany. Having succeeded in this task, by the 1870s the chief goal for a Germany unified under Prussia's leadership was to ensure that its newfound strength did not provoke others to combine against it. China's period of precarious security, as noted below, was the cold war era; in the post–cold war world, its strategic purposes are closer to those of Germany during the last two decades of Bismarck's era.[9]

Second, Bismarck employed an exquisitely complex strategy of careful alliance building designed to check potential enemies while Germany grew from one among several European great powers to become the dominant actor on the continent. After 1871, Bismarck claimed that Germany was a "saturated power" and eschewed expansionism that might have united rivals or stimulated the only real peer competitor (naval power Britain) from a determined effort to offset Berlin's growing strength in Europe.[10] Bismarck's diplomacy was strikingly successful during the latter decades of the nineteenth century. It subsequently broke down, however, as the complexity of the conservative cross-cutting alliances he had managed with much difficulty proved too difficult for his less capable and more ambitious successors to sustain.[11]

Beijing, too, claims that it harbors no hegemonic ambitions. But as it seeks to prevent the hardening of a hostile alliance network while its own capabilities grow, it has not reprised the alliance-based strategy of Bismarck. Instead, as explained below, it has devised a distinctive set of policies that emphasize reassurance, linkage, and flexibility in its interaction with other states, especially cultivating more ambiguous partnerships rather than formal alliances. While differing from Bismarck's alliance-based diplomacy, the complex network of conditional partnerships China has sought to cultivate, like Bismarck's complex web of alliances, demands similarly sophisticated management and promises to test the talents of Beijing's present and future leaders.

Third, important military-strategic differences distinguish the late nineteenth century from the era in which China is a rising power. Foreign policy in Bismarck's age and after was made in circumstances where it was a question of "when," not "whether," great power war would occur. Expectations today are much different. The role of force endures, a reflection of the permissive environment of international anarchy, but its use is now more tightly constrained. Most importantly, the advent of nuclear weapons has clarified the consequences of general war among the great powers and provided strong incentives for managing those crises and conflicts that cannot be avoided.[12] In addition, the presence of nuclear weapons diminishes the plausibility of dominating by achieving military superiority (even outgunned nuclear adversaries can dissuade aspiring hegemons with threats of retaliation). This difference alters the relative importance placed on the military and economic aspects of grand strategy. While military competition continues, in the contemporary era international economic rivalry is more intense than ever before. Economic strength has always been the foundation for great power, but by the end of the twentieth century the increased significance of science and rapidly changing technology as determinants of relative power, including military clout, mean that security is better served by a strategy that facilitates economic development rather than one that seeks to accumulate foreign territory, resources, and population.[13] As a result, the costs and benefits of the use of force as a means to advance national interests are much different in the present era than they were in Bismarck's.

These sorts of differences in fact raise cautions about the usefulness of looking for lessons in almost any historical example. The broad analogy between contemporary China and Bismarck's Germany is imperfect at best and identifies only a few important similarities in the two countries' circumstances that lead to some similarities in strategic design. The comparison does, however, seem more apt than others that have been suggested. Unlike Wilhelmine Germany, China is not eagerly pursuing imperialist glory; unlike Imperial Japan,

China is not bereft of resources to the point that it is driven to minimize its dependence through expansion; unlike Nazi Germany, China does not have an ideology of racial superiority and a need for lebensraum to motivate it to conquer neighbors; unlike the Soviet Union, China no longer sees itself as the champion of a universally relevant way of life whose dissemination justifies an unremitting effort to erode that championed by its rival.[14] China is instead, like Bismarck's Germany, a nationalist rising power whose interests sometimes conflict with others', but one that so far lacks any obvious ambition or reason to indulge a thirst for international expansion, let alone dominance.

Two final points of clarification about my use of the neo-Bismarckian label are in order before proceeding. First, I am not claiming that China's leaders are self-consciously imitating Bismarck's approach (though the historical bent of Chinese strategists makes it impossible to rule out this possibility). Instead, I am simply suggesting that as a consequence of international constraints, national circumstances, and the hard lessons of China's experience in the early post–cold war years, a de facto grand strategy has begun to emerge. Second, some might argue that the term "grand strategy" overstates the coherence I identify in China's foreign policy. To be sure, in China as elsewhere, the numerous individuals and organizations responsible for formulating and implementing policy ensures something short of full coherence. Nevertheless, even though the power of the paramount leader in Beijing today is less than it was under Mao or Deng, the Chinese Communist regime's Leninist structure endures and, especially on major foreign policy matters, enables the party center to provide the broad direction within which actors must operate. It is the strategic content of this framework that I examine here.

CHINA'S GRAND STRATEGIES

China's grand strategy during the cold war. During the cold war China pursued its foreign policy interests within the tight constraints and resulting clear incentives bipolarity provided. Given the country's meager national wealth and the scope of the threat each of the superpowers posed, Beijing's foreign policy for almost four decades after 1949 was driven by a survivalist logic that frequently trumped other regime preferences. The imperatives of international structure derived not merely from the relatively clear implications of bipolarity, but also from the tightness of its constraints for a state so closely involved in the system's superpower-dominated competitive politics.[15] Any Chinese government with the limited capabilities Beijing commanded would have behaved in much the same way, relying on one superpower to counter the threat the other represented (a consequence of bipolarity), even as it sought to improve the prospects for self-reliance because of worries about the wisdom of depending on foreigners (a consequence of anarchy).[16] International-structural causes clearly illuminated the broad logic of China's strategy during the cold war, and did so better for the China case than for many others (e.g., Japan, Germany, Sweden, India).

The PRC's cold war approach of counter-hegemonic coalition building was manifest after 1949 in its initial "lean to one side" grand strategy. Strong disagreements with Stalin and a sense of resentment about his tepid economic and military support for Mao's CCP notwithstanding, the Sino-Soviet alliance provided the PRC with the only available counter to a globally dominant U.S. whose deployments in the Western Pacific and track record of hostility toward the Chinese communist movement made it the principal external threat to the newly founded PRC. Counter-hegemonic balancing also informed Mao's subsequent "lean to the other side" grand strategy of Sino-American rapprochement initiated in the early 1970s. As the Soviet military buildup along its Asian frontier compounded the deep-seated political and ideological disputes between Beijing and Moscow, and as Washington demonstrated the limits of its military ambitions in Southeast Asia and then previewed its plans for retrenchment (Nixon Doctrine), China's leaders determined that the Soviet Union was the superpower posing the more serious threat. This new principal strategic concern dictated China's flexibility in improving relations with the United States (and other advanced industrial states) so that the counter-Soviet coalition would include partners more weighty than the handful of third world regimes and revolutionary movements who sided with Beijing against the USSR.

After Mao's death in 1976, China's grand strategy retained its basic orientation, identifying the Soviet Union as the main adversary and the United States as the essential member of a countervailing coalition of diverse states. Indeed, in the immediate post-Mao years (1976–1980), China's anti-Soviet diplomacy was at its zenith. Beijing basically dropped the ideological fig leaf (neo-Leninist claims about the "revisionist" roots of Soviet "socialist imperialism") that had been required in the era of radical socialism and simply sought to build a global anti-Soviet United Front based on naked claims about power and threats. During the early 1980s, however, the character of the Sino-American strategic alignment began to change as a consequence of three developments.[17] First, China's perception of the level of Soviet threat began to decline.[18] Second, after years denouncing détente as a delusion and encouraging the West to arm against the dangerous Soviet hegemon, Beijing saw its wishes more than fulfilled in the massive military buildup undertaken by President Reagan's U.S. and other leading NATO countries. Third, by the 1980s Beijing was finally deploying small numbers of nuclear delivery systems that forced Soviet planners to confront the risk of devastating retaliatory punishment should a confrontation over vital interests escalate uncontrollably. The "existential deterrence" benefits of China's nuclear arsenal reinforced the "existential alliance" benefits of the Sino-American relationship that China had enjoyed since the Nixon opening of 1972.

As a result of these developments, Deng's counter-Soviet balancing grand strategy after 1980, differed from Mao's in being less tightly constrained by the need to cultivate a de facto alliance with the United States. It also differed from Mao's insofar as the political, economic, and military content of the strategy changed along with the domestic transformation Deng and his reformers initiated in 1979. Politically, with the end of class-struggle rhetoric, China no longer relied on the Marxist categories of "revisionism" vs. "revolution" to explain the reasons for threatening Soviet behavior. Economically, with the abandonment of the Maoist development model, China sought to combine institutional changes at home with an "opening to the outside" world to stimulate rapid economic growth that might eventually provide a foundation for national strength. Such growth would in turn reduce the need in the future to depend on powerful patrons when facing international threats. Militarily, with the demythologization of Mao, the People's Liberation Army was able to reduce, if not eliminate, the longstanding emphasis on adhering to the techniques that had proved helpful in the 1930s and 1940s, the doctrine of people's war, and begin the arduous process of creating a professional army with the personnel and equipment required on the modern battlefield.[19]

During the 1980s, then, China's grand strategy was characterized by continuity in its fundamental purpose, but its content was changing. Beijing viewed the advanced West, especially the United States, less as a military partner essential to China's short-term interest in coping with a pressing security threat and more as an economic partner essential to China's long-term interest in modernization. Although China still hedged against the unlikely contingency of a Soviet challenge, it also pursued improved relations with its northern neighbor.[20] As Soviet "new thinking" under Gorbachev's leadership heralded an inward turn by the country whose expansionist tendencies China had feared, a flurry of diplomacy quickly moved Sino-Soviet relations from the phase of reduced tension and dialogue that had begun in the early 1980s, to an era of full normalization capped by the Gorbachev visit to Beijing in May 1989.

By the end of the 1980s, China's international situation could hardly have seemed brighter. Neither superpower any longer posed a serious threat to its security, and both were eager to nurture good relations with an economically awakening China. But the apparent dawn of a golden age for Chinese foreign policy in the "new world order" was not to be. Political and economic countercurrents were at work within China and abroad that soon required Beijing to scramble for a strategy that was more than "status quo plus."

China's initial post–cold war strategic challenge. China's spectacular economic performance during the early 1980s had taken a turn for the worse after 1986. Heightened job insecurity and raging inflation, together with political dissatisfaction among China's intellectuals and broad-based frustration with official corruption, created a volatile mix that produced nationwide demonstrations when a window of opportunity opened in spring 1989.[21] This unanticipated challenge to the CCP's monopoly on political power emerged just as China's leaders were attempting to consolidate their newly favorable position in the post–cold war world. President Bush had visited Beijing two months before the demonstrations began and General Secretary Gorbachev arrived when they peaked in early May.[22] The brutal crackdown that followed in June transformed Western perceptions of the PRC and ended the era in which cold war strategic interests had greased the skids for the West's favorable economic and political treatment of the Chinese regime, its communist moniker notwithstanding.

Beijing's security environment was dramatically altered. To be sure, neither the U.S. nor the Soviet Union posed an immediate *military* threat (as had been the case during most of the cold war). Yet from Beijing's perspective, both posed a challenge to China's national security. The United States threatened China not only because it spearheaded the initial post-Tiananmen effort to isolate China and impose sanctions, but also because its subsequent effort at resuming constructive engagement carried the risk (for Americans, the promise) of "peaceful evolution" that might precipitate pressures for political change and domestic unrest, if not regime collapse.[23] The Soviet Union, its successor states, and former satellites threatened China by example, at least during the years of early enthusiasm for the newly democratic regimes.[24]

As if the "democratic threat" from abroad were not enough, at the same time Beijing also faced a frustrating new challenge on a matter it had long defined as an absolutely vital national interest—its sovereignty over Taiwan. After decades of harsh liberation rhetoric, beginning in 1979 the CCP had floated a series of proposals that emphasized patience on timing and tolerance of differences (ultimately permitting Taiwan to maintain its own political, economic, and military institutions if it would only acknowledge Beijing's sovereignty). During the early post-Mao era, this more generous approach may have seemed promising since it was directed at an authoritarian Kuomintang (KMT) regime that, however ideologically hostile, was at least committed to the idea that Taiwan was part of China. As Taiwan began to democratize in the late 1980s, this commitment was in jeopardy. Younger KMT politicians with roots on the island and newly active opposition politicians, especially in the Democratic Progressive Party (DPP), envisioned a continuation of the island's de facto independence indefinitely and, increasingly, moves toward de jure independence. If time meant greater democratization on Taiwan, and increased democratization meant an end to Taipei's traditional commitment to reunification, a policy of patience and tolerance was no longer so appealing in Beijing. Moreover, the end of the cold war had revived the importance of ideology as a driving force in U.S. foreign policy that sought to advance the spread of liberal democracy and free markets. Thus, the likelihood of American support for democratic, capitalist Taiwan against authoritarian, semi-socialist China, especially in the wake of the brutal 1989 crackdown, increased to levels unmatched since Nixon's historic visit in 1972.[25]

As the 1990s opened, Beijing found itself in a precarious position. Its cold war grand strategy was dead, but a new direction was not yet clear. Until 1992, China focused mainly on its internal political and economic problems. Foreign policy was limited essentially to small steps to undo the setbacks in international economic and diplomatic relations that had followed the outrage about Tiananmen Square.[26] By 1992, apparently satisfied that it had weathered the political storm of communist collapses and had righted its own economic ship, the regime began to evince greater self-confidence at home and abroad.[27] With a decisive push provided by Deng Xiaoping, and sustained by his designated successor Jiang Zemin, aggressive economic reforms re-ignited rapid growth catalyzed by large-scale foreign trade and investment.[28] The economic attractiveness of China, whose communist regime was no longer deemed to be on the verge of collapse, led others to seize the opportunity China's new openness provided. China's booming growth rates even had political spillover effects on the delicate matter of relations with Taiwan. In 1993 the two sides opened unofficial talks and began to establish a framework for expanding economic, social, and academic exchanges. Then, in 1994, as memories of the CCP's brutal 1989 crackdown faded, U.S. President Clinton, despite his earlier campaign trail rhetoric against "coddling Chinese dictators," called for an end to the annual effort to link MFN with Beijing's domestic and foreign policy behavior. China's international prospects were clearly brightening.

As the PRC re-emerged from the shadow of Tiananmen and became more internationally active, however, it confronted a less forgiving world than the one it faced in the 1980s. Remarkably quickly, China's international position began to deteriorate during 1995–1996 as others reacted with alarm to what they saw as an increasingly powerful Beijing more assertively staking its claims to disputed territory in the South China Sea and to sovereignty over Taiwan. By the time the PRC concluded military exercises aimed at influencing the March 1996 presidential election on Taiwan, it faced an international environment more hostile and potentially dangerous than at any time since the late 1970s. China's regional activism had successively antagonized the ASEAN states, crystallized the view of an important segment of the U.S. foreign policy elite that the PRC represented a new threat to American international interests, and aroused Japanese fears about Beijing's regional intentions.[29] Thus, although rapid economic growth was enabling China to increase its military capabilities, these capabilities and China's actions were triggering responses that seemed likely to undermine the country's security.[30]

Growing threats: Stimuli for a new strategy. In this context, analysts in Beijing were especially concerned about the implications for China of unprecedented American capabilities combined with Washington's belief that U.S. national security frontiers are unlimited. In the post–cold war era this expansive definition of interests was allegedly leading an unchecked U.S. to undertake repeated military interventions around the globe, to engage in "frequent crude interferences in the internal affairs of other countries," and to attempt to upgrade its anachronistic network of cold war alliances as a vehicle for ensuring continued American dominance. The East Asian facet of the U.S. post–cold war strategy was to use the theory of a "China threat" to "sow divisions [among the region's states and] . . . to prevent China from becoming developed and powerful."[31] Particularly worrisome was the nearly simultaneous strengthening of two U.S.-led Pacific alliances that Beijing believed were acquiring an anti-China focus.[32]

The July 1996 declaration on the "Relations of Strategic Partners of the 21st Century between Australia and the United States" troubled China. Australia's "security outlook" embraced a belief "that potential security risks existed in its area . . . that countries in that area were building up their militaries," and that instability in "the Korean Peninsula . . . the Taiwan Strait . . . and the Nansha Islands" required the "forward deployment of the U.S. military in Australia . . . to effectively handle future regional and global challenges." Beijing clearly understood this declaration to reflect concerns about a rising China. It included not only plans for joint U.S.-Australian military exercises, and intelligence and logistical cooperation, but also permission for the U.S. "to build a ground relay station in Australia" as part of its advanced warning system necessary for ballistic missile defenses. This last item especially rankled Beijing because it raised the prospect of deployments that could vitiate one of the PRC's few areas of regional military strength. Defense Secretary William Perry's assertion that Australia was one of two U.S. "anchors in the Asia-Pacific Region," Australia in the south and Japan in the north, further reinforced Beijing's perception that the U.S. was cultivating a "triangular security framework in the Asia Pacific region" as part of an incipient anti-China containment policy, Australia's protestations to the contrary notwithstanding.[33]

While Beijing worried about the potential threat of changes in the U.S.-Australia link, it was the prospect of a changing U.S.-Japan security relationship that most alarmed China. Its fears were aroused not just by the content of the revised guidelines for U.S.-Japan military cooperation being hammered out in 1996 and 1997, but also by a continuing skepticism about Japan's commitment to a peaceful foreign policy that colored Beijing's interpretation of the new arrangements.[34] Washington and Tokyo portrayed the revised policy on U.S.-Japan defense cooperation as merely an updating of longstanding security ties in light of the end of the cold war while Beijing saw in it an ominous portent. China asserted that the heart of the revision was contained in the agreement's fourth section, "outline of the new policy," which called for Japan to assume greater responsibilities in the event a crisis emerged in regions on Japan's periphery. Although the limited support activities to which Tokyo committed itself, and the absence of collective self-defense language suggested marginal adjustments, China strongly objected on the following grounds:

> [1] While small, the change was a continuation of a disturbing trend in Japan's military policy. In half a century Japan had progressed "from having no army to having a modernized 'self-defense force'; and from only protecting Japan's own territory to the possibility of entering 'Japan's peripheral regions'." At best, the change is a turn for the worse, a possible deviation from Japan's postwar path of peace and development; at worst it is an attempt to provide legal cover for "edgeballing" (a Ping-Pong equivalent for "salami tactics") the constitutional proscriptions on Japan's international military activity.
>
> [2] Because the concept "Japan's peripheral regions (*Riben zhoubian diqu*)" is vague, and because the guidelines state that the concept is not defined geographically, but is determined by considering the nature of the situation, at any time the periphery could be arbitrarily expanded.
>
> [3] The pretext for this change (that in Japan's peripheral regions after the cold war there are still unstable and untrustworthy factors) reveals that the real motive for the change is a concern about China[35]

Beijing was determined to minimize the anti-China potential of a shifting U.S.-Japan alliance. Most importantly, this meant ensuring that the peripheral regions for joint action did not include Taiwan and its surrounding waters. China repeatedly sought clarification on this point, but found Japanese statements less than fully reassuring. In September 1997, Koichi Kato, Secretary General of Japan's Liberal Democratic Party, for example, offered the following mixed message about Taiwan: "Our position is that the Taiwan issue is a Chinese domestic issue. But it is an important question whether, in the event military action is taken from Mainland China toward Taiwan, against the residents' will, whether we can remain unconcerned."[36]

During his February 1998 trip to Japan, China's Defense Minister Chi Haotian asked again for clarification.[37] His Japanese hosts responded by stating that the security treaty is a bilateral matter not targeting any third country, that it does not aim at interfering in other countries' internal politics, and that Japan's stance on Taiwan is already set forth in a Sino-Japanese joint declaration—Japan will not change its policy of maintaining only informal relations with Taiwan. Though diplomatically proper, this position again fell short of what China wanted to hear, since the absence of formal links to Taipei in no way rules out the possibility that Japan could, under the terms of the revised relationship support U.S. military operations in the area around Taiwan if a crisis developed. In any case, given the inherent uncertainty about promises in an anarchic international realm, even more forthcoming statements from Tokyo could not have eliminated China's lingering fear that Japan will assist the U.S. in the event of a renewed military confrontation in the Taiwan Straits.[38]

Responding to the threats: Strategic alternatives. China's growing capabilities and assertive behavior in the mid-1990s seemed to be nurturing an increasingly hostile, potentially dangerous, international environment. What could China do about it? One alternative would be a determined effort to rapidly augment the PLA's capabilities in the hope that it would more than offset any countermeasure others might adopt. Essentially, this would have represented a bet against the logic of the security dilemma, or at least a gamble on the inefficiency of others' attempts to counterbalance China's efforts via arming or alliance formation. Such "internal balancing" might at first glance seem to have been more plausible than ever in light of China's improving economic situation in the 1990s. But the experience of the early nineties cast doubt on the viability of this approach. Beijing's accelerated military modernization after 1989, a serious effort but one exaggerated in foreign analysts' great leaps of faith about the operational significance of equipment purchases and changes in military doctrine, was not quickly transforming the PLA into a first-class, great power fighting force able to take on all comers.[39] China's economy was simply not yet able to provide the quantity and, more importantly, the quality of resources necessary for a serious effort at militarily outracing its chief competitors who were already demonstrating a determination to respond in kind.[40]

Resource constraints aside, a self-reliant military buildup may have been unattractive because China's leaders were wary of repeating what they understood to be the Soviet Union's foreign policy mistakes. China's economic reforms were enabling the PRC to avoid the "Soviet disease" at home, but its foreign policy in the mid-1990s already seemed to be increasing the risk of suffering the "Soviet disease" abroad.[41] By this I mean a lesser great power whose international behavior, political character, and geographic location lead a broad coalition to view it as more threatening than the world's most powerful state.[42] As the 1990s unfolded and others worried about what they saw as the PRC's disturbing program of military modernization and assertive regional behavior, China faced a real risk that it could find itself, like the cold war Soviet Union, surrounded by states that had decided to align with, rather than balance against, the hegemonic U.S.[43] Indeed, Beijing's foreign policy shift described below specifically sought to discourage others from embracing calls for a new strategy of containment, aimed this time at China.[44]

Because China's leaders believed that the underlying problem they faced in the mid-1990s was others' exaggerated threat perceptions, an attempt to discredit such views was another possible response to their country's deteriorating security situation. Official spokesmen did in fact consistently denounce the "China threat theory" as absurd—arguing that the PRC's national defense buildup was purely defensive.[45] Chinese analysts emphasized three points—shortcomings in the country's economic and military capabilities,[46] its benign intentions,[47] and the risk that threat exaggeration and attempts to contain an imaginary China threat could result in a tragic self-fulfilling prophecy.[48] By itself, however, Beijing's well articulated effort to discredit "China-threat theory" failed to effectively reassure regional and global actors; "cheap talk" predictably mattered less than uncertainties created by an increasingly powerful China's assertive actions.

A third alternative for the PRC would be to secure an ally (or allies) thereby combining its clout with others to deal with the heightened insecurity it faced in the mid-1990s. But the lack of sufficiently capable partners sharing China's concerns limited the feasibility of this approach. It is true that the one significant bright spot for China's diplomacy early in the decade was an improving relationship with the new Russia, especially as a vendor of military hardware that the PRC could not produce for itself. But the purchase of limited amounts of Russian weaponry could not provide a sufficient counter to the more advanced, and potentially larger military forces that seemed to be arraying themselves against China on issues ranging from the Spratlys to Taiwan to the Diaoyus. Nor would close relations with a struggling Russia enable China to pursue its chief international economic goal—further integration into the global economy (especially accession to the WTO) to ensure that foreign trade and investment would continue to play its role in keeping the country's national engine running. On the contrary, the opportunity costs of cultivating an alliance against the U.S. and its Pacific partners were too high. A turn toward hostile alliance systems would jeopardize the benefits of participation in the relatively open post–cold war international economic system essential to China (and Russia's) continued modernization.[49]

Shared resentment of U.S. international dominance (in Russia over having to accept NATO's eastward expansion, in China over refocused U.S. bilateral alliances in Asia and American leadership of the West's demands that China meet the standards set by the developed industrial states on matters from human rights to market access) did produce rhetoric condemning U.S. hegemony. However, this shared *welt angst* would be no more effective in dealing with the tangible challenges to China's interests in the 1990s than Maoist rhetoric about unity with the third world had been in the 1960s. A militarily and economically ineffectual Russia could not even provide the sort of security benefits that the quasi-alliance ties to the U.S had in the last two decades of the cold war. In short, a Sino-Russian alliance was not a viable option.

The unattractiveness or infeasibility of the obvious alternatives led China instead to adopt policies that, taken together, I label their neo-Bismarckian strategy. These policies aimed to reverse the trend of the mid-1990s whose continuation might have resulted in China confronting an encircling coalition incorporating virtually all of the major and minor powers in the region as well as the heavily involved U.S. They represent a pragmatic attempt to deal with the consequences of "China-threat" perceptions that an increasingly sophisticated leadership began to view as understandable, though misguided.[50] From mid-1996, China's foreign policy focused on two broad efforts. The first entailed actions, and not just words, to reassure China's neighbors by enhancing the PRC's reputation as a more responsible and cooperative player. The key to this component of China's new approach was a more active embrace of multilateralism and Beijing's widely touted self-restraint during the wave of currency devaluations that accompanied the Asian financial crisis. The second aspect of the new policy turn aimed to reduce the likelihood that others would unite to prevent China's slow but steady rise to the ranks of the great powers. Most importantly by cultivating "strategic partnerships" in its bilateral relations with the world's major states, Beijing hoped to increase the benefits they perceived in working with China and to underscore the opportunity costs of working against it. The following section discusses these two distinctive components of China's grand strategy that emerged most clearly after 1996.

CHINA'S NEO-BISMARCKIAN TURN: REASSURANCE

Multilateralism. China was skeptical of multilateralism in the early post–cold war period. Beijing valued participation in multilateral institutions mainly as a symbol of the PRC's status as an actor that must be included in deliberating matters of regional or global importance. Its skepticism reflected a concern that these forums were subject to manipulation by the United States and Japan to put pressure on China.[51] For solving issues touching on its vital interests, Beijing instead preferred bilateral diplomacy (or unilateral action) backed by the country's growing capabilities. Experience soon suggested, however, that the original calculation of the costs and benefits of multilateralism, and the advantages for China of the bilateral emphasis, was misguided. Even in its dealings with relatively small powers in the South China Sea disputes, bilateralism was not providing Beijing with the leverage it hoped for; when disputes intensified, regional adversaries, whose unity China feared would be manifest in multilateral settings, united anyway.

In the mid-1990s, then, China began to evince a new appreciation of the benefits of multilateralism.[52] Beijing apparently concluded that accepting the constraints that come with working in multilateral settings was preferable to the risk of isolation and encirclement that its aloof stance and assertive behavior were creating.[53] The shift to a more receptive posture on multilateralism was expected to help dampen the "China-threat" perceptions that so worried Beijing; continued participation was expected to further the perception of responsible international behavior more convincingly than the repeated official denunciations of "China-threat theory." Agreeing to the CTBT, cooperating with the effort to promote peace on the Korean peninsula, joining with other leading members of the nonproliferation regime in condemning the South Asian nuclear tests of 1998, more flexibly engaging the ASEAN states, and negotiating agreements on the disputed borders with its former Soviet neighbors, have been part of an embrace of multilateralism that serves China's national interest in countering fears of its unilateral assertiveness.[54] Indeed, multilateral forums, once seen as a potential vehicle for outside pressure, are now seen as offering an opportunity to counter some of the threats to China that were developing in the mid-1990s. Beijing has touted multilateral security arrangements, including arms control, as an alternative to regional developments it saw as dangerous—specifically the strengthening bilateral military alliances (i.e., U.S. ties to Japan and Australia) and deployment of increasingly advanced weapons systems (especially ballistic missile defenses).[55]

Beijing's warmer embrace of multilateralism represents, as Iain Johnston and Paul Evans suggest, a significant shift from past practice.[56] But it should not be mistaken for a conversion to supranational values. Instead, it represents a component of China's neo-Bismarckian grand strategy designed to advance national interests, in this case by reassuring those who might otherwise collaborate against a putative China threat. However real, the embrace is partial and conditional; China continues to resist efforts to place on the multilateral agenda sovereignty disputes it insists can only be resolved through bilateral negotiations.[57]

Currency responsibility. As with the change in its position on multilateralism, China's policy on currency devaluation while the East Asian financial crisis deepened and threatened to spread around the globe since 1997 reflected the broader foreign policy goal of transforming the reputation China was acquiring in 1995–1996 as an irredentist, revisionist, rising power, into the reputation China was cultivating in 1997–1998 as paragon of international responsibility. What would have constituted an economically sensible Chinese reaction to the currency devaluations undertaken by major trading states in East Asia is debatable. Economic considerations aside, however, Beijing expected its announcement and repeated assurances that it was not going to devalue the yuan to maintain the competitiveness of Chinese exports, to pay significant international political dividends. It worked. Foreign analysts intermittently predicted that China would devalue because declining exports were hurting national economic growth at a moment when the regime was undertaking painful domestic reforms. The more they speculated, the greater the payoff for Beijing in terms of a reputation for responsible internationalism that seemed to contrast with the narrowly self-interested approaches of others in the region, and the greater the payoff for Beijing in terms of the increased credibility of its international promises that seemed to contrast with the unfilled or broken promises of others as well. Even if devaluation of the yuan had ultimately become an economic necessity, the longer China could delay the decision the more likely it would have been able to portray the step as a result of the others' failure to assume their responsibilities for regional economic health (especially Japan) while China had shouldered more than its share.[58] In the event, Beijing did not devalue during the financial crisis. Although a few analysts argued that the decision reflected not altruism but rather economic self-interest, China had nevertheless succeeded in reaping a significant political benefit.

CHINA'S NEO-BISMARCKIAN TURN: GREAT POWER DIPLOMACY

Actions to reassure others and transform China's international reputation are important features of Beijing's current grand strategy, but China's principal focus remains its bilateral relations with the world's other major powers. In this respect, the neo-Bismarckian turn in the PRC's foreign policy gradually emerged in 1996 when Beijing began to label its preferred arrangement with major powers "strategic partnerships."[59] Although the invocation of this precise term would vary, the approach to bilateral diplomacy it represented endured. China has attempted to build a series of relationships with the other major powers that enhance its attractiveness as a partner while maximizing its own leverage and flexibility by not firmly aligning with any particular state or group of states. Rather than explicitly identifying friends and enemies among principal actors on the international scene, China sought to establish partnerships with each as a way of binding their interests to China's and reducing the likelihood that any would be able to cobble together a hostile coalition. Asserting that the old categories of ally and adversary were a relic of power politics that prevailed until the end of the cold war, Beijing attempted to link itself to each of the world's other major powers in order to increase the costs they would face if they took actions that ran contrary to China's interests.[60] Cooperation in improving the opportunities for foreigners to benefit from trade with and investment in the China market, and Beijing's cooperation on managing the security problems of weapons proliferation and terrorism, are among some of the more important benefits that great power partners would put at risk if they opted to press China on matters sensitive enough to sour bilateral relations.[61]

Great-power partnerships were not only hailed as a force for international peace, stability, and mutually beneficial economic relations. As repeatedly emphasized in discussing the first one established with Russia, they were also expected to serve as a vehicle for fostering the emergence of a multipolar international system in which the U.S. would no longer be so dominant—a result that China sought to hasten.[62] This partnership approach had the added value for China of enabling it to pursue its interest in offsetting American dominance without resorting to the directly confrontational (and given the current power distribution, probably futile) alternative of straightforward counterhegemonic balancing. Indeed, by eschewing alliances and instead cultivating strategic partnerships, Beijing not only hoped to avoid antagonizing others, and perhaps exacerbating concerns about its international intentions. It also anticipated a propaganda advantage insofar as it could portray U.S. foreign policy as stubbornly anachronistic, criticizing Washington's effort to reinvigorate, expand, and redirect its alliances in Asia and Europe as reflecting a cold war mentality that others were discarding.[63]

What is the content of a strategic partnership, and with whom are they being established? In practice, the essential elements are a commitment to promoting stable relationships and extensive economic intercourse, muting disagreements about domestic politics in the interest of working together on matters of shared concern in international diplomacy, and routinizing the frequent exchange of official visits, especially those by representatives of each country's military and regular summit meetings between top government leaders. Although resting on some of the same principles of mutual respect and noninterference that constituted the "Five Principles of Peaceful Coexistence" set forth in the mid-1950s, strategic partnerships are arrangements that go well beyond mere tolerance. Beginning in 1996, China has pursued such partnerships with Russia and the United States, but developments in bilateral relations with Europe and Japan suggest that it may expect others to follow.

China-Russia. The formation of a strategic partnership with Russia set the pattern for China's preferred approach to bilateral relations with the major powers. Boris Yeltsin's initial state visit to China in December 1992 had laid the groundwork for improving Sino-Russian ties in the post-Soviet era and resulted in the September 1994 joint announcement during Jiang Zemin's return visit that China and Russia were establishing a "constructive partnership." At a third summit meeting in Beijing in April 1996, the relationship was redefined as a "strategic cooperative partnership."[64] The broader significance of the term used was not immediately obvious, and some wondered whether the arrangement was in fact simply a step toward an old-fashioned alliance, especially since it emerged amidst sharpening Sino-Russian concerns about U.S. international dominance in Europe and Asia (NATO's eastward expansion; Washington's recommitment to a broad security role in the Western Pacific as well as the March 1996 aircraft carrier maneuvers demonstrating an enduring unofficial U.S. support for Taiwan). For reasons outlined above, however, an alliance targeting the U.S. was not particularly attractive to China or Russia.[65] Nevertheless, their shared anxiety about the role of an unchecked American superpower provided a solid foundation for this most stable of the partnerships that Beijing would cultivate.[66] Indeed, during the first decade of the post–cold war era, Sino-Russian anxiety about U.S. capabilities and intentions deepened, not only in response to NATO expansion and Washington's strengthened ties to American allies in East

Asia, but also in response to what these partners saw as the U.S. penchant for foreign military intervention and its ever clearer determination to deploy ballistic missile defenses.[67]

Because Moscow and Beijing each have territories over which they seek to secure sovereign control (for Russia, Chechnya; for China, Taiwan and perhaps someday Tibet or Xinjiang), both have become increasingly wary of the role that a more fearless U.S. might decide to play.[68] U.S. missile defense plans reinforced the Sino-Russian concerns about continued "hegemony" that American interventionist behavior nurtured.[69] Ballistic missile defenses pose a serious challenge for Russia and China insofar as they raise the possibility of altering the military-strategic context in ways that would be distinctly disadvantageous for both. In the present strategic setting, Russian and Chinese missile forces offer an affordable offset to the advantages the U.S. military enjoys on the modern battlefield. In a world with extensive missile defenses, Russia and China would have to worry about the possibility that great power strategic competition would be decided in an arena of expensive, advanced, conventional armaments where U.S. economic and technological strengths give it a huge and, for the foreseeable future, enduring advantage. If so, both Russia and China might have to shoulder a much heavier military burden simply to maintain their current levels of security in an extended era of American unipolarity.[70]

Such shared security concerns have become the basis for a robust Sino-Russian strategic partnership despite problems that plague their bilateral relations (most prominently, profoundly disappointing economic ties and recurrent tensions over the high profile of Chinese nationals in Russia's far eastern regions).[71] President Putin's July 2000 state visit to Beijing repeated a pattern Yeltsin and Jiang established in the mid-1990s—reemphasis on the countries' interest in opposing and hastening the end of American-led unipolarity (warning against outside intervention in others' internal affairs and against deploying allegedly destabilizing missile defenses) but no breakthrough on deepening a bilateral economic relationship that continues to be limited by Russia's enduring weakness.[72] Because its ties to Russia provide military-strategic benefits (permitting China to turn its attention to security concerns in the East and South, complicating U.S. attempts to isolate Beijing on matters such as arms control and the hard sovereignty principle behind its claim to Taiwan) and also access to weapons it can neither produce itself nor purchase elsewhere, the Sino-Russian strategic partnership remains vital to the PRC.[73] But because the relationship does not provide the economic benefits necessary for China to sustain its great-power aspirations, and because of remaining mutual suspicions rooted in recent history as well as the belief that rivalry between big neighbors is natural and will be hard to avoid once Russia recovers from its economic downturn, the PRC hedges its bets. China limits its ties to Russia by drawing the line short of alliance while also working to build partnerships with other great powers, especially those that can better serve its immediate grand-strategic interest in economic modernization.[74] In this effort, managing China's relations with the potentially threatening U.S. remains the top priority.[75]

China-U.S. At the October 1997 summit in Washington, the PRC and the U.S. agreed to work toward a "constructive strategic partnership." The term had been chosen, after some haggling, in order to [1] indicate that the countries would work together to solve problems threatening peace and stability (thus, a partnership); [2] underscore the significance of this bilateral relationship for broader regional and international security (thus, strategic); and, [3] distinguish it from the closer ties already in place with Russia (thus, the need to work on making strained bilateral relations more constructive).[76] The announcement and subsequent discussion emphasized the mutual economic benefits of exchange between the world's largest developed and developing countries, the advantages of close consultation on political and security issues (including establishing a Beijing-Washington hotline, regular meetings between cabinet level officials, exchange visits by military personnel, joint efforts on counter-proliferation, environmental protection, and drug enforcement) as well as the importance of not permitting differences on any single issue (e.g., human rights, trade disputes) to obscure the big picture of common strategic interests.[77]

Just as some observers at first misinterpreted the Sino-Russian strategic partnership as a way station to an alliance, some mistakenly anticipated that the Sino-American strategic partnership was intended to herald an era of close cooperation that would preclude traditional great power conflict. Some who viewed the U.S. as a counterweight to China, worried that Washington might subordinate their interests to the exigencies of a Sinocentric Asia policy. Diplomatic pleasantries and lofty summit rhetoric aside, however, the announced effort to build a Sino-American strategic partnership was actually a search for a workable framework to manage the significant differences and conflicts of interest between the two most active major powers in Asia after the cold war. For its part, China had no intention of abandoning its aspiration for increased international influence, even if that conflicted with an American interest in preserving its primacy. Instead, strategic partnership with the U.S. was designed to better enable China to cope with the potentially dangerous constraints of American hegemony during China's rise to great-power status. Partnership made cooperation conditional, linking it to American behavior that did not infringe on core Chinese security interests and clarifying the benefits a hostile U.S. might forfeit.

Since 1997 Beijing has indicated that a souring of the relationship might lead it to: (1) give preferential economic treatment to other partners (Japan or Europe); (2) complicate U.S. diplomacy by exercising the Chinese veto in the UN Security Council; (3) be less circumspect in its export controls on sensitive military technologies (especially nuclear and missile technologies) to states about which the U.S. has strong concerns; (4) delay its participation in agreements that comprise the nonproliferation regime, especially the Missile Technology Control Regime and the proposed agreement to cut off fissile material production; (5) limit its cooperation in the fight against international terrorism, especially in Central Asia; (6) play a less helpful role in containing regional tension in Korea or South Asia.[78] China, in short, saw partnership as a way to realize its strategic interest in linkage—highlighting the price the U.S. may incur if its actions reduce Beijing's willingness to play a constructive role on economically, diplomatically, or militarily important matters. Given the material advantages of the U.S., such costs may not much constrain American policymakers. But for now, limited leverage may simply be the best of a bad lot of options available to a relatively weak China.[79]

During Jiang Zemin's 1997 visit to Washington, Chinese and U.S. leaders both expressed the hope that in working toward the constructive strategic partnership bilateral relations would evolve in a positive direction. At first, however, the priority was on avoiding renewed confrontation (such as that in the Taiwan Strait during 1995–96) rather than finally resolving existing conflicts or promoting still more ambitious cooperation.[80] Yet even with this modest aim, and despite a successful follow-up return visit to China by President Clinton in June 1998, events soon began to pose a stiff test of the still "under construction" Sino-American strategic partnership that prompted a reconsideration of its value both in Beijing and Washington.

American support for the partnership began to erode dramatically by late 1998. Disillusionment followed from disappointment with China's renewed clampdown on political and religious dissidents, accusations of Chinese corporate and military espionage aimed at acquiring advanced missile and nuclear warhead technologies, and the belief that after the accidental U.S. bombing of China's embassy in Belgrade the Communist Party leaders had cynically fanned the flames of anti-Americanism resulting in violent demonstrations targeting the U.S. embassy in Beijing. Although high-level American envoys to China still privately invoked the term "strategic partnership" during their meetings with PRC leaders, in the U.S. the phrase virtually disappeared as a public way to refer to Sino-American relations, except when used pejoratively by critics of Clinton administration policy.[81]

In China, however, the upshot of the ongoing turmoil in Sino-American relations after 1998 was different. Although the unexpected downturn in relations with the U.S. so soon after the two successful Jiang-Clinton summits provoked a sharp internal debate, by late summer 1999 China's top-level leaders apparently decided that the grand strategy in which great power partnerships were a central feature would remain in place.[82]

The different reactions in Beijing and Washington to the troubles that beset bilateral relations after late 1998 are partly explained by contrasting visions of the strategic partnership. The American understanding of a "constructive" relationship included not only the anticipation of growing international cooperation, but also the expectation that in the interest of good relations China's leaders would at least temper their domestic political practices in ways that the U.S. would find more palatable. China's expectations were quite different, however. Strategic partnership with the U.S. was a means for advancing China's own interests. In this view, because China's interests paralleled those of the U.S. on some major international issues, the partnership appropriately facilitated cooperation. Parallel interests led to joint condemnation of India's nuclear tests in 1998 (for Washington, a general interest in nonproliferation; for Beijing, specific concerns about a potential military rivalry with India).[83]

Parallel interests also led to coordinated efforts to restrain North Korea's missile program (for Washington, an interest in limiting the capabilities of a "rogue" state; for Beijing, an interest in reducing the risks of war on its border and eliminating the rationale Pyongyang was providing for advocates of early U.S. deployment of theater and national ballistic missile defenses). But since a central purpose of partnership with the U.S. was also to facilitate continued economic development necessary for China to become a genuine great power, Beijing was not willing to sacrifice what it saw as a vital national interest in preserving a key aspect of the foundation for growth—the domestic political stability it associated with the one-party communist rule that so troubled Americans.[84] Simply put, China's understanding of strategic partnership was that it meant a relationship both sides viewed as important enough to sustain despite such areas of disagreement.[85]

Given this Chinese understanding, among the small group of relatively insulated Communist Party leaders who determine the country's foreign policy, support for working toward a constructive strategic partnership with the U.S. endured. It did so despite the intensifying American criticism of China's human rights record, the release of the Cox Committee report alleging a long history of Chinese espionage in the U.S., the double embarrassment for Premier Zhu Rongji of first having the proposed terms for China's accession to WTO that he carried with him to Washington in April 1999 rejected, and then having its major concessions to the U.S. revealed before he even returned to China, and finally the May 1999 American bombing of the Chinese embassy in Belgrade.[86]

To be sure, these troubling events did spur a vigorous debate among China's foreign policy elite about the feasibility of working toward a constructive strategic partnership with the U.S. Indeed, after the May 1999 embassy bombing there was at least brief consideration of shifting to a new line that emphasized straightforward opposition to American hegemony by uniting closely with Russia and the developing world.[87] Such a shift would have amounted to a change of grand strategy for China. By late summer 1999, however, a consensus had formed. While China's leaders embraced the internal critics' more suspicious view of U.S. intentions, they also acknowledged that an important lesson of the war in Kosovo was that the American advantage in relative capabilities was proving remarkably robust and, therefore, that the transition to a multipolar world would take longer than previously anticipated.[88] Under such circumstances, China's own interests led them back to the simple conclusion that there was simply no feasible substitute for developing a positive working relationship with the U.S.[89]

In part this conclusion was based on the bracing realities of relative military power and the enduring economic importance of the U.S. for China's modernization. In part, however, it was also a reaction to newly troublesome developments on the Taiwan front during the summer of 1999, when the island's president, Lee Teng-hui, publicly floated his idea that ties with the PRC should be viewed as "special state-to-state" relations. This stance seemed to inch the island further in the direction of independence and predictably elicited a strong reaction from the mainland.[90] The mini-crisis that resulted had the potential to drive a final nail in the coffin of the Sino-American partnership that seemed to be on the verge of total collapse following the Belgrade bombing just one month earlier. In the event, the Clinton administration's carefully calculated reaction contributed to the PRC's decision to salvage the Sino-American strategic partnership. President Clinton sent envoys to both Beijing and Taipei who not only urged Beijing to act with restraint, but also warned Taipei that there were limits to the conditions under which it could count on support from Washington—a tacit warning against provocative moves toward independence.[91]

With a presidential election on Taiwan looming in March 2000, and the possibility it could trigger a serious crisis if it led to the victory of a candidate committed to independence, China could ill afford to sacrifice the sort of leverage its working relationship with the U.S. seemed to provide. Writing off the strategic partnership with the U.S. would not only complicate China's ability to enjoy the full fruits of participation in the international economy and clearly put China in the cross-hairs of an incomparably more powerful U.S. military. It would also free the U.S. to further upgrade its security ties with Taiwan since there would no longer be valued links with China on matters such as proliferation or Korea that would be put at risk. By the time the CCP's top leaders gathered at the seaside resort of Beidaihe in August 1999 for their annual policy review, they evidently concluded that the partnership approach to relations with the U.S. and the opportunities for linkage that it created still served their nation's vital interests in development and unification; it therefore would remain a central feature of the foreign policy approach China had embraced since 1996.[92]

China-Europe. In order to further reduce the likelihood of confronting a broad coalition united by its hostility toward China, after April 1996 Beijing also intensified its efforts to build partnerships with other actors it envisions as key players in a future multipolar world—the European states and especially nearby Japan. As a practical matter, however, China's cultivation of bilateral relations with these partners has differed from its approach to Russia or the United States. And apparently because it views the broader effects on international security as smaller than those obtained through its relations with Russia and the U.S., Beijing refrained from using the term "strategic" to describe these partnerships, though in practice they establish many of the same linkages (e.g., the lure of mutually beneficial economic arrangements and the promise of constructive efforts to address major international problems such as the Asian financial crisis and tensions on the Korean peninsula). China has in fact chosen a distinct label for its ties with each of these other major powers—"long-term comprehensive partnership" with France; "comprehensive cooperative partnership" with Britain; "trustworthy partnership" with Germany; "long-term stable and constructive partnership" with the EU; "friendly and cooperative partnership" with Japan.[93]

Because a united Europe does not yet formulate a single foreign policy, China has worked separately on partnerships with its leading states (France, Britain, Germany) while also dealing with the representatives of the EU as a whole.[94] The lure of upgrading bilateral relations with China and especially the interest in improving economic ties, induced first France (1997), and then each of the other leading European powers to stake out a less confrontational posture on the PRC's human rights policy and agree to ease the conditions for China's trade with Europe.[95] While cultivating its partnerships with France, Britain, and Germany, in 1998 the tempo of building China's links with the EU also accelerated. The fanfare that accompanied the first China-EU summit in April 1998 (labeled the beginning of "a new era" in relations with China), the announced plans "to intensify high-level contacts, including possible annual summits,"[96] the EU's June 29, 1998 meeting that approved a new China policy "establishing a comprehensive partnership,"[97] and a series of visits to Europe by China's top three leaders (Jiang Zemin, Li Peng, and Zhu Rongji) suggest that Beijing may be laying the groundwork to use the term "strategic partnership" to describe its relations with the EU if it is ever convinced that the entity is able to speak with a weighty single voice in international affairs.

China-Japan. In comparison to its ties with the major European states, China's political relationship with Japan, though recently improving, has advanced more slowly. Because Japan does not yet play an international political or military role commensurate with its capabilities and because China remains nervous about the uncertain prospect of Japan departing from its familiar role as a limited and constrained junior ally of the U.S., the approach to a partnership with Japan has been somewhat ambivalent. In 1997, when Beijing was celebrating smooth cooperation with Britain on the reversion of Hong Kong to Chinese rule, and issuing joint statements with France's President Chirac about shared interests in building a multipolar world, China was still expressing its displeasure with what it saw as signs of an anti-China undercurrent in Japan—renewed controversy about the disputed Diaoyu/Senkaku Islands, thinly veiled China-threat references inserted in Tokyo's Defense White Papers, and especially the revised guidelines for the U.S.-Japan security relationship.[98] Even so, China also emphasized Japan's self-interest in fostering better bilateral relations in an increasingly competitive global economy, an argument given a fillip as the spreading Asian financial crisis after summer 1997 compounded the challenges already confronting a stalled Japanese economy.[99] In 1998, as the twentieth anniversary of the Sino-Japanese Peace and Friendship Treaty loomed, China indicated its own expectation that "[t]he two sides will construct from the high plane of orienting to the 21st Century a new framework of relations of the two big neighboring nations."[100] Yet, because of the historical legacy of Sino-Japanese animosity and because China either believes Japan cannot or should not play a leadership role on most international-strategic matters, Beijing reportedly resisted Tokyo's private suggestions that their extensive bilateral ties be described as a "strategic" partnership.[101]

In early 1998 China's asking price for announcing any sort of Sino-Japanese partnership seemed to be a more convincing display of contrition for Japan's behavior in China during WWII, and ironclad assurances that Tokyo would not become involved in any future Taiwan Straits crisis under the terms of the revised U.S.-Japan security guidelines. Beijing may have anticipated that an economically troubled Japan, needing a viable partner in the region, would so covet improved ties that it would be willing to accommodate China. Japan resisted. At the November 1998 Tokyo summit meeting between President Jiang and Prime Minister Obuchi, Japan refused to go beyond previous public apologies for its wartime role in China.[102] It also refused to go beyond its basic Taiwan policy recognizing Beijing as the sole government of China or to offer promises about actions it might decide to take in unforeseeable future circumstances. The result was that no ceremony was held to sign a communiqué. Instead, in his post-summit speech Jiang simply announced that the two countries had "agreed that we should establish a friendly and cooperative partnership in which we make efforts together for peace and development."[103] Observers immediately labeled the Chinese president's visit to Japan a disappointment, contrasting with his highly publicized successes in other countries.

Yet the apparent setback at the 1998 summit seems to have been small and temporary. Indeed, in substance if not in name the Sino-Japanese relationship continued to develop most of the characteristics of a strategic partnership—extensive economic ties, regular summit meetings including reciprocal visits by top government officials, and even military-to-military exchanges. Chinese Premier Zhu Rongji's visit to Japan in October 2000 seemed to represent a renewed effort to boost the partnership and to further mute some of the problems that had marred Jiang's 1998 trip.[104] To the extent the two sides are able to move beyond their differences about dealing with the historical legacy of Japan's aggression in the mid-twentieth century, it becomes easier for Beijing to establish the sorts of linkages it hopes will influence Japan's readiness to cooperate with any American regional effort to promote policies that are deemed "anti-China." Of course, even a robust Sino-Japanese partnership cannot enable Beijing to shape debates in Tokyo about matters such as missile defenses and Taiwan as effectively as Japan's long-standing ally in Washington. But to the extent China succeeds in cultivating a sound working relationship with Japan on important regional security concerns and offers attractive economic opportunities to vested Japanese interests, it expects to at least alter the cost-benefit calculations underlying Tokyo's foreign policy choices.

CONCLUSION

China's emerging grand strategy links political, economic and military means in an effort to advance the PRC's twin goals of security and great-power status. Politically, China pursues multilateral and bilateral diplomacy to mute threat perceptions and to convince others of the benefits of engagement and the counterproductive consequences of containment. Economically, China nurtures relations with diverse trading partners and sources of foreign investment, weaving a network of economic relations to limit the leverage of any single partner in setting the terms of China's international economic involvement. Militarily, China seeks to create some breathing space for modernization of its armed forces. To the extent the strategy mitigates perceptions of an overly assertive China, it mutes the security dilemma dynamics that might otherwise (as in the mid-1990s) lead others to respond in ways that offset even measured improvement in the quantity and quality of the PLA's capabilities. And to the extent the strategy facilitates the country's economic development through integration with the global economy, it promises to increase access to advanced technologies essential for China's military if it hopes to move beyond the short-term, second-best solution of importing Russian equipment (most of which falls short of the best available) and attempting to reverse engineer Chinese versions.[105]

China's emerging grand strategy, then, integrates available means with preferred ends. Yet the short period in which its logic has been evident raises the question of the strategy's durability. As noted above, the approach has already survived at least one tough test—the challenge serious Sino-American conflicts posed to one of its central features (great power partnerships) during the first half of 1999. Whether it can survive the repeated tests it will surely face in coming years, such as the tensions following the collision between a U.S. reconnaissance aircraft and a Chinese fighter in April 2001, remains to be seen. There are, however, broad domestic-political and international-power considerations that suggest the strategy may have staying power.

Elite support. First, China's current grand strategy seems politically sustainable within the elite coalition that shapes China's foreign policy. The new approach arguably represents a viable compromise between more exclusively "soft" and "hard" lines, each of which were partly discredited by the events of the mid-1990s generally, and the Taiwan Straits crisis of 1995–96 in particular. After Washington had surprised and angered Beijing by granting Lee Teng-hui a visa in May 1995 that enabled him to continue his campaign to raise Taiwan's international profile, China's leaders quickly coalesced behind a decision to more clearly warn Taiwan (and the U.S.) about the dangers inherent in even small steps toward independence. Beijing shifted from the softer reunification line emphasizing cross-strait dialogue set forth in Jiang Zemin's January 1995 speech to a harder line emphasizing action (including military exercises and missile tests).[106]

As noted above, however, the international ramifications of China's heavy emphasis on coercion proved troubling. By March 1996, "soft" diplomacy and "hard" coercion had each revealed their limited usefulness. Against this background, China's subsequent, more nuanced foreign policy line has obvious attractions. Insofar as it steers a middle course, the present approach appeals to those, especially among the military elite, who worry not only about the willingness of the Foreign Ministry to compromise in the face of foreign, especially American, pressure but who also recognize the difficulties China faces in developing a capability to offset potentially threatening U.S. power.[107] For others, especially younger civilian elites affiliated with the Foreign Ministry, the strategy's emphasis on more active diplomacy, including multilateralism and great power partnerships, provides an alternative to relying too heavily on coercive power as a tool to ensure China's interests, an approach that experience suggested would evoke a clearly counterproductive international reaction.

International-power realities. As has often been noted, China's contemporary leaders, like their predecessors, prize the practice of realpolitik.[108] Beijing's keen sensitivity to the importance of relative capabilities is a second reason to anticipate the durability of the current strategy. Because China's ability to improve its international power position is sharply limited both by the burden of a still developing economy and by the long head start of its advanced industrial rivals, the foreign policy line Beijing has pursued since 1996 is likely continue for at least several more decades. Contemplating the sorts of changes in China's circumstances that would lead Beijing to discard its present grand strategy any sooner suggests why.

The current approach might be abandoned under two scenarios—one in which external constraints became much tighter, and one in which they became much looser.[109] If China, while still relatively weak, found itself facing dire threats from one or more great powers, a situation similar to that which the PRC faced during much of the cold war, Beijing would be constrained to reprise that era's simple balancing strategy—relying on China's nuclear deterrent as the ultimate security guarantee while attempting to secure the backing of a powerful ally, perhaps transforming one or more of its strategic partnerships into a straightforward security entente.[110] Alternatively, if China's relative capabilities were to increase dramatically, or if Beijing concluded that the system's other most capable actors no longer posed much of a constraint on action, it might believe that it no longer needed to reassure others or prevent their collaboration. China might then shift to a strategy that more assertively attempted to reshape the international system according to its own preferences. Such a relaxation of the external constraints on China's foreign policy could result if unexpectedly successful economic and military modernization rapidly elevated the PRC to superpower status or if China's most capable competitors proved unable or unwilling to remain internationally engaged. Under such circumstances, China would not be free to do as it pleased on the world scene, but it would have greater latitude than it now does to follow preference rather than necessity.[111]

For the foreseeable future, however, neither of these more extreme alternatives seems as plausible as a slow but steady increase in China's economic and military clout within an East Asian region where rivals remain vigilant.[112] Indeed, China's analysts prudently anticipate a protracted and multifaceted struggle between American efforts to prolong the present era of unipolarity and other countries (especially China, Russia, and France) attempting to hasten the transition to a multipolar world.[113] China's leaders understand that their country's military capabilities will lag significantly behind those of the U.S. for at least several decades[114] They now also understand more clearly than in the early 1990s that even though the PLA's growing capabilities remain limited and even if, as Beijing insists, its intentions are benign, neighboring countries naturally harbor doubts about China's future international role that the U.S. can decide to exploit if it wants to hem China in.[115] The need to minimize the likelihood of provoking such a dangerous deterioration in its international environment is an important reason why some variation of China's current grand strategy is likely to endure. Beijing faces strong incentives to continue to rely on policies that strive to advance its interests without relying on methods (unrestrained military armament or explicit alliance) that would alarm potential military rivals and alienate valued economic partners.[116]

China's current grand strategy may well remain attractive to leaders in Beijing. What, then, are its implications for international security? The process by which a similarly complex and subtle approach, crafted by Bismarck, came unraveled in Europe at the turn of the last century suggests that there may be reason to worry about the hidden weaknesses and dangers of what currently seems to be a benign a policy that benefits both China and its neighbors. The chief danger, as noted above, is not likely to be an echo of the sort of aggressive nationalism that reared its head in late Imperial and Nazi Germany. Chinese nationalism is a potent force to which the country's legitimacy-challenged leaders must attend, but it is a nationalism that focuses on protecting the territorial and political integrity of the country as delimited at the close of World War II. Whatever the bitterness about the ravages of imperialism China suffered during the Qing dynasty, this has not resulted in demands to redress such historically distant grievances. China's principal claims to territory in the South and East China Seas (the Spratlys, Taiwan, the Diaoyus) are not evidence of a revisionist, expansionist mentality, but rather Beijing's determination to restore what it believes are the outlines of the de jure status quo. As Thomas Christensen's chapter about the dynamics of the security dilemma in the China-U.S.-Japan triangle suggests, however, even policies to preserve the status quo may contribute to confrontational relations (especially when the unavoidable consequences of anarchy are compounded by historically grounded mutual suspicion, as in the Sino-Japanese relationship he describes). Yet China's behavior since the mid-1990s suggests that its leaders have attempted to mute the intensity of the counterproductive security dilemma its behavior had been exacerbating. Since the security dilemma can be managed, but not eliminated as long as the condition of anarchy endures, even self-interested efforts to cope with its effects should be welcomed.

The real danger, or more troubling possibility, is not that China will abandon its neo-Bismarckian strategy in favor of an ambitious, expansionist crusade but that unintended consequences might follow from the strategy's success. Like its nineteenth-century forerunner, the neo-Bismarckian approach entails extensive and intensive linkages among states with competing and common interests. As long as relations are more cooperative than conflictive, fostering tight interdependence may be attractive. But the risk in this sort of arrangement is that when problems emerge they ripple through the system in unpredictable ways that defy efforts at management. Should China's relations with any of the major powers significantly deteriorate, especially if the international system finally does become truly multipolar, the remaining partnerships might be reinterpreted as de facto alliances. States intimately entangled, unable to remain aloof, might feel compelled to choose sides. As noted above, because international norms, economic self-interest, and the advent of nuclear weapons have dramatically altered the role of force for resolving interstate dispute, a disastrous "fail deadly," scenario—a twenty-first-century version of July 1914—seems implausible. An era of renewed international division into rival economic and military blocs would be unfortunate enough. The largely benign consequences of a prudently self-interested China's adherence to its neo-Bismarckian grand strategy in the present era of low tension should not obscure the complexity and challenges such an approach poses for all drawn into its orbit.

ACKNOWLEDGMENT

I thank Cheng Chen and Tang Wei for their research assistance. I also thank the Smith Richardson Foundation as well as the Center for East Asian Studies and the Research Foundation at the University of Pennsylvania for their financial support.

In addition to cited publications, this chapter draws on approximately 80 hours of interviews the author conducted in Beijing (65 hours in June–July 1998, March–April and October, 2000), Tokyo (15 hours in March 1999). The interview subjects (promised confidentiality) were civilian officials and military officers, as well as advisers and independent analysts. In Tokyo, these included individuals affiliated with the Ministry of Foreign Affairs, the Nomura Institute, the Okazaki Institute, Japan's self-defense forces, journalists, and academics. In Beijing, these included individuals affiliated with the Ministry of Foreign Affairs; Ministry of National Defense; the PLA's Academy of Military Sciences; the PLA's National Defense University; the China Institute for International Strategic Studies; the China Institute for Contemporary International Relations, the Foundation for International and Strategic Studies, the China Institute of International Studies, the China Society for Strategy and Management Research; four institutes within the Chinese Academy of Social Sciences (Institute of American Studies, Institute for the Study of World Politics and Economics, Institute for Asian-Pacific Studies, Institute of East European, Russian, and Central Asian Studies), and scholars at Beijing University, Qinghua University, and the Foreign Affairs College.

ENDNOTES

1. Grand strategy here refers to the distinctive combination of military, political, and economic means a state employs to pursue its goals within the constraints posed by the international environment. national goals, as well as the means to pursue them, vary. at a minimum, states seek "to survive and flourish in an anarchic and often threatening international order that oscillates between peace and war." see Paul Kennedy, "Grand Strategy in War and Peace: Toward a Broader Definition," in Paul Kennedy, ed., *Grand Strategies in War and Peace* (New Haven: Yale University Press, 1991), p. 6; see also Kenneth N. Waltz, *Theory of International Politics* (Menlo Park, CA: Addison-Wesley, 1979): 91–92. Some states, however, have interests that are more expansive. Although few are as ambitious as history's aspiring hegemons (Napoleon's France, Hitler's Germany, Hirohito's Japan), the world's leading states have usually sought to shape, and not just survive in, their international environment, typically in ways that will further enhance the wealth, power, and status of their country.

2. Christopher Layne, "The Unipolar Illusion: Why New Great Powers Will Arise," *International Security* 17, no. 4 (Spring 1993): 5–51; Kenneth N. Waltz, "The Emerging Structure of International Politics," *International Security* 18 , no. 2 (Fall 1993); Waltz, "Intimations of Multipolarity," typescript, March 1998.

3. Moreover, minority peoples, whose loyalty to Beijing is questionable, populate China's border regions (especially Tibet, Xinjiang, and Inner Mongolia). This raises concerns about neighboring countries exploiting ethnic unrest if relations with China deteriorate.

4. Swaine and Tellis refer to China's current grand strategy as "the calculative strategy," also emphasizing that China's approach is one for a state that faces a very tough challenge in trying to become a peer competitor of the currently dominant U.S. See Michael D. Swaine and Ashley J. Tellis, *Interpreting China's Grand Strategy: Past, Present, and Future*. (Santa Monica, CA: RAND, 2000), p. xi. On the alternative possibilities for adjusting relations between a dominant and rising power, see Robert Powell, *In the Shadow of Power: States and Strategies in International Politics* (Princeton: Princeton University Press, 1999); A.F.K. Organski and Jacek Kugler, *The War Ledger* (Chicago: University of Chicago Press, 1980); Robert Gilpin, *War and Change in World Politics* (New York: Cambridge University Press, 1981).

5. For an application of Bismarckian strategy to the case of the U.S. in the post–cold war world, see Josef Joffe, "'Bismarck or Britain'? Toward an American Grand Strategy after Bipolarity," *International Security* 19, no. 4 (Spring 1995): 94–117. Joffe discusses the strategy's appropriateness for a dominant, geopolitically insulated state. China may be a better candidate for analogy with Bismarck's Germany, since it lacks the geographical separation of the U.S. and is a rising, but not yet dominant state.

6. For a more detailed discussion of these theoretical expectations and China's role in the post–cold war world, see Avery Goldstein, "Great Expectations: Interpreting China's Arrival," *International Security*, 22, no. 3 (Winter 1997/98): 36–73.

7. See, for example, Arthur Waldron, "Statement of Dr. Arthur Waldron." *House Armed Services Committee*, June 21 2000, http://www.house.gov/hasc/testimony/106thcongress/00–06–21waldron.html. See also Edward Friedman. "The Challenge of a Rising China: Another Germany?" In *Eagle Adrift: American Foreign Policy at the End of the Century*, edited by Robert J. Lieber. (New York: Addison Wesley, 1997).

8. I thank Walter McDougall and Marc Trachtenberg for their criticisms that helped me refine my thinking about the China-Bismarck analogy. On the usefulness of historical analogies applied to China, see Richard Baum and Alexei Shevchenko, "Will China Join an Encompassing Coalition with Other Great Powers?," in Richard N. Rosecrance, ed., *Creating an Encompassing Coalition to Prevent International Conflict* (Lanham, MD: Rowman and Littlefield, 2001), pp. 298–314. For a less sanguine view of China embracing a Bismarckian approach, see comments of U.S. Admiral Dennis C. Blair, Commander in Chief of the U.S. Pacific Command, in "The Role of Armed Forces in Regional Security Cooperation." *Pacific Forum, CSIS, PacNet* 34, August 25 2000, http://taiwansecurity.org/IS/PacNet-082500.htm.

9. Kissinger's characterization of post–Franco-Prussian War Germany might well be applied to post–cold war China: "Once Germany was transformed from a potential victim of aggression to a threat to the European equilibrium, the remote contingency of the other states of Europe uniting against Germany became a real possibility." (*Diplomacy*, p. 134). For an overview of these themes, see Henry Kissinger, *Diplomacy* (New York: Touchstsone, 1994): 122–123, 125, 134, 158. On Bismarck's diplomatic efforts, see also W. N. Medlicott, and Dorothy K. Covney, (eds.), *Bismarck and Europe* (New York: St. Martin's Press, 1972); D. G. Williamson, *Bismarck and Germany, 1862–1890* (New York: Longman, 1986); Theodore S. Hamerow. "Introduction." In *Otto Von Bismarck: A Historical Assessment*, edited by Theodore S. Hamerow, xxii–xix (Lexington,

MA: D.C. Heath and Company, 1972); George O. Kent, *Bismarck and His Times* (Carbondale: Southern Illinois University Press, 1978).

10. Medlicott and Covney, *Bismarck and Europe*, pp. 178–179 ; Williamson, *Bismarck and Germany, 1862–1890*, p. 65; Hamerow, *Otto Von Bismarck: A Historical Assessment*, p. xv; Kent, *Bismarck and His Times*, p. 104.

11. Kissinger argues that the strategy ultimately proved unsustainable even for Bismarck. See *Diplomacy*, pp. 127–128, 136, 146, 160–161, 166.

12. On the nuclear revolution, see Robert Jervis, *The Meaning of the Nuclear Revolution* (Ithaca: Cornell University Press, 1989); Avery Goldstein, *Deterrence and Security in the 21st Century: China, Britain, France and the Enduring Legacy of the Nuclear Revolution* (Stanford: Stanford University Press, 2000). In addition, and only partly related to the advent of nuclear weapons, norms against the use of military force to achieve political objectives are stronger today than in Bismarck's era. Although such norms are no guarantee that states will refrain from warfighting, among the great powers the brutal lessons of twentieth-century military conflicts reinforce normative pressures, making it a less attractive option than in earlier eras and one that increasingly demands extensive justification before both domestic and international audiences.

13. For the strong form of this argument, see Richard N. Rosecrance, *The Rise of the Trading State: Commerce and Conquest in the Modern World* (New York: Basic Books, 1985); see also Steven Van Evera, "Why Europe Matters, Why the Third World Doesn't: American Grand Strategy after the cold war," *Journal of Strategic Studies* 13, no. 2 (1990): 1–51. Cf. Peter Liberman, "The Spoils of Conquest," *International Security* 18 no. 2 (Fall 1993): 125–153. The collapse of the Soviet Union may provide the clearest evidence of the importance of economic competitiveness rather than control of resources in the contemporary era.

14. My Chinese interlocutors noted, and some lamented, the lack of any universal appeal in their country's current pragmatic, eclectic socioeconomic program that is tailored to its particular problems. They explicitly contrast this with the revolutionary socialist paradigms of the Soviet Union and Maoist China, as well as with the universality of political and economic principles that underpin what Joseph Nye labels contemporary America's "soft power." See Joseph S. Nye Jr. and William A. Owens. "America's Information Edge," *Foreign Affairs* 75, no. 3 (March/April 1996): 20–36; Samuel P. Huntington, "The U.S.-Decline or Renewal," *Foreign Affairs* 67, no. 2 (Winter 1988): 76–96.

15. China's borders served as the venue for the superpowers' three biggest foreign military operations of the cold war era (Korea, Vietnam, Afghanistan) as well as the site for several escalation-threatening crises between Beijing and the system's duopolists (the Taiwan Straits during the 1950s, the Sino-Soviet border in 1969, and perhaps Indochina in 1979). China's international behavior suggested it was the unusual case where structural constraints are so tight, that personality and national attributes need play only a distant secondary role in analyzing its foreign policy. For a debate about the usefulness and limitations of structural-realist explanations of foreign policy, see Colin Elman, "Horses for Courses: Why *Not* Neorealist Theories of Foreign Policy?" *Security Studies* 6, no. 1 (Autumn 1996): 7–53; Kenneth N. Waltz, "International Politics Is not Foreign Policy," *Security Studies* 6, no. 1 (Autumn 1996): 54–57; and Elman's re-

sponse, pp. 58–61. See also the debate about the neorealist research program contained in the *American Political Science Review* 91, no. 4 (December 1997).

16. See Avery Goldstein, "Discounting the Free Ride: Alliances and Security in the Postwar World," *International Organization* 49, no. 1 (Winter 1995): 39–72.

17. For a survey of China's varying willingness to set aside differences in its negotiations with the U.S. see Robert S. Ross, *Negotiating Cooperation: The United States and China, 1969–1989* (Stanford: Stanford University Press, 1995).

18. As indigenous resistance efforts garnered international support that hamstrung Moscow's position in Afghanistan and the efforts of its ally, Hanoi, to consolidate its position in Cambodia, Beijing's sense of alarm about events on its periphery ebbed. Ahead of their western counterparts, some Chinese analysts even began to argue that the Soviets had, to use Paul Kennedy's term, entered the phase of imperial overstretch, suggesting that the shortcomings of the Soviet economy were finally limiting Moscow's ability to meet the ever-escalating demands (quantitative and qualitative) of military competition in the bipolar world. See Paul Kennedy, *The Rise and Fall of the Great Powers* (New York: Vintage, 1987); Wenqing Xie, "U.S.-Soviet Military Contention in the Asia-Pacific Region, *Shijie Zhishi*, 16 (March 1987), in Foreign Broadcast Information Service [hereafter FBIS], March 31, 1987, pp. A2, A5; Bei Jia, "Gorbachev's Policy Toward the Asian Pacific Region," *Guoji Yanti Yanjiu*, April 13, 1987, FBIS, May 14, 1987, pp. C8-C14.

19. For literature on the initial wave of post-Mao military modernization, see Paul H. B. Godwin, *The Chinese Defense Establishment: Continuity and Change in the 1980s* (Boulder, CO: Westview Press, 1983); Ellis Joffe, *The Chinese Army after Mao* (Cambridge: Harvard University Press, 1987); Charles D. Lovejoy and Bruce W. Watson, eds., *China's Military Reforms* (Boulder, CO: Westview Press, 1986); Larry M. Wortzell, ed. *China's Military Modernization* (New York: Greenwood Press, 1988).

20. On some of these changes, see Liu Di, "Deng Xiaoping's Thinking on Diplomatic Work—Interview with Liang Shoude, Dean for College of International Relations for Beijing University." *Ta Kung Pao*, November 2, 1997, p. A6, FBIS. See also Liu Huaqiu, "Strive for a Peaceful International Environment," *Jiefang Ribao*, November 3, 1997, p. 5, FBIS.

21. Three circumstances created a "window" for the airing of grievances: the death of sacked CCP General Secretary Hu Yaobang in April 1989 created an opportunity for students to take to the streets under cover of mourning activities; the arrival soon afterward of the international press corps to cover the May Sino-Soviet summit provided a degree of protection from police repression; and the seventieth anniversary of the May 4th movement's most celebrated demonstrations offered a thematic focus on the issues of patriotic demands for political modernization. See Andrew J. Nathan, and Perry Link, (eds.), *The Tiananmen Papers* (New York: Public Affairs, 2001).

22. China welcomed Gorbachev's visit as decisively ending the cold war in Asia, but fretted over the "blowback" from political reforms in the Soviet bloc that were more ambitious than those the PRC had initiated a decade earlier. Author's interviews, Beijing June–July 1998.

23. Indeed, one analyst labeled peaceful evolution "the theory of China's collapse." See Liu, "Strive for a Peaceful International Environment."

24. See John W. Garver, "The Chinese Communist Party and the Collapse of Soviet Communism," *The China Quarterly*, no. 133 (March 1993): 1–26.

25. Several of my Chinese interlocutors stressed the importance of the contrasting images of "democratizing Taiwan" and "Tiananmen China" that prevailed in the U.S. after 1989, arguing that these conditioned the American reaction to Taipei's mid-1990s initiatives to elevate its independent international profile.

26. China's cooperation, or at least acquiescence, at the United Nations during the Persian Gulf crisis of 1990–1991, was a noteworthy part of Beijing's effort to rebuild Sino-American relations. Deng Xiaoping called for China to maintain a low profile during this troubled time. See "Beijing Urged to Keep Regional Power Focus," *South China Morning Post*, September 29, 1998, available online, http://www.taiwansecurity.org/SCMP-980929.htm and interview #66c.

27. In retrospect, it was asserted that China had "withstood the impact from the drastic changes in Eastern Europe and the disintegration of the Soviet Union, smashed Western sanctions." (Liu, "Strive for a Peaceful International Environment.")

28. See Suisheng Zhao, "Deng Xiaoping's Southern Tour: Elite Politics in Post-Tiananmen China," *Asian Survey* 33, no. 8 (1993): 739–756. Nicholas R. Lardy, *China in the World Economy* (Washington, DC: Institute for International Economics, 1994).

29. Author's interviews, Beijing, June–July 1998. As a research analyst on Chinese politics at the National Institute of Defense Studies in Japan's Defense Agency suggested: "[O]ne must question why we hear 'arguments of a China threat.' In that respect, we can point not only to China's assertion of territorial rights without the approval of concerned nations, rapid economic growth, justification of the use of military capabilities, modernization of weapons, and lack of transparency in military spending, but China's erstwhile about-face in diplomatic stances . . . When one deals with any country that is prone to about-faces, one cannot avoid a sense of insecurity." (Nobuyuki Ito, "Reading the World: The Strategic Environment in the 21st Century," *Tokyo Asagumo*, January 8, 1998, p. 1, FBIS) For assessments in the early 1990s that anticipated some of these concerns, see Aaron Friedberg, "Ripe for Rivalry: Prospects for Peace in a Multipolar Asia," *International Security* 18, no. 3 (Winter 1993/1994): 5–33; Denny Roy, "Hegemon on the Horizon? China's Threat to East Asian Security," *International Security* 19, no. 1 (Summer 1994): 149–168; cf. Michael G. Gallagher, "China's Illusory Threat to the South China Sea," *International Security* 19, no. 1 (Summer 1994): 169–194.

30. The pattern, of course, reflects the familiar logic of the security dilemma. See Robert Jervis, "Cooperation under the Security Dilemma," *World Politics* 30, no. 2 (1978): 167–214.

31. Fu Liqun, "Several Basic Ideas in U.S. Strategic Thinking," *Beijing Zhongguo Junshi Kexue*, 1 (February 20, 1997): 28–37, FBIS. See also Zhang De Zhen, "Qianghua Junshi Tongmeng Buhe Shidai Chaoliu," *Renmin Ribao*, January 31, 1997. (*Renmin Ribao* articles available online at http://www.snweb.com/gb/people_daily/gbrm.htm.)

32. Bilateral security cooperation between the U.S. and ASEAN states, including joint military exercises, and Indonesia's security agreement with Australia were also driven by worried perceptions of China's growing power and assertive regional behav-

ior. See Masashi Nishihara, "Aiming at New Order for Regional Security—Current State of ARF," *Gaiko Forum*, November 1997, pp. 35–40, FBIS.

33. By April 1997 Japan and Australia were engaged in a dialogue to expand their bilateral defense ties, and to cooperate in facilitating U.S. military presence in the region. "Australia, Japan: Hashimoto, Howard Discuss Security Issues, Environment," *Tokyo Kyodo*, April 29, 1997, FBIS. See also Tang Guanghui, "Behind the Warming of Australian-U.S. Relations," *Beijing Shijie Zhishi*, 20 (October 16, 1996): 19–21, FBIS; "Australia: PRC Criticism Over Security Pact With U.S. Noted," *Melbourne Radio Australia*, August, 7, 1996, FBIS; Zhang Dezhen, "Qianghua Junshi Tongmeng Buhe Shidai Chaoliu," *Renmin Ribao*, January 31, 1997. In addition New Zealand doubled the power of its Waihopai spy station to facilitate intelligence-gathering efforts with the U.S., Australia, and Britain, allegedly to maintain the ability to monitor China that was forfeited when Hong Kong reverted to PRC rule. See "New Zealand: Spying Capacity Upgrade in New Zealand Linked to China," *Agence France-Presse*, July 30, 1997, FBIS.

34. See, for example, the analysis by Lt. General and Deputy Commandant of the Academy of Military Sciences, Li Jun: "A half century has passed, and facts show that Japan's strategic culture has really made no appreciable progress." Li contrasted Japan's refusal to confront its militarist past with "the kind of self-introspection" the Germans had undertaken and that had "promoted European reconciliation." Li Jun, "On Strategic Culture," *Zhongguo Junshi Kexue*, no. 1 (February 1997): 8–15, FBIS. Another analysis argued: "In recent years, the 'pacifist' trend in Japan that has dominated for a long time in the post-war period has weakened, with an obvious rightist political trend developing through such things as the glorification of aggressive wars, requesting revision of the peace constitution, and advocating the 'right to collective defense' in joint operations with the United States." (Ma Junwei, "Political Trends in Japan Following the General Election," *Xiandai Guoji Guanxi*, February 20, 1997, no. 2, pp. 11, 14–16, FBIS.) See also a similarly alarmist assessment, focusing especially on Japan's military modernization in Xia Liping, "Some Views on Multilateral Security Cooperation in Northeast Asia," *Xiandai Guoji Guanxi*, December 20, 1996, no. 12, pp. 12–15, FBIS.

35. Zhang Guocheng, "Ling Ren Guanzhu de Xin Dongxiang—Rimei Xiugai Fangwei Hezuo Fangzhen Chuxi," *Renmin Ribao*, June 14, 1997; Zhang Guocheng, "Hewei 'Zhoubian You Shi'?—Xie Zai Xin 'Rimei Fangwei Hezuo Fangzhen' Qiaoding Zhi Shi" *Renmin Ribao, September 25, 1997* My Chinese interlocutors dismissed as unbelievable the idea that the revisions were not undertaken with China in mind. They gave little credence to the U.S. and Japanese argument that the main reason for the revision was the need to better prepare for joint response to a possible military crisis on the Korean peninsula. Author's interviews, June–July 1998.

36. "Japan: Kato on Domestic, International Politics," Interview by Columbia University Professor Gerald Curtis *Tokyo Chuo Koron*, September 1997, pp. 28–43, FBIS.

37. "Chi Haotian yu Riben Fanwei Tingzhang Guanhuitan, Huijian Riben Zimindang Ganshizhang he Zhengtiaohuizhang," *Renmin Ribao*, February 5, 1998.

38. When the *Yomiuri Shimbun* reported that the peripheral region to be covered under the revised guidelines "would be 'the Far East and its vicinity,' including the Tai-

wan Strait and the Spratly Islands, the Government immediately denied that it would decide in advance which areas should be covered by the guidelines. Instead, said Kanezo Muranoka, the Government's chief Cabinet Secretary, a decision will be deferred until an emergency arises." *New York Times*, April 29, 1998, p. A6. In late summer 1998, press reports suggested that Jiang Zemin postponed his state visit to Japan not because of the massive floods in China (as officially asserted), but because Japan's leaders were rejecting a summit communiqué that would include the sort of firm pledges (the "three noes") about one-China that President Clinton had issued during his 1998 trip to the PRC. See "Chinese President Jiang's Visit to Japan May Be Delayed to Next Year," *Agence France-Presse*, September 10, 1998, from clari.world.asia.China, ClariNet Communications Corp. [hereafter clari.China]; see also "Japan Rejects Any Chinese Pressure Over Taiwan," *Agence France-Presse*, October 28, 1998, clari.China. My Chinese interlocutors expressed very strong skepticism about Japan's intentions toward China's claim over Taiwan. Many Chinese assert there are close ties between (allegedly influential) Japanese "rightists" and Taiwan's independence movement. One Chinese analyst who plays an important advisory role on Beijing's Taiwan policy argued that Japan's leaders are not less meddlesome on the Taiwan matter than the U.S., but only much more "cunning." (Author's interview, Beijing, June–July 1998).

39. See Goldstein, "Great Expectations"; Andrew J. Nathan and Robert S. Ross, *The Great Wall and the Empty Fortress: China's Search for Security* (New York: Norton, 1997); cf. Richard Bernstein and Ross H. Munro, *The Coming Conflict with China* (New York: Knopf, 1997).

40. Armed aloofness was feasible if China wanted only to ensure that its homeland was free from foreign occupation forces and safe from damaging military strikes (China's modest nuclear arsenal served this dissuasive purpose). But armed aloofness would not serve an internationally active and engaged China with a more ambitious agenda, but limited resources. Authors interviews, Beijing, June–July 1998; also "Beijing Urged to Keep Regional Power Focus."

41. Since 1978, China's communist leaders have aggressively addressed the domestic strain of the Soviet disease, a stagnant planned economy along with vested political interests that block serious attempts at reform.

42. Walt has described how such perceptions of the Soviet threat induced patterns of alignment that were anomalous from the perspective of balance-of-power theory. Stephen M. Walt, "Alliance Formation and the Balance of World Power," *International Security* 9, no. 4 (Spring 1985): 3–43; Stephen M. Walt, *The Origins of Alliances* (Ithaca: Cornell University Press, 1988).

43. Author's interviews, Beijing, June–July 1998.

44. For overviews of the containment vs. engagement debate, see David Shambaugh, "Containment or Engagement of China: Calculating Beijing's Responses," *International Security*, 21, no. 2 (Fall 1996): 202; Gerald Segal, "East Asia and the 'Containment' of China," *International Security*, 20, no. 4 (Spring 1996): 107–135.

45. Chi Haotian, "Zou Fuhe Woguo Guoqing Bing Fanying Shidai Tezheng de Guofang Xiandaihua Jianshe Daolu," *Qiushi* 188:8 (April 1996), p. 10. For an attack on "China threat theory" as a latter day version of the "yellow peril theory," labeling it a

"'threat to China' theory," and a "trick to intimidate and hold China back," see Li Jun, "On Strategic Culture," *Zhongguo Junshi Kexue*, no. 1 (February 1997): 8–15, FBIS. A lack of sensitivity to others' worries is not unique to Chinese leaders. See Robert Jervis, "Hypotheses on Misperception," *World Politics*, 20, no. 3 (April 1968).

46. Assessments of China's aggregate, rather than per capita, capabilities overlook the country's huge, largely rural population. Satisfying demands for improved living standards as well as national development, it was asserted, both limits the resources Beijing can allocate to the military (whose budgets are claimed to be small compared with those of other major powers, especially the U.S.) and requires a peaceful international environment. ("Jieshou Meiguo Youxian Xinwen Dianshiwang Jizhe Caifang, Jiang Zemin Changtan Zhongmei Guanxi ji Taiwan Deng Wenti," *Renmin Ribao*, May 10, 1997; "Tulao de Wudao," *Renmin Ribao*, January 22, 1997; Liu, "Strive for a Peaceful International Environment," p. 5; "Jundui Yao Shiying Gaige he Fazhan de Xin Xingshi, Gengjia Zijue Fucong Fuwu Dang he Guojia Da Ju," *Renmin Ribao*, March 11, 1998.

47. China's own bitter historical experience of exploitation at the hands of imperialist powers after 1800, it was asserted, has taught it to treasure independence and peace, and to oppose power politics—that is why others should believe its pledge never to seek hegemony ("Jiu Zhongmei Guanxi, Taiwan Wenti, Zhongguo Renda Zhidu deng Wenti: Qiao Shi Jieshou Meiguo Jizhe Caifang," *Renmin Ribao*, January 17, 1997; "Chi Haotian Zai Riben Fabiao Yanjiang, Zhuozhong Chanshu Zhongguo Guofang Zhengce," *Renmin Ribao*, February 5, 1998).

48. See Wang Jisi, "Shiji Zhi Jiao de Zhongmei Guanxi," *Renmin Ribao*, March 1, 1997.

49. Author's interviews, Beijing, June–July 1998.

50. Many of my interlocutors discussed the changing reaction within China to "China-threat" arguments during the mid-1990s—from righteous indignation to a sense that they reflected the sort of anxiety that normally accompanies the emergence of a new great power on the international scene, especially as the Soviet threat that had previously led others to subordinate many secondary disagreements with China evaporated. (Author's interviews, Beijing, June–July , 1998).

51. See "Analyst Interviewed on APEC's Prospects," *Chuon Koron*, December 1995, pp. 30–44, FBIS. Han Hua, "Zhang Yishan [Chinese Foreign Ministry Official] on China's Multilateral Diplomacy," *Wen Wei Po*, January 7, 1997, p. A2, FBIS.

52. A shift many of my interlocutors emphasized (Beijing, June–July 1998). At the Fifteenth CCP Congress in September 1997, General Secretary Jiang's report placed a new emphasis on multilateral diplomacy, "the first time China has announced that it would take vigorous part in multilateral diplomatic activities. It is a major change in China's diplomacy." (Liu, "Deng Xiaoping's Thinking on Diplomatic Work and China's Diplomatic Policy.")

53. In a review of China's position reflected in the ASEAN Regional Forum, Masashi Nishihara of Japan's Defense University noted that when China first took part in 1994 it was "cautious about multilateral diplomacy," but gradually began to change its position when "pressed by participating countries." Nishihara argued that "[t]he reason that China has become active in multilateral security cooperation is that it must

have concluded that it was more advantageous to pursue its national interests from the inside, rather than remaining outside of multilateral diplomacy." ("Aiming at New Order for Regional Security—Current State of ARF," *Gaiko Forum*, November 1997, pp. 35–40, FBIS. See also Alastair Iain Johnston and Paul Evans, "China's Engagement with Multilateral Security Institutions," in Alastair Iain Johnston and Robert S. Ross, (eds.), *Engaging China* (London and New York: Routledge, 1999), pp. 258–261.

54. At every opportunity China proudly points to the April 1996 five-nation treaty (among China, Russia, Kazakhstan, Kyrgyzstan, and Tajikistan) as "the first multilateral treaty signed to build confidence in the Asia-Pacific region" and cites it as a "powerful rebuttal of the 'China threat theory'," evidence that "instead of being a 'threat,' China actually plays a constructive role in preserving peace and stability in its peripheral areas." (Xia, "Some Views on Multilateral Security Cooperation in Northeast Asia"; "Five-nation Agreement Provides Model in Peaceful Conflict Resolution," *Jiefang Ribao*, April 27, 1996, p. 4, FBIS.) In March 1997, when the "Inter-sessional Support Group on confidence-building measures of the ASEAN Regional Forum (ARF)" was held in Beijing, it was emphasized that "China has placed importance to [*sic*] this three day meeting because it's the first on multilateral dialogue and cooperation hosted by China." "ARF Support Group Meeting Ends in Beijing," *Xinhua*, March 8, 1997, FBIS. See also "Roundup: China Becoming Active Force in Multilateral Cooperation," *Xinhua*, January 2, 1997, FBIS. China has also cautiously endorsed the idea of multilateral security cooperation in Northeast Asia, though it argues for substantial preliminary discussions, and "track-two" initiatives prior to convening formal meetings. (Han Hua, "It is Better for Multilateral Dialogue to be Started by Scholars," *Wen Wei Po*, November 13, 1997, FBIS.) The idea of relying on unofficial "track-two" diplomacy was touted by several of my interlocutors, who saw it as a way to expedite the exploration of options about which powerful elements of Chinese officialdom are skeptical.

55. Xia, "Some Views on Multilateral Security Cooperation in Northeast Asia"; see also Johnston and Evans, "China's Engagement with Multilateral Security Institutions." There are other benefits from multilateralism as well. Because an influential segment of China's foreign policy elite now see multilateralism as an integral part of the diplomatic portfolio that true great powers now possess, it has become important to those who expect their country to fill such an international role. See also Thomas J. Christensen, "Parsimony is no Simple Matter: International Relations Theory, Area Studies, and the Rise of China," unpublished ms., February 26, 1998, pp. 35–36; Johnston and Evans, "China's Engagement with Multilateral Security Institutions." Multilateralism also provides China with forums within which representatives of the developing world are likely to support Beijing's "hard sovereignty" views. See "Quanmian Kaichuang Jiushi Niandai Waijiao Xin Jumian—Dang de Shisida Yilai Woguo Waijiao Gongzuo Shuping," *Renmin Ribao*, September 6, 1997. This is not only reflected in upholding the "noninterference" principle in disputes about human rights, but also arms control, when China positions itself as the champion of developing states' preference that the terms of multilateral agreements remain sensitive to their sovereignty concerns, rather than enshrining absolute principles, such as maximum transparency, that advantage the advanced states. See "Wo Caijun Dashi Zai Lianda

Yiwei Qiangdiao, Ying Fangzhi Ba Caijun Mubiao Yinxiang Fazhanzhong Guojia," *Renmin Ribao*, October 16, 1997; "Wo Daibiao Tan Junshi Touming Wenti, Chanshu Kongzhi Xiao Wuqi Wenti Lichang," *Renmin Ribao*, November 18, 1997; "Wo Dashi Zai Lianheguo Caijun Weiyuanhui Zhichu, Jianli Wuhequ Youli Heping," *Renmin Ribao*, April 10, 1998.

56. Johnston and Evans, "China's Engagement with Multilateral Security Institutions."

57. Author's interviews, Beijing, June–July 1998.. On the instrumental value of participation (China gains access and say-so) as well as the image value (avoiding opprobrium but also creating opportunities for "backpatting"), see Johnston and Evans, "China's Engagement with Multilateral Security Institutions," pp. 237, 251–253, 261. China's instrumental use of multilateralism indicates that its understanding differs from the more expansive definition of multilateralism articulated by Ruggie. See John Gerard Ruggie, "Multilateralism: The Anatomy of an Institution," in Ruggie, *Multilateralism Matters* (New York: Columbia University Press, 1993).

58. During the visit of EC President Jacques Santer, China's central bank governor promised to hold the line on the yuan in 1999, "as part of [China's] 'responsible attitude' to the Asian financial crisis." ("Yuan must Remain Stable, says China's Central Bank Governor," *Agence France-Presse*, October 30, 1998, clari.world.europe.union, ClariNet Communications Corp.) Santer in turn referred to China as "the pillar for the region's economic and financial stability." See "EU Chief Congratulates China As Pillar of Asian Economy," *Agence France-Presse*, October 26, 1998, clari. China; "China's New Premier Takes Centre Stage But Avoids Limelight," *Agence France-Presse*, April 4, 1998, clari. China.

59. Whatever other adjectives are used to label these relationships (e.g., constructive or cooperative) "strategic" is the key adjective. Though China uses the "partnership" label for good relations with smaller states, it reserves the term "strategic partnership" to define a "new way of handling relations between major countries in the post–cold war period." See "China: Qian Qichen on 'Constructive' Strategic Partnerships," *Xinhua*, November 3, 1997, FBIS; Lu Jin and Liu Yunfei, "New Analysis: From Beijing to Washington and From Moscow to Beijing—a Revelation of New-Type relations Between Major Powers," *Xinhua*, November 9, 1997, FBIS; Zhang Yifan, "From 'Playing Card' to Establishing Strategic Partnership," Special interview with Yang Chengxu, Director of the China Institute of International Studies, *Hsin Pao*, December 25, 1997, p. 5, FBIS. Bilateral ties with smaller states are also designed to cultivate mutual interests in ways that raise the costs of severing the relationship by embracing policies hostile to China. Unlike those with major powers, these partnerships are not seen as strategically crucial for determining the fundamental nature of international relations. See "Quanmian Kaichuang Jiushi Niandai Waijiao Xin Jumian—Dang de Shisida Yilai Woguo Waijiao Gongzuo Shuping," *Renmin Ribao*, September 6, 1997; Han Hua, "Jiang Zemin to Go to Kuala Lumpur in Mid-December to attend East Asia-ASEAN Summit, China to Establish Partnership with ASEAN," *Wen Wei Po*, December 3, 1997, p. A1, FBIS; "Chinese President Tells ASEAN Summit Of Hopes For "Good-Neighbourly Partnership," *Xinhua*, BBC Summary of World Broadcasts, December 18, 1997.

60. See "Prospects of China's Diplomatic Activities in 1998," *Beijing Central People's Radio*, January 25, 1998, FBIS. On the alleged obsolescence of alliances in the post–cold war world, see "Gouzhu Xin Shiji de Xinxing Guojia Guanxi" *Renmin Ribao*, December 8, 1997, p. 6. On China's refusal to pursue its interests by traditional means, see Liu, "Deng Xiaoping's Thinking on Diplomatic Work." As for the character of the different type of relations China is now cultivating: "In these partnerships we won't find a clearly us-against-them characteristic . . . . These new strategic partnerships often have a two-fold nature. More often than not, the two sides are both partners and competitors." ("Interview with Song Baotian, Deputy Director of the China Institute for International Relations," *New Report and Current Events, Beijing China Radio International*, November 13, 1997, FBIS.)

61. As an official review of China's diplomacy put it: "Indeed, 1997 is a year of great success. China's booming economy should be put at the top of all supporting factors. . . . [N]o one living in today's integrated global economy can afford to neglect such an enormous and dynamic economic powerhouse. Therefore, as foreign companies flooded into the country, business contacts entailed comprehensive dialogues and deeper understanding, which gave China an upper hand both in advancing confidence, coordination and cooperation and in reversing bias, antagonism and menace which may be the result of legacy, ignorance or, simply, malice." See Shi Nangen, "1997: A Fruitful Year in China's Multi-Dimensional Diplomacy," *Beijing Review*, no. 7, February 16–22, 1998, p. 7, FBIS. Several interlocutors frankly noted that the transfer of arms or dual-use technology to states like Iran was one of the few "cards" in China's hand when dealing with the world's other great powers.

62. Multipolarity is seen as a desirable goal, not an imminent reality. Some analysts finesse (or muddle) this point by referring to the foreseeable future as a multipolar world with only one superpower (Author's interviews, Beijing, June–July, 1998). In practice this seems to mean an international system with one true great power (i.e., unipolar), but several regional powers. In the late 1990s, Chinese analysts (echoing the declinist arguments set forth in the West during the late 1980s) emphasized evidence of the shrinking U.S. share of the international economy and predicted that this would contribute to an increase in resistance to American foreign policy leadership. See Fu Fuyuan, "Zhiyi Shidai de Qiwen," *Renmin Ribao*, September 9, 1997; "Iraq Crisis Revealed Collapse of U.S. Global Authority: Chinese Analysts," *Agence France-Presse*, March 9, 1998, clari. China.; "Yici Yiyi Zhongda Yingxiang shenyuan de Fanwen—Zhuhe Jiang Zhuxi Fang E Yuanman Chenggong," *Renmin Ribao*, April 27, 1997; Liu, "Strive for a Peaceful International Environment"; Tang Tianri, "Relations Between Major Powers Are Being Readjusted," *Xinhua*, December 15, 1997, FBIS; "Jiu Zhong'E Liangguo Zui Gaoji Huiwu, Shuangbian Guanxi Deng Wenti, Jiang Zhuxi Jieshou Eluosi Zizhe Caifang," *Renmin Ribao*, April 18, 1997; "Li Peng Zai Mosike Jishou Zizhe Fangwen," *Renmin Ribao*, February, 19, 1998. At the turn of the century, especially after the U.S. military operation in Kosovo, Chinese analysts became more pessimistic about the pace of America's decline. Multipolarity was still deemed an inevitable outcome, but one that might be more distant than originally anticipated.

63. See Zhao Gangzhen, "Daguo Guanxi, 'Huoban Re'," *Renmin Ribao*, April 21, 1998. Chinese Defense Minister Chi Haotian told U.S. Defense Secretary William

Cohen during his January 1998 visit to Beijing "that at present, relations between major powers are undergoing a strategic readjustment. In the new situation, neither expanding military alliances [i.e., NATO] nor strengthening military alliances [i.e., U.S. alliances with Japan and Australia] is conducive to maintenance of peace and security." ("China: Expanding Military contacts part of Diplomatic Strategy," *Xinhua*, February 20, 1998, FBIS.)

64. See Yinwan Fang and Guojun Yang, "Beneficial Enlightenment for Large Countries to Build a New Type of Relationship," *Xinhua*, April 25, 1996, FBIS; Wu Songzhi and Yi Shuguang, "Gongzhu Mulin Youhao Hezuo Guanxi," *Renmin Ribao*, April 22, 1997; "Zhong'E Zui Gaoji Huiwu," *Renmin Ribao*, November 7, 1997. Some of my interlocutors attribute the precise phrasing to Yeltsin.

65. Zhou Guiyin, "Xin Shiji De Guoji Anquan," p. 71; Ye Zicheng, "Zhongguo Shixing Daguo Waijiao Zhanlüe," pp. 9–10. When Russian Premier Primakov floated a trial balloon (subsequently disavowed by President Yeltsin) about a Russia-India-China defense alliance, China (and India) rejected the idea. See "China Cautious on Primakov Plan," *The Hindu*, December 23, 1998, LEXIS-NEXIS, Read-Elsevier Inc. [hereafter LEXIS-NEXIS]; "Russia, India Reject Three-way Strategic Axis with China," *Agence France Presse*, May 25, 1999, LEXIS-NEXIS; Tyler Marshall, "A China-India-Russia Axis: Within The Realm Of Possibility," *Los Angeles Times*, September 22, 1999, p. 11, LEXIS-NEXIS.

66. Several of my interlocutors doubted the robustness of the Sino-Russian partnership and argued that it was little more than a formality originally sustained by the close personal relationship between Boris Yeltsin and Jiang Zemin. Others emphasized that on most practical matters, that bilateral ties have steadily deteriorated since 1994. See also Zhao Longgeng, "Zhong'E Zhanlüe Xiezuo Huoban Guanxi Maixiang Jianshi Zhi Lu," *Xiandai Guoji Guanxi*, no. 5 (1999): 32–33; Li Jingjie, "Pillars of the Sino-Russian Partnership," *Orbis* 44, no. 4 (2000): 527–539. These concerns, however, seem at least overstated. It is difficult to identify hard evidence that the partnership actually weakened during the final years of Yeltsin's rule and, if anything, it has seemed to strengthen in President Putin's administration. When the Russian premier visited Beijing in November 2000, China's premier claimed that "Sino-Russian relations are enjoying their best period ever." (Francesco Sisci, "Neighbours Push For Better Ties With Russia—CHINA: Military Transfers Get Boost After Talks," *The Straits Times* (Singapore) November 4, 2000, p. 39, LEXIS-NEXIS.) See also Ye Zicheng, "Zhongguo Shixing Daguo Waijiao Zhanlüe"; "Joint Statement by the PRC President and the Russian Federation President on the Antimissile Issue," *Xinhua*, July 18, 2000, FBIS. And on the Russian side, a December 2000 Gallup poll revealed that a "majority of Russian politicians, journalists and business leaders view China as Moscow's most important strategic partner" ("China Is Russia's Most Important Partner: Poll," *Agence France-Presse*, December 4, 2000, clari.China).

67. See Huang Zongliang, "Miandui Beiyue Xin Zhanlüe Chonggu," *Xin Shiye*, no. 5 (1999), reprinted in *Zhongguo Waijiao* (2000), no. 1, pp. 25–28.

68. "PRC: More on Sino-Russian Strategic Partnership," *Xinhua*, April 25, 1996, FBIS; "PRC: Qian Qichen, Primakov Hold Breakfast Meeting," *Xinhua*, April 25, 1996, FBIS; "Joint Statement by the PRC President and the Russian Federation Presi-

dent on the Antimissile Issue." For a Chinese view questioning Russia's real interests in the Taiwan Strait, see Yiwei Wang, "Dui Tai Junshi Douzheng," p. 28.

69. Their concerns are clearly manifest in the Sino-Russian Presidential joint statement on missiles defense, see "Joint Statement by the PRC President and the Russian Federation President on the Antimissile Issue." See also Chen Ying, "Zhanqu Daodan Fangyu Xitong Yu Dongya Anquan Xingshi," *Shijie Jingji yu Zhengzhi Luntan*, no. 4 (1999): 28, 30; Zhu Feng, "TMD Yu Dangqian Zhongmei Guanxi," *Shijie Jingji yu Zhengzhi*, no. 5 (1999), p. 10.

70. See Lu Youzhi, "Chongxin Shenshi Zhongguo De Anquan Huanjing," *Shijie Jingji yu Zhengzhi*, no. 1 (2000): 59; Chen Ying, "Zhanqu Daodan Fangyu Xitong," p. 28. The political cross-pressures are already evident in Moscow and Beijing as leaders disagree about how best to invest scarce military resources as U.S. missile defense loom. See "Political Scientist Criticizes Planned Reform Of Russian Missile Forces," *Interfax News Agency*, July 26, 2000, LEXIS-NEXIS; Fred Weir, "Putin Tries Big Shift in Military Strategy, " *The Christian Science Monitor*, August 2, 2000, p. 1, LEXIS-NEXIS; "Chuanwen Jiang Zemin Zhishi Gaibian Zhonggong de Guofang Zhengce." Many Chinese go further, explicitly arguing that missile defenses are intended to be part of the U.S. effort to prevent the rise of China. See Zhu Feng, "TMD Yu Dangqian Zhongmei Guanxi," p. 12. For an American view that the most important purpose for U.S. missile defenses is indeed to cope with a more powerful China, see the comments by Peter Brookes, a leading Congressional adviser in Gay Alcorn, "China 'Real Reason' for Missile Shield," *Sydney Morning Herald*, July 28, 2000, http://www.smh.com.au/news/0007/28/text/world03.html; also Peter Brookes, "The Case for Missile Defense," *Far Eastern Economic Review*," September 7, 2000.

71. See Chen Xiaoqin, "Buru 21 Shiji De Zhong'E Guanxi," *Zhongguo Waijiao*, no. 3 (2000): 31–35; Zhao Longgeng, "Zhong'E Zhanlüe Xiezuo Huoban Guanxi." In the mid-1990s, Russia and China set the target for two-way trade volume at $20 billion by the turn of the century. As the new millennium dawned, trade volumes remained in the $5–6 billion range, with Russian sales of raw materials and modern weapons the only real bright spots.

72. See "New Agency Interviews Russian President on Visit to China," *BBC Summary of World Broadcasts*, July 18, 2000, LEXIS-NEXIS; "China, Russia Issue Beijing Declaration," *Xinhua New Agency*, July 18, 2000, LEXIS-NEXIS; "Joint Statement by the PRC President and the Russian Federation President on the Antimissile Issue." See also Gilbert Rozman, "Sino-Russian Relations in the 1990s: A Balance Sheet," *Post-Soviet Affairs* 14, no. 2 (April–June 1998): 93–113; "PRC Academics Interviewed on Putin's Visit to China," *Hong Kong Ming Pao*, July 19, 2000, p. A15, FBIS.

73. Michael Pillsbury, *China Debates the Future Security Environment* (Washington, D.C.: National Defense University Press, 2000), p. 155.

74. See Huang Zongliang, "Miandui Beiyue Xin Zhanlüe Chonggu"; Ye Zicheng, "Zhongguo Shixing Daguo Waijiao Zhanlüe," p. 7. One of my interlocutors insisted that the push for still closer Sino-Russian relations since Putin's ascent has come mainly from the Russian side, with some Russian scholars advocating open alliance with China, and even (in a throwback to a proposal the Chinese rejected in 1958) sug-

gestions to establish a joint naval fleet based in Dalian. Author's interview, October 2000.

75. Ye Zicheng, "Zhongguo Shixing Daguo Waijiao Zhanlüe," p. 7; Zalmay M. Khalilzad, Abram N. Shulsky, Daniel L. Byman, Roger Cliff, David Orletsky, David Shlapak, and Ashley J. Tellis, *The United States and a Rising China: Strategic and Military Implications* (Santa Monica, CA: RAND, 1999): xiii-xiv, 3–5.

76. Discussions about announcing plans to work towards such a partnership were initiated in July 1997 when China's foreign minister and the U.S. secretary of state met in Malaysia. See Liu Huorong, Wu Dingbao, and Yang Zhongyi, "China: Qian Qichen Holds Talks with Albright," *Xinhua*, July 26, 1997, FBIS; "China: Further on Qian-Albright Comments after Talks," *Xinhua*, July 26, 1997, FBIS; Guo Jian, and Su Xiangxin, "China: Shen Guofang Hails Jiang Zemin's Us Trip," *Zhongguo Xinwenshe*, November 2, 1997, FBIS; He Chong, "China and the United States Declare Their Endeavor to Build a Constructive and Strategic Partnership Relationship," *Zhongguo Tongxunshe*, November 3, 1997, FBIS. This marked the last stages of negotiations about holding the 1997 and 1998 summits. Serious talks about the summits began during July 1996, in the wake of the 1995–96 Sino-American tensions over Taiwan. See Ross, "The 1995–96 Taiwan Strait Confrontation," p. 113.

77. Gu Ping, "Sino-Us Relations Are Facing Historic Opportunity," *Renmin Ribao*, October 19, 1997, FBIS; He Chong, "China and the United States Are Exploring the Possibility of Establishing a 'Strategic Partnership'—First in a Series on Prospects of Jiang Zemin's U.S. Visit," *Zhongguo Tongxunshe*, October 22, 1997, FBIS; "Jiu Zhongmei Guanxi, Taiwan Wenti, Zhongguo Renda Zhidu Deng Wenti: Qiao Shi Jieshou Meiguo Jizhe Caifang," *Renmin Ribao*, January 17, 1997; He Chong, "China and the United States Declare Their Endeavor to Build a Constructive and Strategic Partnership Relationship"; "Interview with Song Baotian"; "China: Pact to Prevent Naval Accidents Initialed," *Xinhua*, December 12, 1997, FBIS; Chi Haotian, "A Year of Our Army's Active Foreign Contacts," *Renmin Ribao*, December 26, 1997, p. 7, FBIS; "China: Expanding Military contacts part of Diplomatic Strategy," *Xinhua*, February 20, 1998, FBIS. The U.S. was eager to expand such exchanges not only to lessen the chance of inadvertent conflict, but also to counter an allegedly dangerous Chinese overestimation of American hostility and underestimation of American military capabilities that it can bring to bear in a war in Asia. See Jim Mannion, "Pentagon Study Sees Danger in Chinese View of U.S. Power," *Agence France-Presse*, March 7, 1998, clari.China. On common interests in Korea, Zhou Guiyin, "Xin Shiji De Guoji Anquan," p. 70.

78. On China's role as a "balancing" force in the UN, see Teng Xiaodong, "Dialogue on 1996 International Situation: China in the United Nations," *Jiefangjun Bao*, December 26, 1996, p. 5, FBIS. Since 1999, Beijing has indicated the link it sees between U.S. decisions to share TMD technology with Asian states, especially Taiwan, and the efforts to institutionalize the Missile Technology Control Regime. China's view is that joint work on TMD amounts to the spread of missile technology to Japan and Taiwan. Author's interviews, June–July, 1998, March–April, October, 2000. See also Jin Xin, "Meiguo Yanfa TMD De Yitu Ji Dui Quanqiu He Woguo Anquan De Yingxiang," *Guoji Guancha*, no. 4 (1999): 24; Monte R. Bullard, "Undiscussed Link-

ages: Implications of Taiwan Straits Security Activity on Global Arms Control and Nonproliferation," *CNS Reports*, October 11, 2000, Available at the website of Center for Nonproliferation Studies, Monterey Institute of International Studies, http://cns.miis.edu/.

79. Wise tactics can enhance the effectiveness of its linkage strategy. China's cultivation of ties to the U.S. business community, for example, helps it to maximize the political appeal of maintaining good Sino-American relations. See Swaine and Tellis, *Interpreting China's Grand Strategy*, p. 117.

80. A point my interlocutors emphasized. After Lee Teng-hui's visit to the U.S. in May 1995, Beijing was especially interested getting the U.S. to reiterate the one-China philosophy that informed three joint communiqués (Shanghai 1972, Normalization 1978, Arms Sales 1981). See "Jiang Zemin Zhuxi Huijian Ge'er Fuzontong Shi Tichu Fazhan Zhongmei Guanxi," *Renmin Ribao*, March 27, 1997; Gu Ping, "Zhongmei Guanxi Mianlin Lishi Jiyu," *Renmin Ribao*, November 5, 1997, p. 1.

81. In the U.S., by late 1998, the phrase was increasingly viewed as a symbol of the Clinton administration's naivete in dealing with China, much as conservative critics of Nixon-Ford foreign policy saw "détente" as a symbol of naivete in U.S. policy towards the Soviet Union in the mid-1970s. Early in the 2000 U.S. electoral cycle, key advisers to the Republican Party explicitly argued that China should be viewed as a strategic competitor, rather than a strategic partner, a position criticized by Chinese analysts. See Condoleeza Rice, "Campaign 2000—Promoting The National Interest," *Foreign Affairs*, January-February, 2000, 79, no. 1, pp. 45–62; "Commenting on Recent U.S. Policy toward China" *Hong Kong Wen Wei Po*, July 27, 2000, FBIS. One well-informed Chinese interlocutor emphasized that following the Belgrade bombing, every high-level U.S. visitor privately emphasized the American interest in continuing to work toward the "constructive strategic partnership." Though not rejecting the phrase, the Chinese side did not echo the American invocation until Tang Jiaxuan's meeting with Albright in June 2000 at which they discussed plans for a Jiang-Clinton meeting at the September 2000 UN millenium summit. Jiang's use of the term in a speech on the eve of his meeting with Clinton was intended both as a way of punctuating the end of the post-bombing bilateral tensions and also as a signal to the U.S. public that China remained interested in working toward a constructive strategic partnership after the Clinton era. ("Jiang Zemin on Sino-U.S. Ties, Taiwan, WTO, Tibet: Text of Speech by President Jiang Zemin at Luncheon Held by U.S. Amity Group in New York," *Xinhua*, September 8, 2000, FBIS.) For China's press coverage that continued to highlight the term "strategic partnership" as a goal for Sino-American relations even if the term was not attributed to Chinese leaders, see "Wrap-Up: Jiang Zemin Meets U.S. National Security Adviser," *Xinhua*, March 30, 2000, FBIS; "Tang, Albright Say Sino-U.S. Ties Can Move Forward; Discuss PNTR, Taiwan, NMD," *Xinhua*, June 22, 2000, FBIS; Erik Eckholm, "U.S. and Top Chinese Officials Try to Smooth Over Differences," *New York Times*, July 14, 2000, p. 7.

82. For examples of the calls for a more explicitly anti-American line in China's foreign policy, see Chu Shulong and Wang Zaibang, "Guanyu Guoji Xingshi," p. 21; Lu Youzhi, "Chongxin Shenshi Zhongguo De Anquan Huanjing," p. 60. On the debate's unusually wide range of views and its resolution see Tao Wenzhao, "A Foreign Policy

Debate in China after the Tragic Bombing of the Chinese Embassy in Belgrade," unpublished ms., Institute of American Studies, Chinese Academy of Social Sciences; Willy Wo-Lap Lam, "Jiang To Pressure Clinton Over Taiwan Stance," *South China Morning Post*, August 14, 1999, p. 1, LEXIS-NEXIS; Ching Cheong, "Cross-Strait Dispute: China Gives Peace A Chance," *The Straits Times (Singapore)*, August 25, 1999, p. 40, LEXIS-NEXIS.

83. Zhang Wenmu, "Heshihou Nanya Xingshi Ji Zouxiang," *Zhanlüe yu Guanli*, no. 2 (1999): 46–49; Zhou Guiyin, "Xin Shiji De Guoji Anquan Yu Anquan Zhanlüe," p. 70; Peng Shujie and Liu Yunfei, "Partnership Promotes China's All around Diplomacy."

84. Swaine and Tellis, *Interpreting China's Grand Strategy*, pp. 9–20, ch. 2.

85. Ye Zicheng, "Zhongguo Shixing Daguo Waijiao Zhanlüe," p. 7; Chen Demin, "90 Niandai Zhongmei Guanxi Tanxi," *Xiandai Guoji Guanxi*, no. 9 (1999), reprinted in *Zhongguo Waijiao* (2000) no. 1, pp. 20–24; Jin Canrong, "Zhongmei Guanxi De Bian Yu Bubian," *Guoji Jingji Pinglun*, no. 11/12 (1999), reprinted in *Zhongguo Waijiao* no. 2 (2000): 21–25.

86. For Chinese comments on the series of problems in bilateral relations, see Lu Youzhi, "Chongxin Shenshi Zhongguo De Anquan Huanjing," p. 60; Fang Hua, "Yatai Anquan Jiagou De Xianzhuang," p. 13.

87. Author's interviews March–April 2000; See also Zhou Guiyin, "Xin Shiji De Guoji Anquan Yu Anquan Zhanlüe," p. 71; Lu Youzhi, "Chongxin Shenshi Zhongguo De Anquan Huanjing," p. 60; Pillsbury, *China Debates the Future Security Environment*, p. xl. For a more strident view of the U.S. as enemy even before the Belgrade bombing, see Zhang Wenmu, "Kesuowo Zhanzheng Yu Zhongguo Xin Shiji Anquan Zhanlüe," *Zhanlüe yu Guanli* no. 3 (1999): 3.

88. Pillsbury *China Debates the Future Security Environment*, pp. 13–15, 25, 27–28, 58; Chu Shulong and Wang Zaibang, "Guanyu Guoji Xingshi," p. 17; Xiao Feng, "Dui Guoji Xingshizhong," p. 3.

89. Author's interviews March–April, October, 2000; Sun Jianshe, "Shiji Zhijiao," pp. 21, 22; Chu Shulong and Wang Zaibang, "Guanyu Guoji Xingshi," p. 21; Ye Zicheng, "Zhongguo Shixing Daguo Waijiao Zhanlüe."

90. See "President Lee's Deutsche Welle Interview," July 9, 1999, in http://taiwansecurity.org/TS/SS-990709-Deutsche-Welle-Interview.htm. For the many interpretations, clarifications, and criticisms his statement provoked, see the articles and papers collected at http://taiwansecurity.org/TSR-State-to-State.htm.

91. Ross, "The 1995–96 Taiwan Strait Confrontation," p. 116.

92. On reports that Jiang and the other top CCP leaders decided at their August 1999 Beidaihe gathering to clearly signal the U.S. that continued cooperation required Washington's help in trying to rein in Taiwan's Lee Teng-hui, see "'Source' Says PRC to Pressure U.S. over Taiwan Issue," *Agence France-Presse*, August 14, 1999, FBIS. See also Zhou Guiyin, "Xin Shiji De Guoji Anquan Yu Anquan Zhanlüe," pp. 69–70. Sensitive to the internal criticism that had surfaced over the previous year from ideological conservatives worried about the disruptive consequences of further exposing the country to the forces of globalization and from military conservatives who preferred a more bluntly coercive Taiwan policy, China's top leaders moved slowly in re-

pairing its relations with Washington. The initial steps came at the informal Jiang-Clinton talks during the Auckland APEC meetings in September 1999. See Xu Hongzhi and Huang Qing, "Advancing Toward Multipolarization Amid Turbulence," *Renmin Ribao* December 16, 1999, p. 7, FBIS; also Chen Jian, "Jiang Zemin Talks With Former U.S. President George Bush in Beijing on March 2 About Bilateral Ties, WTO," *Zhongguo Xinwen She*, March 2, 2000, FBIS; "PRC Vice Premier Qian Qichen Meets Albright on Sino-U.S. Ties, Taiwan," *Xinhua*, June 22, 2000, FBIS; "Sino-Us Military Exchanges Resume Gradually." *Hong Kong Wen Wei Po*, November 4, 2000, FBIS; Tong Ying. "PRC Expert Views Us Elections, Explains Why Beijing Feels Relieved," *Hong Kong Wen Wei Po*, November 10, 2000, FBIS. For a skeptical Chinese view about U.S. sincerity in salvaging the partnership, see Ding Kuisong, "Zongjie Guoqu Mianxiang Weilai," *Xiandai Guoji Guanxi*, no. 10 (1999), reprinted in *Zhongguo Waijiao* no. 2 (2000): 12–13. On China's limited willingness to compromise in order to foster the strategic partnership, see Khalilzad, et. al, *The United States and a Rising China*, pp. 5–9.

93. See Xue Longgen, "Zhengzai Shenhua Fazhan De Zhongfa Quanmian Huoban Guanxi," *Shijie Jingji yu Zhengzhi Luntan* no. 5 (1999): 26.

94. "Prospects of China's Diplomatic Activities in 1998." Chinese analysts, like their foreign counterparts, disagree about the chances for the EU to develop a common foreign policy. Of the EU members, France and Germany are viewed as important international powers in their own right. Britain, however, is often viewed as simply following the American lead (Author's interviews, June–July, 1998).

95. "Presidents Jiang and Chirac Agree to Build 'Comprehensive Partnership'," *Xinhua*, May 15, 1997, BBC Summary of World Broadcasts; "China: France's Foreign Minister Gives Press Conference," *Xinhua*, January 23, 1998, FBIS; Han Hua, "Four Keys in 1998 Chinese Diplomacy," *Wen Wei Po*, March 4, 1998, FBIS; "Editorial: Great Success in China's Big-Nation Diplomacy"; "China's International Status Is in the Ascendance," *Ta Kung Pao*, July 6, 1998, FBIS; Wang Xingqiao, "A Positive Step Taken by the European Union to Promote Relations with China," *Xinhua*, July 10, 1998, FBIS; Peng Shujie and Liu Yunfei, "Partnership Promotes China's All around Diplomacy"; Huang Xingwei, "Sino-British Relations Develop Steadily," *Xinhua*, October 18, 1999, FBIS; "Diplomatic News Highlights for 23–29 Oct.," *Xinhua*, October 30, 1999, FBIS; Si Jiuyue and Huang Yong, "Zhu Rongji Held Talks with Schroeder, and Delivered Important Speech to German Industry and Trade Council," *Xinhua*, June 30, 2000, FBIS.

96. See "China and EU To Step Up Dialogue, May Hold Annual Summits," *Agence France-Presse*, April 2, 1998, clari.China; "Chinese Premier's First European Trip Crowned with Glory," *Agence France-Presse*, April 8, 1998, clari.China; "EU Adopts New Anti-Dumping Rules for China," *Agence France-Presse*, April 28, 1998, clari.world.asia.China.biz, ClariNet Communications; "European Union Calls for New Partnership with China," *Agence France-Presse*, October 29, 1998, clari.China; "President Jiang Zemin To Tour Italy, Switzerland, Austria Next March," *Agence France-Presse*, October 28, 1998, clari.China; Ren Xin, "1996: A Year of Diplomatic Feats for China," *Beijing Review* no. 1,(January 6–12, 1997): 9–13, FBIS. China sees ASEM itself as a potential counterbalance to U.S. dominance, particularly on eco-

nomic affairs, in the emerging multipolar world. See Huang Qing, "Ya'Ou Huiyi he Duojihua," *Renmin Ribao*, April 9, 1998.

97. "China's International Status Is in the Ascendance"; Wang Xingqiao, "A Positive Step Taken by the European Union to Promote Relations with China."

98. Zhang Guocheng, "Riben de Daguo Waijiao," *Renmin Ribao*, December 19, 1997.

99. See Avery Goldstein, "The Political Implications of a Slowdown," *Orbis* 43, no. 2 (Spring 1999): 203–221; Liu, "Deng Xiaoping's Thinking on Diplomatic Work"; "Editorial: Great Success in China's Big-Nation Diplomacy."

100. "Prospects of China's Diplomatic Activities in 1998." See also Shi Nangen, "1997: A Fruitful Year in China's Multi-Dimensional Diplomacy."

101. As noted above, China and Japan ultimately agreed to the term "friendly and cooperative partnership." Despite the passing years, and regardless of generation, most of my interlocutors continued to note the persistent historical impediments to completely normalizing Sino-Japanese relations. Author's interviews, June–July, 1998, March–April, October, 2000. See also Thomas J. Christensen, "China, the U.S.-Japan Alliance, and the Security Dilemma in East Asia," *International Security* 23 no. 4 (Spring 1999): 49–80.

102. For the continuing tension in China's approach to Japan, compare "Japan, China Agree On Mutual Visits By Warships: Report," *Agence France-Presse*, April 26, 1998, clari.China; and "China Wary of U.S.-Japan Military Pact," *UPI*, April 28, 1998, clari.China. Prior to President Jiang's late 1998 trip to Tokyo, a Japanese foreign ministry official indicated that there would be no strengthening of Japan's noninterventionist commitments regarding Taiwan, and Prime Minister Obuchi refused to commit himself to issue a formal written apology for Japan's wartime aggression against China. "Japan Rejects Any Chinese Pressure Over Taiwan," *Agence France-Presse*, October 28, 1998, clari.China. My Japanese interlocutors familiar with the internal and bilateral negotiations prior to Jiang's visit to Tokyo, stated that Obuchi's decision not to offer Jiang the sort of explicit public apology South Korea's Kim Dae-jung had just received reflected (1) the belief that Japanese leaders had more than once expressed remorse about Japan's behavior in China (but not Korea) during WWII; and, (2) the conviction that China's leaders would never be satisfied, accept a proffered apology, and consider the matter closed (a promise Kim Dae-jung made in advance of his summit with Obuchi). Author's interviews, Tokyo, March, 1999.

103. Yumiko Miyai, and Mami Tsukahara, "Jiang Hails New Era in Japan-China Ties; 3 Hecklers Held for Interrupting Waseda Speech," *Yomiuri Shimbun*, November 29, 1998, LEXIS-NEXIS; Willy Wo-Lap Lam, "China, Japan Struggle on Accord; Leaders Fail to Sign Joint Statement after Disagreement over Apology for War Atrocities," *South China Morning Post*, November 27, 1998, from LEXIS-NEXIS. See also "Chinese President Jiang's Visit to Japan May Be Delayed to Next Year"; Michael Zielenziger, "Talks Fall Short for China, Japan," *Philadelphia Inquirer*, November 27, 1998, p. A1, A4. For an official characterization of the state of Sino-Japanese ties after the Jiang visit see "China-Japan: Bilateral Political Relations," available at Regions link of the Foreign Ministry of the PRC website, http://www.fmprc.gov.cn/eng/4278.html.

104. On Tokyo's mixed interests, see Jiang Lifeng, "Zhongri Guanxi De Xianzhuang Yu Weilai," *Riben Yanjiu* no. 3 (1998): 6–15. One of my interlocutors famil-

iar with the Chinese Foreign Ministry's deliberations, insisted that Premier Zhu's visit represented a victory for those advisers who believed that China should emphasize the importance of Japan's integration within a regional economic community, and that this meant de-emphasizing, though not forgetting, disputes over issues "left over from history" on which Jiang had focused attention in 1998 (Author's interviews October 2000). Indeed, Zhu subsequently advanced this general idea of fostering region-wide cooperation at the ASEAN plus three summit meetings in November 2000 (Robert J. Saiget, "China Pushes Higher Profile for ASEAN Talks with Japan, South Korea." *Agence France-Presse*, November 22, 2000, clari.China).

105. The controversy about how much the Chinese learned about rocket guidance from working with the U.S. company Loral in investigating a failed satellite launch, suggests other potentially fruitful linkages between the economic and military aspects of the grand strategy. See Jeff Gerth, "Congress Investigating Sales of Satellite Technology to China," *New York Times*, April 16, 1998, p. A5; "The Sanctity of Missile Secrets," *New York Times*, April 15, 1998, p. A24; See also Michael Hirsch, "The Great Technology Giveaway?" *Foreign Affairs* 77, no. 5 (September/October 1998): 2–9.

106. See "President's Speech On Taiwan Reunification" *New China News Agency*, BBC Summary of World Broadcasts, January 31, 1995, LEXIS-NEXIS; Author's interviews, June–July, 1998; Ross, "The 1995–96 Taiwan Strait Confrontation." For arguments emphasizing basic consensus on core security questions such as Taiwan, see Paul Heer, "A House United." For an assessment that sets forward multiple reasons why China views Taiwan as a core security interest, see also Wang Yiwei, "Dui Tai Junshi Douzheng," p. 29.

107. Christensen's interviews suggest the military's strong disdain for Foreign Ministry officials. See Thomas J. Christensen, "Realism with Chinese Characteristics: Beijing's Perceptions of Japan, the United States, and the Future of East Asian Security," Research report submitted to the Asia Security Project, Olin Institute for Strategic Studies, Harvard University, November 28, 1996, typescript, p. 16.

108. See Alastair Iain Johnston, *Cultural Realism: Strategic Culture and Grand Strategy in Chinese History* (Princeton: Princeton University Press, 1995); Alastair Iain Johnston, "Cultural Realism and Strategy in Maoist China" in Peter J. Katzenstein, ed., *The Culture Of National Security: Norms And Identity In World Politics* (New York: Columbia University Press, 1996): 219–220, 247; Thomas J. Christensen, "Chinese Realpolitik," *Foreign Affairs* 75, no. 5 (1996): 37–52; Pillsbury *China Debates the Future Security Environment*, pp. xxxv, xxxvix; Swaine and Tellis, *Interpreting China's Grand Strategy*, pp. xii; 231, 233, 236.

109. See Swaine and Tellis, *Interpreting China's Grand Strategy*, pp. 152, 153–179; 183–97.

110. See Yan Xuetong, "Dui Zhongguo Anquan Huanjing," pp. 7, 8; Chu Shulong and Wang Zaibang, "Guanyu Guoji Xingshi," pp. 18–19

111. See Swaine and Tellis, *Interpreting China's Grand Strategy*, pp. 231, 233, 236.

112. See Brzezinski *The Grand Chessboard*, pp. 164, 165–167; Goldstein, "Great Expectations." For Chinese views that anticipate a more threatening environment, see Sun Jianshe, "Shiji Zhijiao Dui Woguo Anquan Huanjing De Sikao, pp. 20, 21; Yan Xuetong, "Dui Zhongguo Anquan Huanjing," pp. 5, 6. For assessments of the power

trajectories of various countries, including discussions of "comprehensive national power," see Yan Xuetong, *Zhongguo Guojia Liyi Fenxi* (Tianjin: Tianjin Renmin Chubanshe, 1997): 87–95; Gao Heng, (ed.), 2020 *Daguo Zhanlüe* (Shijiazhuang: Hebei Renmin Chubanshe, 2000); Pillsbury, *China Debates the Future Security Environment.*

113. Lu Youzhi, "Chongxin Shenshi Zhongguo De Anquan Huanjing," pp. 57–58; Sun Jianshe, "Shiji Zhijiao Dui Woguo Anquan Huanjing De Sikao," p. 19; Pillsbury, *China Debates the Future Security Environment*, pp. 13, 15, 25, 28, 58; Ye Zicheng, "Zhongguo Shixing Daguo Waijiao Zhanlüe," pp. 6, 7; Chu Shulong and Wang Zaibang, "Guanyu Guoji Xingshi," p. 17; Xiao (12/99), p. 3; Xiao Feng, "Dui Guoji Xingshizhong," pp. 1, 2. On China's confidence in the inevitability of multipolarity, however slow its arrival may be, see Pillsbury, *China Debates the Future Security Environment*, pp. 65–72, 73–76.

114. Yan Xuetong, "Dui Zhongguo Anquan Huanjing," pp. 7, 9. For a Chinese vision of naval modernization consistent with the notion that the first three decades of the twentyh-first century are a period in which China must strive simply to catch up with the world-class military powers, see Liu Yijian, "Zhongguo Weilai De Haijun Jianshe Yu Haijun Zhanlüe," *Zhanlüe yu Guanli* no. 5 (1999): 99, 100. Consequently, at the turn of the century, China's most innovative military strategists have focused on the need to cope with their country's present material disadvantage by emphasizing investment in improving the technological quality of selected forces and by developing clever varieties of asymmetric warfare. See Mark Burles and Abram N. Shulsky, *Patterns in China's Use of Force: Evidence from History and Doctrinal Writings* (Santa Monica, CA: RAND, 2000). Pillsbury, *China Debates the Future Security Environment*, ch. 6; Zhang Wenmu, "Kesuowo Zhanzheng Yu Zhongguo Xin Shiji Anquan Zhanlüe," p. 4; Yan Xuetong, "Dui Zhongguo Anquan Huanjing," p. 10; Chu Shulong, "Lengzhanhou Zhongguo Anquan Zhanlüe Sixiang De Fazhan," p. 13; "Chuanwen Jiang Zemin Zhishi Gaibian Zhonggong De Guofang Zhengce"; Khalilzad, et. al., *The United States and a Rising China: Strategic and Military Implications* (Santa Monica, CA: RAND, 1999)pp. 39–44, 48–59. For China's method of calculating comprehensive national power, see Pillsbury, *China Debates the Future Security Environment*, p. 203, ch. 5.

115. Yan Xuetong, "Dui Zhongguo Anquan Huanjing," pp. 8, 9; Chu Shulong and Wang Zaibang, "Guanyu Guoji Xingshi," p. 20.

116. See Pillsbury, *China Debates the Future Security Environment*, pp. xxxvix. As noted above, China understands this assertive approach to be the self-defeating path the Soviet Union followed. See Guo Shuyong, "21 Shiji Qianye Zhongguo Waijiao," pp. 92–93, 94.

Chapter 3

SOCIALIZATION IN INTERNATIONAL INSTITUTIONS

The ASEAN Way and International Relations Theory

Alastair Iain Johnston

INTRODUCTION[1]

I think it is fair to say that for most IR theorists there are two main ways in which involvement in international institutions changes state behavior in more cooperative directions. The first is through material rewards and punishments: in pursuit of a (mostly) constant set of interests or preferences a state responds to positive and negative sanctions provided exogenously by the institution (rules, membership requirements, etc.) or by certain actors within the institution. The second is through changes in the domestic distributions of power among social groups pursuing (mostly) a constant set of interests or preferences such that different distributions lead to different aggregated state preferences.

Few would deny that these are plausible, observable and probably quite frequent ways in which policies change direction after a state enters an international institution. But are these the only or even primary ways in which this change occurs? The ASEAN Way discourse explicitly challenges the "hegemony" of these two processes in IR theory and practice. The discourse stresses that the way in which the social milieu is created inside formally weak institutions—the effects of familiarity, consensus building, consultation, non-coercive argumentation, the avoidance of legalistic solutions to distribution problems, etc.,—the process itself, is a critical variable in explaining cooperative outcomes

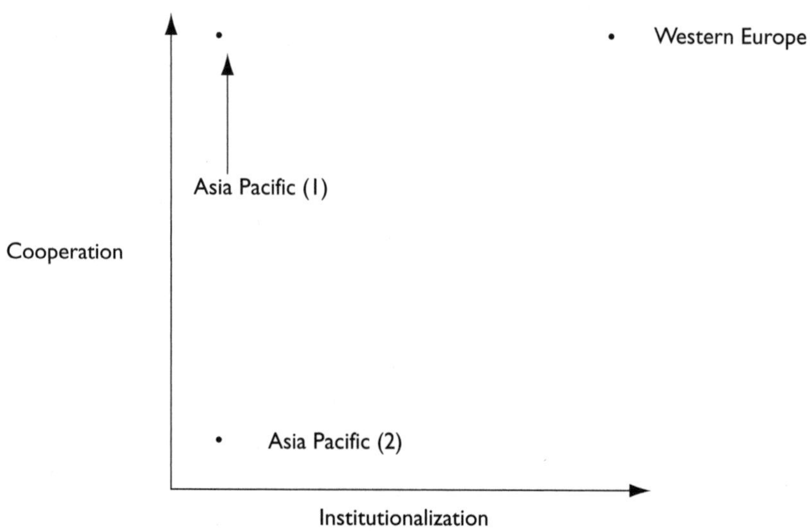

FIGURE 3.1 Comparative Regional Subsystem Contexts.

in institutions.[2] Thus, proponents of the ASEAN Way argue that, in contrast to the pessimism of realist theory and its variants, and to the "follow-me" hubris of European institutionalization and integration, the Asia-Pacific is developing patterns of institutional form and content that can lead to high levels of cooperation even with low levels of formality and intrusiveness. That is to say, the discourse suggests that there is a third way in which state behavior changes, namely, through socialization inside international institutions such that state behavior changes in the absence of these two conditions and, instead, in the presence of the endogenous "social" effects of institutions.

One of the most important of these effects is persuasion.[3] Indeed, the explicit purpose of the ASEAN Way as manifested in the only multilateral security institution in the region—the ARF—is to develop "habits" of cooperation.[4] A habit (according to Webster's) is, among other things, an "acquired mode of behavior that has become nearly or completely involuntary." Thus the ARF aims, in part, at socializing its participants in "modes of behavior" (in this case cooperation) that become taken-for-granted, pursued on the basis of appropriateness. The ASEAN Way, and the ARF, then, are explicitly trying to create what constructivists argue are central processes in IR, namely, processes of social interaction that lead to the internalization of normative understandings which, in turn, create new definitions of interest independent of exogenous material constraints (whether these be material power structures or institutional rules). Putting it crudely and visually (fig. 3.1), the ASEAN Way discourse might suggest that the Asia-Pacific is situated in or moving toward the northwest corner of the x and y axes (1), unlike Western Europe situated in the northeast corner, and unlike the dire predictions of the neo-and traditional realists who would argue that the region is mired in the realpolitik southwest corner (2).[5]

It is one thing to claim this is what the ASEAN Way is doing in Asia-Pacific IR and altogether another to show that this is in fact happening. How would one know it if these social effects were indeed critical for understanding cooperation inside institutions? And why it is important for IR theory to find an answer to these questions? Interestingly enough, the claim that the ASEAN Way is, at least in part, responsible for this evolution in Asia-Pacific IR parallels the "sociological turn" in IR theory led by social constructivist work. Social constructivists in particular focus on the link between the presence of particular normative structures at the international level (mostly in international institutions) and the incorporation of these norms in behavior by the actor/agent at the unit-level. Indeed, socialization is *the* central "causal" process for constructivists that links structures to agents and back again. And a subset of socialization, a critical microprocess, is persuasion—their trump card.

But constructivists, as Jeff Checkel has pointed out, have not been very successful in explaining the microprocesses under which actors are exposed to, receive, process, and then act upon the normative arguments that predominate in particular social environments—particularly in the so-called hard case area of security.[6] Given the claims about socialization embedded in the ASEAN Way discourse, a focus on precisely how an institution allegedly modeled off this discourse does affect cooperation might be useful in testing the valued added of this sociological turn in IR.

So what I propose to do here is to ask, first, is there space for a socialization argument in IR theory? And if so, what might such an argument look like? That is, if one were to treat institutions as social environments rather than only as a set of exogenous rule-based constraints on actors, what might the implications be for thinking about institutional design and cooperation?[7] Finally I'll try to test for the effects of socialization—persuasion in particular—in explaining the evolution of Chinese approaches to the ARF, and to multilateral security dialogues in the Asia-Pacific in general.

SOCIALIZATION IN IR THEORY

Socialization is a fairly common analytical concept in a range of social sciences where social interaction and the impact of group processes on individual behavior is a critical research focus: linguistics and the acquisition of language; sociology and social psychology and theories of in-group identity formation and compliance with group norms; political science and the acquisition of basic political orientations among young people or explanations of social movements; international law and the role of shaming and social opprobrium in eliciting treaty compliance; anthropology and the diffusion of cultural practices, among other fields and topics. It ought to be a vibrant area in IR as well since socialization would seem to be central to some of the major topics in IR theory today: preference formation and change;[8] national identity formation; the creation and diffusion of, and compliance with, international norms; the effects of international institutions, etc.[9]

But while most noncoercive diplomatic efforts have been aimed at persuasion—"changing the minds of others"—only recently has IR theory begun to engage the concept of socialization. The Clinton administration, as did many ASEAN states, for example, viewed the engagement of China as a way of "teaching" Beijing about allegedly predominant norms and rules of international relations (free trade; non-use of force in the resolution of disputes; nonproliferation; multilateralism, etc.). Clinton officials in particular spoke about bringing China into the international normative community, an enculturation discourse if ever there was one. Defense Secretary William Perry noted in a speech in Seattle in 1995 that engagement was a strategy for getting China to act like a "responsible world power."[10] In March 1997, in outlining national security policy for Clinton's second term National Security Advisor Sandy Berger referred to engagement as designed to pull China "in the direction of the international community."[11] Stanley Roth, Assistant Secretary of State for East Asian and Pacific Affairs, noted in a speech to the World Economic Forum in October 1997 that "We want China to take its place as an active and responsible member of the international community."[12] Secretary of State Madeline Albright wrote in an op ed in the Miami paper Diario *Las Americas* in July 1998: "The manner in which the United States engages China now and in the future will influence whether China *becomes* a constructive participant in the international arena. . . . We seek a China that embraces universally recognized human rights and global norms of conduct and one that works with us to build a secure international order."[13]

Even if, in the end, many attempts to use diplomacy to effect the internalization of new ways of thinking and behaving fail,[14] it still makes sense to try to explain why actors (state and non-state) engage in this kind of activity in the first place. But of course, we don't really know how many of these attempts do fail because we haven't really tried to define, isolate, and measure the effects of socialization processes in IR.

This is not to say that predominant IR theories ignore the term socialization completely. Neorealism uses the term to describe the homogenization of self-help balancing behavior among security-seeking states interacting under conditions of anarchy.[15] But in neorealism homogenization is not really socialization in common-sense usage. Rather it is imitation and selection leads to similarities in behavior of actors through interaction: states that do not emulate the self-help balancing behavior of the most successful actors in the system will be selected out of it, while those remaining (assuming there are no new entrants into the system—a problematic assumption that I will come to in a moment) will tend to share behavioral traits. It is unclear as to whether the theory assumes states will also share epiphenomenal realpolitik foreign policy ideologies, because the theory is unclear as to whether states are conscious agents pursuing balancing outcomes or simply unconscious participants in the creation of unintended systemic balances.

In any event, it is simply not empirically obvious that this kind of selection even occurs. As Dan Reiter has argued, historical experience rather than some search for obvious transhistorical exemplars is often the criteria states have used when deciding when and what type of balancing is appropriate (Reiter 1996). Indeed, one could legitimately question whether material structure plus anarchy does any selecting out at all, given the empirical frequency and significance of failures to balance.[16] The death rates of states declined dramatically in the latter half of the twentieth century. Unsuccessful states—those that eschew self-help, that fail to balance internally or externally—simply do not disappear anymore.[17] New states emerged in the late twentieth century in an era when failed or unsuccessful states were not routinely eliminated, and thus, presumably, could retain heterogeneous traits and characteristics, supported in some respects by institutions and rules analogous to those that support socially weak, "deviant," and failed individuals in domestic societies. This being the case, the characteristics of the system structure must, by definition, be much more varied and complex than the simple tending-toward-balances anarchy of a neorealist world. Thus, the social environment in which these new states are socialized must be one that not only rewards or selects states that copy 'successful" self-help balancers, but one that may also reward or support "deviant," heterodox behavior. If so, then so much for the homogenizing effects of social interaction—socialization—in anarchy.[18]

Contractual institutionalism generally does not use the term socialization. For most contractual institutionalists, true to their micro-economic and game theoretic predelictions, the notion that social interaction can change preferences and interests is not a central concern (or they are divided as to its theoretical possibility and empirical frequency). Social interaction inside institutions is assumed to have no effect on the "identities" or "interests" of actors, or at least institutionalists are divided as to whether there are any effects.[19] That is, actors emerge from interaction inside institutions with the same attributes, traits, and characteristics with which they entered. These characteristics in turn have no effect on the attributes, traits or characteristics of the institution itself—an efficient institution reflects the nature of the cooperation problem, not the nature of the actors themselves—and these characteristics, in turn, have no impact on actor identities. Iteration, the intensity of interaction, or the provision of new information about the beliefs of other actors, etc., do not seem to have any effect on the basic preferences of actors. The quality or quantity of prior social interaction among players should be irrelevant to the calculus of whether or not to defect.[20]

Instead, prosocial or cooperative behavior in institutions is a function of such things as material side payments or sanctions provided by institution or other actors; the desire for a good reputation portable to other exchange relationships; and reassurance information. Contractual institutionalism generally does not treat institutions as agent-like entities, nor does it examine the affect relationships created through interaction inside institutions.

For contractual institutionalists, or those sympathetic to the approach, there are sound methodological reasons for downplaying socialization.[21] For one thing, socialization opens the door to unstable or rapidly changing preferences, depending on how interactive the agent-structure relationship is. This makes modeling hard because it makes it difficult to hold preferences fixed to determine the independent effects of strategic environment on behavior. For another, observing preferences is hard; it is particularly difficult to determine whether external manifestations (e.g. speech act or action) of what is "inside heads" are in fact strategic. This leads to a methodological tendency to deduce preferences from theoretically based characteristics of actors (e.g. militaries prefer large budgets because they prefer offensive doctrines because they prefer efficiency and minimal uncertainty).[22]

Institutionalists do not rule out changes in preferences or behavior that are not exogenously constrained: There is no *a priori* reason why information, say, might change not only beliefs about the strategic environment, but also the preferences of extant decisionmakers. But if preferences do change as a result of interaction in an institution, institutionalists usually look for a change in distribution of power among political elites/decisionmakers (elite replacement—due to some effect of an institution—e.g information about policy failure; sanctions; distribution of institutions benefits).[23]

This uninterest in socialization is somewhat surprising, though. Given the prominence of coordination games and focal points in institutionalist theorizing about social norms, habits, customs, and conventions that constrain rationally optimizing behavior one might expect more curiosity about the social-historical origins, and the stability, of focal points. Institutionalists admit that focal points can be products of shared culture and experience.[24] Martin notes that bargaining inside institutions may allow states to establish focal points in a coordination game. But the origins of these focal points in IR are not of central concern, and institutionalists do not explicate the microprocesses by which bargaining reveals or creates (or convinces actors to accept) a focal point.[25] This is acceptable if one assumes relative stability in focal points and conventions. But this is an assumption, not an empirical claim. It is an assumption challenged by constructivist or complex adaptive systems, agent-based ontologies that assume that continuous interaction between multiple agents over time can lead to rapidly changing social structural contexts (emergent properties) that, in turn, affect how agents define their interests. In macrohistorical terms, this means that social conventions and focal points can evolve and change rather dramatically, non-linearly, and in path-dependent ways.

Needless to say, for social constructivists socialization is a central concept: The constructivists' focus on the "logics of appropriateness"—pro-norm behavior that is so deeply internalized as to be unquestioned, automatic, and taken-for-granted—naturally motivates questions about which norms are internalized by agents, how, and to what degree. The empirical work in this regard has tended to follow the sociological institutionalists' focus on macrohistorical diffusion of values and practices (e.g. rationalism, bureaucracy, market economics), measured by correlations between the presence of a global norm and the presence of corresponding local practices. Finnemore goes beyond correlation to causation by focusing on how international agents (e.g. international organizations, ideas entrepreneurs, etc.) have actually gone about "teaching" values and constructing domestic institutions and procedures that reflect emergent international norms and practices and that states pursue even if these seem inconsistent with its material welfare or security interests.

The problems with constructivist work so far, however, are fairly basic. First, inheriting much of the epistemology of sociological institutionalism, constructivists have tended to leave the microprocesses of socialization underexplained.[26] They tend to assume that agents at the systemic level have relatively unobstructed access to states and sub-state actors for diffusing new normative understandings. This leaves variation in the degree of socialization across units—the degree of contestation, normative "retardation," etc.—unexplained. And it leaves the causal processes unexplicated.[27] Even Finnemore's story of "teaching" stops essentially at the point where agents at the international level deliver norm-based lessons to rather passive students. There is less attention paid to the processes by which units or unit-level actors understand, process, interpret, and act upon these "lessons." It is unclear how exactly pro-normative behavior is elicited once the models of "appropriate behavior" are displayed or communicated to agents at the unit-level. This neglect is surprising, given constructivists' focus on reflective action by multiple agents: if this kind of agency exists in the diffusion of norms, what happens when "teaching" efforts run into reflective action by multiple agents at the receiving end?[28] The result is, however, that the "constitutive" effects of systemic normative structures are mostly assumed, rather than shown.

Second, when constructivists do begin to look at these microprocesses of socialization and the constitutive effects of social interaction, the focus is almost exclusively on persuasion. Yet here there are two issues. One is that persuasion and shaming or social opprobrium (often termed normative "pressure") are conflated.[29] These are, in fact, distinct microprocesses. Persuasion involves the noncoercive communication of normative understandings that is internalized by actors such that new courses of action are viewed as entirely reasonable and appropriate. Social pressure, opprobrium—also termed social influence—is different. The actor desires to maximize social status and image as ends in themselves. This leads to a sensitivity to the accumulation of status markers that are bestowed only by a relevant audience with which the actor has at least a modicum of identification. The process of choosing to act in prosocial ways is an instrumental or "consequentialist" one, not one governed by appropriateness per se.[30]

A second issue is that when talking about persuasion constructivist-oriented research has tended to borrow in some form or another from Habermas' theory of communicative action. The argument is that social interaction is not all strategic bargaining. That is, bargaining is often not simply a process of manipulating exogenous incentives to elicit desired behavior from the other side. Rather it involves argument and deliberation all in an effort to change the minds of others. As Hasenclever et al., put it, "parties enter into a debate in which they try to agree on the relevant features of a social situation and then advance reasons why certain behaviors should be chosen. These reasons—in so far as they are *convincing*—internally motivate the parties to behave in accordance with the mutually arrived at interpretation."[31]

The main problem here is that it is not obvious, when actually doing empirical research, what the value added of using Habermas is to the neglect of a very rich research tradition on persuasion in communications theory, social psychology, and political socialization. It is not clear how the application of the communicative theory of action would go about showing whether persuasion or coercion explained behavior that was more pro-social over time, which is what makes communicative action in and of itself "convincing." How are actors convinced to agree on a "mutually arrived at interpretation" of social facts. Under what social or material conditions is "communicative action" more likely to be successful? How would one know? Constructivists seem to rely on an identity argument that hints at an infinite regress problem: that is persuasion is more likely to occur when two actors trust one another such that each accepts the "veracity of an enormous range of evidence, concepts and conclusions drawn by others."[32]

SOCIALIZATION: DEFINITION AND PROCESSES

Social scientists generally agree that socialization is a process by which social interaction leads novices to endorse "expected ways of thinking, feeling, and acting." For Stryker and Statham 'socialization is the generic term used to refer to the processes by which the newcomer—the infant, rookie, trainee for example—becomes incorporated into organized patterns of interaction."[33] Berger and Luckmann define the term as "the comprehensive and consistent induction of an individual into the objective world of a society or sector of it." Socialization, then, involves the development of shared identification such that people become members in a society where the intersubjective understandings of the society become "objective facticities" that are taken for granted.[34] Political scientists generally agree with the sociologists: Ichilov refers to political socialization as "the universal processes of induction into any type of regime." These processes focus on "how citizenship orientations emerge."[35] Siegal refers to political socialization as the "process by which people learn to adopt the norms, values, attitudes and behaviors accepted and practiced by the ongoing system."[36] IR theorists have generally simplified socialization to processes "resulting in the internalization of norms so that they assume their 'taken for granted' nature."[37] Ikenberry and Kupchan evoke a Gramscian-like image when they define socialization as a process whereby states internalize "the norms and value orientations espoused by the hegemon and, as a consequence, become socialized into the community formed by the hegemon and other nations accept its leadership position." This hegemonic order "comes to possess a 'quality of oughtness.' "[38]

There are a couple of common themes here: The first is that socialization is most evidently directed at, or experienced by, novices, newcomers, whether they be children, inductees into a military, immigrants, or "new" states. That is, "noviceness" is an important characteristic that affects the pace and outcome of socialization processes.[39]

The second theme is the internalization of the values, roles, and understandings held by a group that constitutes the society of which the actor becomes a member. Internalization implies, further, that these values, roles, and understandings take on a character of "taken-for-grantedness" so that not only are they hard to change, but also the benefits of behavior are calculated in very abstract social terms rather than concrete consequentialist terms. Why should one do X? "Because, . . . " or "because it is the right thing to do . . . " rather than "Why should one do X? Because it will lead to Y, and Y benefits me."[40] To date, however, constructivism has been vague on how persuasion leads to internalization and why.

Persuasion has to do with cognition and the active assessment of the content of a particular message. As a microprocess of socialization, it involves changing minds, opinions, and attitudes about causality and affect in the absence of overtly material or mental coercion. It can lead to common knowledge, or "epistemic conventions" (that may or may not be cooperative) or it can lead to a homogenization of interests. That is, actors can be persuaded that they are indeed in competition with each other, or that they share may cooperative interests. The point is, however, that the gap or distance between actors' basic causal understandings closes as a result of successful persuasion.

Persuasion is a common tool in social relationships. People tend to rank changing other's opinions very high in a list of influence strategies, regardless of whether the other is considered a friend or an enemy.[41] Communications theorists have argued that all social interaction involves communications that alter people's "perceptions, attitudes, beliefs and motivations."[42] How persuasion works therefore is a focus of a great deal of research in communications theory, social psychology, and sociology, and there is no obvious way of summarizing a disparate and complex literature.[43] But let me try.

Essentially there are three ways in which an actor is persuaded. First, s/he can engage in a high intensity process of cognition, reflection, and argument about the content of new information (what Bar-Tal and Saxe call cognitive capacity).[44] Also known by some as the "central route" to persuasion, the actor weighs evidence, puzzles through "counterattitudinal" arguments, and comes to conclusions different from those h/she began with. That is the "merits" of the argument are persuasive, *given* internalized standards for evaluating truth claims. Arguments are more persuasive and more likely to affect behavior when they are considered systematically and, thus, linked to other attitudes and schema in a complex network of causal connections and cognitive cues.[45] This process of cognition, linking one set of attitudes to another, is more likely to occur when the environment cues and allows for the actor to consider these connections. That is, it is less likely to be spontaneous than it is promoted.

Thus the probability of some change in attitudes through cognition increases in an iterated, cognition-rich environment (where there is lots of new information that cues linkages to other attitudes and interests). As a general rule the probability goes down if the initial attitudes are already linked to a larger, internally consistent "network of supportive beliefs," particularly if these beliefs are about potential enemies and other high-threat outgroups. In small, but high affect in-groups, the content and volume of new information is likely to favor the existing dominant preferences of the group. Thus, even if the actorgives rational consideration to the available information, s/he is more likely to support the groups' conclusions if s/he is from outside the group.[46]

This relates to a second route to persuasion. An actor is persuaded because of her/his affect relationship to the persuader: Sometimes called the "peripheral" route to persuasion, here the persuadee looks for cues about the nature of this relationship to judge the legitimacy of counterattitudinal arguments. Thus information from in-groups is more convincing than that from outgroups. Information from culturally recognized authorities (e.g. scientists, doctors, religious leaders) is more convincing than that from less authoritative sources. This will be especially true for novices who have little information about an issue on which to rely for guidance.[47] Information from sources that are "liked" is more convincing than that from sources that are disliked. Liking will increase with more exposure, contact, and familiarity. The desire for social proofing means that information accepted through consensus or supermajority in a valued group will be more convincing than if the group were divided about how to interpret the message.[48]

Third the persuasiveness of a message may be a function of characteristics of the persuadee her/himself. This can refer to a range of variables from cognitive processing abilities, to the strength of existing attitudes (usually these are stronger if developed through personal experience than if based on hearsay or indirect experience, for example), to what appears to be an deeply internalized desire to avoid appearing inconsistent, to the degree of independence an agent might have in relation to a principal. Thus, for example, an attitude associated with an explicit behavioral commitment made earlier will be more resistant to change later because actors experience discomfort at being viewed as hypocritical and inconsistent. Conversely, a new set of attitudes will be more persuasive if associated with a new, high-profile behavioral commitment.[49] Thus a focus on the characteristics of the persuadee means looking at the individual features that can either retard or propel persuasion. All this means is that actors entering a social interaction bring with them particular prior traits that, interacting with the features of the social environment and other actors, leads to variation in the degree of attitudinal change.[50]

Obviously persuasion in the end is a combination of all three processes above and it is hard to run controls that might isolate the effects of any one process. People are more likely to think hard and favorably about a proposition, for instance, when it comes from a high affect source, in part because affect helps kick in cognitive processes that include resistances to information from other sources.[51] On the other hand, one can identify ideal combinations that could, in principle be tested. Given these processes, then, there are certain kinds of social environments that ought to be especially conducive to persuasion.

- when the actor is highly cognitively motivated to analyze counterattitudinal information (e.g. a very novel or potentially threatening environment);
- when the persuader is a highly authoritative member of a small, intimate, high affect in-group to which the also persuadee belongs or wants to belong
- when the actor has few prior, ingrained attitudes that are inconsistent with the counterattitudinal message,
- when the agent is relatively autonomous from principal (e.g. when issue is technical or issue is ignored by principal).[52]

TESTING FOR SOCIALIZATION EFFECTS: RESEARCH DESIGN ISSUES

For the most part, when IR specialists or sociological institutionalists look for the effects of socialization the unit of analysis has tended to be the state—or state elites in a fairly aggregated way.[53] This presents obvious problems when examining particular institutions as social environments since states as unitary actors don't participate in institutions; rather, state agents do, e.g. diplomats, decisionmakers, analysts, policy specialists, as well as nongovernmental agents of state principals. Secondly, it presents problems when applying the most-developed literature on socialization typically found in social psychology, sociology, communications theory, and even political socialization theory. Most of this literature examines the effects of socialization on individuals or small groups. Thirdly, a constructivist ontology, in a sense, allows (even demands) that the unit of socialization be the individual or small group. As Cederman points out, constructivism's ontology can best be captured by the notion of complex adaptive systems whereby social structures and agent characteristics are mutually constitutive, or locked in tight feedback loops, where small perturbations in the characteristics of agents interacting with each other can have large, nonlinear effects on social structures.[54] Thus it matters how individual agents or small groups are socialized because their impacts on larger emergent properties of the social environment can be quite dramatic.[55] Finally, constructivists have to deal with the choice theoretic critique that what is observed as the normatively motivated behavior of a group at one level may be the aggregation of the strategic behavior of many subactors comprising that group at a lower level.[56] There are good reasons, then, for studies of socialization to "go micro" and focus on the socialization of individuals, small groups and, in turn, the effects of these agents on the foreign policy processes of states.[57]

But if these are appropriate units of analysis why choose international institutions as the "agentic environments" of socialization? After all, state actors experience a myriad of socializing environments from bilateral interactions at the state level, to intrabureaucratic environments at the policy level, to training and work environments inside bureaucratic organizations themselves. Let me try to make the case. One of the critical claims constructivists make is that "anarchy is what states make of it." In other words, material power structures do not determine state interests or practices, and thus the practice of realpolitik by unitary rational actors is not an immutable "fact" of international politics. In order to make this case, constructivists and their fellow-travelers have, for the most part, underscored the empirical "deviations" from realist or material power-interests theories (such as weapons taboos, "autistic" military doctrines, and cultural limits on the conduct of war, 1996), etc.[58] These have been important cases that have chipped away at the realist edifice. But the durability of constructivism depends, I believe, on going beyond so-called deviant cases to look at cases and phenomena that realist theories claim they can explain; that is, constructivists are going to have to make the argument that realpolitik practice is a reflection of ideology and realpolitik norms.

If this is done, then by definition one has the conditions for a critical test.[59] In a critical test one spins out additional alternative but *competitive* propositions, predictions, and expectations from the two sets of explanations to see which additional set of empirical observations is confirmed or disconfirmed. One such additional empirical implication that could provide an important test of constructivist versus material realist explanations of realpolitik is as follows: if constructivists are right, realpolitik discourse and practice ought to be changeable, independent of material power distributions and "anarchy," when actors are exposed to or socialized in counter-realpolitik ideology. If materialist realist theories are right, realpolitik discourse is epiphenomenal to realpolitik practice and neither should change in the presence of counter-realpolitik ideology because for rational security seeking actors no counterrealpolitik argument about how to achieve security should be convincing or persuasive.

This is where international institutions come in. Constructivists suggest that international institutions in particular are often agents of counter-realpolitik socialization. They posit a link between the presence of particular normative structures embodied in institutions and the incorporation of these norms in behavior by the actor/agent at the unit-level. It is in institutions where the interaction of activists, so-called norm entrepreneurs, is most likely, and where social conformity pressures are most concentrated. Institutions often have corporate identities, traits, missions, normative cores, and official discourses[60] at odds with realpolitik axioms. So, for example, some arms control institutions expose actors to an ideology where multilateral transparency is normatively better than unilateral nontransparency; where disarming is better than arming as basis of security; where common security is better than unilateral security; and where evidence of the potential for cooperative, joint gains in security in the international system is greater than evidence that the environment is a fixed, conflictual one. All of these axioms and assumptions challenge the core assumptions of realpolitik ideology. So, if there is any counterattitudinal socialization going on, it ought to be happening in particular kinds of security institutions.[61]

Precisely because counter-realpolitik institutions may be critical environments for counter-realpolitik socialization, an easy case can be made for studying the ASEAN Way and the ARF in particular. As I will discuss, in *content* the ASEAN Way and the ARF embody a non-realpolitik ideology centered on the notion of common security (though, admittedly, in uneasy tensions with sovereignty-centric axioms as well). In *form*, the ARF's loose and informal features best fit the kind of institutional ideal type environment most conducive to persuasion as a socialization process. Moreover, crucial for testing the constructivist case, the ARF is, in part, aimed explicitly at socializing a large, deeply realpolitik actor, but one that is nonetheless as much as a novice to international institutional life as one can find among major powers—the PRC. I treat the PRC as a novice in the sense that China has moved more rapidly into interna-

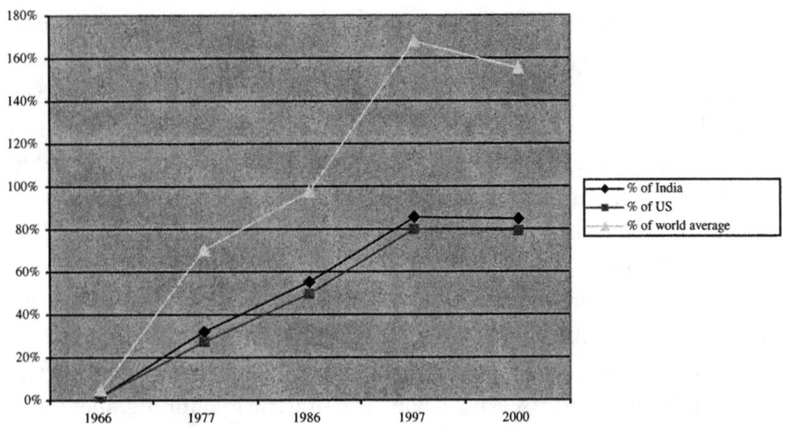

FIGURE 3.2 China's IGO memberships as % of US, Indian and average world memberships. *Source*: *Yearbook of International Organizations* (2000/2001), Appendix 3: Table 3.

tional institutional life starting from a lower baseline of participation than any other major power or even most minor powers in perhaps this century. Figures 3.2 and 3.3 illustrate both the China's "laggard" participation profile and its rapid move into institutions in the 1990s.

On the ARF specifically, one senior Chinese analyst involved in the interagency process told me that prior to participation in the ARF China didn't know what its interests were on many regional security issues, having never had to do the research on things such as transparency, military observer CBMs, and preventive diplomacy.[62]

Together, a "novice" and hard-realpolitik state(s) is ideal for testing for socialization since this is precisely the kind of state where the effects of socialization (if there are any) are easiest to observe. If constructivists are right, any prosocial or cooperative behavior that emerges from China's involvement in the ARF should be a function either of changes in a preference for multilateralist outcomes (in which case there should be a convergence in the security ideology that Chinese decisionmakers take to the ARF and that promoted by the institution itself). Those substate actors most directly exposed to this ideology should be the strongest proponents of it.[63] If materialist realist theories are right, there should be no socialization effects of a non-realpolitik kind on the PRC. Indeed, China's suspicions about entrapment in multilateral security commitments should not change. At best, all relevant actors in China should see the ARF as a tool for balancing against U.S. power. There should not be much internal debate on this score. If contractual institutionalist arguments are right, then prosocial or cooperative Chinese behavior should be either a product of exogenous incentives or disincentives constraining China from pursuing its prisoner's

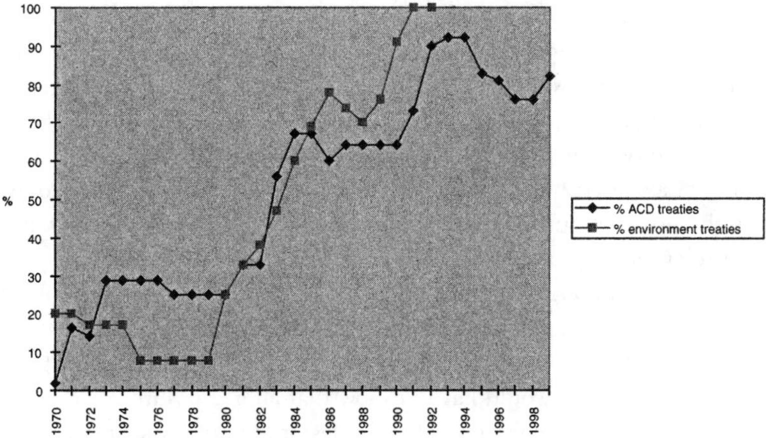

FIGURE 3.3 China's Accessions to Multilateral Arms Control and Environmental Treaties as % of Eligible Accessions.

dilemma (or worse, deadlock) preferences, or perhaps new information that reassures a PD or deadlock China that it cannot be exploited or entrapped in the ARF (e.g. that participation is essentially costless).

Note, however, that treating institutions as social environments means positing that different social environments vary in terms of their persuasiveness. This means asking how institutions as social environments vary in ways conducive to socialization. We need, then, a typology of institutional forms or institutional social environments. Unfortunately, we don't have one. One could imagine, though, at least several dimensions for coding institutions as social environments. Here I am borrowing and expanding on the typology of domestic institutions developed by Rogowski:[64]

1. membership: e.g. small and exclusive or large and inclusive
2. franchise: e.g. where the authoritativeness of members is equally allocated, or unevenly (though legitimately) allocated
3. decision rules: e.g. unanimity, consensus, majority, supermajority
4. mandate: e.g. to provide information, to deliberate and resolve, to negotiate and legislate
5. autonomy of agents from principals: low through high.

Different institutional designs (combinations of measures on these five dimensions) would thus create different kinds of social environments, leading to differences in the likelihood and degree of persuasion. For instance, persuasion is likely to be the most prevalent and powerful socialization process when membership is small (social liking, in-group identity effects on persuasiveness of counterattitudinal message); when franchise recognizes the special authoritativeness of a couple of actors (authoritativeness of messenger); when decision rules are based on consensus (requires deliberation–cognition effects); when the institution's mandate is deliberative (requires cognition, agents may be more autonomous since there is no obvious distribution of benefits at stake so there is less pressure to represent principal); and when autonomy of agents is high, e.g. when the issue is a narrow technical one or when the principal just doesn't care much (when the principal is less attentive or relevant).[65]

But how would one know if persuasion had led to prosocial/pronormative behavior in international institutions? First, as I noted above, one would have to show that social environments in institutions are conducive to persuasion. Second, one would have to show that after exposure to or involvement in a new social environment, attitudes or arguments for participation have indeed changed, converging with the normative/causal arguments that predominate in a particular social environment. Third one would have to show that behavior had changed in ways consistent with prior attitudinal change. Finally, one would have to show that material side payment or threats were not present, nor were they part of the decision to conform to prosocial norms.

Together, these design issues suggest a set of empirical referents. Assuming an actor enters the institution and its particular social environment with realpolitik preferences and causal and principled beliefs, and assuming the institution embodies causal and principled beliefs that are generally inconsistent with realpolitik ones, if persuasion is at work, one should expect to see (after exposure to this environment): arguments about participation should include declining concern about detrimental effects of participation on relative capabilities and security; heightened concern about beneficial effects for global, regional and national security; and conformist behavior later in the process that could not be expected earlier on. In short, you should get increasing "comfort" levels even as the process becomes more intrusive. Unfortunately, there simply is not enough variation in security institutions in the Asia-Pacific at the moment to systematically test for the socialization effects of variation in institutional social environments.[66] Thus, as a test for the "plausibility" of the persuasion, I will look at an institution that ought to be highly conducive to counter-realpolitik persuasion (ARF), and examine what socialization effects, if any, it has had on a relatively novice realpolitik state (China). This constitutes, interestingly enough, both a most likely AND a least likely test of socialization. It is a most likely test because conditions are ideal for determining and isolating the independent effects of socialization (in this case persuasion, the "purest" form of socialization). It is a least likely test as well because China's long-time hard realpolitik, unilateralist approach to regional security would seem to be least susceptible to change.

THE ARF AS A COUNTER-REALPOLITIK INSTITUTION

The first thing is to establish is that the ASEAN Way as embodied in the ARF does indeed constitute a counter-realpolitik ideology that is, in some sense, "diffusable." Acharya identifies at least four key elements of this ideology: open regionalism, soft-regionalism, flexible consensus, cooperative/common security. The first three refer to the "structure" and form of the ARF, a variable that matters when discussing whether the ARF creates conditions conducive to persuasion (and perhaps social influence). I will come back to these features in a moment. Cooperative and/or common security, however, is the normative core of the ARF.[67] First enunciated by the Palme Commission for Europe in the early 1980s, the concept embodies a number of principles: the nonlegitimacy of military force for resolving disputes, security through reassurance rather than unilateral military superiority, nonprovocative defense, transparency. Behavior that is reassuring rather than threatening should be the rule, such that the ARF can "develop a more predictable and constructive pattern of relations for the Asia-Pacific region."[68]

The security philosophy here implicitly assumes states are essentially status quo (or can be socialized to accept the status quo) and as such it is both normatively and empirically "true" that reassurance behavior is a better route to security than traditional realpolitik strategies. Security is positive sum. As such, traditional axioms like "if you want peace, prepare for war" are outmoded or counterproductive.[69] To this end, the normatively appropriate and empirically effective means for achieving security involve the building of trust through confidence-building measures, and the diffusion of security problems through preventive diplomacy and conflict management. This is not to say that all members of the ARF, even the strongest backers of the institution, behave in ways perfectly consistent with the injunctive norms. The point is that these are the articulated, and formal, if sometimes implicit, "theories" of security that are supposed to serve as the basis of "habits of cooperation."

For a social environment to have a socializing effect, obviously an actor has to be a participant. The ARF is explicitly designed to be maximally attractive to states. The principles of open regionalism, soft-regionalism, and flexible consensus are critical in this regard. Together they reflect the nondiscriminatory goals of the ARF. While there are evolving rules for participation, the principle of open regionalism means the institution should be as inclusive as possible, combining multilateralist activists and skeptics such that there is no aggrieved actor left out to undermine the efficacy or legitimacy of the institution.[70]

Moreover, the institution should be as attractive to states as possible (in this case, China). Soft-regionalism, therefore, emphasizes the informality, nonintrusiveness of the institution, and explicitly endorses the codes of conduct in the

ASEAN Treaty of Amity and Cooperation (TAC), which emphasizes sovereignty-preserving principles such as the noninterference in the internal affairs of states, respect for territorial integrity, the right to chose domestic social systems, etc.[71]

At first glance this would appear to be inconsistent with counter-realpolitik socialization. I don't think there is any easy way of squaring this circle. What this principle does do, however, is send reassurance signals toreassure participants that the institution will not undermine basic interests, that it will not be used by powerful states to exploit or influence less powerful or influence ones. That is, it makes the institution attractive, or at least nonthreatening from the perspective of the most skeptical potential participant.[72]

Flexible consensus ensures not only that the institution doesn't move far ahead of the interests of the most skeptical state but also that the most skeptical state cannot veto its evolution. Consensus decisionmaking is a logical mechanism for reassuring member states that the institution will not threaten sovereignty or national unity. The rule was expressly written into the Chair's Statement summarizing the consensus at the Second ARF meeting in Brunei in 1995: "Decisions of the ARF shall be made through consensus after careful and extensive consultations among all participants."[73]

Consensus decisionmaking might appear to be a suboptimal decision making rule for a diverse group of actors: while it is more efficient than a unanimity rule, there is always the risk that individual actors can acquire informal veto power.[74] Studies of consensus decisionmaking among political parties in Swiss canton governments suggest, however, that consensus rules are likely to reduce intergroup conflicts in systems with "strong subcultural segmentation"—e.g. diverse subgroups as in the ARF.[75] In addition, as Chigas et al. argue in their analysis of consensus rules in the OSCE, consensus means all states have a greater stake in the implementation of decisions because they are collectively identified with a decision in ways that they would not be had they been defeated in an on-the-record vote over a particular course of action. Efforts to buck or shirk consensus decisions will generate more negative "peer pressure" than had clear opposition been registered through a vote.[76] Put differently, consensus rules make obstinacy costly in ways that up-and-down voting rules do not: obstinacy threatens to undermine the effectiveness of the entire institution because its effectiveness is premised on consensus. It portrays the obstinate actor as one whose behavior is fundamentally at odds with the purposes of the institution. "Principled stands" against efforts to declare consensus are viewed as less principled that had they been expressed in a losing vote. Moreover, a consensus decision reduces the risk of ending up on the losing side. Losing internationally can have domestic political costs. It could be harder to maintain a domestic consensus for an international institution if one appears to lose badly from time to time.[77]

The ARF's consensus decision rule was an attractive feature for China. Consensus ensures that China will not be on the losing side in any majoritarian voting system. This was probably important for those in the Ministry of Foreign Affairs handling ARF diplomacy: It would have been much harder to sell the benefits of the ARF in the policy process in Beijing if China's leaders had evidence that China was losing in recorded voting procedures.

A subcomponent of consensus decisionmaking rules in the ARF is a norm of avoiding particularly controversial issues that might end up preventing consensus. This is where Track II activities have been instrumental to the functioning of the ARF, both as a source of ideas and as a channel for defusing potentially volatile issues. These track II activities come in three forms: ARF-sponsored Track II meetings;[78] activities undertaken parallel to, or in support of, the ARF without the ARF's prior formal endorsement;[79] and the Council on Security Cooperation in the Asia-Pacific, an umbrella organization created in 1993 of 13 national CSCAP committees. While it is not the only Track II process around, CSCAP is the largest and most organized, with national CSCAP committees collaborating in working groups on topics such as CBMs.[80]

Whether or not by design, the evolving relationship to Track II contributes to the ARF's stability and legitimacy as an institution for states in the region. Issues that are too controversial for Track I can be moved into Track II rather than being discarded entirely. This sustains the momentum behind issues that the ARF might otherwise be compelled to abandon at the Track I level. Given that many Track II participants are government officials who also participate in Track I activities,[81] an issue is never really not within Track I's sphere of attention. This means that states are more likely to get used to an issue being part of their interaction than if it were initially considered illegitimate. Track II can also "filter," or sanitize proposals that would otherwise be deemed more controversial by dint of who made them. *Who* makes a proposal can sometimes be more controversial than the *content* of the proposal itself.[82] But if proposals are "de-personalized" through the Track II consensus process, and then again through the ARF Chair's determination of consensus in the Track I level, much of the controversiality can be filtered out. Thus Track II can help define a Track I agenda that might not have otherwise appeared. As long as this myth of difference is not explicitly challenged, then the destabilizing effect of controversial issues is reduced. Chinese officials have stated openly that CSCAP's unofficial nature was a fiction because of the presence of so many government officials in their "personal capacities." Nonetheless the Chinese government has played along: In a statement of support for links to Track II, it noted, "Issues not discussed or needing further discussions because of disagreement" can be put into Track II fora.

The form of the ARF, then, exhibits some of the features of an institution that may be likely to create a social environment conducive to persuasion:

membership is relatively small (22 states) with some consistency over time in the participants at both the senior minister and functional specialists levels.[83] The decision rule is consensus; the mandate is deliberative and, partly as a result, this lowers the perception that highly threatening states can control the outcomes of the institution; and initially at least there was a certain amount of autonomy for China's representatives to the extent that the ARF was not central to Beijing's regional diplomacy, and the most likely repository of opponents, the PLA, was not fully involved in policymaking.[84]

We have, then, two key features of the ARF: a counter-realpolitik ideology and an institutional structure with features conducive, in part, to maximize opportunities to develop "habits of cooperation" in the absence of material threats and punishments. On top of this, the institution is seen explicitly by many of its participants as a tool for socializing China to accept the legitimacy of multilateralism, transparency and reassurance as a basis for security.[85]

Put differently, some participants in the regional security discourse see the ARF as a tool for increasing China's "comfort level" with multilateralism. Comfort level is another way of saying that an actor's utility level changes positively with changing levels of institutionalization. An actor has a particular distribution of utility associated with particular levels of institutionalization. Different actors may have different distributions of utility. Skeptics of multilateralism would have low values of utility at high levels of institutionalization. Committed multilateral activists would have high values of utility at high levels of institutionalization. Greater willingness to accept institutionalization would be indicated by an increase in an actor's utility whereby it comes to believe that the absence of an institution is a less valued than before and the presence of one becomes more valued than before.

The question is what might cause a shift in this comfort level, in this distribution of utility?

Mainstream institutionalist theory would probably focus on things such as reassurance (information underscores that fears of even small amounts of institutionalization are exaggerated) or the distributional effects of the institution (leading to change in domestic political balances of power). Socialization arguments would focus on persuasive arguments that more institutionalization is a "good" in and of itself, or on social backpatting and opprobrium effects that link the utility of involvement in the institution to the utility of social status and diffuse image.[86]

Here I want to focus on evidence for persuasion. Recall the required indicators of persuasion: that social environments in the institution are conducive to persuasion; that after exposure to or involvement in a new social environment, attitudes or arguments for participation converge with the normative/causal arguments that predominate in the social environment; that behavior had changed in ways consistent with prior attitudinal change; and that that material side payment or threats were not present, nor were any part of the decision to conform to prosocial norms.

Having established that the institutional form of the ARF meets the criteria for an environment conducive for persuasion the question becomes whether attitudes or arguments in China have converged with the normative/causal arguments at the core of the ARF "ideology." Clearly, the public and internal discourse in China on multilateral security dialogues in the Asia-Pacific prior to China's entry into the ARF in 1994 was highly skeptical of their value. Indeed, in internal circulation (*neibu*) and open materials alike, the discourse stressed that bilateral relations, particularly among the great powers, were the basis of stability or instability in IR; that there was no urgent need to build multilateral security mechanisms, indeed that multilateralism was "largely irrelevant"; that such institutions would be dominated by the U.S. or Japan while China would be outnumbered, and sensitive bilateral disputes where China might have an advantage in bargaining power might be internationalized.[87] The skepticism of multilateralism was rooted in even deeper realpolitik assumptions about international relations where structurally (and sometimes ideologically) induced zero-sum competition among sovereign states necessitates unilateral security strategies.[88]

Since entering the ARF, however, there have been some noticeable changes in the discourse. Initial statements made to the ARF (e.g. Foreign Minister Ian Lichen's comments at the first ARF in 1994) stressed what can only be seen as traditional "rules of the road" for the management of relations among sovereign, autonomous states. These included the five principles of peaceful coexistence, economic ties on the basis of equality and mutual benefit, the peaceful settlement of disputes, adherence to the principle that military power should only be used for defensive purposes (Yuan 1996: 11). Terms, concepts, and phrases associated with common or cooperative security were absent.[89]

By late 1996, however, Chinese working level officials directly involved in ARF-related affairs began to articulate concepts that were, to a degree, in tension with traditional realpolitik arguments. Shu Chunlai (a former Ambassador to India, and a key figure in China's CSCAP committee) appears to have been China's first authoritative participant in ARF-related activities to have used the term "common security." In a paper originally presented at the ARF sponsored Paris workshop on preventive diplomacy (November 1996), Shi and a co-author Xu Jian noted that common security was central to the post-cold war need for a "renewal" of old security concepts. This renewal, they argued, entailed abandoning "old" concepts, "based on the dangerous game of balance of power." There was not much more on the subject, and paper went on to stress, somewhat in tension with common security, that preventive diplomacy should be handled strictly in accordance with the five principles of peaceful coexistence.[90]

By early 1997, however, ARF-involved analysts and officials *unofficially* floated a better developed concept of "mutual security" at the first Canada-

China Multilateral Training Seminar (the seminar brought together a small number of key officials handling the ARF in the MOFA Asia Department, and a couple of analysts from China's intelligence institution (CICIR) who were also in the ARF "interagency" process. The term meant, according to one Chinese participant, that "for you to be secure, your neighbor had to be secure," a common security concept based on the notion of "win-win." It is possible the Chinese may have felt under pressure to develop an original Chinese contribution to the multilateral security discourse: "common security" was perhaps too closely identified the CSCE process, and thus might have been too provocative inside the Chinese policy process.

One of the participants in the seminar (a participant in interagency discussions on the ARF, and an analyst in CICIR) also submitted a paper in which he listed three types of security systems: hegemonic systems, alliance or military-bloc systems, and multilateral systems. The latter he called an "encouraging development," and noted that mutual security, like common security, cooperative security, and comprehensive security were traditionally unfamiliar concepts in China. But these were now "taking place in the minds of policymakers and scholars and in the actions of Chinese policies," though he didn't elaborate beyond this.[91]

Around the time of the seminar, another analyst involved in ARF-related work in a think tank attached to the State Council, Liu Xuecheng, wrote a paper on confidence building in the Asia-Pacific. The paper provided a sophisticated explanation of Western theories of CBMs, noting for example their military reassurance purposes. The author also elaborated a bit on "mutual security," noting that the concept was embodied in the April 1996 Five-Power (China, Russia, Kazakhstan, Kyrgyzstan, Tajikistan) Treaty on CBMs.[92] (One of the Chinese participants at the Canada-China seminar in Toronto had also noted that mutual security had come from the Chinese discourse on the Five-Power Treaty.)

The invocation of the Five Power Treaty in this common-security influenced discourse on mutual security is important. The Treaty comes as close to a CSCE-type CBM agreement as anything in the Asia-Pacific region, with provisions for limits on the size and type of military maneuvers allowed within certain distances of borders, provisions for military observers and military exercises, etc.[93] In internal Chinese debates over multilateralism, whether or not one believed the principles of the treaty had broader applicability to the region was an indicator of sorts about one's skepticism toward multilateralism in general.[94] The initial idea for the treaty grew out of bilateral PRC-Soviet negotiations over the border in the early 1990s. The Soviets had introduced the idea of a formal CBM agreement, using the various conventional weapons CBMs that it had negotiated with Western Europe as a template. Initially, Chinese negotiators were unsure of the meaning of the terms the Soviets were bringing over from the European experience. The terminology had to be translated into Chinese with explanation so that MoFA officials understood the implications of certain CBM terminology. Thus the Five Power Treaty emerged fairly directly from European CBM experiences tabled by the Soviets.[95]That those articulating the concept of mutual security would do so by invoking the Five-Power treaty as an example/precedent/exemplar suggests that the term signified an acceptance of more intrusive and formal security institutions. Indeed, the earliest analyses of the ARF tended to explicitly reject the CSCE as a model for the Asia-Pacific.[96]

Interestingly enough, in June of 1997 at the first CSCAP General Meeting, where China's national committee participated for the first time, China's representative, Chen Jian (Assistant Foreign Minister, and formally in charge of multilateral security issues at the MOFA), explicitly extolled the Five Power CBM treaty as contributing to confidence and security in the region. He did not mention "mutual security," however—nor indeed the term "new security concept."[97] This suggested that there was still probably some internal debate about the legitimacy of the concept and whether China should be formally and publicly associated with it. The term had not yet made it into the official policy discourse.

This changed by November 1997. The Chinese paper presented to the ARF Intersessional Support Group on CBMs in Brunei explicitly noted that the Five-Power Treaty embodied the notion of "mutual security" and could be used as a source of ideas for the rest of the Asia-Pacific. Mutual security was defined as an environment where the "security interests of one side should not undermine those of the other side . . . . This kind of security is a win-win rather than zero-sum game."[98] We shouldn't underestimate the significance of the incorporation of this loosely game-theoretic terminology in the Chinese discourse (and another "positive sum"—*zheng he*—used more recently by multilateralists in China)—terms borrowed, one assumes, from interactions with multilateralists in ARF-related activities. The origins are hard to pinpoint, but it doesn't seem to have been used prior to 1997: one of its earliest appearances was in comments that some Chinese participants made in the Canada-China seminar in January 1997. The term "win-win," of course, stands in distinct tension with traditional realpolitik notions of security and reflects core assumptions of common security.

Then in December 1997 at the Third CSCAP North Pacific Meeting, the Chinese delegate, Ambassador Shi Chunlai, developed the "new security concept" further, linking it to "mutual security" and, by implication, to common security: The concept, he argued, was "one that is not based on the cold war mentality featuring zero-sum game, but on mutual and equal security." Rather it meant "not creating winners and losers."[99] Both "the new security concept" and its component "mutual security" received the highest level endorsement when they were included in remarks by China's Foreign Minister Ian Qichen at the Private Sector's Salute to ASEAN's 30th Anniversary in December 1997.

Since then official Chinese commentary has pushed the discourse further to include rather bald attacks on realpolitik: An analysis broadcast by China Radio International in late December argued, for instance, that the Five Power CBM treaty was a good example for the rest of the Asia-Pacific. It had authenticated "a new security concept completely different from the cold war cold war mentality and the traditional security concept, [']If you desire peace, you must prepare for war.['] This saying is a vivid description of the traditional security concept." The traditional realpolitik concepts included such ideas as maximizing military force so as to become stronger than one's opponent, a narrow focus on the security of the nation above all else and the resort to military means in the pursuit of security.[100]

This does not mean that by 1998 mutual security had becomebecame a fully developed concept, nor that it wholly replicated cooperative or common security concepts, nor that the Chinese leadership had converted and rejected realpolitik axioms. Far from it. But it does mean that regional security issues (outside of the Taiwan question) were discussed increasingly within the framework of multilateralism.

Nonetheless, there was still some concern about the underdeveloped nature of these new themes in discourse about regional security. Thus in 1998 MOFA's Asia Department, realizing that it required more sophisticated "theoretical" arguments to bolster and justify the mutual security discourse and policy, began to ask some prominent international relations specialists in government-run think tanks for new ideas about regional security. A number of these thinkers are people one might consider multilateralists and integrationists.[101]

Specifically, through the MoFA's Policy Research Office, the Department commissioned a study by a respected specialist in regional multilateralism from the Chinese Academy of Social Sciences.[102] The report, entitled "The Concept of Comprehensive Security and some theoretical thoughts about China and Asia-Pacific Security," and submitted to MOFA in December 1998, explicitly argued that military power and traditional territorial-based concepts of national security were no longer the most important issues in China's future security in the region. Rather, China faced an increasing array of nontraditional security problems that could not be solved through the augmentation of national military power alone, and thus should focus more energy on developing multilateral cooperative solutions to security problems, including greater activism in the ARF. The report noted—in recognition of security dilemma dynamics—that China's behavior on the ground was one reason for other states' worrying about China's rising power. To deal with this, the report argued, China had to signal that it basically accepted extant rules of international and regional order while trying to moderate these rules and norms through existing international institutions and procedures. In other words, China's rise was a potentially destabilizing element in international relations not only because of perceptions of Chinese power in the past, but also because China had to credibly signal that it was in essence a status quo power. The report explicitly borrowed arguments and concepts from Western, including Canadian, multilateralists and included an appendix that introduced some of the multilateralist lexicon to its audience (e.g. integration theory, interdependence theory, democratic peace theory).[103] The arguments in the report were designed in part to assist the Asia Department and other multilateralists to make more sophisticated internal arguments in favor of greater participation in the ARF, e.g. to persuade others in the policy process, particularly in the PLA, of the value of multilateral diplomacy.[104]

The Chinese discourse on regional security multilateralism, then, has moved quite some distance from public skepticism to informal articulations of mutual security and common security to public affirmation of the concepts. Moreover, the concepts have been explicitly linked to a "real world" institutional exemplar of these principles, the five power CBM treaty, a document that is consistent with, indeed modeled in some ways off of, CSCE-style institutions.

The obvious question is: Is this all cheap talk? A realpolitik actor would have incentives to be deceptive: if one believed one operated in what could be called a prisoners" dilemma (PD) environment, then cooperative cheap talk could encourage others to cooperate, thus creating opportunities to acquire the "temptation" (C, D) payoff. This would, in principle, be especially attractive to an actor in an institution, such as the ARF, with little or no monitoring capacity (except for voluntary and nonstandardized "defense white papers") and no ability to punish defection. Many in the U.S. government view the mutual security discourse precisely as that: a deceptive effort to redirect attention from inconsistencies between Chinese security behavior (sharp increases in military expenditures, provocative military exercises, etc.) and the ideology of the institution, while trying to underscore the inconsistencies between U.S. bilateral alliance strategies in the region and the ideology of the institution.[105]

I am not convinced of the pure deceptiveness of this discourse, however. In principle there is a relatively easy test of this hypothesis. If it is right, then the strongest *proponents* of the mutual security discourse and the Five-Power Treaty as an exemplar agreement for the region should be the strongest *opponents* of U.S. bilateral alliances in the region. In addition, variations in Chinese efforts to undermine support for U.S. alliances (particularly with Japan), should track directly with variations in the strength and prominence of the mutual security discourse. On both these tests the instrumental or deception hypothesis comes up short. A careful tracking of the discourse, as I have tried to do above, suggests that the strongest proponents are precisely those who in private interactions with diplomats and scholars indicate a deeper commitment to multilateralism—multilateral functional specialists in the MOFA and somewhat more "pro-American" voices in the strategic analysis community. While these people are generally opposed to the expansion of U.S.-Japanese security cooperation, and would like to use multilateral diplomacy to pressure the U.S. to limit the scope of its military cooperation with Japan, they also recognize the alliance is a reality and may indeed constrain Japanese remilitarization.[106]

My sense is that those who are less enamored with the mutual security discourse are be found mostly in the military: It is in the PLA where some of the strongest skeptics of the U.S.-Japan alliance are found. One could also imagine that the PLA should be troubled by the anti-realpolitik content of "mutual security" and its use of a potentially militarily intrusive CBM treaty as a model for the region. Moreover the Chinese CBM proposals that were clearly biased against U.S. military power in the region (e.g. observers at joint military exercises, reductions in military reconnaissance activities aimed at ARF members, etc.) appeared first in 1995–1996, well before the "mutual security" concept emerged, and were promoted by the PLA, not the Ministry of Foreign Affairs.[107]

My argument here rests, obviously, on the critical question of whether the mutual security discourse has, in some sense, been internalized among those working most closely in the ARF environment. The evidence that this may be the case is indirect at the moment.[108] But China's involvement in the ARF and related processes seems to have led to the emergence of a small group of policymakers with an emerging, if tension-ridden, normative commitment to multilateralism because it is "good" for Chinese and regional security. ARF policy in China was put in the hands of the Comprehensive Division of the Asia Department of the Foreign Ministry. The Division had perhaps as few as eight or ten overworked officers. A couple of these officers did the preparatory work for ARF meetings and Track II activities. Initially, in ARF activities the Chinese representatives were unaccustomed to the give and take of corridor debate and negotiation. They also came to the discussions with a watchful eye for developments that might impinge on sensitive security or domestic political issues. Over time, however, with experience in informal discussion, familiarity with the ARF norms of interaction, these officers have become much more engaged, relaxed, and flexible. Even Chinese ARF specialists have noted that the institutional culture of the ARF requires them to adjust the tone and tenor of their discourse. While in the UN where vigorous and legalistic defenses of specific positions in negotiations that are often viewed as close to zero-sum are often required, in the ARF there is more give and take, more spontaneous intervention to explain positions, and with some exceptions, an atmosphere that downplays "in your face" defenses of national positions.[109]

Most interesting has been their apparent endorsement, within limits, of multilateralism as being compatible with Chinese security interests. More than one foreign diplomat in Beijing, who has had interactions with these MFA officers extensively, havehas suggested that their agenda is to tie China gradually and innocuously into regional security institutions so that some day China's leaders will be bound by the institutions. They see ARF involvement as a process of educating their own government. The main conduit for the infusion of these sorts of ideas, into this group at least, has tended to be experience in Track I and II, not so much the absorption of academic literature on multilateralism.[110] It seems this group's influence over Chinese ARF policy may be helped by further institutional change in China. In January 1998, the Asia Department set up a separate division just to handle ARF and Track II diplomacy.

There is some intriguing concrete evidence of the commitment these individuals have in protecting the policy from domestic political critics—hence an indication of their growing normative stake in the ARF. A senior Canadian official involved in ARF diplomacy reported that the Chinese delegates to ARF discussions apparently did not report back to Beijing any reference by other delegations to the CSCE as a possible model for the ARF. The CSCE is not just a symbol of a more intrusive, constraining regime; it is also a regime that deals with human rights.[111] Downplaying this information, then, was important to preserve support or acquiescence for further institutionalization of the ARF. Other Canadian diplomats have reported that sometimes the multilateralists in the MFA will help other states frame proposals for ARF-related activities in ways that will make these more acceptable in Beijing. While only anecdotal, this evidence suggests that over time the character of Chinese obstruction or resistance in its ARF diplomacy "on the ground" has shifted from protecting given Chinese "interests" only to protecting, in part, Chinese multilateral diplomacy from potential domestic opposition. When the ARF diplomats are under closer scrutiny from Beijing they have tended to be less conciliatory publicly. During the 1997 ISG on CBMs in Beijing, for instance, Canadian and American diplomats observed that the MOFA diplomats stuck to the proposal for observers at joint military exercises due, possibly, to the large presence of PLA observers in the meetings. The MOFA ARF diplomats had earlier suggested they might drop the position before the Beijing ISG because of the opposition of many ARF states, but apparently had decided against this in the face of the PLA first-hand scrutiny of China's ARF diplomacy in Beijing.[112]

Tentatively speaking, then, one could plausibly see a shift in China's ARF diplomacy to a diplomacy more empathetic with the institution and less empathetic with other PRC constituencies that may have different views of the value of multilateralism. Indeed, as one might expect, the creation of a specialist regional security institution inside the MoFA has also led to an emergent organizational interest in ARF diplomacy. As one MoFA interviewee implied, as the ARF agenda moves toward considering more formal arms-control like CBMs, the Asia Department has had to defend its prerogatives against the Arms Control and Disarmament Department, which handles most other multilateral security diplomacy for the MoFA.[113]

Even if the new "mutual security" discourse is not entirely cheap talk, is it irrelevant talk in the sense that it has little constraining effect on behavior? This question is central, of course, for showing whether or how socialization matters. But it is not central in showing that socialization occurs. Policy outcomes, like international social structures, should also be seen as products of the interaction of multiple actors in bureaucratic social environments where persuasion, social influence, and mimicking, not to mention strategic behavior, may be at work. Indeed one needs to know far more about the highly secretive Chinese foreign policy process than I do now. But a couple of points are worth mentioning.

First, even though I am black boxing part of the policy process (the part where the newly socialized proto-multilateralists then interact with other constituencies and communities and their normative and causal arguments) suppose they have an influence substantially greater than zero, and that the concept of mutual security has enough normative substance such that policy behavior ought to reflect some of its elements. There ought, then, to be some observable empirical implications. First and foremost, one ought to see a greater degree of Chinese "comfort" with the ARF's more institutionalized features and intrusive agenda over time. That is, there ought to be things about the ARF that Chinese decisionmakers accept now that they either opposed, or one could plausibly "counterfactualize" should have opposed in 1993.

Concretely, China's changing comfort level has allowed the following changes in the ARF institution and agenda:

Institutional Structure: The major innovation occurred at the Second ARF in 1995. The ARF agreed to set up two kinds of working groups to undertake intersessional discussions that could not be handled in the annual day-long Foreign Minister's meeting. Canada and Australia had floated proposals at the First ARF in 1994 for Track I intersessional work, but these had been rejected at the time, primarily because of Chinese objections.[114] In 1995 the proposal was put on the ARF agenda again. This time, despite some Chinese grumbling over the terminology and temporal mandate (China objected to the term "working groups" and to an indefinite timeframe because both smacked of thicker institutionalization) the ARF created two intersessional meetings (ISM)—peacekeeping operations; and search and rescue—and one intersessional support group (ISG) on CBMs. Their initial mandate was only to meet once in 1996, and the Third ARF would then decide whether or not to extend their lives, but they have been renewed regularly since then.[115] In 1998, the ARF ISG on CBMs recommended that the ARF convene two meetings of the ISG in 1999, further "regularizing" what is supposed to be an ad hoc process.[116] The ISG and ISMs finally provided the ARF with a process for much more detailed investigation of solutions to security problems in the region. This allowed states with particular expertise and or interest to influence intersessional work (e.g. Canada and PKO) Most surprising to ARF participants, but consistent with the argument about China's increasing comfort levels, China offered at the 1996 ARF to co-chair an ISG on CBMs with the Philippines in March 1997. China is now part of the intersessional process in a way no one imagined possible in 1993.

Agenda: Here there have been a number of innovations that were either rejected in 1993 and 1994, or were viewed as too controversial. All of these reflect some give by the Chinese. On nuclear testing, for example, despite its sensitivity to criticism on this score, the Chinese did not disrupt consensus when the 1995 and 1996 Chair's statements indirectly criticized both China (and France) for their nuclear testing programs.[117]

On preventive diplomacy (e.g. using the Chair's good offices to investigate or mediate disputes, sending ARF special representatives on fact finding missions, moral suasion, and third-party mediation) the PRC has traditionally been very uneasy with a more active ARF role because of the potential for "internationalization" of core security issues.[118] Nonetheless, the ARF formally took up the issue at its Track II working group on preventive diplomacy in November 1996 in Paris. Indeed, the explicit mandate of the Paris working group was to propose a list of relevant preventive diplomacy CBMs for the agenda of the ISG co-hosted by China March 1997. At the time, the main concrete recommendation to come out of the meeting was a proposal to expand the told of the ARF Chair's "good offices."[119] In April 1998 at another ARF Track II working group on PD the group agreed to recommend to the ARF SOM an "enhanced role for the ARF chair or other third parties in providing good offices in certain circumstances," a slight expansion of whose good offices might be called upon in PD activity. Interestingly enough, China's own experience with border CBMs with the Indians and Russians was suggested as possibly relevant for PD in the rest of the region.[120] These CBMs were, on paper at least, "contractual," CSCE-like agreements placing specific limits on the size and movement of military forces along borders.

The issue moved from Track II to Track I at the Sixth Senior Official Meeting in May 1999 where it was agreed that at the CBM ISGs in 2000 the question of the ARF Chair's good offices should be discussed in more detail. A draft paper on PD, prepared by Singapore, was circulated in November 1999 prior to the ISG on CBMs in Singapore in April 2000. The paper on PD outlined the principles and scope of the concept (see ARF 1999). The Singapore meeting authorized more explicit focus on an enhanced role for the Chair and for "Experts/Eminent Persons" (EEP). Papers on these two topics, presented by Japan and Korea respectively, were placed on the table later in 2000.[121] This finally initiated a detailed, Track I debate in the ARF over PD.

The Chinese position has evolved from opposition to PD to a more active, though wary diplomacy. The Chinese delegation officially contributed a working paper on PD in February 2000, prior to the Singapore ISG, in which it staked out key principles. These stressed that the ARF was a forum, not a mechanism "for dissolving specific conflicts."[122] Preventive diplomacy should use peaceful diplomatic means (by implication eschewing military operations such as PKO) to prevent armed conflict and only with the consent of all the parties directly involved. Any PD should also be based on mutual respect for sovereignty, territorial integrity, noninterference in internal affairs, and extant international law. On the basis of this paper, the Chinese suggested changes to the Singapore PD paper that would have, by and large, incorporated substantial portions directly from the Chinese working paper.

Some of these suggestions made their way into a revised Singapore paper in April 2000. Some of these changes were minor deletions of language. One however enshrined the principles of the UN Charter, the FFPC, and the ASEAN TAC in one of the eight principles of PD, giving the PD paper a stronger emphasis on upholding sovereignty and noninterference in internal affairs. China (and other states) also beat back a Canadian effort to dilute this principle with language on respecting human rights and the rule of law. Not all of the Chinese suggestions were incorporated, in particular a proposal to delete language that, in its view, might allow PD in cases of bilateral disputes that had the potential of spreading to other states.[123]

The PD issue is, as of this writing, at a stage where states are agreeing to disagree about some of the principles and modalities of PD. The revised Singapore paper was accepted at an ISG in Kuala Lumpur in April 2001, though as a 'snap shot" of the state of discussions on PD and with acknowledgment that substantial differences remained on virtually all of its components. The fact remains, however, the ARF appears still to be committed to developing a mechanism for more proactive dispute prevention. Chinese diplomacy on PD is no longer aimed at preventing this kind of evolution in the role of the ARF. Rather it has acquiesced to the notion of PD and instead has been essentially aimed at shielding the Taiwan issue and any of its own bilateral territorial disputes from ARF-based PD, and at strengthening language on sovereignty and noninterference in internal affairs.[124] The fact that the ARF took up these issues and is moving the discussion slowly forward, despite Chinese concerns suggests, again, a changing degree of Chinese comfort with the evolving agenda.[125]

On the South China Sea question, China's leaders' long-time preference has been for bilateral discussions with other claimants. They have worried that in multilateral settings China would be out-voted, its bargaining power diluted, leading to the dilution of China's sovereignty claims or, worse, the carving up of China's claims. They have tried assiduously in the past to prevent what they call the "internationalization" of the issue. It was considered a major conceptual breakthrough, then, when the SCS was put on the Second ARF agenda in 1995. Even though internal reports indicated continuing fears of multilateral approaches to resolving the issue, the Chinese delegation did not object to the Chair's declaration of consensus.[126] Nor was China willing (or able) to prevent the Statement from pointedly encouraging all claimants to reaffirm their commitment to ASEAN's 1992 Declaration on the South China Sea, this after China's construction of as small naval post on the disputed Mischief Reef in February 1995. The Third ARF Chair's Statement again touched on the SCS issue—this time welcoming China for its commitment in 1995 to resolve SCS disputes according to international law, but also pointedly commending the Indonesian workshop on the South China Sea for its work on conflict management issues.[127] The workshop was set up in 1992 and is funded by Canada. The Chinese had been unhappy with this and had tried to pressure the Canadians to stop funding. By the Third ARF, apparently, China didn't believe it was necessary to oppose consensus on this issue.

Over time, Chinese civilian analysts have apparently concluded that any hope of establishing control over all the South China Sea islands and surrounding water is for the foreseeable future fairly dim. Even internal analyses suggest that the exclusive use of military power to assert China's claims will probably be counterproductive and that negotiations are the only realistic solution.[128] But they also recognize that the absence of a viable military option has put China in a very difficult spot since it is unlikely that diplomacy alone will convince other states to acknowledge Chinese sovereignty. In the face of this dilemma, China has quietly scaled down its claims, recognizing that any diplomatic formula will probably require the sacrifice of some portion of extant claims. The issue is, according to which principle should territorial claims be pushed and along which part of the periphery. A continental shelf claim that advantages China in one area may not be as advantageous as a mid-line claim in another. In 1995 at the ARF meeting the PRC announced it would settle disputes on the basis of the rules in the UNCLOS. Internally, Chinese decisionmakers realized that in the face of ASEAN opposition, it did China little diplomatic good to refuse to stick to expansive historical claims as the sole basis for negotiation even though under UNCLOS provisions China would probably have to concede territorial claims to the Vietnamese.[129] China also dropped the claim to Indonesia's Natuna Islands.[130]

I am not suggesting that persuasion inside regional security institutions is the sole explanations for these changes in Chinese diplomacy. Indeed, the basic diplomacy of image in the eyes of ASEAN countries played a critical role. But some of the proto-multilateralists involved in regional security policy have supported these arguments. Some have even remarked that involvement in the ARF has reduced the likelihood of China's resort to force over disputes in the South China Sea because there are now more diplomatic, read multilateral, tools at China's disposal.[131]

Finally, on CBMs, China was traditionally skeptical about their value to the extent these are deemed asymmetrically intrusive. Weak states, like China, it claimed, should rightfully be less transparent than strong states like the U.S. In addition, China has criticized the notion that one can transplant CSCE-type CBMs to the Asia-Pacific. The First ARF was relatively silent on CBMs. However, by the Second ARF, under Brunei's leadership, the ARF had endorsed the ARF Concept Paper that laid out a timetable for implementing a wide variety of CBMs. These, all voluntary, would be taken from the Annex A list. Among them were: statements on security perceptions and defense policies; enhanced military-to-military exchanges; observers at military exercises; promotion of the principles of the ASEAN TAC and the ASEAN Declaration on the South China Sea; exchanges of information on PKO activities. At the ISG on CBMs in January 1996, states presented Defense White Papers and statements about security perceptions. But no comments on or criticisms of the content were permitted. There were complaints outside the ARF that the Chinese presentation—a White Paper on Arms Control—was not especially detailed or credible. China followed up in 1998 with a more detailed and sophisticated White Paper on Defense, modeled more or less on the Japanese and British White Papers.[132]

By the Third ARF, with the results in from the ISG on CBMs, the list of CBMs recommended in the Chair's Statement lengthened and deepened. While Defense White Papers and statements on security policies were still voluntary there were hints of an emerging template.[133] "Such papers could also cover defense contacts and exchange programs undertaken by participants." The Statement also hinted that, unlike in the ISG, the content of these papers would also no longer be off-limits to discussion. "Exchanges of views on the information provided in such statements and papers should be encouraged in future ARF dialogues." On military observers at exercises and prior notification of military exercises, the Statement noted that states were encouraged to exchange information about their ongoing observer and prior notification activities "with a view to discussing the possibilities of such measures in selected exercises."[134] The March 1997 ISG on CBMs co-chaired by China and the Philippines pushed this further. The agenda for the meeting called for reaching consensus on the invitation of observers to joint military exercises and the prior notification of joint military exercises.[135] Interestingly, while ASEAN and China tend to decry the validity of a CSCE template for the Asia-Pacific, the CBMs that are now either on the table in the ARF ISG or endorsed in the ARF Concept Paper Annex B (or embodied in the 5 Power Treaty), are not much different in kind from the first generation of CBMs under the CSCE.[136]

By the end of the decade China had proposed or hosted a number of CBMs ranging from the fourth meeting of Heads of Defense Colleges, to a seminar on Defense Conversion Cooperation, to exchanges on military law, to military exchanges on environmental protection.[137] The character of these proposals still reflected an impulse toward unilateralism—that is they were all proposed by China without coordination with other states or without asking other states to co-chair or co-organize. Moreover, some proposals have been frustratingly vague. For instance, in 1997 China proposed that a maritime information center be set up in Tianjin to provide the region with information about climate, ocean conditions, etc. Other delegates had a hard time trying to elicit more specific details about how such a center might be run, how the information might be disseminated (smaller states might be reluctant to rely on information controlled or provided by a great power in the region).[138] In addition, some of the CBM proposals are transparently self-serving, such as the previously discussed CBM on joint military exercises or a proposal for states to cease surveillance operations against each other. But the fact remains that this activity, as constrained as it is, is not viewed as especially duplicitous by most ARF states, and is considered a welcome indication of a growing Chinese sophistication and nuanced commitment to multilateral measures.

Thus change over time in the ARF is a result, in part, of the social effects of its initial form and function on one of the key actors in the institution. The mutual evolution between social environment and actor interests, understandings, and behavior is precisely what, according to constructivism, we should expect to see.

None of this means that China doesn't ever get its way. Clearly, despite the changes, the instititutionalization, and agenda of the ARF, it is not moving as fast as some countries would like. But often the recalcitrant parties are not just the Chinese. Moreover, often the limits to Chinese comfort levels tend to show up in the language adopted, rather than in the concrete content of discussions. While preventive diplomacy is on the agenda, the Chinese have been reluctant to support conflict resolution roles for the ARF. The 1995 ARF Concept Paper had divided the timeline for ARF development into three phases: CBM phase, development of preventive diplomacy phase, and a phase for the development of conflict resolution mechanisms. When the Second ARF Chair's Statement endorsed the Concept Paper, however, "conflict resolution" was changed to "the elaboration of approaches to conflict." The Chinese had objected to "conflict resolution mechanisms" because the term implied giving the ARF a mandate to intervene in conflicts that the Chinese might want to keep bilateral.[139] The slow pace of discussion on preventive diplomacy is, in part, a function of China's worries about its application to bilateral disputes, or conflicts it considers to be internal (e.g. Taiwan, ethnic separatism), though it has to be said that China is not alone in stressing the importance of the principle of sovereignty and independence in the application of PD mechanisms.[140]

The second general point is that the "mutual security" discourse developed through involvement in the ARF and related activities may become even more constraining over time. Borrowing and modifying normative concepts are not cost-free. Alternative normative discourses can affect actors' behavior in at least three ways. First they can underscore a widening gap between discourse and practice.[141] Subjective pressure due to a perceived gap between one's new identity, as embodied in the new discourse on the one hand and identity violating practices on the other, can lead to practices that are more consistent with the new identity (as consistency theory would suggest). Intersubjective pressure due to opprobrium generated when the new pro-group, pro-social discourse is obviously in tension with behavior can also lead to pro-group practices. In the Chinese case, for China's proto-multilateralists, mutual security (at least its common security elements), the rejection of realpolitik *parabellum*, and holding the Five-Power Treaty up as an exemplar of these principals, puts China's behavioral violation of these principles in starker relief. This can have reputational costs in the contractual institutionalist sense, or legitimacy costs in domestic political processes, or social psychological costs in terms of self-legitimation, identity consistency, and status.

Second, new normative discourses can positively sanction behavior that otherwise is unallowed or not seriously considered. For example, before China could enter international economic institutions like the IMF and the World Bank in the early 1980s, it had to revise its long-standing Leninist thesis on the inevitability of war. Early attempts in the late 1970s to do so ran into resistance.[142] Why? Because revisions would mobilize resistance from "true believers," opponents of engagement with global capitalist institutions who could invoke Mao as legitimating their arguments. The "inevitability of war" discourse didn't mean China was actually preparing for an inevitable global war between socialism and capitalism or within capitalism, nor that Chinese leaders necessarily believed it was imminent. But one couldn't be a Maoist and not profess this view. Thus one couldn't reject Maoism in foreign policy without rejecting the discourse. To no longer be a Maoist, to delegitimate Maoism as an obstacle to moving into institutions, required adjustment of the discourse. Revision of the discourse didn't determine China's entry into IMF and World Bank, but it permitted it, allowed action, and delegitimized opposition on Maoist grounds. Similarly, mutual security and its Five-Power power treaty exemplar legitimates common security arguments internally, and permits proponents to operate, argue, and defend their policies in ways that were illegitimate prior to China's entry into the ARF. That is, new discourses can legitimize or empower those who have genuinely internalized these norms to act politically, thus changing interagency balances of power and foreign policy outcomes.

Third the logics and normative values embodied in discourse can constrain even those who use them instrumentally. They do so by narrowing the range of behavioral options that can be proposed or followed. It becomes harder for pro-realpolitik actors to advocate unilateralist noncooperative security strategies if these fall outside of the range of behaviors acceptable in a cooperative security discourse.[143]

This doesn't guarantee the discourse will win out over realpolitik, and it doesn't mean there aren't other considerations that go into the ARF policy process—diffuse image, rivalry with the U.S., the mimicking of unfamiliar but "standard" diplomatic practices, etc. Nor does it mean there aren't realpolitik actions designed to advantage China's relative security in some way while disadvantaging others. But it does suggest there is now one more, legitimate, rival set of arguments—normatively based on elements of common security and committing

China, perhaps unintended, to support more intrusive multilateral security that it would have opposed, indeed did oppose, prior to its entry into the ARF.

Common knowledge (or intersubjective social facts) comes from common language (or intersubjective social discourses).[144] Cooperative or common security are not value-free imports into the Chinese lexicon, to be used entirely instrumentally for purposes wholly different than those for which the terms were originally designed. Even the Sinified form of cooperative security—mutual security, with its residual elements of Westphalian rules for regulating interaction among autonomous sovereigns states—constrains how some Chinese decision-makers can now talk, and thus think, about multilateralism.

OBJECTIONS AND IMPLICATIONS

There are at least four objections to these tentative findings about the socialization of some of those Chinese officials exposed to the ARF and its related processes. The first is that exogenous material side payments or threats may be responsible for China's more constructive, "comfortable" approach to the ARF. This objection is fairly easy to handle: the ARF has no capacity to put any such exogenous sanctions in place. Nor, as far as I am aware, have any other states unilaterally linked any such sanctions to China's participation. Indeed, the most likely sources of these side payments and sanctions—US foreign-policy makers—have themselves been ambivalent about the value of the ARF.

The second possibility is that changes in the nature of China's participation in the ARF reflect a deceptive effort to exploit cooperation from other states. One would expect this from a realpolitik actor with PD preferences. If this were all only deception, however, we would expect that as the ARF handles increasingly intrusive and sensitive issues that may impinge on core interests or relative power issues the PRC should dig in its heels in the face of any further change in the institution and agenda. In other words, the comfort level on the one hand, and the level of institutionalization and intrusiveness of the agenda on the other, should be negatively related. Yet, change in the ARF and change in comfort levels (at least of those participating in the ARF) are, to this point, positively related. That the ARF is already discussing the South China Sea in multilateral terms, intrusive CBMs, and moving, albeit slowly, toward preventive diplomacy mechanisms is evidence of this. Moreover, that there are Chinese (proto)multilateralists who are now holding up the Five Power CBM treaty as a potential model for East Asia suggests that PD preferences are no longer uniform across the agents in the Chinese policy process.

The third objection is that the Chinese multilateralism discourse in the ARF is deceptive because it is linked to an effort to constrain U.S. military power in the region. As I noted earlier, the problem with this argument is that there doesn't seem to be much of a relationship between the advocates of the multilateralism discourse and the more hardline opponents of U.S. military power in the region. That hardliners are *now* using this discourse to challenge the legitimacy of U.S. bilateral alliances is evident. But the genesis of this discourse does not lie with them.

The fourth objection is that China's changing comfort level is, in fact, a function of new information about the benign nature of the ARF. Beliefs about, and hence strategies toward, the ARF have changed; but preferences have not. There are a number of related components to this argument: the ARF has proven to be largely irrelevant to core security interests; most of the other participants have used the ARF to send assurance signals that it will not become an institution that constraints Chinese relative power; thus, the Chinese have discovered over time that it is relatively costless to participate in the ARF. There has been no real change in China's realpolitik, PD preferences. At most, therefore, more cooperative behavior inside the ARF might serve short-term reputational purposes.

This last objection is the most serious and credible one. But I think it, too, has its problems. First, it is unlikely that a short-term concern for reputational benefits applicable to other specific opportunities for exchange was the driving force behind China's *continued* (as opposed to initial) participation in the ARF: No other states, particularly those who could provide the most concrete costs or benefits to China—the U.S. and Japan, for example—were linking ARF participation to other areas of cooperation such as trade. Indeed, the U.S. administration and Congress have been somewhat ambivalent about the value of the ARF. If the argument is that some more diffuse notion of reputation mattered—that some material cost may be incurred, or some material benefit may be acquired somewhere in the indeterminate future from some other player(s)—then the reputational argument becomes virtually unfalsifiable.

Second, the "new information" explanation is problematic because it underestimates the uncertain status of "new information." Information is interpreted, and the same information can be interpreted differently in the context of similar institutional rules and structures. Empirically we know that the same information will be interpreted differently depending on whether it comes from "people like us" (the information is more authoritative and persuasive) or comes from a devalued "other."[145] Economic transactions, for instance bargaining over price where people exchange information relating to their preferences and their "bottom line," vary dramatically depending on whether or not the parties are friends—friends offer higher payments and lower prices than strangers.[146] Social context is an important variable in how well information reduces uncertainty in a transaction, and in which direction this uncertainty is reduced (e.g. clarifying the other as a friend or adversary).

Thus, if all of China's ARF decisionmakers were realpolitik opportunists (that is, if they believed they were playing a prisoners dilemma game in some form in East Asia) and if this basic worldview were fixed, then new information would be interpreted through these lenses. As I noted earlier, there is solid evidence from China's pronouncements and the interpretations of these by other states in the region that China initially looked upon multilateral institutions with a great deal of skepticism, and that its basic preferences were PD ones. It is probably true that the initial signals provided by a underinstitutionalized and nonintrusive ARF in 1994 could have been interpreted as nonthreatening by realpoliticians.[147] But as the ARF agenda and institution evolved, the signals should have been interpreted with increasing alarm by realpoliticians, since the trend lines were toward issues and procedures that could place some limits on relative military power. Yet, for a small group of China's ARF policymakers these signals were reinterpreted in less, not more, threatening ways. The fact that this group of policymakers eventually believed this information *was* reassuring while still expressing concern that others in the policy process (with more realpolitik views of multilateralism) might see this information as less reassuring, suggests that the information provided by the ARF has often not been unproblematically reassuring. Proto-multilateralists did not enter the ARF with this more sanguine interpretation of this "new information." Rather, this interpretation of the information came from socialization inside the ARF.

A focus on institutions as social environments raises interesting implications for institutional design. In general, contractual institutionalists argue that efficient institutional designs depend on the type of cooperation problem, e.g. a PD-type problem requires information (monitoring) and sanctions; an assurance problem primarily requires reassurance information (Martin 1993). The flip side is that one can identify inefficient institutional designs for a particular cooperation problems as well (e.g. an institution that is designed only to provide assurance information but has no monitoring or sanctioning capacity would be inefficient for resolving for PD-type problems). Additionally, Downs et al., argue that so-called transformational institutions (inclusive institutions that bring genuine cooperators and potential defectors together in an effort to instill norms and obligations in the latter) are less likely to provide efficient solutions than a strategic construction approach. This latter approach to institutional design stresses exclusive memberships of true believers where decisions are made on the basis of supermajority rules. The gradual inclusion of potential defectors under these conditions ensures that the preferences of the true believers predominate as the institution evolves. Their critique of the transformational approach rests explicitly on skepticism that the preferences of potential defectors can change through social interaction.[148]

It is not clear whether their skepticism derives from empirical evidence about the absence of state-level socialization, or simply on the methodological difficulties of assuming and then trying to observe preference change.[149] In any event, if one relaxes this assumption then one is compelled to revisit the contractual institutionalists' notions of efficient institutional design. An institution that appears inefficient to contractual institutionalists (e.g. an assurance institution for a PD problem), may actually be efficient for the cooperation problem at hand. If, say, a player (or subactors in a policy process) with PD preferences can internalize stag hunt preferences through interaction in a social environment with no material sanctioning or side payments, then "assurance" institutions may work in PD-like cooperation problems. An efficient institution might then be reconceived as the *design* and *process* most likely to produce the most efficient environments for socializing actors in alternative definitions of interest. In the ARF case it is hard to imagine that the conclusions which China's proto-multilateralists came to about the role of multilateralism in improving China's security would have come from outside the institution or from experience in realpolitik environments.

ENDNOTES

1. Some of the ideas and evidence developed in this paper were first explored in a preliminary fashion in Alastair Iain Johnston, "The Myth of the ASEAN Way? Explaining the Evolution of the ASEAN Regional Forum" in Helga Haftendorn, Robert Keohane and Celeste Wallander eds., *Imperfect Unions: Security Institutions in Time and Space* (London: Oxford University Press, 1999). Portions of the discussion about persuasion theory are reprinted from Johnston "Treating Institutions as Social Environments," in *International Studies Quarterly* 45(3) (December 2001) with permission of Blackwell Publishers.

2. Amitav Acharya, "Ideas, Identity and Institution-building: From the ASEAN Way to the Asia-Pacific Way" *Pacific Review* 10 (1997): 3; Acharya, *Constructing a Security Community in Southeast Asia* (Oxford: Routledge Press, 2001).

3. Countless studies of cooperation in institutions refer to nonmaterial "international pressure" to explain why some recalcitrant states eventually cooperate, but it is remarkable how under-theorized this notion of "pressure" is in IR.

4. ARF "The ASEAN Regional Forum: A Concept Paper" (1995).

5. Aaron Friedberg, "Ripe for Rivalry: Prospects for Peace in a Multipolar Asia." in *International Security* 18(3) (Winter 1993/4); Richard Betts, "Wealth, Power, and Instability: East Asia and the United States After the Cold War." *International Security* 18 (4) (Winter 1993/4).

6. Jeffrey T. Checkel, "The Constructivist Turn in Interational Relations Theory" *World Politics* 50 (January 1998): 324–348; Checkel, "Forum Section: A Constructivist Research Program in EU Studies?" *European Union Politics* 2(2) (2001): 219–249

7. I am not treating institutions as agents of socialization *per se* the way that Finnemore does, for example. While the line between institutions as agents and as environments will often blur, it is important to keep the distinction clear conceptually so as to ensure that one can at least treat institutions as products of social *structures* produced by the interaction of agents. Otherwise, one ends up studying the interaction of agents with agents, rather than agents with agents inside structures. To the extent that

the social environment inside an institution embodies particular sets of norms that are to be diffused to agents, especially new members, one could talk about institutions having agentic properties.

8. This is particularly relevant when trying to explain how new states, "novices," decide on the policy content and institutional structure of their foreign policies, not an unimportant topic when looking at the effects of decolonization or the collapse of the Soviet empire.

9. See on socialization and its various aspects: Bambi B. Schieffelin and Elinor Ochs eds., *Language Socialization Across Cultures* (Cambridge: Cambridge University Press, 1986); John C. Turner, *Rediscovering the Social Group* (Oxford: Basil Blackwell, 1987); Rodney W. Napier and Matti K. Gershenfeld, *Groups: Theory and Experience* (4th ed.) (Boston: Houghton Mifflin, 1987); Robert Cialdini, "Compliance Principles of Compliance Professionals: Psychologists of Necessity," in Mark P. Zanna et al, eds., *Social Influence: The Ontario Symposium on Personality and Social Psychology* (Lawrence, KS: Erlbaum Associates); Paul Allen Beck and M. Kent Jennings "Family Traditions, Political Periods, and the Development of Partisan Orientations" *Journal of Politics* 53(2) (August 1991): 742–763; Abram Chayes and Antonia H. Chayes, *The New Sovereignty: Compliance with International Regulatory Treaties* (Cambridge: Harvard University Press, 1996); Oran Young, "The Effectiveness of International Institutions: Hard Cases and Critical Variables" in James Rosenau and Ernst-Otto Czempiel, eds, *Governance without Government: Order and Change in World Politics* (Cambridge: Cambridge University Press, 1992), pp. 160–194.

10. William Perry, "U.S. Strategy: Engage China, Not Contain," *Defense Issues* 10, no. 109 at http://www.defenselink.mil/speeches/1995/s19951030-kaminski.html.

11. Samuel Berger, "A Foreign Policy Agenda for the Second Term," Center for Strategic and International Studies Washington, D.C. (March 27, 1997) at http://www.whitehouse.gov/WH/EOP/NSC/html/speeches/032797speech.html.

12. Stanley O. Roth, "U.S.-China Relations on the Eve of the Summit," World Economic Forum, Hong Kong, October 14, 1997 at http://www.state.gov/www/policy_remarks/971014_roth_china.html.

13. "The U.S. and China" *Diario Las Americas* Miami, Florida, July 5, 1998 at http://secretary.state.gov/www/statements/1998/980705.html. Emphasis mine.

14. As the hawkish critics of Clinton administration engagement claim. See for example Kagan (2000) and Kaplan (2001).

15. Kenneth Waltz, *Theory of International Politics* (Reading, MA: Addison-Wesley, 1979), pp. 127–128. Classical realism seems torn between its impulse to essentialize the drive for power in a self-help world on the one hand and its sensitivity to historical contingency on the other. Morgenthau, for example, laments the disappearance of a time in European interstate relations when individual kings and absolute rulers with virtual automaticity heeded norms of behavior for fear of the social punishments from violation—e.g. shame, shunning, loss of prestige and status (Hans W. Morgenthau, *Politics Among Nations: The Struggle for Power and Peace* (New York: Knopf, 1978), pp. 251–252). He even leaves open the possibility that definitions of power and interest are culturally contingent, implying at least that there is variation in how actors are socialized to conceptualize legitimate ways of pursuing legitimate interests (p. 9).

16. Dan Reiter, *Crucible of Beliefs: Learning, Alliances, and World Wars* (Ithaca: Cornell University Press, 1996); Randall L. Schweller, "Bandwagoning for Profit: Bringing the Revisionist State Back In," in *International Security* 19(1) (Summer 1994): 72–107; Paul W. Schroeder (1994) "Historial Reality vs. Neorealist Theory," in *International Security* 19(1): 108–148; Alistair Iain Johnston, "Realism(s) and Chinese Security Policy After the Cold War," in Ethan Kapstein and Michael Mastanduno, eds., *Unipolar Politics: Realism and State Strategies After the Cold War* (New York: Columbia University Press, 1998), pp. 261–318.

17. See, for instance, the data in Tanisha M. Fazal "The Origins and Implications of the Territorial Sovereignty Norm" (Paper prepared for the American Political Science Association Annual Meeting, San Francisco, September, 2001).

18. As Wendt puts it, Waltz's use of socialization is surprising, given there is no social content to neorealism's concept of structure—it is the product of material power factors, *not* the product of the nonmaterial traits and characteristics (identities and preferences) of the interacting units. Thus socialization becomes convergence of behavior around balancing and relative gains concerns, not the convergence of actor attributes—e.g. identities, preferences and interests. Alexander Wendt, *Social Theory of International Relations* (Cambridge: Cambridge University Press, 1999), ch. 3.

19. I am grateful to Celeste Wallander for pointing out to me some of the divisions over institutions and preferences in the contractualist camp.

20. Robert Frank, *Passions Within Reason: The Strategic Role of the Emotions* (New York: Norton, 1988).

21. Jeffry Frieden, "Actors and Preferences in International Relations" in David Lake and Robert Powell eds., *Strategic Choice in International Relations* (Princeton: Princeton University Press, 1999) pp. 39–76.

22. This seems to be a reasonable, cautionary argument for a sound methodological choice. It does reveal, however, an implicit disciplining move that constrains efforts to think about how preferences might change through new information acquired from social interaction inside an institution. There are a number of possible responses. First, theoretically deduced or assumed preferences are not so easily juxtaposed with "observed" preferences. Theories do not appear *deus ex machina*. They are almost invariably based on some initial inductive observation about a phenomenon. It is often not logically obvious what the preferences of actors ought to be from observing their position in society, their organizational constitution as actors—as both Kier and Legro point out about military culture. See Elizabeth Kier, *Imagining War: French and British Military doctrine Between the Wars*. (Princeton: Princeton University Press, 1997); Jeffrey Legro, *Cooperation Under Fire: Anglo-German Restraint During World War Two* (Ithaca: Cornell University Press, 1995). Theorizing about preferences, therefore, comes from a process of backing and forthing between initial empirical observations and theoretical hunches, and is itself subject to the same risks and measurement problems that the proponents of fixed preference analysis argue characterize attempts to observe preferences. Thus deducing preferences should not be a priori privileged as a "better" way of figuring out what actor preferences are. Second, the bias against observing preferences seems to exaggerate the difficulty of observing them. To be sure, validity and reliability of measures for "getting inside heads" of actors is problematic

since the only way to observe is to look at some phenomenon external to what's "inside heads," e.g. a speech act, a gesture, a decision. There is always the possibility that these external manifestations are in some sense strategic, not direct representations of preferences. But given the theoretical importance of the question—whether preferences change through social interaction, how stable the preferences are—it seems premature to give up trying to observe. The response should be, how do we reduce the measurement error to the lowest possible level and maximize the internal validity and reliability of indicators of preferences?

23. Robert O. Keohane "The Analysis of International Regimes: Towards a European-American Research Programme" in Volker Rittberger, ed., *Regime Theory and International Relations* (Oxford: Oxford University Press, 1993), p. 35. Abbott and Snidal try to meld rationalist and constructivist perspectives on the role and effect of formal international organizations, and touch on the possibility that IOs can help states "change their mutually constituted environment and, thus, themselves." Kenneth W. Abbott and Duncan Snidal "Why States Act Through Formal International Organizations," *Journal of Conflict Resolution* 42 (1998): 3–32, at p. 25. But the bulk of the article focuses on the uses of IOs by states or on the roles IOs play in mediation, enforcement, and the provision of information. Despite the promising claim at the start to look at IOs as agents which "influence the interests, intersubjective understandings, and environments of states" (p. 9), but in the end the issue is essentially dropped.

24. The "conspicuousness" or "prominence" of some equilibrium outcome in a coordination game that turns it into a focal point can be a function of socialization in a shared "culture." James D. Morrow, *Game Theory for Political Scientists* (Princeton: Princeton University Press, 1994).

25. Lisa L. Martin, "The Rational Choice State of Multilateralism" in John Gerard Ruggie, ed., *Multilateralism Matters: The Theory and Praxis of an Institutional Form* (New York: Columbia University Press, 1993), pp. 91–121, see esp. p. 101. In more sociological terms, bargaining can entail a process of empathetic discovery of shared notions of prominence and conspicuousness about particular outcomes.

26. For a similar critique see Checkel "The Constructivist Turn," p. 335, and Thomas Risse, "Let's Talk" (Paper presented to American Political Science Associate Annual Conference, Washington DC, August 1997), p. 2.

27. Earlier examples of constructivist-influenced work tended to skip over the micro-conditions under which some norms were more persuasive than others. See John W. Meyer et al. "The Structuring of a World Environmental Regime, 1870–1990," *International Organization* 51(4) (Autumn 1997): 623–651 and Peter Haas "Constructing Multilateral Environmental Governance: the Evolution of Multilateral Environmental Governance since 1972" (Paper presented at Center For International Affairs, Harvard University, April 16, 1998), p. 26.. Haas posits that "interpersonal persuasion, communication, exchange and reflection"—socialization—occurs in thick institutional environments where epistemic communities are active, but there is no discussion of microprocesses of persuasion nor conditions under which variation in the effectiveness of persuasion—hence the completeness of socialization—might be observed. Keck and Sikkink go a long way in looking at the microprocesses by which

transnational activist networks "persuade," but international institutions as social environments per se is not the focus of their research. (Margaret E. Keck and Kathryn Sikkink, *Activists Beyond Borders: Advocacy Networks in International Politics* [Ithaca: Cornell University Press, 1998]).Most recently, these lacunae are being filled by some very rich micro-focused research on socialization of new entrants into European institutions. See the work produced from the IDNET project, such as Jeffery Lewis, "Diplomacy in Europe's Polity: Socialization and the EU Permanent Representatives"; Alexandra Gheciu, "NATO, International Socialization and the Politics of State Crafting in Post-Cold War Central and Eastern Europe"; Jan Beyers and Caroline Steensels, "An exploration of some social mechanism affecting domestic political actors: Europeanisation: the Belgian case"; Jarle Trondal, "Why Europeanization Happens: The Transformative Power of EU Committees." (Papers Prepared for the IDNET second project workshop, "International Institutions and Socialization in the New Europe," European University Institute, Florence, May 18–19, 2001.)

28. Similar questions are raised by Checkel, "The Constructivist Turn," p. 332 and Andrew Moravcsik "Taking Preferences Seriously: A Liberal Theory of International Politics," *International Organization* 51(4) (Autumn 1997): 539. There is a tendency to exaggerate the homogeneity of normative structures at the system level. Reus-Smit, for example, argues that "hegemonic beliefs about the moral purposes of the state" help explain the way in which sovereign states justify their behavior—the hegemony of these beliefs being a result of "communicative action" in action. While constructivsts will willingly argue that the beliefs which are hegemonic may change over time, there seems to be less analysis of cross-unit differences at any given point in time. There seems to be a slighting of the reality of contestation and reinterpretation of allegedly hegemonic norms, hence a lack of interest in variation in the degree of socialization at the unit level. See Christian Reus-Smit, "The Constitutive Structure of International Society and the Nation of Fundamental Institutions," *International Organization* 51(4) (Autumn 1997): 555–589. This is also a problem with the exclusively systemic focus on Alex Wendt's *Social Theory of International Relations.* For a recent effort to look at how precisely states resist normative "teaching" see Carlson's work on China's sovereignty discourse in the face of challenges from sovereignty perforating discourses in human rights, arms control verification, and humanitarian intervention Allen Carlson, "The Lock on China's Door: P.R.C. Foreign Policy and the Norm of State Sovereignty in the Reform Period" (Yale University, Department of Political Science, draft PhD dissertation, 1999).

29. Cites to Keck and Sikkink, *Activists Beyond Borders*; Thomas Risse and Kathryn Sikkink, "The Socialization of International Human Rights Norms Into Domestic Practices: Introduction." In Risse and Sikkink, eds., *The Power of Human Rights: International Norms and Domestic Change,* (Cambridge: Cambridge University Press, 1999) pp. 1–38, and to Richard Price, "Reversing the Gunsights: Transnational Civil Society Targets Landmines," *International Organization* 52(3) (Summer 1998): 613–644. (1998). See Johnston, "Treating Institutions as Social Environments" for an explication of the difference between persuasion and social influence.

30. In addition to social influence, another common microprocess is mimicking whereby actors copy pro-normative behavior as an efficient means ("best practice") of

adapting to an uncertain environment prior to any detailed ends-means calculation of the benefits of doing so. Mimicking is only loosely related to socialization since it is not an effect that is generated by the nature of the social environment. Rather it is a survival strategy for a particular social environment. It could come prior to or be seen as an outcome of persuasion and social influence. However, choosing which groups to mimic involves a degree of prior identification. Moreover, mimicking prosocial behavior can lead to internalization through repetition, or by establishing behavioral precedents that actors sensitive to status and image may be loathe to undermine. See Robert Frank, *Choosing the Right Pond: Human Behavior and the Quest for Status* (New York: Oxford University Press, 1985), p. 18; Bruce J. Biddle, "Social Influence, Self-Reference Identity Labels and Behavior," in *The Sociological Quarterly* 26 (2) (1985): 162; Elinor Ochs, "Introduction" in Bambi B. Schieffelin and Elinor Ochs eds. *Language Socialization Across Cultures* (Cambridge: Cambridge University Press 1986), pp. 2–3; R. B. Cialdini et al., "A Focus Theory of Normative Conduct" in *Advances in Experimental Social Psychology* 24 (1991): 203–204.

31. Andreas Hasenclever, et al., "Interests, Power, Knowledge: The Study of International Regimes," *Mershon International Studies Review* 40 Supplement 2 (October 1996): 213, emphasis mine; see also David Knocke, *Political Networks: The Structural Perspective* (Cambridge: Cambridge University Press, 1994), p. 3. For an excellent exegesis of Habermas' theory of communicative action see Thomas Risse, "Let's Argue: Communicative Action in World Politics. *International Organization*, 54 (2000): 1–39.

32. Michael C. Williams, "The Institutions of Security," *Conflict and Cooperation* 32(3) (1997): 287–307.

33. Sheldon Styker and Anne Statham, "Symbolic Interaction and Role Theory" in Gardner Lindzey and Elliot Aronson, eds., *Handbook of Social Psychology* Vol. 1 "Theory and Method" (New York, Random House, 1985) pp. 311–378 at p. 325. See also Ochs, "Introduction" to *Language Socialization*, p. 2.

34. Peter L. Berger and Thomas Luckmann, *The Social Construction of Reality: A Treaties in the Sociology of Knowledge* (New York: Anchor Books, 1966), p. 44.

35. Orit Ichilov, "Introduction" in Orit Ichilov ed., *Political Socialization, Citizenship Education and Democracy* (New York: Teachers College Press, 1990), pp. 1–8, at p. 1.

36. Cited in P. E. Freedman and A. Freedman "Political Learning" in S. Long, ed., *The Handbook of Political Behavior* (New York: Plenum Press, 1981), 1:255–303, at p. 258. See also Beck and Jennings, "Family Traditions," p. 743.

37. Risse, "Let's Talk," p. 16.

38. G. John Ikenberry and Charles Kupchan, "Socialization and Hegemonic Power," in *International Organization* 44(3) (Summer 1990): 283–315, at pp. 289–290.

39. This raises a general research design question, namely, if socialization is to have a profound impact on state or substate actors, it should be most obvious in novices. Who are novices in IR? The obvious candidates are newly liberated or created states, or recently isolated states. This suggest where to look for "most likely cases" for the purposes of theory testing: e.g. China from 1980s on; newly decolonized states from 1950s on; newly independent states that emerged in wake of Soviet Union's collapse. These are states that quite literally have to set up foreign policy institutions, determine

what their foreign policy interests are on a range of novel issue areas, decide in which of a myriad social environments in IR they should participate (e.g. which institutions, which communities of states (middle power, major power, developed, developing) and which competitive and cooperative relations to foster etc. I will come back to this question of research design in a moment.

40. One should assume, however, that there should be degrees of internalization, given that not all actors are always exposed to exactly the same configuration of social pressures nor do they enter into a social interaction with exactly the same prior identifications. Thus, while pro-social behavior because of its "appropriateness" may be the ideal, at the opposite end of the spectrum should be pro-social behavior because of its material consequences (positive and negative). In between is pro-social behavior produced by positive and negative social sanctions (e.g. status rewards, self-esteem based identity-consistent behavior etc.). This latter process could be called second-order socialization process since status rewards can only be bestowed by a group with which an actor identifies as a relevant reference group or audience.

41. Brendon Gail Rule and Gay L. Bisanz, "Goals and Strategies of Persuasion: A Cognitive Schema for Understanding Social Events," in Mark P. Zanna, James M. Olson and C. Peter Herman, eds., *Social Influence: The Ontario Symposium* vol. 5 (Hillsdale NJ: Lawrence Erlbaum Associates, 1987) pp. 185–206, at 192.

42. Berger, "Inscrutable Goals," p. 1.

43. See Philip G. Zimbardo and Michael R Leippe, *The Psychology of Attitude Change and Social Influence* (New York: McGraw Hill, 1991), pp. 127–167. Despite the volume of this literature, "To date there is precious little evidence specifying who can be talked out of what beliefs, and under what conditions" (Berger "Inscrutable Goals," p. 8).

44. Daniel Bar-Tal and Leonard Saxe (1990) "Acquisition of Political Knowledge: A Social-Psychological Analysis," in Orit Ichilov, *Political Socialization, Citizenship Education and Democracy* (New York: Teachers College Press, 1990), p. 122.

45. Chenhuan Wu and David R. Shaffer, "Susceptibility to Persuasive Appeals as a Function of Source Credibility and Prior Experience with Attitudinal Object," in *Journal of Personality and Social Psychology* 52 (4) (1987): 687; Richard E. Petty et al., "Attitudes and Attitude Change," in *Annual Review of Psychology* 48 (1997): 609–647, at 616; Zimbardo and Leippe, *Psychology of Attitude Change*, pp. 192–197.

46. Rupert Brown *Group Processes: Dynamics Within and Between Groups* (Oxford: Blackwell Publishers, 2000), p. 203.

47. Zimbardo and Leippe, *Psychology of Attitude Change*, p. 70.

48. Petty et al., "Attitudes and Attitude Change," pp. 612–629; James H. Kuklinski and Norman L. Hurley, "Its a Matter of Interpretation" in Diana C. Mutz, Paul M. Sniderman, and Richard Brody eds., *Political Persuasion and Attitude Change* (Ann Arbor: University of Michigan Press, 1966) pp. 125–144, at 129–131; Napien and Gershenfeld, *Groups, Thoery and Experience*, p. 159; Alice M. Isen, "Affect, Cognition and Social Behavior," *Advances in Experimental Social Pyschology* 20 (1987): 203–253, esp. 206–211; Danny Axsom et al., "Audience Response Cues as a Heuristic Cue in Persuasion," *Journal of Personality and Social Psychology* 53(1) (1987): 30–40, esp. 30–31. Using different language, Habermasian constructivists make a similar point: "trust in

the authenticity of a speaker is a precondition for the persuasiveness of a moral argument" (Risse, "Let's Talk," p. 16; see also Williams, "Institutions of Security, pp. 291–292).

49. Robert Cialdini, *Influence: The New Psychology of Modern Persuasion* (New York: Quill Books, 1984); Wu and Shaffer, "Susceptibility to Persuasive Appeals," p. 677.

50. Lupia and McCubbins argue that all of these conditions and characteristics are simply indicators of more basic conditions for persuasion, namely, that the persuadee believes the persuader to be knowledgeable about an issue and that his or her intentions are trustworthy (Arthur Lupia and Matthew D. McCubbins *The Democratic Dilemma: Can Citizens Learn What They Need To Know?* [Cambridge: Cambridge University Press, 1998]). The more certain the persuadee is about these beliefs, the more likely the persuader will be persuasive. Both these characteristics can be a function either of familiarity and extensive interaction that, over time, reveals them, *or* of "external forces" that make it difficult or costly for the persuader to hide knowledge (or lack thereof) and trustworthiness (e.g. mechanisms for revealing knowledge, penalities for lying, costly actions that reveal the position of the persuader). Any other factors, such as ideology, identity, culture etc., are only predictors of persuasion to the extent that they reveal information to the persuadee about the persuader's knowledge and trustworthiness. Yet this misses the more interesting question about the empirical frequency with which social variables such as perceived ideology, identity, and/or cultural values are in fact the primary cues that people use to determine the degree of knowledge and trustworthiness of a persuader. That is, on average is perceived shared identity between persuadee and persuader more likely to be used by the persuadee as an authoritative measure of a persuader's knowledge and trustworthiness than other kinds of cues? The answer has important implications for how social interactions lead to socialization and how different institutional designs might lead to different socialization paths. Lupia and McCubbins tend to focus, as befits their interest in signaling games, on the role of external forces in clarifying beliefs about knowledge and trustworthiness of persuaders. Since, they argue, social and political environments are rarely ones where persuader and persuadee interact face to face over long periods of time, the familiarity/personal interaction route to beliefs about the persuader's knowledge and trustworthiness tends to be less common. This may be true at the national level of persuasion (e.g. political messages from politicians aimed at masses of voters), but it is not necessarily true at the level of social interaction in international institutions among diplomats, specialists, and analysts. Here the first route—familiarity, iterated face-to-face social interaction—may be more common, hence affect based on identity, culture, and ideology may be more critical for persuasion than external forces and costly signals. Institutions, therefore, that are "lite" in terms of these external forces, nonetheless may create conditions conducive to persuasion—and convergence around group norms—even though there are few material costs for the persuader to deceive and few material costs for the persuadee to defect from the group.

51. Jorgensen et al. found in a study of televised political debates in Denmark, for example, that the most persuasive debaters were those who used a small number of extended, weighty discussions of specific qualitative examples. The use of these specific, straightforward, and logical examples seemed to accentuate the authoritativeness of

the debater and were easier for viewers to assess and adjudicate. See Charlotte Jorgensen et al., "Rhetoric that Shifts Votes: An Exploratory Study of Persuasion in Issue-Oriented Public Debates." *Political Communication* 15 (1998): 283–299.

52. For a similar list see Checkel "Forum Section."

53. Dana P. Eyre and Mark C. Suchman, "Status, Norms, and the Proliferation of Conventional Weapons," in Peter J. Katzenstein, ed. *The Culture of National Security* (New York: Columbia University Press, 1996), pp. 79–113; Meyer et al., "Structuring of a World Environmental Regime; Waltz, *Thoery of International Politics.*

54. Lars-Eric Cederman, *Emergent Actors in World Politics* (Princeton: Princeton University Press, 1997); see also Robert Axelrod, "Promoting Norms: An Evolutionary Approach to Norms" in Axelrod, *The Complexity of Cooperation* (Princeton: Princeton University Press, 1997), pp. 44–68.

55. This is, after all, the point of much of the work on how transnational networks affect state behavior (Keck and Sikkink, *Activists Beyond Borders*; Mattjew Evangelista, *Unarmed Forces: The Transnational Movement to End the Cold War* [Ithaca: Cornell University Press,1999]; Emanuel Adler, "The Emergence of Cooperation: National Epistemic Communities and the International Evolution of the Idea of Nuclear Arms Control," in *International Organization* 46[1] [Winter 1992]); "teaching" and the diffusion of norms and the creation of national interests (Martha Finnemore, *National Interests in International Society* [Ithaca: Cornell University Press, 1996]).

56. David A. Lake, and Robert Powell, "International Relations: A Strategic-Choice Approach" in Lake and Powell eds., *Strategic Choice and International Relations* (Princeton: Princeton University Press, 1999) pp. 3–38, at 33.

57. For the most part when I use "China" in this paper it is short-hand for the policy behavior taken officially in the name of the state. I am not, *repeat not,* claiming that the state called China is persuaded or socialized, or that all individuals in the policy process are persuaded by or socialized in the norms of the ARF.

58. Richard Price and Nina Tannewald, "Norms and Deterrrence: The Nuclear and Chemical Weapons Taboos" in Peter J. Katzenstein, ed., *The Culture of National Security: Norms and Identity in World Politics* (New York: Columbia University Press, 1996), pp. 114–152; Kier, *Imagining War*; Legro, *Cooperation Under Fire*; Finnemore, *National Interests in International Society.*

59. Parsimony as the tie-breaker is an illegitimate method for adjudicating between two competing explanations for the same phenomenon prior to a critical test.

60. For a discussion of organizations and their "goals" see Gayl D. Ness and Steven R. Brechin, "Bridging the Gap: International Organizations as Organizations," in *International Organization* 42(2) (Spring 1988): 245–273, esp. 247, 263–266.

61. Risse makes a similar point, suggesting that communicative action should be more frequent inside institutions than outside of them. Risse, "Let's Talk, p. 17. For one analysis of the ideology of a security institution that identifies causal and principled believes in the institution that are at odds with power maximization realpolitik see Muller 1993.

62. Interview with senior Chinese intelligence analyst involved in ARF policy process, Beijing July 1996.

63. Alternatively, cooperation should be result of concerns about diffuse reputation, or status as a responsible major player in a security environment increasingly characterized by multilateral security institutions.

64. Ronald Rogowski, "Institutions as Constraints on Strategic Choice," in David A. Lake and Robert Powell eds., *Strategic Choice and International Relations* (Princeton: Princeton University Press, 1999) pp. 115–136.

65. Here Risse and I are, I think, moving along parallel tracks. He notes, for instance, that nonhierarchical and network-like international institutions, "characterized by a height density of mostly informal interactions should allow for discursive and argumentative processes," Risse, "Let's Talk," p. 17. For a similar list of empirical expectations see Checkel, "Forum Section." Moravscik implies that because one can imagine "rationalist" arguments that make similar predictions these kinds of "mid-range" theory hypotheses developed by constructivism are somehow subsumed by rationalist approaches, or are at the very least theoretically undistinguishable from so-called rationalist predictions about persuasion. Andrew Moravcsik, "Forum Section: A Constructivist Research Program in EU Studies?" *European Union Politics* 2(2) (2001): 219–249. This is debatable on a number of grounds. First, even Lupia and McCubbins, the authors of the only systematic contractualist argument about persuasion, acknowledge that there may be different, more affective bases for persuasion in face-to-face interactions that are not captured by contractualist or "rationalist" microprocesses. Second, since the microprocesses in social psychological-derived hypotheses are different, the practical implications for the kinds of institutional designs most conducive to persuasion are meaningfully different. Finally, Moravscik misses the point of critical tests—namely they are set up precisely because two different sets of theoretical arguments make, in a specific instance, similar predications about behavior. The fact that two theories make similar predictions prior to a critical test means nothing about which theory is distinctively superior.

66. There are only two formal multilateral security institutions in East-Asia at the moment—the ASEAN Regional Forum (1994) and the 5-power CBM agreement (1996) The Korean Energy Development Organization might count as a third, since it is designed to eliminate the North Korean nuclear weapons program.

67. Acharya, "Ideas, Identity and Institution-building"; *Constructing a Security Community in Southeast Asia.* Some analysts differentiate between the two, but the differences are relatively minor and have to do with the issues that are considered security threatening (cooperative security uses a looser definition of security issues to embrace so-called nontraditional security—environment, social unrest etc). See Dewitt 1994).

68. Most of these principles are embodied in the ARF Concept Paper for 1995. See also the comments by the Malaysian defense minister Hajib Tun Rajak cited in David Dewitt, "Common, Comprehensive and Cooperative Security in Asia-Pacific" *CANCAPS Papiers* No. 3 (March 1994): 12–13, and Lee Kwan-yew's comments about the ARF as a channel for China's reassuring Southeast Asia about its status quo intentions, cited in Leah Makabenta, "ASEAN: China Looms Large at Security Meet," Interpress Service, July 22, 1994.

69. Si pacem, parabellum" in the Latin. "Ju an si wei, you bei wu huan" in the Chinese. These are the security principles of the OSCE as well. The primary difference between OSCE and ARF definitions of common and cooperative security is that the former includes human rights and liberal domestic governance as a component of interstate security. The ARF, sensitive to the post-colonial sovereign-centric ideologies in ASEAN and China, has excluded this element.

70. In this respect the ARF reflects what Downs et al. call a transformational regime, precisely the type of design that, they argue, is least conducive to effective multilateral constraints on behavior because it seeks out a lowest common deno minator and dilutes the influence of "activists." Their argument holds IF one assumes that preferences are fixed, that socialization does not occur, and that the ideology of the institution is also diluted as the membership includes more "sceptics." It is not clear why this should be so, however, if the ideology is relatively stable and legitimate. See George W. Downs et al., "Designing Multilaterals: The Architecture and Evolution of Environmental Agreements." (Paper presented to American Political Science Associate Annual Conference, Washington DC, August 1997); "Managing the Evolution of Multlateralism," in *International Organization* 52 (1998): 397–419.

71. On the TAC, see Michael Leifer "The ASEAN Regional Forum: Extending ASEAN's Model of Regional Security" *Adelphi Papers* No. 30 (1996): 12–15. As I noted, these stand in contrast to the OSCE definition of common security. It is unclear how long the ASEAN Way discourse about security can resist a turn to the domestic sources of regional insecurity, however. The notion of nontraditional security issues—drugs, crime, refugees, transboundary pollution, etc.—has begun to enter the vocabulary of security specialists there. It is not a huge leap from discussions about how to prevent these kinds of problems to a focus on, e.g., domestic governance, social welfare, negotiated limits, and constraints on pollution emission.

72. These were norms that the Chinese regime, faced in particular with perceived American threats to unity (support for Taiwan) and domestic political order (human rights), wholly endorsed. As one Canadian diplomat noted, the ASEAN Way is a catch phrase for a pace that the PRC is comfortable with. The promise of a slow pace in the ARF is the only reason China came to the table interview with Canadian embassy officials, Beijing China, April 1996).

73. ARF, "Chairman's Statement of the Secondd ASEAN Regional Forum" (Brunei, August 1). This statement, in turn, reflected the ARF Concept Paper, a blueprint for the ARF's institutional and agenda evolution. "The rules of procedure of ARF papers shall be based on prevailing ASEAN norms and practices: Decisions should be made by consensus after careful and extensive consulations. No voting will take place" (ARF Concept Paper, 1995, p. 6).

74. The application of consensus rules in international organization varies quite a great deal from norms where, in practice, consensus is a unanimity rule in which there is informal vote-taking and where one state can veto, to norms where the chair has such legitimacy and latitude that individual opponents to a declaration of consensus are reluctant to challenge. The ARF tends to operate more closely to the latter than the former.

75. Jurg Steiner, *Amicable Agreement versus Majority Rule: Conflict Resolution in Switzerland* (University of North Carolina Press, 1974).

76. Diana Chigas, et al. "Preventive Diplomacy and the Organization for Security Cooperation in Europe: Creating Incentives for Dialogue and Cooperation" in Abram Chayes and Antonia Handler Chayes, eds., *Preventing Conflict in the Post-Communist World: Mobilizing International and Regional Organization* (Washington DC: The Brookings Institution, 1996).

77. Steiner, *Amicable Agreement*, pp. 269–271.

78. For example, a Paris workshop in November 1996 on preventive diplomacy the Chair's statement recommended that the ARF consider taking a more proactive role in preventive diplomacy through the provision of ARF Chair's "good offices."

79. For example, Australia convened a workshop on CBMs in November 1994; Canada and Malaysia co-hosted a workshop on PKO activities in March 1995; and South Korea hosted a workshop on preventive diplomacy in May 1995. The results of the workshops were acknowledged and commended in the Chair's statement at the 1995 ARF, p. 5. See also Gary Smith, "Multilateralism and Regional Security in Asia: The ASEAN Regional Forum and APEC's Geopolitical Value," *Working Paper* no. 97–2 (Center for International Affairs, Harvard University, February, 1996).

80. The relationship between CSCAP and the ARF has been rather ambiguous. Neither the 1995 nor 1996 ARF Chair's statement specifically names CSCAP as the primary forum for ARF Track II activities, although the 1995 Concept Paper does identify it, along with ASEAN ISIS, as two potential brain trusts for the ARF. Its absence from the Chair's statements reflected, most likely, Chinese objections at that time to handing Track II responsibilities to an organization in which China was not a member. China's membership had been held up as the rest of CSCAP debated how to handle Taiwan's application for membership. The PRC refused to set up a national committee until it was satisfied Taiwan could not participate formally. This decision was made in late 1996; the PRC subsequently put together its national committee and formally applied to join CSCAP. CSCAP now appears to be emerging as a potential ideas factory for the ARF, somewhat analogous to the nongovernmental Pacific Economic Cooperation Council's relationship to APEC (Interview with prominent Canadian academic involved in Track II activities, January 1997 and e-mail correspondence with an Australian government official involved in ARF policy making, February 1997).

81. For example, in the late 1990s about 50 percent of the board of directors of the U.S. national committee of CSCAP had worked in government. The U.S. CSCAP also has a category called observers who are current government officials (U.S. CSCAP 1997). The Chinese CSCAP national committee initially consisted almost entirely of government officials. It included an Assistant Foreign Minister, the senior specialist on American, European, and arms control affairs in the PLA General Staff Department, as well as the Foreign Ministry's senior functional level officer handling ARF affairs (PRC CSCAP, "Preliminary List of Members of CSCAP China Committee. 1997). Very recently the Chinese CSCAP was expanded to include academics working on regional security issues.

82. "Filter" is Paul Evans' term. I am indebted to him for his insights into Track II. For an insightful discussion of the social-psychological "theory" behind Track II effec-

tiveness, with application to the Middle East see Dalia Dassa Kaye "Norm-Creation in the Middle East: Arguing in Track Two Security Dialogues" (unpublished manuscript, 2001). For a discussion of the role of Track II in ASEAN politics see Acharya, *Constructing a Security Community in Southeast Asia*, pp. 66–67. For controversy over who makes the proposal see Marie-France Desjardin, "Rethinking Confidence Building Measures: Obstacles to Agreement and the Risk of Overselling the Process" *Adelpi Paper* No. 307.

83. E.g. Qian Qichen, Chen Jian, Fu Ying, Tong Xiaoling.

84. The franchise characteristics of the ARF are hard to code. On the one hand there is no formal recognition of particularly authoritative voices, e.g. there are no scientists working groups, advisory panels etc., that often define the scientific boundaries of policy discourse in, say, environmental institutions. On the other hand, ASEAN states are clearly authorized to take leadership roles in all ARF activities. All ARF intersessionals, for example, must be co-hosted by an ASEAN state. The ASEAN way, therefore, is enshrined as the guiding ideology of the institution. One complicating factor, however, is that often ASEAN states can be quite passive in the promotion of the common security elements of the ASEAN Way, particularly when these conflict with its sovereign-centric elements. Thus on transparency issues or intrusive confidence-building measures, China is not always the only state pushing for a lowest common denominator solution. On certain multilateral issues non-ASEAN activist states take the lead in defining the discourse. Given its experience, in interssessionals on peacekeeping operations, e.g., Canada can speak with a more authoritative voice.

85. I do not want to leave the impression that everyone in ASEAN intended to try to alter Chinese interests. Some were more skeptical about this possibility than others. Even these people, however, do not necessarily have an interest in openly defining the security problem as a suasion game. The concern is that by focusing on a China threat ARF will lose its focal point status and ASEAN will lose its leadership status in regional security affairs.

86. I would call this shift in utility distribution a change in "preference." I realize some contractual institutionalists would debate this, and consider this a change in "strategy." The difference between the two concepts is artificial and depends on the level of ends and means one is examining. For game theorists, the outcome of strategic interaction between two players is the product of a particular strategy pair. States are said to have preferences over outcomes. Yet if an institution is itself a product of a particular strategy pair (or the confluence of more than two strategies in a multilateral institution), then the form and function of the institution itself is a preference. Of course, multilateralism can also be a strategy at a higher level of interaction where the "goal" is some more abstract good, such as security. But since security is a grand preference of most states, to limit preferences to things as abstract as security, welfare, peace etc., means that no outcome below this level can be called a preference. Everything becomes strategy. I think this is reduces the utility of the term preference, and ignores the fact that actors can come to internalize multilateralism, unilateralism and bilateralism as legitimate, taken-for-granted ends in themselves.

87. Banning Garrett and Bonnie Glaser, "Multilateral Security in the Asia-Pacific Region and its Impact on Chinese Interests: Views from Beijing," in *Contemporary*

Southeast Asia 16(1) (June (1994).; Jing-dong Yuan,"Conditional Multilateralism: Chinese Views on Order and Regional Security" *CANCAPS Papiers* No. 9 (March 1996); Xu Weidi, "Ya-Tai diqu anquan huanjing fenxi" [Analysis of the security environment in the Asia-Pacific region] *Neibu canyue* [Internal reference readings] (Beijing: Central Committee Documents Publishing House, 1996), pp. 251–254. See also, interview with senior Chinese intelligence analyst involved in ARF policy process, Beijing July 1996.

88. On Chinese realpolitik see Thomas J. Christensen, "Chinese Realpolitik" *Foreign Affairs* (September/October 1996); Johnston, "Realism(s) and Chinese Security Policy."

89. On military power for defensive purposes see Yuan,"Conditional Multilateralism."

90. Shi Chunlai, Xu Jian, "Preventive Diplomacy Pertinent to the Asia-Pacific," in *International Review* (China Center for International Studies) No. 4 (July 1997).

91. Chu Shulong "Concepts, Structures and Strategies of Security Cooperation in Asia-Pacific" (unpublished manuscript, January 1997).

92. Liu Xuecheng, "Confidence Building Diplomacy in the Asia-Pacific Region" *International Review* (China Center of International Studies, 1997).

93. For a systematic comparison of the five-power CBM agreement and the CSCE Vienna Document of 1994 see Acharya, "Ideas, Idenity and Instituion-building, pp. 16–23.

94. This was the distinct impression I received when interviewing military and civilian specialists on the ARF in 1996.

95. Interview with Chinese arms control specialist (January 1999).

96. Liu, "Confidence Building Diplomacy," p. 18.

97. Jian Chen, "Challenges and Responses in East Asia" (Speech to the First CSCAP General Meeting, Singapore, June 4, 1996).

98. "Chinese Paper at the ARF-ISG-CBMs in Brunei" (ms. November 3–5, 1997), p. 3.

99. Shi Chunlai, Xu Jian, "Preventive Diplomacy Pertinent to the Asia-Pacific" *International Review* (China Center for International Studies) no. 4 (July 1997).

100. China Radio International (1997) "The Taking Shape of a New Securitiy Concept and its Practice in China" (December 29, 1997), BBC-SWB (January 7, 1998). See also interview with senior Chinese think tank analysts close to the Asia-Pacific policy process in the Ministry of Foreign Affairs, Beijing, October 1998; interview with Chinese academic specialist on Asia-Pacific multilateralism, October 1998); interview with senior Chinese think tank analyst specializing in Asia-Pacific regional affairs, Beijing, October 1998; conversation with MOFA official, October 1998.

101. Interiew with senior MoFA official engaged in ARF work, January 1999. These individuals included Yan Xuetong, Wang Yizhou, Zhang Yunling, among other well-respected IR specialists. Yan is considered somewhat more realpolitik in his views of multilateralism than Wang or Zhang. Zhang, an economist, views regional security through the lens of economic integration. Wang is one of China's foremost IR theorists, with a research interest in the process of China's integration into global institutions. His work is influenced by his exposure to liberal institutionalism and social con-

structivism. The effort to develop more sophisticated thinking about multilateralism was given a boost in 2001 with China's first conference on the topic, hosted by the Institute of World Economics and Politics at the Chinese Academy of Social Sciences. Admitting that the topic was still very sensitive in China, one of the organizers, Wang Yizhou, wrote that multilateralist theory requires China to rethink its opposition to participation in everything from the G-8 to formal relations to NATO, to participation in ASEAN-US multilateral military exercises. See Wang Yizhou "Xin shijie de zhongguo yu duobian waijiao" [The new century China and multilateral diplomacy] (Paper presented to a research conference on "Theory of Multilateralism and Multilateral Diplomacy" in 2001).

102. Technically the study was commissioned by the MOFA Policy Research Office, but the primary consumer was the Asia Department.

103. Zhang Yunling, "Zonghe Anquan guan ji dui wo guo anquan de sikao" [The concept of comprehensive security and reflections on China's security] *Dangai Ya Tai* [Contemporary Asia-Pacific studies] No 1. (2000) pp. 1–16.

104. Interview with Chinese academic specialist on Asia-Pacific multilateralism, January 1999). The report was published about a year later in *Dangdai Ya Tai* [Contemporary Asia-Pacific Studies]. See Zhang, ibid. Interestingly, even in the post-Kosovo atmosphere in China where more "liberal" voices had to tread with somewhat more cautious when discussing international relations, there were essentially no significant changes in the wording or argumentation in the published version of the study.

105. The argument is outlined in Banning Garrett and Bonnie Glaser, "Does China Want the US Out of Asia" *PacNet Newsletter* #22 (May 30, 1997). My own conversations with Pentagon officials involved in Asia policy confirm this particular interpretation. What lent this argument credence was that the mutual security discourse emerged around the same time that the Chinese hosted a rather uncharacteristically contentious (for the ARF) intersessional support group meeting on CBMs in March 1997. The Chinese chair (actually co-chairing with the Philippines, though the Philippines played a passive role in the meeting) refused to drop a Chinese agenda item that called for study of CBMs (military observers, prior notification, etc.) at joint military exercises in the region. Since the U.S. and its allies conduct joint exercises while the Chinese do not, the proposal was rightly criticized as being aimed at the U.S. military interests. The agenda item, however, was drafted by the PLA. The chief MOFA ARF policy functionary had privately indicated a willingness to drop the issue in discussions with the Canadians a couple of months before the meeting. But it is plausible that with the meeting in Beijing, and with a large PLA contingent observing the discussions, the MOFA did not feel free to drop the issue. In any event, the Chinese insistence on maintaining the agenda item in the face of opposition from a range of states prevented consensus on this issue and led to a great deal of concern in the U.S. about a Chinese offensive against US military alliances in the region. Conversations with Canadian diplomats (May 1997), and a PLA officer involved in ARF policy process (December 1997).

106. This argument was made by some of the civilian analysts and military officials involved in ARF policymaking I interviewed in 1998 and 1999. Indeed, the MOFA-commissioned report on comprehensive security is explicit in stating that China

should not and need not replace U.S. military superiority in the region, that China needs to balance militarily against U.S. power, in part especially if effective, practical multilateral security institutions can be set up in the region. See Zhang, "Concept of comprehensive security."

107. These proposals came from the Comprehensive Department of the Foreign Affairs Bureau of the General Staff Department, the Department that coordinates PLA positions on the ARF.

108. The following comes from an interview with Canadian embassy officials, Beijing China, April 1996, interview with Singaporean embassy official, Beijing, China, April 1996; interview with senior Chinese intelligence analyst involved in ARF policy process, Beijing July 1996; interview with prominent Canadian academic involved in Track II activities, January 1997; interview with Canadian embassy official, Beijing, October 1998; and Smith, "Multilateralism and Regional Security in Asia."

109. Interview with senior MoFA official involved in ARF diplomacy, January 1999; Interview with Canadian diplomats involved in ARF work, July 2001.

110. Interview with Canadian embassy officials, Beijing China, April 1996; interview with senior Chinese intelligence analyst involved in ARF policy process, Beijing July 1996.

111. Smith, "Multilateralism and Regional Security in Asia," p. 22.

112. Interview with Canadian diplomat involved in ARF policy, May 1997.

113. The interviewee, in response to a question about the ACD Department's interest in Asia-Pacific multilateral security institutions, remarked that the Department "had a big appetite" (January 1999).

114. Leifer "ASEAN Regional Forum," p. 32

115. Much of the above paragraph came from interview with former senior US administration figure involved in Asia Policy, Beijing, June 1996; and Smith 1997; and e-mail with Australian government official involved in ARF policy, January 1997.

116. ARF Regional Forum Concept and Principles of Preventive Diplomacy (ASEAN Draft, November 6, 1999), p. 8.

117. ARF Chairman's Statement of the Second ASEAN Regional Forum (Brunei, August 1, 1995), p. 7; ibid., Concept Paper, p. 3.

118. China is not alone. South Korea apparently is leery of giving the ARF a preventive diplomacy role if this means ASEAN might try to involve itself in Northeast Asian issues. Interview with prominent Canadian academic involved in Track II activities, January 1997.

119. ARF Concept Paper of Co-Chairs: ARF Intersessional Support Group on Confidence Building Measures (Jakarta, July 22, 1996), p. 2

120. ARF 1999 Regional Forum Concept, p. 5.

121. ARF draft paper, "Enhanced Role of ARF Chair"; "Co-chair's Draft Paper on the Terms of Reference for the ARF Experts/Eminent Persons (EEPs)" (October 2000).

122. "China's Position Paper on Preventive Diplomacy in the Asia-Pacific Region (unpublished document submitted to the ARF, February 1, 2000), p. 2.

123. This analysis is based on comparisons of the November 1999 version of the Singapore PD paper, the Chinese comments on this draft submitted to the ARF in 2000,

the revised April 2000 version of the Singapore PD paper, and subsequent Chinese responses to this revised draft, submitted on January 9, 2001.

124. The language on sovereignty and noninterference was already quite strong in the original draft paper. That is to say, China is not an outlier in promoting this kind of language in ARF discourse. The outliers on PD at the moment are the Canadians, who have pressed language that does not subject PD to consensus decisionmaking that includes respect for human rights, and that allows for military actions such as peacekeeping operations. Canadian diplomats have complained that many Western states have raised very few objections to the issues raised by the Chinese and others and have not been strong supporters of the Canadian position, fearing that the relatively fast-track intrusiveness of the Canadian proposals may undermine support for PD in the end. Interview with Canadian diplomats involved in ARF policy, July 2001.

125. The MOFA-commissioned report on comprehensive security explicitly advocates strengthening the PD capabilities of the ARF, though as of this date there has been no concrete manifestation of this argument in China's diplomacy.

126. Sun Xiaoying, "Zhongguo ying bu ying rang chu Nansha qundao?" [Should China give way on the Nansha islands?] *Nansha Wenti Yanjiu Ziliao* [Research materials on the Nansha question] (Beijing: Chinese Academy of Social Sciences, Asia-Pacific Research Center, 1996) pp. 295–302; Shang Guozhen, "Lue lun Nansha wenti guojihua qushi ji women de duice" [An outline discussion of the internationalization trends on the Nansha question and our countermeasures] *Nansha Wenti Yanjiu Ziliao* [Research materials on the Nansha question] (Beijing: Chinese Academy of Social Sciences, Asia-Pacific Research Center, 1996) pp. 288–295.

127. "Chairman's Statement of the Third ASEAN Regional Forum" (Jakarta, July 23, 1996), p. 4.

128. Zhang Zhirong and Wu Chong, "Jiejue Nansha zhengduan de duice xuanze" [Choices in countermeasures for resolving the Nansha dispute] *Nansha Wenti Yanjiu Ziliao* [Research materials on the Nansha question] (Beijing: Chinese Academy of Social Sciences, Asia-Pacific Research Center, 1996) pp. 258–272, at p. 267; Zhou Liangbiao and Ye Hong, "Jiejue Nansha wenti bixu zhongshi jingji kaifa" [To resolve the Nansha problem we must pay attention to economic development] in *Nansha Wenti Yanjiu Ziliao* [Research materials on the Nansha question] (Beijing: Chinese Academy of Social Sciences, Asia-Pacific Research Center, 1996) pp. 313–317, at p. 317.

129. On how UNCLOS constrains China's claims and options see Lu Jianwei, "Nansha wenti zhengduan ji duice" [The conflict over the Nansha problem and countermeasures] *Nansha Wenti Yanjiu Ziliao* [Research materials on the Nansha question] (Beijing: Chinese Academy of Social Sciences, Asia-Pacific Research Center, 1996) pp. 302–313, at 312.

130. Interview with think tank specialists on China and relations with South East Asian, May 1996.

131. Amitav Acharya, "The Impact of Multilateralism on Chinese Regional Security Thinking and Behavior: Snapshot of Beijing Views" (Unpublished paper, 1998). Also interview with Canadian embassy officials, Beijing China, April 1996, and interview with Canadian embassy official, Beijing, October 1998.

132. Evidently the first White Paper was called a white paper on "arms control and disarmament," even though it covered topics included in defense white papers, because top Chinese military leaders did not want it to appear that China was bowing to external pressure to produce a white paper on defense per se. (Comments by senior National Defense University officer, March 1997.) The drafters of the 1998 white paper explicitly examined a range of possible templates, and rejected some South East Asian examples for being too slim and non-transparent.

133. For which activists were pushing hard. See for instance CSCAP 1995: 4.

134. ARF Chairman's Statement, 1996, pp. 4–6.

135. The agenda focus on "joint" exercises had been set by China, and it ran into opposition from the US and its allies, as they are the ones who run "joint exercises." China does not. The ISG failed to reach consensus on the issue. While this was a setback for the CBM process, a range of alternative proposals was floated for implementing other versions of this kind of CBM. The Chinese ran into heavy criticism for this proposal. Subsequently the proposal was dropped. Interview with Canadian diplomat involved in ARF policy, May 5, 1997; interview with PLA officer involved in ARF policy, January 1999.

136. Desjardin, "Rethinking Confidence Building Measures," p. 7.

137. See the ARF Chairman's Summary and "Regional Forum Seminar on Defense Conversion (Beijing, September 2000).

138. Interview with senior US diplomat involved in ARF policy, February 2001; interview with Canadian diplomats involved in ARF diplomacy, July 2001.

139. "Chinese Paper at the ARF-ISG-CBMs in Brunei" (ms. November 3–5, 1996). Also, interview with Singaporean embassy official, Beijing, China, April 1996.

140. Vietnam has been one of the more vocal opponents of efforts by countries such as Canada to dilute the sovereign centric language or to include military options such as PKO in ARF documents on PD. See for instance, "Vietnam's Views on Singapore's Discussion Paper" (Asian Regional Forum submission, January, 2001). Interview with Canadian diplomats involved in ARF diplomacy, July 3, 2001. India also stressed the importance of protecting sovereignty, and opposed military PD mechanisms. See its comments on a paper submitted to the ARF by India in 2000 entitled "Preventive Diplomacy."

141. For a discussion of transnational activist and "accountibility politics" see Kecik and Sikkink, *Activists Beyond Borders; for a* discussion of Durkheim's analysis of morality, see Freidrich Kratochwil, "The Force of Prescriptions" *International Organization* 38(4) (Autumn 1984): 753–775.

142. Conversation with former senior Chinese diplomat and speechwriter for senior officials in the MOFA.

143. This is a point made in Evangelista's study of transnational effects on Soviet arms control policy. See Evangelista, *Unarmed Forces*, ch. 16.

144. See James Jonson, "Is Talk Really Cheap? Prompting Conversation between Critical Theory and Rational Choice," *American Political Science Review* 87(1) (March): 74–86; John Gerard Ruggie, "Multilateralism: The Anatomy of an Institution" in John Gerard Ruggie, ed., *Multilateralism Matters: The Theory and Praxis of an*

Institutional Form (New York: Columbia University Press, 1993), pp. 3–47; Risse, "Let's Argue."

145. Kuklinski and Hurley, "It's a Matter of Interpretation," p. 127.

146. Jennifer J. Halpern, "Elements of a Script for Friendship in Transaction," *Journal of Conflict Resolution* 41(6) (December 1997): 835–868.

147. Though even this is problematic from an institutionalist perspective. As realpoliticians the Chinese should have been especially suspicious of an institution that activist states like Canada, Australia, and to some extent the U.S. supported. The information that their involvement should have supplied, for realpolitician skeptics, was precisely that the ARF was a potentially constraining institution.

148. George W. Downs et al., "Designing Multilaterals: The Architecture and Evolution of Environmental Agreements." (Paper presented to American Political Science Associate Annual Conference, Washington DC, August 1997).

149. Indeed, the dependent variable in Downs et al. is not the interests, preferences, or behavior of any individual state (say, the potentially worst or most important defector). Thus it is possible that the (admittedly lower) observed level of cooperation (as they operationalize it) may still be a function of socialization. It is also possible, counterfactually, that the depth of cooperation might have been even shallower had there been no socialization effect in transformational institutions. Too much is blackboxed in their empirical tests, such that they cannot show one way or the other whether there are any socialization effects in either transformational or strategically and sequentially constructed institutions.

Chapter 4

HIERARCHY AND STABILITY IN ASIAN INTERNATIONAL RELATIONS

David Kang

In the long run it is Asia (and not Europe) that seems far more likely to be the cockpit of great power conflict. The half millennium during which Europe was the world's primary generator of war (and economic growth) is coming to a close. For better and for worse, Europe's past could be Asia's future.

—Aaron Friedberg[1]

THE PUZZLE

A general consensus is emerging among security experts that Asia is a potential source of instability. [2] Whether realist or liberal, most analyses implicitly or explicitly assume that Asian nations conceive of their security in the same way that western nations do. From this perspective, given the wide disparities in economic and military power among nations in the region, the broad range of political systems that range from democracy to totalitarian, and the lack of international institutions, many western analysts see a region "ripe for rivalry." Despite these concerns, and even after the ignominious exit of the U.S. from Vietnam, after the fall of the Soviet Union, after the implementation of economic reforms China, Asia has yet to see any major conflict or instability.

Yet there is another strand of thinking about Asian international relations that is both more optimistic in its conclusions and also poses different challenges to U.S. foreign policy. In this view Asian international relations have historically been hierarchic, more peaceful, and more stable than that of the west.[3] From this perspective, until the intrusion of the western powers in the nineteenth century, Asian international relations were remarkably stable, punctuated only occasionally by conflict between countries. The system was materially based and reinforced through centuries of cultural practice, and consisted of sovereign states defined over geographic areas that functioned under the organizing principle of anarchy. In this view Asian international relations emphasized formal hierarchy among nations, while allowing considerable informal equality. Consisting of China as the central state, and the peripheral states as lesser states or "vassals," as long as hierarchy was observed there was little need for interstate war. This contrasts sharply with the western tradition of international relations that consisted of formal equality between nation-states, informal hierarchy, and almost constant interstate conflict (see the appendix to this article).

With the intrusion of the western powers in the nineteenth century, the old Asian order was demolished as both western and Asian powers scrambled to establish influence. After a century of tumult in Asia, in the late 1990s a strong and confident China emerged, while Vietnam became increasingly more stable. Soon, perhaps, Korea will be reunified. While realists and liberals have tended to view modern Asia as potentially unstable, if the system is reverting to a pattern of hierarchy, the result may be increased stability.

If this is the case, there are important implications for our understanding of the region. Most significantly, a hierarchic view of Asia leads to different implications for U.S. foreign policy. On the one hand, if the U.S. remains tightly engaged in Asia, and if Asian nations do not balance China as realists expect, an American attempt to construct balancing coalitions to contain China using East Asian states will be highly problematic. On the other hand, if the U.S. withdraws significantly from the region, Asia may not become as dangerous or unstable as the conventional wisdom expects.

This leads to the following questions: is the Asian region hierarchic? If so, what are the implications for stability in the future?

This article makes one overarching argument: there is more security and stability in Asia than is generally realized. Especially because the pessimistic realist predictions show little sign of being born out, at a minimum scholars should seriously consider the implications of this alternative explanation. However, scholars have rarely tested this image in any discriminating manner.[4] In this essay I present the logic and implications of Asian international relations built on the hierarchic system. I define stability as the absence of major interstate war and generally calm relations between countries. I argue that hierarchy is more stable than realists have allowed, and often it is the absence of hierarchy that

leads to conflict, while also providing evidence from the last fifteen years that presents us with at least a plausible argument that such a hierarchic system is re-emerging in Asia.

In the first of the paper's three sections I introduce the logic of a hierarchic international or regional system, and show how this view is only a slight modification of realism. In the second section I examine six centuries of Asian international relations, and show how the system historically functioned from the end of the Yuan dynasty to the twentieth century. The final section shows how a hierarchic perspective explains three puzzles from the current era that realism has had difficulty explaining.

I. ANARCHY AND HIERARCHY IN INTERNATIONAL RELATIONS

Kenneth Waltz led us down the wrong path by contrasting hierarchy and anarchy.[5] His argument that anarchy leads to balancing and fear of preponderant power has become widely accepted in the study of international relations. Realists overwhelmingly expect that power is threatening and that nations balance each other whenever possible.[6] The theoretical argument against the possibility of unipolarity has been best adduced by Christopher Layne. He writes that "in a unipolar world, systemic constraints—balancing, uneven growth rates, and the sameness effect—impel eligible states to become great powers."[7] In realism, the principle of self-help forces nations to coalesce against the would-be dominant power. As Stuart Kaufman points out, the logic of self-help under anarchy "encourages strong powers to absorb weak ones when practical, promoting consolidation in the international system."[8]

The hierarchic model I derive here grows out of realism, and the contrasting form of organization I discuss here embodies many of the traits that realists will find familiar, and begins with the standard neorealist assumptions. Nation-states are the unit of analysis, and exist as sovereign entities defined over a geographic area. The system is one of anarchy, where the use of force is always a possibility.[9] Preferences and position are determined by power and geography. Relative position matters in hierarchy—there is one central state and many lesser, peripheral states. Rhetoric, contracts, and laws and are also regarded as being unenforceable, and thus mistrust is high in the international system. Nations are primarily concerned with survival while threats and instability are accepted as a fact of life in international politics. As a result, nation-states are concerned about power and survival first, and economic issues second.

However, realism posits that only two types of organization can occur in the international system: anarchy, with its emphasis on poles and alliances, and hierarchy, consisting of either formal or informal empire.[10] David Lake writes that "in anarchy, each party of the relationship possess full residual rights of control

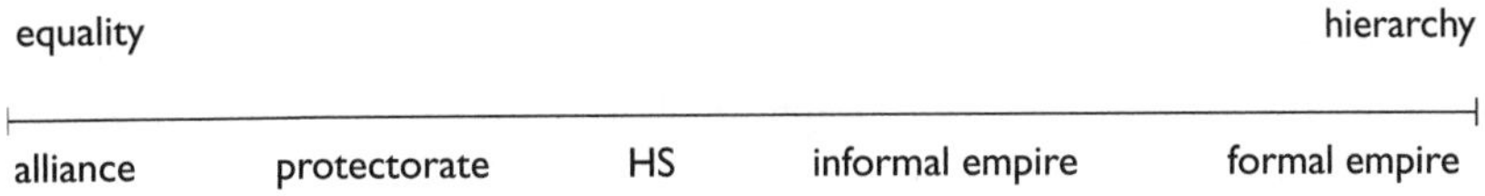

equality				hierarchy
alliance	protectorate	HS	informal empire	formal empire

FIGURE 4.1 A continuum of security relations.

. . . in hierarchy, one party, the dominant member—possess the right to make residual decisions."[11] Lake's conception of hierarchy is hegemony or empire. Yet hierarchy is not the opposite of anarchy; rather, equality is the opposite of hierarchy. Both equality and hierarchy can exist within the larger organizing principle of anarchy.[12] The only major change I make to the standard realist model is to explicitly recognize that nation-states are not equal when acting on the world stage.

Realists have underexplored a hypothetical middle path that involves a central power that still operates in anarchy, but does not cause other nations to balance against the largest power in the system, and does not fold them under its wing in empire. Hierarchy is not hegemony: hegemony is overarching and more intrusive. Hegemony also focuses the bulk of its attention to the largest power, while hierarchy is more concerned with the interaction of states up and down the hierarchy. Hierarchy also accords all states within the system a place and a means of interacting with each other. This middle path is hierarchic (figure 4.1). Hierarchy also allows for substantial autonomy and freedom among the lesser states.

The key issue is whether all nations understand that the central state had no territorial or overweening ambitions, and whether there exists a method for resolving conflicts. If this is the case, all nations in the system can find an equilibrium that involves acquiescence to the dominant state. Equilibrium results because other states know that opposing the central state is impossible, and thus defer to it precisely to the point where expected costs of conquering them slightly exceed the expected benefits. Because conquest has some costs, in hierarchy other states do not need to defer completely to the central state on all issues. They are independent precisely to the degree that they estimate that the central state's expected costs of enforcing deference will exceed benefits. All of this works better to the degree that material power relationships make the expected outcome of conflicts certain. The key insight is that bandwagoning occurs because secondary states have no choice. If they could balance at a bearable costs, they would.

A hierarchic system is also different from informal empire, which exists when a functionally dependent state remains nominally sovereign. Michael Doyle writes "informal imperialism achieves [control] through the collaboration of a legally independent (but actually subordinate) government in the periphery."[13] Wendt and Friedheim distinguish between an informal empire and

the mere concentration of power: "Material inequality is not a sufficient condition [for informal empire], however. . . . The vast majority of materially unequal dyads in the states system are not informal empires. Concentration of capabilities is not equivalent to centralization of control."[14] The contrast with informal empire is important: in informal empire the puppet governments collaborate with the imperial power against the wishes of the populace.[15] In hierarchy, independent sovereign nations accept the central position of the largest power in the system but are fully functional on their own terms.

BEHAVIORAL IMPLICATIONS

There are four major ways in which a hierarchic system differs in its behavioral implications from the Westphalian system of equal nation-states.

1. *Bandwagoning by the lesser states is a central feature of hierarchy.* In contrast to the realist predictions about state behavior that emphasize that lesser states will be fearful of and balance against the central state's capabilities, in hierarchy the lesser states flock to its side with a view toward gaining benefits.[16] This behavior corresponds to Randall Schweller's distinction between balancing for security and bandwagoning for profit, or the "preponderance of power" school.[17] Preponderance-of-power theory argues that a preponderant state will not need to fight, and a smaller state may not wish to fight.

The hierarchy as a system is stable and order is preserved through a combination of benefits and sanctions that the central power provides to the lesser powers. Good relations with the central state ensures survival and even prosperity by the lesser states, through a continual flow of goods trade, and technology. Rejection of the hierarchy brings conflict as the central power intervenes to reestablish the hierarchic order.

When the lesser states challenge the central state, the central state reserves the right to use force to restore order. This hierarchy develops over time and can become a formal or informal pattern of relations among nation-states. Thus order is restored and conflicts resolved through the central state's use of force to impose order on the rest of the lesser states. These states in turn realize that to challenge the hierarchy would be against their own interests. Additionally, internal trouble within the central state does not lead to the lesser states upsetting the existing order; it takes regime change of an enormous amount to disrupt the system from within. Weakness in the foreign relations of the central power invites extensive conflict among the lesser powers, because the organization that stabilized their foreign relations is gone.

2. *A hierarchic system is more stable than a "Westphalian system" in good times, but more chaotic during bad times.* A central state at the top of the hierarchy maintains order and minimizes conflicts between the lesser powers, and also provides a means by which to adjust to unforeseen circumstances. Thus in

"normal" times a hierarchy should see less interstate war and more stability. In the abstract, hierarchy may be more stable than equality. Everyone knows their place, and so there is little misinformation or fear of miscalculation. It is also understood which nations have more responsibility and rights to order the system, and thus they are not viewed with the same suspicion when they do so. However, when the central state experiences trouble and the hierarchy breaks down, order is more easily upset. Thus in times of weakness or major change in the system, we would expect less stability than in a western system.

3. *Material power is at the base of the hierarchy, but other factors also matter.* Nations in the system develop shared norms that allow for communication. Often, these shared cultural norms can serve to mitigate the security dilemma and increase the level of communication between states in the system. Such information is consistent with methods designed to mitigate the problems of asymmetric information that game theorists such as James Fearon have identified.[18] If all states know the rules of the game, they can communicate threats, acceptance of the status quo, and other positions more clearly. Thus, although cultural norms derive *from* the underlying power structure, they are by no means inconsequential or epiphenomenal. As Organski writes: "Everyone comes to know what kind of behavior to expect from the others, habits and patterns are established, and certain rules as to how these relations ought to be carried on grow to be accepted. . . . Trade is conducted along recognized channels . . . diplomatic relations also fall into recognized patterns. Certain nations are even expected to support other nations. . . . There are rules of diplomacy; there are even rules of war."[19] Douglas Lemke and Suzanne Werner also write in this vein: "The status quo of the overall hierarchy is thus the rules, norms, and accepted procedures that govern international relations."[20]

4. *There is little interference by the central power in the affairs of the lesser states in hierarchy.* What makes hierarchy unique is that both the central and the lesser states explicitly recognize the central state's dominant position. And all the states recognize and legitimate the lesser states' positions. As long as the lesser states acknowledge the unrivaled position of the central state, the central state respects the autonomy and sovereignty of the lesser states. The lesser states retain full autonomy of domestic organization and foreign policy, and full authority to order their relations with each other. Indeed, the dominant state in the system does not necessarily care about the lesser states' foreign policies, as long as relations with the dominant state itself are maintained.

CAVEATS

I have developed an inductive, generic model for how hierarchy might function in the international system. It contrasts in some fairly clear ways with the structural realist model developed by Waltz. However, it should be emphasized that the modifications I make to realism here are fairly minor. All I do in this section is add a little complexity to the standard realist view of the world: a pecking order known by all states. This is simple, and derives from a large body of recent literature on international relations. Hierarchy is path dependent, serves to lower transaction costs between actors, is ultimately based on material power but is reified through cultural practices, provides a means by which actors can signal accommodation, deference, and information, and provides an equilibrium focal point around which actor expectations and practices can converge.

II. ASIAN INTERNATIONAL RELATIONS, 1300–1900

Defined as both the absence of major interstate war and the continuity of fixed borders, Asia was more stable than Europe in the period 1300–1900. I define the domain of Asian international relations as ending in Manchuria in the north, the Pacific to the east, the mountains of Tibet to the west, and then running south to the coastal regions of the Mekong delta. In short, this study mainly focuses on the region comprising Japan, Korea, China, and Vietnam. These countries were the major actors in the hierarchic system. Although much more detailed research needs to be conducted, from the decline of the Mongol Yuan dynasty in the late 1300s to the intrusion of the west in the nineteenth century, it appears that the system was relatively stable.

The traditional international order in Asia consisted of an outlook on international relations that yielded substantial stability. In Chinese eyes—and explicitly accepted by the surrounding nations—the world of the past millennium has consisted of civilization (China) and barbarians (all the other states.) In this view, as long as the barbarian states were willing to kowtow to the Chinese emperor, and so demonstrate formal obedience to their lower position in the hierarchy, the Chinese had neither the need to invade these countries nor the desire to so. The Chinese have always known that they are Chinese and not Korean, or Vietnamese. There was extensive knowledge of and interactions among the various countries. This system survived until western encroachment in the early nineteenth century.

The hierarchic world of ancient Asia appears to have incorporated many of the realist assumptions: the ancient Asian world was a self-help system, where anarchy is the organizing principle. Nation-states (broadly defined) are the actors, with position and preferences determined by national power and geographic location. Military power was of potential recourse in dealing with other nations. Yet the hierarchy diverges from the European order in that these fundamental attributes of the system yield hierarchy. The European order consisted of formal equality of sovereign states combined with informal hierarchy since the largest powers have disproportionate influence on the system. In Asia the hierarchy consisted of formal hierarchy and informal equality. As long as the smaller powers paid tribute to China, there was little incentive for China to intervene in local politics. Yet they did not behave the way theories of international relations would predict. The most obvious anomaly is that these nations bandwagoned with, as opposed to balanced against, the largest power in the system.

Asian international relations was distinct from Europe in two other major ways. First, centuries separated major conflict between countries; second, the countries remained essentially the same after the war—there was no shifting and malleable boundaries that were redefined, and nations did not rise and disappear. As seen in the appendix to this article, the major difference between Europe and Asia was that conflicts between the states in the hierarchy were centuries apart, and tended to occur as order within the central power was breaking down. As one Chinese dynasty began to decay internally, conflict along and among the peripheral states would flare up, as the central power's attention was turned inward. As dynasties rose and fell over the centuries movement within the hierarchy took place. Thus in 1274 and 1281, as the Sung and Chin dynasties were crumbling in China, the Mongols under Kublai Khan attempted unsuccessfully to conquer Korea and Japan.[21] As the Ming dynasty weakened, the Japanese general Hideyoshi attempted to invade China through Korea in 1592 and 1598, although he failed to take Korea. But with the restoration of order within China, conflict between the peripheral powers would cease and relations between all powers would be relatively peaceful for centuries.

Borders also remained relatively fixed in Asia. This contrasts sharply with the western experience. In 1500 Europe had some five hundred independent units; by 1900 it had about twenty.[22] In East Asia, the number of countries and boundaries composing the hierarchy have remained essentially the same since 1200 A.D.[23] However, once the hierarchy was upset, it broke apart immediately. In the late nineteenth century both China and Japan became "realist states" almost overnight. Between 1592 and 1895 Japan invaded no country. After that date, it engaged China in a war, annexed Taiwan, and moved into Korea.

The formally hierarchic relationship consisted of a few key acts that communicated information between actors. Most important was kowtow to the Chinese emperor by the sovereigns of the lesser states. Since there could only be one emperor under Heaven, all other sovereigns were known as kings, and on a regular basis would send tribute missions to Beijing to acknowledge the Emperor's central position in the world. In addition, when a new King would take the throne in the lesser states, it was customary to seek the Emperor's approval, a process known as "investiture." Although pro forma, investiture was a necessary component of maintaining stable relations between nations. Korea, Japan, Vietnam, Tibet, and other kingdoms peripheral to China (Jakarta, Malaysia) pursued formal investiture for their own rulers, sent tributary missions, and maintained formal obeisance to China.

This may be opposite of what realists would predict. At a minimum we should see these countries bordering China to be attempting to retain as much independence as possible.

While it is often argued that Japan was outside the Chinese system, the Japanese viewed the world in much the same way as the Chinese: the Japanese described the world as *ka-I no sekai*, or the world of China and the barbarians. As Tashiro Kazui notes, "it was not long before both Japan and Korea had established sovereign-vassal relations (*sakuho kankei*) with China, joining other countries of Northeast Asia as dependent, tributary nations."[24] Kazui notes that "from the time of Queen Himiko's rule over the ancient state of Yamatai to that of the Ashikaga shoguns during the Muromachi period, it was essentially these same international rules that Japan followed."[25] It is true that during the Tokugawa shogunate Japan and China did not resume a tributary relationship. However, trade was still conducted through Nagasaki, although only by private merchants, and indirectly through Korea and the Ryukus. China under the Qing was much more willing to consider private trading relations in the stead of formal tribute relationships.

By the early Ming period (1368–1644), the new Yi dynasty (1392–1910) in Korea was regularly sending three tributary missions per year to China. Until the Tokugawa shogunate (1600–1868), even the Japanese had traditionally given tribute to the Chinese emperor. Key-hiuk Kim writes that:

> In 1404—a year after the ruler of Yi Korea received formal Ming investiture for the first time—Yoshimitsu, the third Ashikaga shogun, received Ming investiture as "King of Japan." The identical status assigned to the rulers of Yi Korea and Ashikaga Japan under the Ming tribute system seems to have facilitated the establishment of formal relations between the two neighbors on the basis of "equality" within the "restored" Confucian world order in East Asia.[26]

Kowtowing to China did not involve much loss of independence, as these states were largely free to run both their internal and foreign affairs independently from China. For example, while Vietnam kowtowed to China it also went on to expand its territory in Southeast Asia. Being a client state had benefits, as well: China helped the Vietnamese fight the French (the Chinese "black flags" troops). In 1592 the Chinese sent troops to Korea to attack Hideyoshi. In the 1800s China sent troops to Tibet to repel an invasion from Nepal. Thus being a client state brought economic, political, and military benefits at a cost lower than arms racing or alliances.

Indeed, after the Hideyoshi invasions of Korea in 1592–1598, the Tokugawa shogunate recognized Japanese-Korean relations as equal. "The Tokugawa rulers understood and accepted the Korean position. Japan after Hideyoshi had no ambition for continental conquest or expansion. They tacitly acknowledged

Chinese supremacy and cultural leadership in the East Asian world. . . . Although Tokugawa Japan maintained no formal ties with China . . . for all intents and purposes it was as much a part of the Chinese world as Ashikaga Japan had been."[27] Japan became known as *sakoku* (closed country). However, it is shown that this is not seen in any Japanese sources, public or private, until a translation of a Dutch paper.[28] These countries, even during Tokugawa and Qing, had extensive relations. During the Tokugawa period, the *bakufu* established formal and equal diplomatic relations with Korea, subordinate relation with the Qing, and superior relations with the Ryukus.

In economic relations, while none of the northeast Asian states were trading states along the lines of the western European powers, China, Japan, and Korea engaged in extensive trade with each other for centuries. Indeed, even "tribute" was more a hypothetical goal than reality, for the tributary nations gained as much in trade and support as they gave to the Chinese emperor. Key-hiuk Kim writes that "Although the total value of Korean tribute exceeded that of Chinese gifts by some 80,000 taels every year, the figure did not represent a net gain for the Chinese government, for it spent at least an equal amount to support the visiting Korean embassy personnel."[29] Tribute in this sense seemed as much a means of trade and transmission of Chinese culture and technology as it was a formal political relationship.

China and its tributaries had far more interaction with each other than is commonly acknowledged. The popular impression of the histories of these countries is that they were virtually autarkic from one another. Recent scholarship, however, is showing that trade, both private and tributary, made up a significant portion of both government revenues and GNP. Under this systme, these countries were a thriving, complex, and vibrant regional order.

During the Tokugawa period, John Lee notes the "undiminished importance of a trade relationship with China and, to a lesser extent, with Korea and the Ryuku."[30] Some scholars estimate that at the height of Japanese trade in the early 1600s, Japanese silver constituted 30 to 40 percent of total world production.[31] Regarding China, John Lee notes that "China since the sixteenth century was even more deeply involved than Japan in trade with the larger world. Few other places produced the commodities that were universally in demand in greater quantity or variety, and few others attracted foreign traders in the same number."[32]

Gang Deng notes that "China is often portrayed as a country isolated from the outside world, self-sufficient and insulated from capitalism . . . with marginal, if not non-existent, foreign trade. In fact, China needed foreign trade, both by land and sea, as much as many other pre-modern societies in Eurasia."[33]

> Zheng Chenggong's Ming loyalist regime in Taiwan (1644–83) took part in triangular trade involving Japan, Vietnam, Cambodia, Indonesia, and

> the Philippines; his fleet to Japan alone comprised fifty ships a year. . . . The total profit from overseas trade each year has been estimated at 2.3–2.7 million *liang* of silver. . . . The tributary system was a form of disguised staple trade. Trade is also shown because of the fighting over the ability by tributary states to pay tribute. Hideyoshi invaded Korea, a Ming vassal state, to force China to allow Japan to resume a tributary relationship, and threatened that a refusal would lead to invasion of China itself.[34]

Culturally the Chinese influence was formative. Although neither the Japanese nor the Korean languages are sinic in origin (generally they are thought to be Ural-Altaic with more similarity to Turkish and Finnish), Vietnam, Korea, and Japan have used Chinese characters and vocabulary for more than 2,000 years. Although the indigenous languages were used for common everyday speech, all educated people, and all formal communications, were written in Chinese. Until the advent of Christian missionaries in Vietnam, the Vietnamese, too, based their writing system on Chinese characters. Family organization, education, cultural, arts and crafts—all were derived from a Chinese influence. Although each country retained its own sense of self, the Chinese influence was pervasive.

In contrast with feudal Europe—and with the intermittent exception of Japan—the nations of Asia have been centrally administered bureaucratic systems for far longer than the European nations. Feudal systems tend to be highly decentralized with government functions delegated to vassals. Centralized bureaucratic administration in China involved a complex system of administration and governance. The entire country was divided into administrative districts down to the province level, with appointments made from the capital for most tax, commercial, and judicial posts. In addition, since the Han dynasty, an examination system was used for selecting government bureaucrats. Passing the exam and going to the capital became the origins of Asia's focus on education—anyone who passed the exam assured both himself and his family a substantial jump in prestige and income.[35]

The demolition of the old order came swiftly in the nineteenth century. The intrusion of western powers and the inherent weaknesses of the Asian nations created a century of chaos. When the hierarchic system broke apart Japan was able to seize the initiative and attempt to become the regional hegemon. Much of Southeast Asia became embroiled in guerrilla wars in an attempt to drive out the western colonizers, from Vietnam to the Philippines to Malaysia and Indonesia. The two world wars and the cold war all muted Asia's inherent dynamism. It was not until the late 1990s that the system began once again to resemble an Asian regional system that is both powered and steered by Asian nations themselves.

III. HIERARCHY IN THE MODERN ERA

More important than whether a hierarchic system existed historically is whether such a system might be reemerging today, and if so what might be the implications. Clearly no modern state will seek investiture from China regarding its chief executive, nor will any country pay tribute to China. Yet modern practices may convey the same shared cultural understanding, and an implicit hierarchy may be reemerging. China is large, growing, and centrally situated, and there is some suggestive evidence that points to the conclusion that Asia is more hierarchic than egalitarian.

In particular, a hierarchic view explains three puzzles that realism has trouble explaining, and presents us with one major contrasting hypothesis. First, hierarchy partially explains why Japan has had a limited reemergence as a great power. Second, why Asian nations have reacted differently to the Taiwan issue than the United States. Third, why Vietnam and Korea are not obviously balancing China. The divergent hypothesis is that the U.S. may face more difficulties creating a balancing coalition against China than is conventionally expected, and that if the U.S. withdraws there may not be the chaos that realism predicts. Each one of these issues is complex, and deserves greater treatment than I can provide here. I will merely sketch out how a hierarchic system explains these issues.

A. *WHY JAPAN IS NOT YET A "NORMAL" POWER*

If Asia—and Japan—were as realist as analysts think, then Japan would have rearmed at least a decade ago, while at the height of its economic growth. Although Japan is very powerful, it has not yet adopted the trappings of a complete great power. Scholars have debated why this has not yet happened. Previously, the debate has been between realists and those who argue "Japan's culture or domestic politics is different, and hence its foreign policy is different."[36] Different from critiques of realism that focus on Japan's domestic politics or culture, the explanation I offer is international in nature. After showing that the two main realist hypotheses for Japan's behavior are suspect, I offer a third hypothesis built on hierarchy. These two realist hypotheses are often conflated in the literature:

1. *The Great Power Hypothesis:* Japan is so rich and large that it will soon want to become a great power once again ("old" realist hypothesis).

2. *The Umbrella Hypothesis:* When the U.S. leaves Japan, it will rearm and become a normal power ("new" realist hypothesis)[37]

These hypotheses have rarely been tested in any discriminating manner. Note as well that these two explanations are mutually incompatible: Japan cannot be a normal great power and yet sit under the U.S. security umbrella.

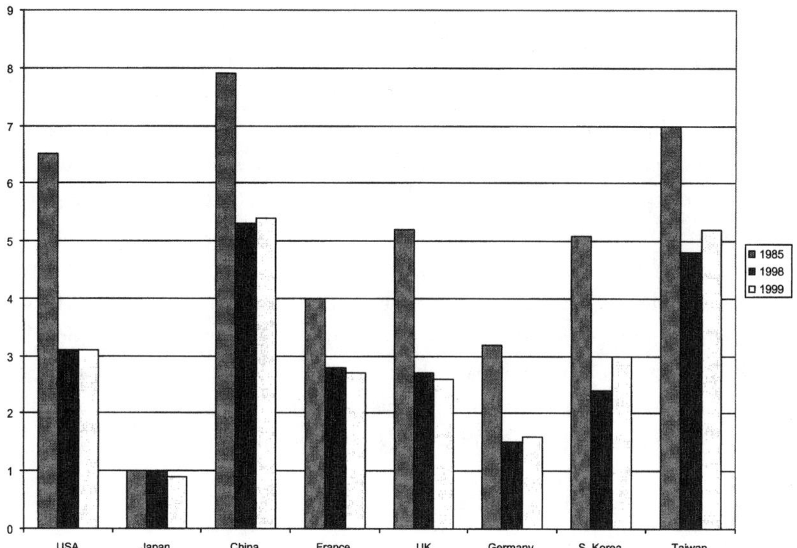

FIGURE 4.2. Defense Spending (% GDP), 1985–1999. *Source*: IISS, the Military Balance 2000–2001.

The first hypothesis, the "Great powers and rising expectations" is most easily falsified. There is no realist explanation for why the second-largest nation in the system does not balance or challenge the largest. Japan has the world's second-largest economy, is arguably the world's finest manufacturing nation, and is certainly one of the most technologically sophisticated countries in the world. Yet Japan lacks aircraft carriers, intercontinental missiles, nuclear weapons, and does not send troops abroad. In sum, Japan is hard to invade, but Japan also evinces almost no significant military or diplomatic strength. So although Japan is relatively strong, it clearly has not rearmed to the extent it could, nor has it rearmed to the extent a "great power" would (figure 4.2).

In support of the great power hypothesis, Michael Desch offers evidence of Japanese intentions: marginally increased defense spending, a virtual nuclear deterrent, and nationalistic rhetoric from selected politicians.[38] Yet this evidence is speculative at best. The key is not the offhand remark from a right-wing politician, but rather that Japan could easily triple its defense budget and still spend only what other powers such as France and Germany spend (figure 4.2). In addition, Japan could modify its constitution, develop nuclear missiles, deploy ICBMs, and build aircraft carriers. It could also forge a foreign policy independent from that of the U.S., and attempt to exert far more influence in diplomatic arenas. This would be convincing evidence that Japan is, or has pretensions to being, a great power. Any discussion of virtual, potential, or nascent power is all an admission that Japan does not yet function as a typical realist nation.

The second hypothesis, regarding the U.S. as keeping the genie in the bottle, is also suspect. First, why would the second-largest power in the system trust the largest power? Threats arise by the mere presence of capabilities—intentions can always change for the worse.[39] As Robert Jervis writes, "Minds can be changed, new leaders can come to power, values can shift, new opportunities and dangers can arise."[40] Even if a nation was peaceful when it was weak, changes in power can bring changes in goals. Second, why has Japan not doubted the U.S. commitment many times before? Arguments about the umbrella implicitly assume that Japan is realist and would rearm if the U.S. leaves. If this is true, and if there is no other factor that keeps Japanese foreign policy from being more assertive, then we should have seen Japan rearm at least a decade ago. From a Japanese perspective, there are only two pieces of information necessary to doubt the trustworthiness of the U.S. commitment:

1. How we treat our allies in Asia
2. How we treat Japan

From a realist perspective, the only information Japan should need to rearm is evidence regarding those two conditions. Yet those two conditions were met in the mid-1980s. From the vantage point of 1985, a Japanese policymaker would have to conclude that it was unlikely that the U.S. would still be defending Japan in 2000. Why? Because Japan had just had 15 years of negative signals. As the Jervis quote above shows, "things change," and if anything, Japanese had every reason to doubt the U.S. commitment. In 1969 President Nixon had called for "Asia for Asians" and began a major drawdown of U.S. troops and commitments to the region. By 1985, Japan had seen the U.S. abandon both South Vietnam and Taiwan. By the mid-1980s, U.S. anger at Japanese trading and economic policies was reaching a crescendo, culminating in the 1985 Plaza Accords and the 1988 Structural Impediments Initiative. In addition, the U.S. had begun to pressure Japan over "burden sharing" and attempted to make the Japanese pay more for the U.S. troops already deployed. All the indicators pointed to the conclusion that the U.S. would not be a reliable ally of Japan in the future. In addition, Japanese economic growth was at its height, Japanese national sentiment about its future was increasingly optimistic, and in 1985 Japan was potentially a better technological and manufacturing country than the U.S.

From a realist perspective, only the most naïve and myopic of leaders would focus only on the present. Indeed, precisely because of the vagaries of international politics, realists see leaders of nations as constantly looking over the horizon and trying to anticipate future trends. Thus, Japan has already had ample reason to doubt the U.S. commitment to its defense.

Yet in 1976 Japan pledged to keep defense spending at 1 percent of GDP, and this has remained virtually unchanged to the present. There was also little

Japanese reaction to the Vietnam or Taiwanese pullout by the U.S. And in the mid-1980s there was not concomitant increase in procurement or personnel policies in the Self-Defense Forces. Japan did not rearm despite real tensions with the United States in the 1980s, and its foreign policy shows almost no behavioral response.

The alternative to the umbrella hypothesis is fairly simple: Japan has not rearmed to the level it could because it has no need to, and it has no intention of challenging China for the central position in Asian politics. Japan can survive right now—it has no need to arm any more. It also has a view that accepts China as big and central. The historic animosities and the lingering mistrust over Japan for its transgressions in the first half of the twentieth century are reasons sometimes cited for a fear of Japanese rearmament. However, the situation has changed dramatically after nearly sixty years. In the late nineteenth century Japan faced decaying and despotic Chinese and Korean monarchies, a significant power vacuum, and extra-regional pressures from the western nations. Today Japan faces the opposite: well-equipped Korean and Chinese militaries with significant economic growth and robust economies, and no significant European or Russian intrusions to its region. It is unlikely that Japan need or will seek to expand its diplomatic and military influence on the Asian landmass.

B. WHY ASIAN NATIONS REACT DIFFERENTLY TO THE TAIWAN ISSUE THAN THE U.S.

Regarding conflict over the status of Taiwan, there are two issues that a hierarchic view of Asia provides us purchase upon. First, why is China so upset? Second, why do the Asian nations seem unconcerned about China's anger? At first glance, the increased tension across the Taiwan Strait in the recent past might seem puzzling: why would China provoke a war over Taiwan that it cannot yet militarily win?[41] Why would China jeopardize its entry into the WTO, risk frightening its neighbors, and severely threaten its economic growth if nations impose sanctions, just to retain Taiwan? The answer lies in China's view of Taiwan as an essential element of its national identity, and China's willingness to bear the real costs of such actions.

A systemic-level view of China and Taiwan would actually point to an increased defensive posture on the part of China. During the cold war China was able to play a middle position between the U.S. and the Soviet Union, and with détente in the 1970s, to become even an ally of sorts with the U.S. against the Soviets. With the collapse of the Soviet Union, the United States emerged as the unquestioned dominant country in the world, and also increasingly turned its attention to a potentially dangerous China.[42] Thus China has come into more directly conflict with the U.S. in the past decade than before, and from a weak position relative to the U.S. A structural view would expect to see China not taking provocative actions against U.S. allies in the region. However, the opposite has occurred.

There are clearly many other factors in addition to hierarchy that affect relations across the Strait. The more Taiwan's identity becomes a mature democracy, the more it exacerbates tension with the mainland. The Taiwan issue is also very much a case of competing identities. The traditional political powers of the KMT and CCP had similar goals and values: both parties want to rule all of China. Taiwan is a case where both sides could potentially coexist: both calling for a unified China, neither one willing to upset the status-quo, and the stalemate undergirded by the physical separation of water and the needs of the two political entities.[43] To that extent the issue is muted, and ironically, these two political entities have been comfortable dealing with each other precisely because they agreed on so many of the basic assumptions regarding what "China" is. But the conflict exists because of issues of identity, and Taiwan's consistently ambiguous historical relationship with China.

Taiwan has always existed uneasily within the shadow of China. Although nominally independent, Taiwan has also traditionally served as a refuge for the losers of mainland strife. Taiwan historically was not a formal province of China, but it was also not a recognized independent state in the manner of Korea, Japan, and Vietnam. In 1644 the Ming loyalists retreated to Taiwan to harass the triumphant Qing.[44] Led by Admiral Koxingga, the Ming loyalists would sally forth from Taiwan. Although the Qing eventually subdued the Ming loyalists, Taiwan was not made a formal province of China until 1886. Before that time Taiwan was considered a part of Fukien province, administered by Manchu officials assigned from Beijing. However, official Chinese records in the eighteenth century also refer to Taiwan as a "frontier area."[45] Although clearly a "part" of China, Taiwan was also not considered a part of Han China, and yet it was also not a separate political entity as were Korea and Vietnam. Thus the issue of China and Taiwan poses an interesting dilemma for realists. Are China and Taiwan nation-states? If not, how do we make sense of them and the conflict?

While the western answer to the question of whether or not Taiwan is a nation-state is obvious, the Chinese answer is exactly the opposite.[46] China may truly view Taiwan as an internal problem. Xu Dunxin, former Chinese ambassador to Japan, expresses a common Chinese refrain: "The Taiwan issue is China's business. It is China's internal affair. No country, including the U.S., has a right to concern itself with this issue."[47] Although such announcements tend to be dismissed in the West, the Chinese have had a consistent policy toward Taiwan, and pretending that China is not sincere in expressing this attitude is perhaps premature.[48] This Chinese perception has two implications for this eassay.

First, imposing a western conception of international relations on China may be missing the point. The nations of Asia have made an implicit pact with

Taiwan: exist as a quasi-nation and enjoy the benefits of the international system. It should be emphasized that this has been the traditional solution to the Taiwan issue.[49] As long as Taiwan was willing to abide by these rules and be a quasi-nation, the benefits of being a nation-state were available to it. Taiwan's leaders could travel the world and play golf and perform quasi-diplomatic functions, Taiwan's firms could trade and invest overseas, and its status was not threatened, even by China. But while Taiwan could act like a nation-state, it could not officially become one.[50]

The furor over the 1996 and 2000 Taiwanese elections, and Lee Teng-hui's 1996 statements in particular, revealed the consequences of breaking the rules. As various Taiwanese leaders became more assertive in their claims to full, sovereign, nation-state status, the rest of the world became increasingly cautious. And the reaction to the Chinese military maneuvers was especially telling.[51] In good realist fashion, United States fury was directly almost exclusively at China for being provocative. However, the rest of the Asian states were muted in their responses to Chinese military intervention, and informally extremely upset at Taiwan for provoking China. The informal feeling among other Asian states has been that "Taiwan broke the pact."[52]

Second, it was only as Taiwan began the transition to a genuine and modern nation-state with democracy that the issues became intractable with China. That is, China has been content to allow Taiwan to act like a normal nation-state and to conduct its affairs with little interference from Beijing.[53] However, a formal declaration of independence would cause China to respond, most likely with a punitive expedition. This should not be considered an idle threat on the Chinese part. The conflict also reveals China's belief that it has the right to order its relations in its surrounding areas.[54]

Indeed, the conflict itself has been exacerbated as Taiwan has consolidated its democratic institutions. While Taiwan was under the control of the KMT and authoritarian governments during the cold war, there was little disagreement between China and Taiwan over the rules of the game and the ultimate place that Taiwan occupied in relation to China: Taiwan was clearly part of mainland China, and the only dispute was who—the KMT or the CCP—were the legitimate rulers of all China.

However, events of the past 15 years have seen Taiwan's identity increasingly shift to that of a modern nation-state. This shift is most notable in the gradual shift to democracy. Taiwan has become a strong, vibrant democracy, where people have the right to voice their opinions, and to elect leaders in contested elections.[55] As such, Taiwan, although not recognized formally as a nation-state by the United States, has become in the eyes of much of the world a legitimate political entity.

And therein lies the heart of the issue. While China's conception of itself remains roughly the same, Taiwan's is changing. And thus there is the clash between a democratic, capitalist, wealthy, and industrialized Taiwan deciding its own fate, and an authoritarian, quasi-capitalist, semi-traditional China attempting to control the fate of Taiwan.[56] Realism has much to say about how the conflict was managed during the cold war, but without understanding these competing visions of the world, it is not possible to understand why the conflict has endured, nor why it has become much more acute in the last decade.

Yet China's view of international relations is considerably more subtle. Although realist in its practices, this view also incorporates many non-Westphalian elements. For its part, China is comfortable with a loose definition of "nation." China has already agreed to a "one nation, two systems" approach with respect to Hong Kong. Although it is too early to draw firm conclusions, China has so far respected in large part the two-systems principle, allowing Hong Kong its own currency, legal system, and even military forces. In addition, the border dispute between India and China has never been formally resolved, both countries agreeing to leave the border undefined, and China's relations with Tibet and its western regions show an acceptance of looser relations than we might expect. The Chinese attempt to derive an identity that allows for the "one-country, two-systems" principle with Hong Kong is one example of how identities can be reconfigured that allow for accommodation. As long as Taiwan would also exist in a traditional, poorly defined, and partial relationship with China, both sides were content. But Taiwan's increasingly democratic domestic political institutions are causing conflict with China.

In a hierarchy, the other Asian nations recognize China's right to order its borders. In addition, other nations see China-Taiwan relations as an internal affair. By this logic, any actions—military or otherwise—that China takes against Taiwan are not indicative of how China would conduct its foreign policy. So we are seeing a China that is flexible in its worldview.

C. WHY VIETNAM AND KOREA ACCEPT CHINA'S CENTRAL POSITION

From a realist perspective, the two countries that should be most fearful of China are Vietnam and Korea, because China can actually invade those countries. Yet both countries, while wary of China, are not behaving in explicitly balancing behavior. Vietnam and Korea must adjust to China,—that has always been the case and will always be the case. One implication of hierarchy is that balancing by equals is impossible. Both Vietnam and Korea have spent centuries adjusting to and resisting China's influence. Indeed, both Vietnam and Korea are known for their stubborn nationalism, gritty pride, and proud history as countries independent from China.[57] Yet at the same time, both Vietnam and Korea must deal with a China that looms large over their countries. From this perspective, it is probably more surprising if these two countries try to balance China by relying on a tenuous U.S. commitment. More reasonable is to adjust, get what you can from China, and not provoke China too much. China for its part realizes invading and holding either Vietnam or Korea would be extremely difficult, and thus hierarchy emerges.

In *Theory of International Politics*, Kenneth Waltz's key escape clause was to argue that "secondary states, *if they are free to choose*, flock to the weaker side."[58] Yet Waltz's implicit argument about alternative forms of organization does not provide us with any understanding of how or when such a situation might occur. In the case of Asia, Korea and Vietnam appear to face much higher costs in balancing China than other nations situated more geographically distant, and they appear to be preparing for a strong China on their borders.

While currently South and North Korea are locked in a zero-sum battle for dominance on the peninsula, there is an increasing possibility that unification could occur.[59] The alliances that a united Korea chooses could tilt the regional balance in any number of ways. A realist view would predict that China would pose the greatest threat to a unified Korea, and that a unified Korea would remain a staunch U.S. and Japanese ally to balance China's power. In contrast, the implication of hierarchy would be that unified Korea will accommodate and coexist with China, and that the U.S. might be the odd man out.

Japan and Korea seem to be natural allies. Both countries are capitalist economies, democracies, allied with the U.S., and they both share rapid economic growth and similar cultural characteristics. Korea and Japan countries would seem ideal as allies, especially put in opposition to a possibly dangerous China. But, as Victor Cha writes, "Throughout the cold war, the two states (Japan and Korea) have been staunch allies of the United States, and hosted the mainstay of the American military presence in East Asia. For most of the period concerned, the two states faced hostile adversaries in China, the Soviet Union, and North Korea. Given this commonalty in allies and enemies, basic balance-of-power dynamics suggest that cooperative relations should ensue. This has been far from the case."[60] Yet a Japan-U.S.-Korea alliance may be more tense, and more difficult to sustain, than we expect.

A unified Korea in a hierarchic world would not necessarily fear a strong China along its border. Instead it would find a way to accommodate and adjust to China. Japan and Korea, being more equal, would have a more difficult time adjusting to each other. There are clearly other factors at work, such as historical animosities between Japan and Korea, but these are also in part endogenous to the collapse of the hierarchic system 150 years ago.

As yet there is little direct evidence that would allow us to discern a hierarchic system on the peninsula, because the division of the peninsula still dominates both North and South Korean strategic considerations. However, there is some suggestive evidence that both Koreas understand China's central position in Asia. First, North Korea has consistently had better relations with China than with any of its other communist patrons. And even after China normalized ties with South Korea in 1991, North Korea and China have managed to have a close relationship. Second, South Korea gleefully rushed to normalize ties with China and the Soviet Union in 1991, and the South has not yet shown any indication that it has fears about the relationship with China. Third, South Korea has shown considerable deference to China, especially in its reluctance to fully support U.S. plans for theater missile defense.[61] Finally, South Korean military planning—even the distant planning for post-unification defense—has been focused on water-borne threats, not the potential threat of a Chinese land invasion.[62] South Korea has not begun to envision China as a potential threat or competitor to national security. This is surprising, given that China can actually invade Korea.

Like the Koreas, Vietnam is not showing any direct signs of being worried about a rising China. Vietnam, like the Koreas, has historically sat in the shadow of China. Although Vietnam and China have a long history of conflict, Vietnam is not currently arming, nor actively defending its border, against China.[63] The past three decades have seen conflict between the two nations: Vietnam fought a brief but sharp war with China in 1979, and then the two countries had a brief naval clash over the Spratley Islands in 1988. However, relations have since then steadily improved. By 1987, border incidents between Vietnam and China had mostly disappeared, and unofficial border trade began to develop.[64]

Full normalization of ties occurred in November 1991. Since then, trade and economic cooperation have developed steadily. By 1997, mutual trade totaled $1.44 billion, and China had invested an estimated total of $102 million in Vietnam.[65] Vietnam and China signed a tourism cooperation plan in April 1999, which allowed Chinese to enter Vietnam without a visa.[66] China also signed an economic-technical agreement with Vietnam in June 2000, which allowed for $55.254 million in upgrading the Thai Nguyen Steel Company and other industrial plants in Vietnam.[67] The indications are that Vietnam and China are developing a stable modus vivendi with each other.

Neither Vietnam nor Korea is obviously balancing China, nor does either country reveal particular concern at China's foreign policies. In fact, they both appear to be adjusting to the reality of a large and relatively rich China. While it is true these countries may have little choice in the matter, it is also true that both countries have options for alliances and defense planning that would be much more focused on deterring or balancing China.

CONCLUSION: U.S. FOREIGN POLICY TO ASIA

A hierarchic view of Asia leads to different predictions about the influence and impact of the U.S. in the region. A hierarchic view would predict that the Aisan states see China's central place in the regional system as inevitable, and have strategies for adjusting to China without provoking it. In addition, China will act within bounds that are acceptable to the other Asian nations. If this is the case, U.S. attempts to form a balancing coalition against China may be counterproductive to the U.S. If forced to choose between the U.S. and China, Asian nations may not make the choice westerners assume that they will. Indeed, recent indications show that South Korea is hesitant about embracing theater missile defense for fears of provoking China and in an attempt to resolve its own peninsular issues.

At the same time, the importance of the U.S. as the lid on the boiling mess of Asian arms-racing and competition may be overstated. If the U.S. pulls out, a hierarchic view would predict that China would take a greater role in organizing the system, and Vietnam, Japan, and Korea adjust, with order preserved. U.S. withdrawal is not nearly so destabilizing for Japan in a hierarchic system as in a realist world. Under this scenario the US might withdraw and Japan will not rearm, because it feels no threat from China. In this case China and Japan know each other's place in the system and respect it. Japanese restraint does not imply that Japan does not fear China. Although there is plenty of concern about China in Japan, hierarchy does not imply warm friendly relations between the powers.[68] Japan can be wary of China and still conduct its foreign policy in a manner that implicitly recognizes China's central position in Asia.

Historically, Chinese weakness has led to chaos in Asia. When China is strong and stable, order has been preserved. The picture of Asia that emerges is one in which China, by virtue of geography and power, is the central player in Asia. And as China's economy continues to develop, it is increasingly a major economic and financial power, as well. In response, Asian nations will adjust to China.

I have attempted in this essay to introduce a focus on hierarchy into the discussion of international relations. I am not arguing that the Asian order may reassert itself, nor am I arguing that an "oriental" way of thinking about the world is simply different from our western ways. My point is rather more cautious: even a slight hierarchic pattern to modern Asian international relations will have different implications for the region than many western scholars predict. There seems to be no *a priori* reason to think that merely because old multipolar Europe was conflictual, modern multipolar Asia must also be conflictual. Rather, since pre-modern Asia was relatively peaceful, perhaps modern Asia can evolve into a similarly peaceful pattern of international relations.

The hierarchic system in Asia is not unique, and is not necessarily cultural in nature. The hierarchy has, of course, Asian forms. But the general pattern of organization is structural, and there are a number of examples that show that this system is neither unique nor completely dated. U.S.-Latin American relations are hierarchic. In fact, many of the same rituals used in Asia appear in a modern

TABLE 4.1. Japan and Evidence of Great Power Status

1.	Modify the constitution	No
2.	nuclear weapons	No
3.	aircraft carriers	No
4.	power projection capabilities	No
5.	intercontinental missiles	No
6.	defense spending equivalent to other great powers	No
7.	procurement strategies	No
8.	attempts to influence the great game (seat on the UN security council, etc.)	No
9.	GDP	Yes
10.	Population	Yes
11.	Per capita GDP	Yes

context in the western hemisphere. The U.S. has generally left the Latin American countries on their own in terms of foreign relations, while explicitly reserving the right to interfere in the foreign relations of Latin American countries if it mattered to us (the Monroe doctrine). As long as foreign leaders come to Washington D.C. (kowtow) and utter the proper phrases (democracy and capitalism), they would reap great rewards from the U.S., and receive investiture (U.S. aid and protection.) However, failure to do so, or uttering certain wrong words meant extensive U.S. pressure, or even punitive expeditions (Haiti, Panama). The U.S. has no territorial goals with these countries, but it does reserve the right to maintain order in its sphere of influence and to punish those that do not explicitly and implicitly follow U.S. cultural guidelines.

More broadly, this essay has argued that hierarchy is compatible with anarchy; the actual contrast for hierarchy is equality. While the Westphalian system that emerged in Europe three centuries ago has spread over the globe, it is neither the only nor a permanent form of organization in international relations.

ACKNOWLEDGMENT

Thanks to Tom Bickford, Stephen Brooks, Victor Cha, Aaron Friedberg, Jim Hentz, Iain Johnston, C.S. Eliot Kang, Chaim Kaufmann, Jenny Lind, Mike Mastanduno, Roger Masters, Bradley Thayer, Alexander Wendt, William Wohlforth, and the participants in the Penn-Dartmouth Conference on the "Future of Asian International Relations" for their helpful comments, and to Dave Moran and Arlene Lim for their research assistance. Particular thanks to Peter Katzenstein for his comments. Earlier versions of this paper were presented at the East-West Center, Honolulu, Hawaii; The *International Political Science* Association, Seoul Korea; and Seoul National University.

ENDNOTES

1. Aaron Friedberg, "Ripe for Rivalry: Prospects for Peace in a Multipolar Asia," *International Security* 18, no. 3 (Winter 1993): 7. For other arguments that overstate the differences between Europe and Asia, see James Goldgeier and Michael McFaul, "A tale of two worlds: core and periphery in the post-cold war era," *International Organization* 46, no. 2 (Spring 1992): 467–491. Goldgeier and McFaul include Japan in the "core" and China in the "periphery." They note that territorial ambition is beyond the core but prevalent in the periphery. It seems that a "regional focus" rather than "core and periphery" would capture these dynamics equally well, with territorial ambition muted in Europe and northeast Asia, yet still potentially useful in other regions.

2. See, for example, Friedberg, "Ripe for Rivalry"; Richard K. Betts, "Wealth, Power, and Instability: East Asia and the United States after the Cold War," *International Security* 18, no. 3 (Winter 1993): 60; Barry Buzan and Gerald Segal, "Rethinking East Asian Security," *Survival* 36, no. 2 (Summer 1994): 3–21; James Goldgeier and Michael McFaul, "A tale of two worlds"; and Kenneth Waltz, "The Emerging Structure of International Politics," *International Security* 18 (Fall 1993): 56, 65. On the China threat, see Gerald Segal, "East Asia and the Constraintment of China," *International Security* 20, no. 4 (Spring 1996): 107–135; Denny Roy, "Hegemon on the Horizon? China's Threat to East Asian Security," *International Security* 19, no. 1 (Summer 1994): 149–168, at 164; and Nicholas D. Kristof, "The Rise of China," *Foreign Affairs* 72, no. 5 (November/December 1993). On Japan see Gerald Segal, "The Coming Confrontation Between China and Japan," *World Policy Journal* 10, no. 2 (Summer 1993); Herman Kahn, *The Emerging Japanese Superstate: Challenge and Response* (Englewood Cliffs, N.J.: Prentice-Hall, 1970); Chalmers Johnson, "Their Behavior, Our Policy," *The National Interest* 17 (Fall 1989); and Clyde Prestowitz, *Trading Places* (New York: Basic Books, 1989). Some of the more frantic concerns over Japan can be found in George Friedman and Meredith Lebard, *The Coming War with Japan* (New York: St. Martin's Press, 1991). For counterarguments, see Thomas U. Berger, "From Sword to Chrysanthemum: Japan's Culture of Anti-Militarism," *International Security* 17 (Spring 1993); and Peter Katzenstein and Nobuo Okawara, "Japan's National Security: structures, norms, and policies," *International Security* 17 (Spring 1993).

3. The classic statement is John Fairbank, ed., *The Chinese World Order* (Cambridge: Harvard University Press, 1968).

4. The best work is by Ian Johnston, *Cultural Realism* (Princeton: Princeton University Press, 1994), although he concentrates exclusively on China and examines neither the Asian region nor the present. See also Victor Cha's discussion in "Defining Security in East Asia: History, Hotspots, and Horizon-gazing," in Eunmee Kim ed., *The Four Asian Tigers: Economic Development and the Global Political Economy* (San Diego: Academic Press, 1998).

5. Kenneth Waltz, *Theory of International Politics* (Reading, MA: Addison-Wesley, 1979), pp. 114–116. The "British school" has been most active in exploring alternative forms of organization . See Evan Luard, *Conflict and Peace in the Modern International System: A Study of the Principles of International Order* (Albany: State University of New York Press, 1988); Adam Watson, *The Evolution of International Society: A*

Comparative Historical Analysis (London : Routledge, 1992); and Barry Buzan, "The Idea of 'International System': Theory Meets History," *International Political Science Review* 15 (July 1994): 231–255.

6. See Christopher Layne, "The Unipolar Illusion: why new great powers will arise," *International Security* 17 (Spring 1993); Charles Krauthammer, "The Unipolar Moment," *Foreign Affairs* 70, no. 1 (Winter 1990/1991): 23–33; and Michael Mastanduno, "Preserving the Unipolar Moment: Realist Theories and U.S. Grand Strategy After the Cold War," *International Security* 21, no. 4 (Spring 1997): 44–98.

7. Layne, "The Unipolar Illusion," p. 7.

8. Stuart Kaufman, "The Fragmentation and Consolidation of International Systems," *International Organization* 51 (Spring 1997): 179.

9. In addition to Waltz, also see John Mearsheimer, "Back to the Future," *International Security* (Spring 1990); and Stephen Walt, *The Origin of Alliances* (Ithaca: Cornell University Press, 1987)

10. See David Lake, "Anarchy, hierarchy, and the variety of international relations," *International Organization* 50, no. 1 (Winter 1996):1–34, Jack Snyder, *Myths of Empire: Domestic politics and international ambition* (Ithaca: Cornell Univeresity Press, 1991); James D. Morrow, "Arms Versus Allies: Trade-offs in the search for security," *International Organization* 47 (1993):207–33; and Michael Doyle, *Empires* (Ithaca: Cornell University Press, 1986).

11. Lake, "Anarchy, Hierarchy, and the Variety of International Relations," p. 7.

12. For arguments compatible with this, see William Wohlforth, "The Stability of a Unipolar World," *International Security* 24, no. 1 (Summer 1999): 5–41; and Katja Weber, "Hierarchy Amidst Anarchy: A Transaction Costs Approach To International Security Cooperation," *International Studies Quarterly* 41 (June 1997): 321–40.

13. Michael Doyle, *Empires* (Ithaca, NY: Cornell University Press, 1986), p. 38.

14. Alexander Wendt and Daniel Friedheim, "Hierarchy Under Anarchy: Informal Empire and the East German State," *International Organization* 49, no. 4 (Autumn 1995): 689–721.

15. Wendt and Friedheim write that "As objects of control, foreign and security policy are almost always regulated from the center . . . another institutional expression [of informal empire] is found in interorganizational linkages." "Hierarchy under anarchy," p. 697.

16. On balancing, see Kenneth Waltz, *Theory of International Politics* (Redding, MA: Addison-Wesley, 1979); Stephen M. Walt, *The Origins of Alliances* (Ithaca: Cornell University Press, 1987); and Eric Labs, "Do Weak States Bandwagon?" *Security Studies* 1, no. 3 (Spring 1992): 409.

17. Randall Schweller, "Bandwagoning for Profit: Bringing the Revisionist State Back In," *International Security* 19, no. 1 (Summer 1994): 72–107.

18. See, for example, James Fearon, "Signaling Foreign Policy Interests: Tying Hands Versus Sinking Costs," *The Journal of Conflict Resolution* 41 (February 1997): 68–90.

19. A.F.K. Organski, *World Politics* (New York: Alfred Knopf, 1958): 315–361.

20. Douglas Lemke and Suzanne Werner, "Power Parity, Commitment to Change, and War," *International Studies Quarterly* 40 (1996): 235–260.

21. See Jeremiah Curtin, *The Mongols: a History* (Westport, CT: Greenwood Press, 1972).

22. Stuart Kaufman, "The Fragmentation and Consolidation of International Systems," *International Organization* 51, no. 2 (Spring 1997): 176.

23. There was conflict in Asia. Often the Chinese fought border wars with the Mongols to the north. However, this was not interstate conflict, and the nomads were considered peripheral to the Asian state system. For more on this period, see Hans J. Van de Ven, "War and the Making of Modern China," *Modern Asian Studies* 30, no. 4 (October 1996): 737; Luc Kwanten, *Imperial Nomads* (Philadelphia: Univeresity of Pennsylvania Press, 1979), and Paul K. Davis, *Encyclopedia of Invasions and Conquests: from Ancient Times to the Present* (Santa Barbara: ABC-CLIO, 1996).

24. Tashiro Kazui, "Foreign Relations During the Edo Period: *Sakoku* Reexamined," *Journal of Japanese Studies* 8, no. 2 (1982): 286.

25. Kazui, "Foreign Relations During the Edo Period," p. 286.

27. Kim, *The Last Phase of the East Asian World Order*, p. 21, 23.

28. Kazui, "Foreign Relations During the Edo Period," pp. 283–306.

29. Kim, *The Last Phase of the East Asian World Order*, p. 10.

30. John Lee, "Trade and Economy in Preindustrial East Asia, c. 1500–1800: East Asia in the Age of Global Integration," *Journal of Asian Studies* 58, no. 1 (February 1999): 7.

31. Dennis O. Flynn and Arturo Giraldez, "Born with a "Silver Spoon": The Origin of World Trade in 1571," *Journal of World History* 6, no. 2 (1995): 202.

32. Lee, "Trade and Economy in Preindustrial East Asia," p. 14.

33. Gang Deng, "The Foreign Staple Trade of China in the Pre-Modern Era," *International History Review* 19, no. 2 (May 1997): 254.

34. Deng, "The Foreign Staple Trade of China in the Pre-Modern Era," pp. 253–285. See also C. I. Beckwith, "The Immpact of the Horse and Silk Trade on the Economies of T'ang China and the Uighur Empire," *Journal of the Economic and Social History of the Orient* 34 (1991): 183–98.

35. On the nascent nation states of Asia, see Keith Taylor, *The Birth of Vietnam* (Berkeley: University of California Press, 1983); and G. Coedes, *The Making of Southeast Asia* trans. H.M. Wright (Berkeley: University of California Press, 1969).

36. See, for example, Peter Katzenstein, *Cultural Norms and National Security: Police and Military in Postwar Japan* (Ithaca, N.Y.: Cornell University Press, 1996); Thomas U. Berger, "From Sword to Chrysanthemum: Japan's Culture of Anti-Militarism," *International Security* 17 (Spring 1993); Eric Heginbotham, "Mercantile Realism and Japanese Foreign Policy," *International Security* 22, no. 4 (Spring 1998) p. 171–203.

37. On great powers, see for example, Waltz, "The Emerging Structure of International Politics," *International Security* 18 (Fall 1993): 56, 65; Betts, "Wealth, Power, and Instability," p. 55; and Michael Desch, "Correspondence," *International Security* 24, no. 1 (Summer 1999): 176. On the U.S. security umbrella, see Betts, "Wealth, Power, and Instability," p. 56; and Friedberg, "Ripe for Rivalry," p. 25.

38. Desch, "Correspondence," p. 177.

39. Christopher Layne, "The Unipolar Illusion: Why New Great Powers Will Rise," *International Security* 17 (Spring 1993): 5–51.

40. Robert Jervis, "Cooperation under the Security Dilemma," *World Politics* (1978): 105.

41. For discussion on this point, see Michael O'Hanlon, "Why China Cannot Conquer Taiwan," *International Security* 25, no. 2 (Fall 2000).

42. See, for example, Richard Bernstein and Ross H. Munro, *The Coming Conflict with China* (New York: Alfred A. Knopf, 1997); and Nicholas D. Kristof, "The Rise of China," *Foreign Affairs* 72, no. 5 (November/December 1993).

43. Christopher Hughes, *Taiwan and Chinese Nationalism: National Identity and Status in International Society* (New York: Routledge, 1997).

44. Jonathan Spence, *The Search for Modern China* (New York: Norton, 1991), p. 50; and John Copper, *Taiwan: Nation-State or Province?* (Boulder, CO: Westview Press, 1990).

45. Copper, *Taiwan*, p. 21.

46. Hughes, *Taiwan and Chinese Nationalism;* and Michael Yahuda, "The International Standing of the Republic of China on Taiwan," *China Quarterly* 148 (December 1996): 1319–39.

47. Quoted in Susan Lawrence, "Yearning to Lead," *Far Eastern Economic Review* September 16, 1999, p. 19.

48. See Thomas Christensen, "China, the U.S.-Japan Alliance, and the Security Dilemma in East Asia," *International Security* 23, no. 4 (Spring 1999):49–80.

49. Michel Oksenberg, "Soveriegnty," in Stephen Krasner, ed., *Sovereignty* (forthcoming).

50. On Chinese-Taiwan relations, see Gary Klintworth, *New Taiwan, New China: Taiwan's Changing Role in the Asia-Pacific Region* (New York : St. Martin's Press, 1995).

51. Taifa Yu, "Relations between Taiwan and China after the Missile Crisis: toward Reconciliation?" *Pacific Affairs* 72, no. 1 (Spring 1999): 39–55.

52. See Shelley Rigger, "Competing Conceptions of Taiwan's Identity," in Suisheng Zhao, ed., *Across the Taiwan Strait: Mainland China, Taiwan, and the 1995–1996 Crisis* (New York: Routledge, 1997).

53. For a good overview of China's recent grand strategy, Avery Goldstein, "Great Expectations: Interpreting China's Arrival," *International Security* 22, no. 3 (Winter 1997–98): 36–73.

54. Hsin-hsing Wu, *Bridging the Strait: Taiwan, China, and the Prospects for Reunification* (Oxford: Oxford University Press, 1994).

55. Tun-Jen Cheng, "Political Regimes and Development Strategies: South Korea and Taiwan," in Gary Gereffi and Donald Wyman, eds., *Manufacturing Miracles: Paths of Industrialization in Latin America and East Asia* (Princeton: Princeton University Press, 1990): 139–178.

56. Hung-mao Tien, "Building democracy in Taiwan," *The China Quarterly* 148 (December 1996): 1141–70.

57. See Stanley Karnow, *Vietnam: A History* (New York: Penguin Books, 1997).

58. Waltz, *Theory of International Politics* (Reading, MA: Addison-Wesley, 1979), p. 127 (emphasis added).

59. For optimists, see Thomas H. Henriksen and Kyongsoo Lho, eds., *One Korea?: Challenges and Prospects for Reunification* (Stanford: Hoover Institution Press, 1994);

and Nicholas Eberstadt, *Korea Approaches Reunification* (Armonk, NY: M.E. Sharpe, 1995). For pessimists, see Marcus Noland, "Why North Korea will muddle through," *Foreign Affairs* 76 (July/August 1997): 105–118.

60. Victor D. Cha, "Alignment Despite Antagonism: Japan and Korea as Quasi-allies," (Georgetown University, unpublished manuscript): 4.

61. See Victor Cha, "TMD and Nuclear Weapons in Asia," paper presented at the conference "Asian Security in Asia," East-West Center, Honolulu, Hawaii, October 21, 1999.

62. For discussion of the normalization of ties, see Dan Sanford, *South Korea and the Socialist Countries : The Politics of Trade* (New York : St. Martin's Press, 1990). On military planning, see Ministry of Foreign Affairs, *Waygyo Baekso (Foreign Policy White Paper)* (Seoul, MFA, 1999).

63. For a review, see Cecil B. Currey, "Vietnam: Foreign and Domestic Policies," *Journal of Third World Studies* 16, no. 2 (Fall 1999) p. 197–198; and Cheng Guan Ang, "Vietnam-China relations since the end of the cold war," *Asian Survey* 38, no. 12 (December 1998): 1122–1141.

64. Carlyle Thayer, "Vietnam: Coping with China," *Southeast Asian Affairs 1994* (Singapore: Institute of Southeast Asian Studies, 1995), p. 353.

65. Gu Xiaosong and Brantly Womack, "Border Cooperation Between China and Vietnam in the 1990s," *Asian Survey* 40, no. 6 (November/December 2000): 1045.

66. Tuyet Minh, "The Chinese are Coming," *Vietnam Economic News*, no. 33 (2000): 24.

67. *Business Vietnam*, vol. 12, no. 6 (2000): 4.

68. The 1997 Japanese Defense White Paper noted with concern China's rising defense expenditures.

Chapter 5

AMBIGUOUS JAPAN: JAPANESE NATIONAL IDENTITY AT CENTURY'S END

Masaru Tamamoto

What follows is not the typical international relations theory paper. While it expresses a way of thinking about Japanese political culture, a set of ideas about how to describe and analyze Japanese behavior toward the outside world, it does so with little explicit effort toward theorizing and generalizing. It is written in a manner more typical of historians and anthropologists than of political scientists. The essay is a "thick description" of the salient features of Japanese political culture which construct the nation's particularities; this emphasis on cultural difference fits somewhat uncomfortably with the dominant impulse of American political science (which claims international relations as its sub-field) to equate scholarship with general theory. Elsewhere in this volume, Thomas Berger presents a more political science approach to Japanese culture and identity and their effects on Japanese international behavior. I leave to the reader the task of determining the pros and cons of the differing approaches.

My essay on culture and identity is sandwiched in this volume of works by political scientists. This situation requires explication for, until recently, culture and identity have been suspect issues in political science. As a general statement, culture and identity matter in the study of international relations. But it is another matter to try to generalize about culture and identity. In the dominant manner of international relations analysis—of the Decartes-Newton mode of thought, of positivism, of scientific theorizing—the impulse is to break down the object of investigation into its components. But culture and identity, by their nature, make sense only as wholes. When one breaks down what constitutes culture and identity into their components, there is little meaning, for it is not the components but the complex relations between them that matter. Culture and identity are organic wholes and seamless webs. The task of scientific theorizing is to achieve simplicity and clarity, and by them, to make general statements. It is problematic to apply this manner of investigation to culture and identity, which are complex and ambiguous; the idea of counting and measuring cultural identity seems improbable. This is why I find the essay form a compelling conduit for analyzing culture and identity.

Political scientists tend to regard the essay form with suspicion for its lack of scientific rigor. Furthermore, they deem thick descriptions to be wanting in scholarly value. Country and area specialists (apart from the Americans who come under different demands) in political science departments are put increasingly on the defensive, forced to justify their academic appointment and tenure by cloaking their work with general theory thereby acquiring scholarly garb and disciplinary legitimacy. Scientific theorizing and generalizing have their merits, yet there also lies the danger of forcing America's parochial values into the investigation of foreign cultures. Rational choice, for example, is a popular and dominant scholarly methodology in the American discipline of political science. Often, so strong is the impulse to generalize that rational choice theorists fail to consider that different cultures harbor different notions of what is rational, that different cultures have different utility curves.

Historians and anthropologists have known the richness of cultural differences, that identities matter in the behavior of nation states and of men. Cultures are possibilities of differences, and they are differences of possibilities. Belatedly, students of international relations are discovering culture and identity in a new way. The conference, which led to the making of this volume, positing that there are distinct international relations in the Asia-Pacific region, is part of the discovery. In another example, the political scientist Yosef Lapid writes, "(T)he global eruption of separatist nationalism set in motion by the abrupt ending of the cold war has directly and inescapably forced the (international relations) scholarly community to rethink the theoretical status of culture and identity in world affairs."[1] Students of international relations are now paying attention to culture and identity making.

The historian David Landes contrasts how the nature of Muslim and European imperialism differed. He contends that Muslim expansion was motivated primarily by their conviction in god and history. This made the Muslim rush more uncompromising and insatiable. Souls mattered to the Europeans, but rarely did souls count enough to get in the way of profit and loss. European motivation, Landes is convinced, was sustainable profit. So, when colonial resistance and the cost of staying rose, they left. Among the Europeans, the

Catholics held greater conviction in God than the Protestants, and that made for differences in behavior, say, between the Portuguese and Dutch. Between the British and French empires, there was a distinct difference in the pride quotient. The British were quick to leave India when the cost of empire rose, while the French lingered in Vietnam and Algeria, suffering increasing costs, driven by greater pride.[2]

Thus, culture and identity have been salient and obvious factors shaping the history of international relations. Then why did the discipline of international relations tend to underplay the relevance of culture and identity? And why is it that the end of the cold war steers the discipline to (re)consider culture and identity? The answers lie in international relations as sociology of knowledge.

I take the discipline of international relations, dominated by discussions of realism and liberalism and their variants, to be, in large measure, a post-1945 American discipline. In this sense, the discipline can be understood as an expression of American culture and identity, expressing particular cultural sensitivities. The discipline tended to separate the realms of the domestic and international, working on the assumption that international relations and foreign policy were somehow distinct from domestic politics, thereby allowing the analyst to underplay cultural and identity issues. With the end of the cold war the mainstream in the discipline came to "discover" there are domestic constraints to foreign policy. This discovery of the obvious—to those whose thinking had not been constrained by socialization into the discipline—revealed the discipline's surprising innocence as it had been constructed in the cold war context.

I posit that underlying the construction of the international relations discipline was fear (though most practitioners of the discipline were not cognizant). The Cuban missile crisis, bringing the world to the brink of nuclear holocaust, accelerated the discipline's tendency toward positivism and scientific theorizing, toward the pretension of value-free analysis, and toward the separation of the international from the domestic. As justification or criticism, the discipline's primary impetus had been how to account for the cold war, for American-Soviet rivalry, for the nuclear predicament, for the world of mutually assured destruction, for America's complicity in the possible end of humanity. Separating the realms of the domestic and international, and the guise of positivism offered the discipline two coveted assurances and an escape from fear. (It should be noted that while American academics tended to separate domestic and international politics, American policymakers really did not. For American officials, Soviet foreign policy was always a function of Soviet domestic politics—the Soviet Union was not simply viewed as another great power, but as a distinctively ideological power.)

First, if one assumed that culture and identity did not matter, this precluded the usefulness of American policy to alter the Soviet domestic order. That is, irrespective of the nature of Soviet culture and identity, interstate rivalry between the two super powers would persist. The temptation to orchestrate a concerted effort to change the Soviet Union was much too risky given the nuclear predicament. Its failure could have resulted in the end of humanity. Thucydides became an icon of proof of the permanency of interstate rivalry, of the validity of realist assumptions since time immemorial; therefore of the continuation of the cold war thus human survival. (The discipline's reading of Thucydides tended to focus on the nature of competition between Athens and Sparta, and less on the termination of the Peloponnesian War.) There was no serious thinking in the discipline of international relations about how to end the cold war or, more passively, because the norms of international relations were often thought to be beyond American or any other actors' will and design how it might come to an end. The concern was balance and stability of terror. So the fall of the Soviet Union took the discipline by surprise.

Second, the separation of the domestic and international realms helped preserve the sense of American innocence; of its sense of democratic virtue meanwhile being complicit in the threat of destruction of humanity. The separation allowed America, in the main, to avoid the question: If American society is so virtuous, how can it partake in the construction of an international world so maddening? American thinking to underplay the fact that the separation also allowed cold war was, in collusion with the Soviet Union, of American making, as if America was merely reacting to a set of "objective" conditions in international relations. As an outside observer of American culture and identity, I have been struck by the generally veiled manner with which America understands its imperial hegemonic place in international affairs, its role as maker of international rules.

Now the end of the cold war has freed the discipline of American international relations to ponder the meaning of culture and identity. But it remains in an awkward state. One recent and representative effort is *The Culture of National Security*, a collection of essays, which argues that security interests are defined by actors who respond to cultural factors, and asking, for one, why the Soviet Union considered it to be in its interest to withdraw from Eastern Europe. The editor Peter Katzenstein defines culture and identity in the book's introduction thus, and I quote in full:

> The essays refer to *identity* as a shorthand label for varying construction of nation and statehood. The process of construction typically is explicitly political and pits conflicting actors against each other. In invoking the concept of identity the authors depict varying national ideologies of collective distinctiveness and purpose. And they refer to variations across countries in the statehood that is enacted domestically and projected internationally.

> The authors in the volume invoke the term *culture* as a broad label that denotes the collective models of nation-state authority or identity, carried by custom or law. Culture refers to both a set of evaluative standards (such as norms and values) and a set of cognitive standards (such as rules and models) that define what social actors exist in a system, how they operate, and how they relate to one another.[3]

I find these definitions not helpful. They are all encompassing and, in themselves, tell us nothing about the substance of particular cultures and identities. What is required and, that is what the many chapters in the Katzenstien volume do, is to offer thick descriptions of the cultures and identities in question.

"Ambiguous Japan," the title of the essay is taken from the Nobel laureate Kenzaburo Oe's speech delivered in Stockholm. The title seems to give the false impression to many that I am arguing that Japan is without identity. Japan certainly has identity. But it is ambiguous. This ambiguity comes mainly from Japan's singular success at Westernization and modernization among the non-Western nations. (Of course, modernization is in itself an ambiguous notion.) Other non-Western nations have their ambiguities, but theirs are different in that their ambiguities are often expressions of either continuing or failing struggles to cope with the question of modernity. In contrast, Japan's ambiguity comes from success recently arrived at. In short time, the Japanese should come to be able to accept the nation's place in the world and shed the kind of ambiguity that comes from the idealized imagining division of the world into the West and other, into the modern and not. Japanese national identity is now framed primarily as a member of the G-7, and this categorization allows Japan to free itself from a sense of separation from the West, from the modern, and allows Japan to assume a place in the club of wealthy and democratic nations.

An ambiguous identity is not a monopoly of the non-West. Is Japanese identity more ambiguous than, say, the United States? In the post-1945 context, Japanese identity is more ambiguous because of the compromised state of sovereignty and independence, which stems from Japan's security relationship with the United States. Post-1945 Japanese sovereignty has been divisible and its independence limited. These are symbolized by the continuing presence of the American military on Japanese soil after the formal conclusion of the post-Second World War military occupation. Japan has willfully accepted this status and, under cover of the American security guarantee, continued to cherish its politically isolationist pacifism. Japan's ambiguity comes from the contradiction between its pacifism—symbolized by the "anti-or post-Westphalia" peace constitution which forever renounces the use or threat of use of force to settle international disputes—and the American use of violent means explicitly renounced by the Japanese constitution to provide for Japan's security.

Post-1945 United States, mindful of the lessons of Munich and Pearl Harbor, posed to guard its peace through strength, through enhanced military preparedness as witnessed by the arms race with the Soviet Union. In contrast, Japan after 1945 fell into a psychology similar to what the United States and Europe embraced following the First World War. Like the United States after Versailles, Japan after Hiroshima sought to distance itself from international politics. Like Europe after Versailles, which sought to guard its peace by goodwill as symbolized by the signing of treaties banning war, note the Kellogg-Briand Pact; Japan after the Second World War has hoped to guard its peace by minimum military preparedness and "by trusting in the peace loving peoples of the world" as dictated in the constitutional preamble. It is the juxtaposition between the divergent American and Japanese lessons of the Second World War, and Japan's dependence on the United States as the final guarantor of its security which help make Japanese identity ambiguous. In essence, Japan has had neither will nor interest to actively identify the country's place by its brand of pacifism. It has been pacifism in one country, obscured from the rest of the world, made more visible by American military protection. This veiled pacifism has done little to dispel the universal suspicion of the possibility of resurgent Japanese militarism.

To the extent that the nation's place in and relationship with the international world, pre-1945 imperial Japan, with its more proactive and expansionist foreign policy shape national identity, possessed a much less ambiguous identity. Japan after 1945, in contrast, has been timid in the international political arena and its foreign policy more reactive, thereby leading to a greater sense of ambiguity. Thus, the air and pretension and will to supremacy help lull ambiguity. The United States possesses this sense of supremacy; therefore it is free of the kind of ambiguity that marks Japan. Japan, as argued above, is quite comfortable in the relationship with the United States reigning supreme. Japan deeply cherishes its pacifism. Ever mindful of America's role in guaranteeing that pacifism, it is hard to imagine the contrasts in Japanese and American cultures leading to conflict in the foreseeable future. I contend, contrary to Robert Gilpin's argument found elsewhere in this volume, that, at each turn, as has been the pattern during the past half century, the Japanese government will continue to bend to avert any serious conflict with the United States. The single, most important source of contemporary Japanese national identity is its relationship with the United States. A radical revision of the constitution or even the abolition of the imperial house will not have as much impact on Japanese national identity as will the abrogation, under dire circumstance, of the U.S-Japan security treaty.

Ambiguous Japan's relationship with Asia has been markedly problematic. It has to do with the enduring uneasiness stemming from Japanese imperial aggression. It has to do with Japan's historical inability to regard other Asian nations as equals. And, more recently, it has to do with Japan's distaste for the Chinese will to supremacy. China and the United States, two most influential countries affecting Japan's place in the world, are driven by a similar will to supremacy. Japan lives comfortably with the American one but is reluctant to acknowledge the Chinese claim. The more China asserts its claim, the more Japan will be driven toward the United States to foil and counter. While, elsewhere in this volume, David Kang argues that a central system, with China at the center, is rising in East Asia, I would contend that, for Japan as well as South Korea, there is already a central system in place with the United States at the center, and that the American centered system will strengthen in proportion to any, especially political and military Chinese claim to supremacy.

To understand any culture and its identity, one must be immersed in its life. Its interpreter must experience a long period of socialization. One must have distance, to figuratively step outside of the cultural realm to be able to recognize and define its identity. It is in the comparison with others, through the ability to identify differences, that definitions of cultures and identities can be made meaningful. A person who knows only one culture has a difficult task trying to identify that culture's identity. As cultures have different pride quotients, they also have different tolerances for ambiguity. What follows is an essay on Japanese ambiguity, about the kind of cultural ambiguity for which America would have little tolerance.

I. REQUIEM FOR JAPANESE THOUGHT

"I live as a novelist marked by the deep wounds of Japan's ambiguity"[4] Kenzaburo Oe told the Swedish Academy in accepting the 1994 Nobel Prize in literature. He depicted how Japan's ambiguity casts a dark shadow over the country's achievements in modernity, and how it traps the intellectual class, a trap from which no modern Japanese intellectual has been able to escape.

This ambiguity, Oe explained, began in the late nineteenth century, when Japan opened itself to the international world, bringing—to an end more than two centuries of seclusion, and embarked on a frenzied path of modernization. To this day, even after Japan's arrival at modernity, this ambiguity wields tremendous power and continues to tear apart the country and its people. In the international realm, Oe fears, Japan's ambiguity means isolation and the inability to relate to the rest of the world.

Japan's modernization posited the West as model, but Japan is situated in Asia, and the Japanese have sought to preserve their traditional culture. On the one hand, this ambiguous path pushed the country and its people into the role of aggressors in Asia. On the other hand, Japanese culture, which is supposed to have become completely open toward the West, remains obscure, if not incomprehensible, to the West. Furthermore, this ambiguity has led to Japan's political, social and cultural isolation in Asia.[5]

In this way, Oe iterated an enduring theme in the history of modern Japanese thought (*Nihon shiso-shi*), which saw its beginning with the country's opening to the world. The primary goal of Japanese thought has been to establish a national identity in an alien world. Torn between the idealized poles of the West and Asia, the Japanese intellectual search for identity has been an elusive affair. Because the search has been framed between two imagined extremes, there is no way to reconcile the two; thus any definition of Japan can only be a paradox. While this sort of dualism has been a common feature of non-Western political thought in the modern era, peculiar is the lack of a structured ideology of native authenticity in Japanese thought. In the Islamic world, in contrast, the glory and purity of the prophet Muhammad stand as the source of native authenticity; for the Muslims, history since Muhammad is understood to be a history of decline, and the idea of recovering a glorious and pure past becomes an important source of selfhood. In Albert Hourani's depiction, "With the full articulation of the message of Muhammad in a universal community obedient to divine command, what was significant in history came to an end."[6] In this sense, there is in Japan an absence of selfhood; there is no past to recover, no tradition to conserve. The modern creation of the emperor myth in the late nineteenth century was an attempt at establishing authenticity, but the very amorphousness of the imperial institution then and now attests to the difficulty of fabricating a tradition to preserve the Japanese self in the quest for modernity. Note that the dominant counter to the West in Japanese thought is not Japan but Asia, a concept, which begs satisfactory definition. Japan, to borrow the imagery of Roland Barthes, is an "empty center."[7]

In 1935, in the midst of Japan's rebellion against the Western international order, when the country ostensibly stood united behind the banner of emperor, philosopher Tetsuro Watsuji, astutely and defiantly observed, everybody knows what the Japanese spirit (*Nihon seishin*) is, but once you question it, you begin to realize that nobody knows what it is.[8] Who are the Japanese? asks and answers social critic Shuichi Kato in a 1957 essay: The Japanese are a people who continuously and tirelessly ask who are the Japanese?[9] Watsuji and Kato were two of the leading thinkers of twentieth-century Japan. Conservative Watsuji spanned the pre-1945 imperial order and the postwar democratic transformation, and liberal Kato has been a champion of postwar democracy. While their political orientations differ, both must agree on the amorphousness of Japanese national identity, for that is the essential quality of modern Japanese thought of which they are part.

To become modern with the West as model has been the core sentiment of Japanese thought. Every piece of thought on national identity, profound and trivial, has had to be a comparison between Japan and the West. Even the urge to reject the West and to establish Japan's distinctiveness necessarily has been framed in terms of the confrontation with the West. Therefore, contribution to

Japanese thought demanded knowledge of Western thought, even if distorted and cursory. Japanese thought generally has been articulated in categories, which are assumed to be intelligible to Western thought. Thinking about national identity, thus, becomes the reification of a Western audience. In this way, Japanese thought has been the "work of translators."[10]

The tragedy for Japanese thought so obsessed with Western thought is that, while Japan looked toward the West, the West cared little about Japan. This is one central reason for the ambiguity of Japanese thought. Given the manner with which Japanese thought addresses a reified Western audience, true legitimacy can be conferred only through recognition by Western thought. Japanese thinkers have been unable to find their images in the eyes of the West. Cultural distance and language barrier are two obvious reasons. But the real problem lay with the essence of Japanese thought: Why would Western thought be interested in investigating "translations" of itself? What universal significance, applicable beyond Japan's narrow concerns, can there be in "translations" which cannot be found in the original?

Oe struggles to break out of the mold of the "translator" and to reach out to the world. He belongs to the category of Japanese writers whom he describes as those who learned from world literature, then created Japanese literature and, if possible, yearn to offer feedback to world literature. As to what is meant by world literature, he identifies French, German, English, and Russian literatures; the "world" in characteristically Japanese fashion emphasizes the West.[11] Oe seeks a sense of totality with the world and universality for Japanese literature and for Japan. Only then can Japan's ambiguity be shed. He is, of course, not so naive as to imagine the transformation of Japan into a part of the West or any other. He notes, Americans and Indians and other peoples have religions which give them the sense of transcendence, and that gives rise to visions of world order in America and to the Gandhi creed in India, but the Japanese who lack religious commitment are bound by the practicalities of reality. He stresses, "I do not have a religion, and I wish to die without being caught by one."[12] What he wants is the ability to relate to the world, and he abhors the Japanese tendency toward nihilism.

Oe's Nobel prize speech, "Japan, the Ambiguous, and Myself," was a deliberate attack on the other Japanese Nobel laureate in literature, Yasunari Kawabata. In 1968, Kawabata, dressed in kimono, spoke in Japanese at the Swedish Academy on "Japan, the Beautiful, and Myself," displaying his personal brand of mysticism, quoting lines from a medieval Zen monk. For his turn, Oe, speaking in English, derided Kawabata's nihilism, pointing out that the Zen poem Kawabata quoted sings of the beauty of the impossibility of representing truth with words. Rejecting this kind of parochialism, Oe identified himself with the humanism of William Yeats, William Blake, W. H. Auden, George Orwell, Milan Kundera, and others, stressing decency, innocence and sanity as desirable values of humanity. This identification was not made as an equal; Oe concluded by depicting himself as a writer from the world's periphery.

Oe's speech would have made a suitable entry in a recent book by Hiroshi Minami, Japan's leading social psychologist. It is a masterful compilation of and commentary on Japanese thinkers on national identity since the mid-nineteenth century.

Minami concludes that one constant in Japan's psychology and national character throughout the turbulent modern experience is uncertainty of the self: The Japanese people lack self-assertiveness and are imbued with the spirit of submissiveness, making them fearful of power yet prone to authoritarian behavior; these characteristics manifest themselves in Japan's particular emperor system and sycophancy, including the admiration of the West.[13] There is no future for Japan by strengthening its national egoism (read the emperor system), argues one of the last entries in Minami's study. It is an argument made in 1991 by a Japanese Christian who posits that the Christian spirit respects human rights and is the necessary antidote to Japan's national egoism.[14] As those familiar with Japanese intellectual history will recognize, it is the kind of argument which could have appeared anywhere in the chronology of modern Japanese thought, the kind of argument which contrasts a "superior" Western idea to an "inferior" Japanese quality, prodding Japan to alter its inadequacy. In a sense, the dominantly self-critical mode of Japanese thought, whose self-criticism rose to elevated heights after the disaster of the Second World War, has served as tonic for national self-improvement and encouraged Japan's achievements in modernity. At the same time, by its incessant revelation of Japan's inadequacies and suspicion of native qualities, Japanese thought, whose task ostensibly is to establish a national identity, has helped perpetuate its ambiguity.

Today, there is great discrepancy between Japan's intellectual ambiguity, on the one hand, and its social achievements and economic power in the world, on the other. There grows a gulf between Japanese thought and the assumptions of society. At the twentieth century's end, Oe's depiction of Japan as the world's periphery struck many Japanese as a curious utterance. Society no longer recognizes the West as model; the one constant in the turbulent history of modernizing Japan had been the assumption that the world would continue to provide models from which it could pick and choose. Now, Japan has arrived at modernity. The West has begun to look toward Japanese thought and literature as well as management and manufacturing techniques. Even Oe admits that Japanese writers are no longer isolated; this admission came naturally after his receipt of the Nobel Prize. When in 1968 Kawabata became the first Japanese recipient of the Nobel Prize in literature, Japan still mindful of Western recognition stood jubilant; it was a moment of national celebration and honor. By 1994, Japan was no longer needy of such national recognition; Oe's honor was more personal and less national. In this can be read the final chapter of Japanese thought as it had been constituted for 120 years.

II. MODERNITY AS TECHNIQUE OVER REASON

"Enlightenment is man's emergence from his self-imposed immaturity. Immaturity is the inability to use one's understanding without guidance from another. This immaturity is self-imposed when its cause lies not in lack of understanding, but in lack of resolve and courage to use it without guidance from another."[15] Thus Immanuel Kant defined Enlightenment in a 1784 essay. The modern West has been framed by the Enlightenment project. Its modernity has been propelled by efforts to implement ideas about progress and reason, and characterized by universalizing and rationalizing impulses. While, with the passage of time, reason tended to disappear into technique in the West, in Japan, modernity has always been about technique.

The pursuit of modernity for Japan, a non-Western latecomer to the concept, has involved, above all, a concern with the nation's status in an alien world. The purpose of technique has been to elevate Japan in world history by generally accepting the universalizing claim of the West and to find the meaning of Japan by imagining an actual context of modernity. By dissociating culture from modernity, non-Western Japan could hope to become modern, that is, to parallel the achievements of the West but not to be of the West.

This Japan is often described by outside observers as goal-oriented, but the nature of Japanese goals is fundamentally incompatible with the transcendent nature of Western Enlightenment. Japanese goals are immediate and defined by particular historical situations. The Japanese are a people who ask "how" and not why. To question why is anti-social and often creates embarrassing situations. *Rikutsu* is one Japanese word for reason; when used to describe a person, it means argumentative, not reasonable. To speak of truths and principles is frowned upon and little understood; at best, it is tolerated as the whim of ivory tower intellectuals. There are always those who wish to inject higher ideals into what they see as a world of compromises. But the essence of society in Japan is compromise; it is a compromise among men and not of principles. Reflexivity marks and distinguishes the West's Enlightenment project, but reflexivity without reason is mere technique.

"He believed that remote ends were a dream, that faith in them was a fatal illusion; that to sacrifice the present . . . to distant ends must always lead to cruel and futile form of human sacrifice. He believed that values were not found in an impersonal, objective realm, but were created by human beings, changed with the generations of men; that suffering was inescapable, and infallible knowledge neither attainable nor needed."[16] This description, which aptly fits Japanese sensibility, is how Isaiah Berlin portrays the skepticism of the nineteenth century Russian publicist Alexander Herzen. Applying this description to Japan today, a rather successful society by world standards, one can recognize the virtue of Japanese flexibility and the achievements this flexibility has accorded.

At the same time, it describes a Japan without core values, a Japan which can swing from liberal internationalism to militarism and imperialism, then to politically isolationist economics—which is a rough description of the swings in Japan's orientation in the world during the twentieth century. Of course, one can readily identify countries within the Western Enlightenment tradition with similarly upsetting international experiences during the turbulent twentieth century. In a comparative evaluation of Western great powers, only the United States and Britain are arguably exempt. Still, what matters in a reflection of contemporary Japanese national identity is the fact that a large proportion of the Japanese intellectual class regards the country's paucity of core values and transcendent reason for the swings, in general, and specifically for Japan's disaster in the Second World War.

Masao Maruyama, a key contributor to post-1945 Japanese thought, whose evaluation of Japanese militarism and ultra-nationalism of the 1930s and early 1940s has helped set the dominant tone with which the country has come to understand that past, argues that the Japanese, despite great dedication and sacrifice, could not even make themselves into good fascists. The social fact of dictatorship is one thing, Maruyama wrote a few months after Japan's unconditional surrender in the Second World War, but this should not be confused with the consciousness of the dictators: "Dictatorship as consciousness ought necessarily be linked to awareness of responsibility, but this awareness was lacking in both the military and bureaucracy."[17] Whether in pursuit of fascism, liberalism or any other political arrangement commonly understood in the West as an "ism," in the Japanese society of compromise where technique suffices for reason, scant is the sense of the philosophical underpinnings of political orders, of the responsibility and fidelity toward an ideal as political goal and social good, and of the need to question why. Even the Russian skeptic Herzen, struggling with life in the periphery of the Enlightenment West, believed in reason.

Echoing Maruyama half a century later, Oe asks why there are so few political leaders with creed in postwar Japan, why Japanese politicians and bureaucrats do not seem to mature through the process of reflection, choice, and design, why they do not struggle with the realities of life to hone for the improvement of their personal creeds and, in the end to see in the quality of their creeds their lives' worth. Japan's bureaucratic mandarins are reputed for their excellence, but when you begin to peel off their layers of excellence which are their bureaucratic techniques, like an onion (bamboo shoot in the Japanese imagery), there is nothing at their cores. You find no creed, no ideal, which ought to be what gives meaning to the life of an individual. Bound by the value of concrete, immediate goals of identifiable living individuals and their organizations, they remain untouched and unmoved by great historical goals such as liberty, equality, human rights, and human solidarity. When such principles are approximated in Japanese society, that is only a coincidental result of the exercise of bureaucratic technique. Oe laments, there is no habit in Japan of seeking out men of upstanding character to shoulder the responsibility of political leadership.[18]

Societies that emphasize technique over reason place great value on the process of how things are done. Observance of socially accepted rules of process often becomes more important than the result of human activity. To have followed procedural rules with sincerity and good faith often excuses less than desirable result. Societies imbued with these characteristics tend to be ceremonial and ritualistic. In Japanese life, rituals acquire authority, and power flows from them. While rituals serve to preserve social order, at the same time, they tend to obscure the purpose of human activity and the reason why. Heavily ritualistic Japan is a society saturated with the logic of technical procedures. The oft heard complaint of a foreigner that Japanese society is closed attests to the importance of rituals in Japanese life. Whether for a foreigner or native, knowledge of rituals and ceremonies that constitute daily life is the prerequisite for acceptance into society. Such knowledge is acquired only through a long and constant process of socialization, for in Japanese society which emphasizes relations among identifiable individuals and their organizations, its rituals and ceremonies are discrete and in constant flux.

There is certain efficiency in societies which emphasize the question how over why. It allows men with conflicting motives to work together. But there are drawbacks. Japanese society at this century's beginning displays an exaggerated dependence on procedural technique as societal norm, and that has diminished the value of honor and morality in public life. Pervasive corruption in politics is manifest; there is neither shame nor guilt among politicians, only the search for technical leeway to prolong their political lives. This amorality extends to how the country deals with the international world. When Korea raises the issue of Koreans forced to serve as "comfort women" for Japanese soldiers during the Second World War, the Japanese government carefully considers which agency, preferably a nongovernmental one, should dispense monetary compensation. In this way the question of accountability is avoided to the extent possible. Korea is raising the issue as a moral problem, Oe blasts, but Japan is reducing it to a technical problem.[19] Exaggerated reliance on technique leads to moral ambiguity.

Societies that discourage personal creed have little room for dissent. Societies unaccustomed to dissent witness little debate. In these societies, there can be no tradition of exile. Japanese society, imbued with these characteristics, has tended to place a high premium on conformity, consensus, and community. For communal men without a strong sense of personal creed, there is no identity outside of community. Such men become adrift morally and psychologically when shunned from community. Banishment from communal life was considered severe punishment in traditional Japan; exile had been the fate of criminals. "Oe is a foreigner!"—this has become the battle cry of Oe's critics, who abhor what they see as Oe's submissiveness toward the West. The critics argue that his writing is incomprehensible, for he is merely using Japanese words to compose foreign language prose; that his political creed of democracy and pacifism is foreign, for these were imposed upon Japan by a foreign conqueror after the defeat in war; that few Japanese had read him before the Nobel prize, and it took this foreign recognition for his discovery in Japan. What is notable about the furor surrounding Oe's Nobel prize is that a real intellectual debate has ensued between supporters of Oe and their critics; furthermore, the act of branding one's enemy a foreigner, the act of banishment from Japanese community, no longer seems to be an effective weapon as it had been not so long ago. Societal norms are changing; values and lifestyles within society are becoming increasingly diverse; and diversity is giving way to the development of personal creed. Dissent and debate are beginning to erode at consensus and conformity. Just as the weak sense of "national" celebration of Oe's award points to the evolution of a new Japanese identity, so too does the weakening of the meaning of banishment from community that is Japan. If communalism has been a source of Japanese ambiguity, dissent and debate are antidotes. A Japan in which morality and honor acquire heightened value may be in the making.

Oe, as we have seen, posits that Japan's ambiguity began with the advent of modernity, after which Japan has been unable to reconcile the meaning of the West and itself. True independence for Japan cannot be attained until every Japanese acquire the spirit of "independent self-esteem" (*dokuritsu lison*), warned Yukichi Fukuzawa, Japan's foremost Enlightenment thinker, writing in 1875 soon after the country's opening to the world. He likened Japan's antimodern character to that of a palace maid, envious, scheming, and sycophantic, struggling for improvement of one's status in a world where objective rules for promotion do not exit, where winning the personal favor and whim of the palace lord is key.[20] Fukuzawa's warning continues to find resonance in contemporary Japan. Returning to Kant, Enlightenment is man's emergence from his self-imposed immaturity.

III. FAREWELL AMERICA

There is no precise equivalent of the word identity in Japanese; some use the English word. Others prefer the word *shutaisei*, whose Japanese-English dictionary definition is commonly given as subjectivity, independence, identity of existence, or the rule of individualism. None of them corresponds exactly with the Japanese term. Most Japanese thinkers are agreed that Japan lacks *shutaisei*, and many argue that Japan is in need of one. But nobody seems to have a satisfactory idea of what a Japan with *shutaisei* may be, or what it takes to bring *shutaisei* to Japan. Still Japanese thinkers see *shutaisei* everywhere in Western political thought and practice: in individualism, liberalism, Marxism, pacifism, autonomy in action, and freedom in thought and expression. Given this muddled Japanese conception of national identity, Masao Miyoshi, a Japanese-born naturalized American arid literary critic, offers clarification: "The uncritical pursuit of *shutaisei* in Japan may be still one more example of Japan's gestures toward Westernization, and thus ironically proof of its lack of *shutaisei*.[21] It takes one with Japanese sensibility but with cultural distance to cut through the mire of Japanese thinking on national identity.

That Japan has no national identity is, of course, a curious proposition. It certainly has values, its own language, and art and literature and customs. Its economic, social and political structures and manners are distinct from those of other countries. It has a national history. Why then do the Japanese today think of their country as lacking in identity? The answer lies with the end of World War II.

August 15, 1945, the day Japan surrendered unconditionally to the United States, is the singular source of contemporary Japanese national identity. The Japanese continue to refer to the era after 1945 as *sengo*, the postwar era. *Sengo* does not simply denote a time frame; it embodies a historical consciousness. The postwar era has been an era in which Japan embraced America as the dominant model. In the Japanese penchant to seek out models in its pursuit of modernity, one hitch has been the inability to recognize models in the abstract; models have necessarily been identified with concrete characteristics of certain countries. Democracy, an important theme in postwar Japanese thought, for example, has held meaning in the context of American democracy and Japan's relation with America. Postwar Japanese national identity has been bound by its images of America, images which, according to Oe, has evoked in the Japanese the feelings of "shame and envy."[22]

It is in the context of America as model, as Kant's "guidance from above" that the Japanese understanding of *shutaisei* holds meaning. The concept of *shutaisei* first arose during the height of the Second World War in the Pacific. It was the Kyoto school of philosophy that coined the term in the search for an ideological justification for the country's pursuit of the Asian co-prosperity sphere. Only in the way that a culture without a firmly articulated native tradition and authenticity can, the Kyoto school imagined Japan's transcendence of modernity (*kindai no chokoku*). Whether the Kyoto school was anything more than a cover for Japan's brute aggression is a topic of continuing debate. It was generally understood that on August 15, 1945, the guns of America defeated Japan, while America's *shutaisei* triumphed over the Japanese one. Henceforth, Japan that opted for willful subservience to America, especially in international politics, looked toward America as the embodiment of *shutaisei*, as the model which points to the full recovery of Japan's *shutaisei*, when time came.

In this sense, we begin to understand what Japan's *shutaisei* has meant in postwar thought. It essentially points to the ideology of great powers, to the ability of one power to impose its ways on others. America possesses *shutaisei*, because of its victory in the Second World War and its consequent ascendance to super power status, and because of its brand of liberalism, its democracy and capitalism, which have acquired global relevance. *Shutaisei* thus is achieved when native ideas expand toward universal significance. So it was that the wartime Kyoto school imagined a world order led by Japanese values. In postwar Japanese thought, *shutaisei* became overlapped with the more enduring question of modernity: To become modern meant the attainment of *shutaisei*.

America as Japan's model has been a paradox. America's highly principled ways, its legalistic tendency, and its faith in the transcendent relevance of its values contrast with the more amorphous, particular, and ambiguous Japanese ways. Between America, whose founding document guarantees the right of the "pursuit of happiness," and Japan, whose constitutional guarantee is mere enjoyment of a "cultured life," there is a gap. The American belief in perfection could not mean much in the Japanese world of compromise.

Furthermore, postwar Japan clearly lost the stomach for the harshness of international politics. If *shutaisei* comes from great power status, Japan's orientation in the world during the past half century has pointed to the explicit denial of such ambition. Japanese society is now one that wants to be a "Denmark" or "Netherlands." It harbors no desire for national greatness in international politics. It wishes to enjoy the material benefits of hard work. It wants to be a wealthy and orderly small power, whose per capita gross national product and equitable distribution of wealth mean more than aggregate gross national product as measure of comparative national power. The psychology of Japanese society today does not match the large proportion of the world's wealth the country commands. Rather than as a source of challenge, as it had been until recently, the world outside increasingly appears as a source of intrusion: Why must Japan continue to dole out large sums for foreign economic aid when the economy is doing badly? Why must the economy be deregulated if the majority of the people are content with things as they are? Why must Japan break its postwar policy of "pacifism in one country" and dispatch troops abroad for United Nations peacekeeping operations and become embroiled once again in international politics?

Caught between society's willful innocence of international politics and America as model of *shutaisei*, Japanese thought on national identity floundered, unable to reconcile the two. Meanwhile, notably since the early 1960s, the meaning of modernity for society at large became increasingly associated with material culture, the production and consumption of things. In this context, modernity could be arrived at when Japanese products based on advanced technology became world competitive. In this context, too, America was the model. Because of the Japanese tendency to associate models with concrete countries, the proof of arrival at modernity had to come from America; it was not something Japan could simply claim. In the late 1930s, Japan's nominal per capita gross national product surpassed that of America. At about the same time, the American government began to deal with Japan Primarily as an economic competitor. When America categorized Japan as a major economic threat, notably under the Clinton administration, that to Japanese eyes was a concession of equality. Japan became modern.

The arrival at modernity is at once intellectually liberating and onerous. As long as modernity was at issue, by definition, Japan could identify models in the outside world. It was through these models that Japanese thought articulated signposts for the nation's future. According to the Japanese understanding of the order of things, Japan arrived at modernity because there are no more outside models; as a result, for now, Japan has lost its image of the future.

The dissipation of America as model leads to the Japanese recognition of the varieties in American life. As long as America was heralded as model, there was a strong tendency to ascribe to America monolithic characteristics. Different Japanese would harbor different images of America, but each image tended to be a gross simplification and reduction, whether it be America as the model for capitalism, democracy, or imperialism. Now, with the arrival at modernity, Japanese views of America are increasingly subtle and complex, reflecting the realities of American life. This recognition, the ability to consider complexity in others, comes in large measure from the growing diversity in Japanese life itself. What this does is to prod Japanese thought to reconsider the plurality of cultures and the plurality of modernity.

The cultural approach to the clarification of national identity in Japanese thought is not new. It has been a distinct feature of Japanese thought since the mid-nineteenth century. One common cultural approach has been the study of poetry, bound by the particularity of language and essentially untranslatable. The cultural approach has aimed to establish Japanese distinctiveness, to locate sources of identity which are not comparable, thus free of value judgments in relation to others, yet as good as any other. This is in one sense a healthy recognition of the plurality of cultures. As long as the Japanese continued to consider their country as less than modern, the cultural approach could not satisfactorily tackle the question of modernity: If Japanese culture is as good as any other, why does Japan lag behind the West in wealth and power? Begging this question, in a less than modern Japan, the cultural approach stood as a failed attempt to escape the burden of world history.

In a modern Japan, an equal in the achievements of modernity, investigation of cultural pluralism begets new life. Japan has become modern, yet it is not the same as America. This simple truth frees Japanese thought to reconsider culture not as an escape from world history but as an effort to forge a world history that is more cognizant and tolerant of cultural differences.

IV. JAPAN AS AN ASIAN COUNTRY

The arrival at modernity brings with it another paradox. Because Japanese national identity had been largely understood as a comparison, in a world without models, Japanese thought loses bearing. Instead of forging an identity with universal and inclusive qualities, in a Japan that has finally achieved the historical pursuit of modernity, in a Japan that has approximated the West's claim to universality, Japanese thought tends to retreat toward specifics. Without a comparison to gauge its status in the world, Japanese thought as it has been constituted will tend to claim the singularity of its experience.

Who are the Japanese? It is time for Japanese thought to stop seeing the country in comparative terms and ask what it is that the country and its people want to be in the world. While many thinkers no doubt will continue to be bound by old categories and habits, henceforth any socially and politically meaningful contribution to Japanese thought will add to the invention of a new set of categories and assumptions. There has occurred a "paradigm shift."

Looking foward, it seems clear that Japan's relations with Asia will play a critical role in forging a new national identity. Much of this will be led by the internationalization of economic activities in the Asian region. For Japan, whose dominant impulse for over a century had been to "escape Asia," to borrow the nineteenth-century Enlightenment thinker Fukuzawa's imagery, the old question of equality resurfaces. Many of the problems of Japan in Asia have been results of the inequality of power between Japan and the rest of the Asian countries since the late nineteenth century. The history of the region, in one sense, has been one of Japanese domination and Asian rebellion. Even today, there is no regionalism akin to that of Europe where Germany, France, Italy, and Britain hold relatively equal power. Asian regionalism is more like the North American Free Trade Agreement in which the United States dominates Canada and Mexico.

The last time Japan was seriously and fully engaged with Asia was during the Second World War. It was raw imperialism. The ideology of Japan's Asian co-prosperity sphere as articulated by the Kyoto school of philosophy had at its core the notion of equality. The war was understood to be that between "haves" and "have-nots," its purpose to bring equality to the international world of inequality. As things turned out, Japan was interested only in equality between itself and the Western imperial powers. In the way Japan treated Asia, the co-prosperity slogan of equality among Asians was a brutal joke. A country can only present to others values that it possesses. Japanese society during the Second World War was an unequal place, divided by social class, its distribution of opportunities, wealth, and power rather skewed. This Japan could not understand the meaning of equality.

Japan today is a rather equal place. The class system was abolished after the war; opportunities and wealth are fairly evenly distributed. This Japan has the chance to forge an Asian regionalism based on the idea of equality. But there is still a hitch. The Japanese sense of equality is predominantly that of sameness, not the equality of rights. In a society that emphasizes consensus and conformity, the lowest common denominator is the measure of equality. It continues to be shaped by Fukuzawa's "envy of the palace maid." To be like others is understood as equality. Until Japanese society further develops the idea of equality of rights and recognizes the value of diversity, Japan in Asia will continue to face difficulties. What do the Japanese want? Oe wants relativism that is universally tolerant.

Still, when rights are confused with general principles, where rights become ends in themselves, in the absence of guiding principles, there grows a tendency for individualism to run amok and civility to disappear. Oe's Japan needs to identify a set of guiding principles, which capture his desire for decency, innocence, and sanity for our world that is coercive and hierarchical. In Western thought today, there is confusion of rights and principles. So, at last, after more than 120 years, universal significance for Japanese thought moving beyond the struggle with the meaning of modernity can be forged by articulating a set of principles which is authentic in the Japanese context and which disentangles the Western confusion of rights and principles.

CONCLUSION

Japan is certainly not without identity or empty at the center. There is an identity, but its is ambiguous. This ambiguity comes mainly from Japan's singular success at Westernizing and modernizing among the non-Western nations. Other non-Western nations have their ambiguities, but theirs are different in that their ambiguities are often expressions of either continuing or failing struggles to cope with the question of modernity. In contrast, Japan's ambiguity comes from success recently arrived at, and in a short time the Japanese should come to be able to accept the nation's place in the world and shed the kind of ambiguity that comes from the idealized imagining/division of the world into the West and other, into the modern and not. Japanese identity is now framed primarily as a member of the "G-7," and this categorization allows Japan to free itself from a sense of separation from the West, from the modern, and allows Japan to assume a rightful place in a club whose members share the world's highest per capita incomes.

Still an ambiguous identity is not a monopoly of the non-West. Is Japanese identity more ambiguous than that of the United States? In the post-1945 context, Japanese identity is in one sense more ambiguous because of the compromised state of sovereignty and independence that evolves from Japan's relationship with the United States. Post-1945 Japanese sovereignty has been divisible and independence limited. These are symbolized by the continuing presence of the American military on Japanese soil after the formal conclusion of the post-Second World War military occupation. Japan has willfully accepted this status and, under cover of the American security guarantee, hidden behind the United States and cherished its pacifism. This stance in international politics certainly has helped shape Japan's political culture specified in this essay. The ambiguity comes from the contradiction between its pacifism—symbolized by the "anti or post-Westphalia" peace constitution which forever denounces the use or threat of use of force to settle international disputes—and the American use of violent means explicitly denied by the Japanese constitution to provide for Japan's security.

Post-1945 United States, mindful of the lessons of Munich and Pearl Harbor, posed to guard its peace through strength, through enhanced military preparedness as witnessed in the arms race with the Soviet Union. In contrast, Japan after 1945 fell into a psychology similar to what the United States and Europe embraced following the First World War. Like the United States after Versailles, Japan after Hiroshima sought to isolate itself from international politics. And like Europe after Versailles, which sought to guard its peace by goodwill as symbolized by the signing of treaties banning war, note the Kellogg-Briand pact, Japan has hoped to guard its peace by minimum military preparedness and "by trusting in the peace loving peoples of the world," as dictated in the constitutional preamble. It is the juxtaposition between the divergent American and Japanese lessons of the Second World War, and Japan's dependence on the United States as the final guarantor of its security, that helps make Japanese national identity ambiguous. For, in essence, Japan, the people and government, has had neither will nor interest to actively identify the country's place in the world by its brand of pacifism. It has been pacifism in one country obscured from the rest of the world, and more visible has been the logic of American military protection. (In this sense, prewar imperial Japan with its more proactive and clearly expansive foreign policy was a drastically less ambiguous place. Also, this veiled pacifism does little to dispel the universal suspicion of Japanese militarism.)

So deeply cherished and embedded in Japan is pacifism in one country, it is hard to imagine the contrasts in American and Japanese cultures to lead to conflict in the foreseeable future. At each turn, as has been the pattern during the last half century, the Japanese government should bend to avert conflict with the United States, the guarantor of Japan's politically isolationist pacifism. The United States does not trust other countries, but it is convinced that others can and should trust it. The United States has a preponderant military presence in East Asia supported by a network of bilateral security treaties, the American-Japanese being key. The United States is not prepared to leave the region; it cannot trust the countries in the region to forge a workable order that is not detrimental to American interests. So the American-Japanese alliance is not about to erode soon. As the preceding discussion indicates, Japanese political culture is dependent on the security arrangement with the United States, thus will remain ambiguous as long as the United States continues to command preponderance in East Asian security affairs.

Within that framework, given the way regional integration proceeds through growing economic interdependence, Japan will continue to play a major part. In the long run, with economic interdependence and attendant cordiality in relations among states, the efficacy/need for American security guarantee for Japan and the region should diminish. Then, Japan's pacifism in one country will have a chance to expand beyond the border, and that will help clarify Japan's ambiguous identity.

ENDNOTES

1. Yosef Lapid, "Culture's Ship: Returns and Departures in International Relations Theory" in Yosef Lapid and Friedrich Kratochwil, eds., *The Return of Culture and Identity in IR Theory* (Boulder: Lynne Rienner, 1996) p. 4.

2. David Landes, *The Wealth and Poverty of Nations* (New York: W. W. Norton & Co. Inc., 1998) p. 393.

3. Peter J. Katzenstein, ed., *The Culture of National Security: Norms and Identity in World Politics* (New York: Columbia University Press, 1996) p. 6.

4. Kenzaburo Oe, *Aimai na nihon no watashi* (Ambiguous Japan and myself) (Tokyo: Iwanami shinsho, 1995), p. 8.

5. Oe, *Aimai na nihon no watashi*, p. 8.

6. Albert Hourani, *Arabic Thought in the Liberal Age, 1793–1939* (Cambridge: Cambridge University Press, 1983), p. 8.

7. Roland Barthes, *Empire of Signs*, trans. By Richard Howard (New York: Hill and Wang, 1982).

8. Tetsuro Watsuji, "?oku nihon seishin-shi kenkyu" (Study of the Japanese spirit), in *Watsuji Tesssuro senshu*, vol. 4 (Tokyo: Iwanami shoten, 1962), p. 281.

9. Shuichi Kato, "Nihon-jin to wa nanika" (What is a Japanese?), in *Nihon-jin to wa nanika* (Tokyo: Kodansha, 1976), p. 8.

10. Naoki Sakai, "Nihon shakai kagaku hoho josetsu" (Introduction to Japanese social science methodology), in Iwanami Koza. *Shakai kagaku no hoho*, vol. 3. *Nihon shakai kagaku no shiso* (Tokyo: Iwanami shoten, 1993), pp. 1–37.

11. Oe, *Aimai na nihon no watashi*, p. 209.

12. Kenzaburo Oe and Ryosuke Yasui, "Tokubetsu raidan: shoshin kara nigerarezu ni kita," (Dialogue: unable to escape the beginning), *Sekat*, January 1995, p. 39.

13. Hiroshi Minami, *Nihon-jin ron: mesji eara konnichi made* (Theory of the Japanese: from Meiji to the present) (Tokyo: Iwanami shoten, 1994), p. 392.

14. Minami, *Nihon-jin ron*, p. 389.

15. Immanuel Kant, "An Answer to the Question: What is Enlightenment?" in *Perpetual Peace and Other Essays*, trans. Ted Humphrey (Indianapolis: Hackett, 1983), p. 41.

16. Isiah Berlin, "Introduction," in Alexander Herzen, *My Past and Thoughts*, trans. Constance Garnett, abridged by Dwight Macdonald (Berkeley: University of California Press, 1982), p. xiii.

17. Masao Maruyama, Gendai seiji no shiso to kodo (Thought and behavior in contemporary politics) (Tokyo: Miraisha, 1964), p. 24.

18. Oe and Yasui, "Tokubetsu raiden," pp. 36, 42–43.

19. Ibid., p. 44.

20. Yukichi Fukazawa, *Bunmei-ron no gairyaku* (Outline of civilization), 47th printing (Tokyo: Iwanami bunko, 1987), p. 25.

21. Masao Miyoshi, *Off Center: Power and Culture Relations between Japan and the United States* (Cambridge: Harvard University Press, 1991), p. 97.

22. Kenzaburo Oe, Kujira no shimesu suru hi (The day the whale becomes extinct) (Tokyo: Kodansha bungei bunko, 1992), p. 201.

Chapter 6

IDENTITY AND THE BALANCE OF POWER IN ASIA

Henry R. Nau

Two theories of contemporary international relations compete to explain state behavior at the system level. Realist theories explain state behavior primarily in terms of a country's relative position in the international distribution of power. The internal attributes of the country, such as political ideology, economic system, or governmental institutions, are secondary. "State behavior" according to Kenneth Waltz, the preeminent realist theorist, "varies more with differences of power than differences of ideology, internal structure of property relations, or in governmental form."[1] Constructivist theories explain state behavior at the system level in terms of a country's identity or relative position in "the intersubjective understandings and expectations that constitute [states'] conception of self and other."[2] State identities determine whether countries see each other as friends or foes and thus whether relative power differences between countries are threatening or not.

These theories inform current analysis of international relations in Asia. Henry Kissinger, a foremost practitioner of realist theory, interprets Asia's future largely in terms of the position and balancing of rival powers. "The relations of the principal Asian nations to each other," he writes, "bear most of the attributes of the European balance-of-power system of the nineteenth century." "China is on the road to superpower status." "The other Asian nations are likely to seek counterweights to an increasingly powerful China." And "the

American role is the key to helping Japan and China coexist despite their suspicions of each other."[3] Iain Johnston, on the other hand, interprets Chinese foreign policy behavior primarily in terms of its realpolitik strategic culture (identity). This culture, "which generally places offensive strategies before static defense and accommodations strategies," drives Chinese foreign policy whatever the external distribution of power may be. It "reflects a set of characteristics of the external environment as dangerous, adversaries as threatening, and conflict as zero-sum, in which the application of violence is ultimately required to deal with threats."[4] If this interpretation holds, balancing Chinese power is not likely to facilitate coexistence, as Kissinger expects, but may actually intensify conflict as China maneuvers persistently to shift the balance of power in its favor.

Realist theories, which argue that power positioning overrides cultural self-identification, do not deal effectively with revisionist states (such as China, if Johnston is correct) whose self-image rejects the status quo and seeks to maximize, not balance, power.[5] On the other hand, constructivist theories, which argue that national self-images drive foreign policy irrespective of external power positions, do not deal adequately with performance or outcomes. Some self-images work better in the "real world" than others. If self-images interpret power, they may also misinterpret it.[6] In the end, the Soviet Union's self-image as a communist state failed because it did not cope adequately with the exploding power realities of the information age. China, as the last great communist state, may fail for the same reason. Self-images motivate power, but they are also subject to it. To evaluate outcomes, relative power remains a necessary exogenous factor, not a wholly endogenous product of interpretation, as some constructivist approaches maintain.[7]

How might one compensate for the shortcomings of realist and constructivist theories? This essay suggests combining the realist and constructivist variables of power and identity (self-image) to explain present and potential patterns of Asian politics at the systemic (or sub-systemic) level. Each variable becomes an independent influence on outcomes at the system level.[8] The distribution captures relative power differences (from equal/decentralized to unequal/centralized). The distribution of identity maps out threat perceptions based on differences among self-images (friendly vs. unfriendly). Juxtaposed, the two variables define a scatter diagram of four basic models of international systems (or subsystems, if one is looking only at the Asia-Pacific region). I call these models *anarchic* (decentralized/relatively equal power and unfriendly self-images), *security communities* (decentralized/relatively equal power and friendly self-images), *imperial* (unequal power and unfriendly self-images), and *hierarchical* (centralized power and integrated self-images).

The anarchic model captures realist terrain in international politics. But security communities, imperial models, and hierarchical situations illustrate circumstances that realism cannot account for (or, in the case of hierarchy, consigns to domestic politics alone). And, while constructivism claims to account for all of these situations (whatever states make of the situation), it ignores the constraints on collective dialogue imposed by power structures. As I note below, the dialogue in a situation of imperial or unipolar power is likely to be differently constrained than a dialogue in an anarchic situation or within security communities.

A particular international system (or subsystem) may exist anywhere on the scatter diagram (see figure 6.1, below). The axes are continuous, not dichotomous. At each point on the scatter diagram, the structural constraints of power and identity vary, setting various limits on military, economic, and political behavior among actors within that system (or subsystem).[9]

The four models obtained by juxtaposing power and identity variables help to solve a number of puzzles about contemporary and future Asian relations that realism and constructivism alone cannot explain. Two such puzzles are the relative stability of great power politics in Asia and the low level of institutionalization in the region compared to Europe.

Realism predicts only situations of anarchy. Because states balance not maximize power, they do not bandwagon and create imperial or unipolar situations.[10] Similarly, they do not form security communities, even if they share friendly self-images, because internal similarities cannot override external differences in power positions.

Thus, in Asia, realism predicts that great powers will compete and balance against one another. There should be considerable instability. In the near term, Japan and the United States are the two principal and therefore competing powers, and in the longer-term China will join the competition against both Japan and the United States. In fact, however, Japan and the United States are allied with one another and are strengthening their alliance to deal with threats in Asia beyond the borders of Japan (the new defense guidelines). They exist in a security community in which intense economic competition does not escalate readily into international military threats or rivalries. In addition, the United States and Japan dwarf China in military and economic power. They exercise imperial or unipolar power in the region. These two factors—the security community between Japan and the United States, and the unipolar power position of the United States and Japan vis-à-vis China—contribute to greater stability in the region. Thus, an approach combining identity and power predicts existing realities in Asia better than realism can do by itself.

Constructivism tends to predict high levels of institutionalization among states if state identities are cooperative and not competitive. Realism predicts high levels of institutionalization (and hence specialization) if the distribution of power is hierarchical. As all of the papers in this volume confirm, the level of institutionalization and multilateralism in the Asia-Pacific region is low compared to that in Europe. Constructivism would have to account for this outcome by arguing that identities in Asia are more competitive than those in Europe. Asia does include nondemocratic as well as democratic states and multiple world religions, rather than the predominant Judeo-Christian religion of Europe. Yet, historically, as Dave Kang suggests in this volume, Asia has experienced less competition and fewer wars than Europe (at least until Western intrusion in the nineteenth century). Kang attributes this outcome to Chinese imperialism (or the Chinese system) which emphasized formal hierarchy but informal equality (as opposed to the emphasis in Europe on formal equality and informal hierarchy). But Chinese imperialism in Asia does not equate with higher levels of institutionalization.

Considering power and identity simultaneously helps to solve this puzzle. Constructivism ignores the possibility that the distribution of power may exert an independent influence on the construction of social identities.[11] Yet social identities in Asia have been constructed for the most part under an imperial or unipolar distribution of power, with China having been the dominant power for much of the past thousand years. This configuration of power did not lead to higher levels of institutionalization, however, because China's identity emphasized a soft institutional system of tribute and deference, rather than a hard institutional system of international organizations and specialization. China's domestic institutions sufficed to order the realm. In Europe, by contrast, the distribution of power was continuously anarchic, with only very brief moments of imperial conquest. Under the circumstances, no one state was able to impose its domestic institutions on the international realm and higher levels of international institutionalization were required to coordinate interstate affairs.

From the outset of the state system at Westphalia, European states depended upon contractual and eventually legal institutions to guarantee and protect their separate and independent identities. Although the anarchic distribution of power produced much instability, the competitive construction of identities produced a corresponding codification of legal and organizational devices, which ensured the survival of separate and independent states, despite repeated wars. Thus, levels of institutionalization in Asia and Europe are functions of the configuration of both power and identity, not of either one alone.

The rest of the essay divides into two parts. In the first part, I explore the rationale and empirical considerations involved in developing a structural model of international politics that tracks simultaneously both identity and power. In part two, I use the model to explain aspects of contemporary and future interstate relations in Asia that realism and constructivism cannot or do not explain as well.

A STRUCTURAL MODEL OF POWER AND IDENTITY

SOCIAL CONSENSUS AND THE BALANCE OF POWER

The history of the modern state system suggests that both material (realist) and social (constructivist) factors have always combined at the structural level to determine the character of state behavior. The balance of power system that emerged in the sixteenth and seventeenth centuries in Europe involved not just a physical separation of territories and decentralization of power. It also involved the social structure of sovereignty. The critical parameter of that system, as John Ruggie points out, "was not who had how much power, but who could be designated *as* a power."[12] That designation came about through a shared understanding that, although states projected diverging cultural and religious self-images, they would not seek to impose their own culture (at the time, specifically their religion) within the territory of another state. This reciprocal recognition of state sovereignty constrained the use of power. It did not eliminate war, but it did make war illegitimate for the purpose of eradicating another state. In this sense, the European system that emerged after 1500 was not imperial but anarchic.[13]

While the power structure of the European system has remained anarchic to the present day, the social structure has gone through several changes.[14] At the end of the Napoleonic wars, the victorious powers—Great Britain, Prussia, Russia, and Austria—reinstituted the system of state sovereignty. Rather than eliminate the defeated power, they restored the French monarchy. The great powers also agreed to abstain from intervention in internal affairs and to accept a defensive posture—to balance, not maximize, power—in external affairs. From this point on, however, the social consensus unraveled. First, through the Holy Alliance, Prussia, Russia, and Austria sought to legitimate intervention in the affairs of another sovereign (e.g., Spain, Italy, Greece) to prevent the overthrow of the monarchy (that is, to prevent a repetition of the French revolution that led to the Napoleonic wars). This was too much for Great Britain whose domestic politics was moving toward representative institutions. After Britain left the Congress of Vienna system, Prince Metternich of Austria managed to moderate the anti-revolutionary zeal of the Holy Alliance, especially that of the Russian Czar. After Metternich's death, Prussia, under Bismarck, posed a new challenge to the conservative consensus. Bismarck believed it was legitimate to use force offensively to unite independent states under the banner of their common German culture. The great powers now splintered on the critical question of when and for what purposes it was legitimate to use force in interstate affairs. The empires (Russia and Austria-Hungary) sought to use force to conserve the monarchy, Germany to unite and protect a new autocratic nation, and Great Britain and France to defend emerging liberal institutions.[15]

Two world wars and then a cold war followed. Each of these contests was as much about the social basis for managing the balance of power as about the balance of power itself. Was mutual respect of sovereignty compatible with Bismarck's and then the Kaiser's militant nationalism? Did mutual respect of sovereignty extend to Hitler's criminal regime engaged in genocide? Did peaceful coexistence imply the moral equivalence of totalitarian communist states and liberal democracies? The cold war was not only about the social structure that would govern the balance of power in Europe; it was also the first major world conflict that was settled largely by a contest between competing values or self-images rather than an actual test of military arms.[16]

In the wake of the cold war, a new social consensus has emerged among the major industrial countries for managing the balance of power. As mature democracies, these countries subject the legitimate use of force at home to strict constitutional guarantees and appear to reciprocate the expectation that they are not likely to use force in their external relations with one another. The so-called democratic peace, while it is not fully understood by political scientists, is nevertheless a powerful expression of contemporary reality.[17] The Atlantic democracies and Japan do not threaten one another with military force and do not have any strategic plans to do so. Their behavior reflects a pervasive consensus among democratic nations as to when and for what purposes it is legitimate to use force within their individual societies as well as in their relations with one another. In the limited area of human rights, this consensus appears to go beyond democratic countries. Increasingly, all countries accept the notion that it is illegitimate to use force domestically to torture or otherwise abuse the person of each individual citizen. They also appear to accept the idea that international intervention is justified to protect these basic human rights.[18]

DEFINING IDENTITY

How could we model the role of identity without slighting that of power? Identity is a very broad concept. It might refer to ethnicity, culture, religion, politics or any number of other variables. The aspect of identity that appears to be most crucial to international affairs, however, is the orientation countries take toward the use of force. As Robert Powell demonstrates, the issue of the use of force essentially separates realist and neoliberal theories of international relations. "When . . . the use of force actually is at issue," Powell writes, "cooperative outcomes . . . cannot be supported," and "this inability to cooperate is in accord with the expectations of structural realism." On the other hand, "if the use of force is not at issue, . . . the results are more in accord with neoliberal institutionalism."[19] Powell identifies the use of force as a constraint in the system arising from the nature of military technology and the cost of fighting. This constraint also reflects a common evaluation among the states of the costs and benefits of fighting and therefore a shared understanding among them affecting the management of the balance of power.

We can break such a shared understanding or consensus down into the orientation (or identity) of individual states toward the use of force. This orientation has both an internal and an external component. The internal aspect deals with the conditions under which the state considers it legitimate to use force against its own citizens. As Waltz tells us, a state or hierarchical actor is not defined primarily by a monopoly on the use of force but by "a monopoly on the *legitimate* use of force."[20] Internally, each state has an agreed set of rules that legitimates or delegitimates the use of force within that society. These rules have a substantive and a procedural dimension. The substantive dimension concerns the rationale or grounds on which the use of force is legitimate—political ideology (e.g., liberalism, communism, etc.), tradition (e.g., culture, religion, ethnicity, etc.), or charisma (heroic myths, cult of the leader, etc.).[21] The procedural dimension deals with the question of who makes the decision to use legitimate force—a single ruler, an elite or oligarchy, or the people directly or through representative institutions. One measure of internal identity, therefore, may be a typology of regime types, graded in terms of the substantive and procedural mechanisms by which these regimes legitimate the use of force internally against their own citizens. Several data bases exist that provide such a typology of regime types. They make it possible to code the internal dimension of a country's identity and associate an empirical measure of legitimacy with each empirical aggregate or pole of military (and economic) power in the international system (or subsystem).[22]

The external aspect of a state's orientation toward the use of force deals with the conditions under which a state considers it legitimate to use force against another state in the international system. Some states may consider it legitimate to use force only for defensive purposes. These states are called status quo powers or "defensive positionalists."[23] They do not seek offensive gain; they seek only safety. They try to minimize the difference between their gains and the gains of others, not to maximize this difference. Other states may consider it legitimate to use force to achieve offensive gains. These states are called revisionist powers. They seek to maximize the difference between their gains and that of others and to shift the relative distribution of power in their favor. By deposing sovereigns in other states, Bismarck, as Kissinger details, signaled that he no longer accepted the European status quo based on legitimate monarchical states. Bismarck sought to revise the system to accommodate the unification of smaller German states based on more aggressive nationalist principles.[24] What was not clear until World War I was whether other states could or would accommodate the new Germany. Accommodating states fall somewhere between offensive maximizers and defensive positionalists. They consider it legitimate to use offensive force for certain purposes but not ultimately to challenge a multipolar equilibrium.[25]

External and internal orientations toward the legitimate use of force may be related. It would be unusual to expect a government that used force arbitrarily at home against its own citizens to refrain in a principled way from the use of force against citizens of other countries abroad.[26] Conversely, democratic states appear to externalize the reluctance to use force at home in their relations with other countries abroad, at least with other democracies. Not only are states influenced in their external behavior by internal self-images and practices, but they also read the internal self-images of other states to give them a clue about the external behavior of those states. As Thomas Risse-Kappen points out, "threat perceptions do not emerge from a quasi-objective international power structure, but actors infer external behavior from the values and norms governing the domestic political practices that shape the identities of their partners in the international system."[27]

Nevertheless, internal and external orientations of states toward the use of force may also be independent of one another. Democratic states may not be more peaceful in general than other states,[28] and nondemocratic states have formed peaceful alliances throughout history (such as the Holy Alliance from 1815–1850).

COMBINING IDENTITY AND POWER

Identity as defined above is obviously influenced by power. In the crudest cases, power determines identity. Stalin remarked once to an associate, "whoever occupies a territory also imposes on it his own social system."[29] On the other hand, identity sometimes defies power and has significant consequences even when power wins. A Lithuanian parliament guard commented when Soviet troops threatened to storm that country's parliament: "the intention is not to win, because we all know that is impossible. The intention is to die, but by doing so to make sure Moscow can't tell any lies as they did in 1940."[30] Power and identity can and do act independently of one another. As Joe Nye writes, "politics is not merely a struggle for physical power, but also a contest over legitimacy."[31] Something important about international relations is lost particularly in a setting in which notions about the legitimate use of force differ (as they do among the states of the Asian-Pacific region perhaps more so than among European states).

Figure 6.1 juxtaposes identity and power as two independent variables.[32] The distribution of power measures relative *military* capabilities along the y-axis. The distribution of identity measures the differences among states toward the *legitimate* use of military force along the x-axis. The x-axis in figure 6.1 is actually a summation of differences along the two dimensions of a state's orientation toward the use of force—internal and external. It gives us a measure of the polar-

	Identity	
	Convergence	Divergence
Relatively Unequal or Centralized Power	Hierarchy Sector 1	Empire Sector 2
Relatively Equal or Decentralized	Security Community Sector 3	Anarchy Sector 4

FIGURE 6.1 Distribution of Identity and Power.

ity among states in terms of the degree to which they threaten one another by the rules they apply to legitimate the use of force (as distinguished from the capabilities they possess, which is measured by the y-axis). If these rules diverge (right side of the figure), states manage power capabilities competitively; the prospect of physical violence (anarchy) or political oppression (empire) is always present. If the rules converge (left side of the figure), hierarchies and security communities emerge which regulate the use of force on the basis of common rules.

Because legitimacy has two dimensions (internal and external), convergence can lead to more than one type of hierarchy or security community. Figure 6.2 illustrates various types of security communities. Security communities in area A that involve only mature democratic, defensive-oriented republics severely limit the legitimate use of force. For all practical purposes, this type of community eliminates the competition for military power among members. The democratic peace prevails. Security communities in area C include some democracies that are immature or oligarchic and offensive-minded. Relations in this type of security community involve more instability and suspicion. Disputes

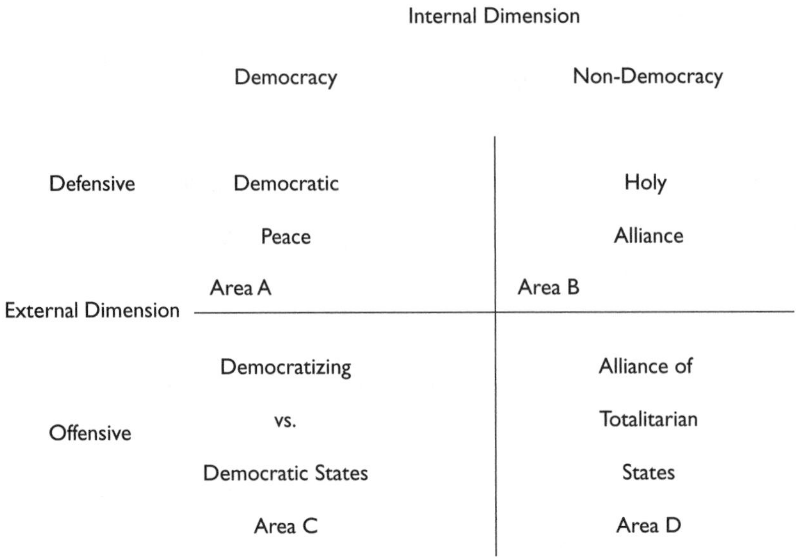

External Dimension	Internal Dimension: Democracy	Internal Dimension: Non-Democracy
Defensive	Democratic Peace Area A	Holy Alliance Area B
Offensive	Democratizing vs. Democratic States Area C	Alliance of Totalitarian States Area D

FIGURE 6.2 Convergence of Identity in Security Communities.

may escalate more easily to the level of military threat. One example is the tension that prevails between mature democratic states and younger, democratizing states.[33] Security communities in area B involve nondemocratic and defensive-minded states. This type of security community legitimates the use of force more often than does a democratic security community. Force is used domestically to repress the rights of a majority of the citizens and externally to assist other members in suppressing internal revolts. The Holy Alliance among Russia, Prussia, and Austria was such a community. Finally, security communities in area D include member states that are nondemocratic and offensive-minded. Such states are mobilized authoritarian or totalitarian governments. They sanction the most invasive and aggressive use of force. Although these states still agree on the internal and external circumstances when it is legitimate to use force (otherwise their relations would not constitute a security community but a traditional alliance under anarchy), the use of force is so arbitrary and unconstrained that such a community is hard to sustain. The troubled alliances between fascist states before World War II (e.g., Germany and Italy) and communist states after World War II (e.g., Sino-Soviet alliance) may be examples.

EXPECTED BEHAVIOR

Combining realist and constructivist variables at the structural level predicts a different range of expected behavior than either realism or constructivism alone.

In sector 1 of figure 6.1, realism predicts hierarchy and specialized behavior. Actors perform different functions and depend upon one another through interdependent or integrated institutions.[34] If identity is included in the analysis, however, behavior may not be specialized. A totalitarian hierarchy, which rules by fear of the use of force, elicits redundant (parallel) and segmented (compartmentalized), not specialized and integrated, behavior.[35] A liberal hierarchy, on the other hand, encourages specialized behavior through exchange-based political and economic institutions.[36] NATO and the former Warsaw Pact do not strictly qualify as hierarchies. They do reflect similar structures of centralized power in the areas of military command and control. Despite these similar material structures, however, they display very different internal and external behavior patterns because the terms on which their hierarchical power is legitimated are very different.[37]

Sector 2 of figure 6.1 predicts different behavior than we expect from realism. As Michael Doyle points out, "imperialism's foundation is not anarchy but order, albeit an order imposed and strained."[38] There is a single center of power, as in the case of hierarchy, but there is no single community or consensus on the legitimate use of force.[39] This imperial or unipolar structure predicts muted military and economic competition because no state or combination of states is capable of challenging the imperial power. Political competition replaces military competition. Asian nations, for example, challenge U.S. and Western values, even while they rely on U.S. military forces for security against each other. Economic relations center bilaterally on the imperial power. They are specialized but not integrated. The form of institutionalization depends upon the content of the rules by which the imperial state legitimates its power. A nondemocratic imperial state may marginalize and exploit smaller states. A democratic one may seek to develop and assimilate them. Examples in the case of U.S. imperial power are the international economic institutions (International Monetary Fund, World Bank, and World Trade Organization) which project America's soft power to promote liberal markets and transparent governments among developing states.

Thus, in a situation of empire, the extent to which the imperial state threatens other states is a function of identity not power. Threat depends, as Michael Mastanduno shows, on whether the challenging states are status-quo, revisionist, or accommodating states and whether the imperial state can successively reassure, confront, and engage these states to perpetuate its dominance. As Mastanduno concludes, U.S. security practices in the unipolar, post–cold war world can be better explained by balance of threat theory, which pays attention to countries' self-images, intentions and soft power, than by balance of power theory, which focuses only on the distribution of capabilities.[40]

Security communities (sector 3 of figure 6.1) predict coordinated, not specialized or ordered, behavior.[41] States apply the same rules to the use of force. If those rules severely restrict the use of force, as they do among mature democratic countries, liberal institutions and trade replace military competition. Institutions such as the European Union and Group-of-Seven (G-7) elevate economic relations and promote absolute economic gains as opposed to relative military power. An apparent firewall separates economic from military competition.[42] If the rules sanction the frequent use of force, state institutions penetrate the society and dominate economic markets as well as nongovernmental relations (i.e. limit civil society). Economic rivalry escalates more easily to military rivalries. This reasoning explains why security communities among nondemocratic states, which sanction the more frequent use of force, tend to be less stable.

Sector 4 of figure 6.1 predicts highly competitive behavior in all areas—political (because rules of legitimacy diverge), military (because power is decentralized), and economic (because competition is zero-sum). No state in this situation can afford to specialize or coordinate, let alone subordinate, its behavior to that of other states. Temporary alliances, entered into warily and exited easily, are the dominant form of behavior observed in this context.[43] This box captures the realist situation of anarchy, but because states compete for advantage as well as security, anarchy may be far more chaotic and dangerous than realists predicted.[44] Stability depends on state identities. If states are revisionist, anarchy is highly unstable; if they are defensive, anarchy might be quite peaceful.

THE MODEL APPLIED TO ASIA

THE ASIA-PACIFIC SUBSYSTEM

What are the structural features of contemporary international relations in Asia and how might they change in the future? Do structural features of identity and power predict great-power relations in this region, principally relations among China, Japan, and the United States, better than alternative models? For this purpose, the Asia-Pacific region will be considered as an insulated or closed subsystem. If necessary, this assumption can be amended to take into account the behavior of the European Union and Russia, the other two major powers of the global system.

Table 6.1 provides some basic indicators of the distribution of power and identity in the Asia-Pacific sub-region and the global system overall. A look at the three major Asian powers suggests several points. First, on the basis of military expenditures as a percentage of GDP (columns 9 and 10), the United States and China devote more of their annual resources to the use of force than Japan. China and the United States are also the only declared nuclear powers in the region (column 11). Given its larger GDP, of course, the United States dwarfs China in absolute military expenditures, as does Japan, even with its lower share of GDP devoted to defense. This is true even though China has sharply increased its absolute military expenditures in recent years, as its GDP rose, while the U.S. and Japan reduced their military spending. In absolute expenditures the United States also dwarfs Japan (spending more than four times as much). The distribution of military power, therefore, is skewed sharply in favor of the United States. From a military power perspective, the United States is imperial, with its principal rival—in terms of nuclear weapons and relative attention paid to military matters—being China.

Second, the distribution of identity indicated in table 6.1 (columns 3 to 5) magnifies the power rivalry between the United States and China. Indicators of regime type provided by Freedom House and Polity III databases offer an empirical measure of the latitude of countries to use force legitimately in internal affairs. These indicators show the United States and China separated from one another as far as the scales measure—1 being most free, 7 least free on the Freedom House scale; and 0 being least free, 10 most free on the Polity III scale. In addition, Japan now lines up very closely with the United States, measuring the same as the United States on the Polity III scale (number of 10) and only slightly below the United States on the Freedom House scale (1 and 2 on political rights and civil liberties respectively compared to 1 and 1). Japan's numbers may overstate the quality of democracy in Japan. As column 6 shows, Japan is a highly homogeneous society with a strong propensity toward consensus and bureaucratic, as opposed to parliamentary, authority. Nevertheless, the distribution of power and identity taken together suggests a very wide gap in the region between the United States and Japan, on the one hand, and China, on the other. If we now consider the external aspects of identity—attitude toward the use of force in external affairs—the gap widens still further. Japan is by constitution a purely defensive-minded country. China maintains the right to use force offensively if necessary to prevent the alienation of Taiwan.[45] China's neighbor and communist friend, North Korea, also asserts the right to use force offensively to attack South Korea. The United States maintains a security alliance with Japan and a large military presence in the region. This presence is too far away from U.S. territory to claim purely defensive purposes, as in the case of Japan's forces. Unlike the forces of China potentially arrayed against Taiwan or those of North Korea aligned against South Korea, U.S. forces have no specific offensive intentions. The U.S. attitude might be considered accommodating, intended to deter the use of force for offensive purposes and to bring about a peaceful resolution of territorial disputes in the region.[46]

A third feature of the Asian subsystem that emerges from Table 1 is the relatively equal economic capabilities of the United States and Japan. In terms of GDP (column 2), the two countries dwarf China and roughly approximate one another.[47] Compared to China, the two countries also have economic freedom and social development ratings (columns 7 and 8) that are roughly comparable.

TABLE 6.1 Identity and Power Indicators

	Population (millions) 1995[1]	GDP (billion dollars) 1995[1]	Political Freedom Rating[2]		Polity III Ranking[3]	Minorities (%)	Econ. Freedom 1988[5]	Social Dev't[6]	Military Budget % GDP)[7]		ABC Weaps[8]
			PR	*CL*					1985	1996	
China	1,200	698	7	7	0	8	3.75	.626	7.9	5.7	ABC
Japan	125	5,109	1	2	10	1	2.05	.940	1.0	1.0	C
United States	263	6,952	1	1	10	12–9–8	1.90	.942	6.5	3.6	AC
S. Korea	45	455	2	2	10	0	2.30	.890	5.1	3.3	C
Taiwan	22	260	2	2	6	14 from Mainland	1.95		7.0	4.9	C
Hong Kong	6	28			5	1.25	.914				
ASEAN	477	633	2-7	3-7	0-8	multiple	1.30–5.00	.900–.348	1.4-19.4	2.0—7.6	C

European Union	372	8,331	1	1–3	8–10	Less than 10	1.95–2.90	.946–.890	3.0	2.1	AC
Russia	148	345	3	4	8		3.45	.792	7.4		ABC

1. *World Development Report* 1997, (Washington: The World Bank 1997), pp. 214–215, 236–237, 248.
2. *Freedom in the World: The Annual Survey of Political Rights and Civil Liberties* 1997–98 (New York: Freedom House, 1998), pp. 600–601.
3. Keith Jaggers and Ted Robert Gurr, *Polity III: Regime Type and Political Authority 1800–1994* (Ann Arbor: Inter-University Consortium for Political and Social Research, September 1996). The numbers in this column are for the democracy variable in year 1994.
4. U.S. Central Intelligence Agency, *The World Fact Book 1996*, World Wide Web: http://www.odci.gov/cia/publications/nsolo/factbook/peo.htm. Single minority groups, defined by ethnic origin, that represent at least 5% of the population are listed separately.
5. Bryan T. Johnson, Kim R. Holmes and Melanie Kirkpatrick, *The 1998 Index of Economic Freedom* (Washington: Heritage Foundation, 1998), pp. xxix–xxxii
6. United Nations, *Human Development Report 1997*, Worldwide Web: http://www.undp.org/undp/hdro/hdil.htm
7. *The Military Balance 1997–98* (Oxford: The International Institute for Strategic Studies, 1997), pp. 293–398.

Countries proven or suspected to have Atomic, Biological and Chemical weapons as cited in following sources and from interviews with government officials. Arms Control and Disarmament Agency, 1996 *Annual Report*, World Wide Web: http//www.acda.gov/reports/annual/comp.htm; Stockholm International Peace Research Institute, World Wide Web: http://www.sipri.se/cbw/cbw-mainpage.html.; U.S. Department of Defense, *Proliferation: Threat and Response*, November 1997, World Wide Web: http://www.defenselink.mil/pubs/prolif97/toc.html.

What this suggests is that the principal economic rivalry in the region is between the United States and Japan. These countries have comparable capabilities and freer access to one another's markets. China is a definite outlier in this configuration.

The picture that emerges from the table is an Asian-Pacific system that sits in the lower left-hand corner of sector 2 in figure 6.1. The structure of identity and power is imperial. The United States dominates the region militarily. What is more, the United States and Japan form a security community subsystem in the region that dominates politically and economically. This security community (a democratic one situated in area A of figure 6.2) mutes the use of force in domestic affairs of both countries; eliminates active military competition in their relations with one another; and underpins a security alliance that defends Japan and possibly other areas of common interest in the region (the subject of current defense guideline talks under the U.S.-Japan Security Treaty). The United States and Japan compete economically, but a firewall prevents their economic competition from escalating to military rivalry. Nevertheless, the level of economic integration between the United States and Japan is lower (more bilateral and sectoral) than U.S. ties in Europe. Trade tensions are also higher, reflecting perhaps a wider gap in political culture (parliamentary versus bureaucratic) between the two countries.

Thus, the United States, alone or with Japan, has an imperial advantage over China in both military and economic terms. Moreover, China, unlike Japan, contests U.S. political identity. China rejects U.S. values of individual human rights and the rule of law. Together with smaller Asian states, it touts Asian values—collective over individual rights, efficient over democratic government, and personal over legal relations. China trades with the United States and Japan, but this relationship is not well balanced or integrated. (The United States and Japan have much less access to China's market than China has to the U.S. or Japanese market.)[48] The firewall between economic and governmental or military disputes is more porous as state-directed agencies play a larger role in the Chinese economy. Political authoritarianism obscures the relationship between economic activities and military intentions.

ALTERNATIVE INTERPRETATIONS

This portrait of contemporary Asian-Pacific relations from a perspective that combines identity and power emphasizes different constraints on state behavior than realism or constructivism. Realism expects the two preeminent, not opposing, powers in the region to balance against one another. Hence, Japan and the United States should be competing against one another, not either one of them or both against China. They should be competing both through internal political and economic differentiation, and through external alignment with lesser powers in the region, such as China and the ASEAN grouping of Southeast Asian nations.[49] Constructivism highlights the social and cultural diversity of the region and anticipates informal, pluralist institutions such as the ASEAN Regional Forum (ARF) and the Asia-Pacific Economic Conference (APEC) to foster higher levels of consensus and cooperation.[50] By contrast, the present analysis highlights neither the balance of power (anarchy) nor the emerging arms control dialogue (security communities). It emphasizes instead imperial structures of U.S. political and military dominance and U.S.-Japan economic dominance.

Which portrait is more accurate? If realism holds, there should be clear signs of growing military conflict between the United States and Japan. There are growing political tensions, to be sure (see later discussion under the section on Scenarios for Change). To date these tensions have not translated into military differences. Quite the contrary, the U.S.-Japan security treaty, although neglected after the fall of the Soviet Union, has if anything been strengthened recently in the wake of Chinese threats in the Taiwan Straits and North Korea's missile firings and clandestine underground nuclear weapons activities.[51] If constructivism holds, regional economic and security dialogues should be progressing more rapidly than regional arms races or territorial disputes. While precise empirical comparisons are beyond the scope of this essay, the rapid increase in arms expenditures in Asia since the 1980s, matched against the snail-like pace and lowest-common-denominator approach of both ARF and APEC, seems to argue against constructivist expectations.[52]

Realist and constructivist perspectives tap real developments in Asia. That much is not disputed in this essay. But because these perspectives track only one structural variable, they pull these developments out of context. Constructivist perspectives that focus on arms control dialogues, for example, fail to link up these dialogues with parallel dialogues that may be intensifying arms races. For every moderating influence on armaments that Chinese negotiations in ARF exert on top Beijing leadership, for example, there may be counter-influences from Chinese defense officials pushing for higher arms expenditures and concerned about relative military balances.[53] Realism risks the opposite distortion. It focuses primarily on arms races and discounts security dialogues that might lead to greater trust.[54] A more complete perspective would track both variables simultaneously.

Imperial structures highlighted by the combined identity and power approach explain several outcomes that realist and constructivist perspectives do not explain. First, imperial structures explain why military conflict in the Asia-Pacific region is currently muted. Under the constraints of an imperial structure, the balance of military power is essentially uncontested. China's military moves in the Taiwan Straits and South China Sea do not challenge American military preeminence directly, as would such moves against South Korea, Japan or the Philippines.[55] The competition takes place primarily in political arenas. In these arenas, China attacks U.S. hegemony ideologically, rejecting U.S. views on human rights and challenging Western values more generally by championing Asian values.

Second, imperial structures predict "ordered" economic relations centered on the imperial power, as opposed to "coordinated" behavior through multilateral institutions. Such structures explain stability in Asia despite low levels of institutionalization. Japan and the United States do not coordinate their trade policies with China or ASEAN countries. Both give priority to bilateral contacts. APEC seeks to change this pattern. But APEC operates on the convoy principle, going only as fast as the slowest member does. Compared to the EU, North American Free Trade Agreement (NAFTA) or ASEAN, APEC is an extremely weak organization.

Third, as suggested earlier, a security community subsystem in Asia mutes military conflicts between the United States and Japan (conflict which realism expects). It is significant that, despite escalating trade and political tensions, the firewall between economic and military threats in U.S.-Japan relations has not been breached. Some studies trace this phenomenon to fundamental cultural changes in Japan centered around "beliefs and values that make [the Japanese] peculiarly reluctant to resort to the use of military force."[56] If this is so, it highlights the importance of tracking identity indicators as well as power rivalries.

Thus, the power and identity approach explains better recent stability in the Asia-Pacific subsystem. It does so without the complacent expectations of constructivist perspectives (equating dialogue with cooperation) or the powder kegs predictions of realist perspectives (expecting imminent military rivalry between preeminent powers). Moreover, because it tracks both political convergence and military conflict, the power and identity approach is better able to anticipate future changes in Asia-Pacific international relations.

SCENARIOS FOR CHANGE

The structural model developed in this paper does not predict sources of change. but given various scenarios for change, it can predict ranges of expected outcomes. Some scenarios for change could build on and reinforce contemporary stability in Asia. China could continue to liberalize internally, particularly in economic areas. While the government would remain authoritarian, the economy and society as a whole would become less vulnerable to arbitrary government intervention and more subject to the rule of law. This modest convergence of China's internal identity toward the United States and Japan might facilitate a marginal reduction of bilateral priorities and greater coordination of policies through multilateral institutions in the region—trade and economic ties in the Asia-Pacific Economic Conference (APEC) and World Trade Organization (WTO), and confidence-building military talks under the ASEAN Regional Forum (ARF). Similarly, on the positive side, the United States and Japan might continue to converge toward more compatible economic and trade regimes. Trade imbalances may persist and competition intensifies, but the possibility that this competition would spill over into greater political tensions would be diminished, not increased as in recent years. In short, the present imperial structure of power and identity would evolve toward a nascent security community with features characteristic of the upper right hand corner of sector 3 in figure 6.1.[57]

However, the theoretical perspective provided by a combination of identity and power would not lead one to expect that security community relations in Asia will take the form of institutional specialization and integration found in Europe. Because some important Asian countries remain nondemocratic, convergence of identities will not be sufficient to support a liberal consensus facilitating specialization and integration. The countries in Europe that are moving toward monetary and economic union sit on the far left hand side of the x-axis in sector 3 of figure 6.1. They are all solidly democratic and endorse global economic institutions and integration. If they succeed in federalizing, they may move progressively up the y-axis toward a hierarchical structure of international affairs in Europe (perhaps entering sector 1 at some point). The countries in Asia, even under the optimistic scenario of convergence toward a security community, are not likely to move in the same direction. They will remain further to the right of the x-axis and toward the top of the y-axis in sector 3, as identities remain more diverse and power more asymmetric in Asia than in Europe.

Even this limited security community scenario may be entirely too optimistic for Asia, however. There are also important instabilities in the present situation. Two factors potentially pull the participants toward anarchy and the more dangerous structural features of sector 4 in figure 6.1. The most important is the military rivalry between the United States and China. If China continues to expand its military capabilities and exhibits greater political tenacity in the region because it cares more about the issues (which are closer to home), and if the United States gradually reduces its imperial military position in the region (either physically, politically or both), the situation will drift toward an anarchic structure of power and identity (sector 4 of figure 6.1). Japan will have to expand its independent military capability, and a triangular balance of power may emerge (which Henry Kissinger believes already exists or is soon inevitable—see earlier text and note 3).[58]

A second source of instability in the region lies in economic and political relations between the United States and Japan. Both Freedom House and Polity III indicate that Japan falls well within the range of peaceful democracies that appear to eschew the use of force or military threats in their relations with one another.[59] Nevertheless, there is persistent debate about how deep and mature Japanese democracy may be.[60] If Japan fails to move forward toward greater political pluralism, transparency, and accountability; it is conceivable that current economic distrust between the two countries may grow.[61] Trade issues will continue to become bitter political issues resolved through contentious governmental negotiations rather than courts or multilateral dispute settlement mechanisms. Inevitably, political friction will generate doubt about security, and Japan may maneuver to attain a technological independence that could at some point support an independent military policy.[62] This estrangement between the United States and Japan could change the character of the security community between the two countries, creating fears that one side might use its material advantages for offensive purposes (moving the security community from area A to area C of figure 6.2). If political identities diverged further, the structure of relations might revert back to anarchy (sector 4 of figure 6.1). Assuming Japan and the United States remained significantly more powerful than China, the Asia-Pacific subsystem would become bipolar. China, even with its lesser power, might play a crucial role as a "swing state," courted vigorously by both the United States and Japan. If the United States withdrew, Japan might occupy an imperial position, at least for a while. Over the longer-run, if China's power grew, Japan and China might become the principal bipolar rivals.

There is a prospect, assuming the United States withdraws and Japan reverts back to non-democratic policies at home, that Japan and China might draw closer together, sharing certain Asian values and common authoritarian ideas about the use of force at home and adopting defensive-minded attitudes toward the use of force abroad. That would place Japan and China in area B of figure 6.2, suggesting a kind of security community among nondemocratic powers, analogous perhaps to the original Congress of Vienna in Europe. This scenario captures the notion of the Asianization of regional politics—a community of authoritarian governments content to accommodate one another, particularly in rivalries against the United States or other outside powers.[63] If Iain Johnston is right about China's strategic culture, however, China is unlikely to forego opportunities to use force offensively.[64] Japan's history offers little optimism that it would be able to do so either.[65] As we noted earlier, unless states are status-quo-oriented, a balance of power is difficult to sustain without early and usually system-wide (or at least subsystem-wide) military rivalries and conflicts.

An equally plausible prospect, therefore, is that China and Japan would compete for imperial dominance. Driven by the internal need to establish social hierarchies (consistent with their nondemocratic identities) and the external opportunity to exploit advantages, the two countries would clash with one another, rather than accommodate differences. Anarchy would replace a nondemocratic security community.

CONCLUSION

The theoretical framework in this paper based on the distribution of power and identity—rather than on power or strategic culture alone—broadens our analytical tools for understanding the Asia-Pacific region. The cold war confrontation between the United States and the Soviet Union effectively froze the distribution of identity in world affairs and conflated it with the distribution of power. In these circumstances, two models—hierarchy and anarchy—sufficed and indeed offered considerable insight into world affairs.

In Asia, for example, the bipolar Soviet–American confrontation created alliances that had everything to do with power and little to do with political identity among the countries involved. To combat the Soviet Union, the United States established a standing military alliance with Japan, an industrial county that had no significant democratic tradition (compared even with Germany, for example, whose people experienced the revolution of 1848 and the Weimar Republic). Subsequently, the United States allied with China against the Soviet Union. At the time China was a totalitarian and violent communist country convulsed in the Cultural Revolution. Balance of power considerations dictated such relationships irrespective of political identities. On the other hand, within the U.S.-Japan (and U.S-European) alliance, the hierarchical model enlightened thinking and practice. A division of labor was established. The United States assumed primary responsibility for security, while Japan committed itself to democratic reforms and economic reconstruction.[66] Similar understandings, but with an emphasis primarily on economic reconstruction, drove U.S. alliance relationships with South Korea, the Philippines and, less formally, Taiwan.

With the end of the cold war, thinking remained locked in these realist manacles. The United States, it was argued, had two choices—to confront and contain China in a new balance of power struggle between democratic and communist states, or to engage China and try to integrate it into hierarchical alliance institutions modeled after the integrated military and economic institutions of NATO and the European Union. To contain China, the United States would strengthen and integrate security alliances with Japan, South Korea, and other Asian states. To engage China the United States would promote free trade and potentially common-market-type arrangements within APEC and the WTO, as well as Helsinki-like arms control and human rights discussions in ARF.

The collapse of the Soviet Union, however, unfroze the identity variable in international affairs. The distribution of identity in the system between communism and democracy, which gave bipolarity its peculiar intensity and danger, no longer coincided with the distribution of power.[67] Although American power declined, the United States became part of a wider association of democratic states. And although the Soviet Union retained its military, especially nuclear, capabilities, it disintegrated into fifteen separate political identities.

Identity factors open up two additional models for thinking about international and particularly Asian-Pacific politics. Because the United States, Japan, and other countries in the region (South Korea, Philippines, the other Chinese political system in Hong Kong, and possibly Taiwan) have converging political identities, they compete in ways that mitigate, if not eliminate, military rivalries among them. They live in a democratic security community, rather than a multipolar balance of power, and resolve competitive issues largely through economic and legal means. Simultaneously, however, these countries face significant internal and external differences vis-à-vis China. Because their military power is preeminent, however, these differences play out more in political and diplomatic terms—human rights, skirmishing over the Taiwan issue, diplomatic maneuvering to deal with North Korea, etc.—than head-on military crises. This imperial system, supplemented by a security community subsystem, is much more stable than a traditional anarchic balance of power. It could achieve even greater stability if the United States remains engaged in the region, China continues to liberalize economically, and the United States and its partners do not expect the levels of specialization and integration that characterize Atlantic institutions. On the other hand, the imperial system may also pull apart. The current relatively stable system might give way to a more fluid, triangular traditional-style balance of power politics among the United States, China, and Japan, or, if the United States withdraws, a competition for imperial power between China and Japan.

ENDNOTES

1. Kenneth N. Waltz, *Theory of International Politics* (New York: Random House, 1979), p. 329. Under realist theories, I include classical and neorealist versions. Both give priority to the struggle for power. Classical realism recognized the relevance of goals, aims, values and domestic politics (identity). It conceptualized these constructivist factors only at the level of relationships, not the level of structure (as this article does). Hans Morgenthau, the preeminent classical realist, made very clear that "whatever the ultimate aims of international politics, power is always the immediate aim." See Hans J. Morgenthau and Kenneth W. Thompson, *Politics Among Nations: The Struggle for Power and Peace*. (New York: Knopf, 6th Edition, 1985), p. 31.

2. Alexander Wendt, "Anarchy Is What States Make of It: The Social Construction of Power Politics," *International Organization*, 46, no. 2 (Spring 1992): 397. Constructivism focuses on identity formation and includes notions of corporate (autonomy), type (rational), and social (interrelational) identity. Social identity dominates, whereas in other traditions, such as liberalism, type identity (i.e. domestic politics) may stand alone and determine social interactions. For a contrast between constructivist and liberal perspectives, see Alexander Wendt, *Social Theory of International Politics* (Cam-

bridge: Cambridge University Press, forthcoming); and Andrew Moravcsik,"Taking Preferences Seriously: A Liberal Theory of Individual Politics," *International Organization*, 51, no. 4 (Autumn 1997): 513–555.

3. Henry Kissinger, *Diplomacy* (New York: Simon and Schuster, 1994), Quotes from pp. 826–828.

4. Alastair Iain Johnston,"Cultural Realism and Strategy in Maoist China," in Peter J. Katzenstein, ed., *The Culture of National Security: Norms and Identity in World Politics* (New York: Columbia University Press, 1996), p. 219. See also Johnston's book, *Cultural Realism* (Princeton: Princeton University Press, 1994).

5. See Randall L. Schweller, "Bandwagoning for Profit: Bringing the Revisionist State Back In," *International Security*, 19, no. 1 (Summer 1994): 72–108.

6. Native Indians in sixteenth-century Mexico, for example, interpreted invading Spanish conquistadors as gods. They obviously misinterpreted the power realities and were subsequently enslaved.

7. As Jeffrey T. Checked points out, "constructivists rely upon the insights of sociological institutionalism, . . . a particular branch of organization theory that systematically excludes questions of agency, interest, and power." See "The Constructivist Turn in International Relations Theory," *World Politics*, 50, no. 2 (January 1998): 341.

8. By contrast, realism and constructivism attempt to subsume the other variable and make it epiphenomenal. As Waltz explains, "the placement of states affects their behavior and even colors their characters." *Theory of International Politics*, p. 127. Conversely, Iain Johnston contends that "structural realpolitik can be subsumed within the cultural realpolitik model." See "Cultural Realism and Strategy in Maoist China," p. 264. Not all constructivist arguments make this strong claim. They seek only to supplement or compete on equal terms with realist perspectives. See Ronald L. Jepperson, Alexander Wendt, and Peter J. Katzenstein,"Norms, Identity, and Culture in National Security,"in Katzenstein, ed. *The Culture of National Security*, pp. 68–70.

9. The logic of structures is not causal but constraining. The distribution of power and identity defines the structures of any particular system or subsystem. Structures, in turn, define ranges of specific preferences, strategies, behaviors and outcomes. See John D. Morrow, "Social Choice and System Structure," *World Politics*, 41, no. 1 (October 1988): 75–97.

10. Classical realists assumed that states did maximize power but still expected balance to prevail over bandwagoning or imperialism. Prudence restrained state objectives. Neorealists substituted the restraint of structure for prudence. As R. Harrison Wagner notes, "Waltz recognized only two types of systems: bipolar and multipolar." See "What was bipolarity?" *International Organization*, 47, no. 1 (Winter 1993): 88. Although Waltz and other neorealists argued belatedly that unipolar situations elicit balancing behavior against the imperial power, other realists point out that "if the hegemon adopts a benevolent strategy and creates a negotiated order based on legitimate influences and management, lesser states will bandwagon with, rather than balance against, it." See Kenneth N. Waltz, "The Emerging Structure of International Politics," *International Security*, 18, no. 2 (Fall 1993): 44–80; and Christopher Layne, "The Unipolar Illusion: Why New Great Powers Will Rise," *International Security*, 17, no. 4 (Spring 1993): 5–52. For the argument that bandwagoning, not balancing, may

characterize behavior in unipolar situations, see Randall L. Schweller and David Priess, "A Tale of Two Realism: Expanding the Institutions Debate," *Mershon International Studies Review*, 41, no. 1 (May 1997): 24.

11. Constructivists do talk about discursive power to influence intersubjective understanding. But they relatively ignore coercive power to *impose* intersubjective understanding. See Ted Hopf, "The Promise of Constructivism in International Relations Theory," *International Security*, 23, no. 1 (Summer 1998), especially pp. 177–180. As John Mearsheimer asks, isn't it possible that a fascist discourse would be more violent than a liberal or realist one? See "The False Promise of International Institutions," *International Security*, 19, no. 3 (Winter 1994/95): 43–44.

12. John Gerard Ruggie, "Territoriality and Beyond," *International Organization*, 47, no. 1 (Winter 1993): 162.

13. According to Paul Kennedy, this was the principal difference between Europe and the empires that persisted in other parts of the world—China, Islam, etc. See *The Rise and Fall of the Great Powers* (New York: Random House, 1987), Chapter 1.

14. See J. Samuel Barkin and Bruce Cronin, "The state and the nation: changing norms and the rules of sovereignty in international relations," *International Organization* 48, no. 1 (Winter 1994): 107–130.

15. For an insightful treatment of this eighteenth and nineteenth century history in terms of the interplay between shared values and power, see Kissinger, *Diplomacy*, chapters 3 and 4.

16. There are many and conflicting interpretations of the end of the cold war. For interpretations attentive to the role of domestic political ideas and self-images as well as that of power, see John Lewis Gaddis, *The United States and the End of the Cold War* (New York: Oxford University Press, 1992); Daniel Deudney and G. John Ikenberry, "The International Sources of Soviet Change," *International Security*, 16, no. 3 (Winter 1991–1992), 74–119; and Thomas Risse-Kappen, "Collective Identity in a Democratic Community: The Case of NATO," in Katzenstein, ed., *The Culture of National Security*, pp. 357–400.

17. For summaries and critiques of the democratic peace, see Bruce Russett, *Grasping the Democratic Peace: Principles of a Post Cold-War World* (Princeton: Princeton University Press, 1993); James Lee Ray, *Democracy and International Conflict* (Columbia: University of South Carolina Press, 1995); the three articles by Christopher Layne, David E. Spiro and John M. Owen in the section, "Give Democratic Peace a Chance?" *International Security*, 19, no. 2 (Fall 1994): 5–126; and Joanne Gowa, "Democratic States and International Disputes," *International Organization*, 49, no. 3 (Summer 1995): 511–523.

18. See Martha Finnemore's discussion of the expanding practice of humanitarian intervention, "Constructing Norms of Humanitarian Intervention," in Katzenstein, ed. *The Culture of National Security*, pp. 153–186.

19. See Robert Powell, "Absolute and Relative Gains in International Relations Theory," in Robert A. Baldwin, ed., *Neorealism and Neoliberalism* (New York: Columbia University Press, 1993): 211.

20. See Waltz, *Theory of International Politics*, pp. 103–104.

21. Max Weber discussed these three sources of substantive legitimacy. See *From Max Weber: Essays in Sociology*, H. H. Gerth and C. Wright Mills, eds. (New York: Oxford University Press, 1946), pp. 78–79.

22. This internal aspect of a state's identity corresponds to what constructivists call type (as opposed to social) identity. It acknowledges that identity is in part intrinsic if actors are to have the capacity to change extrinsic or social identities. To get at this internal dimension of identity, this study uses two data sets of regime type. The Polity III data set, available through the Inter University Consortium for Political and Social Research at the University of Michigan, contains two indicators of regime type (autocracy and democracy) and eight indicators of political authority. All of these indicators measure procedural aspects of government—the competitiveness, openness, and checks and balances (constraints) of electoral and institutional processes. There is no indicator of substantive political ideology or measure of civil liberties. A second data set, the index of political rights and civil liberties, available through Freedom House in New York, ranks countries in terms of both substantive and procedural dimensions. Although the measures focus primarily on procedural dimensions of government, by including the protection of civil liberties, the Freedom House data set incorporates a measure of substantive political ideology—liberalism vs. illiberalism.

23. See Joseph M. Greico, *Cooperation Among Nations* (Ithaca: Cornell University Press, 1990); and "Realist International Theory and the Study of World Politics," in Michael Doyle and G. John Ikenberry, eds., *New Directions In international Relations Theory* (Boulder: Westview Press, 1997).

24. Kissinger, *Diplomacy*, p. 117. Kissinger recounts a fascinating dialogue between Bismarck and his Prussian mentor, Leopold von Gerlach, in which Bismarck demarcates his policy of expedience in the service of his country from that of the Holy Alliance to preserve the status quo. See pp. 120–127.

25. This external dimension of identity corresponds to what constructivists call social identity. I am relating this dimension to a state's willingness to use force against other states, a willingness that depends on designations of friend and foe and hence the social construction of identities. There are well-known difficulties in making distinctions among offensive, accommodationist and defensive attitudes toward the use of force. Nevertheless, thee distinctions are made and form the basis of a substantial school of theorizing about the causes of war. For a recent discussion, see, the two articles by Stephen Van Evera, "Offense, Defense, and the Causes of War" and Charles L. Glaser and Chaim Kaufmann,"What Is the Offense-Defense Balance and How Can We Measure It," in *International Security*, 22, no. 4 (Spring 1998): 5–44 and 44–83 respectively.

26. Ronald Reagan put the point succinctly: "A government which does not respect its citizens rights and its international commitments to protect those rights is not likely to respect its other international undertakings." Quoted in Tony Smith, *America's Mission: The United States and the Worldwide Struggle for Democracy in the Twentieth Century* (Princeton: Princeton University Press, 1994), p. 271.

27. See Thomas Risse-Kappen, "Collective Identity in a Democratic Community," p. 22.

28. The evidence that democratic states are more peaceful in general is not as strong as the evidence that they are peaceful with one another. See David L. Rousseau, et al., "Assessing the Dyadic Nature of the Democratic Peace, 1918–88," *American Political Science Review*, 90, no. 3 (September 1996): 512–534. See also John R. O'Neal and Bruce Russett, "The Classical Liberals Were Right: Democracy, Interdependence, and Conflict, 1950–1985," *International Studies Quarterly*, 41, no. 2 (June 1997): 267–294.

29. Quoted in Milovan Djilas, *Conversations with Stalin*, trans. Michaels B. Petrovich (San Diego: Harcourt Bruce Javanovich, 1962), p. 114.

30. See Anatol Lieven, *The Baltic Revolution: Estonia, Latvia, Lithuania and the Path to Independence* (New Haven: Yale University Press, 1993), p. 253. See also Jeffrey C. Goldfarb, *After the Fall: The Pursuit of Democracy in Central Europe* (New York: Basic Books, 1991), who comments about the dissidents who defied Soviet power during the cold war: "Remember, totalitarian power was brought down by so-called impractical idealists who proved to be the genuine realists; people who were willing to act as if they lived in a free society and often suffered the consequences because in fact they didn't." p. 249.

31. See Joseph S. Nye, Jr. *Understanding International Conflicts: An Introduction to Theory and History* (New York: Harper Collins, 1993), p. 142.

32. For a related attempt to apply both regime types and external power shifts to a discussion of war, see Randall Schweller, "Domestic Structure and Preventive War: Are Democracies more Pacific?" *World Politics*, 44, no. 2 (January 1992): 235–269. Schweller finds that the relationship of regime types defined as challenging or declining powers produces different behavior under similar relative power conditions.

33. In the democratic transition process, elites in democratizing states, some of whom are left over from previous nondemocratic regimes, compete to mobilize mass allies and in the process may unleash aggressive, warlike sentiments against other countries, including democracies. See Edward D. Mansfield and Jack Snyder, "Democratization and the Danger of War," *International Security*, 20, no. 1 (Summer 1995): 5–38. Spencer R. Weart also finds this tendency among ancient republics. Oligarchic republics, which enfranchised about one-third of their population to participate in politics, did not fight against one another. Neither did democratic republics, which enfranchised about two-thirds of their population. However, oligarchic and democratic republics did fight against one another, reflecting the tendency of differences in degree or stage of democracy to produce offensive-minded behavior leading to war. See "Peace among Democratic and Oligarchic Republics," *Journal of Peace Research*, 31, no. 3 (August 1994): 299–316.

34. Waltz, *Theory of International Politics*, pp. 104–105.

35. Fascist and communist societies, for example, construct parallel systems of party and secret police institutions to monitor all aspects of government and private life. Citizen behavior in these circumstances is not specialized and exchange-based but withdrawn (private revolt) or, at the extreme, revolutionary (public revolt). See Timur Kuran, "Now Out of Never: The Element of Surprise in the East European Revolution of 1989," *World Politics*, 44, no. 1 (October 1991): 7–49. See also Jeffrey Berejikian, "Revolutionary Collective Action and the Agent-Structure Problem," *American Political Science Review*, 86, no. 3 (September 1992): 647–658.

36. See Andrew Moravcsik, "Taking Preferences Seriously: A Liberal Theory of International Politics," *International Organization*, 51, no. 4 (Autumn 1997): 513–555.

37. For studies that illustrate the different behaviors (nonhierarchical consultation versus informal empire) induced by NATO and the Warsaw Pact. See, respectively, Thomas Risse-Kappen, *Cooperation Among Democracies: The European Influence on U.S. Foreign Policy*, (Princeton: Princeton University Press, 1995); and Alexander Wendt and Daniel Friedheim, "Hierarchy Under Anarchy: Informal Empire and the East German State," *International Organization*, 49, no. 4 (Autumn 1995): 689–723.

38. Michael W. Doyle, *Empires* (Ithaca: Cornell University Press, 1986), p. 11. See also Charles A. Kupahan, *The Vulnerability of Empire* (Ithaca: Cornell University Press, 1994).

39. As Doyle puts it, "the imperial government is a sovereignty that lacks a community," *Empires*, p. 36. On the different behaviors one might expect in an imperial as opposed to anarchic system, see also Iain Johnston, "Cultural Realism and Strategy in Maoist China," pp. 260–262.

40. See "Preserving the Unipolar Moment: Realist Theories and U.S. Grand Strategy After the Cold War," *International Security*, 21, no. 4 (Spring 1997): 49–89.

41. Karl W. Deutsch developed the concept of security community although he was thinking primarily about relations among democracies. See *Political Community and the North Atlantic Area* (Princeton: Princeton University Press, 1957).

42. For example, Mastanduno finds that balance of power theory explains U.S. post-Cold War economic relations with other countries better than balance of threat theory. This balance of power behavior in economic areas does not translate into balance of power behavior in security relations. The latter are better explained by more muted balance of threat theory. See "Preserving the Unipolar Moment."

43. Bruce Bueno de Mesquita showed why allies remain wary of one another and even fight if one takes policy goals (an identity measure) as well as power capabilities into account. However, Bueno de Mesquita uses an expected utility, not a structural, model. See *The War Trap* (New Haven: Yale University Press, 1981).

44. For Waltz and other realists, the fact that states pursue security and not maximum power is crucial and the main reason that anarchy is not as dangerous as it might otherwise be. See Kenneth N. Waltz, "Realist Thought and Neorealist Theory" in Robert L. Rothstein, ed., *The Evolution of Theory in International Relations* (Columbia, S.C.: University of South Carolina Press, 1992), p. 37.

45. Although China claims that the use of force against Taiwan is not external but internal, that claim is not a consensus view in the region. Hence China's reservation to use force against Taiwan may be coded as offensive.

46. In fairness to China, its intention to use force offensively against Taiwan might also be coded if China intends to use such force only if this can be done without disrupting the general equilibrium or balance of power in Asia. (See earlier definition of accommodationist behavior in text.) It is doubtful, however, that China could use force against Taiwan and presumably (assuming such force is unprovoked) against the United States as well without challenging the general balance of power in Asia.

47. The Table shows GDP at nominal exchange rates in 1995. It appears that Japan has a significantly higher per capita GDP then the United States. This relationship

changes when GDP is measured in terms of purchasing power parity. On that basis in 1990, Japan had a GDP per capita about 80 percent that of the United States. See McKinsey and Company, Inc., McKinsey Global Institute, *Manufacturing Productivity*, Washington, DC, October 1993.

48. China is the one of the few countries in Asia with which Japan runs a trade deficit. In 1996, Japan exported $22b. of goods and services to China and imported $40b. from China. See *Direction of Trade Statistics* 1997 (Washington: IMF, 1997) p. 271.

49. Eric Heginbotham and Richard J. Samuels find evidence of such competitive alignments. They argue that mercantile realism, which emphasizes techno-economic rather than military power, explains patterns of Japanese economic alignment with China and other Asian countries, as well as Japanese military commitments to multilateral peacekeeping operations. These patterns, they contend, are designed to counter long-run dependency on U.S. security guarantees. See "Mercantile Realism and Japanese Foreign Policy," *International Security*, 22, no. 4 (Spring 1998): 171–203.

50. For an analysis along these lines, see Alastair Johnston's contribution to this volume.

51. Realists acknowledge the absence of U.S.-Japan military conflict but then argue, contrary to realist logic, that military power no longer matters because "the efficacy of appeals to arms has . . . declined dramatically during the course of the twentieth century." See Heginbotham and Samuels, "Mercantile Realism," p. 190.

52. What is more, as Thomas Christensen suggests in his contribution to this volume, the multilateral security cooperation that exists in ARF may actually be driven in part by arms competition. China, normally unfriendly to multilateralism, participates in ARF as a way to dilute U.S.-Japan bilateral defense moves, which may restrict China's military options in the Taiwan Straits and South China Sea.

53. See the contribution in this volume by Alastair Iain Johnston.

54. Heginbotham and Samuels, for example, discount existing U.S.-Japan security ties by arguing that "Japan is doing little substantively . . . to make the alliance more appealing to its American ally." They focus primarily on growing technoeconomic conflicts, assuming rather than demonstrating that these conflicts trump already substantial security cooperation. See "Mercantile Realism," p. 185.

55. The United States has no explicit commitments to defend Taiwan or islands in the South China Sea, as it does, for example, to defend South Korea, Japan or the Philippines.

56. See the contribution in this volume by Thomas U. Berger and his article, "Norms, Identity and National Security in Germany and Japan," in *Katzenstein* (ed.), *The Culture of National Security*. p. 318.

57. This scenario is equivalent to Joe Nye's strategy for the United States in Asia of "deep engagement." See "East Asian Security: The Case for Deep Engagement," *Foreign Affairs*, 74, no. 4 (July/August 1995): 90–103.

58. Revisionist scholars of Japan envision this scenario. See Chalmers Johnson and E. B. Keehm, "The Pentagon's Ossified Strategy," *Foreign Affairs*, 74, no. 4 (July/August 1995): 103–116.

59. On the Freedom House scale, Japan ranks no worst than five European countries—Belgium, Germany, Italy, Spain and the United Kingdom—and better than

Greece. On the Polity III scale (which does not include measures of civil liberties), it ranks the same as other Western countries and better than Spain and France (which rank 9 and 8 respectively on the democracy scale).

60. For the two sides of this debate, see Karel van Wolferen, *The Enigma of Japanese Power* (New York: Knopf, 1989); and Kent E. Calder, *Strategic Capitalism Private Business and Public Purpose in Japanese Industrial Finance* (Princeton: Princeton University Press, 1993). Karel van Wolferen states bluntly "Japan democracy has not been realized. It exists only in potential." *The New York Times*, June 4, 1995, p. E5.

61. This distrust may already be breaching the firewall between economic and military competition, causing the United States and Japan to worry that relative economic gains may translate into the capacity to do each other political and ultimately military harm. See Michael Mastanduno, "Do Relative Gains Matter? America's Response to Japanese Industrial Policy," *International Security* 16, no. 1 (Summer 1991): 73–113. For a broader discussion of the relationship between economic and military issues, see my essay, *Trade and Security: U.S. Policies at Cross-Purposes* (Washington: America Enterprise Institute Press, 1995).

62. For one analyst who sees clear signs of this development already, see Richard J. Samuels, *Rich Nation, Strong Army: National Security and the Technological Transformation of Japan* (Ithaca: Cornell University Press, 1994).

63. See Yoichi Funabashi, *Asia-Pacific Fusion: Japan's Role in APEC* (Washington, DC: Institute for International Economics, October 1995).

64. See Johnston, "Cultural Realism and Strategy in Maoist China."

65. See Akira Iriye, *China and Japan in the Global Setting* (Cambridge: Harvard University Press, 1992).

66. See J. W. Dower, *Empire and Aftermath: Yoshida Shigeru and the Japanese Experience, no. 1878–1954* (Cambridge: Harvard University Press, 1979).

67. We now know that the cold war was a struggle between two political systems as well as two preeminent powers. As John Lewis Gaddis suggests, "if the Soviet Union had been the superpower that it actually was but with a system of checks and balances that could have constrained Stalin's authoritarian tendencies, a Cold War might have happened, but it could hardly have been as dangerous or as protracted a conflict." See "The Tragedy of Cold War History: Reflections on Revisionism," *Foreign Affairs*, 73, no. 1 (January/February 1994): 145. This view, is not uncontested by strong realists, of course. The noted historian Arthur M. Schlesinger Jr. believes that the Cold War "would have been quite as acute if the United States had been like the Soviet Union, a Marxist-Leninist state"—in short, irrespective of political identities. See *The Cycles of American History* (Boston: Houghton Mifflin, 1986), p. 202.

Chapter 7

ASIA-PACIFIC SECURITY INSTITUTIONS IN COMPARATIVE PERSPECTIVE

John S. Duffield

Since the end of the cold war, the security of the Asia-Pacific region has been the subject of considerable scholarly attention. One reason for this interest is the area's heightened strategic significance, which is itself due in no small part to the rapid economic growth that many of the countries in the region enjoyed in the 1980s and 1990s. At the same time, the post–cold war international politics of the Asia-Pacific have been relatively dynamic and unsettled, especially in comparison with Europe. The breakup of the Soviet Union and subsequent turmoil in Russia, the rise of China, the strategic retrenchment of the United States, uncertainty about Japan, and other developments all have raised questions about the future trajectory of security relations in the region.

Of particular interest to a number of scholars has been the evolving constellation of international security institutions in the Asia-Pacific. One can discern two especially notable sets of recent developments. On the one hand, many long-standing mutual security arrangements have undergone significant changes, ranging from dissolution to revitalization. On the other hand, the last decade has seen efforts to fashion all new international security structures, most importantly the ASEAN Regional Forum (ARF), that, many hope, will be able to address the novel security challenges presented by the post–cold war era.

Despite this recent flurry of activity, however, one cannot help but be struck by the relatively limited nature of the formal institutional security architecture to be found in the Asia-Pacific region throughout the postwar era, at least in comparison, once again, with the Euro-Atlantic. Although both areas have been crisscrossed by large numbers of security ties, those of the Euro-Atlantic have generally been characterized by greater multilateralism, elaboration, and formalization than have those of the Asia-Pacific. Such differences have been emblematic, moreover, of both externally oriented collective defense ties and inclusive collective security arrangements at the regional level. In short, the Asia-Pacific has yet to host anything comparable to the highly developed North Atlantic Treaty Organization (NATO) and Organization for Security and Cooperation in Europe (OSCE), respectively.[1]

The striking nature of these differences is only intensified when one considers that, at least from a global perspective, the two regions have possessed many common features since World War II. In both cases, the postwar era began with the defeat of a regional power that had aspired to hegemony, leaving a profound power vacuum. Subsequent years witnessed an increasingly intense struggle for influence and control by the two emergent superpowers, the United States and the Soviet Union, a competition that culminated in the formation of numerous formal alliances between them and local partners. Within its own spheres of influence, the United States exhibited, at least initially, a pronounced preference for multilateral security arrangements. And both regions have been characterized in more recent decades, but especially since 1990, by a growing degree of multipolarity as the cold war competition has abated and the power of the United States and the Soviet Union has declined in comparison with that of important regional actors.

How, then, is one to explain the contrasting nature of the security institutionalization that has occurred in the two regions? The answer to this question is of potentially great policy relevance. Prominent analysts have argued that the absence in the Asia-Pacific of a dense network of security institutions like that of Europe is one condition that makes the former area more "ripe for rivalry" after the cold war.[2] Thus a better understanding of the determinants of regional security institutions should help to illuminate the prospects—and perhaps even to suggest concrete strategies—for creating and strengthening those of the Asia-Pacific as part of a more comprehensive program for promoting peace and stability in the region.[3]

At the same time, a comparative analysis of the formal security arrangements of the Asia-Pacific regions promises to make a contribution to the more general theoretical literature on international security institutions.[4] Although a substantial number of works on the sources of alliances already exists, scholars have yet to ask why such institutions are formalized and elaborated to varying degrees and why they assume bilateral versus multilateral forms (when more than two potential partners are available).[5] Likewise, no systematic attempts have been made to understand variations in regional collective security institutions.[6]

The use of an explicitly comparative approach should help to illuminate the causes of such differences. Nevertheless, the purpose of this essay is not theory testing per se. Rather, the goal is simply to identify factors that would seem to account for the variation in regional security institutionalization that has been observed. To this end, I borrow freely from several well-established theoretical perspectives in the international relations literature. The first of these, neorealism, seeks to explain variations in international outcomes primarily in terms of the structure of the international system, which is typically defined as the distribution of material capabilities among states. Neorealist analyses may differ depending on whether the focus is on global structures or those at the regional level. But for all neorealists, the intrinsic nature of states as well as the international institutions they may create are relatively unimportant.[7]

In contrast, two other important theoretical perspectives stress precisely those factors that neorealism deemphasizes. State-level or "second-image" theories seek to explain international outcomes primarily in terms of state characteristics. Over the years, such theories have proliferated, and there is no consensus on precisely which state characteristics—political system, level of development, national identity, political culture, ideology, etc.—are most consequential. But second-image theorists would agree that such factors are determinative of whether or not state preferences and strategies are compatible and, just as importantly, whether or not states perceive them as being so. Finally, institutional theories seek to highlight the role that international institutions play in shaping international outcomes. The problem for the present analysis is that variations in institutionalization are precisely the outcomes we are seeking to explain. Nevertheless, institutional theory can be useful by sensitizing us to the possibility of path dependence as a result of sunk costs and altered incentive structures.

In fact, this analysis finds that all three of these theoretical perspectives help to account for the differences in security institutionalization observed between the Asia-Pacific and the Euro-Atlantic areas. But some appear to be more helpful than others. In particular, differences in regional structural factors, especially the relative capabilities and geographical dispersion of the states in each area, appear to have been leading determinants of this cross-regional variation. Such factors, which are emphasized by fine-grained versions of neorealism, tended to promote the creation of multilateral alliances and stronger institutional forms in the Euro-Atlantic while favoring bilateralism and less elaborate and formalized institutions in the Asia-Pacific, especially in the early postwar years. Until relatively recently, moreover, the effects of these regional structural differences appear to have been significantly reinforced by differences in the patterns of state characteristics, especially those concerning historical animosities and levels of development, to be found in the two regions. In addition, the nature of the institutions established (or not, as the case may be) at one point in time has restricted the range of institutional possibilities at later junctures. Arguably, the constraining effect of the regional structural factors that inhibited the creation of strong multilateral security institutions in the Asia-Pacific has attenuated with the passage of time, but the state-level obstacles remain significant.

The following section surveys the empirical record of security institutions in the Asia-Pacific and Euro-Atlantic regions, highlighting the most important differences. A second section discusses the inadequacy of a global structural perspective for explaining these differences. The third section explores the role of regional structural factors in producing the contrasting institutional outcomes. A fourth section explicates the reinforcing effects of state characteristics and the role of institutional path-dependence. In a conclusion, I draw upon the preceding analysis to consider the future prospects for security institutionalization in the Asia-Pacific.

THE EMPIRICAL RECORD

Since World War II, both the Euro-Atlantic and Asia-Pacific have hosted large numbers of security institutions. Most prominent among these have been strong—by historical standards—alliances linking the United States to regional actors, but there have also been some modest regional collective security arrangements.[8] What distinguishes the regions is not so much the sheer number of security institutions as it is the greater elaboration and formalization of those ties and the more multilateral nature of alliances in the Euro-Atlantic area.

ALLIANCE FORMATION DURING THE EARLY COLD WAR YEARS, 1945–1955

These differences emerged by the early 1950s. By that time, the countries of the Euro-Atlantic area had formed a highly institutionalized 12-member alliance, NATO, which included both an elaborate political apparatus for consultation, policy coordination, and joint decisionmaking and an integrated military planning and command structure. Grounded in the North Atlantic Treaty of 1949, NATO also built on the preexisting Western Union, which six West European states had established the previous year. In the early 1950s, moreover, five of the original continental members of NATO in combination with the Federal Republic of Germany (FRG) elaborated plans for a supranational European Defense Community (EDC), which, however, never came to fruition.[9]

In contrast, the security institutions of the Asia-Pacific region in the early postwar years consisted primarily of a series of bilateral agreements concluded by the United States and individual countries: the Philippines (August 1951), Japan (September 1951), South Korea (October 1953), and Nationalist China (December 1954). The only—and still modest—departure from this initial pattern was the trilateral security treaty signed by the United States, Australia, and New Zealand (ANZUS) in September 1951. It was not until 1954 that a multilateral arrangement bearing any resemblance to NATO was born with the signing of the Manila Pact that led to the creation of the eight-member Southeast Asian Treaty Organization (SEATO) the following year.[10]

Especially in comparison with NATO, moreover, most of these U.S.-sponsored arrangements were only weakly institutionalized. As a general rule, they involved less binding security guarantees, few if any common policymaking structures, little joint military planning, and minimal or no integrated command bodies and military infrastructure.[11] In addition, they failed to include some important noncommunist regional actors, such as Indonesia, Burma, and India, all of which had been mooted as potential members of SEATO, and, after its independence in 1957, Malaya.[12] It is also noteworthy that, in contrast to the Western Union and NATO, none of these alliances were established until after the outbreak of the Korean War and that no comparable formal security arrangements of any kind—bilateral or multilateral—were concluded among the many U.S. allies in the region.

THE EMERGENCE OF REGIONAL COLLECTIVE SECURITY INSTITUTIONS

A second distinct phase of regional security institution-building took place in the late 1960s and 1970s. In the Euro-Atlantic area, the principal development during this period was the establishment of the bloc-transcending Conference on Security and Cooperation in Europe (CSCE) in 1973 and the signing two years later of the Helsinki Final Act, which included a set of principles concerning the behavior of participating states and several confidence-building measures (CBMs).[13] Although the CSCE was better characterized as a process than as an organization, through the 1980s it nevertheless served as the pan-European forum for the negotiation of arms control agreements and additional CBMs.

In the Asia-Pacific region, in contrast, there was no comparable movement, however modest, toward the establishment of an all-inclusive regional collective security system.[14] What little activity of this nature that did take place occurred at the subregional level, with the founding of the Association of Southeast Asian Nations (ASEAN) in 1967.[15] Yet even ASEAN could be characterized as a security institution in only the most limited terms. Indeed, only in 1992 did its leaders explicitly agree for the first time that security cooperation was a worthy goal and begin to address security issues directly.[16] In addition, ASEAN contained only very general behavioral prescriptions, such as noninterference in the internal affairs of other members and renunciation of the threat or use of force; few formal mechanisms, which have seen little or no use; and no military component. Instead, ASEAN consisted primarily of regular dialogues and consultation, leading on occasion to consensual ad hoc agreements that placed few constraints on its members.[17] SEATO, for its part, rather than grow, began to lose members and was finally disbanded in 1977, although the Manila Pact on which it was based remained in force.[18]

THE POST-COLD WAR PERIOD, 1990–PRESENT

It was not until the 1990s that either region witnessed a degree of security institution-building that was in any way comparable to that of the early postwar years. In the Euro-Atlantic area, this activity has assumed a wide variety of regional and subregional forms. The CSCE has been transformed from a process into a formal organization consisting of several permanent bodies, and it has acquired a growing number of security-related mechanisms as well as a new name (OSCE). NATO has been streamlined and has developed new appendages—the North Atlantic Cooperation Council (NACC), the Partnership for Peace (PFP), the Euro-Atlantic Partnership Council, and the NATO-Russia Permanent Joint Council—that have joined it and its members with erstwhile adversaries and European neutrals. The members of the European Union (EU) have sought to fashion a new European security and defense identity (ESDI) based on a revitalized WEU and the EU's own new Common Foreign and Security Policy (CFSP).[19] And the countries of the region have forged several important pan-European agreements concerning arms control and CBMs.

Although not insignificant, the level of post–cold war institution building in the Asia-Pacific region has not been nearly as great. Here, the most important development has been the initiation, in July 1994, of the ASEAN Regional Forum.[20] By bringing together virtually all the states in the area, including the major powers, the ARF represents the potential kernel of a regional collective security system. So far, however, it remains only minimally institutionalized, possessing few formal structures or procedures. Instead, it continues to emphasize dialogue, consultation, and informal consensus in lieu of decisive action, with the most noteworthy achievements taking the form of modest CBMs. As a result, it has not yet helped to resolve any actual conflicts or yielded any concrete institutional measures that might significantly enhance the security of its participants.[21]

In addition, the end of the cold war has been followed by considerable activity in the area of bilateral security relationships. The closure of the last U.S. bases in the Philippines in 1992 was offset by the conclusion of modest military support arrangements between the United States and Singapore, Malaysia, Indonesia, and Brunei.[22] In December 1995, Australia and Indonesia signed a very general agreement on security cooperation, although this was subsequently suspended.[23] The United States and Japan have taken steps, most notably the issuance of a revised set of defense cooperation guidelines, to reaffirm and strengthen their long-standing security ties.[24] And even Vietnam has moved toward establishing military ties with the United States.[25] None of these bilateral developments, however, have notably altered the overall security architecture of the region. Even the U.S.-Japan alliance, which is the strongest of these bilateral arrangements, remains far less elaborated than NATO.

In sum, both the Asia-Pacific and the Euro-Atlantic areas have hosted large numbers of security institutions since shortly after World War II, and both have seen a renewal of institution-building activity in the post–cold war era. Nevertheless, the security institutions of the two regions have been characterized by important differences concerning the degree of formalization, elaborateness, and multilateralism. How might we best make sense of these regional patterns of security institutionalization, in terms of both their similarities and their differences?

THE INADEQUACY OF A GLOBAL STRUCTURAL PERSPECTIVE

A common starting point for the analysis of security affairs is neorealist theory. Neorealist explanations typically emphasize the basic structure of the international system, as defined primarily by the number and relative capabilities of major powers. In fact, a global structural perspective does help to explain the rapid proliferation of security institutions in both the Asia-Pacific and the Euro-Atlantic during the decade after World War II as well as the emergence of proto-collective security institutions in later years. It is much less able, however, to account for the important differences across the two regions that are identified above.

From a global perspective, the Euro-Atlantic and Asia-Pacific areas shared a number of important structural features during the early postwar years. In each case, a would-be regional hegemon lay in ruins, defeated and occupied. Although both Germany and Japan continued to represent potential threats, should their war-making potentials ever be revived without adequate controls, the dominant powers then vying for influence in each region were the United States and the Soviet Union, a situation that reflected the highly bipolar nature of the new global power structure. Increasingly, moreover, and perhaps quite naturally in view of this bipolar structure, relations between the two superpowers were marked by tension and hostility. As a result, the United States became ever more inclined to seek the rapid political and economic rehabilitation of the defeated regional powers, or at least those parts of their former territories lying within its sphere of influence. From the U.S. perspective, it was imperative to deny the Soviet Union control over the industrial and military resources of Germany and Japan.[26] And ideally, their energies could be enlisted in the emerging global competition for influence between Soviet communism and the West.

These common factors go far toward explaining the emergence of formal U.S. security ties to states in both regions. American efforts to hasten the restoration of sovereignty, the economic recovery, and the rearmament of the defeated powers raised acute security concerns among their regional neighbors, which had so recently been the victims of German and Japanese aggression. Consequently, the United States found it expedient to offer formal security guarantees to Western-oriented states in both areas in order to obtain their acquiescence in its lenient policies toward Germany and Japan.[27] Otherwise, the erection of strong regional bulwarks against Soviet influence would have been much more problematic.[28]

Although a global structural perspective yields important insights, it does not begin to provide a fully satisfactory account of the security institutionalization that has occurred in the Asia-Pacific and Euro-Atlantic regions. Several of the leading motives for the creation and maintenance of security institutions do not fit easily with such an analytical framework. Above all, there is the rather awkward fact that many of the initial postwar security arrangements were directed at least as much against Germany and Japan as they were against the Soviet Union, notwithstanding the severely weakened positions of the defeated powers.

In addition, the structural similarities cannot explain the important variations identified above in the nature of security institutionalization across the two regions. The difference in the degree of multilateralism is even more puzzling when one considers U.S. preferences. Although these are often portrayed as fundamentally different in the two regions, they were in fact quite similar. The Truman administration was not enthusiastic about incurring formal security obligations in either area, but its natural inclination and initial predisposition, once the need to extend security guarantees became clear, was to seek multilateral solutions. In the Euro-Atlantic area, U.S. officials never gave any serious consideration to purely bilateral arrangements. In the Asia-Pacific as well, the original U.S. conception was of a multilateral Pacific Pact that would include the United States, Japan, the Philippines, Australia, New Zealand, and possibly Indonesia.[29] Yet this proposal was never realized. And the primarily bilateral nature of the institutional outcome in the Asia-Pacific would seem to be rendered yet more problematic by the fact that, given the differences in timing, an attractive multilateral model already existed in the form of NATO.[30]

A global structural perspective is no more satisfactory for explaining subsequent institutional developments in the two regions. Clearly, the emergence of the CSCE was facilitated by the considerable improvement in U.S.-Soviet relations that began in the 1960s, just as the end of the cold war set the stage for the further institutionalization of the CSCE and the first steps toward the possible erection of a collective security system in the Asia-Pacific that have occurred in the 1990s. In Northeast Asia in particular, recent concerns among American allies that the United States might reduce its security role in the region has done much to prompt interest in multilateral alternatives.[31] Yet the decline and, later, the disappearance of cold war antagonisms cannot account for the important differences that mark the two regions—above all the fact that inclusive collective security arrangements appeared much earlier and have attained much higher levels of institutionalization in the Euro-Atlantic area—or for the precise character of the institutional outcomes, given the wide range of possibilities.

THE IMPORTANCE OF REGIONAL STRUCTURAL FACTORS

The limitations of a global structural perspective suggests the need, at least as a first step, for a more fine-grained neorealist analysis that is sensitive to regional characteristics. Such an approach directs our attention to subsystemic structural conditions, such as the number, relative capabilities, and location of regional actors, that can serve as important additional incentives for and impediments to security institutionalization.[32] For example, one important factor that a focus limited to the power and policies of the United States and Soviet Union fails to capture is the leading role that lingering concerns about potential German and Japanese power played well after the end of World War II in shaping regional security cooperation. After all, it was those countries, not the Soviet Union, that had just waged unsuccessful campaigns of aggression against many of their neighbors. Consequently, it was natural for surrounding countries to continue to fear and to seek assurances against them, even though they had been eclipsed in terms of actual capabilities by the new superpowers. Indeed, Asia-Pacific states initially demanded U.S. security assurances almost exclusively out of concerns about a possible resurgence of Japanese power once the United States began to press for a liberal peace treaty.[33] Likewise, France, in seeking alliance ties with the United States, was motivated at least as much by the anxieties triggered by Western moves to create a separate German state out of the western zones of occupation.[34] Several years would have to pass before the Soviet Union and its satellites would replace them in the eyes of many as the principal regional threat. Only the last early cold war security institutions to be erected in the Asia-Pacific can be viewed principally as attempts to block the expansion of communist influence.[35]

The employment of a regional structural perspective is even more useful for highlighting dissimilarities across the two areas under consideration that can serve as the basis for a more satisfactory explanation. At least two differences in the geostrategic circumstances of the U.S. spheres of influence in the Asia-Pacific and Euro-Atlantic help to account for the disparate institutional outcomes, especially during the early postwar years.[36] The first is differences in the relative sizes of the extant regional actors. The construction of security institutions in Western Europe benefited from the presence of two major—if no longer great—powers, Britain and France, which were willing and able to take the initiative and play leading roles in this process. In the Asia-Pacific, in contrast, no countries of comparable rank existed.[37] As a result, although even a country as large as France frequently evinced fears of German domination, Japan's potential regional partners had even more reason to be concerned and thus to eschew security ties with the former hegemon for fear of being dominated.[38]

At least as important, however, are the geographic characteristics that have set the two regions apart. For example, one finds considerable differences in the proximity of regional states to one another. In the Euro-Atlantic area, many countries shared a common border with or lay only a short distance from the former enemy. As a result, it was not difficult to imagine that a serious military threat could quickly materialize if and when the shackles of the occupation were removed. In the Asia-Pacific, in contrast, most regional actors were located far enough from Japan that they had somewhat less (although still good) reason to be concerned. Japan would have to acquire a substantial power projection capability before it could once again threaten them, and it would be relatively easy to interpose the U.S. navy. Consequently, they had less incentive to erect strong institutional security structures—beyond bilateral ties with the United States—as a hedge against a possible revival of Japanese militarism. This situation may also help to explain the lack of institution building prior to the outbreak of the Korean War.

Geographic proximity also made it more natural and easier for West European states to work together. Proximity meant a greater degree of security interdependence; an external threat to one country often represented a threat to others. In addition, considerable gains were to be had through cooperation, since the security of one country could often be enhanced by strengthening the defenses of its contiguous neighbors.

In the Asia-Pacific, by contrast, greater distances meant that threats to one country did not necessarily translate into common security concerns requiring joint solutions. As a result, less was to be gained through multilateralism, and the obstacles to collective military preparations were greater. The assumption of defense obligations to other countries in the region was unlikely to enhance a state's security and might well, in the event of actual hostilities, have the effect of tying down scarce defense resources that would be needed elsewhere.[39]

Finally, the nature of the respective institutional security arrangements was importantly shaped by the geographical circumstances of the regional power center. In Europe, the industrial resources of western Germany were located hard on the dividing line between the two emerging blocs. Consequently, the task of deterring and defending against possible attacks on German territory, especially once the outbreak of the Korean War convinced Western leaders that

Soviet military restraint could no longer be assumed, was a highly demanding one. It required the active participation of all of western Germany's neighbors as well as that of the Federal Republic itself. This requirement in turn necessitated the establishment of elaborate political and military structures to determine and coordinate the myriad activities of the allies and to ensure that German armed forces, once formed, would be under tight allied supervision and control.[40]

In the Asia-Pacific, by contrast, the vital center of regional power, Japan, although actually closer to the territory of the Soviet Union than was Germany, lay off the Eurasian mainland. As a result, the United States, by virtue of its substantial naval and air capabilities, could defend Japanese territory almost single-handedly. There was no compelling need to involve other countries, and since relatively few Japanese resources, in addition to U.S. basing rights, were required, there was little need for elaborate bilateral structures either. By the same token, because of their distance from the Soviet threat and the availability of U.S. naval protection, other island states in the region had little to gain from military ties with Japan. It was simply a less important potential security partner than was the Federal Republic in Europe.

A further consequence of the relatively low level of security interdependence in the Asia-Pacific resulting from the geography of the region was that the United States initially had little interest in making security commitments to noncommunist territories that bordered directly on or that lay just overland from the Soviet Union and its Chinese ally, e.g., South Korea, Hong Kong, Indochina, Thailand, and Burma. Not only were these areas of relatively little strategic importance, but they seemed highly vulnerable to attack. As special envoy and soon to be Secretary of State John Foster Dulles noted in early 1952, "the United States should not assume formal commitments which overstrain its present capabilities and give rise to military expectations we could not fulfill, particularly in terms of land forces."[41] Consequently, the Pacific Pact proposal proffered by the United States was limited to offshore island states.

The initial U.S. inclination to exclude mainland territories from its formal security sphere in the Asia-Pacific had yet another important consequence. From London's perspective, not only would it leave the British colonies of Hong Kong and Malaya unprotected, but it would suggest that Britain was renouncing its responsibilities in the region. Thus the British voiced strong objections to the U.S. proposal. Primarily as a result of this opposition, the multilateral Pacific Plan quickly dissolved into bilateral arrangements with Japan and the Philippines and the trilateral ANZUS treaty.[42]

In more recent years, the arguably higher level of security interdependence bred by greater geographical proximity in Europe as a whole has fostered the development of stronger collective security institutions there than in the Asia-Pacific. One might also expect the growth of Chinese power to have had a stultifying impact in this regard, but it has thus far had, in fact, the opposite effect.

An important motive for the formation of the ARF was the desire to constrain China by engaging it in a constructive manner.[43] Nevertheless, although China has not (yet) posed enough of a threat to provoke strong balancing behavior by its neighbors, the creation and strengthening of many bilateral security arrangements in the region as well as the ARF itself represent attempts to respond to the rise of Chinese by ensuring continued U.S. engagement.[44]

REINFORCING STATE-LEVEL AND INSTITUTIONAL FACTORS

Differences in regional structural factors appear to account to a considerable extent for postwar differences in security institutionalization in the Asia-Pacific and Euro-Atlantic areas, especially during the early cold war years. Nevertheless, two other sets of factors seem to have importantly reinforced and sometimes supplemented the effects of local geostrategic circumstances. These are the characteristics of the states in the region and their perceptions of one another, and the path-determining effects of preexisting international institutions.[45]

STATE CHARACTERISTICS

In contrast to neorealist theory and other systemic or "third image" approaches, a number of theoretical attempts to explain international relations have emphasized the characteristics of the units, in this case nation-states. Notwithstanding its structural "neorealist" turn of the past two decades, even realist theory has traditionally placed considerable weight on the nature of states and their perceptions of one another.[46] And over the years, an almost bewildering array of other unit-level theories, concerning everything from class and social structure to political institutions to ideology and culture, have been developed and advanced. Despite their significant differences, these approaches are united in agreement on the importance of the intrinsic behavioral and perceptual dispositions of states, whatever their origins. In particular, such factors can greatly shape the possibilities for security cooperation.

Among other things, this state-level perspective directs our attention to differences in the character of Germany and Japan and in regional perceptions of them, differences which have had important institutional consequences. Although there was little love lost between Germany and her western neighbors after World War II, the especially brutal nature of Japan's wartime behavior (and, before that, its colonial practices) erected unusually high obstacles to postwar cooperation with potential regional partners, obstacles that in fact have still not been overcome. These differing legacies of the conflict were subsequently reinforced by the types of policies pursued by the defeated powers. Once established in 1949, the FRG aggressively pursued reconciliation with its neighbors, championing novel schemes for European integration that might even involve the sacrifice of important aspects of state sovereignty. Japan, in contrast, had minimal dealings with nearby countries, focusing instead on its bilateral relationship with the United States.[47]

Consequently, fears of Japanese intentions and anti-Japanese sentiment more generally remained strong long after the war. Shortly after the failure of the American Pacific Pact proposal, Dulles, who had been the chief U.S. negotiator, wrote that many prospective members of any Asian alliance "have memories of Japanese aggression which are so vivid that they are reluctant to create a Mutual Security Pact which will include Japan."[48] In 1954, when the members of the Western Union and NATO were willing to add Germany to their ranks, Australia and New Zealand opposed the inclusion of Japan in the relatively inconsequential SEATO on the grounds that to do so would be provocative in areas where the physical or psychological scars of the war remained unhealed.[49] And South Korea and Japan, both close U.S. allies with several nearby common enemies, did not even normalize their political relations until 1965 because of historical animosities.[50]

Nor have intra-regional obstacles to security cooperation been limited to lingering attitudes of enmity toward defeated would-be hegemons, especially in the Asia-Pacific region. Another important unit-level factor, especially in the early postwar years, has been the legacy of imperialism, especially distrust, and in some cases outright hostility, on the part of former colonies toward the former imperial powers. As Dulles observed in the language of the time, "Many Orientals fear that Westerners are incapable of cooperating with them on a basis of political, economic, and social equality."[51] As a result, newly independent states were often hesitant or unwilling to enter into the security arrangements proffered by the United States, especially where doing so meant compromising their neutrality.[52] In particular, Indonesia, Burma, and India had no interest in joining SEATO.[53] Indeed, Indonesia under Sukarno pursued a foreign policy based on confrontation against all forms (both real and imagined) of colonialism and imperialism, opposing in particular the U.S. and British military presence in the Philippines, Malaysia, and Singapore.[54]

More generally, the fact that the countries of the Euro-Atlantic area have been characterized by a high degree of political, economic, and cultural homogeneity has arguably contributed to a natural cohesiveness and mutual identification that facilitated the emergence of multilateral security arrangements independently of any favorable geographical circumstances.[55] In the Asia-Pacific region, by contrast, security cooperation has often been impeded by significant differences in the level of political and economic development, not to mention the possibility of racist attitudes. Thus, in the early 1950s, Australia and New Zealand were reluctant to assume defense obligations to the Philippines, which they viewed as politically unstable and, in any case, unable to make much of a contribution to their common security.[56] As Dulles noted in his post-mortem on the Pacific Pact negotiations, "some countries are as yet unable or unwilling to qualify for definitive security arrangements under the 'Vandenberg formula' of 'continuous and effective self-help and mutual aid.' "[57]

Occasionally, other dyadic tensions and conflicts rooted in state characteristics have interfered with institution building or precluded greater multilateralism. For example, in the early 1950s, Australia, because of the risk that communists might come to power in Jakarta as well as revisionist Indonesian claims to western New Guinea, opposed its inclusion in U.S. proposals for multilateral security arrangements.[58] By the same token, Indonesia's decision to jettison its policy of confrontation with Malaysia and adopt a more conciliatory attitude in the mid-1960s following Sukarno's replacement by Suharto was a necessary condition for the establishment of ASEAN.[59]

Curiously, these unit-level differences could on occasion serve as a fillip to multilateralism. One consideration that influenced the initial U.S. design for a Pacific Pact was the desire to have Asiatic representation in the form of the Philippines and possibly Indonesia.[60] Later, the imperative to avoid the taint of imperialism was an important U.S. motive for resisting the expansion of ANZUS to include Britain, notwithstanding entreaties from London, and for creating SEATO.[61] A primary purpose of Indonesia's support for ASEAN was to alter its neighbors' negative perceptions of its intentions.[62] Likewise, an important Japanese motive for promoting multilateral security cooperation in the region after the cold war has been to reassure others.[63]

INSTITUTIONAL PATH-DEPENDENCE

Consideration of institutional factors themselves as possible explanatory variables can further enrich our understanding of the patterns of security institutionalization considered in this essay. The principal conceptual contribution of an institutional perspective in this context is that of path dependence.[64] The choice of institutional arrangements at one point in time can have an important bearing on institutional (and other) possibilities and outcomes at subsequent junctures. Although this perspective would thus seem to be most useful for explaining later rather than earlier developments in a temporal sequence, it also helps to justify the considerable attention paid so far to the initial phase of security institutionalization in the two regions.

In fact, the search for institutional determinants of the postwar security outcomes in the Asia-Pacific and the Euro-Atlantic must go back at least to the institutional legacies of World War II, especially the occupation regimes imposed on Germany and Japan. Differences in those regimes contributed to the different regional configurations of power and interest that in turn influenced the timing and nature of the initial postwar regional security institutions.

In Japan, the United States effectively enjoyed total control over the administration of the occupation. It was dependent on other countries primarily to legitimize its policies, especially when it sought to reach a peace agreement with Tokyo at the beginning of the 1950s.[65] In Germany, in contrast, power was divided, both de jure and de facto, among the United States, the Soviet Union, Britain, and France.

This power-sharing arrangement had several important consequences. First, it hastened the unfolding of the cold war in the European theater. Conflicting objectives with regard to Germany contributed to a rapid breakdown of four-power cooperation and early decisions by the three western powers to proceed jointly with the political and economic rehabilitation of their zones of occupation. These moves helped in turn to put the issue of U.S. security guarantees to the countries of Western Europe on the agenda as early as 1948, some two years sooner than occurred in the Asia-Pacific.

Second, the multilateral nature of the occupation regime meant that, even after attempts to find a common solution with the Soviet Union to the German problem had ceased, the United States could not easily pursue its objectives in the western part of Germany unilaterally. Rather, it still needed to obtain the cooperation of Britain and France. Thus these two European powers enjoyed greater leverage over U.S. policy than did any Asia-Pacific state. This leverage helped Britain and France to extract American security guarantees at an earlier date than was possible in the Asia-Pacific.

Finally, the presence of British and French as well as U.S. military forces in Western Germany meant that the territory of the FRG was covered by NATO security guarantees. As a result of this situation, France in particular was spared the need to agree to early German membership in the alliance. In contrast, a comparable Asia-Pacific security arrangement involving Japan could have been truly multilateral only if Japan had been included as a formal party from the outset. This, of course, was a requirement that all potential members of the proposed Pacific Pact other than the United States found highly objectionable.

Once the first postwar security institutions began to form in Europe, further institutional consequences followed. The multilateral Western Union offered a logical and compelling model for NATO, which can be understood primarily as an expansion of the former to include the United States and Canada.[66] In fact, given the prior existence of the Western Union, it would probably have been difficult for the United States to insist on organizing its security ties to Europe on a purely bilateral basis, even if it had wanted to.[67] In contrast, no such regional institutional template existed in the Asia-Pacific prior to the U.S. decision to offer security guarantees to countries in the area.

The early experience with NATO had a different set of consequences for the shape of the security institutions that were to emerge in the Asia-Pacific. Most importantly, objections to Article 5 of the North Atlantic Treaty that arose in the Senate during the ratification process led Truman administration negotiators, especially Dulles, to press for the inclusion of more open-ended, and thus less controversial, language in the guarantee clauses of the treaties concluded with allies in the Asia-Pacific.[68] In addition, prior military commitments in Europe made in the context of NATO caused the U.S. Joint Chiefs of Staff to object strongly to the assumption of any comparable obligations in the Asia-Pacific, especially while large numbers of forces were tied down in Korea. And later, it has been suggested, preexisting alliance arrangements were at least partly responsible for the lack of effort to develop true collective security or collective defense schemes in Southeast Asia.[69]

One can point to additional examples of institutional path dependence in the wake of the cold war. In both the Euro-Atlantic and Asia-Pacific regions, most of the institution building that has taken place since 1990 has centered on international institutions erected during previous decades. Few, if any, of the new security institutions have been created entirely from scratch. Consequently, one might legitimately wonder whether the OSCE, the NACC and the PFP, the CFSP, and the ARF might ever have emerged but for the prior existence of the CSCE, NATO, the EC, and ASEAN, respectively. Indeed, in the absence of ASEAN, something even as modest as the ARF might have been difficult to set up, given the continuing level of mistrust among the major powers in Northeast Asia.[70]

Moreover, the new institutions have strongly reflected the strengths and limitations of their predecessors. To continue with the example of the ARF, its extremely low level of formalization and elaboration is not surprising given the nature of ASEAN. In contrast, the architects of the new European security architecture have benefited in general from the prior existence of a much stronger and more diversified institutional basis on which to build. Of course, the degree to which the potential of preexisting institutional infrastructures is actually exploited will depend on a range of other factors, not least of which are the interests of their participants and the degree of amity and enmity that prevails among them, as suggested by the case of the ARF. Nevertheless, one can say that such institutional legacies will be especially determinative when the structure of the international system offers few clear imperatives, as has been the case since the end of the cold war.

CONCLUSION

This analysis has found that, using familiar theoretical approaches to the study of international relations, one can offer a highly satisfactory account of postwar patterns of security institutionalization in the Asia-Pacific and Euro-Atlantic regions. Commonplace analytical perspectives help to explain both the similarities and the differences in the institutional outcomes that have characterized the two regions. At the most general level, a global structural perspective helps to account for the rapid proliferation of security institutions in both regions during the decade after World War II and, to a lesser extent, the institution building that has taken place since 1990. It cannot explain, however, the much greater degrees of multilateralism and of institutional formalization and elaborateness to be found in the Euro-Atlantic area throughout the postwar era.

In order to understand these differences, it is necessary to consider structural factors of a primarily regional nature, such as the relative sizes and the geographical dispersion of relevant regional state actors. In particular, the absence of potential regional counterweights to Japan, the relatively great distances between Japan and other U.S. allies in the Asia-Pacific, and Japan's greater defensibility in comparison with West Germany resulted in fewer opportunities and incentives for security cooperation than existed in the Euro-Atlantic area during the early postwar years. These unfavorable structural circumstances were reinforced by state characteristics, such as enduring enmity toward Japan, mistrust of the former colonial powers, and disparate levels of development, that erected additional obstacles to the construction of strong multilateral security institutions in the region. Finally, we have seen how the presence (or absence) of regional institutions at one point in time has importantly shaped the possibilities for further institutional development at later junctures.

Missing, perhaps conspicuously so, from this analysis has been a search for internal motives for the formation of regional security institutions. Important recent studies of the sources of alliances have shown that weak regimes sometimes seek security ties with other states in order to shore up their positions vis-à-vis domestic opponents.[71] In fact, considerations of this nature have not been entirely absent from the calculations of postwar national leaders in the Euro-Atlantic and Asia-Pacific areas. For example, an important initial purpose of the North Atlantic Treaty was to raise confidence and boost morale in the countries of Western Europe.[72] And SEATO was set up as much to counter the danger of internal subversion in the countries of Southeast Asia as it was to deter more traditional external forms of aggression. In later years, Indonesia at least viewed ASEAN largely as a means to address internal threats by preventing external interference in its domestic affairs.[73]

Overall, however, domestic security concerns appear to have done relatively little, in comparison with the other factors identified in this paper, to promote or hinder the formation of security institutions in both regions. In Western Europe, apprehensions about the durability of the democratic orientation of several countries immediately after World War II were short-lived. And although domestic instability in some of the postcolonial Asia-Pacific states due to a lack of strong central political institutions or the presence of serious internal challenges sometimes served to obstruct the establishment of alliance ties by diminishing the appetite of potential partners for greater security cooperation, this does not seem to have been the dominant determinant.

THE FUTURE OF SECURITY INSTITUTIONS IN THE ASIA-PACIFIC

On the basis of the preceding analysis, one might derive several conclusions about the prospects for further security institutionalization in the Asia-Pacific. In important respects, the obstacles to multilateralism and the development of more elaborate and formalized institutions have been reduced. Other significant impediments remain, however, and some new ones have emerged. Thus the further development of regional security institutions, especially those of an inclusive nature, is possible, but progress is not likely to come as easily as it has in Europe.

Turning first to conclusions that follow from the global structural perspective, the end of the East-West ideological conflict that marked the cold war should, on balance, facilitate the formation of inclusive regional collective security institutions, as has already begun to occur with the formation of the ARF. At the same time, however, it renders problematic the preservation of existing alliances—primarily those involving the United States—predicated on the Soviet threat and precludes the creation of strong new ones, absent the emergence of compelling new security rationales.

A second structural development of a global nature, the steady erosion, if not the definitive end, of U.S. hegemony in its former spheres of influence, has ambiguous implications. In some respects, it complicates the task of institution building and maintenance. In theory, the existence of an effective hegemon can compensate to a considerable extent for the absence of common interests and even the presence of significant conflicts among other regional actors.[74] During the decades since World War II, and especially in recent years, however, both the relative power of the United States and the size of its military presence in the Far East has declined, reducing its previously unrivaled potential for inducing or coercing security cooperation.[75]

Nevertheless, as suggested above, one should not exaggerate the ability—or at least the willingness—of the United States to impose multilateral institutions where they are not wanted. Its most ambitious proposal, the ill-fated Pacific Pact, was blocked by the opposition of much smaller regional actors. Paradoxically, moreover, the risk of U.S. disengagement and the desire to prevent it has served as a leading motive for the creation of new security ties in the Asia-Pacific. Thus perhaps the most that can be said is that American policy preferences will play an important role in shaping institutional outcomes in the region, notwithstanding the relative decline of U.S. power.

To the extent that global structural conditions have become yet less determinative of regional security arrangements, local structural circumstances should be even more so in the future. And from this perspective, the conditions for institutionalization are perhaps more auspicious than at any time since World War II. First, and paralleling the relative decline of U.S. power, the Asia-Pacific has seen since the 1940s the steady emergence of a number of important regional actors with the potential, in principle, to play leadership roles, thanks to a combination of successful postwar economic recovery and development. These include Japan, Canada, South Korea, Australia, the ASEAN group, and, if one brings in former adversaries, China. Indeed, Australia, Canada, and ASEAN have been the sources of the most important multilateral institutional initiatives since the late 1980s.

One caveat is nevertheless in order. The regional distribution of power remains highly skewed in favor of Japan and, increasingly, China. Consequently, the smaller countries may well continue to fear the possible domination of regional security arrangements by those countries. In addition, the rise of China may continue to help to breathe new life into the bilateral alliances forged by the United States in Northeast Asia during the cold war, and it could even overcome the traditional obstacles to closer Japan-Korea security cooperation.[76]

Second, the implications of the geography of the Asia-Pacific, which previously militated against multilateralism, may have been altered by advances in military technology. The protection previously afforded by the great distances between many regional actors and, in a number of cases, their offshore locations has been eroded by increases in power projection capabilities through such mechanisms as the proliferation of ballistic missiles and advances in naval technology. The resulting higher levels of security interdependence should, other things being equal, provide incentives for greater security cooperation.

These reasons for expecting further security institutionalization, especially of a collective nature, must be tempered, however, by a recognition of the enduring obstacles to institution building presented by the characteristics of the states in the region and their perceptions of one another. Rather than reinforcing the effects of regional geostrategic circumstances, as they did during the cold war, these unit-level factors may tend to work counter to the favorable structural trends identified above. In contrast to Europe, the Asia-Pacific remains fractured by tensions and conflicts stemming largely from state characteristics that can hinder the development of collective security institutions even as they provide reasons for maintaining old alliances and creating new ones.[77]

Chief among these are enduring historical animosities. To some extent, security cooperation may also continue to be hampered by the legacy of colonialism, especially the mistrust that it has generated on the part of former colonies toward former colonizers, a hindrance that is absent in the Euro-Atlantic area. Perhaps more importantly, Japan's otherwise substantial potential to exert political leadership in the region continues to be crippled by strongly held memories in other countries of its actions as a colonial power and during World War II and its perceived failure, in marked contrast to Germany, to accept its responsibility and apologize for past misdeeds. It may still be many years, if not decades, before Japan can earn the confidence of potential regional security partners.[78] For its part, Japan will find it difficult to assume security commitments involving military obligations to other countries, even where they are welcome, because of deeply rooted anti-militarist sentiments.[79]

More generally, the region's diverse state characteristics and practices raise fears and create frictions that are not conducive to progress on international issues.[80] The actual and potential political and economic instability of many states, such as Russia, China, Indonesia, India, and Pakistan, generates uncertainty about their future intentions and behavior. Beyond that, substantial differences in political and economic systems and levels of development may simply make it more difficult to find common ground on security issues.[81] And some close observers have pointed to a deeply rooted Chinese preference for bilateralism and suspicion of multilateral institutions, which has served as a principal brake on the development of the ARF.[82]

Not to be overlooked are the places, such as Korea, Taiwan, the South China Sea, and the Kurile Islands, where one can still find revisionist attitudes toward basic questions of political jurisdiction and territorial boundaries. Such fundamental conflicts can complicate even the mere task of initiating and maintaining a dialogue on security issues, not to mention the actual creation of formal security ties. The trend toward democracy in several states, most notably South Korea, offers some grounds for optimism, since pairs of liberal democracies are less likely than other types of dyads to engage in military conflict.[83] But this trend is not yet sufficiently widespread or far enough advanced to promise a fundamental change in overall regional security relations.

Finally, security institutionalization will continue to be constrained by the lack of a strong base of preexisting regional institutions, especially institutions of a multilateral character, on which to build.[84] To be sure, the presence of old institutions can sometimes stand in the way of creating new, more functional structures. For example, the initially cool American responses to proposals in the late 1980s and early 1990s for an Asia-Pacific cooperative security structure reflected concerns that such a body would undermine the U.S. alliances in the region.[85] As suggested above, however, much of the recent activity in Europe has been facilitated by the presence of considerable institutional raw material with which to work. The other consequence of the absence of an elaborate and multilateral institutional infrastructure in the Asia-Pacific is that it may represent a lost opportunity for promoting reconciliation among past and present adversaries in the region. Although the historic improvement that has occurred in Germany's relations with its neighbors owes first and foremost to a conscious

German strategy to effect such change, it was certainly facilitated by the presence of security institutions such as NATO that, although created for other purposes, could be used to burnish the country's image in the eyes of its partners.[86]

Nevertheless, there is at least one institutional cause for optimism. Recent institutional developments in Europe, especially those of a pan-European nature, can serve as valuable sources of ideas for possible Asia-Pacific experiments. Indeed, some recent proposals have been explicitly modeled after aspects of the CSCE and OCSE.[87] Although too close an association with European structures can also taint an initiative in the eyes of some states in the region, their relatively successful track record may ultimately imbue derivative proposals for the Asia-Pacific with an appeal that can overcome parochial resistance.

ACKNOWLEDGMENT

I would like to thank John Ikenberry, Michael Mastanduno, Oran Young, Thomas Berger, and other participants in the project on "The Emerging International Relations of the Asia-Pacific Region" for helpful comments and suggestions.

ENDNOTES

1. This analysis emphasizes those parts of Asia that are contiguous with the Pacific ocean, namely northeast and southeast Asia.

2. Richard K. Betts, "Wealth, Power, and Instability: East Asia and the United States after the Cold War," *International Security* 18, no. 3 (Winter 1993/94): 34–77, and Aaron Friedberg, "Ripe for Rivalry: Prospects for Peace in a Multipolar Asia," *International Security* 19, no. 3 (Winter 19993/94): 5–33.

3. It should be noted that this paper does not attempt to undertake the equally important task of evaluating the effects and effectiveness of different types of regional security institutions.

4. For recent overviews of this literature, see Steven Weber, "Institutions and Change," in Michael W. Doyle and G. John Ikenberry, eds., *New Thinking in International Relations Theory* (Boulder, CO: Westview, 1997), pp. 229–65, and Lisa L. Martin and Beth Simmons, "Theories and Empirical Studies of International Institutions," *International Organization* 52, no. 4 (Autumn 1998): 729–57. Most of the extant theoretically informed works on international institutions in the Asia-Pacific focus on nonsecurity issue areas. See, for example, Vinod K. Aggarwal, "Building International Institutions in the Asia-Pacific," *Asian Survey* 33, no. 11 (Nov. 1993): 1029–42; Joseph M. Grieco, "Realism and Regionalism: American Power and German and Japanese Institutional Strategies during and after the Cold War," in Ethan B. Kapstein and Michael Mastanduno, eds., *Unipolar Politics: Realism and State Strategies after the Cold War* (New York: Columbia University Press, 1999), pp. 319–53; and Peter J. Katzenstein, "Regionalism in Comparative Perspective," *Cooperation and Conflict* Vol. 31, no. 2 (1996): 129–59. The principle exception to this generalization is Andrew Mack and

John Ravenhill, eds., *Pacific Cooperation: Building Economic and Security Regimes in the Asia-Pacific Region* (St. Leonards, Australia: Allen & Unwin, 1994), which examines both economic and security regimes.

5. One might justifiably question whether much of alliance theory actually considers alliances *qua* institutions rather than merely as alignments. For example, one particularly influential study, Stephen M. Walt, *The Origins of Alliances* (Ithaca, NY: Cornell University Press, 1987), defines alliance as any formal or informal relationship of security cooperation between sovereign states. This definition would not seem to preclude purely ad hoc, one-shot arrangements growing out of a transitory alignment of interests.

6. Two recent books employ a theoretically informed, comparative approach to study regional security. Emanuel Adler and Michael Barnett, eds., *Security Communities* (Cambridge: Cambridge University Press, 1998), focuses on security communities, which are ideational constructs, while David A. Lake and Patrick M. Morgan, eds., *Regional Orders: Building Security in a New World* (University Park: Pennsylvania State University Press, 1997), examines what are termed "regional orders," which refer to modes of conflict management. Neither, however, is explicitly concerned with formal collective security organizations per se, although there are likely to be important links between the three phenomena.

7. The seminal neorealist work is Kenneth N. Waltz, *Theory of International Politics* (Reading, MA: Addison-Wesley, 1979).

8. The analysis will exclude the security institutions such as the Warsaw Treaty Organization that linked the Soviet Union to its respective regional allies.

9. In 1955, the FRG was admitted to both NATO and the WU, and the latter was renamed the Western European Union (WEU).

10. The signatories included the United States, Britain, France, Australia, New Zealand, the Philippines, Thailand, and Pakistan.

11. For descriptions of the limitations of SEATO, see Ralph Braibanti, "International Implications of the Manila Pact," American I.P.R. Paper No. 1 (New York: American Institute of Pacific Relations, Inc., December 1957), and George Modelski, "SEATO: Its Functions and Organization," in Modelski, ed., *SEATO: Six Studies* (Vancouver: University of British Columbia, 1962), pp. 1–45 at 38–9.

12. In 1957, Britain agreed to guarantee the security of Malaya (later Malaysia), its former colony, under the terms of the Anglo-Malayan Defense Agreement (AMDA), with which Australia and New Zealand associated themselves in 1959.

13. Also of note is the 1971 Four-Power Agreement on Berlin, signed by the United States, Soviet Union, Britain, and France, which codified the status of the divided city.

14. As for alliance-like arrangements, the Anglo-Malaysian Defense Agreement was replaced in 1971 by the Five Power Defense Arrangements (FPDA) linking Britain, Australia, New Zealand, Malaysia, and Singapore. These new arrangements, however, were merely consultative in nature. See Muthia Alagappa, "Asian Practice of Security: Key Features and Explanations," in Alagappa, *Asian Security Practice: Material and Ideational Influences* (Stanford, CA: Stanford University Press, 1999), pp. 611–76 at 634.

15. The five original members were Indonesia, Malaysia, the Philippines, Singapore, and Thailand. Brunei joined on attaining independence in 1984.

16. Alice Ba, "The ASEAN Regional Forum: Maintaining the Regional Idea in Southeast Asia," *International Journal* 52, no. 4 (Autumn 1997): 635–56 at 648. The 1976 "Declaration of ASEAN Accord' explicitly excluded security as one of the subjects to be addressed within the framework of ASEAN cooperation.

17. See, for example, Michael Leifer, *ASEAN and the Security of South-East Asia* (London: Routledge, 1989), Michael Leifer, "The ASEAN Regional Forum," Adelphi Paper, no. 302 (Oxford: Oxford University Press, 1996), and Sheldon W. Simon, "Security Prospects in Southeast Asia: Collaborative Efforts and the ASEAN Regional Forum," *Pacific Review* 11, no. 2 (Feb. 1998): 195–212.

18. France ceased to participate in 1966, and Pakistan withdrew in 1973. See Michael Haas, *The Asian Way to Peace: A Story of Regional Cooperation* (New York: Praeger, 1989), pp. 32–39.

19. All of the WEU's original military structures had been absorbed by NATO by the mid-1950s. In the 1990s, however, it added a planning cell, a situation center, and a range of military and politico-military committees and working groups. (See Western European Union, "WEU's Structure," available from http://www.weu.int/eng/info/structure.htm; accessed 1 Oct. 1998.) And at the end of the decade, the EU took its first steps toward the acquisition of an autonomous capability for military action, including the creation of a Military Staff.

20. As of 2001, the membership of the ARF consisted of the ten ASEAN states, Brunei, Cambodia, Indonesia, Laos, Malaysia, Myanmar, the Philippines, Singapore, Thailand, Vietnam, and 12 other countries: Australia, Canada, China, India, Japan, South Korea, North Korea, Mongolia, New Zealand, Papua New Guinea, Russia, and the United States. In addition, a representative of the EU participates.

21. Leifer, "ASEAN Regional Forum," pp. 31 and 40; Jörn Dosch, "PMC, ARF and CSCAP: Foundations for a Security Architecture in the Asia-Pacific?" Working Paper, no. 307 (Canberra: Australian National University, Strategic and Defence Studies Centre, June 1997), p. 10; Jörn Dosch, "The United States and the New Security Architecture of the Asia-Pacific: A European View (Asia/Pacific Research Center, April 1998); Simon, "Security Prospects"; Amitav Acharya, "A Concert of Asia?" *Survival* 41, no. 3 (Autumn 1999): 84–101 at 99; Alagappa, "Asian Practice," p. 637; and Alastair Iain Johnston, "The Myth of the ASEAN Way? Explaining the Evolution of the ASEAN Regional Forum," in Helga Haftendorn, Robert O. Keohane, and Celeste A. Wallander, eds., *Imperfect Unions: Security Institutions over Time and Space* (New York: Oxford University Press, 1999), pp. 287–324. South Korea has proposed several times the creation of a distinct Northeast Asia security cooperation forum, but nothing has yet come of this idea. See Sheldon W. Simon, "The Parallel Tracks of Asian Multilateralism,"in Richard J. Ellings and Sheldon W. Simon, eds., *Southeast Asian Security in the New Millenium* (Armonk, NY: M.E. Sharpe, 1996), pp. 13–33 at 28, and Acharya, "A Concert of Asia?" p. 94.

22. Leifer, "ASEAN Regional Forum," pp. 7 and 15, and Donald K. Emmerson, "Indonesia, Malaysia, Singapore: A Regional Security Core?" in Ellings and Simon, eds., *Southeast Asian Security*, pp. 34–88 at 76.

23. The most comprehensive discussion of the Australia-Indonesia agreement is Bob Lowry, "Australia-Indonesia Security Cooperation: For Better or Worse?" Working

Paper, no. 299 (Canberra: Australian National University, Strategic and Defence Studies Centre, Aug. 1996).

24. *New York Times*, 24 Sept. 1997, A7. Among other things, the new guidelines provide for the first time for Japanese support U.S. military operations in areas surrounding Japan. See *New York Times*, 29 April 1998, A6, and "Interim Report on the Review of the Guidelines for U.S.-Japan Defense Cooperation," available from http://www.mofa.go.jp/region/n-america/us/security, accessed 2 March 1999. See also Alagappa, "Asian Practice," p. 634.

25. *New York Times*, 27 April 2000; available at http://www.nytimes.com/library/world/asia/042700vietnam-us.html.

26. As early as 1948, George Kennan had defined them, along with the United States, the Soviet Union, and Great Britain, as the five most vital power centers in the world from the standpoint of U.S. national security. See John Lewis Gaddis, *Strategies of Containment: A Critical Appraisal of Postwar American National Security Policy* (New York: Oxford University Press, 1982), pp. 30ff.

27. David W. Mabon describes the early postwar Asia-Pacific treaties as being "largely extorted from the United States' in "Elusive Agreements: The Pacific Pact Proposals of 1949–1951," *Pacific Historical Review* 57, no. 2 (May 1988): 147–77 at 175.

28. On the role played by fears of Germany in the origins of NATO, see Timothy P. Ireland, *Creating the Entangling Alliance: The Origins of the North Atlantic Treaty Organization* (Westport, CT: Greenwood, 1981). On the situation in the Asia-Pacific, see W. David McIntyre, *Background to the Anzus Pact: Policy-making, Strategy and Diplomacy, 1945–55* (New York: St. Martin's, 1995).

29. McIntyre, *Background to the Anzus Pact*, and David McLean, "Anzus Origins: A Reassessment," *Australian Historical Studies* 24, no. 94 (April 1990): 64–82 at 68. In fact, the first serious discussion within the Department of State concerning possible multilateral security arrangements in the Asia-Pacific contemplated the inclusion of Britain, France, the Netherlands, and Canada as well (McIntyre, *Background to the Anzus Pact*, 265–66). This history conflicts with Peter Katzenstein's contention that "after 1945 the United States enshrined the principle of bilateralism in its dealing with Japan and other Asian states" and Miles Kahler's suggestion (1994, 20) that the United States resisted multilateral security schemes desired by its allies in Asia. See Katzenstein, "Regionalism," p. 143, and Miles Kahler, "Institution-building in the Asia-Pacific," in Mack and Ravenhill, eds., *Pacific Cooperation*, pp. 16–39 at 20.

30. Also rather problematic from a global perspective is the fact the United States did not simply impose its policy preferences for a multilateral arrangement on the states within its sphere of influence, much as the Soviet Union did in Europe. To explain such variations in superpower behavior requires acknowledging the existence of important sources of state interests that are not merely derivative of the material structure of the international system, an analytical move that is certainly inconsistent with the tenets of neorealism.

31. Alagappa, "Asian Practice," p. 631; Chung-in Moon, "South Korea: Recasting Security Paradigms," in Alagappa, ed., *Asian Security Practice*, pp. 264–87; and Yoshihide Soeya, "Japan: Normative Constraints Versus Structural Imperatives," in Alagappa, ed., *Asian Security Practice*, pp. 198–233 at 222.

32. Such factors play a role in balance of threat theory (Walt, *Origins of Alliances*) and offense-defense theory, see Stephen Van Evera, "Offense, Defense, and the Causes of War," *International Security* 22, no. 4 (Spring 1988): 5–43. These approaches, however, depart from the original tenets of neorealism by including variables that are not strictly structural in nature. By contrast, geography is often neglected in purely structural realist analyses of world politics. See in particular Waltz, *Theory of International Politics.*

33. See, for example, Mabon, "Elusive Agreements," p. 149; Melvyn Leffler, *A Preponderance of Power: National Security, the Truman Administration, and the Cold War* (Stanford, CA: Stanford University Press, 1992), p. 394; and McIntyre, *Background to the Anzus Pact.*

34. Ireland, *Creating the Entangling Alliance.*

35. See, for example, McIntyre, *Background to the Anzus Pact*, p. 381.

36. Joseph Grieco has successfully used a similar approach for explaining differences in the degree of regional economic institutionalization (Grieco, "Realism and Regionalism," esp. pp. 336–40). Nevertheless, Grieco places primary emphasis on differences in German and Japanese preferences, which he in turn explains in terms of U.S. power.

37. In 1965, Japan's gross domestic product was equal to those of Australia, New Zealand, South Korea, the Philippines, Singapore, Thailand, Malaysia, and Indonesia combined. In 1989, it was more than three times as large. Figures derived from Table 4 in Donald Crone, "Does Hegemony Matter? The Reorganization of the Pacific Political Economy," *World Politics* 45, no. 4 (July 1993): 501–25 at 510.

38. For similar reasons, Western-oriented Asian countries were reluctant to establish economic ties with Japan in the 1950s. See Grieco, "Realism and Regionalism," p. 339.

39. In fact, the principal military commitments of Australia and New Zealand in the early postwar years lay in the Middle East. See McIntyre, *Background to the Anzus Pact*, p. 304.

40. For a detailed discussion, see John S. Duffield, *Power Rules: The Evolution of NATO's Conventional Force Posture* (Stanford, CA: Stanford University Press, 1995), ch. 2. See also Grieco, "Realism and Regionalism," pp. 337–40.

41. John Foster Dulles, "Security in the Pacific," *Foreign Affairs* 30, no. 2 (Spring 1952): 175–87 at 183.

42. Mabon, "Elusive Agreements," pp. 169–71, and McIntyre, *Background to the Anzus Pact.*

43. Alagappa, "Asian Practice," p. 636, and Johnston, "Myth of the ASEAN Way?" p. 292.

44. Lowry, "Australia-Indonesia Security Cooperation," pp. 11–12; Ba, "ASEAN Regional Forum"; Alagappa, "Asian Practice," p. 636; and Muthiah Alagappa, "International Politics in Asia: The Historical Context," in Alagappa, ed., *Asian Security Practice*: 65–111 at 98.

45. Similarly, Peter Katzenstein ("Regionalism") has identified differences in domestic structures, especially the character of state institutions, as an important determinant of differences in the forms of regionalism pursued in Asia and in Europe.

46. For example, Walt, *Origins of Alliances*, highlights the role of perceptions of intentions in determining patterns of alliance formation. Randall Schweller, "Tripolarity

and the Second World War," *International Studies Quarterly* 37, no. 1 (March 1993): 73–103, following Hans J. Morgenthau, *Politics Among Nations: The Struggle for Power and Peace* (New York: Knopf, 1967), emphasizes state interests or power preferences, although he includes, for the sake of parsimony, only status quo and revisionist states in his typology.

47. Of course, it is important to recognize the structural and institutional reasons for these different policies. For geographical and economic reasons, Germany was much more dependent upon the goodwill and cooperation of its regional neighbors. In contrast, Japan had to rely primarily on the United States for its economic redevelopment as well as its security. In addition, the FRG began its life deprived of many of the traditional perquisites of sovereignty, not least of which was the right to make its own foreign policy. Thus it still had to overcome the mistrust of its neighbors before it could be fully rehabilitated politically.

48. Dulles, "Security in the Pacific," pp. 182 and 184.

49. Henry W. Brands, Jr., "From ANZUS to SEATO: United States Strategic Policy towards Australia and New Zealand, 1952–1954," *The International History Review* 9, no. 2 (May 1987): 250–70 at 268. For a glimpse of the intensity of anti-Japanese sentiment in Australia, a country that had not even been occupied by Japan, see Robert Gordon Menzies, "The Pacific Settlement Seen from Australia," *Foreign Affairs* 30, no. 2 (Jan. 1952): 188–96.

50. Victor D. Cha, *Alignment Despite Antagonism: The United States-Korea-Japan Security Triangle* (Stanford, CA: Stanford University Press, 1999). Although Japan and South Korea have engaged in a number of practical forms of security cooperation since 1965, they have never concluded a formal alliance.

51. Dulles, "Security in the Pacific," p. 185.

52. Dulles, "Security in the Pacific," p. 183

53. Braibanti, "International Implications," p. 37; Brands, "From ANZUS to SEATO," p. 268; and McIntyre, *Background to the Anzus Pact*, p. 383. The inability of the United States to impose its multilateral preferences on the countries of the region sits uncomfortably with Katzenstein's characterization ("Regionalism," p. 142) of the period as one of "extreme hegemony."

54. Dewi Fortuna Anwar, "Indonesia: Domestic Priorities Define Foreign Policy," in Alagappa, ed., *Asian Security Practice*, pp. 477–512 at 478–81.

55. See also Christopher Hemmer and Peter J. Katzenstein, "Collective Identities and the Origins of Multilateralism in Europe but not in Asia in the Early Cold War," paper prepared for delivery at the 2000 annual meeting of the American Political Science Association, Washington, D.C., 31 Aug.–3 Sept. 2000. Katzenstein, "Regionalism," p. 142, offers similar reasons for the greater degree of political-economic institutionalization in the North Atlantic area.

56. McIntyre, *Background to the Anzus Pact*, pp. 302 and 306–7.

57. Dulles, "Security in the Pacific," p. 183.

58. McLean, "Anzus Origins," p. 78.

59. Leifer, "ASEAN Regional Forum," p. 13.

60. McIntyre, *Background to the Anzus Pact*, pp. 332–35.

61. Brands, "From ANZUS to SEATO," pp. 263 and 270.

62. Anwar, "Indonesia," p. 508.

63. Soeya, "Japan," p. 222, and Alagappa, "Asian Practice," p. 636.

64. Institutional path dependence is a central theme of the "new institutionalism." See, for example, Thomas A. Koelble, "The New Institutionalism in Political Science and Sociology," *Comparative Politics* 27, no. 2 (Jan. 1995): 231–43, and Peter A. Hall and Rosemary C.R. Taylor, "Political Science and the Three New Institutionalisms," *Political Studies* 44, no. 5 (Dec. 1996): 936–57. Thus far, however, this concept has seen little application in the study of international relations. For an exception, see Grieco, "Realism and Regionalism," p. 342.

65. Michael Schaller, *The American Occupation of Japan: The Origins of the Cold War in Asia* (New York: Oxford University Press, 1985), and Leffler, *Preponderance of Power.*

66. Iceland, Denmark, Portugal, and Norway were invited to be charter members primarily because of the strategic importance attached to their North Atlantic territories, including Greenland and the Azores, for ensuring the unimpeded flow of U.S. reinforcements to Europe in the event of a conflict. See Lawrence S. Kaplan, *The United States and NATO: The Formative Years* (Lexington: University Press of Kentucky, 1984), pp. 82–83.

67. This discussion of institutional path dependence is not meant to deny the importance of realist factors in precipitating the formation of the Western Union and in motivating the conclusion of some form of transatlantic security ties.

68. Dulles, "Security in the Pacific," p. 180. More generally, one is struck by how often diplomats and negotiators borrowed language from existing treaties in order to facilitate the conclusion of new agreements.

69. Alagappa, "Asian Practice," p. 635.

70. Likewise, the primary reliance of the United States on bilateral security agreements during the cold war caused Bush administration officials to be suspicious of new multilateral arrangements, which they feared might undermine existing U.S. ties. See Leifer, "ASEAN Regional Forum," p. 23. It is not clear, however, whether this initial skepticism had any lasting consequences.

71. Michael Barnett and Jack Levy, "Domestic Sources of Alliances and Alignments," *International Organization* 45, no. 3 (Summer 1991), pp. 369–95, and Stephen David, *Choosing Sides* (Baltimore: The Johns Hopkins University Press, 1991).

72. John S. Duffield, "Explaining the Long Peace in Europe: The Contributions of Regional Security Regimes," *Review of International Studies* 20, no. 4 (October 1994): 369–88.

73. Anwar, "Indonesia," pp. 477–79 and 483.

74. See, for example, Robert O. Keohane, "The Theory of Hegemonic Stability and Changes in International Economic Regimes, 1967–1977," in Ole R. Hosti, Randolph M. Siverson, and Alexander L. George, eds., *Change in the International System* (Boulder, CO: Westview, 1980), pp. 131–62.

75. In this connection, it is also worth mentioning the long-term trend of growing strains in U.S. economic relations with some of its Asian allies, which occasionally spill over into security relations.

76. Alagappa, "Asian Practice," pp. 633–34, and Cha, *Alignment Despite Antagonism*, p. 209.

77. See also James H. Nolt, "Liberalizing Asia," *World Policy Journal* 16, no. 2 (Summer 1999), pp. 94–110 at 96–7.

78. Kenneth B. Pyle, "Japan's Emerging Strategy in Asia," in Ellings and Simon, eds., *Southeast Asian Security*, pp. 123–48 at 133, and Ellings and Simon, eds., *Southeast Asian Security*, p. 9. In October 1998, the Japanese prime minister offered an unusually forthright apology to the Korean people (*New York Times*, 9. Oct. 1998). Whether that and possible future gestures of atonement will be sufficient to overcome enduring regional resentments and suspicions remains to be seen, however. Just the following month, the President of China sharply criticized Japan for its unwillingness to apologize for its acts of aggression against that country in the 1930s and 1940s (*New York Times*, 30 Nov. 1998). And Japan has continued to resist international demands that it compensate the victims of its use of germ warfare or make records of the atrocities public (*New York Times*, 4 March 1999).

79. Thomas U. Berger, *Cultures of Antimilitarism: National Security in Germany and Japan* (Baltimore: The Johns Hopkins University Press, 1998). For doubts about how quickly and how fully Japan would respond to a regional crisis involving U.S. forces even under the new bilateral defense guidelines, see *New York Times*, 28 April 1999.

80. Aaron Friedberg has cited the lack of a common culture and of a shared identity in the Asia-Pacific, in comparison with the Euro-Atlantic, in "Ripe for Rivalry," p. 24. The impact of such differences on security institutionalization, however, is relatively difficult to trace.

81. Nolt, "Liberalizing Asia," p. 97.

82. Acharya, "A Concert of Asia?" pp. 88 and 96; Johnston, "Myth of the ASEAN Way?"; and Wu Xinbo, "China: Security Practice of a Modernizing and Ascending Power," in Alagappa, *Asian Security Practice*, pp. 115–56 at 149 and 151.

83. See Cha, *Alignment Despite Antagonism*, pp. 223–29, for an application of this argument to Japan-Korea relations.

84. See also Friedberg, "Ripe for Rivalry," p. 23, and Betts, "Wealth, Power, and Instability," p. 73.

85. See, for example, David Youtz and Paul Midford, *A Northeast Asian Security Regime: Prospects after the Cold War*, Public Policy Paper 5 (New York: Institute for EastWest Studies, 1992), pp. 18–20.

86. See, for example, Christian Tuschhoff, in Haftendorn, Keohane, and Wallander, eds., *Imperfect Unions*, pp. 140–61.

87. See, for example, Johnston, "Myth of the ASEAN Way," pp. 314–15.

PART II

Politics, Economics, and Stability

Chapter 8

STATES, MARKETS, AND GREAT POWER RELATIONS IN THE PACIFIC

Some Realist Expectations

Jonathan Kirshner

What will explain the emerging pattern of economic relations among the great powers in the Pacific? This essay applies a realist political economy framework to deduce expectations regarding the trade, monetary, and financial relations in the region with an emphasis on the United States, China, and Japan. It will consider the expectations of specific realist *theories*, not realism itself. Realist theories of political economy, some of which may in fact deduce competing predictions, derive from a common framework. The first section of this essay will establish that framework, which, it should be emphasized, is an approach, not a theory, and as such can not be falsified. Successive sections will then derive or review specific realist theories regarding trade, money, and finance and apply them to contemporary politics. These issue areas are addressed in increasing order of their practical significance. This underscores an implicit argument that trade issues have attracted a disproportionate amount of attention in debates surrounding realist analysis, at the expense of more consequential developments in the monetary and financial spheres.

THE POLITICAL ECONOMY OF REALISM[1]

Realist theories of political economy share three foundations, regarding the relationship between wealth and power, expectations of war, and the nature of the state. The first foundation—that *economic growth and capacity are the underlying source of power; economic and political goals are complementary in the long run*—is not unique to realism. It is clearly associated with Adam Smith, and most aspects of realist political economy can be traced to the neomercantilist response to Smith's devastating critique of classical mercantilism. Those neomercantilists, however, did not refute Smith's arguments. Rather, they integrated parts of his doctrine into the reformulation of their own.[2] Thus, while liberals and realists have always shared the view that both power and plenty were crucial and complementary aims of state action,[3] modern realists have integrated the liberal argument that power flows from productive capability and productive capability from economic growth. These are core assumptions upon which realism draws, but they are not uniquely realist positions.

What distinguishes realism from other schools of thought, and particularly from liberalism, are the two additional foundational assumptions, which regard war and the state. These also fundamentally shape the distinct way in which realists have interpreted the consequences of the assumption regarding economic growth. Realists expect states to prefer high rates of economic growth, but they also assume that *states must anticipate the possibility of war*. It is important to stress that the concern for war is best conceptualized as a dimension. Realists need not see a constant "state of war," nor do liberals consider war impossible. What distinguishes realists is that they can be placed on that end of a continuum which stresses the likelihood of war, threats of war, and the need for states to shape their policies in the light of this consideration. For E. H. Carr, for example, "Potential war" is "a dominant factor in international politics."[4] This prevents states, realists argue, from pursuing policies that, while optimal from an economic perspective, threaten national security.

Realists are also distinguished by their view that *the state is a distinct actor with its own interests*. As with the significance of war, assumptions regarding states rights are not absolute, but are held to varying degrees. Thus, non-realists do not deny the existence of an autonomous state; they simply differ as to the extent and consequence of that autonomy. Realists stress the state as a distinct entity from the sum of particular interests; as an entity with the capability and inclination to pursue its own agenda; and as the principal actor in international relations.[5] Significantly, the interests of the state will often diverge markedly from the sum of particular interests within society, and the state will act to defend its interests.

These three foundations combine in ways that define some of the broader contours of realist expectations. Divergences between state and societal interests, for example, can come from a number of sources but are most likely to arise in regard to issues related to security. This is because in a world where war is possible, states are likely to be very sensitive to national security issues, while, due to a collective action dynamic, individual actors within society are likely to be suboptimally concerned with the common defense. Thus, while power and plenty are complementary in the long run, the state will often be willing to sacrifice short- and medium-term economic gains when tradeoffs present themselves. Indeed, states may routinely make economic sacrifices in order to further international political goals.

Concerns for war also catalyze the instinct of the state for autonomy from all quarters (domestic interests, other states, and economic forces) resulting in a preference for national self-sufficiency. Limiting international exposure reduces vulnerabilities, which would result from the disruption of peacetime patterns of international economic flows. Given these preferences, realists tend to discount the benefits of interdependence, stressing instead how it may be an irritant for states, and as such a source of friction between them.[6]

Realist political economy thus presents states with a delicate balancing act. Given the possibility of war, states would prefer to limit interdependence, retain a reservoir of resources, and forgo a number of beneficial transactions. But such behavior will direct economic activity along suboptimal paths, and this in turn threatens economic growth, which provides the basis for long-run power. Thus complete autarky will rarely be sought—the state must mediate between its desire for autonomy and its need to assure adequate long run economic growth.[7]

REALIST TRADE CONFLICTS? THE BATTLE OVERSTATED

The realist perspective tends to be pessimistic about the prospects for international cooperation, and in no sphere is this more obvious than with regard to trade. Since economic growth determines long-run military capability, and given concerns for the possibility of war, states will find it difficult to cooperate. Even with the recognition that mutual gains exist, states must still be concerned with the distribution of those gains, lest potential adversaries become relatively more powerful.[8]

Realists do not deny the existence of mutual economic gains from trade, but rather question whether the existence of such shared gains are sufficient to assure that they will be reached. One barrier to cooperation is the question of dynamic comparative advantage: whether the pattern of specialization imposed by international market forces would put a nation on a trajectory of relatively low growth. Economically rational specialization might also make the state less able to defend itself, causing a contraction of the steel industry, for example, in favor of expanded agricultural cultivation.

In the latter case, concerns for security will force states to include noneconomic factors in their calculations of the costs and benefits of efficient specialization, and deviate indefinitely from economically optimal patterns of production.[9] More subtly, in the former instance, if temporary protection or other measures, which, when removed, would allow for specialization in more attractive products, then free trade would not be the optimal policy in the short run. Again, the gains from trade are not denied—rather, this is a classic case of the state imposing short-term costs on society for greater benefits in the long run.[10] It is important to note that the realist concern is for the *composition* of trade, and not its overall balance. This one way in which realists can be distinguished from crude protectionists.

Even in the absence of concerns for dynamic comparative advantage, realists would still expect cooperation to founder over the distribution of gains in a static setting. As Gilpin noted, "the distinction between absolute and relative gains" is "a fundamental difference in emphasis" which distinguishes realism. In contemporary international relations theory, this issue has received a disproportionate share of attention. While the concern for the distribution of mutual gains (the "relative gains" issue) is significant for realist political economy, what ultimately distinguishes realism is not the pursuit of relative gains, but the *motives* behind that pursuit: the existence of anarchy and the concern for security. Actors in the absence of anarchy routinely seek relative, not just absolute, gains in their interactions. Thus while realists offer a fundamental motivational difference for state behavior, the behavior itself (pursuit of relative gains) is not incompatible with other approaches to political economy.[11]

Liberals, for example, do not deny the possibility of conflicts about the distribution of relative gains—these take place in many instances between friendly partners in the absence of threats of force, readily seen, for example in most transactions between actors within a domestic economy. In international trade, and especially in the high-technology sectors, oligopoly competition, strategic behavior, economies of scale, high start-up costs, and other deviations from the "classical" model may stimulate trade conflict and provide the grounds for government intervention in commercial policy. These conflicts need not be rooted in concerns for security, but solely for optimal economic growth.[12]

Realist motives simply raise the stakes in these conflicts, supplying an additional source of friction. Actors are not concerned simply with others reneging on promises, a sense of distributive justice, or the need to establish a tough reputation for future negotiations, but rather, as Grieco argues, "states in anarchy must fear that others may seek to destroy or enslave them."[13] Thus what distinguishes realists' expectations in practice are not conflicts over relative gains, but *sharper* conflicts over relative gains; with partners walking away from *a significant number* of deals with mutual gains left on the table. For both liberals and realists, then, the "core" of agreements is smaller than the set of mutually beneficial deals. The realist subset is simply smaller still. Distinguishing between these subsets in practice is extremely difficult, since the simple illustration of relative gains conflicts will not be sufficient.[14]

As a result there are no distinct realist expectations with regard to trade between the U.S and Japan and between the U.S. and China. While there may be good realist reasons to expect trade conflicts between the U.S. and Japan, there are good liberal reasons to expect the same thing.[15] While many analysts expect increasing trade frictions to emerge between the U.S. and China,[16] there is no theoretical justification in liberal *or* realist theory for placing the *balance* of trade into the first (or even second) rank of policy concerns. Thus we are likely to witness trade conflicts that are overdetermined—consistent with both liberal and realist expectations, and other disputes that neither perspective can productively address.

There is, however, one distinct realist theory of international trade, articulated by Hirschman, in his book *National Power and the Structure of Foreign Trade*.[17] Hirschman focused on German interwar trading relations, demonstrating how Germany cultivated a series of asymmetric trading relationships with the small states of southeastern Europe, as part of its pre–World War II grand strategy to secure needed raw materials and increase German leverage there. Although inefficient from an economic perspective, redirecting trade enhanced Germany's autonomy. Focusing on small states increased Germany's political leverage in these relationships by making exit more costly for others. This asymmetry, plus the relatively sweet deals offered by Germany, exerted, as Hirschman noted, "a powerful influence in favor of a 'friendly' attitude towards the state to the imports of which they owe their interests."[18]

But there is much more to Hirschman's story than coercion: there is also a story about influence, and in practice this is almost certainly the more significant of the two.[19] Simply put, *National Power* shows that the pattern of international economic relations affects domestic politics, which in turn shape the orientation of foreign policy. This effect is always present but most consequential in asymmetric relations, where the effects are typically large, visible, and almost wholly found within the smaller economy. Consider, for example, a free trade agreement between a large and a small state. The likely result is a change in the smaller state's self-perception of its own interest: it will converge toward that of the larger. Why? Because the simple act of participation in the arrangement strengthens those who benefit from it relative to those who, by definition, do not. This strength should translate into political power.[20] Further, because firms and sectors engage in patterns of activity based on economic incentives, and since this constellation of incentives will be transformed by the trade agreement, the subsequent reshuffling of behavior will lead to new interests and the formation of political coalitions to advance those interests.[21] Most important, decisions based on these new incentives give firms a stake in their country's continued participation, and they will direct their political energies to that end. In Hirschman's words, "these regions or industries will exert a powerful influence in favor of a 'friendly' attitude towards the state to the imports of which they owe their interests."[22] Finally, the central government can find its own interests reshaped, above and beyond that which results from domestic political pressures.[23]

In practice, Hirschmanesque effects are more profoundly felt with regard to influence than coercion. They are about the fact, to paraphrase one report, "a salesman of [country A's] exports in his own market" becomes "a spokesman of [country A's] interests with his own government."[24] Resulting changes in international political behavior do not occur because of pressure, but because new incentives alter perceptions of interest. This is akin to what Nye has called "soft power." Rather than forcing others to do what you want them to do, soft power, or influence, is about "getting others to want what you want"[25]

The trade strategies that flow from a Hirschmanesque strategy are uniquely realist. Such strategies employ economic means to advance political goals. Small states in this setting typically gain in an economic sense, often handsomely, as large states attempting to enhance their influence make overly generous concessions. Thus asymmetric economic relations offer an exception to, and in fact a reversal of, the concern for relative gains. This expands the core of mutually acceptable bargains and makes cooperation between them even more likely. Such behavior cannot be explained from a liberal perspective, since the states with greater economic leverage and less to gain from exchange are the ones making the greater concessions to assure the bargain. It is the converse of the radical conception of asymmetric trade, where large states use their political power to enforce economic extraction. From the radical perspective, then, power is a means to achieve an economic end. In the realist strategy described by Hirschman, wealth is used to advance a political goal.

In contemporary Asian international politics, then, realist theory will expect that in the context of asymmetric economic relations, great powers will likely tailor their trade strategies to cultivate political influence with smaller states.[26] Of the three, Japan would appear to be the most ideally situated to practice Hirschmanesque diplomacy. The U.S., distant and with the most broadly global interests, may be less inclined to introduce the regionally discriminatory tactics that such a strategy would require. Compared with China, Japan is better placed to follow such a strategy, given the larger size of its economy, its relative economic development, and potential as a financial center. Further, given that Japanese policy is still viewed with suspicion by many states in the region, Japan should be more likely to employ tools designed to increase its influence in order to advance its political goals, rather than introduce baldly coercive policies, which could easily backfire. China's employment of Hirschmanesque devices is thus likely to be more limited and often responsive to Japanese measures.

INTERNATIONAL MONETARY RELATIONS: THE BATTLE POSTPONED

A REALIST THEORY OF MONETARY RELATIONS

The principal general theory that has been employed to explain the pattern of monetary relations is the hegemonic stability thesis.[27] While its story is superficially appealing, there are several compelling challenges to this interpretation. First, it is now clear that in the nineteenth century, Britain was not a monetary hegemon, nor did it behave in the way that the theory would predict. While cooperation was common in this era, the Bank of England was often the *borrower* of last resort, dependent on the support of other central banks in times of crisis.[28] Second, recent investigations of interwar monetary politics have countered that the great depression was not the result of absent hegemony (not to mention that the U.S. may have been "hegemonic" at this time), but was transmitted and exacerbated by the interwar gold standard. According to this interpretation, hegemony was not necessary to overcome the collective action problem of competitive devaluation. Instead, each state held the key to its own recovery through the abandonment of the gold standard and the adoption of expansionary policies.[29] Finally, a state at the center of an international monetary system can also be a source of *instability* in the system. Such states, especially if they provide the "world's currency," are less constrained than other states and may fall prey to temptation, or even purposefully choose to exploit their position.[30]

The concentration of power, then, does not appear to be a good explanation of monetary cooperation.[31] Liberal theories have adapted and now stress the importance of ideological consensus, rather than the provision of public goods, to explain when such cooperation will occur.[32] Realists have yet to articulate a clear alternative; I suggest one possible approach.

While realists tend to be pessimistic regarding the prospects for international cooperation in general, a close look suggests that from any perspective monetary cooperation should be especially difficult. Explaining such cooperation thus requires elucidating under what conditions the formidable barriers to cooperation can be overcome. Those barriers are the complexity of international monetary arrangements, the public nature of macroeconomic externalities, and the distinct nature of the salience of monetary commitments.

The complexity of international monetary arrangements poses unique challenges to monetary cooperation. Even if states believe that such cooperation would be appealing in theory, they may still disagree over practical issues regarding the "rules of the game."[33] Even if these problems are overcome, difficulties associated with complexity of international money remain. Given the existence of large private currency and financial markets, adherence to agreements can be difficult to monitor. Since state intervention may be ineffective against countervailing market forces, there is no way to assure that states are in fact living up to their obligations.[34] Trade agreements, on the other hand, typically require public legislation and such laws are not subject to competing market pressures.

Monetary cooperation is also difficult, as Oye has argued, because of the public nature of macroeconomic externalities.[35] Externalities in international relations result from the fact that states adopt policies that have "spillover" effects: consequences felt beyond a state's borders. These are externalities because they are not part of the cost calculation of the state that transmits them. As a result, there is a tendency toward the over-provision of negative spillover effects in the international system. If injured states punish the producers of the negative spillovers, then those policies will be perceived as costly and curtailed. For example, if one nation raises its tariffs, even if it does so universally, other states can raise tariffs that directly target the protectionist. Each can then bargain for market share, and are the sole beneficiaries of their efforts. While states can discriminate in their trade policies, macroeconomic policies regarding interest and exchange rates are almost inherently standard. Thus producers of macroeconomic bads (say, for example, very high interest rates) will tend to go unpunished, because injured states face a collective-action dilemma: all will benefit from the elimination of the public bad, no matter who bears the cost. Because of the free rider problem (private costs and public benefits), negative externalities in this case will not be significantly reduced.

Finally, monetary cooperation is difficult because it involves the abdication of national macroeconomic policy autonomy. The essence of this problem can be traced to Keynes, who wrote extensively about the difficulty states faces in balancing their preferences for internal and external price stability. Monetary cooperation links the national with the international economy. This is "the dilemma of an international monetary system": the difficulty in providing both stability in external monetary relations while assuring "at the same time an adequate local autonomy for each member over its domestic rate of interest" and other macroeconomic policies.[36]

As a result, even if states are able to reach monetary agreements, those agreements are likely to be fragile. All states gain from international monetary stability. To contribute to that stability, by adherence to agreements of monetary cooperation, governments are often forced to engage in unpleasant acts: austerity budgets, deflationary monetary policy, costly and compulsory intervention in exchange markets, and a number of other initiatives such governments would otherwise not undertake. These pressures often arise at the worst possible time: a state may be in a recession, but to fulfill its commitments to an international monetary agreement it might be forced to engage in deflationary policies. The costs of these actions are often severe and are associated by the general public with the ruling administration.[37]

The problems of externalities and autonomy suggest that monetary cooperation should be extremely difficult to *sustain*. On the other hand, in the absence of economic distress, state autonomy (vis-à-vis domestic actors) with regard to international macroeconomic policymaking is likely to be quite high.[38] Given the typical degree of insulation of exchange rate policy from the domestic political process, monetary cooperation may be relatively easy to establish. Trade agreements, on the other hand, may be more difficult to reach, but easier to keep. This may help explain the different fates of postwar trade and monetary regimes.

A baseline expectation with regard to monetary relations, then, should be that monetary agreements will be reached, but will tend to break down. The relatively free reign of governments over monetary affairs should provide the political space necessary to overcome the problems of complexity in reaching monetary accords. Difficulties in monitoring compliance, dis-incentives to challenge producers of negative macroeconomic externalities, and intense pressure to renounce painful and counter-intuitive pro-cyclical commitments suggest that such agreements will fail when challenged by the course of economic events.

When can these problems be overcome? One realist answer is that monetary cooperation is likely to be sustained to the extent to which potential participants have *shared, salient security concerns*. The greater the consensus that exists on core security issues and their significance, the more likely it is that "high politics" will dominate "low politics." Simply put—states will be more willing to bear the costs of monetary cooperation when they share a common security vision. When states have similar security concerns and shared threat perception, the costs of monetary cooperation remain the same while the benefits are increased to the extent that monetary cooperation facilitates and enhances overall political cooperation. Additionally, states may refrain from abrogating monetary agreements because of the fear that such action might cause a larger set of political understandings to unravel, or signal dissension to common adversaries.[39]

PROSPECTS FOR MONETARY CONFLICT

Realist analysis is quite pessimistic about the prospects for monetary cooperation in general, and with the end of the cold war the most important element in preventing monetary conflicts from looming even larger than they have has disappeared. The underlying tensions in U.S.-Japan monetary relations have existed almost from the beginning of the cold war, although they only became salient in the 1970s. Only a serious and mutually perceived threat, that might result, for example, should China become both assertive and belligerent, can prevent serious monetary conflict from erupting between the U.S. and Japan. Moreover, if Chinese behavior does not serve to facilitate monetary cooperation between the U.S. and Japan, then it will likely contribute to an even more complex triangular currency relationship, which will only further confound efforts at monetary cooperation. In most circumstances, monetary relations are likely to be characterized in a stop-go pattern where agreements are repeatedly reached and then collapse.

In retrospect, sources of underlying frictions in money matters can be observed even in the 1940s. On August 25, 1949, an exchange rate of 360 yen to the dollar was introduced, replacing Japan's multiple exchange rate system which featured rates raging from 100 to 1500 yen per dollar. The 360 figure was a compromise between American authorities who preferred a rate of 300, and Japanese businessmen who had hoped for an even weaker level for the yen.[40] It should be underscored that from an economic perspective any fixed rate chosen would be arbitrary, and reflected a political compromise. Worse, since crucial economic conditions like relative rates of inflation, growth, and productivity would vary over time, whatever economic logic was captured by the 360 rate would likely erode over time.

In practice, of course, open monetary conflict in the first two decades of the cold war was muted by the primacy of the U.S. goal of nurturing the Japanese economy to counter the Soviet Union, and by the relative insignificance of the Japanese economy. Even in the 1950s Japanese officials were acutely aware of the relationship between the international monetary system and the performance of the Japanese economy. Growth in Japan repeatedly hit a "balance of payments ceiling," in that as growth surged, domestic demand for imports would outstrip foreign demand for Japanese products, which drained Japan's foreign exchange reserves. In 1953–54, 1957–58, 1961–62, the government was forced to slow the economy's rate of growth through monetary and fiscal tightening in order to defend the country's reserves.[41]

This phenomenon continued into the 1960s, when monetary policy was tightened to reduce growth not only in 1961, but also in 1964 and 1967, in response to balance of payments pressures. This would have become a more serious problem but for two considerations. First, Japan enjoyed a real annual growth rate of over 10 percent in the 1960s, taking some of the sting out of monetary tightening. Second, near the close of the decade the Japanese economy shifted toward a structural balance of payments surplus, rather then deficit. Cumulative increases in Japanese productivity meant that its unchanged exchange rate left the yen increasingly undervalued, while at the same time, macroeconomic policies in the U.S. meant that the dollar was increasingly overvalued.[42]

This set the stage for the open monetary conflict of the 1970s. President Nixon, who, unwilling to swallow the deflationary medicine necessary to defend the dollar, instead closed the gold window of August 15, 1971.[43] Nowhere were the "Nixon shocks" felt more acutely than in Japan. The government had been following an "eight point program to avoid yen revaluation" and was "absolutely opposed even to consideration of a parity change." Japan was so committed to the 360 figure that while all other states closed their exchanges and prepared to revalue their currencies vis-à-vis the dollar, Japan kept its foreign exchange markets open and continued to buy dollars at that rate for almost two weeks. Finally, as part of the Smithsonian agreement in December, the yen was repegged at 308 to the dollar, a revaluation of almost 17 percent.[44]

Although Prime Minister Kakuei Tanaka insisted that the new peg would be defended, the Smithsonian agreement was ultimately a stepping-stone en route to a system of floating exchange rates, and when it collapsed in March 1973 the yen appreciated to 260. The floating provided a continual source of tension. From January 1976 to October 1978, the yen again appreciated, from 305 to 180. Fred Bergsten, writing in 1982, saw three "episodes of major economic conflict" between the U.S. and Japan in the preceding dozen years, each of which he attributed to disputes over the dollar/yen rate. Typically, the U.S. pressed for yen appreciation to ease the growing trade imbalance between the two countries. Japan often intervened to limit yen appreciation, much to the consternation of the Americans.[45]

At that particular moment, however, U.S. pressure for yen appreciation receded. While the easing of cold war tensions during the Nixon and Carter Administrations allowed simmering monetary conflicts to bubble to the surface, the escalating bipolar conflict in the early 1980s reordered foreign policy priorities. When the macroeconomic policies of the first Reagan administration sent the dollar soaring, the free-market instincts of U.S. officials limited pressure on Japan to negotiations over financial liberalization.[46]

By 1985, however, the dollar had appreciated to a level well above what could be considered its "equilibrium" rate. Surging Japanese imports increased the salience of currency issues between the two states. Fears within the U.S. of a "hard landing" for the overvalued dollar coincided with Japan's fear that the exchange rate issue would lead to increased American protectionism. This led to a window of cooperation on monetary issues, from September 1985 February 1987, where the major industrialized nations agreed to oversee an orderly depreciation of the dollar, in practice from about 260 to 150 yen to the dollar.[47]

However, this coordination was closer to harmony than true cooperation, and soon after the successful depreciation of the dollar, traditional lines of disagreement reemerged, with the U.S, in favor of further yen appreciation in order to address imbalances in trade between the two states. In the 1990s, the Bush and Clinton administrations favored further yen appreciation, and the Japanese currency appreciated from 160 to 80.[48]

Since 1995, although the yen has depreciated considerably, conflict over monetary issues has essentially been on hold. The American economy's continued expansion, coupled with serious fears about the fundamental fragility of the Japanese economy, have forced a suspension of U.S. pressure on Japanese currency policy. When these exceptional circumstances fade from view, and the U.S. economy slows and Japan finally recovers, conditions will be ripe for sharp monetary conflict between the two states. Barring a mutually perceived and salient threat from China, the security ties that have bound the U.S. and Japan are looser than at any time since World War II. Further, as McKinnon and Ohno have forcefully argued, yen appreciation in Japan has a relatively deflationary effect on the Japanese economy. This was less consequential decades ago when U.S. inflation rates were high and Japanese growth spectacular. With lower U.S. inflation and the likelihood that growth, when it returns to Japan, will be more "normal," there will be less space for Japan to tolerate yen appreciation and attendant "high yen induced recessions" (endaka fukyo).[49]

In sum, with regard to monetary cooperation in the Pacific, the future offers fewer incentives and greater barriers. Excepting a dramatic change in Chinese foreign policy, the problems raised by the U.S.-Japan bilateral relationship are only exacerbated when considered in the context of a broader regional perspective. By the criteria established above (public externalities, divergent security perceptions, etc.), exchange rate conflict between Japan, China, and other states of South and Northeast Asia would appear to be almost inevitable.[50] These battles, however, await the recovery of Japan's economy, the convertibility of China's currency, and eventual recession in the United States.

FINANCIAL FLOWS AND STATE AUTONOMY: THE BATTLE ENGAGED

One of the defining characteristics of the international economy over the past quarter-century has been its dramatic expansion. These changes in the nature of international trade, investment, and especially finance, pose threats to state autonomy.[51] Market forces undermine state capacity, while private actors may engage in patterns of activity that can diverge from the goals of government policy, creating domestic political barriers to some preferred policies.[52] The unregulated flow of financial capital is the most significant of these phenomena, routinely, but often spectacularly, forcing states to abandon strongly favored policies, as illustrated by the well known French episode of the early 1980s. Unable to contain capital flight and following three devaluations of the franc within eighteen months, the socialist government of François Mitterrand was forced to reverse course, abandon its expansionary macroeconomic policies, and introduce austerity measures that were more restrictive than those of its conservative predecessor.[53]

Realists must expect states to find these challenges to autonomy intolerable, or at least highly objectionable, and anticipate that states will attempt to constrain these forces. It is not sufficient for realists to note, however accurately, that there have been periods of history where the international economy imposed even greater constraints on states.[54] The absence of clear efforts by states to reassert control over many of these flows will challenge fundamental realist conceptions.[55] This issue area also provides a clear contrast between liberal and realist expectations, since a liberal perspective would be to expect that these changes are irreversible, or at least highly likely to continue.

Ironically, the collapse of the Bretton Woods system, which ushered in the era of unregulated capital, was a reassertion of autonomy by states. Large countries, most notably the U.S., were no longer willing to play by the constraints imposed by the fixed-exchange rate system. Flexible exchange rate systems were thought to afford macroeconomic policy autonomy following the logic that states could select only two items from the following menu: free capital flows, fixed exchange rates, and autonomous monetary policy.[56] States thought that by abandoning fixed rates, they could pursue the monetary policies of their choice. This did not turn out to be the case. In theory, given flexible rates, policy disparities should be mediated at the border. Thus if a state's policies resulted in an inflation rate that was 5 percent above the international average, its currency would depreciate by 5 percent and that would be that. But if capital mobility is accompanied by a consensus with regard to what is a "correct" monetary policy, then the depreciation will not stop at 5 percent. Capital flight in this case will punish the state for pursuing a deviant policy. Failure to reverse that policy in the wake of a sustained depreciation will stimulate even further capital flight and depreciation, and so on. Thus a state that preferred to pursue a more expansionist monetary policy than average, even one that was willing to tolerate the depreciation necessary to restore equilibrium in international prices, may be unable to chart such a course in the face of punishing (as opposed to equilibrating) capital flows. Thus the "holy trinity" is a myth: if there is an ideological consensus regarding macroeconomic policy, it is not possible to have capital mobility and policy autonomy at the same time. Given this realization, the same motives that led states to break with the fixed exchange rate system should, for realists, lead them to abandon capital mobility as well.

One manifestation of realist expectations should be calls from states in the system to somehow limit the mobility of financial capital. How might this occur? A minimalist avenue, perhaps most plausible given the power of the neoliberal consensus, will be that calls for new regulations will be phrased in the language of "market failure," in order to provide a theoretical justification for regulatory intervention.[57]

In fact, unregulated capital flows can easily be considered a case of market failure, for three reasons. First, contemporary technology allows investors to move huge amounts of money almost instantaneously, at very little cost. Thus the value of assets, including national currencies, can change significantly, literally overnight, undermining the basic price stability that economies need to function smoothly. Second, to an important extent, financial assets are worth what people think they are worth. Fears regarding what other people are thinking can cause herding behavior, unleashing financial stampedes with economic consequences that veer far from the path suggested by any reading of the economic "fundamentals." Third, states face diverse economic conditions, and need to tailor their economic policies accordingly. Investors, scanning the globe for the best rates of return, create pressures for conformity across countries' macroeconomic policies. Nations that deviate from the international norm, even when pursuing policies appropriate for local needs, are "punished" by capital flight.[58]

States can seize upon this logic to apply the standard policy prescription for dealing with externalities: tax the externality in order to force producers to consider the full range of its costs, so that pursuit of narrow self-interests and the social optimum again converge. Right now, there is clear evidence that there is "too much" short term capital movement. The data suggest that 80 percent of all foreign exchange transactions involve round trips that take place in less than a week—and more than half of those in under two days.[59] A small uniform tax on foreign exchange transactions, known as the "Tobin Tax," would have a much larger effect on short- as opposed to long-term capital flows.[60] It is a very modest measure, and not the only way that states can reassert control over international finance. It does represent a minimalist threshold—if states are unable to impose a Tobin Tax, which would not "control" capital but simply afford some modest policy autonomy—then there is good reason to question how well states are able to pursue their interests in the contemporary international economy.

Regardless of the specific measure, realists must anticipate that states will try to reassert control over capital flows. If international reform does not occur, then individual states should be expected to take more dramatic measures. A few short years ago there was no evidence to support any conclusion other than the liberal view that financial liberalization was irreversible, and that international institutions were important forces in driving these changes further.[61] However, in the wake of the Asian financial crisis, an emerging battle is increasingly visible.

The first sign that the tide has turned—that there will be, at least, a debate over unmitigated financial globalization—is the emergence of a literature that has challenged the efficiency of completely unregulated financial capital. The credentials of some of these new critics of unlimited capital mobility are formidable, and this will make them difficult to ignore. Jagdish Bhagwati, the distinguished Columbia University economist and noted champion of free trade, argues in "The Capital Myth" that while proponents of free trade have provided evidence to support their claims, the supporters of free capital have not: :"The weight of evidence and the force of logic point in the opposite direction, toward restraints on capital flows. It is time to shift the burden of proof from those who oppose to those who favor liberated capital."[62]

Harvard's Dani Rodrik, whose analysis from a 100-country sample finds "no evidence that countries without capital controls have grown faster, invested more, or experienced lower inflation," underscores Bhagwati's challenge.[63]

These arguments have taken on added weight with the unexpected spread and depth of the Asian financial crisis. Efforts by states in Asia to defend their currencies in an environment of capital mobility required interest rate increases that exacerbated economic distress. This stimulated new interest in capital controls, which, as Paul Krugman argued, would give states the ability to lower interest rates and stimulate their economies. While still a minority position, there is now, for the first time in many years, a debate over capital mobility.[64]

Possibly influenced by this debate, Malaysia introduced strict controls over capital movements on September 1, 1998.[65] Trade in the ringgit was banned and new restrictions on foreign stock investors introduced.[66] While the proponents of capital controls might have preferred another champion than Malaysia's Prime Minister Mahathir, a reckless figure engaged in a bitter domestic political struggle, Malaysia is the front line in the battle over capital control. It has been noted that those countries which had controls in place before the crisis emerged, such as Taiwan, have to date fared well, while those without controls are closely monitoring the Malaysian experiment. It is still much too early to tell, but initial signs are promising. The exchange rate has stabilized, making business planning more feasible, the stock market rebounded quickly, gaining 50 percent in the first week, and the government has announced interest rate cuts in support of an aggressive pro-growth policy. While the foreign business community has been less enthusiastic, this has not yet translated into action. Intel recently reaffirmed its plans to spend $400 million to expand its Malaysian operation.[67]

The world is clearly watching, and those with ringside seats: Thailand, Indonesia, and the Philippines, are paying particularly close attention. If the Malaysian experiment does not fail quickly, it is quite likely that Indonesia, whose economy has been hard hit by high interest rates, will be the first to follow Malaysia's lead.[68]

The proponents of unregulated capital, however, are not merely spectators in this drama. Stressing the "fundamentals" of an economy, their credo remains "get the pricing right and hot money will take care of itself."[69] The fundamentalists remain in vogue in the business and academic community, and in control of international institutions such as the International Monetary Fund.[70] In September 1996, IMF asserted that "international capital markets appear to have become more resilient and are less likely to be a source of disturbances."[71] Following this assumption, the Fund embarked upon a fundamental revision of its charter, and in May 1997 announced plans to amend its constitution—the Articles of Agreement—"to make the promotion of capital account liberalization a specific purpose of the IMF and give it jurisdiction over capital movements."[72] This would be a profound change in the very nature of the international economy. It is the *opposite* what the founding fathers of the IMF intended. They thought that capital controls were necessary to assure the smooth functioning of an open international economy, and the Bretton Woods era, the "golden age of capitalism," was a period of ubiquitous capital control. Now, however, the IMF has declared explicitly that "Forces of Globalization Must Be Embraced." Its new policy was has been repeatedly characterized as a proposition "to make unrestricted capital flows a condition of membership in the global economy."[73]

The position of the IMF has profound practical consequences. It is also of interest to IR theorists. The amended IMF articles of agreement, once in place, would be a dramatic change in the balance of power between states and international market forces, in an arena where the state has already experienced a withering away of its autonomy. They represent triumphant liberalism spearheaded by an international institution, a one-two punch that realists can not easily shrug off. The alternative path is marked by some form of controls, coordinated or not, on the mobility of short-term capital. What happens in response to the Asian financial crisis may be decisive in determining which path is chosen. This is clear to the guardians of the neoliberal consensus, some of whom, according to the *New York Times*, have "quietly expressed the hope that his experiment would fail so spectacularly that the smoldering ruins of the Malaysian economy would act as a caution to other countries." In particular, the nature of China's financial liberalization is at stake, and that in turn will have a formative effect on the evolution of finance in the Asian region.[74]

REALIST POLITICAL ECONOMY IN THE PACIFIC RIM

This essay has addressed some realist expectations with regard to the trajectory of great-power relations in the Pacific. It is not intended as a comprehensive survey of the relevant issue areas, or a "test" of the realist approach to political economy. Rather, it is an effort to elucidate and provide the criteria to evaluate three specific theories that derive from a realist tradition, ones that yield distinct expectations in the spheres of international trade, monetary, and financial relations. With regard to trade, it has been argued that while realist approaches stress different motivations for state behavior, there are no distinct realist expectations with regard to trade between the U.S and Japan and the between the U.S. and China. Distinctly realist trade strategies do exist with regard to asymmetric relations, and these should be relevant, especially in explaining Japanese trade policy. One argument of this essay is that trade relations will not the best place to look to gauge realist behavioral expectations, for three reasons. First, while the international economy continues its broad expansion, trade is of relatively decreasing significance. Second, arguments based on realist assumptions require highly complex assessments of the relations between trade and the differential rates of and composition of economic growth across states, and then of the translation of those changes into military prowess and intentions. Third, realist expectations with regard to trade are likely to be overdetermined—that is, consistent with theories derived from other traditions as well.

On the other hand, the monetary and financial spheres pose increasing challenges to state autonomy, and yield distinct realist behavioral expectations. Realists must expect states to reassert greater control over these matters. Thus while current conditions (Japan's fragility, China's inconvertibility, America's robust economy) have postponed monetary conflict, such conflict is likely to characterize trans-Pacific monetary relations in the future. More imminent is the realist prediction that states will re-regulate international capital flows.

Finally, speaking more broadly and speculatively about the prospects for relations in region as a whole, two other realist theories yield some intriguing expectations. First, realist theories expect that China's growing economic strength will translate into greater external ambition.[75] But that "ambition" is underdefined. If China becomes highly assertive and belligerent, we have, of course, a very pessimistic assessment of the region's prospects. But if China's increasing might is coupled with more subtle tactics, then the net result might be to facilitate greater cooperation among the other states in trade and money, following the theories discussed above.

Second, realist expectations with regard to money and finance might also leave room for optimism. The claims of some realists that trade interdependence leads to war has always sounded like a rhetorical overreaction to the liberal argument that such ties promote peace.[76] But shift the discussion—from war to economic relations, from trade to money and finance and from interdependence to globalization—and the realist view that states crave autonomy yields another glimmer of optimism. Here the argument that increased economic exposure leads to greater friction between states makes more sense. If the realists are right, and states reassert some control over monetary and financial flows, greater economic stability in the region might allow for enhanced economic cooperation.

ENDNOTES

1. This section draws on Jonathan Kirshner, "The Political Economy of Realism," in Ethan Kapstein and Michael Mastanduno, eds., *Unipolar Politics: Realism and State Strategies After the Cold War* (New York: Columbia University Press, 1999).

2. See Adam Smith, *An Inquiry into the Nature and Causes of The Wealth of Nations* (Chicago: University of Chicago Press, 1976 [1776]); Alexander Hamilton, "Report on the Subject of Manufactures" (1791), in Harold C. Syrett, ed., *The Papers of Alexander Hamilton—Volume* X (New York: Columbia University Press, 1966); Edward G. Bourne, "Alexander Hamilton and Adam Smith" *Quarterly Journal of Economics* 8:, no. 3 (April 1894): 329–48; Friedrich List, *The National System of Political Economy* (London, Longmans, Green and Co., 1885).

3. Jacob Viner, "Power Versus Plenty as Objectives of Statecraft in the Seventeenth and Eighteenth Centuries," *World Politics* 1, no.1 (October 1948): 1–29. esp. p. 10.

4. E. H. Carr, The Twenty Year's Crisis, 1919–1939 (2nd edition) (New York: Harper Row, 1964), p. 109. List emphasized these differences repeatedly, arguing that "The idea of a perpetual state of peace forms the foundation of all [Smith's] arguments." National System, p. 120 see also pp. 316, 347.

5. As one realist study concluded, "This investigation has shown that the state has purposes of its own." Stephen Krasner, *Defending the National Interest* (Princeton: Princeton University Press, 1978), p. 300. See also Robert Gilpin, *U.S. Power and the Multinational Corporation* (New York: Basic Books, 1975), esp. pp. 26–32.

6. See Kenneth Waltz, "The Myth of National Interdependence," in Charles Kindleberger, ed., *The International Corporation* (Cambridge: MIT Press, 1970); also Waltz, *Theory of International Politics* (New York: Random House, 1979), ch. 7; Katherine Barbieri, "Economic Interdependence: A Path to Peace or a Source of Interstate Conflict?" *Journal of Peace Research* 33, no. 1 (February 1996): 29–49; and Norrin Ripsman and Jean-Marc Blanchard, "Commercial Liberalism Under Fire: Evidence From 1914 and 1936" *Security Studies* 6, no. 2 (Winter 1996/97): 4–50.

7. Carr, *Twenty Year's Crisis*, pp. 120–24. For a contemporary example of the trade-offs sometimes faced by states, see Irving Lachow, "The GPS Dilemma: Balancing Military Risks and Economic Benefits," *International Security* 20, no. 1 (Summer 1995): 126–48.

8. Given the concern for empowering adversaries, some barriers to trade can be overcome between partners in a military alliance that is expected to endure indefinitely. It has been suggested that a bipolar structure will be likely to feature stable military alliances, muting state concerns for the consequences of relative gains that result from trade within each pole. See Joanne Gowa, "Bipolarity, Multipolarity, and Free Trade," *American Political Science Review* 83, no. 4 (December 1989). This is not likely to be a factor in Pacific Rim trade for the foreseeable future.

9. Again, the divergence from the economic optimum will have to be balanced against the costs to long-run growth, which states seeking security must also be concerned about.

10. See, for example, Halford J. Mackinder, *Money Power and Man Power: The Underlying Principles Rather than the Statistics of Tariff Reform* (London: Sompkin, Marshall, Hamilton, Kent, 1906), esp. pp. 18–20; also pp. 2, 15, 17, 22.

11. On the absolute/relative gains debate, see for example Robert Powell, "Anarchy in International Relations Theory: The Neorealist-Neoliberal Debate," *International Organization* 48, no. 2 (Spring 1994): 313–44; Powell, "Absolute and Relative Gains in International Relations Theory," *American Political Science Review* 85, no. 4 (December 1991): 1303–20; Duncan Snidal, "Relative Gains and the Pattern of International Cooperation," *American Political Science Review* 85, no. 3 (September 1991): 701–26; Robert Keohane, "Institutional Theory and the Realist Challenge After the Cold War," in David Baldwin, ed., *Neorealism and Neoliberalism: The Contemporary Debate* (New York: Columbia University Press, 1993) and Joseph Grieco, "Understanding the Problem of International Cooperation: The Limits of Neoliberal Institutionalism and the Future of Realist Theory," also in Baldwin, *Neorealism and Neoliberalism*. For an example of how difficult it is to distinguish these behaviors in practice, see Peter

Liberman, "Trading With the Enemy: Security and Relative Economic Gains," *International Security* 21, no. 1 (Summer 1996): 147–75.

12. Laura D'Andrea Tyson, *Who's Bashing Whom? Trade Conflict in High Technology Industries* (Washington: Institute for International Economics, 1992). See esp. pp. 3–4, 12, 17, 31, on deviations from the classical model. See also Paul Krugman, ed., *Strategic Trade Policy and the New International Economics* (Cambridge: MIT Press, 1986); Gene Grossman, ed., *Imperfect Competition and International Trade* (Cambridge: MIT Press 1992).

13. Grieco, *Cooperation Among Nations*, p. 217.

14. For investigations into this question, see Michael Mastanduno, "Do Relative Gains Matter?" *International Security* 16, no. 1 (Summer 1991): 73–113; Joseph Grieco, *Cooperation Among Nations: Europe, America, and Non-Tariff Barriers to Trade* (Ithaca: Cornell University Press, 1990).

15. See for example Tyson, *Who's Bashing Whom*; Kenneth Flam, *Mismanaged Trade? Strategic Policy and the Semiconductor Industry* (Washington: Brookings, 1996); Sylvia Ostry and Richard Nelson, *Techno-Nationalism and Techno-Globalism* (Washington: Brookings, 1995); C. Fred Bergsten and Marcus Noland, *Reconcilable Differences? United States-Japan Economic Conflict* (Washington: Institute for International Economics, 1993).

16. Julia Chang Bloch, "Commercial Diplomacy," in Ezra F. Vogel , ed., *Living With China: U.S.-China Relations in the Twenty-First Century* (New York: Norton, 1997); Lardy, *China in the World Economy*.

17. (Berkeley: University of California Press, 1980 [1945]).

18. Hirschman, *National Power*, p. 29. See also Allan G. B. Fisher, "The German Trade Drive in South-Eastern Europe," *International Affairs* 18, no. 2 (March 1939): 143–70; Antonín Basch, *The Danube Basin and the German Economic Sphere* (New York: Columbia University Press, 1943), esp. p. 178.

19. See Rawi Abdelal and Jonathan Kirshner, "Strategy, Economic Relations, and the Definition on National Interests," *Security Studies*, 9, nos. 1–2 (Autumn 1999–Winter 2000): 119–156.

20. Gary S. Becker, "A Theory of Competition Among Pressure Groups for Political Influence" *Quarterly Journal of Economics* 98, no. 3 (August 1983).

21. Charles P. Kindleberger, "Group Behavior and International Trade" *Journal of Political Economy* 59, no. 1 (Feb 1959): 30–47; Peter Gourevitch, *Politics in Hard Times* (Ithaca: Cornell University Press, 1986); Jeffry Frieden and Ronald Rogowski, "The Impact of the National Economy on Domestic Politics," in Robert Keohane and Helen Milner, *Internationalization and Domestic Politics* (Cambridge: Cambridge University Press, 1996). Kindleberger emphasizes sectors, Gourevitch coalitions, Frieden and Rogowski factors and price incentives. Hirschman demonstrates the consequences for power politics of economic incentives and group conflict.

22. Hirschman, *National Power*, p. 29.

23. This can result from concerns regarding the overall balance of trade, revenue from tariffs, or trade undertaken or controlled by the government.

24. "The Aski Mark," *The Economist*, 8/12/39, p. 322 (Referring to Latin American importers of German products).

25. Joseph S. Nye Jr., *Bound to Lead: The Changing Nature of American Power* (New York: Basic Books, 1990), p. 188. Nye argues that "trends today are making . . . soft power resources more important." See also pp. 189–201.

26. On these issues, see Mark Selden, "China, Japan, and the Political Economy of East Asia," in Peter Katzenstein and Takashi Shiraishi , eds., *Network Power: Japan and Asia* (Ithaca: Cornell University Press, 1997); Walter Hatch and Kozo Yamamura, *Asia in Japan's Embrace: Building a Regional Production Alliance* (New York: Cambridge University Press, 1996); Richard Doner, "Japanese Foreign Investment and the Creation of a Pacific Asian Region," in Jeffrey Frankel and Miles Kahler, eds., *Regionalism and Rivalry: Japan and the United States in Pacific Asia* (Chicago: University of Chicago Press, 1993); Peter Katzenstein and Martin Rouse, "Japan as a Regional Power in Asia," in Frankel and Kahler; Robert Ash and Y. Y. Kueh, "Economic Integration Within Greater China: Trade and Investment Flows Between China, Hong Kong, and Taiwan," *The China Quarterly* 136 (December 1993); Wayne Bert, "Chinese Policies and U.S. Interests in Southeast Asia," *Asian Survey* 33, no. 3 (March 1993).

27. Considerations of the hegemonic stability theory as it applies to money include: Benjamin M. Rowland , ed., *Balance of Power or Hegemony: The Inter-war Monetary System* (New York: Lehrman Institute, 1976); John Odell, "Bretton Woods and International Political Disintegration: Implications for Monetary Diplomacy," in R. E. Lombra and W. E. White, eds., *Political Economy of International and Domestic Monetary Relations* (Ames: Iowa State University Press, 1982); Joanne Gowa, "Hegemons, IOs, Markets: the Case of the Substitution Account," *International Organization* 38, no. 4 (Autumn 1984) Kenneth Oye, "The Sterling-Dollar-Franc Triangle: Monetary Diplomacy 1929–1937," in Oye, ed., *Cooperation Under Anarchy* (Princeton: Princeton University Press, 1986); Barry Eichengreen, "Hegemonic Stability Theories of the International Monetary System," in Richard N. Cooper, et al., *Can Nations Agree?* (Brookings: Washington DC, 1989).

28. For example, the evidence does not support the contention that Britain, or even the Bank of England, purposefully managed the international monetary system. Britain did not foster the formation of the international monetary regime, encourage policy coordination, or enforce rules. Nor is it clear that Britain's lending in this period was countercyclical. On these points, see Giulio M. Gallarotti, *The Anatomy of an International Monetary Regime: The Classical Gold Standard, 1880–1914* (New York: Oxford University Press, 1995); Barry Eichengreen, *Golden Fetters: The Gold Standard and the Great Depression 1919–1939* (New York: Oxford University Press, 1992); Andrew Walter, *World Power and World Money: The Role of Hegemony and International Monetary Order* (New York: St. Martin's Press, 1991).

29. See Eichengreen, *Golden Fetters*.

30. That a predatory hegemon can be an important source of instability in the international monetary system is emphasized by Walter, *World Power and World Money*, see esp. pp. 180. This argument is also advanced by Susan Strange, in "Still an Extraordinary Power: America's Role in a Global Monetary System," in Lombra and White, eds., esp. p. 74; see also David P. Calleo, *The Imperious Economy* (Cambridge: Harvard University Press, 1982).

31. Even if the hegemonic stability theory does not hold in its basic form, it should be noted that the existence of a distinct monetary leader may make cooperation more likely, ceteris paribus. A monetary leader can provide the international public good of a stable numeraire—a currency around which other actors can base their expectations. It also provides a "focal point" around which states can coordinate their monetary policies. See Jonathan Kirshner, "Cooperation and Consequence: The Politics of International Monetary Relations," *Journal of European Economic History*, forthcoming; also Gustav Cassel, *The World's Monetary Problems* (London: Constable and Co., 1921), p. 80; Eichengreen, "Hegemonic Stability Theories," p. 272.

32. See G. John Ikenberry, "A World Economy : Expert Consensus and the Anglo-American Postwar Settlement" *International Organization* 46, no. 1 (Winter 1992); Kathleen McNamara, *The Currency of Ideas: Monetary Politics in the European Union* (Ithaca: Cornell University Press, 1998).

33. On possible disagreements over distribution, preferences, circumstances, see Richard Cooper, "Prolegomena to the Choice of an International Monetary System," *International Organization* 29, no. 1 (Winter 1975): 63–98. For a discussion of various possible objectives and alternative organizing principles, see Benjamin J. Cohen, *Organizing the World's Money* (New York: Basic Books, 1977).

34. On the effectiveness of intervention, see Kathryn M. Dominguez and Jeffrey A. Frankel, *Does Foreign Exchange Intervention Work?* (Washington DC: Institute for International Economics, 1993); Hali J. Edison, "The Effectiveness of Central Bank Intervention: A Survey of the Literature After 1982," *Special Papers in International Economics*, (International Finance Section, Princeton University) No. 18, July 1993.

35. Kenneth A. Oye, *Economic Discrimination and Political Exchange: World Political Economy in the* 1930s *and* 1980s (Princeton: Princeton University Press, 1992).

36. John Maynard Keynes, A *Treatise on Money: The Applied Theory of Money* (Cambridge: Cambridge University Press, 1971 [1930]), p. 272.

37. The saliency of monetary commitments further undermine their sustainability. Cooperation in this sphere requires actions, such as interest rate hikes during a recession, that appear to be clearly at odds with domestic interests. Sticking to a trade agreement, however, even in the face of domestic pressure during a recession, only requires maintenance of the policy status-quo—not passing new protectionist legislation.

38. See Joanne Gowa, "Public Goods and Political Institutions: Trade and Monetary Policy Processes in the United States," *International Organization* 42, no. 1 (Winter 1988); Stephen Krasner, "United States Commercial and Monetary Policy: Unraveling the Paradox of External Strength and Internal Weakness," *International Organization* 31, no. 4 (Autumn 1977); I. M. Destler and C. Randall Henning, *Dollar Politics: Exchange Rate Policymaking in the United States* (Washington: Institute for International Economics, 1989). C. F. Jeffry Frieden, who expects increased interest group conflict over the exchange rate, "Invested Interests: the Politics of National Economic Policies in a World of Global Finance," *International Organization* 45, no. 4 (1991): 425–51.

39. Note that this is distinct from arguments that use security to explain economic cooperation but stress concern for "relative gains." See Joanne Gowa, "Bipolarity, Multipolarity, and Free Trade," and the discussion on trade below.

40. Robert V. Roosa, *The United States and Japan in the International Monetary System, 1946–1985* (New York: Group of Thirty, 1986), p. 1; Robert C. Angel, *Explaining Economic Policy Failure: Japan in the 1969–71 International Monetary Crisis* (New York: Columbia University Press, 1991), p. 38.

41. Thomas F. Cargill, Michael M. Hutchison and Takatoshi Ito, *The Political Economy of Japanese Monetary Policy*, (Cambridge: MIT Press, 1997), pp. 61–62; Angel, *Explaining Economic Policy Failure*, p. 45; Roosa, *The United States and Japan*, pp. 2–3.

42. Kozo Yamamura, "The Legacies of a Bargain: The Reagan Deficits and Japan's "Bubble," in Yukio Noguchi and Kozo Yamamura, eds., *U.S.-Japan Macroeconomic Relations* (Seattle: University of Washington Press, 1996), p. 32; C. Randall Henning, *Currencies and Politics in the United States, Germany, and Japan* (Washington: Institute for International Economics, 1994), p. 123. On Japan's post-war business cycles with an emphasis on interest rate policy, see. Hiroshi Yoshikawa, "Monetary Policy and the Real Economy in Japan," in Kenneth Singleton, ed., *Japanese Monetary Policy* (Chicago: University of Chicago Press, 1993).

43. See Calleo, *Imperious Economy*, esp. p. 30; also Joanne Gowa, *Closing the Gold Window: Domestic Politics and the End of Bretton Woods* (Ithaca: Cornell University Press, 1983); also John S. Odell, *U.S. International Monetary Policy: Markets, Power, and Ideas as Sources of Change* (Princeton: Princeton University Press, 1982).

44. See Angel,*Explaining Economic Policy Failure*, esp. pp. 104 (quote), 115; also Paul Volcker and Toyoo Gyohten, *Changing Fortunes* (New York: Times Books, 1992), pp. 92–100.

45. C. Fred Bergsten, "What to Do about the U.S.-Japan Economic Conflict," *Foreign Affairs* 60:5 (Summer 1982), pp. 1059, 1065–6; On techniques Japan used to mask its interventions, see Dean Taylor, "The Mismanaged Float: Official Intervention by Industrialized Countries," in Michael B. Connolly, ed., *The International Monetary System: Choices for the Future* (New York: Praeger, 1982), pp. 70–72; see also Koichi Hamada and Hugh Patrick, "Japan and the International Monetary Regime," in Takashi Inoguchi and Daniel Okimoto, eds., *The Political Economy of Japan* (Vol. II) (Stanford: Stanford University Press, 1988), pp. 118–19; Cargill, Hutchison, and Ito, *The Political Economy of Japanese Monetary Policy*, 65–6.

46. On the appreciation of the dollar and U.S. opposition to policy coordination, see Martin Feldstein, "Thinking about International Economic Cooperation, *Journal of Economic Perspectives* 2, no. 2 (Spring 1988), esp. p. 12, and Jeffrey A. Frankel, "Exchange Rate Policy," in Martin Feldstein , ed., *American Economic Policy in the 1980s* (Chicago: University of Chicago Press, 1994). See also Jeffrey A. Frankel, *The Yen/Dollar Agreement: Liberalizing Japanese Capital Markets* (Washington: Institute for International Economics, 1984).

47. Volcker and Gyohten, *Changing Fortunes*, pp. 244, 268, 285; Yoichi Funabashi, *Managing the Dollar: From the Plaza to the Louvre* (Washington DC: Institute for International Economics, 1988).

48. Ronald McKinnon and Kenichi Ohno, *Dollar and Yen: Resolving Economic Conflict Between the U.S. and Japan* (Cambridge: MIT Press, 1997), pp. 10, 205 on successive U.S. pressure for yen appreciation.

49. McKinnon and Ohno, *Dollar and Yen*, esp. chapters. 3, 5. For more on the relationship between yen appreciation and recession in the Japanese economy, see Volcker and Gyohten, *Changing Fortunes*, p. 92; Yoshikawa, "Monetary Policy and the Real Economy in Japan," p. 140; Yamamura, "Legacies of a Bargain," p. 36.

50. For an illustration of the differential regional effects of changes in the yen-dollar rate on other Asian economies, see K. C. Kwan, *Economic Interdependence in the Asia-Pacific Region: Towards a Yen Bloc* (London: Routledge, 1994); esp. chapter 3.

51. J. Goodman and L. Pauly, "The Obsolescence of Capital Controls? Economic Management in an Age of Global Markets," *World Politics* 46, no. 1 (October 1993): 50–82; Andrew D. Cosh, Alan Hughes, and Ajit Singh, "Openness, Financial Innovation, Changing Patters of Ownership, and the Structure of Financial Markets," in Tariq Banuri and Juliet B. Schor , eds., *Financial Openness and National Autonomy: Opportunities and Constraints* (Oxford: Clarendon Press, 1992); Raymond Vernon, *Sovereignty at Bay* (New York: Basic Books, 1971); P. Cohey and J. Aronson, "A New Trade Order" *Foreign Affairs* 72, no. 1 (Supplement 1992–93); Ethan Kapstein, *Governing the Global Economy: International Finance and the State* (Cambridge: Harvard University Press, 1994).

52. On these issues, see Benjamin J. Cohen, *In Who's Interest? International Banking and American Foreign Policy* (New Haven: Yale University Press, 1986), esp. Part I.

53. Jeffrey Sachs and Charles Wyplosz, "The Economic Consequences of President Mitterrand," *Economic Policy* (April 1986) 262–306; Michael Loriaux, *France After Hegemony: International Change and Financial Reform* (Ithaca: Cornell University Press, 1991); See also Paulette Kurzer, *Business and Banking: Political Change and Economic Integration in Western Europe* (Ithaca: Cornell University Press, 1993).

54. See for example, Robert Zevin, "Are World Financial Markets More Open? If So, Why and With What Effects," in Banuri and Schor.

55. For an illustration of how capital mobility imposes a structural constraint on state capacity, see David Andrews, "Capital Mobility and State Autonomy: Toward a Structural Theory of International Monetary Relations," *International Studies Quarterly* 38, no. 2 (June 1994): 193–218. Eric Helleiner argues that de-regulation was state led, not market driven, but even if one accepts his interpretation the constraints imposed by high capital mobility remain. See his *States and the Reemergence of Global Finance* (Ithaca: Cornell University Press, 1994).

56. Robert Mundell, "The Monetary Dynamics of International Adjustment under Fixed Capital," *Quarterly Journal of Economics* 74 (1960): 227–57.

57. Liberals hold that the market system works because the effort of each actor in pursuit of his or her particular (selfish) interest generally results in the outcome that is optimal for society as a whole. Adam Smith's "invisible hand" assures this outcome, not government policy. However, Smith and the classical economists recognized that there are some instances when the sum of individual actions does not produce socially optimal results. These are cases of market failure, and as such provide justification for government intervention to correct the imbalance. It is interesting to note that Smith himself saw the financial system as an illustration of such a market failure, and called for the regulation of interest rates. *Wealth of Nations*, pp. 379–80.

58. On these issues, see Jonathan Kirshner, "Disinflation, Structural Change, and Distribution," *Review of Radical Political Economics* 30, no. 1 (March 1998): 52–89.

59. Mahbub ul Haq, Inge Kaul, and Isabelle Grunberg , eds., *The Tobin Tax: Coping With Financial Volatility* (New York: Oxford University Press, 1996), p. 3.

60. For a recent statement in favor of the Tobin Tax, see Barry Eichengreen, James Tobin, and Charles Wyplosz, "Two Cases for Sand in the Wheels of International Finance," *The Economic Journal* 105 (January 1995): 162–72.

61. See the assessment in Kirshner, "Political Economy of Realism.

62. Jagdish Bhagwati, "The Capital Myth," *Foreign Affairs* 77, no. 3 (May/June 1998), pp. 9, 12 (quote).

63. Dani Rodrik, "Who Needs Capital Account Convertibility?" in *Should the IMF Pursue Capital Account Convertibility*? Essays in International Finance, International Finance Section, Princeton University, no 207, May 1998, p. 61.

64. Paul Krugman, "Saving Asia: It's Time to Get Radical," *Fortune*, Sept 7, 1998; esp. "Part 5: What is Plan B?" See also Jonathan Kirshner, "Culprit is Unregulated Capital," *Los Angeles Times*, Sunday, September 13, 1998; David Wessel and Bob Davis, "Cash Cowed: Currency Controls Debated As Asian Crisis Takes Toll." *Asian Wall Street Journal* Sept. 7, 1998; Karen Pennar, "Is the Global Currency Crisis Greek to You?" *Business Week* Sept. 21 1998, p. 33; Peter Coy, Manjeet Kripalani, and Mark Clifford, "Capital Controls: Lifeline or Noose?" *Business Week*, Sept. 28, 1998, pp. 36–37; Robert Reich, "The Real Policy Makers," *New York Times*, Sept. 29, 1998.

65. It has been suggested that Mahathir was particularly influenced by Krugman's *Fortune* essay. In response, Krugman wrote "An Open Letter to Prime Minister Mahathir from Paul Krugman" on *Fortune*'s Web site (Sept. 1, 1998), in which he qualified his support for controls. Controls will create space for needed economic stimulus and reform, he explained, but are "risky," and "the distortions they impose on the economy are serious, and tend to get worse over time.'

66. "Malaysia Imposes Controls on the Ringgit—Mahathir's Hope is to Insulate Currency From Any Easing of Credit," *Asian Wall Street Journal*, Sept. 2, 1998; "Malaysia's Self-Isolation," *Asian Wall Street Journal*, Sept. 3, 1998; Mark Clifford and Pete Engardio, "Renegade Economy," *Business Week*, Sept. 21, 1998, 46–47.

67. Murray Hiebert and Andrew Sherry, "After the Fall," *Far Eastern Economic Review*, Sept. 17, 1998, p. 11; S. Jayasankaran, "Business as Usual?" *Far Eastern Economic Review*, Sept. 24, 1998; Clifford and Engardio, "Renegade Economy," p. 47. Of course, some sectors of Malaysia have been hit very hard: there have been severe cutbacks at local offices of foreign security firms. Douglas Appell: "Foreign Brokers face Malaysian Struggle—They Stop Equity Purchases under Currency Controls, and Job Cuts Start." *Asian Wall Street Journal*, Sept. 17, 1998.

68. Tom Holland, "Rupiah Advances in Asia as Talk of Capital Controls Spurs Buying," *Asian Wall Street Journal*, Sept. 16, 1998; Grainne McCarthy, "Indonesia hit by talk of Curbs on Capital Flow—Stock Market Slides Despite Denials by President Habibie," *Asian Wall Street Journal*, Sept. 16, 1998; "Indonesia Limits Offshore Banks to Minimize Rupia Outflows," *Asian Wall Street Journal*, Sept. 18, 1998. For relevant background detail and analysis, see Natasha Hamilton-Hart, *States and Capital Mo-*

bility: Indonesia, Malaysia, and Singapore in the Asian Region, Ph.D. Dissertation, Department of Government, Cornell University, 1998.

69. This was how the *Far Eastern Economic Review* expressed its skepticism of any scheme to control capital. "Some Like it Hot: The Mahathir-Soros Complex," July 16, 1998, p. 29.

70. In its retrospective analyses of the crisis, the IMF remains unrepentant, focused on the domestic sources of the crisis and highly suspicious of any forms of capital control. See International Monetary Fund, *International Capital Markets: Developments, Prospects, and Key Policy Issues* (Washington: IMF, September 1998), esp. pp. 6, 11, 57, 63, 73, 148–50; See also International Monetary Fund, *World Economic Outlook: Financial Turbulence and the World Economy* (Washington: IMF, October 1998), esp. pp. 16–18; 101–2. It should be noted, however, that in the wake of the crisis the World Bank has been willing to at least address the issue of the possible benefits of some control over short-term capital flows. See The World Bank, *Global Economic Prospects and the Developing Countries, 1998/99: Beyond Financial Crisis* (Washington: The World Bank, 1999), esp. pp. xi–xii, xxi, 4, 123–24, 128, 142–52; see also the World Bank, *East Asia: The Road to Recovery* (Washington: The World Bank, 1998), esp. pp. 9–10, 16, 34.

71. *IMF Survey*, September 23, 1996, p. 294. Under the headline "International Capital Markets charting a Steadier Course," the Fund also noted that "Although the scale of financial activity continues to grow, market participants—including high-risk high-return investment funds—are more disciplined, cautious, and sensitive to market fundamentals" (p. 293).

72. *IMF Survey*, May 12, 1997, pp. 131–32. Under the headline "IMF Wins Mandate to Cover Capital Accounts," the Survey reported "Managing Director, Michael Camdessus, remarked that global economic prospects warranted 'rational exuberance'." Economic prospects were "bright," and "overheating pressures have abated in many emerging market economies, especially in Asia—where growth has stayed string for several years." (pp. 129–30)

73. *IMF Survey*, May 26, 1997 (1st quote); Darren Mcdermott and Leslie Lopez, "Malaysia Imposes Sweeping Currency Controls—Such Capital Restrictions Win Credence in Wake of Financial Turmoil," *Wall Street Journal* September 2, 1998, G. Pierre Goad, "Acceptance of Capital Controls Is Spreading," *Asian Wall Street Journal*, September 2, 1998 ("condition of membership" quotes).

74. David E. Sanger, "Gaining Currency: The Invisible Hand's New Strong Arm," *New York Times*, Sept. 9, 1998 (quote); Sanger also notes a suspension of U.S. pressure on China to make their currency completely convertible. See also Richard Saludo: "Cold War Over Hot Money," *Asiaweek*, Sept. 18, 1998, who characterizes the struggle between liberalism a la the IMF and state control of the economy as "Cold War 2."

75. See Robert Gilpin, *War and Change in World Politics* (Cambridge: Cambridge University Press, 1981). This also contrasts with many baseline liberal expectations, which expect contemporary economic change to reduce China's aggressiveness, as economic growth and international trade decentralizes power within China and creates vested interests in continued peace. See also Miles Kahler, "External Ambition and Economic Performance," *World Politics* 40, no. 4 (July 1988), p. 451; Denny Roy, "Hegemon on the Horizon? China's Threat to East Asian Security," *International Se-*

curity 19, no. 1 (1994), 149–68; Aaron Friedberg, "Ripe for Rivalry: Prospects for Peace in a Multipolar Asia," *International Security* 18, no. 3 (Winter 1993/4), 5–33; and Alastair Iain Johnston, "Realism's and Chinese Security Policy in the Post-Cold War Period," in Kapstein and Mastanduno.

76. In my experience, realist scholars, when pressed, are not able to come up with a case where *interdependence* caused war. That is, instances when a high level of trade between two states was, *ceteris paribus*, an important cause of war between then.

Chapter 9

SOURCES OF AMERICAN-JAPANESE ECONOMIC CONFLICT

Robert Gilpin

An important issue raised by "revisionist" scholars such as Chalmers Johnson and Clyde Prestowitz is whether the clash between communism and capitalism has been replaced by conflict among rival models of capitalism. In a provocative article, Samuel Huntington declared that, with the end of the cold war, Japan had become a "security" threat to the United States.[1] According to these revisionists, whereas Western "regulatory" capitalism is consumer- and market-oriented, Asian "developmental" capitalism is characterized by a powerful role of the state and emphasis on production. High officials in both the Bush Administration (1989–1992) and the first Clinton Administration (1993–1997) shared this belief that Japan's distinctive capitalist system and trade pattern were responsible for America's huge trade deficit and the deindustrialization of the American economy. On the basis of this belief, President Bush launched the Structural Impediments Initiative (1989) whose purpose was to transform the nature of Japanese capitalism and President Clinton pursued a "managed trade" policy to open Japanese markets to American goods. These revisionist views have also been prevalent in Western Europe. A number of French intellectuals and business executives such as Albert Breton, Jacques Attali, and James Goldsmith have shared these revisionist opinions and have argued that the Western and Asian modes of capitalism are inherently incompatible.

Neoclassical economists tend to ignore the structural or systemic differences among national economies in the functioning of the world economy. Every economy, or at least every efficient one, is assumed to function according to the universal laws of the self-regulating market. International economists, for example, regard national economies as dimensionless points or as "empty boxes" connected by exchange rates and trade/financial flows. What is important, according to economic orthodoxy, is "getting the prices right" and letting unfettered markets work. For this position, the American trade/payments imbalance especially in manufacturing can be explained by the well-established theories of conventional economics. Although the tendency of economists to downplay the importance of national systemic differences has been modified with the increasing openness and interdependence of national economies, economists continue to neglect the important role of domestic institutions and structures in the functioning of the international economy.

The purpose of this article is to assess these conflicting explanations of the American-Japanese trade conflict that arose in the 1980s in response to the immense American trade/payments deficit. Although this conflict abated in the early 1990s due in large part to the economic revival of the American economy, the revisionist charges against Japan have not disappeared from the American political agenda and, in fact, resurfaced in the late 1990s as a consequence of the East Asian (including Japan) economic crisis. This crisis has given rise to the fear that the United States will be flooded by Asian imports. As I shall discuss below, this crisis and the failure of Japan to respond adequately to it are alleged to be responsible for a resurgence of the American trade/payments deficit with Pacific Asia. The place to begin this consideration of the sources of the American-Japanese trade conflict is with a discussion of the fundamental differences between the two economies.

DIFFERENCES AMONG NATIONAL ECONOMIES

Every national economy is embedded in a larger sociopolitical system. A nation's culture, social mores, and political system affect every aspect of economic affairs such as what is considered to be "fair" and "unfair" economic behavior. Although national systems of political economy differ from one another in many important respects, I shall focus on three principal differences: the primary purposes of economic activity, the role of the state in the economy, and the mechanism of corporate governance and private business practices. Although every modern economy must promote the welfare of its citizenry, different societies vary in the emphasis given to particular objectives. These objectives, which range from promoting consumer welfare to the pursuit of national power, strongly influence other features of an economy such as the role of the state in the economy and the structure of the economy. The role of the state in the economy differs in every market economy ranging from the generally laissez-faire, noninterventionist stance of the United States to the central role of the state in the overall management of the Japanese economy. The mechanisms of corporate governance and private business practices also differ; the relatively fragmented American business structure and the Japanese system of tightly integrated industrial groupings (*keiretsu*) provide the most dramatic contrast. Very different national systems of political economy result from variations in these three components of an economy.

The purpose of economic activity can differ considerable across national economies. As Karl Polanyi pointed out in *The Great Transformation*, the purpose of economic activities is culturally or politically determined.[2] The Western notion of individualism and of the market as an autonomous entity is unique and historically recent. Throughout history, Polanyi argues, economic activities have been deeply embedded in social arrangements and subordinated to more communal goals. The economy has seldom, if ever, been conceived as an end in itself or regarded as something separate and independent from the rest of society. Although the welfare of the consumer and the identity of the economy with the free market have become increasingly prominent in many analyses in the modern era, Japan, Germany, and many other societies continue to give a high priority to communal or collective purposes.

The role of the state in the economy is determined primarily by a society's conception of the purpose of economic activity. In those "liberal" societies where the welfare of the consumer and the autonomy of the market are emphasized, the role of the state tends to be minimal. Although liberal societies obviously differ in the extent to which they may pursue social welfare goals and some may be classified as "welfare states," the predominant responsibility of the state is to correct market failures and to provide public goods. On the other hand, in those societies where more communal or collective purposes prevail, the role of the state is much more intrusive and interventionist in the economy. Thus, the role of such states can range from provision of what the Japanese call "administrative guidance" to a command economy like that of the former Soviet Union.

Another important component of a national political economy is the system of corporate governance and the nature of private business practices. The major corporations of Japan, Germany, and the United States have very different systems of corporate governance, and they organize their economic activities (production, marketing, etc.) in distinctive ways. For example, whereas stockholders and their representatives have an important role in the governance of American business, banks play a more important role in both Japan and Germany. Although these national differences in corporate structure and business practices have evolved largely in response to economic and technological forces, the state has played an essential role in shaping the nature of business enterprise and business behavior through its regulatory, industrial, and other policies.

THE AMERICAN SYSTEM OF MANAGERIAL CAPITALISM

The American system of political economy is founded on the premise that the primary purpose of economic activity is to benefit consumers while maximizing wealth creation (regardless of its distribution domestically or internationally). Despite innumerable lapses, the American economy, which incorporates the fundamental principles of neoclassical economics as an ideal goal, approaches the neoclassical model of a competitive market economy. In the American conception of the economy, individuals are assumed to maximize their own private interests ("utility"), and business corporations are expected to maximize profits. The American model of the economy rests on the assumption that markets are competitive and that, where they are not,, competition should be promoted. Almost any economic activity is permitted unless explicitly forbidden. The economy is also assumed to be open to the outside world unless specifically closed. Such an emphasis on consumerism and wealth creation results in a powerful pro-consumption bias and a greater insensitivity (at least when compared to Japan and Germany) to the social welfare impact of economic activities. Although Americans pride themselves on their pragmatism, the American economy is founded upon the abstract theory of economic science to a greater degree than is any other economy.

At the same time, however, the American economy is well characterized as a system of "managerial" capitalism. The American economy was profoundly transformed by the emergence in the closing decades of the nineteenth century of huge corporations and the accompanying shift from a "proprietary" capitalism to one dominated by large, oligopolistic corporations. Management was separated from ownership and the corporate elite became virtually a law unto itself. Subsequently, with the New Deal of the 1930s, the balance shifted to some degree away from big business with the creation of a strong regulatory bureaucracy and the empowerment of organized labor. In effect the neoclassical laissez-faire ideal was diluted by the notion that the federal government had a responsibility to promote economic equity and social welfare. The economic ideal of a self-regulating economy was further undermined by the passage of the Full Employment Act of 1945 and by the Kennedy Administration's implementation of that Act when it accepted the Keynesian idea that the federal government had a responsibility to maintain full employment through its use of macroeconomic (fiscal and monetary) policies.

Commitments to the welfare of individual consumers and the realities of corporate power have been strong in American economic life, but there has been no persistently strong sense of business responsibility to the society or to the individual citizen. Japanese corporations, as will be shown below, have long been committed to the interests of their "stake holders" including labor and subcontractors, while German firms are more accepting than are American firms of the welfare state. American corporations are more detached from the welfare concerns of the other components of society than either Germany or Japan. For example, Japanese and German firms are much more reluctant to shift industrial production to other countries than are their American rivals. However, over time, the balance between the ideal and the reality of the American economy has shifted back and forth. In the 1980s, with the election of Ronald Reagan, emphasis on the unfettered market eclipsed the welfare ideal of the earlier post World War II era.

ECONOMIC ROLE OF THE STATE

The role of the American government in the economy is determined not only by the influence of the neoclassical model on American economic thinking but also by fundamental features of the American political system. The fact that authority over the economy is divided among the executive, legislative, and judicial branches of the federal government is vitally important. As Jeffrey Garten points out, whereas the Japanese Ministry of Finance has virtual monopoly power over the Japanese financial system, in the United States this responsibility is shared by the Treasury, the Federal Reserve, and several other powerful and independent federal agencies; furthermore, all of those agencies are strongly affected by actions of the legislative and judicial branches of government.[3]

The other important structural feature of the American political economy is the federal system itself, which fragments authority over the economy between Washington and each of the 50 states. Conflicts between the federal government and the individual states over economic policy occur again and again in the American system. Moreover, this fragmentation causes great consternation among America's economic partners, as it is extremely difficult for foreign nationals to know who has the last word in their dealings with the United States. A prime example of these complexities is found in the questionable attempts by individual states to tax the profits of the American subsidiaries of foreign firms. In addition, the U.S. constitutional system of checks and balances also greatly inhibits the fashioning of an effective role for the government in the economy. Added to these structural features is a weak civil service which cannot provide the independent leadership expected from Japanese and German officials.

Another restraining influence on the role of the American state in the economy is the opposition between the private and public sectors. The adversarial relationship between government and business in the United States make cooperation very difficult, while their mutual suspicions are reflected in American politics. Whereas political conservatives reject, at least in principle, any strong role for the state in the economy, political liberals are fearful that private business interests will capture government programs in order to "feather their own nests." A political stalemate frequently results from this situation. At the same time, however, the fragmented structure of the American government and its many points of access make it easier than in some other systems for private interests to challenge government actions. These ideological, structural, and public versus private aspects of the American political economy have restricted greatly the capacity of the American government to develop a coherent national economic strategy.

Macroeconomic policymaking does provide a major exception to the generally limited role of the American government in the economy. Yet, even in this area, the responsibility for macroeconomic policy has, in actual practice, been divided. Although passage of the Full Employment Act acknowledged that the federal government had an overall responsibility for maintaining full employment, both the Congress and the Executive Branch are responsible for fiscal policy. The control over monetary policy has rested with the Federal Reserve which functions largely independent of the rest of the Federal Government. However, starting with the fiscal policy excesses of the Reagan Administration in the early 1980s and the accumulation of an immense federal debt, the role of fiscal policy declined and the Federal Reserve, through its control over monetary policy, has become the principal manager of the American economy.

While there is general acceptance that the American state has a major role in the economy at the macroeconomic level, its role at the microeconomic level is highly controversial. The society generally assumes that the government should establish a neutral environment for business and should not involve itself in business affairs. From this perspective, the primary responsibility of the government is the regulation of the economy and to overcome "market failures." Among "market failures" that justify an active government role in the economy are the need to control monopoly power, to correct negative "externalities," and to compensate for inadequate consumer information. While economists and others differ over the definition of market failure and the proper scope of government regulatory policy, the legitimacy of a significant role for the government in this area is well established.

There are several implications that flow from this regulatory yet severely limited role for the American government in the economy. In the first place, this task means that the American government frequently assumes a role as an adversary to business. Indeed, American business and government seldom cooperate to increase the international competitiveness of the economy. Second, emphasis is placed on protecting American consumers even when this may weaken the competitiveness of American firms against their foreign rivals; for example, the strict application of anti-trust laws to prohibit monopoly prevents the type of cooperative research projects frequently found in Japan and Western Europe. Third, the government is inhibited from pursuing industrial and other policies that might develop or strengthen industries considered to be of competitive importance; instead, the role of trade or commercial policy is to create a "level playing field" on which American and foreign firms can compete fairly and not to favor American firms. In brief, the federal government is assumed to have only a limited role in promoting the international competitiveness of American business.

Industrial policy is an area of important differences between the U.S. and Japan. The term refers to the deliberate efforts by a government to determine the structure of the economy through such devices as financial subsidies, trade protectionism, or government procurement. Interventionist activity is justified by the assumption that some industries are more important than others for the overall economy, and that certain strategic industries create higher quality jobs (such as manufacturing jobs which are generally considered better than service jobs). Favored industries may also produce technological or other "spillovers" (externalities) that have a beneficial effect on the rest of the economy; frequently cited examples are the computer industry and other high tech industries. Those industries and technologies judged to be important to national security and to economic independence are also in this special category.

A high degree of consensus exists among professional economists and within the American business community (except of course among those industries demanding special treatment) that the American government should not and, in fact, cannot "pick winners." Most contend that the structure and distribution of industries in the United States should be left up to the market. In effect, the basic belief is that all industries are created equal and that there are no strategic sectors. In the oft-paraphrased expression of Michael Boskin, Chairman of President George H. W. Bush's Council of Economic Advisers, a chip is a chip, whether it be a potato or a computer chip, and there is no legitimate reason for the government to favor one or the other. There are, however, three major exceptions to this consensus against industrial policy: in the areas of agriculture, national security, and research and development. Since the mid-nineteenth century, the federal government has funded agricultural research. Under the rubric of national security, the Pentagon, as foreign governments charge, has long carried out an extensive industrial policy supporting technological advance on a broad front. Although government financing of research and development is generic and seldom attempts to promote specific industries, one can legitimately classify this activity also as a form of industrial policy.

CORPORATE GOVERNANCE AND PRIVATE BUSINESS PRACTICES

In important ways the American system of corporate governance and industrial structure parallels the national system of political governance and political structure. U.S. corporate governance and organization are characterized by fragmentation and an overall lack of policy coordination at both the corporate and national levels. Indeed, the strong American anti-trust tradition and competition policy are intended to prevent concentration of corporate power. American business is much more constrained than its rivals in its ability to share business information, to pool technological and other resources, and to develop joint strategies. As many observers have charged, such restrictions disadvantage American firms in global competition.

Control of American business is much more dispersed than in Japan or Germany. Whereas the largest stockholders in many of America's large corporations may own only one or two percent of the stock, it is not infrequent in Japan for ownership of seventy percent or more of the stock to reside in a cooperative business grouping (*keiretsu*). Also industry and finance are more completely separated from one another in the United States; this has meant higher capital costs than those enjoyed by foreign rivals and also frequent conflicts of interest between industry and finance that have been detrimental to national policymaking. At the national level, the National Association of Manufacturers, Chamber of Commerce, and other business organizations play no role commensurate with that of the *keidanren* in Japan or the Federation of German Industries. These Japanese and German organizations can speak with one strong voice and frequently act on behalf of business interests.

Underlying many of these contrasts between American and Japanese/German business is a fundamentally different conception of the corporation and of its role in society. In the United States, a business corporation is regarded as a commodity that is bought and sold like any other commodity regardless of the social consequences of such transactions. The 1980s wave of leveraged buyouts and corporate takeovers was a grotesque exaggeration of this mentality. In both Japan and Germany, on the other hand, the corporation tends to be regarded more as a semi-public institution with a responsibility to society and to a broard range of stake holders; it is expected to promote larger social and political objectives than just the bottom line of profitability. Japanese firms in particular are expected to increase the power and independence of Japanese society; while Germany places a high premium on social welfare. American law is designed to ensure neutrality and fair play in the competitive market for corporate control. In contrast to the United Sates, Japan, and Germany attempt to limit the struggle for corporate control.

THE JAPANESE SYSTEM OF COLLECTIVE CAPITALISM

G. C. Allen, the distinguished British authority on Japanese economic history, tells a story that provides an important insight into Japanese economic psychology. At the end of World War II, American economists and officials advised the Japanese that they should follow the theory of comparative advantage as they rebuilt their war-torn economy and that Japan's advantage lay with labor-intensive products. The Japanese bureaucratic elite, however, had quite different ideas and would have nothing to do with what they considered to be an American effort to relegate Japan to the low end of the economic and technological spectrum. Instead, the Japanese Ministry of International Trade and Industry (MITI) and other agencies of the Japanese economic high command set their sights on making vanquished Japan into the economic and technological equal, and perhaps the superior, of the West. This objective remains the driving force of Japanese society.

In the Japanese scheme of things, the economy is subordinate to the political objectives of society. Ever since the Meiji Restoration (1868) the overriding goals of Japan have been to make the economy self-sufficient and to catch up with the West. In the pre–World War II years, this national ambition meant building a strong army as well as becoming an industrial power. Since its disastrous defeat in World War II, however, Japan has abandoned militarism and has focused on becoming a powerful industrial and technological nation while also promoting internal social harmony among the Japanese people. There has been a concerted effort by the Japanese state to guide the evolution and functioning of the Japanese economy in order to pursue these two basic objectives.

These political goals have resulted in a national economic policy best characterized as neomercantilism. This policy has involved state assistance, extensive regulation, and protection of specific industrial sectors in order to increase their international competitiveness and thereby achieve national preeminence over the leading high tech sectors of the world economy. This economic objective of achieving industrial and technological supremacy over other countries arose from Japan's experience as a late developer and also from its strong sense of economic and political vulnerability. Another very important source of this powerful economic drive is the Japanese people's overwhelming belief in their uniqueness, in the superiority of their culture, and in their manifest destiny to become a great power.

Many terms have been used to characterize the distinctive nature of the Japanese system of political economy: developmental capitalism, tribal capitalism, collective capitalism, network capitalism, companyism, producer capitalism, stake holder capitalism, and, perhaps most famous or infamous, "Japan, Inc." Each expression connotes particularly important elements of the Japanese economic system such as: (1) its overwhelming emphasis on economic development, (2) the key role of large corporations in the organization of the economy and society, (3) emphasis on the group rather than the individual, (4) primacy of the producer over the consumer, and (5) the close cooperation among government, business, and labor. I believe that the term, "collective capitalism" best captures the essence of the system because this characterization conveys the priority that the Japanese give to working together to achieve the overriding national purposes of catching up with the West while also achieving domestic social stability and national harmony.

Perhaps more than any other advanced economy, the Japanese are willing to subordinate the pursuit of economic efficiency to social equity and fairness. The Japanese strive mightily to preserve their unity, independence, and uniqueness in a highly competitive and, at times, dangerous international system. These fundamental goals undoubtedly reflect the fact that the Japanese are as much a race as a nation. However, the uniqueness of Japan increases the difficulties of integrating that dynamic and important nation into the larger world economy.

THE ECONOMIC ROLE OF THE STATE

The role of the Japanese state in the economy is something of an enigma. Few Japanese or foreign commentators would deny that the Japanese state has played an extremely important role in Japanese economic development or that it continues to be an important factor in managing the economy. It is frequently asserted that the Japanese state, in American political science terminology, is a "strong" state with a pervasive presence in every aspect of Japanese economic life. Who could possibly doubt, for example, the powerful influence of MITI or of the even more powerful Ministry of Finance (MOF)! Yet, the size and the cost of the Japanese state are really quite small, particularly when compared to the American government. Moreover, the Japanese government is frequently stalemated and incapable of decisive action. Despite these important qualifications, however, the Japanese state has had and continues to have a profound influence over the direction of the economy.

It is very important to recognize that Japan, throughout most of the postwar era, has been ruled by a tripartite alliance of government bureaucracies, the ruling Liberal Democratic Party (LDP), and big business. This alliance achieved a consensus that Japan's primary objective should be rapid industrialization. Moreover, the state should play a central role in achieving this objective. In addition, the Japanese people themselves believe that the state has a legitimate and important economic function in promoting economic growth and international competitiveness. The government bureaucracy and the private sector, with the former taking the lead, are expected to work together for the greater collective good of Japanese society. Pursuing this goal, MITI and other Japanese bureaucracies have developed a number of policy instruments ranging from "administrative guidance" to financial support and trade protection to promote the development of specific industries.

Perhaps even more importantly, the Japanese state has supported aspects of Japanese society such as hard work, a skilled labor force, and a high savings rate, characteristics that account perhaps more than anything else for Japanese economic success. As an example, Japan's extraordinarily high savings rate has reduced the cost of investment and contributed to Japanese competitiveness. The Japanese state has also played an important role in supporting social, political, and legal aspects of Japanese society that make Japanese society frequently inhospitable to foreign firms and limit the importation of foreign goods.

An important and distinctive feature of Japanese society is that many of the "public" responsibilities of the American or German governments are delegated to the private sector. For example, corporations have a major responsibility for the social welfare of a substantial portion of the Japanese population. Whereas the American government delegates regulatory authority to quasi-autonomous public agencies, Japanese delegate much of the responsibility for the policing of business activities to private associations. This has been a highly pragmatic practice based on the close ties and mutual trust between private business and government. A remarkable example of this practice of delegating public functions is the privatizing of "law and order." One reason for the low level of street crime in Japan is that the Japanese Mafia (*yakuza*) police the streets in exchange for police toleration of their businesses.

At least in part, this practice of self-regulation and self-policing by business and other private associations is intended to provide social stability and to ensure fairness. However, it can and does lead to special treatment of particular groups, seemingly arbitrary decisions, and discriminatory behavior designed to protect the weak. This practice is directly counter to the American concept of universal rules that apply equally to everyone regardless of their status. This cultural difference in the definition of "fairness" has been a major source of American-Japanese economic tension and has, on occasion, erupted into open conflict. The Japanese practice of delegating what are considered in the U.S. to be essentially public responsibilities to private associations has raised significant problems for a Japan increasingly integrated into the world economy. For cultural and other reasons, it is virtually impossible for Japan to incorporate outsiders into the self-regulating associations that set the rules governing competitive behavior and other aspects of the conduct of business in Japan, and foreign companies seeking entry into the Japanese market naturally regard the practice of self-regulation as discriminatory, which it most assuredly is. The self-policing system with its emphasis on fairness and on tailor-made rules enforced in self-regulatory associations conflicts directly with the concept of universal and nondiscriminatory rules embodied in the General Agreement on Tariffs and Trade and is thus an immense hurdle to be cleared in opening the Japanese market and internationalizing Japan.

Japan's political and bureaucratic fragmentation also set the state apart. The economic and other bureaucracies of the government are virtually lords unto themselves in their own areas of responsibility. Johnson has made the point that the three major economic agencies responsible for foreign affairs at times have had different and conflicting foreign economic policies. Every Japanese bureaucracy tends to believe that it has a responsibility to protect a particular segment of Japanese society. Disputes over policy and conflicts over areas of responsibility are frequent.

Although bureaucratic struggles exist in every country, in Japan there is no effective way to resolve such conflicts because there is no powerful chief executive. In addition, the strong Japanese belief in consensus decisionmaking encourages stalemate and indecision. The one great exception to this generalization is a major crisis, especially one that originates elsewhere, and forces Japan to resolve its internal divisions. Although such external pressures (*gaiatsu*) are deeply resented by the Japanese, the outcomes produced by such pressures, as many Japanese will admit, are frequently beneficial to Japanese consumers and other groups. For example, reform of the "big store law" facilitated establishment of discount stores (both American and Japanese) with greater variety and lower costs than the traditional Japanese "Mom and Pop" stores.

The area of industrial policy is the most controversial aspect of the Japanese political economy. As I have already noted, industrial policy refers to the extensive and deliberate efforts of the government to guide and shape the development of the economy. Through such policy devices as trade protection, industrial subsidies, and "administrative guidance," the government attempts to determine the nation's economic and industrial structure. In the Japanese case, the government has sought to promote high value-added and internationally competitive industries.

The debate over the role and effectiveness of industrial policy in the postwar economic success of Japan has been extensive and contentious. The debate has centered on three questions: Did the Japanese state play a crucial and central role in the postwar development of the Japanese economy? Was Japanese industrial policy a major factor in Japan's outstanding economic success or was it, as some economists charge, an utter failure? Even if industrial policy did contribute to Japan's earlier postwar achievements, is it still relevant in an economically mature and technologically advanced Japanese economy?

On one side of this debate have been those revisionist scholars and commentators who have argued that MITI and other key Japanese bureaucracies have in large part been responsible for Japan's outstanding technological achievements and unsurpassed international competitiveness. The *locus classicus* of this positive assessment of Japanese industrial policy is Johnson's *MITI and the Japanese Miracle: The Growth of Industrial Policy. 1925–1975* (1982).[4] Johnson credits MITI for having orchestrated Japan's postwar economic and technological success.

On the other side of the debate are neoclassical economists and other detractors of MITI's role who argue that MITI's efforts to channel resources into specific industrial projects such as aircraft, shipbuilding, and fifth-generation computers were not only unsuccessful, but actually resulted in huge costs and were detrimental to the Japanese economy. These economists attribute Japan's postwar success entirely to such market-conforming policies of the Japanese government as stable macroeconomic policies, public investments in human capital, and the decisions of Japan's private sector that conformed to Japan's comparative advantage as a resource-poor and capital/skilled labor-rich economy.

Much of the debate over Japanese industrial policy has obscured the most important aspect of the role of the Japanese state in Japan's postwar economic and technological success. Even though neoclassical economists are essentially correct that Japanese bureaucrats have seldom been successful in picking winners and have made many mistakes this interpretation overlooks the critical and unique role of the Japanese state in facilitating and supporting the entrepreneurial efforts of Japanese business. The policies of MITI and other Japanese economic bureaucracies were very important in enabling Japanese firms to close the technological gap with American and other Western high tech industries.

The Japanese government has generally pursued a highly successful policy of "infant industry protection." It is important to recognize that the Japanese government was most successful when it supported those industrial sectors whose economic significance had already been proven in the United States and that the government was much less successful when it attempted to "pick winners." In addition, throughout most of the postwar era, the Japanese government has pursued a number of policies that significantly increased the economic and competitive success of Japanese business. These beneficial policies have included:

1. Taxation, financial, and other policies that encouraged extraordinarily high savings and investment rates.
2. Fiscal and other policies that kept consumer prices high, corporate earnings up, and discouraged consumption, especially of foreign goods.
3. Strategic trade policies that protected infant Japanese industries against both imported goods and the subsidiaries of foreign firms.
4. Government support for basic industries and such generic technology as materials research.
5. Competitive (anti-trust) and other policies favorable to the *keiretsu* and inter-firm cooperation.

However, in the 1990s, as Japan has closed the technological gap with the United States, as its corporations became among the most competitive in the world, and as its economy has opened, many of the long-term policies have become both ineffective and unnecessary.

CORPORATE GOVERNANCE AND INDUSTRIAL STRUCTURE

Although many American neoclassical economists deny it, the Japanese system of political economy differs significantly from Western economic models. While it is true that some of the distinctive features of the Japanese system are now changing, fundamental differences between the Japanese and Western economic systems continue. Certain important features of the Japanese system deserve particular study. The Japanese system of industrial organization with large closely connected industrial groups *keiretsu* and long-term relationships between major firms and their suppliers sets the Japanese system apart from the American and, to a lesser extent, from the German system of industrial organization.

The dualistic nature of the Japanese labor market is also distinctive. Some workers (primarily males working in Japan's major corporations) enjoy lifetime employment and are considered to be stake holders to whom Japanese firms have a responsibility. Simultaneously, however, a large portion of the work force (especially women and workers in smaller firms) has little job security and does not share equally in the benefits of the system. The distribution system is also unique; although Japan has a few large independent stores, the distribution system is generally dualistic. It is largely composed of major outlets controlled by the *keiretsu* and an enormous number of very small "mom and pop" stores. In this discussion, I shall concentrate on the *keiretsu* because of their central importance in the functioning of the Japanese economy.

The members of a *keiretsu* are bound together by mutual trust and long-term relationships among a number of firms. Informal ties are reinforced by overlapping memberships on governing boards, mutual stock ownership, and other mechanisms. The purpose of these structures is to serve the interests of stake holders rather than stockholders, and it is important to remember that those stake holders include not only the corporate members of the *keiretsu* but also labor and suppliers of components to those corporate members. The horizontal *keiretsu*, enterprise groups such as Mitsui, Mitsubishi, and Sumitomo, are composed of a few dozen members and include a large bank, manufacturing firms, and a distribution network along with other elements. The vertical *keiretsu* are composed of a parent manufacturing company and a large network of long-standing subcontractors and suppliers of services. The approximately two dozen vertical *keiretsu* include the leading Japanese manufacturing corporations in the automotive and consumer electronics industries such as Toyota and Matsushita. Together, the vertical and horizontal *keiretsu* control much of Japanese business. Dominant firms in a *keiretsu* may both exploit and promote the strengths of their junior partners. For example, the parent firms work with their extensive stable of long-term and trusted subcontractors to increase the latter's technological capabilities and to improve the quality of the components supplied to the parent. The parent even shares exclusive information with its affiliates, greatly enhancing the overall efficiency of the *keiretsu*.

The extensive presence of the *keiretsu* in the Japanese economy has profound consequences for the nature of Japanese domestic and international economic competition and for the dynamics of the Japanese economy. Contrary to the frequently issued charge leveled by some revisionist writers that the Japanese domestic market is noncompetitive, this market is in fact extraordinarily competitive. For example, Japan has a number of important automobile companies, whereas the United States has only three. However, competition in Japan does tend to be oligopolistic and Schumpeterian; that is, it is based on technological innovation and is quality-driven rather than based mainly on price competition. Furthermore, consumer prices in Japan are kept high by government policies in order to benefit the corporate sector.

In addition, whereas American consumers tend to be price-sensitive, Japanese consumers tend to be more quality-sensitive; they have a strong bias toward buying either "Japanese"or expensive and quite prestigious foreign goods. Market share (rather than the profit maximization familiar to Western industry) is the driving force behind Japanese competition; a large market share increases economies of scale and benefits the firm's stake holders. Paradoxically, the Japanese economy is highly regulated, compartmentalized and overprotected, yet it is also the most fiercely competitive market in the world.

In his book on the governance of Japanese corporations, W. Carl Kester makes the convincing argument that the *keiretsu* is a highly efficient and rational mechanism for organizing economic activities.[5] Its distinctive characteristics make it a formidable competitor in world markets. Mutual trust, for example, substantially reduces transaction costs. Information exchange within the *keiretsu* decreases uncertainties and is conducive to innovative activities. Intragroup cross-shareholding protects members against "hostile" takeovers and significantly reduces the cost of capital. The system is a mutual assistance society; when a member firm gets into trouble, other members come to its rescue.

Corporate leadership's independence from outside stockholders permits the firm, unlike American management, to pursue a corporate strategy based on maximizing market share rather than short-term profit maximization. The *keiretsu* is a crucial element in Japan's remarkable capacity to adjust to economic, technological, and other changes; no other country was as successful as Japan in adjusting to the two oil price rises (1973–74 and 1979–80). Despite the troubles of the Japanese economy in the 1990s, the Japanese *keiretsu* has proved to be a successful innovator of new products and production techniques because of its immense internal resources and long-term perspective. The *keiretsu* appears to have effectively joined the financial and other comparative advantages of the large firm with the flexibility and innovativeness of the small firm.

Although (or perhaps because) the *keiretsu* is a highly effective means of industrial organization, it is deeply resented by non-Japanese. One reason for this resentment is that the *keiretsu* is a closed system and excludes all "outsiders." By outsider, I mean any firm, including any Japanese firm, that is not a member of the alliance of stake holders who share the monopolistic rents generated by this oligopolistic form of business organization. This exclusive nature of the *keiretsu* system significantly limits the access of foreign firms to the Japanese market. The *keiretsu* also makes takeovers of Japanese firms by foreign firms extremely difficult and gives Japanese firms a huge advantage in corporate expansion. Whereas Japanese firms can easily purchase a non-Japanese firm in order to acquire its technology or to gain market access, it is seldom possible for non-Japanese firms to purchase Japanese firms for the same purposes.

Furthermore, control by a *keiretsu* over distribution channels effectively shuts non-Japanese firms out of the Japanese market; this issue was at the heart of the Clinton Administration's conflict with Japan over automotive trade in the early 1990s. Non-Japanese firms and other governments regard *keiretsu* as significant barriers both to exporting goods to the Japanese market and to investment in Japan. The Japanese, on the other hand, regard the *keiretsu* as key elements in their economic success. The problem of differential or asymmetrical access was a major cause of conflict between Japan and its trading partners in the 1980s.

THE AMERICAN–JAPANESE TRADE CONFLICT

The issue of Japan's uniqueness and allegedly "unfair" behavior has been joined in the debate between revisionist scholars and neoclassical economists over Japanese trade.[6] This debate has centered on Japan's persistent and large trade/payments surplus and its alleged distinctive trade pattern. Although the tension between Japan and the United States abated somewhat during the 1990s, its underlying causes remain, and serious American-Japanese conflicts over trade and investment are very likely to arise again in the future unless radical changes are made in the economic systems and policies of both countries.

JAPAN'S TRADE SURPLUS/AMERICAN TRADE DEFICIT

Revisionists attribute Japan's continuing trade surplus to that country's neomercantilist economic strategy. They argue that the purpose of Japanese policy has been to generate a trade/payments surplus and to make Japan the world's dominant industrial and technological power. Japan's large trade surplus is cited as ipso facto proof that Japan has unfairly kept its economy closed to non-Japanese goods, protected its domestic market, and employed many devices like export subsidies and dumping to achieve a surplus vis-à-vis its trading partners. Even though Japan has lowered its formal tariff barriers and, in fact, has the lowest overall tariffs of any industrialized economy, both the government and business maintain a number of informal and nontransparent barriers that are continuing to keep imports out of the Japanese market. The mechanisms used as informal trade barriers include detailed specific product standards, the distribution system, and government procurement policies.

In opposition to the revisionist position, most neoclassical economists and the Japanese themselves argue that Japan's trade surplus and America's corresponding trade deficit can be explained entirely by macroeconomic factors. They remind us that a nation's trade surplus or deficit is primarily a function of the difference between its savings and investment rates; thus, a nation like Japan, with a high savings rate that exceeds its investment rate, will inevitably have a trade surplus whereas a nation like the United States with an exceedingly low savings rate and a high consumption rate will inevitably have a trade deficit. These differing macroeconomic situations, according to neoclassical analysts, clearly explain the Japanese trade/payments surplus and America's trade/payments deficit; for this reason, they argue, it is inaccurate to blame Japan for America's trade deficit. If the United States stopped all imports from Japan, the overall American trade deficit with the rest of the world would increase unless Americans decided to save more and invest/consume less. Stated succinctly, the neoclassical interpretation is that the American trade deficit originates in the United States itself.

JAPAN'S TRADE PATTERN

The other major issue in the American-Japanese trade dispute is Japan's distinctive trade pattern. Japan imports remarkably few of the manufactured goods that it consumes. Or, to put the matter another way, only a small fraction of Japanese trade is two-way trade within particular industries. Stated more formally, whereas a substantial portion of American and European trade has been intra-industry trade, Japanese trade has been largely inter-industry.[7] Japan imports mainly commodities (food, raw materials, and fuels) while exporting primarily manufactured goods (motor vehicles, electronics, and other high tech products). Although Japan did begin to import more manufactured goods following revaluation of the yen in 1986, many of the imports were from overseas subsidiaries of Japan's large multinational corporations.

Japan's unusual trading pattern contrasts with the more "normal" German pattern of intra-industry trade. Germany, which has traditionally been a much larger exporter than Japan and which has generally had an overall trade surplus in manufactured goods (at least before reunification) still imports many of the manufactured goods that it consumes. For example, Germany both imports and exports automobiles. Whereas German exports from many industrial sectors reach diverse foreign markets, Japan's exports are concentrated in relatively few markets, especially the American, and in relatively few industrial sectors, especially automobiles, consumer electronics, and auto parts. The United States, the world's largest exporter, has an intra-industry trade pattern similar to that of the Germans. These fundamental differences between trans-Atlantic and trans-Pacific trade are important in explaining why Americans and Germans, for example, have had little trade friction with one another and why many Americans and Europeans have been irritated by Japan's peculiar trade pattern.

For the revisionists, Japan's distinctive trade policy provides convincing evidence of Japan's neomercantilist economic strategy. Tyson has maintained that conventional trade theory does not apply to Japanese trade behavior. Instead, Japan's trade surplus and distinctive trade pattern are due to its policies of protection, preclusive investment, and industrial targeting.[8] Foreign manufacturers, it is charged, have been systematically denied access to the Japanese market at the very same time that Japan has carried out a trade offensive against other countries. Japan, revisionists contend, should be importing substantially more foreign manufactured goods. In addition, they point out, Japan has pursued a strategy of "preemptive investment" excluding foreign goods and investment from its domestic market until Japanese firms have become sufficiently strong to defeat foreign competition anywhere in the world.

Through governmental support of economies of scale and movement down the learning curve, it is alleged, Japan has been able to reduce its production costs and increase its international competitiveness. As Edward Lincoln pointed out in *Japan's Unequal Trade* (1990), the Japanese consider their distinctive trade pattern to be perfectly natural due to the noncompetitive nature of foreign products.[9] He charges that the Japanese government has deliberately promoted policies to limit manufactured and many other imports into its economy. In effect, Japan's trade surplus and distinctive pattern of trade are due to official state policy rather than to factor endowment alone. Japan's broad array of economic policies has been planned to make Japan the world's foremost industrial and technological power.

Rejecting such charges, neoclassical economists note that the Heckscher-Ohlin trade theory tells us that Japan's trade pattern is a product of its factor endowments, e.g., a shortage of raw materials, a highly skilled labor force, and abundant capital. Other countries with similar endowments, such as Italy, exhibit a similar trading pattern, and it is thus quite natural for Japan to export automobiles, consumer electronics, and auto parts and to import only a small percentage of the manufactured goods that it consumes. The impact of such inter-industry trading is magnified by Japan's concentration of its exports on the huge American consumer market. Neoclassicists are, therefore, convinced that Japan's distinctive trade pattern can be explained by economic science and does not result from the economic policies of the Japanese government.[10]

THE AMERICAN-JAPANESE TRADE PROBLEM: AN ASSESSMENT

Both the revisionist and the neoclassical positions provide important insights into the American-Japanese trade conflict; in some ways, they are more complementary than contradictory due in part to different levels of analysis. As the neoclassical interpretation correctly asserts, America's low and Japan's high saving rates do indeed account for America's trade deficit and Japan's trade surplus. Similarly, the neoclassical position is correct that Japan's distinctive pattern of inter-industry trade can be explained largely in terms of Japan's comparative advantage, namely, the fact that Japan is capital-rich and resource-poor. However, one must go behind these explanations and inquire why Japan's has such an extraordinary high savings rate in the first place and has a comparative advantage in high tech products and imports so few non-Japanese manufactured goods. As the revisionists argue, these distinctive features of the Japanese economy have more to do with Japan's neomercantilistic economic policies than with economic theories.

Why does America have such a low and Japan such a high savings rate? The extraordinarily low American savings rate has been due to a number of economic policies and a national psychology that encourages consumption rather than savings; for example, as Martin Feldstein and other economists have pointed out, Social Security tends to assure Americans that they need not save for their retirement. Similarly, the extremely high savings rate in Japan is due to government policies that have deliberately suppressed domestic demand and, thereby, encouraged saving. In this section, I shall concentrate on Japan's pro-savings policies.

The Japanese government for decades has pursued policies to reduce consumption and promote savings. Restrictive macroeconomic policies have suppressed Japanese domestic consumption. Consumer spending in Japan has reached only 56 percent of GNP compared to 64 percent for Europe and 68 percent for the USA; this helps to explain the more than 30-year-long Japanese trade surplus.[11] An Organization for Economic Cooperation report in 1989, noted that in Japan "there is still a substantial discrepancy between the country's economic strength and the relatively poor quality of life."[12] The report pointed out that the Japanese government and corporations have suppressed the Japanese standard of living far below what it should be in relation to its accumulated wealth resulting in a large trade/payments surplus with the United States and nearly every one of its trading partners. In addition, strict capital controls and the postal savings system along with no adequate national system of social security have also encouraged a high savings rate; the principal purpose of policies supporting high savings and underconsumption has been to promote Japan's overall strategy of export-led economic growth and a rapid industrialization.

In summary, well-established economic theory supports the neoclassical argument that Japan's trade/payments surplus is not responsible for the America's trade/payments; the answer lies in Japan's high and America's low savings rates.[13] However, Japan's high savings rate is due principally to the economic policies of the Japanese government that support a mercantile trade policy. On political grounds, this mercantilism has become increasingly unsustainable. At the very least, Japanese "free riding" on the international trading system does not make Japan a promising partner in the leadership of the world economy.

The neoclassical argument that Japan as a capital rich and resource poor nation has a comparative advantage in manufacturing is most certainly correct. However, the revisionist argument that the Japanese state has promoted manufacturing and has discriminated against non-Japanese imports through its industrial and protectionist policies are well-grounded. As the revisionists have argued, underlying the national emphasis on industrial production has been the strong and undoubtedly justified Japanese belief that Japan's comparative advantage is and must continue to be in the manufacture of quality goods in high volume at competitive prices. Behind this commitment is the fact that an increase in productivity in manufacturing is much more easily attained than in services. For this reason, the Japanese have been extremely reluctant to become a service economy as has been rapidly taking place in the United States and Western Europe. In addition, a strategy of export-led growth and a trade surplus enable Japanese manufacturing firms to reach a high volume of output and, thus, to achieve economies of scale that increase their competitiveness in high tech industries. If Japanese business is to have a high rate of productivity and economic growth, according to this analysis, then it must maintain a strong manufacturing base.

As neoclassicists correctly observe, Japan has the lowest level of formal tariff protection in manufacturing. However, even as formal Japanese trade barriers have been lowered or removed, excessive bureaucratic regulations, xenophobic consumer attitudes, and private business practices have continued to limit foreign goods entering the Japanese market. The most important obstacle to foreign-made imports has been the *keiretsu* system of business organization. This system of cooperative business arrangements has been nourished by a lax antitrust and other supportive policies of the Japanese state. The interlocking web of relationships composed of a *keiretsu*'s powerful firms and their "captive" supplier and distribution networks has constituted an almost unbreachable wall against foreign penetration of the Japanese economy.

In summary, while it is true that Japan's comparative advantage lies in manufacturing, this comparative, or rather competitive, advantage has been strongly influenced by the quite visible hand of the Japanese state rather than by the invisible hand of the market alone. The American government, on the other hand, has done very little to increase the U.S. savings rate and, thus, to decrease the trade deficit. Instead, one American Administration after another has pressured Japan to pursue a more expansionary economic policy and to shift from an export-led to a domestic-led growth strategy. In Japan itself, following collapse of the "bubble economy" in the early 1990s and the recession that followed, more and more Japanese, and even many large firms, have advocated a more open, deregulated, and expansive economy. The lengthy recession that began in 1991 has increased pressures to reform and stimulate the Japanese economy. The overall low level of Japanese productivity has also caused concern; a much higher rate must be achieved if Japan is to meet the challenges ahead, including the rapid aging of its population. Solution of the very serious aging problem will require significant reform of the Japanese economy and a more expansionary economic policy. However, as these policy changes are taking place very slowly, they may not prevent another America-Japanese trade dispute.

A RESURGENCE OF THE AMERICAN-JAPANESE ECONOMIC CONFLICT?

The United States abandoned its attack on Japanese trade and economic policies in the early 1990s. Although the United States continued to have a large albeit declining trade deficit with Japan, the strengthening of the American economy and the negative impact of the trade conflict on American-Japanese security ties convinced the Administration that it should cease "Japan bashing." However, the East Asian financial crisis and its consequences have raised once again the strong possibility of a powerful negative reaction by the United States not only to Japan but also to China and other Asian countries. The increasing trade/payments imbalance between the United States and East Asia including Japan is expected to rise dramatically. Such an imbalance is politically unsustainable. If recent history is any guide these imbalances will produce a powerful political reaction in the United States.

The trade/payments surplus or deficit of a country, as already noted, is due to a nation's spending patterns and in particular to the difference between national savings and investment. For nearly two decades, the United States has been spending much more than its national income and Japan has been spending much less. Over the course of the 1990s, this situation significantly worsened as the savings behavior of both the United States and that of Japan and the other East Asian economies changed dramatically. Throughout the decade, the overall American savings rate dropped considerably and the personal rate even became negative. The diversion of national savings into consumption helped fuel the extraordinary growth of the American economy throughout this period. At the same time, the long recession in Japan and, since late 1997, the recession in much of East Asia, has increased in relative terms the saving rates of these usually high saving economies. This imbalance in rates of national savings across the Pacific is primarily responsible for America's huge trade/payments deficit and the huge trade/payments surplus of Japan and East Asia.

It should be emphasized that the United States, given its extraordinarily low savings and high consumption rates, will inevitably have a huge trade/payments deficit regardless of what the Japanese and the East Asians do. The United States in the late 1990s, for example, had a large trade deficit with West Europe about which few Americans complained. Among the possible reasons for the contrasting negative American reaction to East Asia surplus are the immense size of their trade imbalance with the United States, the alleged effects of their closed economies on the trade balance, and the composition of their exports. Even if Japan and these other countries were to open their economies, as the United States demands, it would not change the situation unless they also decreased their rates of savings. Thus, even though the American trade deficit is not the fault of Japan and other Asian countries, these considerations do make these countries highly vulnerable to attack by American protectionists.

In addition to having high savings rates, the Pacific Asian economies are very competitive and have long targeted the American economy. Due to their depressed currencies, their exports will also displace some goods from other exporters that otherwise would have been imported into the United States. The overall result is a huge trade/payments imbalance. American concerns over the this imbalance are reinforced by the false belief that the trade imbalance is due to the closed nature of these economies. The Clinton Administration proclaimed over and over again the doctrine of "fair trade" and warned that these nations must either liberalize their economies and reduce their exports to the United States or else face increased trade barriers. In addition, the pattern of East Asian imports intensifies the negative political response in the United States. As I pointed out earlier, the industrial policies of the countries concentrated on a few key sectors such as steel, electronics, and automobiles. As the in the case of the increasing demands for protection against rising steel imports into the United States, these sectors are politically very sensitive ones with important domestic support. In effect, the United States in becoming the "importer of last resort" for the East Asian economies can be said to be performing a vital role in their economic recovery. However, this role will inevitably lead to increased protectionist sentiments in the United States. In the event of a prolonged American recession, these calls for protectionism against "unfair" Asian producers could become irresistible.

CONCLUSION

The resolution of the American-Japanese trade/payments requires fundamental changes in both economies. As I have shown, both sides must bear part of the responsibility. Although America's consumer-led economic growth has benefited the entire world, this policy is both politically and economically enviable over the long-term; there is a limit to how long Americans can borrow the savings of others to finance their high level of consumption. Americans must shift away from consumption toward saving; it would also be helpful (but highly unlikely) that Americans come to appreciate the extent to which they themselves are responsible for the huge American trade/payments deficit. The task facing Japan may be even more daunting. Japan must make a fundamental shift in the purpose of economic activities from an export-led to a domestic-led economic growth strategy. This would mean that Japan would consume more and save less. The achievement of this goal will require a more open and deregulated economy as well as more expansive macroeconomic policies. Unless fundamental changes in both economies are forthcoming, Japan and the United States will continue to be very uneasy trading partners.

ENDNOTES

1. Samuel P. Huntington, "America's Changing Strategic Interests." *Survival* 33, no. 1 (January/February 1991): 3–17.

2. Karl Polanyi, *The Great Transformation: The Political and Economic Origins of Our Time* (Boston: Beacon Hill Press, 1957).

3. Jeffrey Garten, A *Cold Peace: America, Japan, Germany and the Struggle for Supremacy* (New York: Times Books, 1992).

4. Chalmers Johnson, *MITI and the Japanese Miracle: The Growth of Industrial Policy 1925–1975* (Stanford: Stanford University Press, 1982).

5. W. Carl Kester, *Japanese Takeovers: The Global Contest for Corporate Control* (Boston: Harvard Business School), 1991.

6. According to the revisionist position, Japan plays by different rules of economic behavior than those associated with Western economic science.

7. Intra-industry trade entails the exporting and importing of goods in the same economic sectors such as the exportation of one type of consumer electronics and the importation of another type of consumer electronics. Inter-industry trade, on the other hand, entails the exporting and importing of goods in different economic sectors such as the exporting of manufactured goods and the importing of raw materials.

8. Laura Tyson in Robert Z. Lawrence and Charles L. Schultze, *An American Trade Policy: Options for the 1990s* (Washington: The Brookings Institution, 1990). Tyson held high positions in the Clinton Administration and was a principal author of the Administration's "result-oriented" trade strategy toward Japan.

9. Edward J. Lincoln, *Japan's Unequal Trade* (Washington, DC: The Brookings Institution, 1990).

10. Gary A. Saxonhouse, "Differerentiated Products, Economies of Scale, and Access to the Japanese Market," in Robert C. Feenstra, ed., *Trade Polices for International Competitiveness* (Chicago: University of Chicago Press, 1989).

11. Kenneth S. Courtis, *The Nikkei Weekly*, May 17, 1993, p. 6.

12. Reported in *The New York Times*, December 27, 1989, p. D2.

13. An excellent discussion of these matters is Gary Burtless, et al., *Globaphobia: Confronting Fears About Open Trade* (Washington, DC: The Brookings Institution, 1998, pp. 103–9).

Chapter 10

ECONOMIC INTERDEPENDENCE AND THE FUTURE OF U.S.-CHINESE RELATIONS

Dale Copeland

As the states of East Asia become increasingly integrated into the world economy, the question of whether economic interdependence is a force for peace or a force for war takes on renewed significance. This chapter focuses on how such interdependence will likely affect the state that seems most destined to achieve superpower status: China. Scholars, policy analysts, and government officials are currently locked in a heated debate over whether the United States should "engage" or "contain" China. Those in favor of engagement argue, among other things, that drawing China into the global economy will encourage it to be peaceful.[1] This argument is founded on the liberal thesis that trade fosters peaceful relations by giving states an economic incentive to avoid war: the benefits received from trade make continued peace more advantageous than war.[2] Those in favor of containment, aside from fearing China's relative growth through trade, would fall back on another realist principle: that interdependence only increases the likelihood of war as dependent states struggle to ensure continued access to vital goods.[3]

This essay shows that both theoretical perspectives have a part of the puzzle right. Yet by not specifying the conditions under which their causal logic should apply, they are incomplete as guides to understanding foreign policymaking in the East Asian region. Elsewhere, I have provided an argument to bridge the liberal and realist views. By introducing a second variable in addition to dependence—namely, a state's expectations for future trade—we can determine when interdependence will drive actors either to peace or to conflict. If trade expectations are positive, dependent states will expect to realize the positive benefits of trade into the future, and thus be more inclined toward peace. If, however, such states are pessimistic about future trade, fearing a cutoff of vital goods or the continuation of current restrictions, the negative expected value for trade will push them toward aggression. This argument not only provides a better logical foundation for thinking about interdependence and conflict, but also helps clear up the empirical anomalies both liberalism and realism face in dealing with two important cases: the outbreak of major war in Europe in 1914 and again in 1939.[4]

The present article builds on the trade expectations argument in three ways. In the first section, I extend its theoretical logic through an examination of how the expected values of peaceful trade versus war shift with changes in an important boundary condition: relative power. The analysis thus considers how interdependence, trade expectations, and relative power interact to shape a state's rational foreign policy. In dealing with China, for example, the United States faces a clear problem. Continued engagement will help China grow in relative economic power. This increased power, if translated into military power, reduces the costs of Chinese expansion. Yet even more significantly, China's growing dependence also means severe costs to its economy should trade be cut off. Thus, while interdependence will provide an incentive for peace when China's trade expectations are optimistic, should these expectations become pessimistic due to foreign trade restrictions, China's dependence could drive it into conflict and war.

In the second section, to illustrate the dilemma, I briefly outline the history of U.S.-Japanese relations from 1920 to December 1941. Because of the potential parallels to future U.S.-China relations, the lessons from the U.S.-Japan case are worth noting. Japan in the 1920s, like China today, was eager to trade extensively with America and the outside world. In the 1930s, however, as the world became increasingly protectionist, Japan shifted to the building of an East Asian "Co-prosperity Sphere" to minimize the impact of protectionism on its economy. Washington eventually retaliated by imposing harsh sanctions. As Japanese trade expectations fell even further, given Japan's high dependence its leaders felt they had no option other than war.

Although there are some obvious differences between the 1930s and today's situation—in particular, the presence of nuclear weapons—the risks of a repeat of this scenario over the next two decades, with China now playing the lead role, cannot be easily dismissed. China has already extended its military influence into the South China Sea to control the area's potential oil and gas reserves and its trade routes. In face of U.S. and western trade restrictions, a co-prosperity sphere in Southeast Asia—based on hegemonic influence if not formal imperial control—would seem not only attractive to Chinese leaders, but also critical to national security. Needless to say, such expansionism would greatly increase the likelihood of a direct clash of U.S. and Chinese forces, possibly leading to all-out war.

The final section of this paper addresses the ways to avoid such a tragic repeat of history. I make an argument for what I call "realist(ic) engagement."[5] Maintaining American superiority in overall power and in power projection capability is essential to reducing Chinese incentives for expansion. Equally critical, however, is the building and sustaining of positive Chinese trade expectations both now and into the future. Adopting CoCom-type restrictions as part of an overall containment policy would only make a cold war inevitable by undermining Chinese confidence in future trade.

This means that U.S. leaders now and into the future must maintain a consistent economic policy emphasizing America's strong commitment to extensive trade with China. This does not mean, as I discuss, that American leaders should never seek to use trade as a tool to encourage good behavior. Rather, they should avoid sanctioning techniques that seem arbitrary, inflexible, or overly driven by parochial domestic interests. Washington must nurture the expectation in Beijing that while the United States seeks free and open trade, this trade will only be forthcoming if China remains committed to maintaining the territorial status quo. In this way, the U.S. military presence and China's economic dependence, working in tandem, will serve to keep the peace in East Asia.

ECONOMIC INTERDEPENDENCE, RELATIVE POWER, AND THE PROBABILITY OF WAR

This section analyzes the relationship between changes in relative power and changes in the expected values of both aggression and peaceful trade. The section has three components. To establish a basis for grappling with the concept of dependence, the argument begins by bringing together in one framework the liberal emphasis on the benefits of trade with the realist sense of the potential costs of severed trade. I then show how a dependent state's expectations of future trade, when taken as an exogenous variable, will determine whether its expected value of trade is positive, inclining it toward peace, or negative, inclining it toward aggressive policies. Finally, I consider relative power as a parameter shaping both the expected values of peace and war.

The deductive logic of the argument, as with liberalism and realism, centers on an individual state's efforts to manage its own situation of dependence.[6] For sake of simplicity, I focus on a two-actor scenario of asymmetrical dependence, where state A needs trade with state B far more than B needs trade with A. The assumption of asymmetry means that changes in the trading environment are much more likely to affect A's decision for peace or war than B's. This allows us to focus on state A as the decisionmaking unit in the model: its responses to changes in the specified variables and parameters will drive the probability of war in the system (i.e., the system of two states).[7]

If state A moves away from the initial position of autarchy to begin trading, and trade is free and open, it will expect to receive the benefits of trade stressed by liberals. These benefits can be conceptualized as the incremental increase in A's total welfare due to trade, as measured, say, by growth in the GNP.[8] Logically, if A's economy is extremely large in comparison to B's, the absolute benefits of trade are likely to be quite small, all other things being equal: even if B is doing almost all its trade just with A, and trading very heavily, B's small size puts a limit on the benefits of that trade for A. Accordingly, as A and B begin to approach each other in relative size, we should expect that the benefits of trade that A receives will rise (again, all other things being equal),[9] and this is confirmed by econometric studies.[10]

When a state trades, it specializes in and exports goods where it enjoys a comparative advantage, while foregoing the production of other goods, which it then imports. The very process of specialization, however, entails potentially large "costs of adjustment" should trade be subsequently cut off. This is especially so if the state becomes dependent on foreign oil and certain raw materials. With the economy's capital infrastructure (machines, factories, transportation systems, etc.) geared to function only with such vital goods, a severing of trade would impose huge costs as the economy struggles to cope with the new no-trade situation. In short, the severing of trade, as realists would argue, would put the state in a situation which was far worse than if it had never specialized in the first place. For a similar reason to the above, when state B is extremely small, state A will likely not suffer large costs of adjustment from a cut off of trade, given the upper limit on A's dependence on B. These costs should rise, however, as A and B move closer together in relative economic power.

This analysis provides a clearer sense of state A's true level of "dependence" on B. On a bilateral basis, that level is represented by the sum of the benefits that state A would receive from free and open trade with B (versus autarchy), and the costs to A of being cut off from that trade after having specialized (versus autarchy). If state A started with an economy of 100 units of GNP before any trade with B (the autarchic position), and open trade with B would mean economic expansion to a level of 110 units of GNP on an ongoing basis, then the "benefits of trade" could be considered as 10 units. If the specialization that trade entails, however, would mean the economy would fall to 85 units should B sever trade ties, then the "costs of severed trade" would be 15 units versus autarchy. State A's total dependence would thus be the benefits of trade plus the costs of severed trade after specialization, or 25 units.

This dependence level, as noted, will be affected by the relative size of the two economies. The more equal the two states are in GNP, the greater the potential benefits of open trade for state A, but also the greater the likely costs of being cut off after specialization. When A is extremely large relative to B, however, A's dependence should be low both in terms of potential benefits and costs of severed trade.[11] (Other parameters will of course affect the level of dependence independent of relative power, including the overall compatibility of the two economies for trade, A's need for vital goods such as oil and raw materials, and the availability of alternative suppliers and markets.[12])

In deciding between an aggressive or peaceful foreign policy, however, state A can not refer simply to its dependence level. Rather, it must determine the overall expected value of trade and therefore the value of continued peace into the foreseeable future. The benefits of trade and the costs of no trade on their own say nothing about this expected value. Dynamic expectations of future trade must be brought in. In determining the expected value of trade, state A will try to arrive at an estimate of how likely state B is to trade with it over the foreseeable future. If it has positive expectations that the other will maintain free and open trade over the long term, then the expected value of trade will be close to the value of the benefits of trade. On the other hand, if state A, after having specialized, comes to expect that state B will sever all trade with A, or continue present restrictions on trade with A, then state A's expected value of trade may be highly negative, that is, close to the value of the costs of severed trade. In essence, the expected value of trade may be anywhere between the two extremes, depending on the estimate of the expected probability of securing open trade, or of being cut off.

This leads to the first important hypothesis. For any given expected value of war, we can predict that the lower the expectations of future trade, the lower the expected value of trade, and therefore the more likely it is that war will be accepted as the rational option.

In making the final decision between aggression and peace, however, state A will have to compare the expected value of trade to the expected value of conflict and war with the other state. The expected value of war, as a realist would emphasize, cannot be ascertained without considering the relative power balance. Intuitively, we can expect that as one state moves from a position of relative inferiority in economic and military power to relative superiority, the expected value of war should move from being negative to being perhaps positive, or even highly positive. Thus, if Saddam Hussein were to invade both Iran and Kuwait again, and to be unopposed by third parties, we might expect that war would "pay" only in the latter case.

The logic behind this intuition can be unpacked more explicitly. We should expect three factors in particular, each influenced by relative power, to shape the expected value of war: the potential gains from defeating an opponent, the costs of war, and the probability of victory. Clearly, as state A moves from parity to great preponderance over state B, the benefits of victory should diminish, since the defeat of a smaller opponent provides a smaller prize. At the same time, as A grows in relative size, the likelihood of victory should increase while the costs of war should decrease.[13]

Bringing these three factors together would suggest that the expected value of war is likely to be greatest for some moderately high level of relative power for state A.[14] Germany's *ex ante* expected value for war in 1938, for example, was undoubtedly greater against a state like Czechoslovakia than against a state like Luxembourg; while the costs of war could have been foreseen to be low and the probability of victory high for war against Luxembourg, this tiny nation simply did not constitute much of a prize (i.e., the benefits of victory were very low).[15] On the other hand, war between more equal great powers is certainly likely to have a much lower, and usually negative, expected value. The Spartan leadership took Sparta into war against Athens in 431 B.C., for example, under no illusions that war would be a profitable venture.[16] Expressed in the above terms, while the Athenian economy presented a large prize should victory be attained, war with a near-equal adversary could be expected, *ex ante*, to be very costly, with a low likelihood of victory.

This discussion suggests that great powers, when they are relatively equal, will tend to attach a low or negative expected value to the option of war. In this context, the expectations of future trade will have a determinant effect on the likelihood of war. If state A has positive expectations for future trade with B, and A and B are roughly equal in relative power, then state A will estimate a high and positive expected value to continued peaceful trade, compare this to the low or negative expected value for war, and choose peace as the rational strategy. The higher A's dependence and the higher the expectations for future trade, the higher the expected value for peaceful trade, and therefore the more likely A is to avoid war. But if state A has negative expectations for future trade with B, then the expected value of trade will be low or negative. If the expected value for trade is lower than the expected value for aggression, war becomes the rational choice, and this is so even when the expected value of aggression is itself negative: war becomes the lesser of two evils.

Two additional points need to be mentioned. First, the above discussion has focused for simplicity on the situation of two great powers, states A and B. Yet in considering A's broader incentives for aggression, the value of A attacking a small third party, state C, should be factored in. If war against C pays, A's overall expected value for aggression would have to incorporate the probability that B will fight an all-out war to defend C. That is, in addition to relative power, we must keep in mind the issue of A's perception of B's resolve (the credibility of B's extended deterrence).[17] The more A doubts that B will defend C, the higher the expected value of the aggression option. This has relevance in considering China's strategy versus Southeast Asian states: the lower Beijing's estimate of U.S. willingness to defend these states against Chinese power projection, the more conflict makes sense.

Second, the analysis has been built on the assumption that war would be largely a conventional affair. When nuclear weapons are introduced, it is clearly more difficult to make war "pay" in any meaningful sense. In the East Asian context, for example, current U.S. nuclear preponderance undoubtedly has a restraining effect on Chinese behavior, while the lack of such weapons in the 1930s gave Japan greater confidence in its expansionist strategy. Yet it is worth remembering that war between China and the United States could still occur through two mechanisms: Beijing's doubt that Washington would actually use nuclear weapons in a dispute over third parties, such as in Southeast Asia; and the willingness of both sides to run the risk of an inadvertent slide into nuclear war to achieve their respective ends (as occurred in the Cuban missile crisis). Hence while nuclear weapons may qualify the conclusions of this paper's argument, the basic logic for how trade expectations and relative power interact to shape the probability of war still stands.[18]

JAPAN AND THE START OF MAJOR WAR IN THE FAR EAST

The period of U.S.-Japanese relations from 1920 to 1941 illustrates the significance of economic dependence and trade expectations when considered simultaneously. In the 1920s, in a parallel to China's current policy, Japan practiced "Shidehara diplomacy," focusing on peaceful trade designed to help Japan modernize and grow as a great power. The key puzzle therefore is to explain Japan's shift to imperial expansionism after 1930. The most common argument is that of unbridled militarism: the military gradually usurped power, highjacking the state for its own aims; in the process, civilian leaders who could have moderated policy were shunted aside.[19] This view faces two problems. First, the closer Japan came to actual war from 1938 to 1941, the greater was civilian intervention against military, particularly by the emperor.[20] Second, the military was not always the most in favor of war. The foreign ministry was often more hardline than the navy, while by 1940–41, almost all civilian leaders as well as the emperor accepted the necessity of major war. Through a series of "Liaison Conferences" coordinating military and civilian views, Japan moved by consensus toward total war, despite the recognized risks and costs.

Once Japan began modernizing after 1857, it had one major limitation: critical vital goods needed to build an industrial great power lay outside of national boundaries. While the colonial acquisitions of Korea and Taiwan helped reduce agricultural dependency from 1910 to 1940, they proved of little value as sources of raw materials.[21] For these goods, Japan was almost totally dependent on trade with U.S. and European powers: America for oil and iron ore; British Malaysia, French Indochina, and Dutch East Indies for rubber, oil, tin, tungsten, and other minerals.

In the 1920s, it made sense for Japan to act cautiously so as not to alienate these critical trading partners. But what differentiates this Shidehara diplomacy from later policies is not the ends of statecraft—since 1857, security was seen to require economic growth, territorial expansion, and a strong military[22]—but rather the means, that is, the degree of emphasis on trade (promoting growth but requiring a more peaceful diplomacy) versus military expansion (in which diplomatic costs would be paid). The shift to a more aggressive policy after 1929 is directly connected to the impact of the Great Depression and the subsequent trade restrictions by other great powers.[23] U.S. and European protectionist policies internally undermined the argument that economic growth through trade was the best means to Japanese security: pessimistic expectations for future trade lowered the expected value of trade, making military options more attractive. In this environment, the value of such areas as Manchuria, occupied in 1931, was manifest. As one government publication put it, the "shortage of the prime necessities of life in Japan, and the instability of their supply" made Manchuria essential to national security. Even if others wanted to supply Japan, their own expanding needs meant that Japan was reasonable to

> fear as to whether advanced industrial countries will long continue to supply the material to our industries which compete with their own . . . if the economic policies of advanced industrial countries should be directed toward the prohibition or restriction of the export of raw materials to this country, the blow dealt to us would be very heavy.[24]

If high dependence and a lower probability of continued trade promote aggression, why did Japan not fight America and Britain at this time? One basic reason stands out: while expectations of future trade were lower by the early 1930s, they were not yet so pessimistic as to make major war against other great powers more attractive than peace. The truly precipitous decline in expectations would only come with American policies after 1939.

Still, the lower expected value for trade meant the opportunity cost of expansion against *smaller* powers after 1930 was reduced; Japan now had less to lose should the other great powers react to this expansion. Moreover, Japan had to worry about the ominous growth of the Soviet Union and the United States. Since these powers possessed huge land masses and resource bases, they would not be as relatively hurt by the closed trading environment, leading to Japan's decline in relative power. Hence, like the German dilemma before both World Wars,[25] long-term security would be hard to maintain unless Japan created a large economic realm to match the other great powers. After 1932, therefore, Japanese leaders sought to dominate East and Southeast Asia—by peaceful means if possible, and by force if necessary—to secure the control over the raw materials and markets needed for national survival.

From 1934 to 1937, civilian and military advocates of "total war," if necessary for Japanese security, rose in influence.[26] Although the Navy showed constant concern about provoking America, there was agreement that Japan needed to increase its economic dominance in Asia. The question by early 1936 was which direction to take. Navy commander Oikawa argued that Japan should expand north first, develop Manchuria, and then turn south. His argument showed the impact of diminishing trade expectations on Japanese policy:

> No problem would arise if we [could proceed] . . . peacefully in all directions, but when the powers are raising high tariff barriers as they are today and are preventing artificially the peaceful advance of other countries, we must of necessity be prepared and determined to use force in some areas and eliminate the barriers.[27]

In April 1936, with Manchuria unable to compensate for Japan's high dependence on oil, Navy Minister Nagano argued that the only solution was expansion southward, where oil was plenty (i.e., the Dutch East Indies).[28]

By 1936, plans for the creation of a Japanese hegemonic sphere were put in place, driven by economic necessity.[29] Should war become necessary—that is, should economic restrictions on Japan increase any further—the military had to be ready to act. In August 1936, cabinet and military consensus was codified in a document entitled "Fundamentals of Our National Policy," which approved an army and navy buildup to secure Japan's position in East Asia "and at the same time advance and develop in the Southern area."[30] Importantly, however, expansion southward was to be "by gradual peaceful means" if possible, to avoid alienating the West.[31]

Trade expectations declined further after 1937. In June 1938, Washington initiated the first in a series of trade sanctions: a "moral embargo" on military equipment.[32] The Japanese government reacted quickly. In November, it proclaimed that Japan must become more self-sufficient through "economic national defense."[33] In April 1939, the navy circulated its "Policy for the South," which emphasized "securing materials necessary to promote productive capacity."[34] Oil was now the key concern; eighty percent of Japan's oil still came from the U.S., and the synthetic oil program had been a dismal failure.[35] In 1939, Japanese trade expectations plummeted further after the U.S. announcement in July that the 1911 trade treaty with Japan would not be renewed. By that summer, Japanese plans for a mission to the Dutch East Indies (DEI) to secure additional oil supplies were drawn up.[36]

The outbreak of war in Europe greatly altered the East Asian situation, providing a short-term opportunity to seize territory to overcome dependence: British and French forces were drawn home, while the U.S. fleet was divided between Atlantic and Pacific theaters. The Japanese also recognized that the war would further exacerbate the raw materials situation, with powers like the United States curtailing exports to conserve supplies for their own military buildups.[37] Pessimism increased even more when, in January 1940, Washington allowed the 1911 trade treaty to expire. That month, the Japanese proposed to the Dutch that the DEI be incorporated into Japan's "Coprosperity Sphere." The Dutch not only refused, but actually increased restrictions on exports to Japan. With the DEI the only other major source of oil, the situation was becoming critical.[38]

In July 1940, the economic situation pushed the army, as evidenced by its report "Main Principles for Coping with the Changing World Situation," into abandoning its goal of moving north. Indeed, the army, supported by civilian leaders, was actually pressing the reluctant navy into striking south. The navy again warned that this might lead to war with the United States, and was able to secure agreement that war should be avoided if at all possible. Still, Japan would take "positive steps" to incorporate the colonies of Southeast Asia into its realm.[39] Trade expectations continued their downward spiral. In July, a U.S. embargo on exports of scrap iron and aviation fuel to Japan was announced. Japan's navy, by August, now sought an immediate move against French Indochina to provide rice, rubber, and iron.[40] This was done with full awareness of the consequences: additional embargoes on scrap iron and oil, should they be forthcoming, would be "a matter of life and death for the empire;" if imposed, Japan would need "will inevitably have to make a firm decision to invade the Dutch East Indies in order to acquire its oil fields."[41]

A vicious dilemma was developing: if Japan did nothing, difficulties in securing supplies would exacerbate its declining position; if, however, Japan expanded in Southeast Asia by force, or even by political means, America would tighten its embargo and simply accelerate the decline. Moreover, the diminishing expectations for trade that had been pushing Japanese leaders to build regional military superiority—enough to acquire raw materials by force should trade relations not improve—was leading to further economic restrictions by the Americans, British, and Dutch, which only made trade expectations more pessimistic. In short, by late 1940 and early 1941, Japan had reached the worst of all scenarios, namely high dependence on others for vital goods but low expectations for future trade. With temporary military superiority, Japanese leaders felt they had to attack soon, before economic decline had progressed too far.

At the September 19, 1940 Imperial Conference, Prime Minister Konoye summarized his view of the future: "We can anticipate that trade relations with Britain and the United States will deteriorate even more. If worst comes to worst, it may be impossible to obtain any imported goods."[42] By April 1941, with peaceful means of ensuring supply still preferred, the army and the navy emphasized that force would have to be used "if the empire's self-existence is threatened by embargoes" imposed by America, Britain, and others.[43] Such an embargo came at the end of July 1941, when the Americans froze all Japanese assets and ended shipments of oil. Earlier that month, leaders had argued in Liaison Conferences that Japan should attempt to increase trade with America if at all possible.[44] Now the possibility of a complete cutoff in trade loomed large. In late July and then again in early September, Navy Chief of Staff Nagano argued that Japan was losing strength versus its main adversaries, particularly the United States, and therefore the time to go to war was now.[45]

This view was carried into the critical Imperial Conference of September 6, 1941, when a consensus civilian-military plan was presented to Hirohito. Regarding upcoming U.S.-Japan negotiations, the plan sought U.S. and British agreement to restore commercial relations with Japan "and [to] supply those goods from their territories in the South West Pacific that our empire urgently needs to sustain herself."[46] Prime Minister Konoye opened the conference, stating that

> If we allow [the present] situation to continue, it is inevitable that our empire will gradually lose the ability to maintain its national power. . . . If the diplomatic measures should fail to bring about a favorable result within a certain period, I believe we cannot help but take the ultimate step in order to defend ourselves.[47]

Suzuki, the Director of the Planning Board, reinforced this, noting that Japan's primary problem was that "we depend on foreign sources to supply many of our vital materials."[48] In particular, the stockpile of oil would reach critical levels within a year; hence, "it is vitally important for the survival of our Empire that we make up our minds to establish and stabilize a firm economic base."[49]

In the conference, the emperor secured the cabinet's assurance that all efforts to solve the crisis through diplomatic means would be attempted. The negotiations with Washington that followed, however, did not go well, the key sticking point being China. In the reexamination of the September decisions at Liaison Conferences in late October, the main issue remained "the prospects for the acquisition of vital materials," which would dry up by the end of 1942.[50] In the historic seventeen-hour November 1 conference, despite the army's demand for immediate war, a collective decision was made to extend negotiations until midnight November 30; "if diplomacy was successful by then, war would be called off."[51] There were no illusions as to what war might entail. As army Vice Chief of Staff Tsukada indicated:

> In general, the prospects if we go to war are not bright. We all wonder if there isn't some way to proceed peacefully. . . . On the other hand, it is not possible to maintain the status quo. Hence, one unavoidably reaches the conclusion that we must go to war.[52]

At the November 5 Imperial conference, Suzuki gave another long extended analysis of the raw materials situation. Regarding expectations of future trade, "the probability that we will experience increased difficulties in obtaining materials . . . is high." In fact, Japan might be drawn into a war, "even though we wish to avoid it," to secure their supply.[53]

At the final Imperial Conference on December 1, Foreign Minister Togo explained that should Japan accept the latest U.S. proposals, which included the demand that Japan withdraw all its forces from China and French Indochina, "our very survival would inevitably be threatened."[54] The president of the Privy Council, Hara, speaking for the emperor, now resigned himself to the tragic reality: "[It] is clear that the existence of our country is being threatened, that the great achievements of the Emperor Meiji would all come to nought [if the demands were accepted], and that there is nothing else we can do."[55] With the nod of the Emperor's head, approval was granted for war. The war in the Pacific would begin six days later.

The above analysis demonstrates the fundamental importance of trade expectations. Japanese leaders had made the decision before World War I to depend on foreign sources of oil and raw materials, given Japan's limited natural resources. In the 1920s, this strategy was working effectively, as other great powers were still willing to trade extensively. But after 1930, with the beginning of highly protectionist British and American policies, Japan saw its national survival tied to expansion against its Asian neighbors—peacefully if possible, by military means if necessary. Although London and Washington had created their own economic realms using less-than-peaceful means, they would not tolerate Japan's use of similar means. By late November 1941, Japanese leaders saw war, despite its high costs and risks, as preferable to the certain destruction that would come if Japan met the new U.S. price for reinstated trade. War had become the tragic lesser of two evils.

TRADE EXPECTATIONS AND THE FUTURE OF U.S.-CHINESE RELATIONS

The previous section indicates that in practical politics, unlike the international relations field, we cannot conveniently separate the realms of international political economy and security. International trade is not simply a question of "low politics" having little to do with the core issues of national survival. Rather, as the Japan case suggests, under certain conditions economic factors push states into conflicts that threaten each nation's very existence.

When considering how America should deal with its most significant long-term concern—China—we must therefore recognize both the upside and the downside of increasing Chinese integration into the global economy. Liberal supporters of engagement are correct to say that interdependence can bind

China in a web of economic constraints. Chinese leaders clearly recognize that they need continued access to the world's markets and resources if they are to modernize their technological base and provide the wealth needed for future great-power status. Yet such an argument ignores the significant potential risks to increasing Chinese dependence. China's trade as a percentage of GNP has gone from 13 percent in 1980 to between 35 and 40 percent by the late 1990s.[56] As China continues to specialize to take advantage of its comparative advantage, any cutoffs of trade will have that much more of a devastating effect on its economy. This is especially so given China's growing need for raw materials and oil, as I discuss below. Moreover, as the paper's argument indicates, even if current trade is high, a dependent state's *anticipation* of cutoffs can drive it to aggression, as the expected value of the trade option falls in comparison to the expected value of conflict.

Proponents of straightforward engagement must also recognize another possible problem with their strategy: that of China's increasing relative power.[57] My argument does suggest that as China grows through trade, one would expect that states like the United States and Japan will become even more valuable trade partners; relatively equal states are more likely to enjoy high benefits of trade. But such states are also likely to face higher potential costs if trade is later severed. They thus have more reason to fear the vulnerability that goes with greater trade. Moreover, as China becomes stronger, the expected value of military expansion rises as the probability of victory increases and the costs of war fall. Vis-à-vis the United States, war would still be an unprofitable and foolhardy venture, to be sure. Yet compared to the smaller states in the region, China's growing economic strength, tied to military modernization, would give it the capability to project both power and influence.

Needless to say, Chinese leaders are well aware that military power projection, say against Southeast Asia, would pose certain costs and risks vis-à-vis its relations with United States and Japan. Yet like Japan in the 1930s, Chinese leaders would be more likely to see these costs and risks as tolerable should their expectations regarding the future trading environment turn pessimistic. As the expected value of continued peaceful trade fell, the creation of a Chinese co-prosperity sphere in east and southeast Asia would become an attractive option, even if only as the lesser of two evils. It is worth remembering that Japan was very reluctant to take on the United States in 1941. It did so only because military conflict, despite its recognized costs and risks, was seen as better than the continuation of the severe economic decline which was undermining Japan's long-term security. China could come to a similar conclusion within the next two decades, should it anticipate trade restrictions.

It is also worth remembering that Japan in 1941 had no desire to defeat and occupy the United States homeland. Rather, it sought to control Southeast Asia, and the oil-rich Dutch East Indies in particular, in order to compensate for U.S.

and British cutoffs. Yet given the United States' presence in the Philippines and U.S. expressions of resolve, Japanese leaders knew that an attack on the Dutch East Indies would lead to conflict with America. Thus it was deemed necessary to strike Pearl Harbor, in order to construct a defense perimeter which would keep the U.S. counterattack as far away as possible from Japan's core interests. Japanese leaders did expect the United States would fight for at least two years. But since the continental United States was not threatened, Tokyo hoped that the Americans would eventually see the costs of continued war as greater than the benefits. Washington would then concede the east Asian sphere to Japan, resting American security on control over North and South America.

Given the presence of nuclear weapons, Chinese leaders over the next few decades have even more reason to avoid a war with America against each others' homelands. Yet Beijing might calculate that the formation of a coprosperity sphere could be achieved without necessarily bringing on major war. As the Chinese navy grows and modernizes, power projection southward might seem to pose acceptable costs and risks should western trading practices turn hostile.[58] The potential for Chinese miscalculation, and a subsequent escalation to militarized conflict or war with the United States, cannot be easily dismissed.

China already feels freer to exercise what it sees to be its legitimate right to control the whole of the South China Sea. In 1995, soon after the U.S. withdrawal from Subik Bay and Clark air force base, the Chinese navy occupied Mischief Reef, a small atoll claimed by Manila and part of the highly contested Spratly Islands. This followed Beijing's use of military force in 1988 and 1991 to seize fifteen islands in the Spratly chain claimed by Vietnam.[59] China's interest in controlling the Spratlys stems in large part from the potential oil and gas reserves of the region.[60] Because of China's phenomenal economic growth and its huge population, in the early 1990s the country moved from energy self-sufficiency to energy dependence. For Beijing, the trends are very unnerving. As a result of stagnant production and phenomenal increases in demand, China is now importing approximately 30 percent of its required oil (after being a net exporter of oil for two decades). If present trends continue, by 2020 almost 60 percent of China's oil requirements will come from abroad.[61] The energy resources of the South China Sea, Malaysia, Brunei, and especially Indonesia will therefore become increasingly attractive as China's oil dependence grows.[62] This does not mean China will necessarily feel the need to occupy and formally control these countries, as did Japan in 1940–41. But Chinese leaders may come to believe that brandishing the military stick can coerce these nations into preferential trading relations with Beijing.[63] Since Washington would likely oppose such moves, the risk of escalation would be significant.

The above analysis in no way implies that military conflict with China is inevitable. If it were, then moving quickly to containment would be the best strategy. Such a policy would at least reduce Chinese economic power and thus its future military power. Yet the problem with containment in the current environment situation is clear: if conflict is not inevitable, containment now will undoubtedly make it much more likely. It will provoke China into a more hostile posture, fueling both its incentive to engage in an arms race and to expand territorially. Indeed, even at China's current level of dependence, a hard-line strategy by Washington, especially one involving a renewal of CoCom-type restrictions, would so reduce Beijing's trade expectations as to make a marked jump in Chinese power projection more likely.

This chapter shows that mere engagement—the increasing integration of China into the world's economy with American help—is not enough. The United States must pursue a policy of realist(ic) engagement. This policy is founded on three interrelated conclusions flowing from the trade expectations argument summarized above. First, the United States should avoid allowing China to achieve significant relative gains through trade, since such gains in power increase China's incentives to expand.[64] As I discuss, U.S. efforts to integrate China into global economic institutions such as the World Trade Organization (WTO) on American terms are critical to the achievement of this end. Second, Washington must act to ensure positive Chinese trade expectations over the long term. Only if Beijing remains confident that trade will continue at high levels into the foreseeable future will it have an incentive to remain peaceful. China's accession to WTO is a crucial means to this objective. Third, the subtle interrelationship between military power, deterrence, and trade expectations must continue to be recognized. Without this recognition, Washington might pursue a political or military policy that ends up damaging Chinese expectations in the economic realm. An inadvertent spiraling to conflict would then be more likely.

Realistic engagement integrates the insights of both the realist and liberal views of world politics. Realists correctly note that relative losses through trade are of concern to great powers, especially when the trade partner is an emerging great power. Washington permitted Japan to gain relative power through trade in the 1920s, and suddenly awoke to a modern industrialized power capable of attacking U.S. interests in the Pacific. China's trade strategy today is deliberately designed to transfer the latest technologies—both economic and military—into Chinese hands. Rules covering joint ventures and foreign investment ensure maximum Chinese access to the technological know-how of global multinationals.[65] The huge trade surplus with America—approximately $60 billion of the total U.S.-China trade of $100 billion[66]—supplies the foreign reserves needed to buy advanced military weapons from Russia, France, and Britain, and to acquire production technology from Japan, South Korea, Singapore, and other advanced states.[67]

The delicate dilemma is clear: Washington must try to minimize the relative losses to China without at the same time undermining Chinese trade expectations. Reestablishing CoCom-type restrictions of the kind used against the Soviet Union during the cold war would be counterproductive. Quite rightly, Beijing will see such a U.S. move as an effort to undermine the Chinese economy. Moreover, should Washington seek, as it did during the cold war, to bring Western Europe and Japan into a new CoCom regime, Beijing would feel not only cut off, but actually surrounded by an emerging anti-China coalition. Such negative trade expectations would drive China to form a counter-economic sphere, using the techniques mentioned above.[68]

The way out of this dilemma is to reduce China's relative gains without simultaneously doing harm to its absolute gains. Instead of cutting China off from the U.S. market, Washington needs to continue to encourage (and compel) Beijing to reduce its significant tariff and non-tariff barriers to U.S. imports. The November 1999 U.S.-China trade agreement, which set the stage for China's accession into the WTO, goes a long way toward achieving this end. The agreement forces China to lower tariffs on key agricultural products from 31 percent to 14 percent by 2004, to cut auto tariffs from 80–100 percent to 25 percent by 2006, and to reduce tariffs on most industrial products from an average of 24.6 percent to an average of 9.4 percent. The agreement also eliminates all tariffs on computers, telecommunications equipment, semiconductors, and other high-tech products.[69]

The significant compromises made by China in this agreement were puzzling to many observers, but are explicable within the framework laid out above. The Chinese leadership understood that without such concessions, it could not achieve two core goals: the ending of the annual review by Congress of China's most favored nation status; and the forging of Washington's support for China's entry into the WTO. The first goal was secured by the Senate's approval of Permanent Normal Trade Relations (PNTR) in September 2000, after the House of Representative's similar vote the previous May. Full implementation of PNTR was contingent upon China's accession to the WTO, which took place on December 11, 2001. With this membership, Chinese leaders have secured a critical benefit: the establishment of stable expectations of long-term future trade with the United States, its most important trading partner. As Yang Donghui, the secretary-general of the China Federation of Textile Industries explained, a fundamental advantage of WTO membership "especially in the long run . . . is that the country will be able to enjoy stable multilateral preferential trade policies in a rules-based market."[70] Thomas Duesterberg notes that China's entry in the WTO will make it much more difficult for the United States to exercise the economic leverage it now enjoys."[71] The Chinese government knows how much China would lose if MFN was ever denied. The fierce Congressional debates over the possible linking of MFN to the improvement in China's human rights record that took place in the early and mid-1990s were especially sobering to Beijing.[72] The 1999 U.S-China trade agreement and WTO membership have ended this uncertainty, thus giving Beijing the confidence that further economic integration could proceed without undue risk.[73]

China's efforts to secure membership in the WTO are part of a broader program of becoming more involved in the world's economic, political, and military institutions. China's membership in international intergovernmental organizations (IGOs) went from 21 in 1977 to 51 in 1996, and its membership in nongovernmental organizations skyrocketed from 71 to 1,079 during the same period.[74] Explaining the joining of the International Monetary Fund and the World Bank in the 1980s is not difficult: China needed massive infusions of capital to fuel its economic reforms.[75] But the Chinese leadership's relatively accommodating stance within international arms control regimes seems on the surface to be more puzzling, given Beijing's past intransigence and the potential restrictions on China's future military growth. The drive to be seen as a "responsible great power"—that is, the drive for international status for its own sake—may be one important motive.[76] Yet Chinese leaders have been historically among the most "realpolitik" of actors out there, rarely indulging in actions that do not further the external or internal security of the nation.[77] Something else, therefore, is likely dominating China's policy of institutionalized integration. Michael Swaine and Ashley Tellis label this policy China's "calculative strategy," namely, the strategy of defusing global suspicions of China's intentions in order to maintain the kind of secure economic relations that will sustain China's rapid growth rates. Good relations with the key players on the global stage will prevent any one of them from effectively forming a counterbalancing coalition that could halt China's development. In short, even if the United States wanted to re-create a CoCom-type regime to prevent trade with China, it would be difficult to get other key powers such as Japan and the European Union to go along with it.[78] Translated into the language of this essay's argument, Beijing's strategy is one of institutionalizing China's economic development in order to sustain and solidify the future trade environment. American efforts to encourage this institutionalization should be applauded, since by building positive expectations for long-term trade in Beijing, peace can indeed be fostered and reinforced.

The U.S. policy of driving a hard bargain on normalized trade relations and WTO accession helps secure two of the elements of realistic engagement—the mitigation of China's relative gains and the stabilizing of positive Chinese trade expectations. The third element of realistic engagement—the interrelationship between deterrence and economic relations—poses perhaps the most difficult problem for U.S. policymakers. We have seen that trade can work with military power to enhance one's deterrence efforts: trade founded on positive expectations increases the other's estimate of the value of peace; military power, credibly projected, reduces the other's value for war. But states face a security dilemma when they try to defend far-flung interests by building military power and projecting their willingness to use it. Other states may be inclined to see such moves as threats to security, requiring a reciprocal response. A spiral of mistrust could then likely arise, which could cause dependent states to wonder about the likelihood of continued trade.[79] The U.S.-Japan case of the 1930s shows how deterrence can backfire. Concern over Japan led Washington to take an increasingly harder line in East Asia—building up the Philippines, projecting the resolve to defend British and American interests, and increasing trade sanctions. These actions ended up destroying Japanese confidence in America's willingness to trade. War soon followed.

The United States must continue to pursue a contingent, but consistent, strategy of deterrence and trade with China. U.S. leaders must show China that while they are more than willing to trade openly, they will not tolerate unilateral changes in the status quo through military force. Maintaining naval forces in the region, but still at some distance from Chinese shores during peacetime, is thus wise. Forces in Guam, for example, can project power when necessary, without causing China to fear imminent attack. Yet if China contemplates an invasion of Taiwan or the coercion of Southeast Asian states, it must know that the United States has the resolve to respond. One of the tools of response, in addition to military action, must remain the possibility of economic sanctions. Indeed, the benefits of trade only create an economic incentive to remain at peace when the dependent state fears an end of those benefits should it aggress. If China were to feel that it could expand in Asia and not suffer any losses in current trade, interdependence would have no restraining effect on its behavior.

The difficult task for policymakers here is projecting the resolve to impose sanctions without at the same time undermining the other's expectations for future trade. This may seem to be an insolvable dilemma, but it is not. The method is to consistently signal that one's policy is contingent on the other's behavior: if it maintains the status quo, trade will be forthcoming; if it threatens the status quo, sanctions will be imposed until the status quo ante is restored.[80] The failure of U.S. policy in the late 1930s stemmed from a lack of consistency. Washington did not respond immediately to the Japanese invasion of China in 1937. Only in mid-1938 did it take some action, and then only in the form of a "moral embargo." When severe trade restrictions were imposed in 1940 and 1941, the Japanese did recognize them as efforts to compel a change in Japanese foreign policy. Yet in late November 1941, Roosevelt proved unwilling to renew trade ties unless Tokyo conceded to a new and larger set of U.S. demands, including the directive that Japan immediately exit China and Manchuria.[81] In today's terms, this would be equivalent to suddenly requiring China to leave Tibet if it hoped to secure continued trade.

Continuity, as opposed to fickleness, is essential to effective U.S. policy. Leaders in Beijing must have a clear idea of those interests that the United

States will defend through military force and economic sanctioning, and those it will not. Vacillating policy only creates uncertainty which reduces the other's ability to know the benefits and costs of alternative paths.[82] It is in this sense that domestic politics can play havoc with U.S. efforts to implement a policy of realistic engagement. Most obviously, the annual congressional review of China's Most Favored Nation status over the past twenty years has held U.S.-Chinese relations hostage to parochial politics and the ideological agendas of specific individuals.[83] The Senate's approval of Permanent Normal Trade Relations and China's accession to WTO have ended much of this uncertainty, thus moderating Chinese leaders' worry that ongoing trade will be disrupted by U.S. domestic struggles.

The future of American policy is clear: the United States must lay down a set of rules and principles, and stick to them. Beijing needs to know that the current trade deficit must be reduced significantly by the ending of unfair Chinese trade practices; rigorous monitoring and enforcement of the principles of the U.S-China trade agreement and of the agreements allowing China's entry into WTO are thus critical. Beijing must also know that America's way of life rests on the principle of free trade with those nations which do not seek to change the status quo through force. China will receive the benefits of trade as long as it is peaceful. But if it is not, it will not only face the might of the U.S. military, but also suffer trade sanctions commensurate with its violations of others' territorial sovereignty. Washington must also signal clearly that these sanctions will last only so long as the violations continue. That is, Washington must foster confidence in Beijing that sanctions do not reflect a permanent state of animosity toward China and the Chinese people, but only a dislike of Chinese behavior. Avoiding any linkage of trade policy to human rights and domestic issues within China is thus crucial; the negative impact of the Jackson-Vanik amendments on the prospects for U.S.-Soviet détente in the 1970s shows the problems with such a policy.[84] The United States as a society must also avoid any "China-bashing" parallel to the Japan-bashing which occurred in the 1980s. Such displays would appear directed toward the Chinese people as a race and civilization. They would create the impression that the United States is fundamentally hostile to China as a country, as is therefore unlikely to trade even if China's foreign policy improves.

One might argue that the policy of realistic engagement, at least in its more ideal-typical form, is ultimately too subtle to be practical over the long term. In particular, its requirement for a nuanced combination of reassuring gestures and firmness seems to place overly stringent demands on the American political system—a system which has exhibited some significant divisions on foreign policy in the past. Yet there is much evidence that the United States, despite continued internal debate, has been moving slowly but surely toward a more cohesive China policy paralleling the principles outlined above. President

Clinton's own attempt to link trade to human rights in his first year in office was abandoned by May 1994, as the White House recognized that it was only alienating Beijing with no concrete results.[85] By the end of his tenure, Clinton had used a combination of economic inducements (particularly the promise of PNTR and WTO accession) and potential counter-tariffs should Beijing not end its unfair trade practices to pry open the Chinese market to U.S. goods and services. The administration of George W. Bush has signaled America's continued commitment to PNTR and to China's entry into the WTO, and thus to the ending of the annual Congressional review of China's MFN status. Even in the midst of April 2001 discussions to bring home U.S. servicemen whose spy plane made an emergency landing in Hainan island after colliding with a Chinese jet, U.S. and Chinese trade negotiators worked out a compromise on allowable Chinese subsidies to farmers that cleared one of the last remaining hurdles to China's accession into the WTO. This signaled that expectations of future trade would not be held hostage to the domestic emotions evoked by a minor diplomatic incident.

Yet when the problem is more severe, such as in the spring of 1996 over the crisis in the Taiwan straits, Washington has demonstrated the ability to project its power and resolve without simultaneously undermining the trading environment. Chinese military exercises and missiles tests around Taiwan were met with the dispatch of two U.S. carrier battle groups into the area. Beijing learned from that episode and what followed that while the United States will oppose China's use of unilateral force against its neighbors, American leaders will be cooperative when China's leaders are cooperative.[86] Within two years of the Taiwan straits crisis, Chinese and American officials were laying the foundation for China's entry into the WTO. Moreover, over the past two decades the United States has effectively signaled that it will continue to defend the commercial sea lanes, to restrain Japan from militarizing, and to deter conflict on the Korean peninsula—activities approved of by Beijing, at least implicitly. But China understands that it must abide by the geopolitical status quo to continue to receive the significant economic benefits that this status quo offers the nation at this critical stage in its development.[87]

Finally, there appears to be broad domestic support for the U.S. Executive's efforts—both under the Clinton administration and now under the Bush administration—to compel China to moderate its trade surplus by reducing its tariff and non-tariff barriers to U.S. exports. Public displays of congressional anger at China's export-led strategy have been relatively muted, perhaps because China's exports to the United States do not threaten American jobs as much as Japanese high-tech exports appeared to do in the 1980s. Moreover, the lack of support for a return to cold-war era trade restrictions seems to reflect the widespread opinion that undermining China's faith in economic integration will only spark a destabilizing rivalry.[88] Given this majority view, Washington can continue to quietly pressure China to open its markets without the U.S. tactics seeming to reflect a groundswell of anti-China sentiment. Indeed, assertive American efforts to pry open Chinese markets, even when it requires coercive bargaining, may actually *improve* Chinese long-term expectations for future trade. Demands for more access, and promises of continued access to U.S. markets in return, send the signal that the United States remains committed to free and open trade as a general principle.[89]

In sum, realistic engagement is a feasible and necessary strategy for dealing with China over the next two decades. It allows the United States to maintain its relative technological and economic dominance, without denying China the opportunity to grow in absolute terms. The resultant optimism of Chinese leaders' regarding the future trading environment will thus enhance their perceptions of Chinese external security, even as it reassures them of their ability to satisfy the rising internal demands of the citizens.

CONCLUSION

This essay has sought to demonstrate the causal ties between relative power, economic interdependence, trade expectations, and interstate conflict. The argument presented allows one to consider the implications of various combinations of these factors for the likelihood of war between states such as the United States and China. The war between Japan and America from 1941 to 1945 is instructive. Inconsistent policy that shifts suddenly from "do-nothing" indifference to severe and inflexible trade sanctions can drive dependent states to war. This chapter has not explored the controversial question of whether Roosevelt deliberately drew the Japanese into war by imposing demands he knew Japan could not meet. But it is clear that his unwillingness to moderate U.S. sanctions in return for a moderation of Japanese policy made conflict in the Pacific inevitable.

U.S. leaders today seem to recognize that they cannot afford to repeat this mistake. They understand that they must specify clear and unequivocal principles that allow Chinese leaders to form positive expectations of future trade contingent on their good behavior. The severity of any trade sanctions that the United States imposes must not only fit the crime. More importantly, the punishment must be seen in Beijing as revokable—parole and rehabilitation into world society must be quickly granted should China mend its ways. Demonizing China as a state will only serve to dash Chinese leaders' hopes that they can ever receive the trade they need on terms compatible with China's sovereignty and its status as an emerging great power. Only by understanding the importance of Chinese trade expectations and their sensitivity to U.S. policy can U.S. policymakers design a strategy that can avoid the tragedy of war.

ACKNOWLEDGMENT

For their insightful comments, I thank Thomas Berger, John Ikenberry, Michael Mastanduno, Robert Pape, Brantly Womack, and the participants of the two workshops on "The Emerging International Relations of the Asia-Pacific Region" at the University of Pennsylvania and at Dartmouth College.

ENDNOTES

1. Robert S. Ross, "Engagement in U.S. China Policy," in Alistair Iain Johnston and Robert S. Ross, eds., *Engaging China: The Management of an Emergent Power* (London: Routledge, 1999), pp. 176–206; Alastair Iain Johnston and Robert S. Ross, "Preface" and "Conclusion," in ibid.; Michel Oksenberg and Elizabeth Economy, "Introduction: China Joins the World," in Economy and Oksenberg, eds., *China Joins the World: Progress and Prospects* (New York: Council on Foreign Relations, 1999), pp. 1–41; David Shambaugh, "Containment or Engagement of China? Calculating Beijing's Responses," *International Security* 21, no. 2 (Fall 1996): 180–209; Shambaugh, "The United States and China: Cooperation or Confrontation," *Current History* 96, no. 611 (September 1997): 241–45; Andrew J. Nathan and Robert S. Ross, *The Great Wall and the Empty Fortress: China's Search for Security* (New York: Norton, 1997); James Shinn, ed., *Weaving the Net: Conditional Engagement with China* (New York: Council on Foreign Relations, 1996); Joseph S. Nye, "China's Re-emergence and the Future of the Asia-Pacific," *Survival* 39, no. 4 (Winter 1997–98): 65–79; Andrey Kurth Cronin and Patrick M. Cronin, "The Realistic Engagement of China," *Washington Quarterly* 19, no. 1 (Winter 1996): 141–170; Kyung-Won Kim, "Maintaining Asia's Current Peace," *Survival* 39, no. 4 (Winter 1997–98); Fei-Ling Wang, "To Incorporate China: A New Policy for a New Era," *Washington Quarterly* 21, no. 1 (Winter 1998): 67–84; Harry Harding, "A Chinese Colossus?" *Journal of Strategic Studies* 18, no. 3 (September 1995): 121; Jose T. Almonte, "Ensuring Security the 'ASEAN way'," *Survival* 39, no. 4 (Winter 1997–98): 91.

2. For a review of the liberal perspective, see Dale Copeland, "Economic Interdependence and War: A Theory of Trade Expectations," *International Security* 20, no. 4 (Spring 1996): 5–41; Susan McMillan, "Interdependence and Conflict," *Mershon International Studies Review* 41, Sup. 1 (May 1997): 33–58; Bruce Russett and John Oneal, *Triangulating Peace: Democracy, Interdependence, and International Organizations* (New York: Norton, 2001), ch. 4; Katherine Barbieri, "Economic Interdependence: A Path to Peace or a Source of Interstate Conflict?" *Journal of Peace Research* 33, no. 7 (1996): 29–49; Arthur R. Stein, "Governments, Economic Interdependence, and International Cooperation," in Philip Tetlock, et al., eds., *Behavior, Society, and International Conflict* 3 (New York: Oxford University Press, 1993); Edward D. Mansfield and Brian M. Pollins, "Economic Interdependence and Political Conflict: A Conceptual and Empirical Overview," paper prepared for the Mershon Center conference on Interdependence and Conflict, September 15–16, 2000. The most extensive modern formulation of the argument, which is rooted in the writings of Kant, Cobden,

and Angell, remains Richard Rosecrance, *The Rise of the Trading State* (New York: Basic Books, 1986).

3. For a review of realist thinking, see Copeland, "Economic Interdependence and War;" McMillan, "Interdependence and Conflict;" Barbieri, "Economic Interdependence;" Mansfield and Pollins, "Economic Interdependence and Political Conflict." Those supporting a hard-line stance against China include Gideon Rachman, "Containing China," *Washington Quarterly* 19, no. 1 (Winter 1998): 129–40; Richard Bernstein, and Ross H. Munro, *The Coming Conflict with China* (New York: Knopf, 1997); Denny Roy, "Hegemon on the Horizon? China's Threat to East Asian Security," *International Security* 10, no. 1 (Summer 1994): 149–68; Gerald Segal, "East Asia and the 'Constrainment' of China," *International Security* 20, no. 4 (Spring 1996): 107–35 [Segal is more inclined to engagement in "Tying China into the International System," *Survival* 37, no. 2 (Summer 1995): 66–73]. These authors do not necessarily focus on interdependence as a cause of conflict, but the realist argument would support their case. For a consideration of the liberal/realist debate on interdependence as it applies to East Asia, see Stuart Harris, "The Economic Aspects of Pacific Security," in *Asia's International Role in the Post-cold War Era: Part I*, Adelphi Paper 275 (London: Brassey's, March 1993).

4. See Copeland, "Economic Interdependence and War."

5. I borrow the term from Cronin and Cronin, "Realistic Engagement of China," but I place more emphasize on realist power politics as critical to maintaining the peace.

6. See Copeland, "Economic Interdependence and War," pp. 12–18.

7. The assumption of asymmetry can of course be later relaxed, to show the effects of symmetrical interdependence on both actors' desire for conflict versus cooperation.

8. See Richard E. Caves and Ronald W. Jones, *World Trade and Payments*, 4th ed. (Boston: Little Brown, 1985), chs. 3–4. Note that state A can still be aware of the benefits of trade even if present trade is nonexistent, since they represent the potential gains from trade that would accrue to the state should trade levels become high in the future.

9. In a two-actor system of 100 units, for example, where A was 99 and B was 1, even trade the equivalent of 100 percent of B's GNP would be only 1 percent of the total system size. On the other hand, in a two-actor system of 100 units where A was 50 and B was 50, if trade represented only say 5 percent of B's size, this would be 2.5 percent of the total system size. Thus we would expect, for example, that Germany today would find France a far more valuable trading partner than Luxembourg or Liechtenstein.

10. See Hans Linnemann, *An Econometric Study of International Trade Flows* (Amsterdam: North-Holland, 1966); Jan Tinbergen, *Shaping the World Economy* (New York: Twentieth Century Fund, 1962), Appendix VI; Brian M. Pollins, "Conflict, Cooperation and Commerce: The Effect of International Political Interactions on Bilateral Trade Flows," *American Journal of Political Science* 33, no. 3 (August 1989): 737–61. These studies show that the level of trade between any two states is a function of the size of one state's GNP multiplied by the other's. That is, if state A's GNP was designated Y_a, and B's GNP designated Y_b, then trade would vary according to the for-

mula $Y_a \times Y_b$ (factored down by some coefficient). We can thus see that a 100-unit two-actor system of 99–1 will expect to have far less trade than a system of 50–50 (for any given coefficient).

11. When A is very small relative to B, the potential benefits and costs will still be small in absolute terms, although they may be very high as a percentage of A's economy.

12. Since the notion of dependence is described in terms of the *potential* benefits and costs of trade given objective factors, leaders' concerns for relative gains and losses are not directly relevant. In practice, of course, such concerns can moderate leaders' willingness to trade with states that are near equals (and are therefore seen as possible military threats). The issue of relative gains is discussed below.

13. The latter two propositions follow directly from the insights of deterrence theory, which suggest that the larger the state in relative size, the higher the probability of winning a victory, while the lower the costs of fighting the war. See, for example, Alexander George and Richard Smoke, *Deterrence in American Foreign Policy* (New York: Columbia University Press, 1974), chs. 2–3.

14. I discuss this logic more formally in Copeland, "Modeling Economic Interdependence and War," paper delivered to the annual meeting of the American Political Science Association, Chicago, September 1995.

15. Evidence does suggest that war for the Nazis was indeed profitable vis-à-vis such nations, and particularly so for the medium-sized states like Czechoslovakia. Peter Liberman, *Does Conquest Pay?* (Princeton: Princeton University Press, 1996).

16. Thucydides, *The Peloponnesian War*, trans. Rex Warner (Harmondsworth: Penguin, 1954), 1: 80–88.

17. For references on the extended deterrence literature, see Dale C. Copeland, "Do Reputations Matter?" *Security Studies* 7, no. 1 (Autumn 1997), fn. 2.

18. I should also note that my argument operates at the systemic level, and therefore does not consider unit-level motives for aggression. Such motives, when present, will clearly intensify state A's likelihood of expanding beyond the constraints and incentives established by relative power, economic interdependence, and trade expectations (the three causal variables of this analysis).

19. While this argument often incorporates many of the external pressures discussed below, it assumes that had the democratic process *not* been undermined, leaders would have chosen another course. For a review of the literature, and an important reworking of the argument, see Jack Snyder, *Myths of Empire: Domestic Politics and International Ambition* (Ithaca: Cornell University Press, 1991).

20. After the failed coup attempt in February 1936, the emperor's crackdown on far-right elements greatly reduced the pressure they could bring to bear on the cabinet (see Edward Behr, *Hirohito: Behind the Myth* (New York: Vintage, 1989)).

21. See Ramon H. Myers and Mark R. Peattie, eds., *The Japanese Colonial Empire, 1895–1945* (Princeton: Princeton University Press, 1984).

22. This is captured in the slogan that defined the elite's objectives since the Meiji restoration: "rich country, strong army" (see W. G. Beasley, *Japanese Imperialism, 1894–1945* (Oxford: Oxford University Press, 1987).

23. Akira Iriye, *After Imperialism: The Search for a New Order in the Far East 1921–31* (Chicago: Imprint, 1990), concluding chapter.

24. Imperial Government of Japan, *Relations of Japan with Manchuria and Mongolia*, Document B, pp. 141–43 (this document was found in the University of Chicago library, without publication house or date, but contents indicate that it was published around 1932–33). While the takeover of Manchuria was executed by the Japanese army, the civilian government in Toyko did not object; after all, it served the economic ends of the nation.

25. See Copeland, "Economic Interdependence and War."

26. Michael A. Barnhart, *Japan Prepares for Total War: The Search for Economic Security, 1919–1941* (Ithaca: Cornell University Press, 1987), p. 37.

27. Stephen E. Petz, *Race to Pearl Harbor The Failure of the Second London Naval Conference and the Onset of World War II* (Cambridge: Harvard University Press, 1974), p. 170.

28. James B. Crowley, *Japan's Quest for Autonomy: National Security and Foreign Policy, 1930–1938* (Princeton: Princeton University Press, 1966), pp. 288, 299.

29. Barnhart's treatment of this (*Japan Prepares*) is the most complete.

30. Joyce C. Lebra, ed. *Japan's Greater East Asia Co-Prosperity Sphere in World War II: Selected Readings and Documents* (Kuala Lumpur: Oxford University Press, 1975), p. 62.

31. Ibid, p. 63.

32. Roosevelt asked firms to voluntarily restrict or halt their imports of such equipment to Japan (*Judgement: International Military Tribunal for the Far East*, Part B, Chap. V–VI (1948), p. 261).

33. Ibid, p. 334.

34. Lebra, *Japan's Coprosperity Sphere*, pp. 64f.

35. Barnhart, *Japan Prepares*.

36. Ibid, p. 146.

37. Ibid, p. 149.

38. Ibid, p. 207.

39. Quoted in Petz, *Race to Pearl Harbor*, p. 215. See also Tsunoda Jun, "The Navy's Role in the Southern Strategy," in James W. Morley, ed., *The Fateful Choice: Japan's Advancement into Southeast Asia*, (New York: Columbia University Press, 1980), p. 247.

40. Barnhart, *Japan Prepares*, pp. 188–191.

41. Petz, *Race to Pearl Harbor*, p. 215.

42. Nobutaka Ike, trans. and ed., *Japan's Decision for War: Records of the 1941 Policy Conferences* (Stanford: Stanford University Press, 1967), p. 5 (cited herein as *JDW*).

43. "Outline of Policy towards the South," in *Fateful Choice*, ed. Morley, p. 303.

44. *JDW*, pp. 96, 101.

45. Ibid, pp. 130–31, 106.

46. Ibid, p. 136.

47. Ibid, p. 138.

48. Ibid, p. 147.

49. Ibid, p. 148.

50. Ibid, p. 191.

51. Ibid, p. 204.

52. Ibid, p. 207. Since the September 6 conference, few believed that war would be short or painless (see ibid, p. 153).

53. Ibid, pp. 221–22.

54. Japan "would be forced to retreat completely from the mainland" (Ibid, pp. 270–71).

55. Ibid, p. 282.

56. International Monetary Fund, *International Financial Statistics* 53, no. 11 (Washington, D.C.: IMF, November 2000), pp. 228–30; Thomas G. Moore, "China and Globalization," *Asian Perspective* 23, no. 4 (1999): 69. China's total trade with the outside world has gone from a mere $21 billion in 1978, at the beginning of reforms, to $360 billion by 1999. By 1997, China had accumulated more than $130 billion in foreign currency reserves, but also had an external debt of $120 billion. See IMF, *International Financial Statistics*, p. 228; Stefan Halper, "Trading with China? Balancing Free Trade with National Security," in Ted Galen Carpenter and James A. Dorn, eds., *China's Future: Constructive Partner or Emerging Threat?* (Washington, D.C.: Cato Institute, 2000), p. 237; Oksenberg and Economy, "Introduction," in Economy and Oksenberg, *China Joins the World*, p. 5; Nicholas Lardy, "China and the International Financial System," in ibid., pp. 206–230.

57. Michael D. Swaine and Ashley J. Tellis, *Interpreting China's Grand Strategy: Past, Present, and Future* (Santa Monica: RAND, 2000); Zalmay M. Khalilzad, et al., *The United States and a Rising China: Strategic and Military Implications* (Santa Monica: RAND, 1999); Roy, "Hegemon on the Horizon;" Roy, "Assessing the Asia-Pacific 'Power Vacuum'," *Survival* 37, no. 3 (Autumn 1995): 45–60; Harding, "A Chinese Colossus?" Nye, "China's Re-emergence and the Future of the Asia-Pacific;" William H. Overholt, *The Rise of China* (New York: Norton, 1993); Nicholas Kristof, "The Rise of China," *Foreign Affairs* 72, no. 5 (November–December 1993); Douglas T. Stuart, "Preparing for Multipolarity in the Asia-Pacific," *Journal of East Asian Affairs* 11, no. 1 (Winter–Spring 1997): 91–120.

58. In the short term, China has reason for caution given the current inferiority of its navy to that of the United States. See Evan A. Feigenbaum, "China's Military Posture and the New Economic Geopolitics," *Survival*, no. 41, no. 2 (Summer 1999): 71–88. Yet there is evidence that many Chinese officials believe that with U.S. forces dispersed around the world, and with the American public apparently unwilling to absorb heavy casualties, China could engage the U.S. military in the region and prevail. See Thomas J. Christensen, "Posing Problems without Catching Up: China's Rise and Challenges for U.S. Security Policy," *International Security* 25, no. 4 (Spring 2001): 4–40.

59. In 1974, China seized the Paracel Islands by force. These islands lie right off Vietnam's coast, and had been claimed and partially occupied by Vietnam. See Mamdouh G. Salameh, "China, Oil, and the Risk of Regional Conflict," *Survival* 37, no. 4 (Winter 1995–96): 143–44; Lee Lai To, *China and the South China Sea Dialogues* (Westport: Praeger, 1999), p. 13.

60. Salameh, "China, Oil, and the Risk of Regional Conflict;" To, *China and the South China Sea Dialogues*, pp. 11, 130–32; Michael Yahuda, "China's Foreign Relations: The Long March, Future Uncertain," *The China Quarterly*, no. 159 (September 1999): 657; Mark J. Valencia, "Energy and Insecurity in Asia," *Survival* 72, no. 3 (Au-

tumn 1997): 85–106; Bernstein and Munro, *Coming Conflict with China*; Michael Leifer, "Chinese Economic Reform and Security Policy: The South China Sea Connection," *Survival* 37, no. 2 (Summer 1997): 44–59; William J. Dobson and M. Taylor Fravel, "Red Herring Hegemon: China in the South China Sea," *Current History* 96, no. 611 (September 1997): 258–69; Aaron Friedberg, "Ripe for Rivalry: Prospects for Peace in a Multipolar Asia," *International Security* 18, no. 3 (Winter 1993–94): 5–33. China's long-term goals apparently extend beyond the Spratlys. In 1995, Indonesia felt compelled to send a diplomatic note to Beijing questioning why certain Chinese maps showed a dotted line around the Spratleys that encompassed Indonesia's natural gas field in the Natuna Islands, 300 miles southwest of the Spratleys. Jakarta was unnerved by the fact that in the previous year, Indonesia's state-owned oil company had signed a $35 billion deal with Exxon to develop the Natuna gas field. To, *China and the South China Sea Dialogues*, p. 131.

61. See Erica Strecker Downs, *China's Quest for Energy Security* (Santa Monica: RAND, 2000), pp. 7–9; Salameh, "China, Oil, and the Risk of Regional Conflict," *Survival*, 137–39. On China's growing oil dependence, see also Vaclav Smil, "China's Energy and Resource Uses: Continuity and Change," *China Quarterly*, no. 156 (December 1998): 943; Mark Burles, *Chinese Policy Toward Russia and the Central Asian Republics* (Santa Monica: RAND, 1999), p. 23; To, *China and the South China Sea Dialogues*, p. 11; Robert B. Zoellick, "Economics and Security in the Changing Asia-Pacific," *Survival* 39, no. 4 (Winter 1997–98): 33; Michael B. McElroy and Chris P. Nielsen, "Energy, Agriculture, and the Environment: Prospects for Sino-American Cooperation," in Ezra F. Vogel, ed., *Living with China: U.S.-China Relations in the Twenty-First Century* (New York: Norton, 1997), pp. 220–21; Segal, "Tying China into the International System," pp. 62–63. Beijing is seeking to diversify its risk by establishing strong economic and political links with the oil-rich countries of Central Asia. Unfortunately, the high costs of transporting oil by pipeline have left China still primarily dependent on oil imports from the Middle East and Southeast Asia, via sea lanes controlled by the U.S. navy. See Burles, *Chinese Policy Toward Russia and the Central Asian Republics*; Downs, *China's Quest for Energy Security*. Frustrations with domestic production and with the Central Asian connection have led China's government-controlled oil companies to participate in the exploration of oil and gas fields in countries as varied as Peru, Thailand, Sudan, Papua New Guinea, and Canada. See ibid., pp. 17–23, and To, *China and the South China Sea Dialogues*, 12.

62. On growing fears within China that future conflicts with other major powers will revolve around natural resources, particularly supplies of oil and gas, see Michael Pillsbury, *China Debates the Future Security Environment* (Washington, D.C.: National Defense University Press, 2000), xxv, 46–47; Moore, "China and Globalization," pp. 76–77.

63. Saddam Hussein, for example, sought to use such a threat up to July 1990 to convince Kuwait to boost the price of oil; the Iraqi economy was devastated by the precipitous fall in world oil prices, due in large part to Kuwaiti and Saudi overproduction above previously-agreed-upon OPEC quotas. When Kuwait refused Iraqi demands, Iraq invaded the country. It seems likely that Saddam would not have taken this risky move had Kuwait abided by OPEC restrictions.

64. On realist arguments that states worry about relative losses through trade, see Joseph Grieco, "Anarchy and the Limits to Cooperation: A Realist Critique of the Newest Liberal Institutionalism," and "Understanding the Problem of International Cooperation: The Limits of Neoliberal Institutionalism and the Future of Realist Theory," in David A. Baldwin, ed., *Neorealism and Neoliberalism* (New York: Columbia University Press, 1993); Michael Mastanduno, "Do Relative Gains Matter? America's Response to Japanese Industrial Policy," *International Security* 16, no. 1 (Summer 1991): 73–113. For critiques of the realist argument, see essays by Duncan Snidal, Robert Keohane, and Robert Powell in Baldwin, *Neorealism and Neoliberalism*.

65. Margaret M. Pearson, "China's Integration into the International Trade and Investment Regime," in Economy and Oksenberg, *China Joins the World*, pp. 161–205.

66. David Shambaugh, "Facing Reality in China Policy," *Foreign Affairs* 80, no. 1 (January/February 2001): 56; Bates Gill, "Limited Engagement," *Foreign Affairs* 78, no. 4 (July/August 1999): 65.

67. Nathan and Ross, *Great Wall and Empty Fortress*; Bernstein and Munro, *Coming Conflict with China*.

68. On the cold-war trade restrictions against China, see Frank Cain, "The U.S.-Led trade Embargo on China: The Origins of CHINCOM, 1947–52," *Journal of Strategic Studies* 18, no. 4 (December 1995): 33–54.

69. Washington Post, September 2000, A1; Jailin Zhang, "Sino-Trade Issues After the WTO Deal: a Chinese Perspective," *Journal of Contemporary China* 9 (July 2000): 310–11.

70. Quoted in Mark A. Groombridge, "China's Accession to the World Trade Organization: Costs and Benefits," in Carpenter and Dorn, *China's Future*, p. 182.

71. Thomas J. Duesterberg, "Zhu Rongji, Political Magician," *Washington Quarterly* 22, no. 4 (Autumn 1999): 17.

72. Julia Chang Block, "Commercial Diplomacy," in Vogel, *Living with China*, pp. 197–210.

73. This is not to say that this was the only reason driving Beijing's desire for WTO membership. Chinese leaders also recognized that integration within the WTO bloc was necessary to the sustaining of China's modernization in the new information-age global economy and to furthering reformers' plans to reduce China's reliance on highly inefficient state-owned enterprises. See Moore, "China and Globalization," pp. 88–92; Edward S. Steinfeld, "Beyond the Transition: China's Economy at Century's End," *Current History* 98, no. 629 (September 1999): 271–75; Elizabeth Economy, "Getting China Right," *Current History* 98, no. 629 (September 1999): 258–59; Groombridge, "China's Accession to the World Trade Organization," in Carpenter and Dorn, *China's Future*, p. 182; Margaret M. Pearson, "The Major Multilateral Economic Institutions Engage China," in Johnston and Ross, *Engaging China*, p. 226.

74. Samuel S. Kim, "China and the United Nations," in Economy and Oksenberg, *China Joins the World*, p. 46.

75. Moore, "China and Globalization," 69; Pearson, "China's Integration into the International Trade and Investment Regime," in Economy and Oksenberg, *China Joins the World*; Lardy, "China and the International Financial System," in

ibid.; Pearson, "The Major Multilateral Economic Institutions Engage China," in Johnston and Ross, *Engaging China*.

76. Alastair Iain Johnston and Paul Evans, "China's Engagement with Multilateral Security Institutions," in Johnston and Ross, *Engaging China*, pp. 235–72; Michael D. Swaine and Alastair Iain Johnston, "China and Arms Control Institutions," in Economy and Oksenberg, *China Joins the World*, pp. 90–135.

77. Thomas J. Christensen, "Chinese Realpolitik," *Foreign Affairs* 75, no. 5 (September/October 1996): 37–52; Alastair Iain Johnston, *Cultural Realism: Strategic Culture and Grand Strategy in Chinese History* (Princeton: Princeton University Press, 1995); Swaine and Tellis, *Interpreting China's Grand Strategy*.

78. Swaine and Tellis, *Interpreting China's Grand Strategy*. On China's strategy of using cooperation in the near term to foster a climate conducive to economic growth and modernization, see Pillsbury, *China Debates the Future Security Environment*, xxxiv; Sheng Lijun, "China and the United States: Asymmetrical Strategic Partners," *Washington Quarterly* 22, no. 3 (Summer 1999): 158; Michael Yahuda, "China's Search for a Global Role," *Current History* 98, no.629 (September 1999): 269; Yahuda, "China's Foreign Relations," pp. 655–56.

79. See Dale C. Copeland, "Trade Expectations and the Outbreak of Peace: Détente 1970–74 and the End of the Cold War 1985–91," *Security Studies* 9, nos. 1–2 (Autumn 1999–Winter 2000): 23–25.

80. For arguments which stress the importance of a contingent U.S. policy, see Shinn, *Weaving the Net*; Segal, "Tying China into the International System," pp. 70–73.

81. It is important to note that internally, the Japanese leaders had agreed that they would be willing to accept a deal to leave China (but not Manchuria) in a staged withdrawal; all recognized the war in China to be a losing battle. As with U.S. negotiations over Vietnam in the late 1960s, Japan in November 1941 was resisting an *immediate* exiting of China which would harm its reputation for resolve and thus its ability to control Korea and Taiwan. Roosevelt, insensitive to Japanese concerns, refused to bargain toward a more modest *modus vivendi* (even though the U.S. military sought such a deal to buy time for the American military buildup). See Ike, *Japan's Decision for War*; Dale Copeland, "Deterrence, Reassurance, and Machiavellian Appeasement," paper presented at conference on enduring rivalries sponsored by *Security Studies*, Washington, D.C., March 1996.

82. The one exception is Taiwan. Here, Washington has wisely pursued a policy of calculated ambiguity—being committed to "One China," yet simultaneously signaling to Beijing that it cannot be sure that the United States would not act to defend Taiwan should China attack.

83. On the need for consistency and the failure of the arbitrary linking of trade to human rights concerns, see Economy, "Getting China Right," p. 259; Bloch, "Commercial Diplomacy," in Vogel, *Living with China*, 196–97.

84. See Copeland, "Trade Expectations and the Outbreak of Peace," pp. 25–40.

85. David M. Lampton, "America's China Policy in the Age of the Finance Minister: Clinton Ends Linkage," *China Quarterly* 139 (September 1994): 597–621.

86. Robert S. Ross, "The 1995–96 Taiwan Straits Confrontation: Coercion, Credibility, and the Use of Force," *International Security* 25, no. 2 (Fall 2000): 87–123.

87. Feigenbaum, "China's Military Posture and the New Economic Geopolitics;" Sheng, "China and the United States."

88. As Assistant Secretary of State Joseph S. Nye told the U.S. House of Representatives International Relations Committee in 1995: "If you treat China as [an] enemy, then you will have an enemy." Quoted in Ross, "Engagement in U.S. China Policy," in Johnston and Ross, *Engaging China*, 184.

89. See ibid., pp. 185–86, on the value of "market access talks" in the 1990s as an alternative to unilateral U.S. protectionism. By embedding the threat of U.S. sanctions with the context of these ongoing talks, Washington was successful in compelling compromises from Beijing on tariffs and non-tariff barriers while simultaneously upholding America's general commitment to the free trade principle.

Chapter 11

INSTITUTIONALIZED INERTIA

Japanese Foreign Policy in the Post-Cold War World

William W. Grimes

Japan is an oddity in the Asia-Pacific, and indeed the world. While it is by far the largest economy in Asia, and a top economic presence throughout the region, its international posture has been unassuming and often inconsistent. Despite a growing potential threat from China and at least the future possibility of U.S. military withdrawal from post–cold war Asia, it has, ironically, made no serious effort to develop an autonomous defense capability even though it now has the world's second most expensive armed forces. And although many observers claim that the state played a key strategic role in the rapid growth of the postwar economy, foreign economic policy appears generally to be uncoordinated and only occasionally strategic.

An equally important puzzle is what effects Japan's inertial tendencies have on regional politics. Does Japan's military constraint promote or corrode peace and stability? Should we be reassured by the low profile of the Japanese state in presenting itself as an economic leader, or should we be concerned that it is not providing essential regional public goods?

In this chapter, I argue that the Japanese state does not produce a coordinated and effective response to many of the actual or potential challenges of its international situation because it *cannot*. Effective foreign policy is constrained by a set of institutions that reflect strategic and political issues of the past. While there is a growing consensus among Japanese policymakers and people that policy changes may be needed to confront a changing world situation, meaningful policy change is virtually impossible without changes in institutions—but by their very nature, institutions usually change only incrementally, except in crises.

In analyzing the institutional bases of Japanese foreign policy behavior, I concentrate on three sets of institutions and organizations. For security issues, the effects of half a century of the "Peace Constitution" and the U.S.-Japan Mutual Security Treaty are apparent in a decisionmaking structure that almost automatically disallows any serious movement toward autonomous strategic thinking. For most economic issues, particularly trade and aid, the lack of coherence reflects the problems of coordination among turf-conscious bureaucracies that are not subject to centralized decisionmaking by the prime minister. One exceptional institutional feature of Japanese foreign economic policymaking stands out, however—the immense pool of capital (in the form of $350 billion dollars in foreign exchange reserves and well over $3 trillion worth of government trust funds) that can be deployed rapidly in the face of perceived emergencies.

This institutional structure helps to define what responses are possible or impossible in the face of a given international challenge. In security matters, nearly superhuman effort is needed to make any change to the low-profile status quo. In most economic matters as well, Japanese policy is highly inertial. When stakes are high enough (for example, in the pressures to liberalize rice imports in the Uruguay Round), change may occur, but it will tend to be incremental. Interestingly, however, Japan has been able to react decisively to certain specific economic challenges—including, as I will demonstrate, the Asian Financial Crisis. The reason is that the institutions of Japanese economic policy allow for rapid mobilization of funds, but not for rapid adjudication of turf battles.

Thus, I argue, Japan's foreign policy inertia is institutionalized. Of course, institutions do change over time, and past and future institutional change is an important focus of this chapter. In Japan, we have seen institutional evolution as incremental policy changes have accumulated over time, but relatively little intentional, forward-looking institutional transformation. To date, the inertia of Japan's policies has often served its interests well, keeping it out of regional arms races and unwanted military engagements abroad, and helping it to insulate its economy from external pressures for liberalization. Since institutional change tends to lag behind change in the international environment, however, if that international environment turns threatening, then Japan may be unable to respond to that threat in an effective way. In this way, institutionalized inertia creates dangers as well for Japan.

Looking beyond Japan's borders, the effects of its domestic institutions on foreign policies either reduce or excite friction, depending on the case. Its low profile in security issues has been at least somewhat reassuring to its neighbors, and has thus contributed to regional security. However, it has also created frictions with its U.S. protectors, and in the long run could threaten the U.S.-Japan alliance. Economic policy inertia has led to sometimes severe disagreements with trading partners, and on occasion has inspired threatened or actual retaliation.

Serious efforts at institutional change in both security and economic management are ongoing, but even the most ambitious of these efforts have been one step up and two steps back. (It is ironic that these have actually accelerated somewhat in the last decade, even as the Japanese economy has stagnated.) Looking ahead, the slow pace at which the institutions of Japanese foreign policy have been changing under pressure from the outside world may mean that it will be unable to respond effectively to future crises. While Japan's institutionalized inertia in the security realm is useful to regional stability in the short term, it raises the longer-term possibility of a dangerous power vacuum that Japan may not be able to fill in time. Conversely, the short-term implications of a more autonomous security policy would likely be destabilizing, even if it proved to have positive effects in the longer term. Thus, whether Japan will become more or less of a force for stability of international relations in the Asia-Pacific depends at least partly on how its institutions of foreign policy evolve.

INTERNATIONAL FORCES, DOMESTIC INSTITUTIONS, AND FOREIGN POLICY

Neither the argument presented in this chapter nor domestic institutions arguments in general offer a "fundamental" explanation in the sense that realism or liberalism does—in other words, making a causal argument about the motive forces of state behavior. Rather, this approach seeks to explain why states do *not* respond to such motive forces in the ways that more fundamental theories, particularly realism, suggest.[1] I argue that domestic institutions can add to a realist approach to provide the best explanation of Japan's international behavior.

REALIST PREDICTIONS

One of the most common starting points for the scholarly study of Japan's international role is that Japan has not met the predictions of realism, and particularly of neorealism. On the security side, Japan has made only limited efforts to balance against China and virtually none at all to break its dependence on U.S. military protection.[2] On the economic side, the movement toward an Asian economic bloc headed by Japan that would rival U.S.-led and European blocs has not come to pass, and if anything, we have seen a resurgence of globalization rather than regionalization.[3]

Certainly, a rational, realist Japan would be wary of the security dilemma that it could cause by increasing its military capabilities dramatically—the billions of dollars of spending that it would take to become a regional military superpower could even purchase it *lower* levels of security than it has now. But we should expect that a realist Japan *would* seek to hedge its bets, by lowering its dependence on the United States, and by gradually improving its capabilities in ways that are not directly threatening to its neighbors. The latter would likely include an expansion of purely defensive capabilities and limited participation in UN peacekeeping operations. On the economic side, an Asian economic bloc would make no sense as long as the economies of North America and Europe remain open; rather, a dual strategy of expanding Asian economic ties and seeking to tie outside powers (especially the United States) to the region would appear to make the most sense. The evolution of Japan's actual policies since the late 1980s is at least broadly consistent with this more modest realist agenda, but it has also been halting, apparently uncoordinated, and occasionally retrograde.

An alternative realist formulation is Heginbotham and Samuels' argument that Japan has followed a "mercantile realist" strategy that stresses relative gains in technological prowess—the primary determinant of power in the long term—rather than military power.[4] In this formulation, Japanese policy is strategic. They argue that "Japan has persistently acted as if its greatest vulnerabilities have been economic and technological" and that "foreign penetration of Japanese markets . . . has been perceived as a threat, whether that penetration was by the firms of a military competitor or ally." In terms of the tradeoff between economic and military security, Japan has thus been able to "bandwagon with the United States politically and balance against it economically."[5]

While suggestive, the idea that Japan has practiced a coherent strategy of "mercantile realism" is difficult to prove. Moreover, Japan's mercantilism has often concentrated on declining, nonstrategic sectors such as construction, distribution, and transportation, in ways that have advantaged some of the least efficient domestic producers. It is not clear how a strategically mercantile state would be helped by maintaining protection of inefficient and strategically unimportant industries—institutional inertia would seem to offer a more reasonable explanation.[6] For now, too many ambiguities persist both in theoretical predictions and actual behavior to allow unequivocal judgments either for or against mercantile realism as an explanation of Japan's foreign policies. Thus, in this chapter, I will address deviations from my more generic realist definition of Japan's interests.

INSTITUTIONS AND POLICY

Before going into specifics about the role of Japan's policymaking institutions in responding to realist pressures, we must consider two questions at the theoretical level: how do domestic institutions shape foreign policy processes and outcomes? And, how do international pressures shape domestic institutions?

The strength of the domestic institutions approach is its ability to add to the realist paradigm by considering the *formation* of state interests and state capabilities, rather than simply assuming them based on a process of natural selection in the anarchic international order. Realism expects states to act in a way that will allow them to survive—for example, by balancing against stronger powers and minimizing economic vulnerability. However, there are many policy choices that have little or nothing to do with the survival of the state, or whose consequences are unclear.[7] Tempting though it may be to predict foreign policy from a realist analysis of a state's needs, in the end the task is essentially impossible.

If no set of priorities is preordained by system structure, then we must look inside states to understand how policies and priorities are actually determined. While the domestic-institutions approach moves away from some of the core assumptions of neorealist theory, it does not require a fundamental rethinking or rejection of realism in the way that some versions of constructivism do.[8] Domestic institutions can be important whether states exist in a Hobbesian state of nature, a liberal world of wealth maximizers, or some other construction altogether. The fact that different types of institutions may lead to different types of worldviews may seem to make for a basically constructivist world.[9] But it is perfectly possible that states will be disciplined in the long run by an unforgiving international system, no matter how their dominant beliefs or institutional arrangements induce them to behave internationally—"realist theories are as much about the *consequences* of behavior as about the *determinants* of behavior."[10]

In discussing institutions at the abstract level, I will follow North's terminology: "Institutions are the rules of the game in a society or, more formally, are the humanly devised constraints that shape human interaction."[11] Institutions can be both formal (laws and legal systems) and informal (extensions of formal rules).[12] Institutions may or may not be embodied in or enforced by organizations, which are "groups of individuals bound by some common purpose to achieve objectives."[13] In looking at Japanese foreign policy, an example of a formal institution is the war-renouncing Article 9 of the Constitution in combination with its subsequent legal interpretations;[14] an example of an informal institution is the "Yoshida doctrine" (discussed below); and organizations include the Ministry of Foreign Affairs, the Self-Defense Forces, and the Prime Minister's Office.

Informal institutions of governance are usually buttressed by formal institutions and organizations. When change in a domestic institution or organization leads to discrepancies with related institutions or organizations, tension arises. Over the long term, such tension should lead to reconvergence, either by a reversal of the original change or by an evolution of related institutions and organizations.[15] Such changes can be triggered by crises, or in some cases can themselves trigger crises.

If policymaking institutions and processes are themselves a crucial determinant of policy outcomes, then we should expect to see distinct patterns of policy outcomes that change more slowly than the objective factors that surround the institutions.[16] Domestic institutions approaches in political science have focused variously on the organizations of the state or society, cultural or historical legacies, or long-term coalitions. The usefulness of concentrating on a given type of institution will generally depend on the issue being considered. In this chapter, I look at institutions more narrowly than do authors such as Risse-Kappen and Milner, who focus on broad questions of state-society relations or parliamentary vs. presidential systems.[17] I do so because I am interested in institutional change as well as stasis—and the basic structure of the Japanese political system is not on the verge of change.

DYNAMICS OF INSTITUTIONAL CHANGE

Large-scale political events can shape states' policies for periods of years or decades.[18] In these enduring political compromises, long-term coalitions affect both domestic and foreign policies by favoring some groups and excluding others from the policy process. Over time, patterns of inclusion and exclusion are actually institutionalized in state structures.[19] State structures can also serve to insulate the state from society more generally, and to strengthen its ability to carry out policies that are either in officials' own interests or in their interpretation of the national interest.[20]

International politics can also have reciprocal effects on domestic institutions in some cases—the so-called "second image reversed" approach.[21] This may be particularly true of major trauma, such as when a state entered the modern state system or international economy, or of war.[22] But state formation and war are not the only points at which the international system can be an engine for transforming state institutions. Changed international conditions can also prompt less far-reaching internal changes, as leaders begin to realize the need to deal with the outside world (if not necessarily domestic politics) with new tools. A good example of this is the reestablishment of U.S. foreign policy institutions at the outset of the cold war.[23] Rather than abandoning wartime coordinative and information-gathering agencies as had been standard after earlier large-scale wars, U.S. authorities acted to give these agencies more permanent status in order to deal more effectively with the rapidly developing cold war. The establishment of the National Security Council, the Central Intelligence Agency, and other security agencies, along with the development of systems of clearances, the "military-industrial complex," etc., transformed the United States' abilities both to coordinate foreign policy and to carry out theretofore impossible (if not necessarily always desirable) policies such as reconstruction in Europe and Japan, counter-revolution in Iran and Vietnam, and support of guerrilla movements in Latin America and Afghanistan.

There are opportunities for less dramatic changes as well. Even if imperfectly, states do attempt to be forward-looking, and to recognize inadequacies in their abilities to deal with foreseeable eventualities. The end of the cold war, globalization, and events such as the Asian Financial Crisis have fundamentally changed perceptions of likely eventualities, perhaps particularly in Asia. In particular, the decline in the cohesiveness of cold war–era political and economic blocs should lead to changing relative valuations of economic and political objectives, the possibility of alternative security arrangements which cross the borders of the old alliances, and, in more concrete terms, the increased likelihood of a future withdrawal of U.S. forces from Asia. Thus, despite the inertia that is intrinsic to institutions, we should expect to see at least initial moves by Asian states to improve their abilities to address the new challenges.

INSTITUTIONS VS. CULTURE

Policy institutions are not the same as culture, preferences, or beliefs. In the latter vein, Berger and Katzenstein have argued that such factors as total defeat in World War II, the resulting revulsion toward the militarism of Japan's wartime regime, and the economic successes of a nonmilitarized Japan in the postwar period have combined to institutionalize a "culture of antimilitarism."[24] For them, the changes in societal norms in turn constrain state actions.

It is hard not to accept that Japanese norms concerning international behavior have changed in generally the ways that these authors describe. My argument differs from theirs in the importance assigned to state institutions and in my assessment of Japan's potential responsiveness to changes in the international environment. If the concept of culture is to have any meaning independent of the political institutions that may reflect it, then it should be that norms and perceptions change more slowly in response to environmental change than those institutions that exist explicitly to deal with the external environment. While I argue that political institutions will produce more inertia in Japan's international behavior than a purely realist analysis would prescribe, I also predict that those institutions will change more rapidly and more predictably than cultural institutions, and that changes in objective conditions will be more important in driving change than policy discourse. This is the major predictive difference between the two approaches.[25]

MAKING POLICY IN JAPAN: STRUCTURES, PROCESSES, AND OUTCOMES

Japan's postwar foreign policy can for the most part be delineated by three themes: (1) alliance with the United States, (2) avoidance of confrontation, and (3) concentration on economic issues. These themes have operated both on the level of actual foreign policy, and on the shaping of the policymaking institutions.

The most singular feature of Japanese foreign policy, especially in traditional "high politics" areas, has been the centrality of the alliance with the United States. Japan's fidelity to its U.S. partner can be seen in a variety of actions which were unpopular at home and/or appeared on their face not to be in its national interest, such as its support of the U.S. position in the Vietnam War and its nonrecognition of the People's Republic of China prior to Nixon's historic visit there in 1971. Followership has not been absolute, as seen particularly in the drive to expand autonomous weapons development and production, but in the end usually trumps other foreign policy interests.[26]

Avoiding confrontation with neighbors has been a second hallmark of Japanese foreign policy.[27] Perhaps the most important manifestation of conflict avoidance has been in the military realm. Japan has chosen not to procure equipment such as bombers, aircraft carriers, and landing craft; also, its joint military exercises with the United States and Korea have not had Japanese forces involved in landings.[28] Avoidance has also extended considerably into the political and economic realms. Japan has proved to be quite sensitive in particular to charges of neocolonialism or atavism by Asian countries. In its foreign economic policy as well, Japan has been careful not to appear to interfere in the affairs of other Asian states—in particular, it has been reluctant to attach policy conditions to its development aid.

The third theme has been an emphasis on foreign economic policy aims over "high politics." This theme emerged perhaps most clearly in the 1970s, when Japanese leaders realized that U.S. protection alone would not guarantee access to essential raw materials. Japan's foreign policy began to stray from complete identification with U.S. global politics in the direction which came to be known as "comprehensive security."[29] Comprehensive security particularly embraced resource-rich states that were geographically close, such as Indonesia, while strengthening ties with Middle Eastern states that were not always in U.S. favor. While comprehensive security was the most explicit statement of the emphasis on foreign economic policy, other examples abound, particularly in trade negotiations. Even Japan's dealings in traditional areas of diplomacy and security have had an economic tinge, from the negotiations for the reversion of Okinawa (partially in exchange for a deal on Japanese textile export restraints) to codevelopment of the FS-X fighter aircraft (shaped by U.S. fears of losing the aircraft industry to Japan).[30]

ENVIRONMENTAL CHANGES

As in many areas of the world, the cold war in Asia created a strong inertia in terms of international incentives. Japan was an ally of the United States, situated in one of the most potentially dangerous of the cold war neighborhoods, and had no good alternatives to U.S. protection. Moreover, neighboring states have remained highly suspicious of Japan's intentions regarding rearmament. In such circumstances, a low-profile, economically oriented policy stance throughout the postwar period seems entirely rational.

Key variables have changed, however. The most obvious of these are the end of the cold war and the decline of the potential threat from the Russian Far East. These events should have reduced the need for U.S. protection, and for reflexive deference to U.S. policy objectives. One might argue that the rise of China in recent and future years should continue to tie Japan to the United States. However, for the moment, China's power projection capabilities remain weak, particularly in naval terms.[31] Given the long-term uncertainties as to Chinese intentions and U.S. commitment, it may be better to see the current situation as an opportunity for a realist Japan to start hedging its bets and preparing for the long-term worst case scenario of U.S. disengagement and Chinese aggressiveness.

Over a longer perspective, the transformation of Japan from war-torn basket case to economic superpower (indeed, one which has the world's second highest military spending, despite maintaining the total at around 1 percent of GDP) and the rise of China are the sorts of power shifts that usually alert us to major changes in world political configurations. Japan has not yet sought to take advantage of that potential power. To better understand this reluctance, we must turn to institutions.

The persistence of cold war–era trends in Japanese foreign policy in the face of major changes in objective conditions suggests that policy preferences have in some way become institutionalized in Japan's political and economic structures. To a remarkable degree, the institutions of Japanese foreign policy making have served to limit flexibility, and to maintain the continuity of policy in terms of the trends I have already identified. I will concentrate here on two key sets of formal and informal institutions, which are associated with the "Yoshida Doctrine" on the one hand and with Japan's economic focus on the other.

INSTITUTIONS OF SECURITY POLICY

The Yoshida Doctrine is named after Shigeru Yoshida, who served as Prime Minister for most of the Occupation period as well as the first two and a half years after Occupation. Yoshida's policies were marked by strong anticommunism and a resistance to military buildup, both made possible by heavy reliance on the United States to ensure Japanese security.[32] Their purpose was to keep Japan as far removed as possible from actual involvement in the cold war, paradoxically by relying on one of its two main protagonists.

The Yoshida Doctrine was confirmed in several formal arrangements, including Article 9 of the Constitution and the U.S.-Japan Mutual Security Treaty. Interpretations of Article 9 have expanded far beyond what most would have imagined possible in 1946, as various Cabinets have stated officially that

Article 9 allows for not only limited self-defense, but also forward self-defense (defense of sea-lanes of communication) and overseas dispatch of peacekeeping troops.[33] As for the Security Treaty, it provides for U.S. basing rights in Japan, but is justified constitutionally on the basis that it only involves Japan in its own self-defense, not collective self-defense. However, the ambiguous use of the term "Far East" in the Treaty itself (Articles 4 and 6) opens up considerable room for interpretation. Indeed, the 1997 revision of the "Guidelines for U.S.-Japan Defense Cooperation" states that "The two Governments will take appropriate measures, to include preventing further deterioration of situations, in response to situations in areas surrounding Japan."[34]

The principles of the Constitution and Security Treaty have been reaffirmed more informally as well. In particular, the Japanese government has publicly espoused (though not legally instated) restrictions on the state's military capabilities, including the Three Non-Nuclear Principles, bans on export of military goods or technology, and the so-called 1 percent limit on military spending.[35] Perhaps more importantly, legal interpretations of Article 9 have consistently denied the possibility of participation in collective self-defense, or any action that could engage SDF troops in fighting outside of Japan. In general, the Self-Defense Forces have been most visible in a disaster relief role. The result has been that, even as Japan has become one of the highest spending militaries in the world, the basic consensus against militarization has been confirmed and institutionalized.[36]

More importantly, the principles are embodied in the organizations of security policy. The Defense Agency remains just an agency, while a number of its officials—including key personnel in procurement and budgeting—come from powerful outside ministries. Moreover, under the Security Treaty, interoperability of equipment and integration of tasks and missions between U.S. and Japanese forces is the basis of Japanese defense planning and doctrine, and this complementarity is nurtured by constant high-level coordination and regular joint exercises.[37] Recent developments have actually pulled Japanese forces into a tighter integration—the extreme case of this would be Theater Missile Defense if it is ever developed, since a TMD system would require seamless, real-time cooperation in the form of unified command.

The anti-military consensus and institutions have been weakened somewhat, especially in the last fifteen to twenty years. Prime Minister Yasuhiro Nakasone deliberately violated the 1 percent limit in 1987 and worked to follow up on his predecessor Zenko Suzuki's 1981 pledge to protect sea-lines of communication out to 1,000 miles; Japanese minesweepers were dispatched to the Persian Gulf in 1991 after hostilities had ended between Iraq and the United States; in 1992 the Diet passed a law allowing overseas dispatch of SDF forces in noncombat roles in U.N. peacekeeping operations (the "PKO Law"), and also in 1992 SDF forces were dispatched to Cambodia under the command of the United Nations.[38] Perhaps even more importantly, Japanese military spending has increased apace with its postwar economic growth, leaving it with military capabilities that could not have been foreseen in Yoshida's time.[39]

The core of the institutions has remained, however. The Defense Agency still lacks ministry status and a strong power base among politicians. The high levels of military spending reflect the high salaries necessary to attract and retain personnel, as well as the high costs of development and short production runs of high-tech weapons made by Japanese firms. In short, it can hardly be said that the second most expensive military in the world is the second most capable. Moreover, Japan's force structure is still designed primarily to be complementary to U.S. forces in Japan and the Pacific. All of these points reinforce the continuing dependence on the United States for Japan's security, as well as the relatively low regard in which the importance of military readiness is held. Thus, despite erosion, the basic principles of the Yoshida Doctrine remain embedded in Japanese government institutions: reliance on the United States, and limited military capabilities that do not pose an credible autonomous threat to any neighbors.

INSTITUTIONS OF FOREIGN ECONOMIC POLICY

An emphasis on economic over military aims has similarly been institutionalized in Japan, as a result of the Yoshida Doctrine's success in escaping from the tradeoff of economic growth versus security by trading foreign policy autonomy for U.S. protection. The tradeoffs embodied in the Yoshida Doctrine were reinforced early on by the existing bureaucratic structure of the Occupation. The Army and Navy, once dominant in foreign policy, were eliminated, and domestically powerful bureaucracies such as the Home Ministry were broken up and many of their leaders purged along with many influential politicians and *zaibatsu* leaders. Into the breach stepped the Ministry of Foreign Affairs (MOFA), and the economic ministries, most notably the Ministry of Commerce and Industry (now the Ministry of Economy, Trade, and Industry, or METI) and the Ministry of Finance (MOF).[40] Many of the tools or policies that would become central to Japanese foreign economic policy (such as the foreign exchange budget) operated either through negotiations between line ministries and Occupation officials, or independently even of the Americans. This way of doing business reinforced the principle of line ministries negotiating within their own areas of jurisdiction.

Today as well, one of the most immediately evident characteristics of Japanese foreign economic policy is its distinct separation from the diplomatic establishment, and its fragmentation along functional lines.[41] This separation has been enshrined in the institutions of economic policy and the practice of international negotiations: trade negotiations are carried out by METI officials, those over ports and air routes by the Ministry of Transportation, and so on. This is, of course, not unusual. However, there is no obvious venue in the Japanese state apparatus for coordination of economic and diplomatic aims—not only are the Ministry of Foreign Affairs and the Defense Agency (JDA) left largely out of the loop in foreign economic policy matters, but also the absence of an effective coordinative body at the cabinet level means that different ministries are largely left to their own devices. Even foreign aid—usually seen as a tool of foreign policy—lies largely outside the control of MOFA. Although it is officially decided in consultation among MOFA, METI, MOF, and the former Economic Planning Agency, MOF and METI have often taken the lead role, despite the program's origins in war reparations agreements.[42]

MOFA and the JDA, with little in the way of political resources, are thus highly circumscribed in their abilities to affect international economic negotiations. The primary places where coordination might be expected to occur are in the Prime Minister's office and in the various advisory councils attached to it. However, each of these suffers from the same weaknesses described above—in particular, turf battles and lack of clear coordinating principles. For example, the Prime Minister is advised by five top-level aides on important international and economic matters. Rather than improving coordination, however, this system has actually perpetuated turf battles—among the five aides, there is one each from MOFA, MOF, METI, and the National Police Agency. All return to their respective bureaucracies after their tours of duty in the Prime Minister's office, thus reinforcing the tendency toward protecting turf. As for advisory councils, even those attached to the Prime Minister's office have relied on ministries to provide staff and information. As the best recent work on Japanese advisory councils argues, "The Prime Minister's Office [Cabinet Office as of 2001] houses a welter of unrelated, extraministerial bodies over which the premier exercises little control."[43]

In theory there is no particular reason why a determined ruling party could not act to coordinate economics and "high politics," but clearly this pattern has not been institutionalized to any meaningful degree. (And in any event, party structures—even of the long-dominant Liberal Democratic Party—have been far too balkanized to provide a sufficient base of support for a prime minister with ambitious or original foreign policy goals.) Thus, the apparent consensus among leaders and the public in favor of the Yoshida Doctrine has been reinforced by the organizational structure that it helped to put into place.

PRACTICAL EFFECTS

The Yoshida Doctrine institutions have served to keep the Japanese military under a tight rein, even as it has grown to be one of the world's most expensive—and in terms of naval and air forces, one of Asia's most capable—

armed forces. In addition to reinforcing Yoshida's original political and economic aims, they have had the side benefit of tempering the anxieties of Japan's neighbors. At the same time, they have reduced the state's flexibility to act in what has often appeared to be its own self-interest. Japan's inability to send even noncombatant SDF personnel and equipment to the Persian Gulf in 1990 and 1991 until after hostilities had ended created considerable ill-will in the United States.[44] Similarly, the lack of coordination at a central level has made it difficult to respond with a coherent voice to a variety of situations.

The most obvious of these is in economic negotiations with the United States and other trade partners. Although foreign policy goals generally trump in the end if disputes become too antagonistic, the lack of coordination has regularly led to contentious relations that end with bad feelings on both sides. This has been a common result in negotiations with the United States.[45] Lack of internal coordination in Japan not only slowed down the completion of the Uruguay Round, but also helped to scuttle the 1998 APEC Early Voluntary Sectoral Liberalization negotiations, as agriculture exercised its traditional veto over trade liberalization.

In regard to Japan's second most important bilateral relationship, its foreign policy institutions have had mixed effects. China policy has been a priority in many ways, as demonstrated by the size of aid and investment flows and by the profound sensitivity of Japan to Chinese criticisms of atavistic textbooks and statements by political leaders.[46] Nevertheless, the domination of China policy by economic interests has impeded serious long-term thinking about the security implications of Chinese economic growth or consideration of the question of whether Japan should be withholding certain technologies. Only since the mid-1990s has Japan even begun to move "from commercial liberalism to reluctant realism" in viewing China.[47] Lack of coordination has also stymied the Japanese government's ability to respond strongly to disturbing Chinese actions such as the 1995 nuclear tests. In that case, as in the Tiananmen Square incident and the 1998 nuclear tests by India and Pakistan, the extent of the reaction was official protest and a partial (and temporary) freeze on grant aid.[48] Ironically, the limited reactions in those cases probably helped to smooth bilateral relations—an example of the potential benefits of Japan's institutionalized inertia.

As a final point, as already noted, aid policymaking has been hobbled by the difficulty of gaining cooperation among four agencies with often different agendas. This occasionally affects the apportionment of aid among recipient countries, in which cases broader foreign policy aims (and thus MOFA) generally win.[49] More often, it leads to disputes over how the money is to be used, with METI particularly pushing for uses that benefit Japanese corporations.[50]

THE ASIAN FINANCIAL CRISIS

The most dramatic international economic crisis faced by Japan in the post–cold war era was clearly the Asian Financial Crisis.[51] The crisis naturally posed a severe challenge for Japanese policymakers. However, the Japanese state is far better equipped to deal with international economic crises than with security or political dilemmas. In fact Japan was impressively responsive to the Asian crisis.[52] Not only were officials of the International Finance Bureau of the Ministry of Finance working by early July 1997 to put together a package for Thailand (well before U.S. officials evinced major concern), but in that fall, Finance Minister Mitsuzuka announced a plan to assemble a $100 billion Asian Monetary Fund to handle short-term liquidity problems of Asian economies. Japan offered to put up the bulk of the capital. In addition, Japan was by far the largest single-country donor to each of the IMF-brokered bailouts, pledging $4 billion to Thailand, $5 billion to Indonesia, and $10 billion to Korea.

Japan also responded to the problem of declining Japanese commercial bank lending to the crisis-affected Asian economies. After the fall of 1997, the Japanese government reversed its earlier budgetary commitment to reduce its aid spending. It also stepped up official nonconcessional loans, particularly to provide trade credits and to allow the completion of partially completed projects.[53] The original *ad hoc* efforts were expanded in the 1998 announcement of the $30 billion New Miyazawa Plan, which has provided both substantial short-term support for currencies facing attacks (through a special facility in the Asian Development Bank) and longer-term support for restructuring and development (through direct lending and guarantees for sovereign borrowing).[54] The amounts did not by any means fully make up for the pullback by private lenders, but they have addressed specific problems caused by the crisis.

In other words, regardless of whether rapid bailouts would have been the best response to the crisis (as I believe), the Japanese government has been a central, credible, and decisive actor in international efforts to address that crisis. That decisiveness stands in stark contrast to Japan's efforts to respond effectively to security-related crises such as the Iraq-Kuwait crisis and the North Korean nuclear crisis. (A partial exception can be seen in its attempts to broker a peace in Cambodia. There, although the outcome has not been unambiguously successful, the outcome was surely as positive as anyone could have expected.)

Japan's domestic problems clearly contributed to the emergence of the Asian crisis by reducing Japan's demands for imports and reducing the amount of lending and investment available for troubled economies, but these are the result primarily of domestic problems which are both economically and politically difficult to handle.[55] The only way Japan could have been much more aggressive in dealing with problems at the international level would have been more assertive *domestic* actions. Japan's domestic economic policy problems have been a result of the same dynamic that hampers most decisionmaking in foreign economic policy—namely the sectionalism and clientelism that has been institutionalized over time in a sort of unmediated balance of power among bureaucracies. Only when it comes to deploying discretionary funds does the Japanese foreign economic policy apparatus look like a well-oiled machine.

ELECTORAL POLITICS

Electoral politics provides a less compelling explanation for much of Japan's postwar foreign policy framework. Despite what might appear to be strongly held views on some aspects of foreign policy, as evidenced in demonstrations against the Security Treaty and the Vietnam War and in regular expressions of outrage concerning the Self-Defense Forces and U.S. policies in the Persian Gulf, the Japanese people have been consistent in not emphasizing those views at the ballot box. Similarly, it is striking how careful the conservative Liberal Democratic Party has generally been about keeping foreign policy and security issues off the public agenda. The main exception has been the voice of the private sector in foreign economic policy over the years. Insofar as that voice has been whispered to policymakers rather than shouted to the winds, it reminds us that institutions regularly include some interests at the expense of others, and that the business of the postwar Japanese state has been business. Only in the late 1990s did politicians again begin to take charge of the policies related to foreign policies, and they have done so through struggles over institutions and state organization.

THE END OF THE COLD WAR: HOW WILL STATE STRUCTURES RESPOND?

The end of the cold war carries innumerable implications for the foreign policies of the Asian countries. Depending on one's analytical proclivities, one might concentrate on the end of the bipolar system, the almost-universal acceptance of capitalism and markets as the means of organizing economies, the spread of democracy, or the globalization of the world economy.[56] What I would like to do in this section is to ask not how these forces will directly shape the international relations of the region, but how state policymaking institutions that were developed in the context of the cold war might or might not change in response to the international environment. More speculatively, I will make some tentative predictions about how these changes may affect Japan's foreign policies, and thus the dynamics of international relations in the Asia-Pacific.

As we have seen, Japan was profoundly affected by the cold war, and its foreign policy establishment is in many ways a relic of that long confrontation. Japan's response was a state structure in which foreign policy was predicated on cooperation with the United States, and in which virtually all of what we might call the state's "discretionary" foreign policy making was carried out by domestically oriented bureaucracies.

In the face of the profound changes that have taken place in Japan's external environment, changes in the state's foreign policies have so far remained marginal. It has not staked out clearly independent positions either in its bilateral relations or in international organizations.[57] Meanwhile, it has continued to hold the U.S.-Japan alliance as the centerpiece of its security arrangements. And despite a few forays into more political aspects of diplomacy, such as its leading role in the negotiations leading to Cambodian elections in the early 1990s, Japan's diplomatic profile is still largely focused on economic matters.

Theory suggests that institutions, which tend to embody the goals and political equilibria of the past, will continue to channel policy outcomes in the usual directions even where the external situation has changed considerably. This certainly appears to be the case in Japan, where career diplomats still complain about being left outside the loop, and foreign economic policy is still marked by vertical cleavages among ministries.[58] As it stands today, and despite the large-scale reorganization of ministries in January 2001, the institutional structure is not very different in these regards from thirty years ago; if anything, the weakness of the various coalition cabinets since 1993 has meant that there is even less coordination among the state's various foreign policy activities.

There are times when such a muddle has served Japan well, as in its inability to respond to the 1996 Taiwan Straits crisis until tensions had blown over. However, in other cases, such as Iraq's invasion of Kuwait, the structure of indecision and inaction did not lead to a very positive outcome for Japan. One can only imagine the problems that would ensue if that structure were to lead to ineffective management of a military crisis on the Korean peninsula, or to nonsupport of U.S. forces involved in combat near Japan.[59]

The exception to this picture is in foreign economic policy, particularly crisis management.[60] In terms of crisis management, the Japanese is—perhaps more than any other state—organized in a way that allows it to move money abroad rapidly and strategically, due to institutions originally focused on domestic policy (trust funds) or as part of a defensive strategy against imports (Japan's massive foreign exchange reserves). When absolutely necessary, we also see decisive action in Japan's foreign economic policy more broadly. In international monetary policy, in the 1985 Plaza Agreement the government overrode the objections of exporters and decades of implicit support for a weak yen to support a radical increase in the value of the yen.[61] Turning to trade, while Japan's stance in negotiations has on many occasions ruffled feathers, it is clear that the state has been able to suppress even important domestic interests in extreme cases, when larger questions of national interest were at stake. Examples include the ultimate decision to tariffize rice imports in order to complete the

Uruguay Round, and the government's ability to compromise over joint design and building of the FS-X fighter-bomber once it became clear that the U.S.-Japan alliance might be jeopardized.

INSTITUTIONAL CHANGE IN JAPAN

The logic of the second-image-reversed argument is that such a situation is bound to change. The question is how. Japan is being forced to confront numerous unfamiliar challenges in the post–cold war world, some of them the result of the end of the cold war, and others the result of Japan's increasingly global economic scope. These include:

1. *The long-term prospect of a diminishing U.S. military presence in Japan.* While the 1997 Status of Forces Agreement (SOFA) revision and establishment of new defense guidelines have confirmed a continuing relationship based on the Security Treaty, the end of the cold war and the eventual likelihood of Korean reunification mean that the rationale for a permanent troop presence is declining. This means that Japan must consider the possibility that it may at some point need to ensure its security through its own efforts, a looser alliance with the United States, some sort of regional security arrangement, or a combination of all three.

2. *The economic rise of China.*[62] China presents a special challenge for Japan for several reasons. One is the long-term possibility that a stronger China might also seek to be a hegemonic China, perhaps someday threatening Japan's autonomy of action. Second, Japanese business has been very interested in China's markets and productive capacities, and the Japanese government has generally taken a more conciliatory stance than the United States. Thus, not only are there potential long-term tradeoffs in terms of Japan's own interests with regard to China, but Japanese officials must also worry about antagonizing the United States, their most likely ally should China become belligerent.

3. *The postwar economic rise of Japan.* Despite economic stagnation since the early 1990s, by virtue of its immense wealth and reserves Japan is positioned to be a major player in many international organizations, and to be courted by individual states as well. At the same time that it has potentially greater capabilities, its far-flung commercial interests offer it greater incentive to get involved in shaping the international system.

4. *Japan's role as an economic leader in Asia.* In terms of aid, investment, private and official lending, and trade, Japan has had the largest role of any in-

dustrialized state in the regional economy of East and Southeast Asia. It has not, however, taken on an explicit role as hegemon or leader.[63] The Asian Financial Crisis thus challenged Japan not only to do something in the short term, but also to establish a more long-term framework for leadership.

In each case, Japan is confronted with new opportunities and new vulnerabilities, but the existing policymaking system is ill-equipped to handle them. Thus, over time, we should expect to see key changes in that system, whether in response to policy failures or in anticipation of such failures. In particular, we should see better coordination of the various areas of foreign policy (particularly vis-à-vis the potentially delicate relations with China and the United States), and development of intelligence and military capabilities that might now appear to be redundant with U.S.-provided services.[64] While there does appear to be some movement in those directions, there is no guarantee that they will be in place if and when they are actually needed.

Even in the economic area, where Japan has shown impressive responsiveness to the Asian Financial Crisis—essentially taking on part of the function of lender of last resort—it has been hard put to establish the institutions required for long-term leadership, as seen in the failure of the 1997 AMF proposal. Debates about the internationalization of the yen remain mired in the internal politics of the Ministry of Finance,[65] and Japan's inability to serve as a market for distressed regional exporters has weakened its leadership capabilities despite its extension of swap lines throughout Asia and its immense regional aid program. If Japan is to become an Asian power, it will need to further transform these institutions.

There have been a number of efforts to make changes over the last couple of decades, although so far they have had only limited impact. One of the first of these was Prime Minister Ohira's establishment of the Study Group on Comprehensive National Security in the late 1970s, which sought primarily to coordinate foreign aid and investment policies to favor development of strong relations with key suppliers of raw materials.[66] The effort was well-thought-out, and it had the backing of a number of influential politicians; but in the end it had little effect on overall Japanese foreign policy making, at least partly because the Prime Minister's Office was unable to impose control over line ministries.

In the early 1980s, the hawkish Prime Minister Nakasone tried to transform the Japanese foreign policy establishment in two ways. One was his determined effort to promote the military, albeit within the framework of the Security Treaty. This effort was most clearly symbolized by his defiance of the "1 percent barrier" in 1987, and his decision to allow the export of "dual-use" technology in order to promote joint weapons development with the United States.[67] Japan's increasing economic strength, pressures for burden-sharing, and the presence of intermediate-range nuclear missiles in the Soviet Far East allowed these institutional taboos to be lifted. Once violated, spending limits lost their almost mystical significance. Nakasone also sought more generally to strengthen the office of the Prime Minister. He made aggressive use of advisory councils in a variety of issue areas to try to circumvent territorially minded bureaucrats and parliamentary inertia. He also sought to improve his coordinative powers over foreign (and, to a lesser extent, other) policy through a set of senior bureaucrats who would work in the Prime Minister's Office and report directly to him.[68]

ACCUMULATING INCREMENTAL CHANGES

Few would argue that these efforts were very successful, but over time, even such incremental changes can become important. In analyzing trends in military capability, Berger concedes that "despite considerable resistance from the media and the opposing parties, the LDP and its bureaucratic allies succeeded in achieving important changes in Japanese security policy."[69] However, he goes on to minimize the importance of those changes by pointing out that they were incremental, and stayed within the Yoshida Doctrine consensus. But that is precisely my point: a "process of low-key, graduated steps and the reinterpretation of policy"[70] is the standard way in which institutions and policies change. Eventually, small quantitative changes can become large or qualitative changes (or set the stage for such changes) as both organizational capabilities and public acceptance ratchet upwards. Although the force of inertia has so far been powerful enough to limit its effects, the second-image reversed dynamic is increasingly noticeable in Japanese policymaking circles. Here I address two examples of accumulating incremental changes, and three efforts at qualitative change in Japan's policy institutions.

To start with incremental changes, since the beginning of the 1980s there have been slow but steady moves to improve the state's intelligence apparatus—an essential part of strategic planning and action. These included the establishment of a security policy group in the MOFA Secretariat in 1980, followed by its upgrade to the Security Policy Office in the Bureau of Information and Research. Since MOFA's 1993 reorganization, intelligence and analysis functions have been promoted to a bureau (the largest subdivision in Japanese ministries).[71] In January 1997, the new Defense Intelligence Headquarters brought together the previously separate intelligence analysis groups from the Land, Air, and Maritime Self-Defense Forces, as well as those attached to the Defense Agency itself and the Joint Staff Council.[72] As yet, the DIH has increased neither manpower nor intelligence gathering capabilities, but it does offer the institutional grounding should the state decide to do so. Moreover, the FY 1999 defense budget for the first time included funds to develop a "multi-purpose" satellite to provide important regional security information.[73] Launch is set for FY 2002.

Beyond the move toward a more autonomous intelligence capability, a variety of other procurement debates have raised questions about the purely defensive nature of the Self-Defense Forces. In recent years, the Diet has authorized the purchase of a landing craft, tanker aircraft, and even a destroyer that could be retrofitted to act as an carrier for short take-off/vertical landing airplanes.[74] Japanese policymakers have approved participation in joint research with the United States on theater missile defense, and the implications of eventual deployment are under debate.[75] (Theater missile defense would presumably be as effective against Chinese missiles as against North Korean ones.) Each of these decisions, though of little strategic importance at the moment, breaks a former taboo, and potentially prepares the Japanese military for power projection and perhaps even autonomous defense. Roles and missions are also changing, as seen especially in the 1997 Guidelines revision, which raises the likelihood of Japanese forces being drawn into a regional conflict.

These changes in policy are important, because they lay the groundwork for new ways in which Japan can address international threats. Certainly, they have occurred within the confines of the U.S.-Japan security alliance. But in meaningful ways, they constitute a hedge against future risks. If the alliance weakens, for example, Japan will need to be prepared to expand its warfighting, intelligence, and crisis-management capabilities. The weapons and defense systems now being procured under the aegis of cooperation with the United States will contribute to the former goal. Increased practical experience for SDF troops in joint operations with the United States, South Korea, and Australia have similarly served to improve their battle readiness, and exposure to actual foreign combat (even in limited doses) in the form of peacekeeping will do the same if it is ever permitted.[76] Moreover, these accumulated changes in capabilities and activities are likely to change public acceptance of what is acceptable, as has already occurred in considerable measure over the postwar period.[77]

QUALITATIVE CHANGES

There have also been important qualitative changes in Japanese policy institutions. The most striking so far has been the movement toward actually allowing SDF troops to carry out overseas operations. The first stroke was the legal finding and subsequent law in 1992 that allowed Japanese troops to participate in UN peacekeeping operations. These decisions were highly controversial in Japan, and a similar bill had already failed the year before.[78] Despite strong antimilitary sentiment, however, both public opinion and leaders of the pacifist Komeito (the swing vote in the Upper House) were persuaded that the changing international situation—particularly the need for Japan to act as a leader in the Cambodian settlement—left little choice. Many analysts had long felt that the constitution prevented overseas dispatch of troops; the PKO Law represents a partial lifting of that restraint.

The conservative coalition government that formed in December 1998 actually accelerated the discourse toward greater use of SDF forces abroad. The coalition's junior partner even tried to force the issue of allowing the SDF into potential combat situations. Also, there were reports in February 1999 that policymakers were seriously considering the legality of preemptive strikes to head off missile attacks (presumably from North Korea).[79] The passage of the PKO Law and related legal changes despite nationwide ambivalence and considerable outright opposition demonstrate the ability of the changing international situation to force changes in long-standing institutions. Nonetheless, those institutions continue to exert a powerful inertial influence on foreign policy outcomes—one would be hard-pressed to describe major changes in the ways in which Japan has behaved toward its neighbors or the United States.

Looking at Japanese government institutions more broadly, the administrative reform activities of 1996–2001 may in the long run have significant effects on the ability of the political leadership to coordinate policies—both foreign and otherwise—in a unified manner. These reforms most famously include a reduction in the number of ministries, but more importantly include an expanded role for politicians within ministries and an expansion of the size of the Cabinet Office (formerly the Prime Minister's Office) to improve centralized policy coordination. Administrative reform and government restructuring have not been primarily focused on foreign policy needs; rather, they seek to address Japan's economic failures of the 1990s and politicians' frustration with their inability to control the bureaucracy. Nonetheless, if the reforms are successful, they will improve political control and coordination over key levers of foreign economic policy. This would, for example, make it less likely that specific sectors would have effective veto power over broad trade agreements, as occurred with agriculture in the 1998 APEC Early Voluntary Sectoral Liberalization negotiations. We should probably be skeptical of the likely effectiveness of such reforms, but they do represent a conscious attempt to make the Japanese government more effective in the face of global political-economic change.

The most dramatic potential qualitative change would be constitutional revision. Some of the first serious calls since the late 1950s for revision of Article 9 and other restraints on Japan being a "normal" nation began after the passage of the PKO Law.[80] So far, such calls have been unsuccessful, but the debate has been heating up. By 1999, leaders of three of Japan's largest political parties, including the two largest (the Liberal Democratic Party and the Democratic Party) were on record as favoring constitutional revision—particularly Article 9—and in May 2001 Japan's new prime minister, Junichiro Koizumi, explicitly called for revising Article 9 and for moving toward a more presidential system. Most important, for the first time since the current constitution was approved in

1946, the Diet has formed a combined Upper and Lower House Constitution Research Committee, which is explicitly charged with proposing revisions to the existing constitution; despite apparent popular support of Article 9, its revision remains one of the committee's main focuses.[81]

Most of the current debate over revising or eliminating Article 9 can be split into two (overlapping) streams. One of these argues that Japan must be better able to fulfill its "international responsibilities"—for example, by being able to participate in the peace maintenance functions of UN peacekeeping operations rather than just providing logistical or engineering contributions. The international contribution perspective is exemplified by Nobuyuki Hanashi, head of the Liberal Democratic Party Constitution Research Committee, who has stated that, "Article 51 of the United Nations Charter recognizes the right of collective self-defense for member countries. It is self-evident that revision of Article 9, paragraph 2 [of the Constitution] is necessary."[82] The other stream advocates greater defense autonomy for Japan, albeit often obliquely. For example, Democratic Party leader Hatoyama Yukio is on record as advocating both constitutional revision and a pull-out of U.S. forces from Japan. While he argues that the alliance will remain effective, and that Japan will not require a major military buildup even in the absence of U.S. bases, the clear implication of his position is greater security autonomy for Japan within a diminished alliance with the United States.

The path of constitutional revision is unclear, although it is certain to be slow and difficult. Nonetheless, a process is in motion for the first time in more than fifty years—and in spite of apparently strong antimilitarist feelings on the part of the population as shown in polling data, many of Japan's most popular politicians have called for revision of Article 9, with no obvious loss in popularity.

TENTATIVE CONCLUSIONS, OR LOOKING TO THE FUTURE

Japan's international stance has been riddled with contradictions in the postwar period. But while many observers have derided that policy as reactive, unassertive, or uncoordinated,[83] it has been remarkably successful in allowing the state and economy to carry on their activities relatively unperturbed by pressures from the outside world. Despite the apparent reactiveness or passivity implied by its position, Japan's position as Asian lynchpin of the U.S. global security system in the cold war world was extremely effective in securing national objectives of nonconfrontation with its neighbors (or its past), access to markets and technology, and stable access to the raw materials without which the country would be helpless.

In looking at likely scenarios for the post–cold war world, Japan is particularly interesting because of the degree to which its postwar foreign policy outside the economic realm has been held in escrow. It was almost uniquely dependent on the United States as a result both of its geographical position in one of the most potentially dangerous neighborhoods of the postwar world and of the historically based suspicions of its neighbors throughout Pacific Asia. With the end of the cold war and the fading of colonial memories,[84] Japan is increasingly open to both new vulnerabilities and new opportunities.

The cold war severely constrained the policy choices of Japan and other U.S. allies in Pacific Asia. Despite major changes in regional conditions, the foreign policy institutions that were built up over those decades have continued to condition post–cold war policies. This is particularly evident in Japan, where traditional areas of diplomacy have mimicked those of its senior partner, while foreign economic policy has generally been free of the constraints of larger foreign policy aims.

The end of the cold war and changes in global economic power have profound implications for all of Pacific Asia, but they are perhaps particularly profound for Japan. While South Korea, for example, still faces the fundamental problems of confrontation with the North and of a geopolitical position where it is surrounded by great powers, its current position is less precarious than at any point in the last hundred or more years. Japan, however, is potentially less defined by its relationship with the United States and has itself developed substantial international interests and capabilities. Nonetheless, it remains ill-prepared to address those changes, as its halting and uncoordinated foreign policy efforts to date demonstrate.

This is fundamentally a problem of inadequate institutions, and many Japanese leaders are aware of that fact. While institutions remain inertial, as is their wont, leaders have tried to grapple with questions of how they should change. Despite the inertia, international pressures are slowly forcing Japan to change its ways of making and implementing policy. The fact that change (or at least serious debate about change) is ongoing in key areas such as military capabilities and constitutional revision even in the face of a decade of economic stagnation is striking in this regard. The prediction of this chapter is that Japan will continue to change in these directions, although many of the pathologies of the present system will surely remain.

The other possibility is that some major cataclysm will force more rapid institutional change, in the way that World War II and the rapid onset of the cold war did in the United States. It is impossible to predict just how institutions will change in the face of crisis, but the above analysis does suggest some of the types of crisis that might lead to drastic change. In general, the crises most likely to force institutional change on Japan are security-related. The termination of its alliance with the United States (whether due to long-run imperial fatigue, the failure of cooperation in a regional conflict, the unification of Korea, or whatever) would likely bring about significant changes in command and control and in rules of engagement for Japan, along with considerable military expansion and perhaps even nuclear weapons development. Similarly, a much more threatening China (evidenced by, for example, an attack on Taiwan, or the use of an expanded navy to blockade Taiwan or enforce disputed territorial claims in the Spratly Islands) might create strong incentives to subordinate economic aims to security aims, to rapidly increase military and intelligence capabilities, and/or to upgrade its alliance with the United States or possibly even to form new ties with South Korea. On the economic side, in the unlikely event that more exclusionary economic blocs in Europe and the Americas were to come to pass, Japan would need to rapidly integrate its various assets in the management of the Asian regional economy, while also building new international institutions.[85]

Institutional changes resulting from threat or crisis are unpredictable, and sometimes dangerous. One hopes for the sake of both Japan and the world that Japan's institutions change rapidly enough to head such a possibility off. The slow pace of change and the long-term institutionalization of inertia allow only guarded optimism, however. In the meantime, Japan's inertial foreign policies should remain generally reassuring to Japan's neighbors on the security side, while slowing regional economic integration. Whether that means a more stable Asia-Pacific remains to be seen.

ENDNOTES

1. Among those authors who emphasize the role of domestic institutions in explaining states' differing responses to similar crises are: G. John, Ikenberry, "Conclusion: An Institutional Approach to American Foreign Policy," in G. John Ikenberry, David A. Lake, and Michael Mastanduno, eds., 1988. *International Organization* (Special Issue: The State and American Foreign Policy Making) 42, no. 1 (Winter 1988): 219–43; Thomas Risse-Kappen, "Public Opinion, Domestic Structure, and Foreign Policy in Liberal Democracies," *World Politics* 43, no. 4 (July 1991): 479–512; Matthew Evangelista, "Domestic Structure and International Change," in Michael Doyle and G. John Ikenberry, eds., *New Thinking in International Relations Theory* (Boulder: Westview Press, 1997), pp. 202–28.

2. For a nice analysis of the failings of neo-realism in helping us to understand Japanese policies, see Eric Heginbotham and Richard J. Samuels, "Mercantile Realism and Japanese Foreign Policy," *International Security* 22, no. 4 (Spring 1998): 171–203. Michael Green concentrates on the dynamic of entrapment vs. abandonment to explain Japanese behavior in its alliance with the United States. See Michael Green, *Arming Japan: Defense Production, Alliance Politics, and the Postwar Search for Autonomy* (New York: Columbia University Press, 1995).

3. The best known prediction of such blocs by a realist or neo-realist author (he has been characterized in both ways) is Robert Gilpin. See Gilpin, *The Political Economy of International Relations* (Princeton: Princeton University Press, 1987).

4. The term is from Heginbotham and Samuels, "Mercantile Realism" and follows on Samuels' 1994 work on "technonationalism." See Richard J. Samuels, *"Rich Nation, Strong Army": National Security and the Technological Transformation of Japan* (Ithaca: Cornell University Press, 1994). Gilpin has also been closely associated with the idea that mercantilism is a realist strategy in international political economy, although his 1987 predictions of regionalization have not proved to be a necessary result of mercantilism (at least so far).

5. Heginbotham and Samuels, "Mercantile Realism," pp. 195, 197.

6. Frances McCall Rosenbluth, "Internationalization and Electoral Politics in Japan," in Robert O. Keohane and Helen V. Milner, eds., *Internationalization and Domestic Politics* (New York: Cambridge University Press, 1996). Richard Katz makes clear the extent to which industrial policy has favored less efficient sectors over the last twenty-five to thirty years. Richard Katz, *Japan, the System that Soured: The Rise and Fall of the Japanese Eocnomic Miracle* (Armonk, NY: M. E. Sharpe, 1998)

7. Milner makes this point as well: "The survival of the state is an important value for decision makers, but most decisions do not directly concern the state's survival." Helen V. Milner, *Interests, Institutions, and Information: Domestic Politics and International Relations* (Princeton: Princeton University Press, 1997).

8. Unlike Legro and Moravcsik (1999), I do not believe that this requires the abandonment of the realist paradigm. Jeffrey Legro and Andrew Moravcsik, "Is Anybody Still a Realist?" *International Security* 24, no. 2 (Fall 1999): 5–55.

9. See, for example, Henry Nau's contribution to this volume.

10. Peter Feaver, "Correspondence: Brother, Can You Spare a Paradigm? (Or Was Anybody Ever a Realist?)." *International Security* 25, no. 1 (Summer 2000): 165–69, at p. 166. Italics in the original.

11. Douglass North, *Institutions, Institutional Change and Economic Performance* (New York: Cambridge University Press, 1990), p. 3.

12. Ibid., chs. 5–6. In his discussion of informal institutions on p. 40, North actually offers three types: "(1) extensions, elaborations, and modifications of formal rules, (2) socially sanctioned norms of behavior, and (3) internally enforced standards of conduct." In this essay, I will stick only with (1), since (2) and (3) head much more deeply into culture than I wish to go. In this regard, my focus differs from authors such as Berger and Katzenstein and Okawara, who approach Japanese security policy from the perspective of norms and culture. See Thomas U. Berger, *Cultures of Antimilitarism: National Security in Germany and Japan* (Baltimore: The Johns Hopkins University Press, 1998); Peter J. Katzenstein and Nobuo Okawara, *Japan's National Security: Structures, Norms and Policy Responses in a Changing World* (Ithaca, NY: East Asia Program, Cornell University, 1993).

13. North, *Institutions, Institutional Change*, p. 5.

14. The U.S.-imposed post-war Japanese Constitution has become known as the "Peace Constitution" because of Article 9, which reads: "Aspiring sincerely to an international peace based on justice and order, the Japanese people forever renounce war as a sovereign right of the nation and the threat or use of force as means of settling international disputes.

"In order to accomplish the aim of the preceding paragraph, land, sea, and air forces, as well as other war potential, will never be maintained. The right of belligerency of the state will not be recognized."

While this statement appears unambiguous, the Japanese version offers slightly more ambiguity, as McNelly explains. In any event, the official Japanese interpretation has changed considerably over time. See Theodore McNelly, *The Origins of Japan's Democratic Constitution* (Lanham, MD: University Press of America, 2000), pp. 20–21.

15. North, *Institutions, Institutional Change*, chs. 9–11.

16. The best way to determine whether domestic structures are shaping outcomes is comparatively. We can ask, as do Ikenberry and Henning, whether different states with similar interests but different institutions deal with similar crises in the same way. We can also try to compare whether different issue areas (but with similar interest cleavages) within the *same* country are treated differently by the state. See G. John Ikenberry, *Reasons of State: Oil Politics and the Capacities of American Government* (Ithaca: Cornell University Press, 1988); C. Randall, Henning, *Currencies and Politics in the United States, Germany, and Japan* (Washington, DC: Institute for International Economics).

17. Risse-Kappen "Public Opinion, Domestic Structure," Milner *Interests, Institutions*. See also Evangelista "Domestic Structure."

18. Peter Gourevitch, *Politics in Hard Times: Comparative Responses to International Economic Crises* (Ithaca: Cornell University Press, 1986); Yoshiko Kojo, "Domestic Sources of International Payments Adjustment: Japan's Policy Choices in the Postwar Period" (Unpublished Ph.D dissertation, Princeton University, 1993) applies the approach to Japanese exchange rate policy from the late 1960s to the mid-1980s.

19. This is the main approach taken in Ikenberry, Lake, and Mastanduno, eds. See particularly the introductory and concluding essays. Milner, *Interests, Institutions*, and Ronald Rogowski, "Institutions as Constraints on Strategic Choice," in David Lake and Robert Powell, eds., *Strategic Choice and International Relations* (Princeton: Princeton University Press, 1999), pp. 115–136 provide more formalized discussions of institutional impacts. Following the distinctions of Peter A. Hall and Rosemary C.R. Taylor, "Political Science and the Three New Institutionalisms." *Political Studies* 44, no. 5 (December 1996): 936–957. (1996), my own take on this a "historical institutionalist" analysis rather than a "rational-choice institutionalist" or "cultural institutionalist" one.

20. The contributors to Peter J. Katzenstein, ed., *Between Power and Plenty: Foreign Economic Policies of Advanced Industrialized States* (Madison: University of Wisconsin Press, 1978), for example, tend to follow more of a statist perspective, often suggesting that greater state autonomy leads to more coherent (implying better) foreign economic policies.

21. Peter Gourevitch gets credit for the name, if not the approach itself in his "The Second Image Reversed: The International Sources of Domestic Politics" *International Organization* 32, no. 4 (Autumn 1978): 881–912. A more recent collection of papers in this vein is Keohane and Milner, *Internationalization and Domestic Politics*—see especially the first three essays, by Milner and Keohane, Frieden and Rogowski, and Garrett and Lange.

22. In addition to Gourevitch, "Second Image," see particularly Alexander Gerschenkron, "Economic Backwardness in Historical Perspective," in *Economic Backwardness in Historical Perspective: A Book of Essays* (Cambridge: Harvard University Press, [1952] 1962), pp. 5–30, and Immanuel Wallerstein *The Modern World System* (New York: The Academic Press, 1974). Robert Wade, *Governing the Market: Economic Theory and the Role of Government in East Asian Industrialization* (Princeton: Princeton University Press, 1990) uses the logic of late development to explain East Asian economic development policies and the types of government structures that carry them out, while Stephan Haggard, *Developing Nations and the Politics of Global Integration* (Washington, DC: Brookings Institution, 1995) turns to economic crises to explain developing countries' moves toward economic openness in the 1980s and 1990s.

23. Charles E. Neu, "The Rise of the National Security Bureaucracy," In Louis Galambos, ed., *The New American State: Bureaucracies and Policies since World War II*. Baltimore: Johns Hopkins University Press, 1987), pp. 85–108 provides a good overview of these changes.

24. Berger *Cultures of Antimilitarism* and Peter J. Katzenstein *Cultural Norms and National Security: Police and Military in Postwar Japan* (Ithaca: Cornell University Press, 1996). For Berger, the "culture of antimilitarism" consists of rejection of the use of force as a means of solving international conflicts, an insistence on tight civilian control over the military, and a particularly powerful aversion to nuclear weapons.

25. To be fair, while these writers would agree that the ultimate check on Japanese state action comes through the electoral process, Katzenstein in particular also points to ways in which cultural norms are reflected in state institutions and structures. Nevertheless, his work concentrates on cultural constraints on security policy.

26. See Green *Arming Japan* on autonomous weapons development and production.

27. This has been particularly true in Japan's relations with China. See Katsumi Sohma "The Process of Foreign Policymaking in Japan: The Case of Its Relations with China" (Unpublished Ph.D dissertation, Boston University, 1999).

28. Recently, Japanese forces did participate in a major landing exercise for the first time since the war. The mock landing in Hokkaido in July 1998 was justified as being practice for the retaking of Japanese territory occupied by an enemy. Nonetheless, it may be a signficant first step away from the longstanding taboo. For more on the landing, "Japan: GSDF Uses Amphibious Ship for Hokkaido Landing Drills," *Tokyo Kyodo*, July 2, 1998. Heginbotham and Samuels, "Mercantile Realism," p. 183, also mention the new landing craft (the Osumi), which can carry a helicopter landing pad in addition to troops and ground weapons.

29. See, for example, J.W.M. Chapman, R. Drifte, and I.T.M. Gow, *Japan's Quest for Comprehensive Security: Defence, Diplomacy, Dependence* (New York: St. Martin's Press, 1982) and Dennis T. Yasutomo, "The Politicization of Japan's 'Post-Cold War' Multilateral Diplomacy," In Gerald L. Curtis, ed., *Japan's Foreign Policy after the Cold War: Coping with Change* (Armonk, NY: M.E. Sharpe, 1986), pp. 323–346.

30. On the FS-X, see Samuels, *"Rich Nation, Strong Army,"* pp. 231–244 and Green, *Arming Japan*, chs. 5–6. On Okinawa reversion, see I. M. Destler, Haruhiro Fukui,

and Hideo Sato, *The Textile Wrangle: Conflict in Japanese-American Relations, 1969–1971* (Ithaca: Cornell University Press, 1979).

31. Robert S. Ross, "China II: Beijing as a Conservative Power." *Foreign Affairs* 76, no. 2 (March/April 1997): 33–44.

32. The standard text in English on the Yoshida Doctrine is John W. Dower, *Empire and Aftermath: Yoshida Shigeru and the Japanese Experience, 1878–1954* (Cambridge: Harvard University Press, 1979). Berger, *Cultures of Antimilitarism* ch. 2, clearly lays out the ways in which confrontations and compromises helped to establish it as the dominant approach to Japan's strategic situation.

33. All we have to go on are official Cabinet interpretations, since the Supreme Court has always managed to avoid comment on the constitutionality of either the existence or activities of the SDF. See James Auer, "Article Nine: Renunciation of War," in Percy Luney and Kazuyuki Takahashi, eds., *Japanese Constitutional Law* (Tokyo: University of Tokyo Press, 1993), pp. 69–86; Shigeru Kozai, "UN Peace-Keeping and Japan: Problems and Prospects," in Nisuke Ando, ed., *Japan and International Law: Past, Present and Future* (The Hague: Kluwer Law International, 1999), pp. 29–42. In 1958, Prime Minister Kishi actually claimed that possession of nuclear weapons would not violate the constitution, but this was never an official interpretation.

34. Paragraph V.2. The Guidelines revision debate reopened the debate over the concepts of "areas surrounding Japan" and "Far East" in the Japanese Diet, with the government arguing that these are not specific geographical spaces. Sasaki Yoshitaka, "*Reisengo anpo o meguru shissei*" (Misgovernment Surrounding the Post-Cold War Security Alliance), *Sekai* (October 1998): 26–29.

35. The Three Non-Nuclear Principles (no development, no possession, no use of nuclear weapons) were announced by Prime Minister Sato Eisaku. Prime Minister Miki Takeo announced the 1 percent ceiling (maximum military spending of 1 percent of GDP) in 1976 as a way of blunting opposition accusations of rearmament. Both of these principles have been violated to some extent—it is generally accepted that some U.S. naval ships docking in Japan during the cold war carried nuclear weapons, and the 1 percent rule (officially breached in 1987) has been met by accounting for some expenditures, such as military pensions, in separate line-items. See Susan J. Pharr, "Japan's Defensive Foreign Policy and the Politics of Burden Sharing," in Gerald L. Curtis, ed., *Japan's Foreign Policy after the Cold War: Coping with Change* (Armonk, NY: M.E. Sharpe, 1993), pp. 235–62, or Glen D. Hook, *Militarization and Demilitarization in Contemporary Japan* (New York: Routledge Press, 1995), ch. 3, for some of the history.

36. Berger, *Cultures of Antimilitarism*.

37. Green, *Arming Japan*, ch. 1; Katzenstein and Okawara, *Japan's National Security*, pp. 172–187.

38. On Suzuki's pledge, see Katzenstein and Okawara, ibid., pp. 179–180. Hook, *Militarization and Demilitarization*, pp. 88–98, provides a good summary of the other points mentioned.

39. By 1995, Japan's defense spending was the second highest in the world, although its actual capabilities are considerably less. A late 1980s U.S. Department of Defense study placed Japanese capabilities at the level of a middling NATO state.

Katzenstein and Okawara, *Japan's National Security*, p. 194. For statistics on its spending and force posture relative to other Asian states, see Anthony H. Cordesman, The Asian Military Balance: An Analytic Overview, Center for Strategic and International Studies, February 26, 2000. http://www.csis.org/burke/mb/index.htm#asian.

40. Chalmers Johnson, *MITI and the Japanese Miracle: The Growth of Industrial Policy, 1925–1975* (Stanford: Stanford University Press, 1982), ch. 2. METI was known as MITI (Ministry of International Trade and Industry) until a ministerial reshuffling in January 2001.

41. T. L. Pempel, "The Unbundling of 'Japan, Inc.': The Changing Dynamics of Japanese Policy Formation," in Kenneth B. Pyle, ed., *The Trade Crisis: How Will Japan Respond?* Seattle: Society for Japanese Studies, 1987), pp. 117–152 is a particularly good discussion of the "unbundling of 'Japan, Inc'"—in other words, the fragmentation of foreign economic policy making along the fault-lines of the various ministries. See also Kent E. Calder, "Japanese Foreign Economic Policy Formation: Explaining the Reactive State," *World Politics* 40, no. 4 (July 1988): 517–541; C. S. Ahn, "Interministry Coordination in Japan's Foreign Policy Making," *Pacific Affairs* 71, no. 1 (Spring 1998): 41–60.

42. Robert M. Orr, *The Emergence of Japan's Foreign Aid Power* (New York: Columbia University Press, 1990). Yanagihara and Emig (1991) take a different view, that "MOFA is arguably the most important among the four ministries in setting the tone and direction of aid policy." Toru Yanagihara and Anne Emig, "An Overview of Japan's Aid," in Shafiqul Islam, ed., *Yen for Development: Japanese Foreign Aid & the Politics of Burden-Sharing* (New York: Council on Foreign Relations 1991), pp. 37–69, at p. 55.

43. Frank J. Schwartz, *Advice and Consent: The Politics of Consultation in Japan* (New York: Cambridge University Press, 1998), p. 108.

44. On Japan's response to the Persian Gulf War, see Takashi Inoguchi, "Japan's Response to the Gulf Crisis: An Analytic Overview," *Journal of Japanese Studies* 17, no. 2 (Summer 1991): 257–74 .and Kenichi Ito, "The Japanese State of Mind: Deliberations on the Gulf Crisis," *Journal of Japanese Studies* 17, no. 2 (Summer 1991): 275–90.

45. For a litany of such complaints, see Clyde V. Prestowitz, *Trading Places: How We Allowed Japan to Take the Lead* (New York: Basic Books, 1988). Another example of U.S. frustration with trade talks can be found in American Chamber of Commerce in Japan, *Making Trade Talks Work: Lessons from Recent History* (Tokyo: The Chamber, 1997), which criticizes the degree to which these hard-fought agreements are implemented by the Japanese side. Perhaps the most complex and difficult to coordinate of all U.S.-Japanese economic negotiations was the two-year, multisector Structural Impediments Initiative. For details, see Leonard Schoppa, *Bargaining with Japan: What American Pressure Can and Cannot Do* (New York: Columbia University Press, 1997).

46. Sohma, "The Process of Foreign Policymaking in Japan"; Saori Katada, "Why Did Japan Suspend Foreign Aid to China? Japan's Foreign Aid Decision-Making and Sources of Aid Sanction," *Social Science Japan Journal* 4, no. 1 (April 2001): 39–58; Leonard Schoppa, *Education Reform in Japan: A Case of Immobilist Politics* (New York: Routledge Press, 1991).

47. Michael Green and Benjamin Self, "Japan's Changing China Policy: From Commercial Liberalism to Reluctant Realism," *Survival* 38, no. 2 (Summer 1996): 35–58.

48. Katada, "Why Did Japan Suspend Foreign Aid to China?"

49. Dennis T. Yasutomo, *The Manner of Giving: Strategic Aid and Japanese Foreign Policy* (Lexington, MA: D.C. Heath); Yanagihara and Emig, "An Overview of Japan's Aid."

50. Orr, *Emergence of Japan's Foreign Aid Power*; Yasutomo, *The Manner of Giving*.

51. See, for example, Stephan Haggard, *The Political Economy of the Asian Financial Crisis* (Washington, DC: Institute for International Economics, 2000); Morris Goldstein, *The Asian Financial Crisis: Causes, Cures, and Systemic Implications* (Washington, DC: Institute for International Economics, 1998).

52. I am aware that this is not the consensus view. For a contrary interpretation, see "Zen and the Art of Demand: Michiyo Nakamoto and Gillian Tett Explain Why Japan Has Been Slow to Respond to Crises in Asia and at Home," *Financial Times*, March 9, 1998, p. 19.

53. See, for example, "Japan Comes to Jakarta's Aid," *Financial Times*, June 19, 1998, p. 7.

54. Information on the New Miyazawa Plan can be found on the Ministry of Finance webpage, at http://www.mof.go.jp/english/if/kousou.htm. Some of the money appears to be double-counting, and not all was disbursed immediately. Nonetheless, it constitutes a substantial official contribution, and is commensurate in size with the Capital Recycling program of the late 1980s. See also Shûhei Kishimoto, "Shin Miyazawa kôsô no shimei to Ajia tsûka kikin" (The Mission of the New Miyazawa Plan and the Asian Monetary Fund), *Fainansu* (May 1999): 31–48.

55. The origins and persistence of Japan's macroeconomic problems are addressed in William W. Grimes, *Unmaking the Japanese Miracle: Macroeconomic Politics, 1985–2000* (Ithaca: Cornell University Press, 2001) and Katz, *Japan: The System That Soured.*

56. For varying perspectives on Asia's post–Cold War prospects, see Amitav Acharya, "Ideas, Identity and Institution-Building: From the ASEAN Way to the Asia-Pacific Way," *Pacific Review* 10, no. 3 (1997); Richard Betts, "Wealth, Power, and Instability: East Asia and the United States after the Cold War," *International Security* 18, no. 4 (Winter 1993/94); Thomas Christensen, "China, the U.S.-Japan and the Security Dilemma in East Asia," *International Security* 23, no. 4 (Spring 1999): 49–80; Aaron Friedberg, "Ripe for Rivalry: Prospects for Peace in a Multipolar Asia," *International Security* 18, no. 3 (Winter 1993/94); Yoichi Funabashi, *Nihon senryaku sengen: Shibirian taikoku o mezashite* (Civilian Manifesto) (Tokyo: Kodansha, 1991); Yoshio Katayama, "Nichibei dômei no kôekisei to Nihon no yakuwari: Nihon wa 'ijô na kuni' ka?" (The Japan-U.S. Alliance as a Public Good and Japan's Role: Is Japan an "Abnormal Country?"), *Shin Bôeironshû* 24, no. 2 (September 1996): 85–98.

57. Yasutomo, "Politicization of Japan's 'Post–Cold War' Multilateral Diplomacy," argues that much of Japan's foreign policy strategy in recent years has focused on strengthening its role in multilateral institutions. See also Reinhard Drifte, *Japan's Foreign Policy for the 21st Century: From Economic Superpower to What Power?* (New York: St. Martin's Press 1998), pp. 133–149.

58. Ahn, "Interministry Coordination," p. 44.

59. This was, of course, the rationale for the 1997 revision of the Guidelines for U.S.-Japanese Defense Cooperation. For a good summary of the issues, see Council on Foreign Relations, *The Tests of War and the Strains of Peace: The U.S.-Japan Security Relationship*. (New York: The Council, 1998).

60. The economic picture tends to support the "mercantile realist" interpretation of Heginbotham and Samuels, "Mercantile Realism."

61. See Funabashi, *Managing the Dollar*; Paul A. Volcker and Toyoo Gyohten, *Changing Fortunes: The World's Money and the Threat to American Leadership* (New York: Times Books, 1992), chs. 8–9; Grimes, *Unmaking the Japanese Miracle*, ch. 4.

62. Green and Self, "Japan's Changing China Policy."

63. Yoichi Funabashi, *Asia Pacific Fusion: Japan's Role in APEC* (Washington, DC: Institute for International Economics, 1995); William W. Grimes, "Internationalization of the Yen and the New Politics of Monetary Insulation," in Jonathan Kirshner, ed., *Governing Money: Ambiguous Economics, Ubiquitous Politics* (under review).

64. This would in some ways mirror the reorganization that took place in the United States following the Second World War, when temporary wartime institutions were reestablished in the form of the CIA, the NSC, etc. Neu, "Rise of the National Security Bureaucracy."

65. Willliam W. Grimes, "Internationalization of the Yen and the Ironies of Insulation," paper presented at "Japan Changes: The New Political Economy of Structural Adjustment and Globalization," University of California, San Diego, Graduate School of International Relations and Pacific Studies, March 3, 2001.

66. For more on this concept, see Chapman, et al., *Japan's Quest*; and Yasutomo, *The Manner of Giving*, ch. 2.

67. On the breaking of the 1 percent barrier, see Katzenstein and Okawara, *Japan's National Security*, pp. 155–160. On dual-use technology, see Peter J. Katzenstein, *Cultural Norms and National Security: Police and Military in Postwar Japan* (Ithaca: Cornell University Press 1996), pp. 138–142. Katzenstein points out that despite the agreement, actual exchange from Japan to the United States was limited.

68. Ahn, "Interministry Coordination," pp. 42–45.

69. Berger, *Cultures of Antimilitarism*, p. 132.

70. Ibid.

71. Katzenstein and Okawara, *Japan's National Security*, p. 26. The 1993 reorganization occurred subsequent to the writing of that book.

72. See, for example, Cameron W. Barr, "Asia Eyes Japan's New Military Intelligence Unit," *Christian Science Monitor*, March 21, 1997, p. 5. The so-called "Armitage Report" maintained a call for improved intelligence capabilities and U.S.-Japanese intelligence sharing. Institute for National Strategic Studies, *The United States and Japan: Advancing Toward a Mature Partnership* (Washington, DC: National Defense University, October 11, 2000). Available at http://www.ndu.edu/ndu/SR_JAPAN.HTM (2000).

73. On the budget announcement, see "Japan Plans Reconnaissance Satellite Launch," *Jane's Defense Weekly*, November 18, 1998, p. 14. Japan has pledged not to militarize space, so in order to have strategic satellite capabilities, it must combine the

strategic functions with commercial or scientific functions in a single multi-purpose satellite.

74. "Briefing: Japan," *Jane's Defense Weekly*, January 24, 2001, pp. 24–25; "Japan: GSDF Uses Amphibious Ship for Hokkaido Landing Drills," *Tokyo Kyodo*, July 2, 1998; Heginbotham and Samuels, "Mercantile Realism," p. 183.

75. "TMD Joint Research Budget Is Formally Requested," *Japan Digest*, November 2, 1998; "Cabinet Rules that TMD Research Won't Violate Military Space Proscription," *Japan Digest*, December 28, 1998, p. 6; "Japan Using North Korean Decoy, Prepares against China," *The Hindu*, January 25, 1999. One author even advanced the paranoid hypothesis that the United States "conspired" with North Korea in order to force the Japanese political world to agree to TMD—see "Intensifying Controversy Concerning TMD Inspired by Launching of Taepodon Missile," *Tokyo Sentaku*, October 1998, pp. 120–123 (FBIS).

76. Giarra (1999) goes so far as to say that "PKO will help to define Japan's international security posture, and become a major determinant of alliance politics and Japanese force structure in the 21st century." Paul Giarra, "Peacekeeping: As Good for the Alliance as It Is for Japan?" *Japan Digest*, February 15, 1999, p. 23. A PKO-driven force structure would have more projection capabilities than a purely defensive structure.

77. Ironically, Berger, *Cultures of Antimilitarism* shows this trend quite effectively. Although he emphasizes the maintenance of Yoshida Doctrine norms, one is equally struck in reading his account at the magnitude of the change in what Japanese society has been willing to accept in terms of the capability and role of the SDF. The same can be said of Katzenstein's argument in *Cultural Norms and National Security*.

78. Drifte, *Japan's Foreign Policy for the 21st Century*, pp. 140–144. To be sure, many opponents of the policy shift feared that it was a first step down a slippery slope, and it certainly makes further incremental changes possible or even likely. That is indeed what my analysis suggests. Just how far down that slope Japan will slide remains to be seen.

79. "LDP Debates Military Strikes Strategy," *Financial Times*, February 26, 1999, p. 4.

80. See especially Ichiro Ozawa, *Blueprint for a New Japan* (New York: Kodansha. 1994).

81. "*Kenpô chôsakai ga hassoku*" (Debut of the Constitution Research Committee), *Asahi Shimbun*, January 21, 2000, p. 2; "*Shûgiin kenpô chôsakai, hatsu no chihô kôdokukai*" (First Regional Hearings for the Constitution Research Committee), *Asahi Shimbun*, April 17, 2001, p. 29.

82. "*Kenpô rongi, nao tesaguri*" (Constitution Debate, Still Groping) *Asahi Shimbun*, May 31, 2000, p. 17.

83. Calder, "Japanese Foreign Economic Policy Formation"; Pempel, "the Unbundling of 'Japan, Inc.' "; Ozawa, *Blueprint for a New Japan*; Chihiro Hosoya, "*Taigai seisaku kettei katei ni okeru Nihon no tokushitsu*" (Characteristics of Japan's Foreign Policy Making Process), in Hosoya Chihiro and Watanuki Joji, eds., *Taigai seisaku kettei katei no Nichibei hikaku* (A Comparison of Japanese and U.S. Foreign Policy Making Processes), (Tokyo: Tokyo University Press, 1977), pp. 1–20.

84. The most important element of this memory is anti-Japanese sentiment in formerly occupied, colonized, or brutalized countries. Heginbotham and Samuels,

"Mercantile Realism," even cite a 1995 poll which found that 69 percent of South Koreans "hate" Japan (p. 180). Despite strong anti-Japanese feelings that are still given vent on a fairly regular basis in China and Korea though, even in those countries cooperation with Japanese interests is no longer automatically seen as collaboration.

85. The efforts to "internationalize" the yen can be seen partly as a preliminary risk-hedging tactic to address that remote possibility. Grimes "Internationalization of the Yen and the Ironies of Insulation"; Grimes "Internationalization of the Yen and the New Politics of Monetary Insulation."

Chapter 12

POWER AND PURPOSE IN PACIFIC EAST ASIA
A Constructivist Interpretation

Thomas U. Berger

If one looks at interstate relations in the East Asian region from a conventional International Relations theory perspective—Neorealism[1] and Neoliberalism[2]—one is bound to be simultaneously intrigued and puzzled. On the one hand some aspects of regional politics appear to bear out, at least on a superficial level, the predictions these mainstream approaches might make. For instance, Neorealist theorists may find comfort in the evidence of a growing rivalry between the United States and the People's Republic of China; whatever the fate of great power competition in the Atlantic region, the potential for hegemonic conflict appears to be alive and well in Asia-Pacific. Likewise Neoliberal institutionalists can note with satisfaction the proliferation of international institutions in the Asian region, most notably in the economic sphere, but—as predicted by the standard Neoliberal model—they increasingly spill over into other areas as well.[3]

On closer examination, however important aspects of interstate relations in the region do not fit the Neoliberal and Neorealist paradigms at all well. For instance, from a Neorealist perspective it is difficult to account for Japan's pronounced unwillingness to pursue a political-military role commensurate with its considerable economic power.[4] Likewise, Neoliberal institutionalists and Neorealists alike should be perturbed by the People's Republic of China's (PRC) readiness to risk a military confrontation with the United States over Taiwan despite the overwhelming preponderance of American maritime and strategic power in the Pacific and despite the damage that such a belligerent policy inflicts on China's international image and the possibilities for international cooperation. Equally perplexing are the severe difficulties that Japan and South Korea have in cooperating militarily, despite their many common economic and security interests.[5] Japan's unwillingness or inability to participate even in a token form in the Gulf War poses a puzzle to both Neoliberal and Neorealist theories since Japan's failure to do so posed a threat to the multilateral institutions upon which it has come to depend.[6]

In short, East Asian regional affairs have been characterized by less great power tension than a classical Neorealist account might suggests.[7] At the same time the potential for conflict and the obstacles to cooperation are greater than what a Neoliberal institutionalist or a more moderate "defensive Realist" might expect, as anyone who has spent time in the region or has discussed security issues with experts form the region soon comes to realize.[8]

This essay argues that the problem with standard accounts of regional relations is that they neglect the way in which the structural, material forces emphasized by both Realism and Neoliberalism are mediated by cultural-ideational factors.[9] The primary source of the tensions that trouble the Asian region today are rooted not in their geo-strategic environment, their level of political economic development, or the character of the international institutions in which they are embedded. Rather they are the products of deep-rooted historically based suspicions and animosities, frustrated nationalism, and distinct conceptions of national identity and their differing understanding of the national mission in international affairs.

This is not to say that such Realist or Neoliberal factors as the balance of power or opportunities for interstate cooperation are irrelevant to the study of region. East Asian governments are keenly sensitive to shifts in the military balance, and are actively engaged in building international institutions in order to improve coordination on issues such as trade and the environment. However, the ways in which Asian nations in the region perceive and respond to these threats and opportunities are strongly conditioned by the manner in which these issues are defined in the context of their domestic political cultures.

In order to explore this dimension of East Asian regional affairs, this essay draws on a third theoretical approach that recently has emerged (or reemerged) in the field of International Relations, the so-called Constructivist school. Constructivism seeks to go beyond the narrow, rational-actor premises of Neorealism and Neoliberalism by problematizing aspects of the international system that traditionally have been largely ignored or taken for granted. In particular Constructivists focus on the ways in which state identity and interests are constructed through social-political processes that are only partially explainable within the rational-actor analytical framework.[10]

The main thesis this essay advances is that the stability of the Asian Pacific region in decades has to be attributed to the emergence of a far-reaching consensus among major countries in the region that economic development should be the overreaching national objective. The reasons for the emergence of this consensus—associated with the rise of what has been called the "East Asian developmental State"[11]—vary from country to country and are closely linked to historically contingent factors. The fact remains that the consensus on growth has become strongly institutionalized in their domestic political systems and has come to serve as the primary basis of governmental legitimacy. Consequently, East Asian nations—with the notable exception of North Korea—have chosen to set aside their traditional political-military rivalries and focus on a more cooperative pattern of relations, at least in the economic sphere.

Unlike Western Europe, however, this decision rested not upon a common sense of identity and (with the important exception of Japan) a profound longing for peace.[12] Asian regional cooperation has been much narrower in character and based on largely instrumental considerations. Consequently, regional cooperation is far more fragile in Asia than in Western Europe. Moreover, there exist various domestic cleavages in the region surrounding issues of national identity (Taiwan, Korea) and historically driven animosities (between the PRC and Japan and between Japan and South Korea) that sharply limit the prospects for cooperation and threatens to destabilize regional security. The recent sharp economic downturn in the region may greatly exacerbate these tensions as it casts into doubt the entire economic and political paradigm on which the existing East Asian order is based. In sum, viewing East Asian affairs through constructivist lenses brings into sharp relief some of the underlying sources of tension in the region and suggests that it may be far more unstable than either Neorealist or Neoliberal analyses might lead us to expect.

On the following pages this essay will outline the main features of the Constructivist approach to international relations and suggest some ways in which it might be applied to the analysis of East Asian regional affairs. The essay then briefly examines the domestic contexts of interstate relations, focusing in particular on the ways in which defense and foreign policy issues are framed in the public debate and linked to national identity and historically based understandings of the international system. Finally the essay concludes with some general reflections on the relative utility of the constructivist approach and the future of the region.

CONSTRUCTIVISM AND REGIONAL RELATIONS

Constructivism, like Realism and Liberalism, is not so much a specific theory per se as a broader theoretical approach to the analysis of politics in general. Many disparate and even contending schools of thought have been associated with constructivism in international relations, including Critical Theory,[13] Post-Modernism,[14] Feminist IR theory,[15] and a less clearly defined, but fast growing school of what can be labeled interpretivists.[16] What these various schools of thought share in common is a view of human behavior, including state actions, as being fundamentally shaped by socially shared understandings of the world, both in terms of how the world is and in terms of the ways it should be.[17] Central to such understandings are actor identity and actor interests.

These understandings—which can be called cultures, mentalités, or discourses—are not simply subjective reflections of an objective, material reality, but rather emerge out of social interaction processes—through socialization, debate, and sometimes coercion. The particular cognitive lenses with which actors are endowed thus mediate the material world, including such features as the balance of military power or opportunities for trade and cooperation. As Alexander Wendt put it, "anarchy is what states make of it."[18] In the interest of theoretical even handedness one can make the same point with reference to conditions of complex interdependence.

From the constructivist perspective it is therefore impossible to analyze political behavior merely by examining the material-structural context in which actors find themselves. It is incumbent upon the social-scientific investigator to enter into the ideational and cultural world of his or her research subjects, seeking to uncover the meanings that they give to their actions and how the ideas and behavior of various actors then interact to produce outcomes. The method used is essentially a Weberian one of interpretation and understanding (*verstehen*).[19]

Three common misconceptions regarding the constructivist approach need to be briefly addressed. The first relates to the impression held by many commentators that constructivism is inherently associated with a progressive view of human affairs, along the lines of the Idealists so excoriated by an earlier generation of international relations scholars such as E. H. Carr.[20] In fact, the ways in which actor identity and interests are constructed can have profoundly illiberal consequences. Nationalism is one such example. Nationalism can be best understood as a particular socially constructed definition of collective identity that emerged in early modern Europe that had a profoundly destructive impact on European and world affairs, fueling interstate conflict, ethnic hatreds, and outright genocide in the first half of the twentieth century.[21] Many of the problems confronting the Asia-Pacific region today are attributable to similar kinds of forces.

A second common assumption holds that constructivism is fundamentally opposed to rational actor models of human behavior. This assumption sets up a false dichotomy between culture and rationality that obscures the extent to which the two are interlinked. Rationality can best be understood as a mode of cognition and standard for action whose application is itself culturally determined. On a certain level all actors at all times are acting rationally, even as they pursue goals that are in large measure determined by the particular roles they have been given in society and within constraints of the culture in which they are embedded.[22] It should be taken as a given that Asian nations are sensitive to shifts in the balance of power and opportunities for cooperation and design their foreign policies accordingly. What goals they chose to pursue and how they assess the risks of their actions, however, is not.

Finally, in a similar vein, it would be a mistake to see constructivism as an approach to international relations that is necessarily at odds with Neorealist and Neoliberal understandings of international relations. From a Constructivist perspective both Neorealism and Neoliberalism are possible ways in which the international system may be structured by actors, and the predictions that either approach makes regarding the future of interstate behavior may prove correct. Constructivism maintains, however, that these responses are neither the inevitable result of the anarchic character of the international system and the distribution of power within it, nor are they the necessary byproduct of the emerging patterns of economic and other forms of interstate interaction that have been institutionalized through the creation of international rules and norms. Rather, these material factors are mediated by the actors' culturally derived cognitive lenses, which determine how the actor interprets these factors and how they chose to respond to them.[23]

Given the variable nature of cultures and collectively held understandings it would be futile to try to define a single, cookie-cutter methodological approach to investigating ideational-cultural structures. Rather, it is possible to speak of a number of common empirical tasks and methodological problems that researchers working within an interpretive framework need to perform. Three in particular will be focused on here: the identification of the relevant realm of discourse; the analysis of the actual contents of these discourses; and finally an exploration of their underlying inner dynamics.

The first task involves identifying those societal beliefs and values that are relevant to the particular set of behaviors or practices that the investigator is trying to explain.[24] In contrast to earlier generations of scholarship, which tended to see culture as discrete and monolithic, contemporary scholars emphasize that groups and individuals participate in a variety of different social contexts,[25] each of which may expose them to quite disparate, even contending, sets of ideas and beliefs about the world.

Constructivists investigating the practices of a given political actor or group of actors thus need to be sensitive to the extent to which those practices emerge out of a interactive process occurring between different subgroups within a given society—each of whom may hold very different conceptions of state identity and state interest—and the extent to which those ideas and behaviors emerge out of communicative processes that transcend the boundaries of the state and may be regional or even global in nature.[26] To put it differently, the Constructivist analyst must first ask, what are the relevant social interactions driving actor behavior?

Second, the analyst must examine the actual contents of the relevant belief systems. How do the actors understand the situationconfronting them? What is their understanding of how the international system works (which necessarily is rooted in their particular interpretation of history)?[27] What do they understand their interests to be? Such cognitive artifacts are not only impossible to measure directly, but often are highly ambiguous and contested in nature.[28] In addition, the putative reasons given for any course of action may not be the real ones, either because of deliberate attempts at deception, because reasons are appended in a post-hoc fashion, or because the actors themselves may be unclear as to their motivations or the reasons for their actions. As a result, any statement analysts make with regard to the link between beliefs and action must itself be treated as a hypothesis and tested in a variety of contexts over time.

Finally, the social scientist must be sensitive to the issue of cultural change and evolution. Some types of belief systems may be highly stable over time and undergo little change. Evidence suggests, however, that many aspects of a belief system evolve constantly in response to internal dynamics within a particular universe of discourse and as a result of interactions with the outside world. In order to avoid falling into the trap of using cultural explanations as a post-hoc, tautological form of explanation,[29] while remaining open to the possibility of change, the analyst must be able to specify why changes in the existing patterns of beliefs occur and trace the process by which such changes take place.

In sum, in order to arrive at an explanation for any particular set of state policies or practices the Constructivist approach requires the investigator to engage in a sustained investigation of the debates surrounding those practices within the community of relevant policymaking actors and to place those debates in the context of the broader societal discourses in domestic and international politics. Such an effort, daunting enough in the context of a single country, obviously is nearly impossible to achieve for an entire region, and would require far more space than allowed for in a single essay. The following is intended simply as a suggestive first stab toward drawing a more comprehensive picture of the way in which constructivist factors influence international relations in contemporary East Asia.

THE FOREIGN POLICY CONSEQUENCES OF THE RISE OF THE EAST ASIAN DEVELOPMENTAL STATE

In surveying the contemporary situation in the East Asian region, it is possible to identify three sets of cultural-ideational factors that appear to be of particular significance for interstate relations. The first is the emergence of a general consensus in the countries in the region giving priority to economic growth and development over the pursuit of political-military power. The second is the power of conflicting nationalism on the Korean peninsula and in the Taiwan Straits. Third and finally there are the diverse and mutually reinforcing fears, prejudices, and historically based animosities among China, Korea and Japan which encourage a sense of military insecurity among them and hamper efforts at cooperation in the military sphere. This section, and the two to follow, explore each of these group of variables in turn.

A single-minded focus on economic growth and development has been one of the dominant characteristics of Asian affairs since the late nineteenth century. Originally, however, economic growth was valued as the necessary complement to military power, rather than as an end in and of itself. After being forced out of their self-imposed isolationist stances in the first part of the nineteenth century, Asian countries, beginning with Meiji Japan, were intent on building a "rich nation, strong army" (*Fukokuky-hei*) in order to avoid being gobbled up by the Western Imperial powers. The fundamental view of international relations, in Japan and elsewhere, remained very much "Realist" in its emphasis on security concerns, and was reinforced by the balance-of-power thinking that dominated Europe at the time.[30]

After World War II, this basically instrumental approach to economic power was gradually displaced by a view of economic development as being of at least equal, or of even greater importance than the development of political-military power. The way in which this point of view developed, however, varied considerably from country to country.

The first nation in which this fundamental shift in thinking took place was Japan. Defeated, disarmed, and occupied by the western powers and the United States, Japan in 1945 was in no position to pursue political-military power. The Imperial elite, and in particular the members of the Japanese military establishment, had been discredited by the disastrous defeat, and the prewar militarist ideology was widely rejected. The United States, including the famous clause—Article 9—in which Japan foreswore the right to use military means to pursue foreign policy objectives, imposed a new constitution on Japan.[31]

Although of foreign origin, Article 9 was embraced by many in Japan, both on the idealistic left, but also by many in the Japanese political mainstream who developed a nearly pathological fear of the military as a potential threat to democracy. After having experienced its own military running amok in the 1930s and 40s, and fearing that right-wing elements in Japanese politics might once again make use of a foreign crisis to overturn the nation's fragile democracy, many Japanese were concerned with finding ways of containing the new, postwar defense establishment.[32]

This underlying fear of the military has remained strong into the present era. For instance, in 1988, when the Iran-Iraq war threatened to cut off the flow of oil from the Persian Gulf, it was the old conservative stalwart Gotoda Masaharu—

former Vice Minister of the Japanese Police Agency, implacable advocate of the death penalty, and one of the chief architects of deregulation of the Japanese economy in the 1980s—who was instrumental in preventing the dispatch of Japanese minesweepers. Likewise, during the Persian Gulf War of 1991–92, the Liberal Democratic Prime Minister of the time (Kaifu Toshiki) refused to allow military personnel to report directly to the cabinet for the first six months after the outbreak of the war for fear that civilian leaders might be "contaminated" by militarist thinking.[33] There are probably few countries in the world today who would deliberately cut themselves off from the advice of their own military experts in the midst of a major national security crisis.

During the 1950s fierce ideological battles were waged over the issue of defense and national security between the left, which advocated a stance of complete, unarmed neutrality, and the right, which was intent on restoring Japan as a great military power.[34] The uneasy compromise that emerged out of these struggles was a minimally armed Japan aligned with the West for the purpose of its own territorial defense, but refusing to take on a broader regional security role. Defense came to be widely viewed as the "third rail" of Japanese politics, and Japan's ruling conservative politicians generally preferred to focus on economic development. If Japan was to be neither the great military power that it had aspired to be in the prewar period, nor to accept the role of an unarmed, neutral "peace nation" advocated by the left during the postwar, than at least it could be a great economic power—a "merchant nation" (*Shonin Kokka*), to use the phrase originally invoked by the conservative Prime Minister Yoshida Shigeru.

Over time this view of Japan's national mission solidified and gained increased legitimacy among both the Japanese public and political elites. In the 1980s the Japanese government codified this view by officially adopting the concept of "Comprehensive Security." National security was no longer seen as merely a matter of defending against military threats, but was now redefined to embrace a broad range of goals, including strengthening U.S.-Japanese relations, fostering diplomatic and economic ties with Japan's Asian neighbors in the Asia-Pacific, ensuring energy security, guaranteeing the supply of food, and contributing to global progress through overseas development assistance.[35]

Underlying this shift in policy was a deeper shift in national identity. In the prewar period Japan had taken pride in its martial heritage, in the tradition of the Samurai and *Bushido*. It was Japan's warrior spirit that distinguished it from other nations and was regarded as the source of its national power. By the early 1980s, however, Japanese commentators and politicians increasingly stressed the nation's economic prowess and the supposedly unique cultural features of the Japanese people, which had made Japan's postwar economic accomplishments possible. So far-reaching was this cognitive transformation that increasingly Japanese intellectuals and policymakers began to deny Japan's martial past altogether. They maintained that Japan differed fundamentally from other parts of the world in being an island nation that had never undergone the successive waves of conquest experienced elsewhere. As a result, even sophisticated and hard-nosed analysts of international affairs such as former Ambassador Okazaki Hisahiko argued that the Japanese people as such were peculiarly unsuited at the game of power politics as practiced by the rest of the world.[36]

In short, the peculiarly modest approach to defense and foreign policy that had been forced upon Japan by the United States and bitterly contested in the 1940s and 50s, by the 1980s had become the basis of a broader philosophy of international relations and was firmly anchored in a new understanding of Japanese national identity. Military weakness and dependency on the United States was not merely tolerated, but had come to be widely viewed as preferable to any of the likely alternatives. As a result, even after the constraints of the cold war fell away, public opinion data suggested that the country Japan most wished to emulate was Switzerland, even though Japan has a population of a 125 million compared to Switzerland's 7 million and the nations' geopolitical circumstances could hardly be more dissimilar.

The shift in the attitudes of other East Asian nations toward national security came at a later date, and has not been accompanied by as far-reaching transformations in their national self-understandings as has been the case in Japan. Nonetheless, substantial changes in attitudes and national priorities are discernible in virtually all of the major East Asian powers and are anchored in the shifting basis of regime legitimacy from ideological purity to economic performance.

South Korea and Taiwan began the cold war as embattled authoritarian regimes ruling over divided nations and confronted with massive security threats posed by their Communist neighbors. Fierce anti-communism combined with equally fierce postcolonial nationalism was the ideological message that South Korean President Synghman Rhee and Taiwanese dictator Chiang Kai-shek sought to propagate. A permanent state of crisis was maintained in both countries (martial law in Taiwan was lifted only in 1987) while all national energies were mobilized in preparation for a widely expected renewal of military hostilities. Not until well into the 1960s did South Korean and Taiwanese leaders abandon hope for a military defeat of their Communist rivals.[37] While fears of Communist attacks had very real foundations, the authoritarian rulers in South Korea and Taiwan to justify the suppression of internal dissent also exploited them.

The domestic and foreign policies of the PRC and North Korea in many respects presented a mirror image of the situation in Taiwan and South Korea. Harsh, dictatorial regimes mobilized their populations for potential conflict by exploiting nationalist longings for reunification and popular fear of foreign invasion.[38] While there were very real differences between the two sides in terms of the ideological basis and the character of their regimes (among other things, the Communist systems in the North and on the Chinese Mainland proved much more destructive of human life and values than their authoritarian counterparts), there were striking similarities between them.

This harshly competitive, militarily oriented approach to international affairs gradually came to an end in the late 1970s and 1980s. In China the key shift came in 1978, after the forces of technocratic reform under Deng Xiaoping decisively defeated those elements in the Chinese political system that sought to perpetuate the Maoist revolutionary legacy. After twenty years of disastrous experiences with "putting politics in command" of the economy,[39] the new leadership was determined to rebuild the nation's economic strength and put an end to the destructive ideological mobilization campaigns that had characterized the Maoist period. Domestically this meant the gradual reintroduction of market mechanisms into the Chinese economy. Internationally it led to an intensification of economic ties with the outside world, as the PRC began to actively pursue trade with the West and to court foreign investment.[40]

The implications for Chinese foreign policy, and for regional affairs in general, were far reaching.[41] Whereas in the past China had frequent confrontational encounters with its neighbors (the PRC is the only country in the world which has deliberately attacked the forces of not one, but both nuclear superpowers—the United States in Korea and the Soviet Union along the Amur-Assuri River), in the 1980s—especially after 1982, it shifted to a far more cooperative stance to international relations.

This does not mean that China's leaders had turned into dewy-eyed idealists. On the contrary, most observers maintain that the PRC continued to view the world through largely Realist lenses.[42] At the same time, however, the Chinese leadership became increasingly technocratic in character, and came to be made up largely of pragmatic economic bureaucrats. For the first time after the changes in the Standing Committee of the Politburo in 1998 the highest level of Chinese government did not include a single member of the Chinese armed forces.[43] With the decline in the strength of Communist ideology, the CCP (Chinese Communist Party) increasingly came to rely for legitimacy on its economic performance and its ability to increase the national living standard. Having declared that "to get rich is glorious," the Chinese leadership's ability to use ideology to mobilize the population militarily has no doubt declined significantly.

In South Korea and Taiwan as well, changes in the political regime have been accompanied by a changing outlook on international relations. During the second half of the 1980s South Korea under Roh Tae Woo and Taiwan under Lee Teng Hui underwent remarkable transitions toward democracy. The reasons for these developments are complex and need not be explored here.[44] What is important to note is that in both countries the shift toward democracy was closely associated with moves toward more conciliatory relations with their neighbors and engagement with potential adversaries through trade and investment.[45] While there remained considerable anxiety in some quarters regarding these moves, they enjoyed strong overall domestic political support.

Although this new emphasis on economic engagement was based on primarily instrumental calculations of national interest, they also contained a strong normative element. The shift toward engagement in South Korea and Taiwan was seen to be intrinsically linked to the liberalization of their domestic political systems. Distrust of Communism remained strong. At the same time there was wide spread suspicion—already long-held by members of the Korean and Taiwanese left—that calls for hard-line policies were tied, directly or indirectly, to conservative efforts to contain, if not roll back, liberal reforms, much in the same way that Japanese liberals suspected that calls for Japan to take on a larger military role could lead to a revival of militarism.

The reasons behind the shift toward increased reliance on economic tools of foreign policy are thus many and complex and vary from country to country. Nonetheless, taken together they had a number of important consequences for the development of interstate relations in the region. East Asian countries after 1978 have become increasingly preoccupied with the pursuit of economic development over and against the classical political military competition and ideological rivalry. Domestic political legitimacy has come to rest increasingly in these countries on their ability to fulfill the expectations of high growth and domestic stability that they have promised, making the diversion of scarce resources to costly foreign policy ventures a risky enterprise.

This development represents a novum in regional affairs that cannot be easily explicable through the reference to standard Realist or Neoliberal theoretical models of the international system. Prior to the spread of the post-1945 Development State model in the region, Asia had been beset by classical balance-of-power rivalries. Before the Second World War East Asia witnessed repeated great power clashes, culminating in the savagery of the Japanese invasion of China and the brutal American-Japanese war in the Pacific. Conflict and strife similarly beset the first few decades after 1945. In addition to the Korean and Vietnamese wars there had been low-intensity conflicts involving Australia, Malaysia, and Indonesia in the 1950s to mid 1960s, the Sino-Soviet confrontation of 1969–1970, the Vietnamese invasion of Laos and Cambodia in 1978, and the subsequent Chinese attack on Vietnam, as well as numerous military crises and savage internal conflicts which often involved some degree of external involvement. Not counting the victims of the wars of colonial independence and such largely internal conflicts as the guerrilla conflicts in Indonesia or Malaysia, in all as many as 5 million people lost their lives as a result of interstate violence, and at least three times—during the Korean war, the Vietnam War, and the Sino-Soviet conflict—serious consideration was given to the use of nuclear weapons.

Since 1978, while tensions have certainly continued to simmer, there has been a remarkable decline in actual armed conflict in the region. This shift is at least in part attributable to the settling of the decolonialization process and the creation of stable domestic political regimes throughout the region. Yet equally as important, however, has been the increased emphasis placed by the major regional powers on economic performance over the development of political military power.

A Neorealist might be inclined to argue that this increased emphasis on economic development was largely a consequence of the predominance of American military power in the region. Countries aligned with the United States such as Japan, Korea, and Taiwan could afford to concentrate on economic development while in effect enjoying a free ride on a security order provided at American expense. The PRC, for its part, chose to accept American hegemony for the time being in order to build up its economy so as to be able to possibly challenge the United States at a later point.

Contrary to the expectations of Neorealist theory, however, this redefinition of the national interest took place despite fundamental, and largely unexpected, shifts in the balance of power, from the bipolar world of the late 1970s through a brief period of apparently increased multipolar fluidity in the late 1980s and early 1990s to the de facto unipolar situation that obtains in the region today. While the United States remained the predominant maritime power in the region, at numerous points American power and commitment appeared to wane and waver. The shift toward giving priority to economic growth, however, continued unabated, regardless of the fluctuations in the distribution of power in the international system.

A Neoliberal institutionalist might argue that the increased emphasis on economic growth was the natural result of the increased sophistication and interdependence of the regions' economies as well as of the proliferation of international institutions that permit increased cooperation. These developments, however, occurred after the shift in actor interests and arguably were a reflection, not a cause, of the fundamental ideational shift taking place in the Asian region.

THE POWER OF NATIONALISM

While certain ideational-cultural developments in the East Asian region have increased stability in the region, others continue to act as considerable, even growing, sources of tension, one of the most readily apparent of which is the clash of nationalism on the Korean peninsula and in the Straits of Taiwan. From the perspective of structural IR theory there is no reason to assume that the North Korean regime should be tempted to risk an attack on the South. The balance of power overwhelmingly favors the United States and South Korea, especially since there is little prospect that China or Russia would come to the aid of the North in the event of its making the first aggressive move. The chances of a military victory appear dim at best, and the risk of an escalation of hostilities that could destroy the regime in the North would seem large.[46]

From a Neoliberal point of view, in the long-term cooperation with the South could offer considerable economic rewards. With careful management of its external ties, the North Korean regime might well manage to sustain itself for decades to come.[47] Yet, the North continues to engage in highly provocative and risky actions that appear to be motivated by a deep-seated commitment to achieving national unity on its own terms, whatever the costs.[48]

In the case of Taiwan and China we are confronted with a case of two apparently irreconcilable nationalisms which, if anything, are growing in strength and virulence with each passing year. Although the Nationalist Kuomintang (KMT) government of Taiwan continues to maintain that Taiwan is an integral part of the Mainland, for the majority of the Taiwanese population unification with the motherland is at best a long-term objective of relatively low priority, and at worst an immediate threat to the nation's hard-earned liberty and prosperity. Moreover, a substantial portion of the Taiwanese population supports an outright break with the country's historical ties with China and favors the cause of Taiwanese independence.

For more than forty years the Taiwanese population were denied democracy and civil liberties because the KMT argued that it represented all of China, of which Taiwan was but one province. Through a variety of institutional means the Taiwanese found themselves a political minority in their own country, dominated by an ethnically distinct Mainland elite who controlled all the levers of political power. As a result, the indigenous democratic movement emerged in opposition to the myth of national unity. Many Taiwanese, particularly those of the younger generation, came to feel that democracy in Taiwan could only finally be consolidated through an outright declaration of independence.[49]

The political expression of these sentiments is the Democratic People's Party (DPP). Over the past decade the DPP has steadily increased its share of the vote and has won control of many important political institutions. The KMT, for its part, has chosen to bow to these pressures. Under the leadership of Taiwan-born Lee Teng Hui the Nationalists have tried to co-opt the Taiwanese nationalist mood by trying to increase *de facto* Taiwanese sovereignty without declaring *de jure* independence. Under these conditions, it is perfectly conceivable that either the DPP eventually will come into office, where it may try to implement its radical agenda regardless of the foreign policy consequences, or that the KMT will move so far toward the DPP's position that from the point of view of an outside observer—including the PRC—the differences between the two will appear irrelevant.

At the same time, as pressures for Taiwanese independence grow, the forces of emotive nationalism would appear to be on the rise on the Mainland. After thirty years of mismanagement and two decades of compromising its Socialist principles, the CCP's domestic legitimacy rests on the relatively narrow grounds of maintaining internal order and achieving high rates of economic growth. In order to find a new ideological glue to hold a vast and disparate nation together, in recent years there have been signs of an increased readiness on the part of Chinese leaders and intellectuals to make use of an emotive, nationalist appeal, one that focuses on China's past humiliations at the hands of external powers—its so-called "Century of humiliation"—and makes the rectification of these past injustices a central mission of the nation.[50] Compounding these sentiments are suspicions that outside forces may seek to weaken and divide China, peeling off its peripheral territories—beginning with Taiwan and Tibet—before closing in to dismember the rest, much as the European powers and Japan did in the in the nineteenth and the first half of the twentieth centuries. These ideological trends threaten to make Taiwan a more sensitive issue for China than ever, and could put China on a collision course with Taiwan, and the United States.

From the point of view of an outside observer, be they either of the Neoliberal or a Neorealist persuasion, all three parties to the Taiwanese situation appear to be behaving in an irrational manner. Why should the PRC threaten military action when it has no hope of mounting a successful invasion of the island and is likely to manage to embroil itself in a potentially dangerous confrontation with the United States? In the long run, if they wait and continue to grow as they have over the past two decades, they will either become strong enough to succeed in an attack or the economies of Taiwan and the Mainland will grow so intertwined that Taiwan will effectively fall into its lap. The KMT as well appears to be more than a bit delusional if it really believes that it will be able to absorb all of China on their terms.[51] Finally the DPP for its part would appear foolhardy in its willingness to provoke Taiwan's giant neighbor by demanding outright independence.

All three sides, it could be argued, seem to be reasonably well served by the status quo of *de jure* unity but *de facto* division. Yet, within the context of their respective political cultures, each actor is not only acting in a perfectly rational manner, but also feels that they have virtually no other option than to behave as they do.

THE IMPACT OF HISTORICAL MEMORY

Constructivism draws our attention to the power of historical memory. Today, decades after the end of the War in the Pacific, the memories of the horrors of the war, and debates over Japan's role, remain as vivid as ever. More than ever, Japanese leaders find themselves under intense pressure to apologize for the atrocities committed during the war by the Japanese military.[52] Controversies continue to rage over the issue of Japanese compensation for the victims of the war,[53] and in the United States books about Japanese war crimes and Japan's alleged historical amnesia continue to make the best seller lists.[54] Meanwhile, in Japan itself, a new generation has begun to confront the grim side of the past more openly.[55]

Conventional international relations theory tends to discount the impact of such memories on actual policy behavior. Yet, as almost any researcher who has done field research in the region can testify, their impact seems almost palpable. An excellent illustration of the way in which these factors influence national security policy can seen in the case of Japanese-Korean relations.

From a Realist point of view, security relations between South Korea and Japan have been determined overwhelmingly by three key factors: the existence of a clearly defined and very imminent security threat from the North; the latent security rivalry between Korea and Japan; and the moderating presence of the two countries' security relationship with the United States.

Throughout the cold war, the United States, South Korea, and Japan were united by their common interest in containing Communism in East Asia. For Seoul, the alliance with the West was a matter of national survival. For Japan's ruling conservative elites, denying control of the strategic Korean peninsula to Communist powers was of only slightly lesser importance. After the U.S.-Soviet rivalry had faded, this concern with Communism was replaced with a common desire to maintain regional stability and regional status quo in which all three powers had a very large stake.

While alignment with the United States might be viewed as inevitable from a Realist point of view, the Realist perspective also allows for the identification of various factors that limited direct military cooperation between the two Asian powers. South Korea, from its point of view, had every reason to be suspicious of a resurgent Japan using the alliance as an excuse to once again intervene in Korean affairs. Japan for its part wished to avoid being dragged into a costly military engagement on the Korean peninsula.[56]

The alliance with the United States provided a perfect solution for both these sets of problems. From Seoul's perspective, Japan's alliance with the United States provided reassurance against the threat of Japanese remilitarization. As long as Japan was dependent on the United States for its security there was little danger that Japan would be allowed to threaten South Korean interests. At the same time, the alliance was convenient for Tokyo because it allowed Japan to pass the costs of providing military protection to Korea onto the United States. From a Realist point of view it is therefore far from surprising that military cooperation between the two countries has been limited, and it was no accident that the security dialog between the two intensified whenever the United States appeared to be wavering in its commitment.[57]

From a Neoliberal perspective as well there exist strong reasons for Korea and Japan to cooperate on security. As resource-poor industrialized nations dependent on exports and access to world markets, the two nations have a strong common interest in maintaining regional security in order to avoid disruption of the vital flow of commerce. At the same time, the two countries' commercial rivalry in such industrial sectors as steel, shipbuilding, and semiconductors is at least partially offset by their burgeoning trade and the substantial flow of Japanese investment in the Korean economy.[58]

In addition, Japan's and Korea's common membership in a broad range of international institutions serves to mitigate their mutual suspicions and distrust by improving the flow of information about each other's capabilities and intentions. Likewise, Neoliberal theorists would argue, Korea's recent democratization should help ameliorate any residual concerns that the two nations might harbor regarding each other's intentions and help to stabilize relations between them.[59]

In sum, while identifying some possible sources of tension between Seoul and Tokyo, a Neoliberal perspective would predict continued and growing cooperation between the two powers and would anticipate their becoming leading contributors to regional stability, especially within the framework of international institutions.

A Constructivist looking at the relationship between South Korea and Japan would, to put it mildly, be far less sanguine about the prospects for cooperation between the two. To be sure, a Constructivist would recognize that to the extent that Realist or Neoliberal ways of thinking influences Japanese decisionmaking the two countries may see strong reasons to cooperate with one another. In addition, a Constructivist might acknowledge that the staunch anti-Communist outlook of Korean and Japanese elites provides some basis for the identification of common national interests.

At the same time, however, despite some ideational bases for cooperation, the two countries remain divided by the legacy of a bitter past. On the Korean side the brutality of the Japanese colonial regime is still vivid in living memory, as most recently reflected in the public outrage triggered by the revelation of the complicity of the Japanese government in organizing the sexual slavery of an estimated 200,000 women, the majority of whom were Korean, during World War II.[60]

Beyond the physical and emotional scars borne by the victims of the Japanese colonial regime, there exists a yet deeper and longer lasting resentment of Japan that resides on the level of the Korean collective conscience. Modern Korean nationalism developed in opposition to Japanese Imperialism, and it survived in defiance of harsh assimilatory policies by the colonial regime. The trials and tribulations of that period play a central role in the Korean national myth and are recorded in countless memorials, books, plays, and histories on both sides of the demilitarized zone (albeit with very different interpretations).[61] Indeed, when North and South Korean military officers met for direct talks in the early 1990s, one of the few things they could agree on was the existence of a potential Japanese military threat!

In Japan, the memories of the colonial period have been long suppressed and there is relatively little recrimination regarding Japan's treatment of Korea outside the circles of the liberal left. Instead of guilt for its own misconduct, the primary focus of Japanese memories of the pre-1945 period has been the suffering of its own people as a result of American fire bombings, the savagery of the campaign in the Pacific, the strangulation of its economy by American submarines, and, most important of all, the atomic bombings of Hiroshima and Nagasaki.[62] Korea as a country occupies a relatively small space in Japan's national consciousness, and Japan's image of Koreans remains colored by a lingering attitude of superiority that is traceable to its prewar self image as the enlightened savior of East Asia.[63]

This does not mean, however, that Japan suffers from a form of historical amnesia—as is often charged—or that it has not drawn any lessons from the past. Rather, as is true of most countries, Japan's memories of the past are highly selective, and the dominant image left from the war can be described as "dual victimization." The Japanese feel first of all victimized by victorious Allied powers, who they feel waged the war with racially motivated ruthlessness and who were equally guilty of colonialism and imperialist expansion before the war. But what is frequently overlooked by Western commentators is that Japanese of all political stripes, left, right and center, also feel victimized by their own military and the ultra-nationalist far right, who they hold responsible for destroying Japan's nascent prewar democracy and who led them into a hopeless war which they should have known Japan could not win.

This image of an out-of-control military dominates both popular and scholarly accounts of the war in Japan, and continues to profoundly influence the Japanese view of national security and the military institution. To put it succinctly, the Japanese feel that they have been bullied and manipulated once in the name of nationalism and national security and they are determined not to allow it to happen again. As a result, there are is a strong consensus in Japan that it should minimize its involvement in security affairs and that the armed forces as an institution must be kept in constant check, so as to prevent it from once again exerting a corrosive influence on Japanese democracy.[64]

Although Korean and Japanese attitudes have evolved considerably over the course of the past fifty years, these features of their domestic political cultures have changed relatively little over time. In many respects they have even reinforced one another. Japanese expressions of superiority vis-à-vis Koreans and periodic statements by leading Japanese politicians that reflect an apparent incomprehension of the reasons for the depth of popular Korean resentment of Japan have time and again provoked outrage in Korea.[65] In turn, Korea's virulent and apparently implacable hatred of Japan makes many Japanese despair of ever being able to find any common ground with their Korean neighbors. From a Constructivist point of view this enduring structure of Korean resentment and Japanese aloofness should make it very difficult to enable the two countries to cooperate with one another even within the framework of the two countries' alliances with the United States.

To what extent do the three models elaborated above provide insight on the actual empirical record? The Neorealist perspective provides an excellent guide to the overall direction that the Japanese-Korean security relationship has followed. In the 1950s, when the prospect of conflict on the peninsula seemed very real and the U.S. commitment to regional security seemed strong, Japan strenuously avoided any military commitment, which could lead to its becoming bogged down in a land war in Asia.[66] On the other hand, especially during both the early and late 1970s, when the threat of a general U.S. withdrawal from East Asia seemed very real, the two countries took steps to strengthen their security ties.[67]

The intensification of security ties between the two nations since the end of the cold war, including Japan's recent commitment to provide support to U.S. forces in the event of a security crisis on the Korean peninsula, becomes perfectly intelligible in this light.[68] The possibility of becoming entangled through Korea in a larger conflict involving both Russia and China has greatly diminished since 1991. At the same time, with the demise of the Communist threat to U.S. global interests, the U.S. stake in maintaining regional security is probably at its lowest point since 1945. In order to preserve the security structure that has been so successful in keeping the peace in the region in the past, Japan and the Republic of Korea have every reason to try to find ways to decrease the costs to the United States of maintaining its forward commitment in Asia.

The Neoliberal perspective also provides some insight on policy between the two countries. The 1965 normalization of relations between the two countries owed a great deal to growing interest among Japanese business leaders in improving economic relations with the Republic of Korea, which was just embarking on its remarkable economic takeoff in that period.[69] Since then trade between the two economies has exploded to the point where by the early 1990s each represented the other country's first or second most important trading partner.[70] The two countries' economies have become increasingly integrated with the economies of other countries in the region, feeding—precisely as Neoliberals would anticipate—the profusion of international institutions which increasingly have begun to spill over into other areas.

At first glance, Neorealism and Neoliberalism might seem to provide a fairly convincing set of explanations for the overall development of security relations between the two countries. A closer examination of how policy actually has been made, however, quickly reveals the extent to which domestic political factors, and in particular historical memories, have shaped foreign policy outcomes.

In the 1950s the intensity of personal animosity between Korean and Japanese leaders frustrated all U.S. efforts at fostering greater reconciliation and closer cooperation between its two chief allies in the region. When in 1953 the United States was able to lure Japanese Prime Minister Yoshida Shigeru into a conversation with his South Korean counterpart, President Synghman Rhee, at U.S. military headquarters in Tokyo, reportedly the two men sat silently without exchanging a word. Finally Yoshida, in order to make some conversation, asked politely, "Are there any tigers in Korea?" "No," Rhee replied, "the Japanese took them all." With that brief exchange all conversation ended.[71]

Only when the more pro-Japanese Park Chung Hee took power in the early 1960s did it begin to become possible to establish closer relations.[72] Even then, Korean resentment of Japan always simmered close to the surface, occasionally bursting forth with virulent fury. In 1974, when a second-generation Korean residing in Japan, and associated with pro-North Korean organizations, attempted to assassinate Park Chung Hee, the brunt of South Korean anger was directed at Japan, not the North. The Japanese embassy in Seoul was ransacked and enraged demonstrators cut off their own fingers and wrote anti-Japanese slogans in blood on the embassy walls. In the end U.S. mediation was required to repair the diplomatic rift and calm the over heated emotions.[73]

While a certain degree of Korean suspicion of Japan might appear perfectly reasonable in light of the power disparities between the two nations, the extent to which historically fed resentments color almost every aspect of their relationship appears less rational when viewed through the pristine lenses of mainstream international relations theory. Although at times military men from the two countries are able to interact in a professional manner, and even build up personal friendships, at other times national animosities flare up between them, complicating efforts to get the two armed forces to engage in even limited joint training away from their national territories and triggering pointless military standoffs.[74] Likewise, the Korean press and media remain highly sensitive to the possibility of Japanese military resurgence.[75]

A prime example of the persistence of animosities can be seen in the recent naval confrontation over the disputed territory of Takeshima/Tokdo Island. Although uninhabited and of relatively little economic value, the two nations dispatched naval forces to the island to underline their claims, and South Korean forces even landed and briefly occupied the islands in a televised show of force. The chance of an actual armed clash was admittedly negligible. Japanese public sensibilities virtually rule out the use of force in such a situation, while the South Korean government is well aware that its limited naval forces would be no match for Japan's in the event of a serious test of strength. Such maneuvers, however, appear to be largely motivated by extreme national passions. They have little chance of actually enhancing the prospect of a diplomatic solution to the problem and hardly help the cause of improving military cooperation between the two nations.

Equally damaging to bilateral security relations has been postwar Japan's overall attitude toward national security. In the early 1960s, with U.S. encouragement, the Japanese Self-Defense Agency quietly began to draw up contingency plans on how to respond a renewal of hostilities on the Korean peninsula. When these plans—the so-called "Three Arrows Plans"—were leaked to the Japanese opposition, however, they provoked a storm of controversy. Although the Japanese government felt that in principle such research was necessary and in the national interest, many Japanese leaders, including apparently Prime Minister Sato Eisaku, feared that the armed forces might be tempted to use such a crisis to undermine civilian control of the armed forces. As a result, the plans were discarded and the uniformed officer formally in charge of the project reprimanded and eventually discharged. Further, Prime Minister Sato forbade the further drafting of such contingency plans indefinitely. This ban was to remain in effect for more than thirteen years and still today has been only partially rescinded.[76]

Even after 1978, when Japan began to cooperate more closely with the United States on security matters, the issue of whether Japan would offer even logistical support in the event of a crisis on the Korean peninsula was left deliberately vague. As a result, in 1993, when the United States was on the brink of taking military action to defuse the potential development of nuclear weapons by the North Korean regime, the Japanese government was unable to provide the United States with any assurance of support. Nor was it willing, because of domestic political opposition, to assist directly in a naval blockade directed at the North. As the United States prepared to evacuate its embassy in Seoul and military reinforcements were rushed to the region, the Japanese government informed the United States that if shooting started it might even be unable to provide medical facilities to wounded U.S. servicemen and women.[77]

From a Neorealist perspective passing the buck might seem a perfectly rational strategy, this utter inability of Japan to act is more than passing strange. Four years earlier, during the Gulf War, the Japanese had been faced with similarly strong demands to contribute to a Western military operation to rope in a rogue regime, and in a similar fashion domestic fears of entanglement and remilitarization had paralyzed government decisionmaking then.

After that crisis had passed, Japan's political leadership concluded that the country had barely avoided disaster. If the United States had taken serious casualties in the Gulf conflict while some of its chief allies had stayed at home, there had been every sign that the domestic backlash in the United States would have been enormous and could have undermined the alliance upon which Japan depends almost totally for its military security. Only the relatively happy outcome of the war, from the U.S. perspective, spared Japan from far more serious political consequences.[78] Yet despite near unanimous agreement among the Japanese foreign and defense policy elite that nation's response to the crisis had been woefully inadequate, only a few years later, faced with a potentially even more serious situation on their doorstep, the Japanese once again lapsed into paralysis.

This time after its near brush with disaster in Korea, the Japanese political elite was at last galvanized to revise the 1978 Guidelines on U.S.-Japanese Security Cooperation. When unveiled in 1998, the new Guidelines appeared to promise a stronger Japanese response in the event of a new regional crisis, with special emphasis on rear area support for U.S. forces operating on the Korean peninsula.[79] To this day, however, direct Japanese participation in combat operations remains out of the question, leaving open the very real possibility that in the event of a costly campaign in Korea popular opinion in the United States would complain that Japan is willing to share the financial costs of the defense of Asia, but not the cost in blood. Moreover, direct cooperation between the Japanese and South Korean armed forces remains limited and greatly complicated by the fundamental divergence in attitudes of the two sides.

In sum, a Neorealist or Neoliberal perspective has no difficulty explaining why Korea and Japan should cooperate with one another militarily, and both provide good explanations for why ties between the two sides should be intensifying. The real puzzle for Neorealists and Neoliberals is why despite, all the good structural reasons for Japanese-Korean cooperation on national security, ties remain so limited and relations are so volatile. After more than forty years of U.S. efforts to bring the two sides together, despite the extensive integration of their economies, their increased integration in regional and global institutions, and all the other changes that have taken place, the legacies of the past make Japan and Korea—at best—hostile partners.

CONCLUSIONS

If a theoretical perspective is to have any utility it has to tell the analyst what factors in the complex and often seemingly chaotic world of empirical reality are important and hence worthy of investigation. By the same token, every theoretical approach must also tell the analyst what elements of his or her research subject can be safely ignored or treated as a residual variable.[80] In this way every theoretical research program both illuminates and occludes different aspects of reality. It is up to the investigator, and by extension to the broader scholarly community, to decide whether a particular approach produces accounts of reality which are more persuasive and/or useful than those produced by other approaches.

The Constructivist approach directs our attention to the ways in which collectively held beliefs and values influence and shape actor behavior. At the same time it tends to divert our attention from the factors that other IR perspectives emphasize, such as the military balance of power, opportunities for trade, and international institutions. The question thus arises, to what extent does a Constructivist interpretation improve our understanding of the dynamics of East Asian regional affairs compared to Neorealism and Neoliberalism? The forgoing analysis suggests that it does so in a number of significant ways.

First, the Constructivist approach offers a convincing explanation for the historical shift of actor preferences from security to economic concerns. It allows us to trace the process whereby Chinese, Japanese, Korean, and Taiwanese elites came to institutionalize an approach to foreign policy which emphasizes economic over security issues, albeit in each case these approaches were based on very different underlying ideational-cultural understandings and emerged under very different circumstances. The account that emerges is at least as persuasive as the ones that might be offered by Neorealism or Neoliberalism, and considerably richer.

Second, Constructivism focuses our attention on aspects of regional politics, which tend to be largely discounted by system level theories such as Neorealism and Neoliberalism. While system theorists tend to treat such factors as nationalism and historic enmities as unexplained givens, Constructivism leads the analyst to take them seriously. Not only does this allow the analyst to account for behavior that appears irrational on a systemic level—such as the willingness of China and Taiwan to risk dangerous military confrontations over relatively minor symbolic issues—it also sensitizes the observer to the ways in which these forces develop dynamics of their own. The rise of the Taiwanese independence movement may appear to be a domestic political development rooted in the particular, but it is one with serious, indeed potentially profound, international political consequences.

The predictions that the Constructivist perspective offers differ markedly from those offered by other approaches in a number of respects. For instance, from a Constructivist perspective the evolution of Chinese and Taiwanese national identity will play a far greater role in determining the level of tensions across the straits than either shifts in the balance of power or the state of economic and formal political ties between the two nations. Similarly, Constructivism underlines the importance of resolving the history question.

Likewise, Constructivism makes rather different predictions from Neoliberalism or Neorealism regarding the probable regional response to structural changes. Many Realists predict that a decline in U.S. power or commitment to the region would lead to increased instability and possibly great-power rivalry between China and Japan.[81] Neoliberals would stress instead international institutions and the spread of democracy as the keys to stability. If institutions such as APEC and ARF grow, and the trend toward democratization in the region continues, a relatively optimistic outlook on the future of the region would be warranted. If these conditions do not obtain, Neoliberals would contend that the prospects for conflict grow correspondingly.

Constructivism eschews such relatively simplistic prognostications. Were the U.S military presence in the region to decline significantly, each East Asian nation would be torn in different directions. On the one hand, there would be strong sentiment in favor of continuing the emphasis on economic growth and international cooperation. On the other hand, historically rooted suspicions and resentments, along with nationalist passions, could be expected to flare up and fuel pressures for competitive rearmament. The way in which these forces might be expected to play out will be different in different countries, depending on historically contingent circumstances as well as the different ways in which these sentiments are embedded in their respective domestic political cultures.

Japan, with its comparatively deeply embedded anti-militarism and traditional propensity for aloofness from regional affairs, might well be inclined to retreat into a hedgehog-like defensive stance. In contrast, on the Korean peninsula and in the Taiwan straits, where nationalist tensions run high, the likelihood of conflict would escalate dramatically, and full-scale military clashes would be likely in either or both cases.

Finally, in light of the theoretical considerations sketched out briefly in this essay the current economic crisis in East Asia takes on a rather different, and arguably deeper, significance than it does when viewed through Neoliberal or Neorealist lenses. What is at stake in the current crisis is not merely a transitory shift in economic power resources or an opportunity to better integrate Asian nations into the global trading order. Rather, the crisis has the potential to throw into question the dominant regional model of state-society relations—the East Asian Developmental State model—and in doing so fundamental issues regarding national identity and national interests are opened up for debate that may provide the most severe test of legitimacy the existing political regimes have faced since 1945. Whether the East Asian states reviewed will take up the alternative Western models offered by the United States and the IMF as a result of this process, or turn to the reformulated versions of their own approaches to these issues remains to be seen. In either case, the Constructivist approach suggests that the process will be contentious and volatile.

ENDNOTES

1. Realism views interstate relations as driven by the distribution of power, and in particular military power, in the international system. Key works that have helped define the realist approach include: Hans Morgenthau, *The Politics among Nations*, 6th edition (New York: Knopf, 1985); Kenneth Waltz, *Man the State and War* (New York: Columbia University Press, 1985); Kenneth Waltz, *Theory of International Politics* (Reading, MA: Addison-Wesley, 1979); and Robert Gilpin, *War and Change in Inter-*

national Politics (New York: Cambridge University Press, 1981). For an interesting, and provocative analysis of the difference between classical Realism and its most recent, and most popular variant, Structural Neorealism, see Richard K. Ashley, "The Poverty of Neorealism," in Robert O. Keohane, ed., *Neorealism and its Critics* (New York: Columbia University Press, 1986).

2. Neoliberalism used here focuses on the ways in which patterns of interaction between states in an increasingly interdependent world gives rise to international institutions that provide a structure in which states can overcome coordination problems and are led to redefine conflicting interests. Central texts in the Neoliberal institutionalist program include Robert O. Keohane and Joseph Nye, *Power and Interdependence* (Boston, MA: Little Brown, 1977); Robert O. Keohane, *After Hegemony* (Princeton: Princeton University Press, 1984); Kenneth Oye, ed., *Cooperation Among Nations* (Princeton: Princeton University Press, 1986); and Robert Axelrod, *The Evolution of Cooperation* (New York: Basic Books, 1986). For an insightful overview of the relationship between modern neoliberalism and other forms of liberal theory in international relations see Andrew Moravcsik, "A Liberal Theory of International Politics," *International Organization* 51, no. 4 (Autumn 1997).

3. For a general overview of the development of international institutions, see Andrew Mack and John Ravenhill, eds., *Pacific Cooperation: Building Economic and Security Regimes in the Asia-Pacific Region* (Boulder, CO: Westview Press, 1995).

4. As has been argued by a growing number of analysts, including Peter Katzenstein, *Cultural Norms and National Security: Police and Military in Postwar Japan* (Ithaca, NY: Cornell University Press, 1996); Peter Katzenstein and Nobuo Okawara, "Japan's National Security: Structures, Norms and Policies," *International Security* 17:4 (1993); Davis B. Bobrow, "Military Security Policy," in R. Kent Weaver and Bert A. Rockman, eds., *Do Institutions Matter: Government Capabilities in the United States and Abroad* (Washington, DC: The Brookings Institution, 1993); Glen Hook, Hans W. Maull, "Germany and Japan: The New Civilian Powers," *Foreign Affairs* 69, no. 5 (Winter 1990–1991); and Yoshihide Soeya, "Japan: Normative Constraints versus Structural Imperatives," in Muthiah Alagappa, ed., *Asian Security Practice: Material and Ideational Influences* (Stanford: Stanford University Press, 1998). See also the author's own work on this subject, Thomas Berger, *Cultures of Antimilitarism: National Security in Germany and Japan* (Baltimore: Johns Hopkins University Press, 1998).

5. This argument is made at greater length in Thomas Berger, "Set for Stability? The Ideational Basis of Conflict in East Asia," *Review of International Studies* (Spring 2000).

6. For a more detailed look at Japanese reactions to the Gulf crisis and its implications for Japanese interests, see Thomas Berger, *Cultures of Antimilitarism*, pp. 171–177. See also Asahi Shimbun "Wangankiki" Shuzaihan, *Wangan Senso to Nihon* (Tokyo, Asahi Shimbunsha, 1991); and Courtney Purrington and K. A., "Tokyo's Policy Responses During the Gulf Crisis," *Asian Survey*, Vol.21, no. 4 (April 1991).

7. See for instance, Aaron Friedberg, "Ripe for Rivalry: Prospects for Peace in a Mutlipolar Asia," and Richard K. Betts, "Wealth Power and Instability: East Asia and the United States after the Cold War," both in *International Security* 18, no.3 (Winter 1993/1994).

8. Realism, like other well-developed schools of thought in international relations, contains many different variants. Defensive Realists differ from classical Neorealists in their view of the underlying motives of states. Classical Neorealists see states as power maximizers, striving to enhance their power at every opportunity. For an insightful discussion, see Fareed Zakaria, "Realism and Domestic Politics" *International Security* 17, no. 1 (Summer 1992): 190–196.

9. Although Neorealism and Neoliberalism differ in may respects, in particular regarding the power of international institutions to shape and guide state action, they share a fundamentally similar view of the international system as composed of state actors rationally seeking to maximize their national interests within the structural constraints imposed by their external environments. One consequence of this understanding of the international system is that both Neorealism and Neoliberalism predict that states are likely to behave in similar ways when confronted with similar external conditions, see Peter Katzenstein, "Introduction: Alternative Perspectives on National Security," in Peter J. Katzenstein, ed., *The Culture of National Security* (New York: Columbia University Press, 1996), pp. 11–17.

10. For recent, prominent exemplars of the constructivist approach see Peter Katzenstein, ed., ibid.; Friedrich Kratochwil, *Rules, Norms and Decisions* (New York: Cambridge University Press, 1989); John Ruggie, *Constructing the World Polity: Essays on International Institutionalization* (New York: Routledge, 1998); and Alexander Wendt, "The Agent-Structure Problem in International-Relations Theory," *International Organization* 1, no. 3 (Summer, 1987); and "Anarchy is what States make of it: the Social Construction of Power Politics," *International Organization* 46, no. 2 (Spring 1992). For reviews of the development of the constructivist approach see the introduction to Ruggie, *Constructing the World Polity*; Jeff Chekel, "The Constructivist Turn in International Relations Theory," *World Politics* 50, no. 2 (January 1998); John Gerard Ruggie, "What makes the World hang together? NeoUtilitarianims and the Social Constructivist Challenge," and Martha Finnemore and Kathryn Sikkink, "International Norms and Political Change," both in *International Organization* 52, no. 4 (Autumn 1998).

11. Chalmers Johnson originally developed the concept. He used it to explain the development of the Japanese approach to industrial policy. See Chalmers Johnson, *MITI and the Japanese Miracle* (Stanford: Stanford University Press, 1982). It has since been used widely to refer to the general pattern of development observable in the East Asian region.

12. For an interpretation of European affairs from this point of view, see Thomas Risse-Kappen, "Collective Identity in a Democratic Community: The Case of NATO," in Peter J. Katzenstein, ed., *The Culture of National Security*; and Ole Weaver, "Insecurity, Security and Asecurity in the West European Non-war Community," in Emanuel Adler and Michael Barnet, *Security Communities* (Cambridge, UK: Cambridge University Press, 1998).

13. Critical theory is closely associated with the Frankfurt school of sociology, dominated by such figures as Theodor Adorno, Max Horkenheimer and Jürgen Habermas. For overviews of the main points advanced by this school see Raymond Geuss, *The Idea of Critical Theory: Habermas and the Frankfurt School* (Boston, MA:

Cambridge University Press, 1981). Applications of this approach to international relations can be seen in the works of Andrew Linklater, *Beyond Realism and Marxism: Critical Theory and International Relations* (London, UK: MacMillan, 1990); Robert Cox, *Production, Power and World Order: Social Forces in the Making of History* (New York: Columbia University Press, 1987); and Mark Hoffman, "Critical Theory and the Inter-paradigm Debate," *Millennium: Journal of International Studies* 16 (1987): 231–249. The earlier writings of Richard Ashley are also clearly influenced by a Critical Theory perspective. See Ashley, "Political Realism and Human Interests," *Political Studies Quarterly* 25 (1981).

14. Inspiration for the post-modernist approach comes from the works of Michel Foucault, Jacques Derrida and Richard Rorty. International Relations scholars working within this approach include David Campbell, *Writing Security: United States Foreign Policy and the Politics of Identity* (Manchester, UK: Manchester University Press, 1992); James Der Derian, *On Diplomacy: A Genealogy of Western Estrangement* (Oxford, UK: Basil Blackwell, 1987); and Rob Walker, *Inside/Outside: International Relations as Critical Theory* (Cambridge, UK: Cambridge University Press, 1993). For an insightful analysis of the relationship between Critical Theory, postmodernism and other theoretical perspectives as applied to international relations, see Jim George, *Discourses of Global Politics: A Critical (Re)Introduction to International Relations* (Boulder, CO: Lynne Rienner, 1994), chapters 7 and 8.

15. The past decade has seen a veritable explosion of Feminist writing on international relations, fueled by the broader interest generated by the growth of gender studies. For important representative works see Jean Elshtain, *Women and War* (New York: Basic Books, 1987); V. Spike Peterson, ed., *Gendered States: Feminist (Re)Visions of International Relations Theory* (Boulder, CO: Lynne Rienner, 1992); Christine Sylvester, *Feminist Theory and International Relations in a Postmodern Era* (New York: Cambridge University Press, 1993); and Ann Tickner, *Gender and International Relations: Feminist Perspectives on Achieving Global Security* (New York: Columbia University Press, 1992).

16. Audie Klotz and Ceclia Lynch offer the term "interpretivist" for this school of thought. See Cecilia Lynch, *Beyond Appeasement: Reinterpreting Interwar British and U.S. Peace Movements* (Ithaca, NY: Cornell University Press, 1998).

17. For an excellent analysis of the basic postulates of a cultural theory of action, which can be applied to constructivist approaches in general, see Harry Eckstein, "A Culturalist Theory of Political change," in Eckstein *Regarding Politics: Essays on Political Theory, Stability and Change* (Berkeley and Los Angeles, CA: University of California Press, 1992), pp. 267–271.

18. See Wendt, "Anarchy Is what States Make of it."

19. See Max Weber, *Economy and Society*. Some Constructivists, especially so called "thick Constructivists," deny that even such a modest positivist approach to social science is possible, arguing that the very categories with which social scientists attempt to analyze the world—modernity, development, stability, democracy, and so forth—are themselves social constructs and correspond not necessarily to what is supposedly being investigated, but rather reflect the particular social, economic and ideological circumstances under which those theories were devised and in which social

scientists operate. Many other Constructivists—the so-called "thin Constructivists"—reject such a radical epistemology. For a brief review of the thick constructivist view of the relationship between power and knowledge, see the chapters by Richard Devetak on Critical Theory and Post-modernism in Scott Burchill and Andrew Linklatter, *Theories of International Relations* (New York: St. Martin's Press, 1995), especially pp. 148–155 and 180–184. On the differences between the different approaches to Constructivism, see John Ruggie, *Constructing the World Polity*, pp.35–37; Thomas Berger, "Ideas, Culture and Foreign Policy Formation: Towards a Constructivist Research Strategy," paper delivered at the annual Meeting of the American Political Science Association in San Francisco, September, 1996.

20. See E. H. Carr, *The Twenty Years Crisis, 1919–1939* (New York: Harper Books, 1946). For an interpretation of contemporary Constructivist IR theory that tends in this direction, see John Mearsheimer, "The False Promise of Institutionalism," *International Security* 19, no.3 (Winter 1994/1995): 37–47.

21. For an interesting discussion of nationalism from a constructivist perspective, see Rodney Bruce Hall, *National Collective Identity* (New York: Columbia University Press, 1998).

22. Bourdieu's notion of the "habitus" and "field" can be seen as one particular approach to culture that tries to capture its dynamic interaction with rational calculations and escape the static character of earlier models of culture. See Pierre Bourdieu, *Distinctions: A Social Critique of the Judgement of Taste* (Cambridge: Harvard University Press, 1984), chapters 3 and 4. Max Weber makes a not altogether dissimilar point through his distinction between "value rationality" and "instrumental rationality."

23. Note, however, that material-situational factors certainly do have an impact on the actual outcomes of interaction between different actors, and may have an impact on the continued development of cultures to the extent that these outcomes are perceived by actors as being different from what they had expected and desired. When cultures fail to allow actors to make sense of the material-situational environment and do not lead to the desired outcomes, actors may be impelled to reconsider the way they think about their environment, and possibly about themselves.

24. For an interesting discussion of some of these issues, see Stephen Welch, *The Concept of Political Culture* (New York: St. Martin's Press, 1993), ch. 4.

25. For a brief review of the ways in which the current generation of international relations theorists' understanding of culture differs from that of their predessors, see Yosef Lapid, "Culture's Ship: Returns and Departures in International Relations Theory," in Yosef Lapid and Friedrich Kratochwil, eds., *The Return of Culture and Identity in IR Theory* (Boulder, CO: Lynne Rienner, 1996), especially pp. 6–9.

26. Many Constructivists focus their attention on the emergence of regimes regarding such issues as human rights, arms control and foreign aid on a global scale. Others privilege domestic level discourses on these and other issues. Both approaches were well represented in the Peter Katzenstein, ed., *The Culture of National Security*. Ideally, both levels need to be integrated. For an interesting discussion of one influential approach to the study of global cultural regimes in international relations, see Martha Finnemore, "The Global Society Norms, Culture and World Politics: Insights from Sociology's Institutionalism," *International Organization* 50, no. 2 (Spring 1996).

27. For a fascinating study of the political uses of history, see Robert Gildea, *The Past in French History* (New Haven: Yale University Press, 1994). See also Ernst May, *Lessons of the Past: On the Use and Misuse of History in American Foreign Policy* (New York: Oxford University Press, 1973).

28. On the essentially contested nature of political concepts, see William E. Connolly, *The Terms of Political Discourse*, 3rd Edition (Princeton: Princeton University Press, 1993).

29. See Brian Barry, *Sociologists, Economists and Democracy* (London: Collier-Macmillan, 1970); Carole Pateman, "Political Culture, Political Structure and Political Change," *British Journal of Sociology* 1, no. 3 (July 1971); and David J. Elkins and Richard E. B. Simeons, "A Cause in Search of Its Effect, or What Does Political Culture Explain?" *Comparative Politics* 11 (1979).

30. On the origins of this view of economic power and its continuities with the present day, see Richard Samuels, *Rich Nation, Strong Army* (Ithaca, NY: Cornell University Press, 1994).

31. On American efforts at demilitarization, see Meirion and Susie Harries, *Sheathing the Sword: The Demilitarization of Postwar Japan* (New York: MacMillan, 1987).

32. I develop this argument at greater length in Thomas Berger, *Cultures of Antimilitarism*. Similar arguments are offered by Peter J. Katzenstein, *Cultural Norms and National Security: Police and Military in Postwar Japan* (Ithaca, NY: Cornell University Press, 1996).

33. According to a high ranking Japanese military official who served in a political liaison function during the crisis.

34. On the linkage of defense and domestic politics during this period, see Take Hideo, *Saigumbi to Nashyonarizumu* (Tokyo: Chuokoshinsho, 1989); George Packard, *Protest in Tokyo: The Security Treaty Crisis of 1960* (Westport, CT: Greenwood Press, 1966); and Yoshihisa Hara, *Sengonihon to Kokusaiseiji: Ampokaitei no Seijirikigaku* (Tokyo: Chuokoronsha, 1988).

35. See the report of the Comprehensive Security Research Group, *Sogoanzenhosho kenkyuu gruupu hokokusho*, delivered to the Prime Minister on July 2, 1980.

36. Hisahiko Okazaki, *Senryakuteki Kangaekata to wa Nani ka* (Tokyo: Chuokoshinsho, 1983), pp. 9–13, 24–26. For a more extended discussion of these issues, see Kenneth B. Pyle, *The Japanese Question: Power and Purpose in a New Era* (Washington, DC: AEI Press, 1992); and Thomas Berger, *Cultures of Antimilitarism*.

37. Kim Kwan-bong, *The Korea-Japan Treaty: Crisis and Instability of the Korean Political System* (New York: Praeger, 1971), pp. 80–82.

38. For a particularly fine analysis of the interrelationship of domestic politics and foreign policy in the PRC of the 1950s see Thomas Christensen, *Useful Adversaries: Grand Strategy, Domestic Mobilization and the Sino-American Conflict, 1947–1958* (Princeton: Princeton University Press, 1996).

39. For a useful discussion of the differences of thought between the Maoists and the Reformers, see Lowell Dittmer, *China Under Reform* (Boulder, CO: Westview, 1994), chapter 2; and Joseph Fewsmith, *Dilemmas of Reform in China* (Armonk, NY: M. E. Sharpe, 1994).

40. For a detailed overview of the Chinese economic reform process, see Barry Naughton, *Growing Out of the Plan: Chinese Economic Reform 1978–1993* (Boston: Cambridge University Press, 1995); and Susan L. Shirk, *The Political Logic of Economic Reform in China* (Berkeley, CA: University of California Press, 1993).

41. For a nuance analysis of the implications of Chinese economic reform for its foreign policies, see Barry Naughton, "The Foreign Policy Implications of China's Economic Development Strategy," in Thomas W. Robinson and David Shambaugh, eds., *Chinese Foreign Policy: Theory and Practice* (New York: Oxford University Press, 1994), pp. 65–69; David Lampton, "China and the Strategic Quadrangle," in Michael Mandelbaum, ed., *The Strategic Quadrangle: Russia, China, Japan and the United States in East Asia* (New York: Council on Foreign Relations, 1995), pp. 65–68.

42. See for instance Alastair Iain Johnston, *Cultural Realism: Strategic Culture and Grand Strategy in Chinese History* (Princeton: Princeton University Press, 1998), and Andrew Nathan and Robert Ross, *The Great Wall and the Empty Fortress: China's Search for Security* (New York: Norton, 1997), as well as Thomas Christensen's and Ian Johnston's contributions to this volume.

43. On the increasingly technocratic character of the Chinese leadership see Lyman Miller, "Overlapping Transitions in China's Leadership," *SAIS Review* 16, no. 2 (Summer-Fall 1996); Kenneth Liberthal, *Governing China: From Revolution through Reform* (New York: Norton, 1995), pp. 230–240.

44. On democratization in Taiwan, see *The Great Transformation* and Jaushieh Joseph Wu, *Taiwan's Democratization* (New York: Oxford University Press, 1995); Yun-han Chu, *Crafting Democracy in Taiwan* (Taipei: Institute for Policy Research, 1992); and Hung Mao Tien, *The Great Transition: Political and Social Change in The Republic of China* (Stanford: The Hoover Institution Press, 1988). For an overview of the South Korean experience with democratization, see Sung-Joo Han and Yung Chul Park, "South Korea: Democratization at Last," in James W. Morley, ed., *Driven by Growth: Political Change in the Asia-Pacific Region* (Armonk, NY: M. E. Sharpe, 1993). For a good overview of the wave of democratization that swept over the region during this period, see Minxin Pei, "The Fall and Rise of Democracy in East Asia," in Larry Diamond and, Marc F. Plattner, eds., *Democracy in East Asia* (Baltimore: Johns Hopkins University Press, 1998).

45. On the growth of Taiwanese investment in the PRC, see Tse-Kang Leng, *The Taiwan-China Connection: Democracy and Development across the Taiwan Straits* (Boulder, CO: Westview Press, 1986); Barry Naughton, "Economic Policy Reform in the PRC and Taiwan," and Chin Chung, "Division of Labor across the Taiwan Strait: Macro Overview and Analysis of the Electronics Industry," in Barry Naughton, ed., *The China Circle: Economics and Technology in the PRC, Taiwan and Hong Kong* (Washington, DC: The Brookings Institution Press, 1997).

46. See for instance Michael O'Hanlon. "Stopping a North Korean Invasion: Why Defending South Korea is Easier than the Pentagon Thinks," *International Security* 22:4 (Spring 1998).

47. Marcus Noland, "North Korea's Staying Power," *Foreign Affairs* 76, no. 4 (July/August 1997).

48. On nationalism as a motivating force in intra-Korean affairs, see Han-Kyo Kim, "Korean Unification in Historical Perspective," in Young Whan Khil, ed., *Korean and the World: Beyond the Cold War* (Boulder, CO: Westview Press, 1994).

49. For a review of these issues, see Alan Wachman, *Taiwan: National Identity and Democratization* (Armonk, NY: M. E. Sharpe, 1994). Reflecting the historically contingent nature of the process of identity creation, in South Korea, the trend has been in precisely the opposite direction, with the pro-democracy movement using nationalist themes of a unified Korea to attack the regime and calling for greater dialog with the North.

50. The rise of Chinese nationalist sentiment has been the focus of much scholarly and media attention. See for instance Lucian Pye, "Memory, Imagination, and National Myths," in Gerrit Gong, ed., *Remembering and Forgetting* (Washington, DC : The Center for Strategic International Studies, 1996), pp. 25–28 Chalmers Johnson, "Nationalism and the Market: China as a Superpower," (Japan Policy Research Institute Working Paper #22, July 1996), and *The Far Eastern Economic Review*, November 9, 1995, pp. 25–28.

51. Until the fairly recent past this was a not entirely uncommon point of view. See Wachman, *Taiwan: National Identity and Democratization*.

52. As reflected most recently by Kim Dae Jung's invitation of the Japanese Emperor to South. See the interview with Takamura Masahio, the new Foreign Minister *Asahi* 8/2/98, p. 2. For more background on the emerging role of the Japanese emperor as the conscience of the nation, see David A. Titus, "Accessing the World: Palace and Foreign Policy in Post-Occupation Japan," in Gerald L. Curtis, ed., *Japan's Foreign Policy After the Cold War: Coping with Change* (Armonk, NY: M. E. Sharpe, 1994), pp. 66–67.

53. Most recently the 200,00 or more women who are estimated to have been pushed into sexual slavery by the Japanese military. See George L. Hick, *The Comfort Women: Japan's Brutal regime of Enforced Prostitution in the Second World War* (New York: Norton, 1995).

54. Most recently Iris Chang, *The Rape of Nanking: The Forgotten Holocaust of World War II* (New York: Basic Books, 1997).

55. For an English-language review of some of the documents and testimony that has become available on Unit 731, especially in recent years, see Hal Gold, *Unit 731 Testimony* (Tokyo: Charles Tuttle, 1996).

56. For a theoretically informed and insightful analysis of post-1945 Japanese alliance behavior as the product of alternating fears of abandonment versus entrapment, see Jitsuo Tsuchiyama, "The End of the Alliance? Dilemmas in the U.S.-Japan Relations," in Peter Gourevich et. al., eds., *United States-Japan Relations and International Institutions after the Cold War* (La Jolla, CA: Graduate School of International Relations and Pacific Studies, University of California, San Diego, 1995).

57. See Victor Cha, *Alignment Despite Antagonism* (Stanford: Stanford University Press, 1999).

58. See Brian Bridges, *Japan and Korea in the 1990s*, ch. 6. This is not to understate the severity of the economic competition between Japan and Korea, especially in such sectors as shipbuilding, steel and the low end of the semiconductor market. See for in-

stance Jin-Young Chung, "The Eagle, the Goose and the Dragon: Cagemates in the Asia-Pacific Trade Order?" in Jonathan D. Pollack and Hyun-Dong Kim, eds., *East Asia's Potential for Instability and Crisis: Implications for the United States and Korea* (Santa Monica, CA: RAND, 1995) or John Ravenhill, "The 'Japan Problem' in Pacific Trade" in R. Higgot, R. Leaver and J. Ravenhill, eds., *Pacific Economic Relations in the 1990s: Cooperation or Conflict?* (Boulder, CO: Lynne Rienner, 1993).

59. A vast literature has developed on the putative tendency of democracies not to war upon one another, following on Michael Doyle's classical article. One strand of this literature argues that the reason democracies do not wage war on one another has to do with their formal institutional arrangements. These arrangements increase both internal and external transparency, prevent the policymaking process from being hijacked by domestic groups which may have an interest in conducting war, and sufficiently slow the decisionmaking process as to preclude the possibility of a surprise attack. See for instance Bruce Bueno de Mesquita and David Lalman, *War and Reason* (New Haven: Yale University Press, 1992). These arguments bear a close family resemblance to the arguments regarding the pacifying effects of international institutions made by Neoliberal institutionalists.

Another strand of the literature emphasizes the way in which the internal norms and values of liberal democratic societies influence their external relations, and is thus far closer to constructivism in its view of nature of the forces that guide state action. See for instance John Owen, "How Liberalism Produces the Democratic Peace," *International Security* 19, no. 2 (Fall 1994). See also Bruce Russet, *Grasping the Democratic Peace: Principles for a Post-Cold War World* (Princeton: Princeton University Press, 1993), chapter 2.

A certain degree of skepticism remains regarding the strength of Korean and Japanese democracy. In Korea the main focus of suspicion is the overweening, centralized power of the executive branch and the continued existence of harsh internal security laws that have continued to be used against political dissidents even under the liberal Kim Dae Jung government. In Japan the chief cause for concern is the excessive power of a fragmented, but only partially accountable bureaucracy. Despite these concerns, however, on the whole the arguments of the institutional strand of the democratic peace hypothesis would appear to hold. On the other hand, the intensity of the popular antagonism between the two countries suggests some important caveats for the liberal normative variant of the democratic peace argument.

60. See George Hicks, *The Comfort Women: Japan's Brutal Regime of Enforced Prostitution in the Second World War* (New York: Norton, 1995).

61. See for instance, Bruce Cummings, *Korea's Place in the Sun* (New York: Norton, 1997), p. 397.

62. For a fascinating discussion of the issue of war guilt in Japan, with comparisons to the dramatically different response in Germany, see Ian Buruma, *The Wages of Guilt* (New York: Farrar, Strauss and Giroux, 1994).

63. For polling data see Tsujimura Akira, "Japanese Perceptions of South Korea," *Japan Echo* 8 pp. 75–78. On the historical background of Japanese views of Korea, see Michael Weiner, ed., *Japan's Ethnic Minorities* (London, UK: Routledge, 1996), ch. 1 for an insightful discussion of these issues. It should be noted that Japanese prejudice

against Koreans has greatly diminished over time, leading to a significant improvement in the legal position of the resident Korean community in Japan and a liberalization of social attitudes. One reflection of this change is the fact that since the late 1970s over 50 percent of the marriages in the resident Korean communities are with Japanese.

64. These themes are developed in much greater detail in Thomas Berger, *Cultures of Antimilitarism.*

65. In 1953, when the United States first placed the two countries under pressure to normalize relations, statements by Kubota Kanichi, head of a Japanese diplomatic delegation to South Korea, about the positive aspects of Japanese colonial rule, helped derail negotiations for four years. See Brian Bridges, *Japan and Korea in the 1990s: from Antagonism to Adjustment* (Brooksfield, VT: Edward Elgar, 1993), p. 10. More recently, in November of 1995, the Director General of the Prime Minister's General Affairs Agency, Eto Takemi, was forced to resign because of strong international and domestic criticism of remarks he made to the effect there "also had been positive aspects to Japan's occupation of Korea." See *Asahi* 11/14/1995, p. 1, 2, 3 and 9.

66. Frank Kowalski, *Nihon no Saigumbi* (Tokyo: Simul Press, 1969), pp. 72–73.

67. See Victor Cha, *Alignment Despite Antagonism.*

68. For a useful English language review of the new Guidelines and their significance for U.S.-Japanese security cooperation, see Richard P. Cronin, "Japan-U.S. Security Cooperation: Implications of the New Defense Cooperation Guidelines," (Washington, DC: Congressional Research Service Report for Congress, October 30, 1997). See also *Asahi* February 13, 1998, pp. 1–2 on recent movement toward even closer cooperation in the event of a crisis.

69. Brian Bridges, *Japan and Korea in the 1990s*, pp. 32–33.

70. Ibid., chapter 6.

71. See John Welfield, *An Empire in Eclipse: Japan in the Postwar American Alliance System* (Atlantic Highlands, NJ: Athlone Press, 1988), pp. 91–93.

72. For an excellent discussion of background behind the normalization of Japanese-Korean relations see Victor Cha, "Bridging the Gap: The Strategic Context of the 1965 Korea-Japan Normalization Treaty," *Korean Studies* 20 (1996).

73. For a brief account of the incident, see Don Oberdorfer, *The Two Koreas* (Reading, MA: Addison-Wesley, 1998), pp. 51–56.

74. Conversations with U.S. government and military personnel who have been involved in efforts to improve relations between the two sides provide a veritably inexhaustible store of anecdotes, which illustrate the difficulties involved. As one organizer of a recent (1997) seminar involving South Korean and Japanese participants put it, we can get the two sides together, they all agree that it was useful to get together, and they are equally unanimous in never wanting to do it again.

75. See for instance, the Korean Times commentary on the new U.S.-Japanese guidelines in *The Japan Times* September 29, 1997, p. 21.

76. For good overviews of the controversy, see Ishikuro Takeo, "Mitsuya Kenkyu to Shiberian Kontroruurongi," in *Rippo to Chosa* (June, 1980); Mammitzch, *Die Entwicklung der Selbsterveteidigungs-Streitkräfte und Aspekte der zivil-militärischen Beziehungen in Japan* (Ph.D. Dissertation, Rheinische Friedrich-Wilhelms-Universität, Bonn, 1985), pp. 156–174.

77. See Don Oberdorfer, *The Two Koreas*, ch. 13.

78. See Thomas Berger, *Cultures of Antimilitarism*, pp. 171–177.

79. Ibid.

80. The influential philosopher of science, Imre Lakatos, refers to these two aspects of theoretical as negative and positive heuristics, which he argues constitute the core of a scientific research program. See Imre Lakatos, "Falsification and the Methodology of Social Scientific Research Programs," in Imre Lakatos and Robert Musgraves, eds., *Criticism and the Growth of Knowledge* (Cambridge, MA: Cambridge University Press, 1970).

81. See for instance Friedberg, "Ripe for Rivalry."

CONCLUSION

Images of Order in the Asia-Pacific and the Role of the United States

G. John Ikenberry and Michael Mastanduno

What will the Asia-Pacific look like in the years ahead? This great question of contemporary world politics will remain widely debated. Will the region take on a more coherent political and economic identity? If so, will it be increasingly an Asian region organized around Japan or China, or a wider Pacific region anchored by the United States? Will the region's relationships be driven by an antagonistic geopolitical rivalry between China and the United States, or will deepening economic interdependence lead political elites to expand cooperative political and security institutions? How will Japan's role in the region be redefined after a decade of economic stagnation? In short, will the Asia-Pacific be a stable core of world politics in the decades ahead or an epicenter of instability and conflict?

The chapters in this volume have addressed these questions individually and collectively. Each chapter has taken a distinctive cut into the policies of and relationships among Japan, China, and the United States, and from an array of theoretical positions. Taken together, they demonstrate that a multiplicity of variables have merit in illuminating the regional dynamics of the Asia-Pacific. In our view, three findings are particularly salient in the volume as a whole.

First, "Western" theoretical frameworks have much to say about international relations in the Asia-Pacific. There may have been a time when political relations among Asians were truly distinctive, and David Kang's paper points provocatively to that possibility. But over the course of the last century the nation-states of the Asia-Pacific have been integrated into the larger international system, and have taken on the behavioral norms and attributes associated with that system. Variables and concepts that are the everyday currency of international relations theory—e.g., hegemony, the distribution of power, international regimes, and political identity—are as relevant in the Asia-Pacific context as anywhere else.

But, the chapters also show that the application of those concepts must be sensitive to the particular historical and cultural dimensions of relations in the Asia-Pacific in order to enjoy full explanatory power. The security dilemma operates differently when historical antagonisms and ethnic hatreds are factored into resource competition. Alleviating the security dilemma is more difficult when political identities are contested; consider the impact on China's calculations when the United States ships purely "defensive" weapons to Taiwan. The deepening of economic interdependence affects relations among "developmental" states differently than it does relations among liberal states. Hegemony has different implications for regional stability depending on whether it is informed by Japanese, Chinese, or United States political culture and historical experience. The analysis in this volume serves as a reminder that the "value-added" in social science explanation often results from the interplay of general theoretical insight and deep knowledge of the particular political and cultural circumstances of a state or region.

Second, the challenges to stability in the Asia-Pacific are multiple and interactive. Security relations, economic relations, and the legacies of history can be mutually reinforcing in positive or negative ways. Traditional security contests can take on smaller significance in a prosperous regional economy. Elites can take credit for successful economic performance and can downplay, for example, unresolved territorial claims. New political identities can take hold—witness Japan's self-image, cultivated postwar until the early 1990s, of a powerful "economic superpower" enjoying prosperity and prestige and being emulated by its smaller neighbors.

In a similar way, all bad things can go together. Security contests disrupt interdependence; slower economic growth encourages security contests by raising the incentives for elites to divert attention from sluggish economies by appealing to base nationalism. Economic stagnation can lead to a reappraisal of the sources of national identity and pride. If a modernizing China with great power ambitions falters economically, does it adjust its ambitions or shift its emphasis to military or political sources of power? To what extent is Japan's remarkably pacific postwar identity tied to its success in the international economic arena? Political, economic, and security challenges can be neither analyzed nor addressed in isolation.

Third, the analyses of this volume demonstrate that the United States is and will remain a crucial determinant of the stability of the Asia-Pacific. The U.S. security commitment to Japan, as well as its bilateral security ties to South Korea, Taiwan, the Philippines, and other countries in Southeast Asia, reassures partners and helps to mitigate security dilemmas. The U.S.-Japan alliance "solves" the problem of Japanese power in the region; it enables Japan to play a constructive role without exacerbating security fears that could jeopardize regional order. As the chapters by Henry Nau, Masaru Tamamoto, and Tom Christensen demonstrate most clearly, the United States is the pivotal actor in the U.S.-China-Japan triangle.

Though perhaps not to the same extent, the same holds true in regional economic relations. The chapters by Dale Copeland, Jonathan Kirshner, and Robert Gilpin show in different ways that U.S. behavior has the potential to make the greatest impact on whether the regional economy heads in the direction of cooperation or conflict. For better or worse, the United States has proved to be the market of last resort, the principal nation-state player in the stabilization of financial crises, and the strongest advocate of deeper interdependence and market liberalization.

It is crucial to recognize that an engaged, leadership role by the United States in regional economic and security affairs can neither be assumed analytically nor taken for granted politically. The role of the United States is itself a variable that merits examination. Variations in assumptions made about the U.S. role in the Asia-Pacific lead to different expectations about the emerging character of the region. In that spirit, our conclusion lays out alternative future orders for the Asia-Pacific. Each order is premised on a different U.S. role. We then go on to examine the major policy choices facing U.S. officials and the factors most likely to influence the path taken by the United States.

FOUR IMAGES OF ORDER IN THE ASIA-PACIFIC

IMAGE #1: U.S.-CENTERED HEGEMONIC ORDER

Our first image anticipates a continuation and consolidation of current patterns. The United States would retain its central role, and would organize regional stability around its bilateral security ties and multilateral economic relations. This image presupposes that the United States remains fully engaged in regional affairs, making good on its commitment to a significant troop presence in the region and intervening diplomatically and even militarily to reduce security tensions and ameliorate territorial disputes.

The organizing principle of this order would remain a "hub and spoke" system of bilateral security relationships. The United States would maintain and strengthen the U.S.-Japan alliance, and U.S. bilateral security ties with South

Korea, Taiwan, and countries in Southeast Asia. U.S. officials would also need to develop further and strengthen the strategic partnership between the United States and China. The U.S. strategy, in effect, would be to have a special relationship with each of the major regional players—even though those players may remain suspicious and resentful of each other.

An underlying premise of this order is that strategic relationships run through Washington, D.C. In light of the tensions in the region described elsewhere in this volume, U.S. officials would need to manage regional relationships through a complex game of deterrence, engagement, and reassurance. They would have to discourage revisionist challenges and reward cooperative behavior, but in a way that did not trigger anxiety in the region. In short, U.S. diplomacy has to ensure that both China and Japan accommodate themselves to U.S. preponderance and continue to integrate themselves into U.S.-centered economic and political institutions.

This image of order anticipates the completion of the U.S. hegemonic project in the region. The most important unfinished task would be to convince China that, despite its size, economic power, or political ambition, it is best served as a partner in a U.S.-centered order. Beyond that, great transformations in the foreign policies of other major states or the development of new regional institutions would not be required. Robust, multilateral security institutions, in fact, would run counter to this image of order—unless they were crafted and dominated by the United States.

The potential durability of any U.S.-centered order rests on several considerations. First, the United States must maintain its dominant position in resources and capabilities. The disparity in power between the United States and other major regional actors is the foundation of a hegemonic order, but by itself is not sufficient. U.S. officials also need to maintain their array of political, economic, and security commitments. Both power and purpose are necessary; in the absence of either the order will unravel.[1] Second, other countries in the region, and in particular China, must view U.S. power in the region as relatively benign and subject to influence.[2] If U.S. power appears overwhelming, or if its foreign policy strikes others as too unilateral, arbitrary, or coercive, the willingness of China and other states to accept U.S. leadership in the region will dissolve. Third, other major powers must find U.S. hegemony not only tolerable but also beneficial. For example, the United States must continue to convince Japan that its security is best served through participation in a U.S.-led alliance. At the same time, U.S. officials must signal China that existing U.S. bilateral ties do not threaten China, and in fact may be a useful way to dampen military competition by discouraging governments in Tokyo, Seoul, and Taipei from pursuing more provocative security policies. U.S. alliances, particularly that with Japan, must serve multiple purposes. They must credibly protect the allied state, and must reassure neighboring states that the allied state is itself restrained.[3]

It should be clear that the durability of the U.S.-centered order depends on more than simply the preservation of a unipolar distribution of power. The effectiveness of U.S. diplomacy—the ability to deter through the exercise of power and reassure by moderating the exercise of power—is equally critical.

IMAGE #2: MULTIPOLAR BALANCE OF POWER

The unipolar distribution of power and U.S. hegemonic order may be enduring or short-lived. Many analysts expect the latter, and foresee the return of a more traditional multipolarity in the Asia-Pacific.[4] Order, instead of resting on a series of special bilateral relationships orchestrated by the United States, would be created the old-fashioned way—through the operation of a fluid balance of power among three or more major players.

The realization of a multipolar Asia would require significant transformations in the foreign policies and power positions of regional actors. Great-power status for China would necessitate steady improvements in economic modernization and military capability, and the maintenance of political stability. Japan would need to evolve a more independent diplomatic posture, including the development and utilization of independent military capabilities. This image of order anticipates the termination, or at least significant weakening, of the U.S.-Japan security alliance. As China and Japan increased their power capabilities, the United States would become in relative terms less an extraordinary superpower and more an ordinary great power. Other states that might plausibly join the great power ranks and round out the multipolar order include a revived Russia, satisfying its traditional ambition as a Pacific as well as European power; a rising India, combining its huge size and population with technological competence and great-power ambition; and a unified Korea no longer beholden to the United States.

Could an Asian multipolar balance endure? The nineteent-century European order maintained itself for roughly a century between two great European wars. Stability rested on the existence and consolidation of an international society. Leaders of the great powers shared an interest in the preservation of the order, and developed informal rules proscribing their behavior and institutions to help make the rules effective.[5] They exercised strategic restraint in fighting limited wars, recognized the principle of compensation in the taking of territory, and maintained flexibility in alliance commitments to reduce the chances of major war or the unambiguous dominance of the order by a single state. World War I, of course, signaled the breakdown of these practices.

The operation of a multipolar balance in contemporary Asia would face significant challenges. The existence of nuclear weapons could dampen the incentives for states to engage in any types of military conflict, while the uneven spread of those capabilities to major and lesser powers in the region would render deterrence and crisis stability less than robust. Smaller conflicts could escalate into larger ones as states perceived temptations to test resolve or gain advantage through preemption. The existence of numerous flashpoints in the region—e.g., the Kashmir dispute between India and Pakistan, the troubled relationship between China and Taiwan, competing territorial claims in the South China Sea, the unresolved division of the Korean peninsula—would increase the chances that conflicts would begin with the potential to escalate and draw in the major powers.

The stability of the nineteenth-century balance was reinforced by flexible alliance commitments. How flexible might a contemporary Asian multipolar system be? Longstanding friendships—e.g., the United States and Japan—and longstanding rivalries—e.g., China and Japan, or Russia and the United States—might inhibit flexibility. The inclination of democratic states to identify with each other might also constrain the multipolar balance in a region containing nondemocratic as well as democratic states.

In the current unipolar context, many analysts tend to accept the spread of globalization and liberal economic practices (i.e., the preferences of the dominant state) as natural occurrences. In a multipolar setting, however, a group of independent great powers may not so readily agree on the most appropriate way to organize their domestic economies and foreign economic relations. The traditional appeal of developmental capitalism in the Asia-Pacific suggests that geopolitical competition in multipolarity might be complemented by geoeconomic competition.[6] High levels of energy and export dependence among some of the major actors would increase the political stakes. Mercantilistic competition could easily become an additional source of instability in the multipolar system.

The longstanding tendency for states to balance power makes multipolarity a plausible future world. Significant changes would be required to get there, however, and once there the prospects for stability are uncertain.

IMAGE #3: BIPOLAR BALANCE OF POWER

It is possible that two major actors will emerge rather than three or more. Although several combinations are plausible, the most likely candidates for a bipolar order in the Asia-Pacific are the United States and China. In this order states with lesser capabilities would have incentives to line up behind one or the other of the major powers. Alliance commitments would be more fixed than flexible. As was the case during the cold war, societal and ideological differences between the two major players would be accentuated in the contest for geopolitical primacy.

Bipolarity would likely emerge as the result of a process of action and reaction. A precondition would be the sustained growth of China's economy and the translation of those resources into more modern military capabilities. Despite China's recent, rapid growth, the United States still enjoys significant relative advantages in traditional great power attributes such as economic size, technological capability, and the sophistication of deployed military systems. China can narrow that gap, but only with sustained performance over time.

An increasingly powerful China might be tempted to "test the waters," that is, probe the willingness of the United States to engage as Chinese officials spread their influence regionally. Tests could occur over Taiwan, the South China Sea, political instability in Indonesia, or perhaps the use of nuclear threats by one party or the other. As China sought to challenge the legitimacy of a U.S.-dominated regional system and propose its own alternative, we could expect it to enlist the support of other states in the region.

The United States, of course, could reinforce this pattern by shifting from a strategy of engagement to one of confrontation against China. Any combination of China's questionable human rights practices, its nuclear espionage, its transfer of chemical and nuclear know-how to "rogue" states in the eyes of the United States, its refusal to recognize U.S.-supported investment and intellectual property regimes, and its frequent use of anti-American rhetoric would provide ample political opportunity to justify the shift to confrontation. In this scenario the United States would likely strengthen its alliances with Japan and South Korea and direct them far more explicitly at the Chinese target. China would counter by soliciting its own regional allies—perhaps even Russia and India, with whom it began conversations after the war in Kosovo to stem what was mutually decried as excessive or hyper U.S. hegemony. It would be plausible to expect regional economic interdependence to be disrupted as states were forced to orient their commercial and financial relationships in the direction of one or the other leading powers.

The bipolar order of the cold war lasted some forty-five years. Whether a U.S.-China system could sustain itself for anywhere near as long is impossible to say. The durability of this order would depend, first and foremost, on the staying power of the two rivals. China is the more vulnerable in this regard. It faces the potential for political upheaval as it continues the difficult experiment of centralized political control combined with decentralized market reform. A generational transition in the ruling elite, the continuation of uneven economic development between the heartland and the coastal regions, and a shaky financial system that has yet to open itself to the full impact of globalization each place additional pressure on Chinese political stability.

Bipolarity also presupposes the primacy of two and only two major powers. If China can develop sufficient capacity to challenge U.S. hegemony, then Japan, with a more powerful and sophisticated economy, is certainly capable of challenging China. Russia and India, major land powers with sizable populations, share many, if not all, of the potential great power attributes of China. A future bipolarity could end with one pole standing or with several more emerging.

Finally, the two major powers would need to manage the risks that made the cold war so predictably dangerous. Bipolarity encourages intense ideological conflict and the tests of resolve associated with brinksmanship. The United States and Soviet Union managed those tests well—or were they simply lucky? China and the United States would face additional challenges as long as their nuclear capabilities remained asymmetrical, and as long as the United States claimed as an ally a political entity that China considers part of its own territory.

IMAGE #4: PLURALISTIC SECURITY COMMUNITY

A fourth image is one of a mature security community. In this order a group of states share interests and values with sufficient commonality that the use of force to settle conflicts among them becomes essentially unthinkable.[7] This regional future would entail, in effect, the "Europeanization" of the Asia-Pacific—a coherent and self-conscious political community organized around shared values, interconnected societies, and effective regional institutions. Political community would become the core organizing principle of regional order, offering to states within it the value of joint membership and a sense of identity beyond their borders. The community would possess institutions and mechanisms to foster integration and resolve political conflict.

The circumstances required for the emergence of pluralistic security communities are difficult to attain, and as a result, this regional order may be the least likely.[8] The existence of a shared and deeply felt sense of political community among peoples across the borders of sovereign states is an elusive condition that cannot easily be engineered by state leaders. Perhaps Western Europe has achieved this outcome, but even in that case a common European identity is still evolving. History and geography in the Asia-Pacific are less congenial to shared political identity. Would that identity be trans-Pacific or East Asian? What are its core values, and on what common cultural, religious, or other type of foundation does it rest? Therefore, the presence of a political community is not likely to be a feature of the Asia-Pacific region anytime soon.

Another characteristic of pluralistic security communities absent in the Asia-Pacific is the universal presence of democratic government. Open, democratic polities are a prerequisite of security communities for several reasons. Democratic states tend to acknowledge the legitimacy of other democratic states and in relations with them are more likely to refrain from the use of force to settle disputes.[9] The like-mindedness of democratic polities provides a common experience around which community can be built. People are not simply citizens of individual countries, but have shared identities as members of the democratic world. The openness of democratic government also allows the complex processes of transnationalism to go forward. The barriers to the development of deep interdependence between democratic states are lower than the barriers to such integration between nondemocratic states.[10]

The Asia-Pacific is marked by a significant diversity of regime types, and many of those that are democracies are still in the early phases of political development. China, in particular, would need to undergo a fundamental political transition toward democracy before a regional security community could be viable. It may be that movement toward democratic government is a trend among states in the region. Nevertheless, that movement is still contested and incomplete, and some prominent leaders in the region continue to argue that democracy and especially Western notions of human rights are incompatible with Asian values.

If there is any leading edge in the development of an Asia-Pacific political community, it is probably the shared aspiration of economic development and integration within the regional and world economy. This aspiration is shared by countries with different political systems and with economies at different stages of industrialization, and it provides the basis for much of the region's contemporary institutional initiatives. More than anything else, this mutual embrace of economic modernization has the potential to spark movement toward political community.[11] This does presuppose that continued economic integration would promote spillover pressures for democratic reform and complementary security institutions, rather than the political divisiveness and conflict that also has the potential to emerge as interdependence intensifies.

Because the emergence of pluralistic security communities requires precise initial conditions, once such a community does emerge it is likely to be quite stable. A community comprised of states with democratic governance and high levels of economic development is not likely to be shaken in the absence of cataclysmic political developments. As one study recently concluded with even stronger confidence, "once a country is sufficiently wealthy, with per capita incomes of more than $6,000 a year, democracy is certain to survive, come hell or high water."[12] States in the Asia-Pacific region would need to sustain a convergence of economic and political development in the decades ahead to foster the necessary preconditions for a security community.

THE ROLE OF THE UNITED STATES

As the dominant actor in both the regional and global settings, the United States will play the pivotal role in determining which of the above described images of regional order will prevail. A U.S. retreat from its alliance commitments in the Asia-Pacific would likely drive the emergence of a new multipolarity by forcing Japan to reconsider its security strategy and other states to respond in kind. A U.S. decision to shift its strategy toward China from engagement to confrontation would increase significantly the probability of a new bipolar order. The successful continuation of what Assistant Secretary of Defense Joseph Nye termed a U.S. strategy of "deep engagement" in the region would improve the prospects for a consolidation of the current hegemonic order.[13]

In the years ahead the United States will face three critical choices in crafting its strategy for the Asia-Pacific. The first and broadest issue will be whether to continue deep engagement or to disentangle itself from its alliance commitments and forward military presence. A second issue, directed specifically at the relationship with China, will involve whether to continue what Clinton administration officials have called comprehensive engagement or shift to a more confrontational posture. The third issue, obviously related to the other two, is whether to continue to support a "hub and spoke" security architecture of bilateral alliances centered on Washington, or to promote a regional security community even if that implied a diminished role in the region for the United States.

These choices will be driven by the complex interplay of U.S. state strategy, U.S. domestic politics, and the reactions and behavior of other states. U.S. officials, in effect, will be forced to play an ongoing set of two-level games, crafting and pursuing their own preferred strategies while simultaneously managing domestic political constraints and the reactions of the Japanese, Chinese, and other major governments in the region.

ENGAGE OR PULL BACK?

By the middle of the 1990s it became clear that U.S. officials preferred a strategy of deep engagement in Asia. But, in the absence of the cold war and a readily identifiable security threat, a gradual disentanglement from Asian commitments remains a viable option for the United States as well. Area specialists who believe that the U.S. role in Asia is outdated, and who fear that Asian resentment of U.S. occupying forces will result eventually in a rupture on bad terms, have made the case for withdrawal. They argue, in effect, that it is better for the United States to bow out gracefully than to be thrown out.[14] A similar line of argument is made by geopolitical strategists who cite the advantages of the United States adopting the role of "offshore balancer"—extricating itself from permanent security commitments and focusing instead on the revitalization of the domestic economy and political system.[15] These analysts consider the transition to multipolarity to be imminent and inevitable, and believe there is little the United States can do to forestall it. Proponents of deep engagement counter that there are multiple responses to U.S. hegemony and that U.S. behavior can help to forestall the emergence of a balancing coalition. U.S. hegemony and the unipolar moment can be prolonged significantly if not indefinitely.[16]

What will drive the choice of U.S. strategy? U.S. officials clearly prefer engagement and the effort to prolong hegemony, but they face several sets of interrelated challenges. One set is domestic. During the cold war, the U.S. public could be easily mobilized for the grand strategic purpose of containing communism. But mobilization to preserve "stability," or to freeze the geopolitical status quo in the absence of any well-defined threat, is difficult. It is especially so because U.S. public opinion has become highly sensitive to the costs of maintaining hegemony, whether they be in national lives or in national treasure.

The strategy of U.S. officials, in Asia as well as generally, has been to pursue hegemony as cheaply and as quietly as possible. They have sought to satisfy geopolitical objectives in Asia and Europe while avoiding direct military intervention. When they have judged intervention necessary, they have tried to circumscribe missions so that casualties are minimized and exit strategies are emphasized. To manage the economic costs of hegemony, they have pursued burden-sharing aggressively, prodding allies to bear the costs of U.S.-led initiatives such as the Persian Gulf War, the reconstruction of Bosnia after the Dayton Accords, and the North Korean nuclear arrangement.

A military crisis in the Taiwan Straits or the Korean peninsula would strain and possibly undermine domestic support for this hegemonic strategy in Asia. The test would be most severe if the United States found itself intervening militarily and taking casualties, while its closest ally in the region, Japan, begged off a direct role for political or constitutional reasons. State Department officials have sought assiduously to head off this "nightmare scenario" by resolving conflicts prior to military escalation and by strengthening and clarifying the responsibilities of Japan under the U.S.-Japan Security Treaty. Whether these tactics will work indefinitely remains to be seen.

A prolonged economic downturn in the United States would similarly complicate U.S. strategy. The remarkably long expansion of the U.S. economy during the 1990s served to minimize the domestic political significance of U.S. trade deficits in general and sizable bilateral ones with Japan and China in particular.[17] It is important to recognize that the export strategies of many Asian states hinge on the willingness of the United States to absorb their goods and run chronic trade deficits. The incentives for Asian trading states to embrace a U.S.-centered security order are increased to the extent U.S. officials tolerate these deficits.[18] Slower growth in the United States, however, could rekindle both protectionist pressures and the resentment directed at Asian trading partners perceived to benefit unfairly from the asymmetrical openness of the U.S. market. In relations with Japan and Korea, the politically charged issues of whether the United States should be defending states with prosperous economies, and that are perfectly capable of defending themselves, would be raised anew. Any strategic partnership with China—a potential adversary perceived to be taking advantage of the United States economically—would similarly come under strain.

The broad choice of whether to engage or withdraw will also be affected by how others react to U.S. diplomacy. Other major states in the region could tolerate, or even embrace, the U.S.-centered order. Or they could defy and challenge it. This decision, of course, will be driven in part by their respective geopolitical ambitions. China, Russia, and India, and to a lesser extent Japan, seek status and international recognition commensurate with their self-perception as great powers. Subordination to the United States runs counter to this goal. On the other hand, each of these states is a seeker of material benefits as well as status. To the extent the U.S.-centered order can help to provide those benefits, U.S. hegemony may seem less objectionable.

These choices will not be made in isolation, but will be affected significantly by U.S. behavior. To the extent the United States is perceived as arbitrary or coercive—in effect, viewed as a malign hegemonic power—others will be inclined to challenge and balance U.S. preponderance, individually or collectively. Evidence of this reaction was apparent during the late 1990s and early into the current decade. A series of U.S. initiatives—NATO expansion, the bombing of Kosovo, the failure to ratify the Comprehensive Test Ban Treaty, National Missile Defense, and the announced intention to modify or abandon the ABM Treaty—combined to stress the U.S.-Russia relationship and prompt Russia to explore "anti-hegemonic" diplomatic options. Similarly Chinese officials reacted negatively to what they perceived as U.S. heavy-handedness in the May 1999 bombing of the Chinese embassy in Belgrade, the scandal over Chinese nuclear espionage, the 2001 American spy plane incident, U.S. arms sales to Taiwan, and renewed public criticism from the United States over China's human rights practices. By the end of 1999, Russian arms exports to China increased substantially, and China and Russia moved closer together diplomatically and militarily.[19]

The management challenge faced by U.S. officials is exacerbated by the fact that their responses to these domestic and foreign challenges sometimes work at cross-purposes. The typical state response to public or congressional criticism is to get tough with other states, whether it be over trade, human rights practices, or arms control. Lashing out at the foreigners sells well at home but reinforces the view of the United States as unilateral and coercive abroad. Accommodating policies work better abroad, but they expose U.S. officials in domestic political discourse to the charge of appeasement.

CHINA: PARTNERSHIP OR CONFRONTATION?

The relationship between the United States and China will shape the Asia-Pacific region profoundly in the years ahead. That relationship is still evolving and its prospects remain uncertain.

The U.S. strategy of comprehensive engagement toward China was premised on the expectation that U.S. officials could employ a series of positive economic and diplomatic incentives, combined with deterrence when necessary, to convince China to be a responsible partner in a U.S.-centered order. The underlying logic is that China is not unalterably committed to mounting a revisionist challenge to U.S. hegemony. U.S. behavior can steer China to a more accommodating posture. Trade and technology transfers, in particular, can strengthen Chinese reformers, further open the Chinese economy, and help to steer Chinese foreign policy in a more peaceful direction.[20] Policies associated with this overall strategy have included moderating criticism of China's human rights abuses, delinking trade relations from human rights, lobbying for China's accession to the World Trade Organization, and developing closer communication and partnerships between the U.S. and Chinese militaries.

Although comprehensive engagement characterized U.S. policy through the 1990s, an alternative perspective began to crystallize by the end of the decade. Members of the so-called "Blue Team"—a loose collection of academics, members of Congress and their staffers, and some intelligence and military officials—promote the view that China is a rising and hostile power destined to threaten U.S. vital interests.[21] Blue Team advocates call for the United States to take a harder line on China's human rights and unfair trade practices, restrict technology transfers with military significance, and provide more vigorous support for Taiwan. In short, they support a more confrontational stance against what they view as an adversary with whom future conflict is probable if not inevitable. The second Bush administration, while not committed to depicting China as an enemy, has been far more eager than was the Clinton team to treat China with suspicion and adopt more hard-nosed policies.

U.S. China policy is tied intimately to U.S. domestic politics. During the 1990s, U.S. corporate interests provided key political support for comprehensive engagement in general, and trade-promoting policies such as delinking Most-Favored-Nation status from human rights concerns in particular.[22] Human rights activists, the Taiwan lobby, opponents of religious persecution, and conservative foreign policy analysts were arrayed in favor of a harder line. The business view, shared by the foreign policy establishment in Washington, generally prevailed. Even conservative legislators who were skeptical of China, such as House Majority Leader Richard Armey, tended to support the expansion of bilateral economic relations and Chinese accession to the WTO. By the end of the decade, however, the harder line position clearly had gained momentum, and U.S. China policy had become ripe for serious political debate.

China's own behavior has had and will continue to have a significant effect on that U.S. debate. The proponents of engagement are bolstered when China makes progress on privatization and the decentralization of economic authority. When Chinese authorities increase pressure on Taiwan or crack down on domestic dissidents, advocates of a U.S. strategy of confrontation gain ground. If China were to initiate military conflicts in the region, it is likely that U.S. policy would shift decisively to confrontation.

China's behavior is both a function of the regime's own domestic political calculations and a response to U.S. behavior.[23] It is not surprising that as U.S. officials push China harder on human rights or sell advanced weapons to Taiwan, Chinese officials react with the kind of intransigent behavior that reinforces the perspective of U.S. hardliners. The U.S.-led intervention in Kosovo in 1999, which took place without UN Security Council authorization and which Chinese leaders perceived as an unlawful attack on the territory of a sovereign country, seemed to reinforce in China a view of the United States as unpredictable and a unipolar world as dangerous. Chinese officials reacted with similar alarm to U.S. plans to develop theater missile defenses in Asia. U.S. officials may intend these systems as protection against a "rogue" North Korean attack; the Chinese view them more ominously, as having the potential to undermine the credibility of their own nuclear deterrent.

It is likely to become more difficult for U.S. officials to sustain domestic support for comprehensive engagement in the years ahead. First, as long as Chinese economic growth continues to stall, China's reformers will find themselves on the political defensive against conservatives who question the prudence of close economic integration with the West and who advocate more forceful Chinese military and diplomatic strategies against Taiwan and in the region more generally. The adoption of those strategies reinforces the appeal of more confrontational U.S. policies and the view of China as America's new enemy. Second, the U.S. domestic consensus on comprehensive engagement may continue to erode. That consensus, formed during the Nixon years, was ruptured by the end of the cold war, the loss of the Soviet threat, which drove the United States and China closer together, and the harsh crackdown at Tiananmen Square. It has been further strained by revelations of Chinese nuclear espionage, the escalation of China's rhetoric against Taiwan, the veiled nuclear threats against the United States made by Chinese military officials in 1995 and again in 2000.[24] U.S. supporters of comprehensive engagement will be hard pressed to regain the political initiative. They can take some comfort in the fact that the most vocal opponents of the engagement strategy are found on the far right of the Republican Party and far left of the Democratic Party, and thus are not as potent politically as they would be if unified. Proponents of engagement can also count on broader international constraints to limit the appeal of confrontation. U.S. allies in Europe and Japan will remain reluctant to isolate China economically or diplomatically—unless Chinese leaders act in a far more provocative manner than they have thus far.

The divisiveness of the U.S. debate over China reflects the uncertain future of China itself. On the one hand, China is well-positioned to assume the role of "new enemy" to the United States. It combines a dynamic economy with longstanding great-power ambition and a sense that the West has failed to grant it the political status and recognition it deserves. On the other hand, China is preoccupied with its difficult political and economic transition. And, it is far more dependent on the world economy than the previous hegemonic challenger, the Soviet Union, ever was. China has based its economic growth strategy on deeper integration with the West, and in so doing has granted the West in general and the United States in particular potential sources of strategic leverage through the use of economic statecraft.[25]

BILATERAL ALLIANCES OR REGIONAL SECURITY COMMUNITY?

America's bilateral security relationships with Japan, South Korea, and Taiwan proved to be the centerpiece of U.S. grand strategy in Asia during the cold war. U.S. officials have continued to rely on these constructs after the cold war to promote regional stability and inhibit what they perceive as disruptive geopolitical change. The system of hub and spoke security relations has become, in effect, a way to freeze the cold war status quo with U.S. allies. At the same time, it offers the opportunity to broaden the U.S. hegemonic system by incorporating former adversaries such as China and Russia.

An alternative strategy for the United States would be to encourage the multilateralization of security relations in Asia.[26] U.S. officials promoted this type of system in postwar Europe. They prompted West European states to band together in NATO and reinforced that effort in the economic realm by supporting European cooperation in the OEEC, the EC, and recently the EU. As John Duffield's chapter notes, U.S. officials explored the possibility of a regional security system in Asia early in the postwar era, but eventually defaulted to the bilateral security arrangements that remain in place today.

The promotion of a regional security community would have several advantages. The bilateral security relationships are essentially a holding operation, a *realpolitik* effort to prevent the deterioration of the Asian security environment. Pushing for a regional security community, in contrast, would be a progressive step, an attempt to improve security conditions. As such, it would complement more comfortably the U.S. ideological inclination to "make the world a better place," i.e., promote peace and democracy through multilateral institutions. Working to create a security community would be an effort to resolve, rather than simply contain, the historical animosities among states in the region. A multilateral security system would also provide a robust political foundation for the regional economic interdependence that is expanding so rapidly in the Asia-Pacific. And, multilateralism might help to ease the political tensions that naturally arise in asymmetrical bilateral relationships.

Despite these advantages, it is difficult to anticipate that U.S. officials will push for a multilateral security community at the expense of their bilateral arrangements. As noted earlier, the prospects for the success of a security community in the Asia-Pacific are currently remote. The region lacks uniformity of political regime type and a shared sense of political identity. One of its major powers, Japan, seems less comfortable in multilateral settings than in bilateral or otherwise hierarchical political arrangements. A democratic revolution in China would improve the prospects for a regional security community, but in the short or medium term that event itself is uncertain at best. U.S. officials are unlikely to abandon a set of security arrangements that have worked well—and, that have afforded the United States a considerable measure of hegemonic control—in favor of a security experiment that is appealing ideologically but unlikely to bear fruit in the near term politically.

We should expect U.S. officials to focus instead on what might be called "bilateral arrangements plus." That is, the maintenance of bilateral alliances and special relationships, reinforced by attempts at multilateral or minilateral cooperation where practical. The North Korean nuclear arrangement, institutionalized through KEDO and involving cooperation among the United States, Japan, and South Korea, is an apt example of a minilateral agreement on a specific security issue. Similar efforts—the strengthening of the Asian Regional Forum, for example—might help to tilt the Asia-Pacific, in the absence of hegemony, in the direction of a security community rather than to the more widely anticipated order of a multipolar balance of power.

CONCLUSION

Much of international relations theory, in particular realist theory, has focused over the past twenty years on the role of international structure in the determination of international order and stability. The analysis of this volume, with an eye on the volatile region of the Asia-Pacific, reinforces the view of many scholars that structure is not enough. Future stability in the Asia-Pacific will be informed by structure, but will depend as much on the old-fashioned interplay of diplomacy and statecraft among the major powers. U.S. officials will need to be especially deft in managing domestic constraints and international responses in order to maintain and expand their hegemonic order.

Both the United States and Japan have powerful reasons to maintain the U.S.-centered system, and it does have stabilizing features. The binding character of the alliances works to restrain and reassure the various states in the region. The United States is connected to the region in a way that makes its preponderant power less threatening and uncertain. Japan gains predictability for its own position in the region. Other states can be less fearful of the remilitarization of Japan's foreign policy. To be sure, China may not find this bilateral arrangement, with itself on the outside, as the most desirable security arrangement. But it does have the advantage of restraining the outbreak of serious military competition between itself and Japan.

There is one further reason to maintain the U.S. hegemonic order while striving to make it more acceptable to China and other states in the region. Perhaps the most dynamic agent of regional integration that will set the stage for greater multilateral security cooperation is the "new economy" that is emerging globally. South Korea, Japan, China, the United States, and others in the region are embracing, in varying degrees, the technology and information revolutions that are washing over the globe. The common embrace of internet capitalism may eventually pave the way for a more ambitious security community. But, as during the cold war, a stable political and security foundation is needed in the first place for that economic interdependence to advance.

ENDNOTES

1. See Michael Mastanduno, "Preserving the Unipolar Moment: Realist Theories and U.S. Grand Strategy after the Cold War," *International Security* 21, no. 4 (Spring 1997): 49–88.

2. On the importance of restrained U.S. hegemony for the maintenance of international order, see G. John Ikenberry, "Institutions, Strategic Restraint, and the Persistence of American Postwar Order," *International Security* 23, no. 3 (Winter 1998–99): 43–78. See also Ikenberry, *After Victory: Institutions, Strategic Restraint, and the Rebuilding of Order after Major War* (Princeton: Princeton University Press, 2001).

3. In much the same way, the NATO alliance has both protected German security and reassured Germany's neighbors that German foreign policy would be less provocative and more predictable. For an elaboration of this argument see G. John Ikenberry, *After Victory*.

4. See, for example, Aaron Friedberg, "Ripe for Rivalry: Prospects for Peace in a Multipolar Asia," and Richard K. Betts, "Wealth, Power, and Instability: East Asia and the United States After the Cold War," *International Security* 18, no. 3 (Winter 1993/94): 5–33, and 34–77.

5. Hedley Bull, *The Anarchical Society: A Study of Order in World Politics* (New York: Columbia University Press, 1977), especially ch. 3.

6. It is not surprising that the anticipation of multipolarity right at the end of the Cold War inspired numerous forecasts of geoeconomic competition among major powers. See, for example, Jeffrey E. Garten, *A Cold Peace: America, Japan, Germany, and the Struggle for Supremacy* (New York: Times Books, 1992, and Lester Thurow, *Head to Head: The Coming Economic Battle Among Japan, Europe, and America* (New York: Morrow, 1992).

7. See Emmanuel Adler and Michael Barnett, eds., *Security Communities* (Cambridge: Cambridge University Press, 1998), and Karl Deutsch, et al., *Political Community in the North Atlantic Area* (Princeton: Princeton University Press, 1956).

8. For a discussion of community-based security orders and their prerequisites, see Bruce Cronin, *Community Under Anarchy: Transnational Identity and the Evolution of International Cooperation* (New York: Columbia University Press, 1999).

9. For an overview of the democratic peace literature, see Michael Brown, Sean Lynn-Jones, and Steven Miller, eds., *Debating the Democratic Peace* (Cambridge: The MIT Press, 1996); and Bruce Russett and John Oneal, *Triangulating Peace: Democracy, Interdependence, and International Organizations* (New York: Norton, 2001).

10. Bruce Russett, "A Neo-Kantian Perspective: Democracy, Interdependence, and International Organization in Building Security Communities," in Adler and Barnett, *Security Communities*, pp. 368–96.

11. There is some evidence that Asia as a whole is moving to embrace the internet and other features of the "new economy." See Peter Montagnon, "Catching the New Wave," *Financial Times*, December 28, 1999. The emerging vision of regional community articulated by the ASEAN + 3 grouping—the ten ASEAN countries together with Japan, China, and Korea—is based primarily on the shared embrace of economic modernization.

12. Adam Przeworski, et al., "What Makes Democracies Endure?", *Journal of Democracy* 7, no. 1 (January 1996): 49.

13. Joseph S. Nye, Jr., "The Case for Deep Engagement," *Foreign Affairs* 74, no. 4 (July/August 1995): 90–102. For a later reflection, see Joseph S. Nye, "The 'Nye Report': Six Years Later," *International Relations of the Asia-Pacific* 1, no. 1 (2001).

14. For example, Chalmers Johnson and E.B. Keehn, "The Pentagon's Ossified Strategy," *Foreign Affairs* 74, no. 4 (July/August 1995): 103–114. This theme is also developed in Johnson, *Blowback: The Costs and Consequences of American Empire* (New York: Metropolitan Books, 2000).

15. See Charles William Maynes, "The Perils of (and for) an Imperial America," *Foreign Policy*, no. 111 (Summer 1998): 36–48, and Christopher Layne, "The Unipolar Illusion: Why New Great Powers Will Rise," *International Security* 17, no. 4 (Spring 1993).

16. See Mastanduno, "Preserving the Unipolar Moment: Realist Theories and U.S. Grand Strategy after the Cold War," and Ikenberry, "Institutions, Strategic Restraint, and the Persistence of American Postwar Order."

17. The U.S. merchandise trade deficit in 1999 was a record $271 billion. In 1989, at the height of U.S. economic conflict with Japan, the overall deficit was only $92 billion. John Burgess, "It's a Record: A $271 Billion Deficit," *Washington Post National Weekly Edition*, February 28, 2000.

18. The link between security commitments and trade arrangements is emphasized by Robert G. Gilpin, most recently in *The Challenge of Global Capitalism: The World Economy in the 21st Century* (Princeton: Princeton University Press, 2000).

19. See, for example, James Hackett, "A New Anti-American Axis?" *Washington Times*, February 24, 2000. In the summer of 2001, China and Russia further revived their relationship and signed a Good Neighbor Treaty of Friendship and Cooperation. See Reuters, "Russia and China Sign Friendship Agreement," *New York Times* web edition, July 16, 2001.

20. President Clinton articulated this view in an important speech on China in October 1997: "China's economic growth has made it more and more dependent on the outside world for investment, markets, and energy. Last year it was the second largest recipient of foreign direct investment in the world. These linkages bring with them

powerful forces for change. Computers and the Internet, fax machines and photocopiers, modems and satellites all increase the exposure to people, ideas, and the world beyond China's borders. The effect is only just beginning to be felt." Remarks by the President in Address on China and the National Interest, White House Press Release, October 24, 1997.

21. Robert G. Kaiser and Steven Mufson, "Blue Team Draws a Hard Line on Beijing," *Washington Post*, February 22, 2000. Popular writings that reflect this perspective include Richard Bernstein and Ross H. Munro, *The Coming Conflict with China* (New York: Knopf, 1997), and Arthur Waldron, "How Not to Deal with China," *Commentary*, March 1997.

22. For example, David Sanger, "Diplomats Trail US Business on China Links," *New York Times*, October 28, 1977.

23. David Shambaugh, "Containment or Engagement of China? Calculating Beijing's Responses," *International Security* 21, No (Fall 1996).

24. Bill Gertz, "China Threatens U.S. With Missile Strike," *Washington Times*, February 29, 2000.

25. Good recent discussions include Paul Papayounou and Scott Kastner, "Sleeping with the Potential Enemy: Assessing the U.S. Policy of Engagement with China," *Security Studies* 9, no. 1 (Fall 1999): 164–195, and William J. Long, "Trade and Technology Incentives and Bilateral Cooperation," *International Studies Quarterly* 40, no. 1 (March 1996): 77–106.

26. Discussions of multilateral security arrangements in East Asia include David Dewitt, "Common, Comprehensive, and Cooperative Security," *Pacific Review* 7, no. 1 (1994); Young Sun Song, "Prospects for a New Asia-Pacific Multilateral Security Arrangement," *Korean Journal of Defense Analysis* 5, no. 1 (Summer 1993); Paul Evans, "Reinventing East Asia: Multilateral Security Cooperation and Regional Order," *Harvard International Review* 18, no. 2 (Spring 1996); and Amitav Archarya, "A Concert for Asia?" *Survival* (Autumn 1999).

APPENDIX

Asia and Europe Over Six Centuries

	Europe	Asia
1492	Expulsion of Moors from Spain	(1392–1573) Ashikaga (Muromachi) Shogunate, Japan (1368–1644) Ming Dynasty, China (1392–1910) Yi Dynasty, Korea
1494	Charles VIII of France invades Italy. Beginning of struggle over Italian peninsula by Spain and France	(1467) Onin War, Japan. Beginning of "The Age of the Country at War."
1526	Bohemia and Hungary under Habsburg rule	
1527	sack of Rome	
1552	Maurice of Saxony revolts against the Emperor	
1556	German-Spanish division of the Habsburg possession	
1562	French Wars of Religion	
1572	Revolt of the Netherlands	
1580	Portugual united with Spain	

Asia and Europe Over Six Centuries *(continued)*

	Europe	**Asia**
1588	Spanish Armada defeated	(1592, 1596) Hideyoshi invades Korea
1618	Thirty Years War begins	(1600–1868) Tokugawa Shogunate, Japan (1618) Manchus declare war on the Ming
1630	countermoves by France and Sweden begin	(1627) Manchus invade northern Korea
1640	Portugual breaks away from Spain	
1642	English Civil War	(1644) Ch'ing Dynasty (Manchu)
1648	Peace of Westphalia	
1652	First Naval War between Britain and Holland	
1667	War of Devolution: Louis XIV against Spain in the Netherlands	
1672	Second War, France against Holland and Spain	
1672	Second Naval War between Britain and Holland	
1681	Vienna besieged by Turks	
1688	Third War (League of Augsburg)	
1710	War of the Spanish Succession	
1720	Prussia acquires Western Pomerania from Sweden	
1722	Peter's War against Persia	
1733	War of the Polish Succession	
1735	Annexation of Lorraine to France assured	
1739	Britain at War with Spain in West Indies	
1740	First Silesian War, War of the Austrian Succession	
1744	Second Silesian War	
1755	Britain attacked France at sea	
1756	Seven Year's War	
1774	Crimea annexed to Russia	
1772	First Partition of Poland	(1788) Chinese punitive expedition against Vietnam
1792	France declares war on Austria	
1793	Britain declares war on France, Second Partition of Poland	

Asia and Europe Over Six Centuries *(continued)*

	Europe	Asia
1795	Third Partition of Poland	
1799	War between France and the Second Coalition	
1801	Nelson's victory at Copenhagen	
1805	Trafalgar	
1806	Jena	
1808	Insurrection in Spain	
1812	Napoleon's Russian Campaign	
1815	Waterloo	
1815	Congress of Vienna	
1823	Absolute rule restored in Spain by France	
1830	July Revolution in France, Polish Revolution	(1839, 1856) Opium Wars in China
1848	Revolution in France, Italy, Germany	(1853) Commodore Perry lands in Japan
1859	War for Unification of Italy	
1864	Denmark's war against Prussia and Austria	
1866	Austro-Prussian War	
1870	Franco-Prussian War	(1868) Meiji Restoration
1878	Congress of Berlin	(1874) Japan annexes Taiwan
1899	Boer War	(1894) Sino-Japanese War
		(1900) Boxer Rebellion, China
1904	Russo-Japanese War	(1904) Russo-Japanese War

INDEX